P9-AQC-162

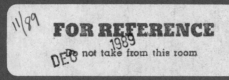

GREAT LIVES
FROM
HISTORY

GREAT LIVES FROM HISTORY

Renaissance
to 1900
Series

Volume 3
Ibs-Mic

Edited by

FRANK N. MAGILL

SALEM PRESS

Pasadena, California   Englewood Cliffs, New Jersey

Copyright © 1989, by FRANK N. MAGILL
All rights in this book are reserved. No part of this work
may be used or reproduced in any manner whatsoever or
transmitted in any form or by any means, electronic or
mechanical, including photocopy, recording, or any information storage and retrieval system, without written
permission from the copyright owner except in the case
of brief quotations embodied in critical articles and
reviews. For information address the publisher, Salem
Press, Inc., P. O. Box 50062, Pasadena, California 91105.

∞ The paper used in these volumes conforms to the
American National Standard for Permanence of Paper
for Printed Library Materials, Z39.48-1984.

Library of Congress Cataloging-in-Publication Data
Great lives from history. Renaissance to 1900 series /
edited by Frank N. Magill.
    p.   cm.
  Includes bibliographical references.
  Summary: This five-volume work examines the lives
of 495 individuals whose contributions greatly influenced the world's cultures that flourished from the Renaissance through 1900. An annotated bibliography accompanies each entry.
  1. Biography. 2. World history [1. Biography. 2. World
history.] I. Magill, Frank Northen, 1907-
CT104.G68   1989
920′.009′03—dc20
[B]
[920]   89-24039
ISBN 0-89356-551-2 (set)   CIP
ISBN 0-89356-554-7 (volume 3)   AC

PRINTED IN THE UNITED STATES OF AMERICA

LIST OF BIOGRAPHIES IN VOLUME THREE

LIST OF BIOGRAPHIES IN VOLUME THREE

GREAT LIVES
FROM
HISTORY

HENRIK IBSEN

Born: March 20, 1828; Skien, Norway
Died: May 23, 1906; Christiana, Norway
Areas of Achievement: Theater and drama
Contribution: Ibsen is one of the leading figures in modern drama. Moving beyond the melodramas of the nineteenth century, Ibsen created a drama of psychological realism. His dramas helped to create modern realistic theater.

Early Life

Henrik Ibsen was born on March 20, 1828, in Skien, Norway, the second child of Knud Ibsen, a well-to-do merchant, and his wife, Marchinen, née Altenburg. Ibsen's house, which faced the town square, was across from a church and a town hall that housed lunatics in its cellar. Early in life, Ibsen was faced with what he would later see as the symbol of spiritual freedom (the church spire) countered by the forces of confinement (the town hall). When his father went bankrupt and the family was forced to move to a small farm, Ibsen felt the pressures of being socially ostracized. Also, rumors that he was illegitimate haunted the young Ibsen.

Theater was one of Ibsen's outlets, and by the age of twelve Ibsen had seen six plays by Augustin-Eugène Scribe and had read Friedrich Schiller. As a child, Ibsen amused himself by staging puppet shows, magic acts, and ventriloquist's routines. In 1843, Ibsen went as an apothecary's apprentice to Grimstead, where he fathered an illegitimate child by a servant girl. This event would account for the themes of guilt, fear, and burdensome responsibility attached to sexual relationships in his works. At Grimstead, Ibsen absorbed himself in the realism of Charles Dickens, the biting satire of Voltaire, the explosive dramas of William Shakespeare, and the Romantic tragedies of Schiller. Also, he began to develop his skill as a social critic by writing lampoons and satires. In addition, he wrote poetry which ranged from introspective meditations to political propaganda, and he published *Catalina* (1850; *Catiline*, 1921), his first play. It focused on one of his favorite themes: the conflict between the lone individual and the forces of power. That same year, Ibsen moved to Christiana to study medicine, but he paid more attention to his literary pursuits and never finished his degree. His play *Kjæmpehøien* (1850; *Burial Mound*, 1912) was produced by the Christiana Theater. Ibsen continued to sharpen his skill as a poet, ventured into political journalism, and wrote perceptive theatrical criticism. Active in leftist political movements, he barely escaped being arrested. From then on, Ibsen distanced himself from political activism.

In 1851, Ibsen became stage manager and playwright-in-residence at Ole Bull's Norwegian Theater in Bergen. Having received a travel grant, he toured Denmark and Germany to learn the latest developments in theater. Overworked, underpaid, and unable to produce innovative works, Ibsen left Bergen to become the artistic director of the Norwegian Theater in Christiana. This job was no less frustrating, however, and Ibsen was eventually driven to bouts of depression and alcoholism. Given a small travel grant and aided by friends, Ibsen finally left Norway for Italy. He was to spend the better part of his career in exile from family and country.

During Ibsen's career in Norwegian theater, he wrote nationalistic sagas and satirical comedies. His experience as a director taught him how to structure his dramas and how to make effective use of visual and poetic imagery. Although the dramas of this early period are full of bombast and mechanical contrivances, Ibsen was starting to formulate a new kind of drama.

Life's Work

Ibsen's career as a major world dramatist began in Rome. Exiled from a Norway whose narrow provincialism had stifled him, and infuriated over his country's refusal to aid Denmark, Ibsen created *Brand* (1866; English translation, 1891), a monumental poetic drama delving into the spiritual crisis of a romantic idealist. Ibsen had now gone beyond the aestheticism of his earlier nationalistic sagas to write a profound drama which would rouse his countrymen from their complacency and force them to face the great issues of life. Widely discussed and hotly debated, *Brand* became a best-seller and won for Ibsen a pension from his government. Ibsen countered *Brand* with another massive poetic drama, *Peer Gynt* (1867; English translation, 1892), the story of an opportunistic double-dealer who compromises his inner self to achieve material gains. These two dramas established Ibsen's reputation.

In 1868, Ibsen moved to Dresden. He was lionized by the king of Sweden and later represented Norway at the opening of the Suez Canal. By 1869, Ibsen started to move in the direction of modern realistic drama. *De unges forbund* (1869; *The League of Youth*, 1890) focused on a contemporary setting, employed colloquial speech patterns, and satirized political chicanery. In *Kejeser og Galilæer* (1873; *Emperor and Galilean*, 1876), Ibsen created an epic tragedy in prose. In this drama, Ibsen tried to reconcile the Christian call for self-sacrifice with the pagan command to enjoy the pleasures of life to the fullest, thereby exposing the underlying dilemma of the late nineteenth century.

Ibsen now began to dissociate himself from political reform movements in favor of a spiritual revolution based on a radical individualism bordering on anarchy. Influenced by the Danish critic George Brandes and the realist director George II, Duke of Saxe-Meiningen, Ibsen shifted away from historical plays and poetic epics to concentrate on prose dramas set in contemporary Norway. Eventually, he also helped to give form and depth to the modern realistic problem play. In *Et dukkehjem* (1879; *A Doll's House*,

1880) and *Gengangere* (1881; *Ghosts*, 1885), Ibsen helped to shape the path of modern drama. Both plays treat contemporary issues, center on a small ensemble of characters, and take place in confined settings. They are crafted around tightly constructed plots which are based on the careful unraveling of past events. Their terse, choppy dialogue is loaded with double meanings, their decor is reflective of the moods and shifts of the characters, and their conflicts are intensely psychological. Both plays deal with women who are asked to sacrifice their duty to themselves in order to meet social obligations. Nora in *A Doll's House* leaves her husband and children, whereas Mrs. Alving in *Ghosts* settles for a loveless marriage, wreaking destruction on her entire family.

In these two dramas, Ibsen exploded both the form and content of the contrived, sentimental, and moralistic melodramas of his time and considered such taboo subjects as venereal disease, incest, and mercy killing. Ibsen even attacked the cherished institution of marriage. On the legitimate stage, his plays were banned or rewritten, but in the new avant-garde theaters of Europe, Ibsen's works became staples of the new repertory. Ibsen created plays that attacked bourgeois values at the same time as he elevated domestic drama to the status of high tragedy.

Soon Ibsen would go beyond social drama to probe the recesses of the unconscious in such plays as *Rosmersholm* (1886; English translation, 1889). Ibsen now began to show that an individual's repressed drives can bring about his or her destruction. In *Hedda Gabler* (1890; English translation, 1891), Ibsen combined realistic techniques with psychological drama. He dropped the standard exposition, eliminated long monologues, and created broken dialogue infused with underlying meanings. Hedda is a middle-class woman with no purpose in life. She tries to release her pent-up drives by controlling the destinies of the men around her. Failing in this, she shoots herself in the head.

After wandering back and forth between Italy and Germany, Ibsen returned to Norway a national hero. He was given the Grand Cross in Denmark, honored by royalty, and celebrated in torchlight parades. Frightened and fascinated by the new generation, Ibsen passed through a series of platonic affairs with young girls such as Émile Bardach, Helene Raff, and Hildur Andersen. The theme of a young girl beckoning an aging architect to create a masterpiece appears in the first of his final plays, *Bygmester Solness* (1892; *The Master Builder*, 1893). In these plays, Ibsen experiments with a form of mystic and visionary drama. Ibsen now focuses on the artist and his relationship to art. These short, narrowly focused dramas have a somber, poetic quality laden with symbolic overtones. Their claustrophobic, intense, and anxious mood of finality foreshadows the techniques of the modernist dramas of the twentieth century.

In 1901, Ibsen suffered the first of a series of strokes, which would eventually lead to his death on May 23, 1906. His last words were "On the contrary!"—an appropriate exit line for a man who celebrated the individual's right to define himself contrary to both the wishes of the establishment and the pressures of the crowd.

Summary

Henrik Ibsen was one of the first playwrights to create tragic dramas about ordinary people caught in the webs of fate and forced to choose between their self-fulfillment and their responsibility to others. Ibsen helped to create the modern psychological drama which probes the recesses of the unconscious. His scenic details, suggestive imagery, poetic symbols, and double-edged dialogue created a dramatic technique that would help to revolutionize the modern theater. His dramas depended on a subtle, truthful form of acting which inspired ensemble productions free from rhetoric, bombast, and posturing. Ibsen's plays challenged avant-garde directors such as André Antoiné, Otto Brahm, and Konstantin Stanislavsky. Ibsen also influenced a diverse group of dramatists. George Bernard Shaw saw him as the champion of the propaganda drama. Arthur Miller centered on Ibsen's social dramas, whereas Luigi Pirandello and Harold Pinter focused on Ibsen's existential pieces.

Ibsen defies classification. He sought to go beyond photographic realism, yet he shunned symbolism. He attacked the hypocrisy of social and political establishments but refused to attach himself to any liberal reform movements. He probed deeply into the problems of women but dissociated himself from feminist causes. Ibsen, the true existentialist, had his characters ask two questions which would become the focal questions of modern drama: Who am I? and How can I be true to myself?

Bibliography

Beyer, Edvard. *Ibsen: The Man and His Work*. Translated by Marie Wells. New York: Taplinger, 1978. A biographical, critical study of Ibsen which relates Ibsen's works to cultural and political events in Norway at the same time as it establishes his place in world literature. Profusely illustrated with drawings, editorial cartoons, and production photographs. Contains a substantial bibliography of critical works in English.

Chamberlain, John S. *Ibsen: The Open Vision*. London: Athlone Press, 1982. Analyzes *Peer Gynt, Ghosts, The Wild Duck*, and *The Master Builder*. Uses significant plays from the major periods in Ibsen's career to show how Ibsen creates dramatic tension by pitting a variety of intellectual positions against one another without settling on a single resolution. Offers detailed analysis of seminal works.

Clurman, Harold. *Ibsen*. New York: Macmillan, 1977. A very readable introduction to Ibsen's plays, covering his early works as well as his major plays. A theatrical director, Clurman pays careful attention to production values. Places Ibsen in perspective with other major dramatists. The appendix provides director's notes for several plays.

Fjelde, Rolf, ed. *Ibsen: A Collection of Critical Essays*. Englewood Cliffs, N.J.: Prentice-Hall, 1965. A sampling of articles covering a wide variety of plays. Focuses on both Ibsen's major themes and his techniques. Contains a balanced sample of the works of important Ibsen scholars.

Haugen, Einar. *Ibsen's Drama: Author to Audience*. Minneapolis: University of Minnesota Press, 1979. Uses current communication theories to demonstrate how Ibsen's work can be decoded by a modern audience. Highlights a variety of themes, styles, and production techniques. The appendix includes a chronology of Ibsen's life and brief plot summaries of his works. Also has a detailed bibliography of foreign and English sources, plus a checklist of Ibsen's works using Norwegian titles.

Hurt, James. *Cataline's Dream: An Essay on Ibsen's Plays*. Urbana: University of Illinois Press, 1972. Using the techniques of depth psychology, Hurt traces the mythic pattern of ascent, descent, and transformation throughout Ibsen's works. Focuses on recurring motifs, characters, and symbols.

Meyer, Michael. *Ibsen: A Biography*. Garden City, N.Y.: Doubleday, 1978. A lengthy and exhaustive biography detailing Ibsen's personal and professional life. It not only documents Ibsen's development as a dramatist, his working methods, and his philosophical shifts but also gives a detailed account of the production history of his plays in Germany, France, and England.

Northam, John. *Ibsen: A Critical Study*. Cambridge: Cambridge University Press, 1973. Covers Ibsen's major work, concentrating on the evolution of Ibsen's later prose plays from the themes of his earlier poetic works. Pays careful attention to Ibsen's imagery.

Thomas, David. *Henrik Ibsen*. New York: Grove Press, 1983. An excellent, concise introduction to Ibsen's work. Thomas offers a brief biographical sketch and discusses literary and theatrical influences. Analyzes selected plays using a thematic approach that highlights the role of women in Ibsen's plays as well as his use of symbolism. Also gives a brief production history of major dramas and a review of critical works in English.

Paul Rosefeldt

II NAOSUKE

Born: November 29, 1815; Hikone, Japan
Died: March 24, 1860; Edo, Japan
Areas of Achievement: Statecraft, government, and politics
Contribution: Ii was a conservative but pragmatic defender of the Tokugawa
family's rule (*bakufu*) in nineteenth century Japan. While he temporarily
slowed the decline of the *bakufu*, his policies in the long run were ineffective in dealing with either the growing domestic hostility toward the
shogun or the Western pressures to open Japan to full participation in
world trade and politics.

Early Life

Ii Naosuke was born into the very large family of the domain (*han*) lord
(daimyo) of Hikone, in central Japan. As the fourteenth son, he had little
prospect of a major political career, since hereditary succession determined
domain leadership. Lacking favorable prospects within the domain's administration, he realistically could expect only that his father would secure his
fortunes by arranging his adoption into a suitable family. A common practice
in Japan, adoption was a principal means of solidifying a family's political
and military ties to other important families. His limited expectations were
further restricted by the death of his mother when he was only five years old.
Her passing left him without an adult to argue that he might be uniquely
suited to participate in domain administration. It was largely chance that
ultimately saved Ii from sharing with many of his elder brothers this fate as
an adoptee and provided him with the opportunity to play a leading role in
the national politics and diplomacy of a Japan that faced grave crises.

There was little in Ii's upbringing that specifically prepared him to direct
domain, much less national, policy in these tumultuous times. Reared with
his younger brother in a small house by the castle moat, he trained until age
seventeen in the traditional fashion of upper-class samurai. He studied poetry, religion (Zen Buddhism), the arts, and such traditional disciplines as
tea ceremony. He also diligently practiced martial arts (fencing, archery,
horsemanship, and gunnery) and studied strategy. As a young adult, the
focus of his studies came to include discussion of current political and administrative matters. Among his acquaintances was Nagano Shuzen, who
beame a lifelong teacher, adviser, and friend.

Following custom, Ii's elder brother, Naoaki, became daimyo, succeeding
their father in 1834. By this time, some of Ii's other brothers had died and
the rest had been placed as adoptees in other prominent families. With the
passage of time, it became clear that Naoaki would have no heirs, so Ii, in
his early thirties, unexpectedly became the heir to the family headship. In
1850, when Naoaki died, Ii was installed as Daimyo of Hikone.

Life's Work

With his rise to daimyo status, Ii was thrust onto the national political stage for the first time. In part, Ii would make his mark by dint of his forceful personality and his willingness to become the leader of the political faction that defended the Tokugawa shogunate. He was also virtually guaranteed a measure of prominence solely by virtue of the fact that his family was one of the very few who could provide candidates for the very powerful office of great councilor (*tairō*), a post he would assume in 1858.

When Ii took on the responsibilities for domain administration, he also joined the ranks of the highest class of warriors and political figures in Japan, the daimyo. During the mid-nineteenth century, these men came to exert uncharacteristic influence on national policies and actions. Since the daimyo as a group were not formally incorporated into the *bakufu*'s policy-making organization, there was no effective means for resolving disputes among the factions that arose among them. During the preceding two hundred years, when Japan had faced no major foreign threat or internal crisis, this absence mattered little. The arrival of Europeans, who pressed Japan to open her ports to trade, sparked a controversy that the *bakufu* could not control. In this setting, some daimyo sought to challenge *bakufu* authority and Ii rose to defend that authority.

A key issue in disputes among daimyo factions was the question of how Japan should respond to Western entreaties to open its ports. Should Japan open its ports to trade with the West, and if so, under what conditions? Should Japan keep its traditional policy of trading only with the Dutch on a very limited basis? As early as 1846, the emperor, encouraged by those who sought a means to intrude on the traditional authority of the *bakufu*, urged the shogun to keep these "barbarians" out of Japan. (That was the first of several important efforts by this faction to use the emperor's antiforeign opinions as a means to compromise shogunal authority.) Others, especially the students of the so-called Dutch Studies (actually, studies of Western nations), were aware of the growing technological and military power of the West. Some of these men argued that Japan could benefit from contact with the West. All suspected that Japan would have a very difficult, if not impossible, time keeping Westerners at bay for very much longer.

Commodore Matthew C. Perry's arrival in Japanese waters in July of 1853 brought urgency to the debate. Accompanied by several large and powerful steamships, the Perry mission was intentionally designed to impress, even to intimidate, the Japanese. Yet, at the same time, Perry brought examples of Western technology designed to entice the Japanese to trade with the United States. Perry's visit was brief, but, before he left, he told the Japanese that he would return in a year to sign a treaty of friendship.

Perry's visit caused substantial consternation among the Japanese. The nation had not confronted a foreign crisis of this magnitude for two centuries. In order to develop a response to Perry that would enjoy the broadest possible support from domain lords, Abe Masahiro, the most important shogunal adviser, requested all the daimyo to submit their opinions on the matter. Abe's hopes of developing a consensus policy were dashed by the lack of agreement among the daimyo and the strident tone of many of those opposed to dealing further with Perry. Tokugawa Nariaki, who was to be the leading opponent of contact with the West, argued that Japan should refuse the American demands, strengthen the nation's defenses, and be prepared for war. Ii, who soon became the leading advocate for a more restrained and pragmatic approach, agreed that Japan should strengthen its defenses but went on to argue that minimum concessions should be granted to Perry in order to avoid war. His proposals included extending the trading privileges granted to the Dutch to other Westerners.

Despite the division of opinion among the domain lords, the shogunate did sign a treaty of friendship with Perry when he returned in 1854. This treaty was very limited in scope, but it contained one provision that would keep the foreign policy dispute alive for several years—a provision to negotiate a full-scale commercial treaty with the United States. Townsend Harris was sent to Japan as ambassador, with the specific charge of completing the commercial treaty. From the time of his arrival in 1856, Harris was beset by Japanese attempts to limit the performance of his ambassadorial duties. Among the Japanese, his presence and his mission were always a source of contention, even an object of violent attack. Abe attempted to deal even-handedly with each side in the debate. Ii was appointed to guard the emperor and to protect him from the Western barbarians. Ii's antiforeign nemesis, Tokugawa Nariaki, was placed in charge of coastal defenses. In the end, attempts to be fair only provoked heated reactions from each faction.

Between late 1855 and Ii's death in 1860, however, Ii was able to engineer the appointment of a number of his supporters to high positions. Beginning with the appointment of Hotta Masayoshi to the rank of senior councillor, the pragmatic defenders of the Tokugawa rule gained preeminence in that most powerful advisory body. This development would have put Ii's supporters in control under normal circumstances, but Nariaki was able to open another arena of competition which, if successful, would allow him to gain direct control of the shogunate itself.

The key issue was who would become the next shogun. Among the anti-foreign faction, the preferred candidate was Nariaki's son, Keiki. If Keiki were to become the heir and eventually the shogun, Nariaki and his fol-lowers could dominate the councillors, reform the shogunate, make efforts to keep the West at bay, and generally guide national policy. Ii and his allies naturally opposed this effort.

In early 1858, the domestic and foreign policy disputes between these two factions came to a head. Hotta presented the emperor with a commercial treaty (the Harris Treaty with the United States) for his approval. Usually, the emperor's consent was automatic, but by this time the antiforeign faction and other supporters of Keiki had been able to convince the emperor that signing the treaty was not in Japan's best interests. They convinced him to refuse to approve the treaty. Rebuffed and embarrassed, Hotta fell from power.

Now Ii was given a special opportunity: He was appointed to the position of great councillor in early June. This office was not a regular one in the Tokugawa administration. Someone was appointed to this position only in great crises, and the authority to act decisively accompanied the title. Ii's actions were forceful, even impolitic. By July, Ii determined to push ahead with the signing of the Harris Treaty. He also agreed to sign similar treaties with other Western nations. Determined to protect his political flank, he appointed his own candidate, the Daimyo of Kii, heir to the shogunate. He also filled as many offices with his supporters as opportunity and his authority to force resignations allowed.

Finally, to remove further threats to his authority from Nariaki and others, he began a purge of his opponents. By 1860, he placed Nariaki under house arrest. About seventy people were arrested in all; seven were sentenced to death, and a number of others were either given short-term imprisonment or sentenced to exile. He dismissed other officials who disagreed with him. This aggressive assault on Ii's opponents created an atmosphere of retribution. Although Ii sought to close the rift between the court and the *bakufu*, his opponents moved quickly to secure their own position at the imperial court. They created situations to embarrass Ii politically. Each of these efforts failed and frustration rose among Ii's enemies. His agressive attempts to support his own position created new foes.

Finally, opposition to Ii peaked in the spring of 1860. As he approached the Sakurada Gate of Edo on March 24, his carriage was attacked by a band of dissatisfied warriors, allies of Nariaki. Ii was hauled from his carriage and beheaded on the spot.

Summary

With Ii Naosuke's death, the last major attempt to preserve the traditional Tokugawa political order ended. In the arena of foreign affairs, he had tried to preserve Japan's independence by bending to Western demands enough to keep Westerners from invading Japan. Domestically, Ii sought to protect the traditional authority of the shogun, and he refused to grant additional authority to the emperor or the domains.

All Ii's efforts failed to stem the crescendo of anti-*bakufu* criticism. Had Ii defended the *bakufu's* prerogatives less vigorously, the Tokugawa shogunate ultimately might have been able to compromise effectively with its critics and Tokugawa rule might have continued for more than another decade.

Contrary to his expectations, Ii's purges did not still the opposition but merely created more and deeper opposition to his policies. By 1868, four domains led a direct military assault on the *bakufu* and established a new, fully centralized government, which set Japan on the road to international preeminence.

Bibliography
Alcock, Rutherford. *The Capital of the Tycoon: A Narrative of a Three Years' Residence in Japan.* 2 vols. Reprint. Westport, Conn.: Greenwood Press, 1969. A widely available account of life and politics in late Tokugawa Japan by a British diplomat.
Lee, Edwin Borden. *The Political Career of Ii Naosuke.* New York: Columbia University Press, 1960. Lee argues that Ii was a patriot who temporarily fought off those who sought to compromise the authority of the *bakufu* and who pragmatically dealt with the problems posed by Perry's arrival and the advent of the "unequal treaty" system.
McMaster, John. "Alcock and Harris: Foreign Diplomacy in *Bakumatsu* Japan." *Monumenta Nipponica* 22 (1967): 305-367. Diplomatic negotiations from the Western side, as seen by a British and an American ambassador. McMaster discusses the broader international context (economic and political) in which the negotiations took place and provides some sense of the military threat Japan faced.
Totman, Conrad. "From *Sakoku* to *Kaikoku*: The Transformation of Foreign-Policy Attitudes, 1853-1868." *Monumenta Nipponica* 35 (1980): 1-19. A general reassessment of Japanese attitudes toward intercourse with the West. Totman suggests that at first loyalists and defenders of the *bakufu* shared the same goal for Japanese foreign policy—keeping foreign contacts to a minimum—but that they disagreed over the means. The ultimate victory of internationalization was the result of a change in fundamental Japanese perceptions of what was good for Japan, not the result of the ascendancy of a favorably disposed faction over isolationists.
Webb, Herschel. *The Japanese Imperial Institution in the Tokugawa Period.* New York: Columbia University Press, 1968. Chapter 4, "The Throne in Politics," analyzes the increased use of the emperor by the anti-Tokugawa forces. Ii's conflict with the imperial loyalists is discussed.

Philip C. Brown

JEAN-AUGUSTE-DOMINIQUE INGRES

Born: August 29, 1780; Montauban, near Toulouse, France
Died: January 14, 1867; Paris, France
Area of Achievement: Art
Contribution: Ingres championed sound draftsmanship and inspiration from
  Greek civilization. His idealized figures and flawless surfaces set an un-
  equaled standard in the first half of the nineteenth century. In elevating
  aesthetic form and personal expression above orthodoxy, Ingres inadver-
  tently became one of the earliest examples of art for art's sake, a concept
  which became important for the later modern movements.

Early Life

Jean-August-Dominique Ingres was born into a family of modest means in
Montauban in southern France. Ingres' father, Joseph, originally from nearby
Toulouse, practiced painting, sculpture, and architecture, but without much
notice. He encouraged his young son to study the arts in general and gave
him lessons in drawing, voice, and violin. By the age of eleven, Ingres was
taking instruction in art at the Museum-du-Midi, Toulouse, under Jean Briant,
a landscape painter. Not long after that, he entered the Académie de Toulouse to study painting with Guillaume-Joseph Roques and sculpture from
Jean-Pierre Vigan. During this period, Ingres did not neglect his music
studies.

In 1797, when barely seventeen, Ingres left Toulouse with the son of his
first instructor and traveled to Paris. Once there, Ingres was no doubt immediately recognizable as coming from the south of France, since he was short,
round-faced, and had an olive complexion. Eventually, his stiff posture and
deliberate walk suggested a slight arrogance. Ingres entered the studio of
Jacques-Louis David, the greatest French talent of the time. This formal
association lasted at least three years, wherein Ingres was thoroughly exposed to David's brand of neoclassicism in both topical works and commissioned portraits. Their approaches to eighteenth century classicism in art
diverged when Ingres' studio apprenticeship ended. David subscribed to a
type of painting activity whose content addressed contemporary issues and
moral questions, as he hoped to influence political action. His figures and
their settings, however, recalled the Greek republican era. Ingres, by contrast, was generally apolitical and content to explore and alter classical form
as a satisfying concept in itself.

In 1800, he competed unsuccessfully for a Prix de Rome. The following
year, he earned the coveted award, only to wait five more years in Paris as a
result of unfavorable political events in Rome. Nevertheless, Ingres did not
languish. Provided with studio space and a modest stipend, he delved into
the art of past eras, especially antiquity. Surprisingly, Ingres' classical edu-

cation to that point was poor, including a near-total deficiency in Greek and Latin. He began to correct his shortcomings by accumulating a modest library, including Greek and Latin poetry and books whose illustrations attracted him because of their special qualities of line.

Ingres traveled to Rome in 1806 to begin his postponed official stay of four years, but remained at the École de Rome for an additional ten years. The sixteen-year period was productive and was marked by several large commissions from Napoleon I for the Quirinale Palace, paintings sent from Rome as submissions to the annual Paris Salon, and stunning portraits of the French colony in Rome, which were characterized by stylization and purity.

Serious financial constraints, however, developed with the fall of the French Empire, the withdrawal of many in the French colony, and Ingres' first marriage. Collectively, these factors led to Ingres' initiation of graphite portraits as a speculative enterprise. This time, the resident English population in Rome provided Ingres with the majority of models, a number of whom were set in family compositions using a vitalistic line and almost no modeling. Already evident in these works is his preference for refined and delicate contour lines verging on the precious.

Ingres spent the years 1820 to 1824 in Florence, gathering data for a religious commission. While there, he came upon the works of Italian primitives which were either unknown or disdained in official circles at the time. These paintings, and the refinement he found in those of the centuries-earlier School of Fountainbleau, surfaced as influences in several quasi-historical genre paintings of that time, such as *Roger Freeing Angelica* (1819), *The Death of Leonardo da Vinci in the Arms of Francis I* (c. 1819), and *The Vow of Louis XIII* (1824).

Life's Work

Ingres returned to Paris at the end of 1824 and opened a studio which welcomed both commissions and students. He received both quickly. The return was a triumph, and official recognition, which he courted, came quickly too. By 1825, Ingres was awarded the Legion of Honor after experiencing salon success the previous year with *The Vow of Louis XIII*. The next year, he received a major commission for a ceiling painting in the new extension of the Louvre. It was known as *The Apotheosis of Homer*; its format conception was unusual, since it was destined for a ceiling but painted as an upright easel picture since Ingres sought to avoid traditional Baroque foreshortening devices.

Though this painting was received without enthusiasm in the 1827 Salon, it was quite important to the artist as a defense of the classical tradition in art and, more acutely, as his participation in the neoclassical movement was threatened by the rise of the Romantic movement in painting. In *The Apotheosis of Homer*, Ingres assembled great men of the past and present, paying tribute to the ancient Greek poet Homer. In fact, it is a group portrait of fine arts luminaries most admired by Ingres, a catalog of his tastes, and, hence, his influences.

Ancient admirers of Homer occupy a raised forecourt in a handsome Ionic peripteral colonnaded temple. At the center of that assembly sits Homer, being crowned by a winged victory figure, enthroned atop a stone base. Seated respectfully below Homer are personifications of the *Iliad* and the *Odyssey.* More recent homage bearers occupy the steps and orchestra pit and include Dante, Raphael, Michelangelo, Nicolas Poussin, Jean Racine, William Shakespeare, Wolfgang Amadeus Mozart, and Joseph Haydn. The overall composition was derived from Raphael's *Parnassus* and confirms Ingres' clear debt to the High Renaissance master. Just as important, Ingres valued Raphael as the last of a line of Italian Renaissance primitives, including Fra Filippo Lippi, Sandro Botticelli, and Petro Perugino, in whose art he saw naïveté and mannered grace in contrast to artists after Raphael, in whom Ingres perceived decadence.

The artist's fear concerning the rise of Romanticism and the decline of classicism did not subside upon completion of *The Apotheosis of Homer.* Ingres immediately assessed the varied directions in his oeuvre and returned to ideas explored in his École de Rome period. One resulting desire was to reinstate academic studies of the nude to a position of official and critical acceptance, but the climate for that had passed. Ingres did the next best thing; he added figures and occasionally drama to early works and amplified projects once shelved. A brief examination of the artist's reworked themes easily establishes his intentions for the nude.

Prominent among the rethought paintings is *Oedipus Solving the Riddle of the Sphinx* (1808), an appealing study of a male nude in an acceptable antique pose with a respectably engaging myth as a foil for the artist's interest in human form. By 1827, it was enlarged and altered by the addition of a Theban in the background fleeing Oedipus' audacity in terror. The Theban's fright contrasts dramatically to the poise and concentration of Oedipus. The work was a salon success in 1827, but it typified a problem in European academic art of the time. Serious artists attached to the human form had to place their figures in historical, biblical, or mythological scenes lest the compositions be criticized as vulgar by salon juries. The attitude became entrenched, discouraging innovation while demanding technical excellence. Almost by default, it encouraged a glut of uninspired formula art. Fortunately, Ingres avoided academic mediocrity by building a career of fresh invention.

Even more of a testament to Ingres' faith in classicism was the ambitious work *Antiochus and Stratonice*, begun in 1807 and thoroughly transformed in the 1830's. The subject, originally told by Plutarch, was familiar to Ingres and his contemporaries in painting and theater during their student years in

Paris and Rome. Ingres' second version illustrated the moment when a physician diagnosed the bedridden Antiochus' illness (by a racing pulse) as passion for his stepmother, Stratonice.

Ingres spent six years on the painting in Italy, where he had accepted the directorship of the École de Rome. The artist did so after being rejected by the Salon of 1834, vowing not to submit again. He researched the correct period setting, documented local color, constructed the convincing illusion of a three-dimensional interior with an air of gravity yet style, and tested forty-five times the gesture of Antiochus shielding himself from the near-fatal view of Stratonice. In 1840, the tenaciously constructed painting was shown privately in Paris at the Palais Royal, where it was a critical success, one which set the stage for Ingres' triumphant return to the capital city the next year.

Throughout his career, Ingres was obsessed with the potential of the female form for serene grace, especially the undraped female form. By the 1830's and 1840's, he was reworking single figures and groups devoted to sensuality. *The Bathing Woman*, a small half-torso study of 1807, and *The Valpincon Bather* of 1808 were the first of a long series of those expressions. In both pictures, the models are viewed discreetly, with turned heads and long, curved backs. A full-length, reclining nude also viewed from the back was used in 1814 for *The Grand Odalisque*, a statement of languid beauty and fantasized oriental exoticism, complete with feathers, silks, fur, jewelry, and incense.

In 1839, Ingres returned to the motif of the reposing nude in an oriental world. Entitled *Odalisque with the Slave*, the work benefited from a study of Persian miniatures and exotic bric-a-brac. Ingres' careerlong obsession with pliant female nudes culminated with *The Turkish Bath* of 1863, four years before the artist's death. The tondo-framed painting presents some two dozen nudes in a harem, bathing, lounging aimlessly, or admiring themselves.

There was at least one more vital aspect to Ingres' fascination with women, namely portraiture, especially of the rising middle class that dominated French society by the mid-1850's. As with the nudes, Ingres found helpful precedents in his own early work, for example, the 1805 portraits of Madame and Mademoiselle Rivière. Ingres' major portraits of the last phase of his career include the *Vicomtesse d'Haussonville* (1845), the *Baronne de Rothschild* (1848), two interpretations of Madame Moitessier in 1851 and 1856, and *Princess de Broglie* (1856). Collectively, the portraits project sensuality, a sense of power, the deceit of informality borrowed from David, and certainly the artist's love of flesh, hair, lush fabrics, patterns, and jewelry. These captivating women seem suitably dressed to receive visitors or to attend a ball.

When Ingres returned to Paris in 1841, he was immediately the honoree of a banquet with 426 guests presided over by the Marquis de Pastoret, plus a concert organized by the composer Hector Berlioz. More honors and commissions followed. One year before his death, Ingres bequeathed to the city of Montauban a collection of his own paintings and drawings, plus prints, books, Etruscan sarcophagi, Greek vases, and musical scores. In return, the city of his birth established the Musée Ingres in 1869 in his honor.

Summary

Jean-Auguste-Dominique Ingres reached a position of prestige and professional success enjoyed by few other artists active from the Renaissance through the nineteenth century. Yet his life and art were full of contradictions and paradoxes. For example, constantly acclaimed as the chief exponent of neoclassicism, he was actually one player in a larger heterogeneous artistic and literary community known as Romanticism. Furthermore, despite his adamant positions supporting classicism and academic techniques, his art could be just as arbitrary as that of his primary rival, Eugène Delacroix, leader of the Romantic movement in painting. Ingres, the neoclassicist, mastered historical genre painting, religious themes, and realistic portraiture. He managed to stay in official favor through the successive regimes of Napoleon I, the Bourbon Restoration, the Civil Wars of 1830 and 1848 and Napoleon III, though he detested change. Perhaps part of his genius is tied to his refusal to be locked into historical time. After all, he refused to change with the prevailing winds of art throughout his life.

The artist professed to copy nature, stressing drawing as the first commandment of high art, using live models, and emphasizing the contours of forms. Yet, as if he were blinded by an obsession for human form, his figures frequently had suspect proportions, extra vertebrae, and rubbery necks. To Ingres, distortions and a mannered anatomy were justified in the service of his uppermost aims: first, the expression of mankind's feelings and situations, second, the attempt to place hybrid people in an idealized nature at once divine and within the measure of contemporary existence.

Bibliography

Condon, Patricia, et al. *Ingres, in Pursuit of Perfection: The Art of J.-A.-D. Ingres*. Louisville: J. B. Speed Art Museum, 1983. A superbly crafted and highly didactic exhibition catalog. Draws together many versions and studies of works unlikely to have been seen in the United States until this exhibit and publication. Illustrations are of excellent quality and satisfying in number. The thoughtful appendix summarizing the artist's ancient and contemporary themes, plus the exhaustive separate indexes listing the artist's works by subject, location, medium, date provenance, and exhibition, are extraordinary.

Cummings, Frederick J., et al. *French Painting, 1774-1830: The Age of*

Revolution. Detroit: Wayne State University Press, 1975. This 712-page
book serves as a necessary aid in comprehending a blockbuster exhibition
devoted to major and minor painters grouped under four historical periods:
Louis XVI, Napoleon I, the Bourbon Restoration, and Napoleon III. Cummings and other authors weave events in art, politics, and intellectual
thought and re-create the concept of period styles.
Ingres, Jean-Auguste-Dominique. *Ingres*. Text by Jon Whiteley. London:
Oresko Books, 1977. A relatively brief but well-prepared and well-
illustrated overview of the artist's major themes. Seventy carefully chosen
works representing Ingres' lengthy career comprise the plate portion.
Eight appear in acceptable color. Most valuable are the well-researched
and easily read notes adjacent to the illustrations.
_____. *Ingres*. Text by Georges Wildenstein. London: Phaidon
Press, 1954, 2d ed. 1956. Part of Phaidon's French Art series, this work
contains a concise examination of the artist's natural gifts and the goals he
set for them as well as a discussion of his techniques. The chronology of
Ingres' life is lengthy and detailed. The plate section of two hundred
images, including good details, is highlighted by six key works in color.
Picon, Gaëton. *Ingres: A Biographical and Critical Study*. Translated by
Stuart Gilbert. 2d ed. New York: Rizzoli, 1980. A large-format, hand-
somely produced monograph. Easily understood by professionals outside
the field of art. The selected bibliography is extensive. The chronologically thorough listing of Ingres' exhibitions up to 1980 will assist serious
students.

Tom Dewey II

IVAN THE GREAT

Born: January 22, 1440; Moscow, Russia
Died: October 27, 1505; Moscow, Russia
Areas of Achievement: Government and politics
Contribution: Ivan the Great laid the foundation for the political centraliza-
tion and territorial unification of the Russian national state and the consol-
idation and growth of imperial autocracy. Known in the history of Russia
as "the gatherer of the Russian lands," he united all the Slavic independent and semi-independent principalities and cities under the aegis of the
Muscovite rulers and began the long struggle with Poland-Lithuania and
Sweden for recovering Russia's "historical" lands of the Ukraine, White
Russia, and the Baltic States. Ivan was also the Grand Prince of Muscovy
who ended Russia's 240 years of Mongol or Tatar rule and proclaimed the
independence of his country.

Early Life

Ivan III Vasilyevich, better known as Ivan the Great, Grand Prince of
Muscovy, was born in Moscow on January 22, 1440. He was the son of
Grand Prince Vasily II and Maria Yaroslavna. Vasily's reign was beset from
the beginning by a series of savage civil wars with his rebellious uncles and
cousins, who contested the throne of Muscovy. One of Vasily's uncles,
Prince Yury, defeated him in 1433 and assumed the title of grand prince.
When Yury died in 1434, one of his sons, Dmitri Shemyaka, claimed the
throne, arrested Vasily, blinded him, and sent him into exile. The young
Ivan, only six years old, was also seized by agents of Shemyaka and jailed
with his father. Vasily, however, recovered his throne in 1447 and, despite
being blind, ruled for another fifteen years.

Throughout the remainder of Vasily's reign, Ivan was closely associated
with his father's administration. The blind Vasily assigned to him many of
the daily duties and tasks of his government, providing him with valuable
experience and political training in the affairs of the state. At the age of
nine, Ivan was proclaimed grand prince and coruler in order to eliminate any
question as to the succession to the throne. When Ivan was twelve years old,
his father arranged, perhaps for political considerations, the marriage of his
son to Maria, the daughter of the Grand Prince of Tver. In 1452, Ivan was at
the head of an army that defeated his father's enemy, Shemyaka. In 1458,
Ivan was in charge of a successful military campaign against the Tatars to
the south. Upon the death of his father on March 27, 1462, Ivan ascended
the throne as Grand Prince and Sovereign of Moscow at age twenty-two.

Life's Work

Ivan's reign was characterized by a series of foreign and domestic threats, all of which he was able to overcome. He proved to be a remarkable ruler of Russia, a man of unusual political foresight and bold accomplishments. Ivan was endowed with extraordinary energy and native intelligence. He was persistent, calculating, and, at the same time, excessively cautious, secretive, and cunning to the extreme. He often avoided taking chances and was hesitant of drastic measures. Instead, he preferred to achieve his goal within the limits of his own power and resources. He employed discretion, calmly tolerated delays—often breaking his word—and used sinuous diplomacy, of which he proved to be a Machiavellian master. These attributes made him secure of himself and brought him many victories, for which he earned the appellation "the Great."

Ivan's major objective was to transform the small and often contested role of the principality of Moscow into the political center of a unified Russian state. He achieved this task through conquest, diplomacy, the purchasing of land, annexation, and voluntary surrender of independent and semi-independent Russian principalities and free cities. He replaced the regional political fragmentation with a strong centralized administrative state. By the end of Ivan's reign, he had gathered all the Russian territories under the rule of the Muscovite grand prince and had incorporated them into the Muscovite state, increasing its territory from 150,000 square miles to nearly 400,000 square miles at the beginning of the sixteenth century.

At the time of Ivan's accession to the throne, there were four major principalities independent of Moscow—Yaroslavl, Rostov, Tver, and Ryazan—and three city-states—the republic of Novgorod the Great, Vyatka, and Pskov. The principalities of Yaroslavl and Rostov were among the least independent Russian lands. By the treaties of 1463 and 1474, they were both formally annexed to Moscow.

Ivan's most important acquisition was the ancient city-republic of Novgorod the Great and its extensive colonies to the northeast. The republic of Novgorod preserved its independence for many centuries from both the Mongols and the Teutonic knights. Since the fifteenth century, however, Novgorod vacillated between Moscow and Poland-Lithuania. The Princes of Moscow viewed Novgorod's relations with these Catholic states with suspicion and distrust. When a pro-Lithuanian party turned to Casimir IV, King of Poland and Grand Prince of Lithuania, seeking to select as their prince a Lithuanian, Ivan III turned against the Novgorodians, accused them of apostasy, invaded the city in the spring of 1471, and imposed upon them a treaty that bound the city closer to Moscow. Within a few years, however, the Novgorodians broke the terms of the treaty and a pro-Polish party turned again to Poland-Lithuania. This new development forced Ivan to attack the city in 1478 for a second time, and to order the annexation of its territory to Moscow, the confiscation of church lands, and finally the deportation and exile of hundreds of prominent noble families, confiscation of their estates, and parceling out of these lands to individuals of lower classes conditional on military service. Ivan's acts signaled the end of Novgorod's independence.

The principality of Tver was the second most important of Ivan's acquisitions. For centuries, Tver had been Moscow's chief contender for control of Russia. When the Grand Prince of Tver, Mikhail, concluded a political alliance with Lithuania in 1483, Ivan used this act as an excuse to invade Tver and officially annex it. The city of Vyatka, a former colony of Novgorod, was annexed in 1489. Finally, the principalities of Ryazan and Pskov came under Moscow's control, but they were annexed by Ivan's son and successor, Vasily III, in 1521.

In the area of foreign affairs, Ivan was successful against both the Tatars to the east and the Poles and Lithuanians to the west. The Tatars, who established the Golden Horde in the southeastern part of Russia, remained potentially the most dangerous adversaries since the thirteenth century. Yet in the second half of the fifteenth century, the Golden Horde broke up into the independent khanates of Kazan, Astrakhan, and the Crimea. Ivan's goal was not only to terminate Moscow's nominal subservience to the Khan of the Golden Horde but also to secure the southeastern boundaries of his realm from further attacks and incursions by the Tatar forces, and to allow him to focus his attention on his principal task: the recovery of the Russian historical lands from Poland-Lithuania.

The friction between Moscow and the Golden Horde came to a head in 1480, when Khan Akhmed concluded an alliance with Poland-Lithuania and staged an attack on Moscow on the grounds that Ivan refused to pay him the customary annual tribute. The Russian and Tatar armies met on the opposite banks of the Ugra River in the fall of 1480. For more than two months, neither Akhmed nor the Russians attempted to attack each other. After waiting for the arrival of the Lithuanian and the Polish armies (who failed to appear), Akhmed suddenly withdrew his troops without giving a battle. In this rather unheroic manner, Ivan terminated Moscow's 240 years of Mongol domination. Ivan also organized military campaigns against the Tatar khanate of Kazan to the southeast of Moscow. In 1487, Ivan captured the khanate and placed on its throne a Tatar vassal ruler, further stabilizing the southeastern boundaries of his realm for some time to come, until it was finally annexed by Ivan IV in the 1550's. Ivan maintained friendly relations with the Tatar khan of Crimea and the Ottoman sultan. In 1480, he signed a treaty with the Crimean leader, Mengli Giray, against the Golden Horde and Poland. Though the Crimean Tatars remained unreliable allies, their hostility toward Lithuania and Poland helped Ivan in his plan to recover the ancient territory of Kievan Russia. In 1494, Ivan seized the town of Vyazma and annexed it to Moscow. A year later, he concluded a truce and entered into dynastic relations with the Grand Prince Alexander of Lithuania by offering his daughter in marriage. This arrangement, however, did not prevent Ivan from going to war with his son-in-law in 1500, on the grounds that his Orthodox subjects had allegedly been persecuted by the Catholic church. When the war ended in 1503, Ivan captured much of the western Russian lands, except the cities of Kiev and Smolensk.

Finally, Ivan faced the growing power of Sweden, a perennial adversary of the Russians since the thirteenth century. In 1493, Ivan and the King of Denmark signed an alliance against Sweden. The same year, Ivan went to war against Sweden, trying to gain control of Finland and the Baltic States. The Swedes, however, retaliated and attacked northern Russia, forcing Ivan to sign a truce in 1497. It was left to Peter the Great to break the power of Sweden in the eighteenth century.

Ivan's successes to the east against the Tatar khanates made Moscow the most powerful state on the Eurasia steppes by replacing the Golden Horde. His victories over Lithuania brought him into direct contact with Europe, and its sovereigns began to view him as a powerful and independent ruler. At the same time, Moscow gradually increased its economic and cultural ties with the West. In 1472, after the death of his first wife, Ivan married Zoë Palaeologus, better known by her Orthodox name of Sophia, the niece of the last Byzantine emperor. The marriage of Sophia to Ivan was arranged, strangely enough, by Pope Paul II, who hoped to bring the Russian Orthodox church under the orbit of the Roman Catholic church. Ivan remained faithful to his orthodoxy, however, and used the marriage to the Byzantine princess to buttress the prestige and power of the Muscovite ruler. To underscore the importance of his new position, he adopted the double-headed black eagle of Byzantium to his family coat of arms, called himself autocrat, or *samoder-zhets*—an imitation of the Byzantine emperors—and added the complex Byzantine court ceremonies to his own. Ivan was also the first Russian ruler to use the title of "czar" (Latin caesar) and "sovereign of all Russia." Moscow would henceforth claim to be the "Third Rome" after the fall of Constantinople in 1453, and the imperial idea became part of Russia's messianic tradition to modern times.

In his internal policy, Ivan was largely responsible for the administrative system he introduced, which lasted until the seventeenth century. He reformed the local government by introducing the system known as *kormlenie*, or "feeding" system. This administrative innovation called for the appointment of district and provincial governors, who were charged with collecting taxes and custom duties for the grand prince, running the army and local militia, and administering justice. The governors were practically supported by taxes they extracted from the local population, thus the meaning of the term "feeding."

Ivan further suppressed and weakened the power of appanage princes, eliminated their separatist tendencies, and confiscated their landholdings. He replaced the hereditary aristocracy and created a new service system, known as *pomestie*. Under this system the officials of the grand prince were granted land in return for military service. This new development led, in turn, to the formation of a new social class, the service gentry, or *dvorianstvo*. This service class became the core of Russia's military power and the staunch supporter of autocracy. Ivan reformed the executive organs of the central government. At the end of the fifteenth century, the first bureaus, known as *prikazy*, were established and were in charge of the various departments of the grand prince's government and run by secretaries. Ivan also improved the system of justice. In 1497, he issued the first code of law, called *Sudebnik*. The code provided a uniform legal system and court procedure for the entire territory of the Muscovite realm. The law also outlined the rules and obligations of the peasants to their landlords, placing the first restrictions on their freedom to move about the land, as the gentry class demanded more peasant labor to till their land. These restrictions foreshadowed the beginning of serfdom in Russia.

During the last years of Ivan's reign, the Russian Orthodox church underwent a serious inner crisis. There was growing opposition to the vast accumulation of wealth and land by the Church and by monasteries. A group, called *strigolniki*, a religious sect known as Judaizers, and a minority of churchmen called the Trans-Volga Elders or "Non-Possessors," led by Nil Sorsky, criticized high prelates, monastic life, rituals, liturgy, icon worship, moral corruption, and simony within the Church. The majority of the conservative hierarchy of the Church, led by Joseph Sanin, defended the church and monastic lands, condemned the reformers, supported the divine right of autocracy, and asked Ivan to suppress and persecute the reformers as heretics. Ivan pondered for some time upon the growing power of the Church that appeared a rival of the state and would have sided with the Trans-Volga Elders and secularized the church lands, but, at the Church Council of 1503, he yielded to the demands of the Josephites and condemned the critics as heretics. At that point, Ivan was greatly concerned with family rivalry over the question of succession to the throne. He yielded to his wife, Sophia, and bestowed upon his son Vasily the title grand prince and asked the boyars to swear allegiance to him. In the meantime, the khanate of Kazan broke away from Moscow's subservience, and the Lithuanian War ended in 1503 rather inconclusively, as Ivan failed to recover all the Russian historical lands in the West. Two years later, on October 27, 1505, Ivan died at the age of sixty-five, unlamented and apparently unloved by his own people. He was succeeded by his son Vasily.

Summary

Ivan the Great was an outstanding ruler. His reign marked a turning point in the history of Russia from the medieval to the modern age. He built up and created modern Russia. By gathering the Russian lands around the principality of Moscow, Ivan strengthened the power of the central government and increased the role and prestige of the Muscovite state and its ruler, both at home and abroad. Indeed, Ivan's diplomatic, political, military, and administrative achievements were comparable to those of his contemporaries Louis IX of France, Henry VII of England, and Ferdinand II and Isabella I of Spain. Ivan was the first to encourage economic and cultural relations with the West and invited foreign craftsmen and artisans to Moscow, among them the noted Italian architect Aristotle Fioravanti, who built the famous Assumption (Uspenski) Cathedral in the Kremlin and other Italian-style palaces. Contacts with the Europeans convinced Ivan that Russia could learn from the West and that Russia could borrow its technical knowledge in order to strengthen its new position and compete successfully with other states. At the same time, Ivan protected and defended the Orthodox faith from Roman Catholicism and made the institution of the Church the loyal supporter and advocate of Russian autocracy. In more than one way, Ivan's accomplishments determined the course that Russia was to follow. He was the first to forge the great beginnings of Russia, which was destined to become a great European power. His appellation of "the Great" is deserved.

Bibliography
Fennel, J. L. I. "The Attitude of the Josephians and the Trans-Volga Elders to the Heresy of the Judaisers." In *Slavonic and East European Review* 29 (June, 1951): 486-509. An inquiry into the different views of supporters of Sanin and the reformers of Sorsky toward the religious sect of the Judaizers.
_____. *Ivan the Great of Moscow*. New York: St. Martin's Press, 1962. The most complete and detailed study of all aspects of Ivan's reign in any language. The author emphasizes Ivan's foreign policy, diplomatic methods, and military campaigns in the Russo-Lithuanian War. Contains an extensive and valuable bibliography.
Grey, Ian. *Ivan III and the Unification of Russia*. New York: Collier, 1964. This is a well-written, detailed biography by a writer and biographer whose other work includes an account of Ivan the Terrible. Discusses the process of the unification of the Russian lands under the Muscovite princes, the wars and military campaigns against domestic and foreign enemies, and the emergence of the Grand Prince of Moscow as the leader of a strong and unified Russian state. Contains an index and brief bibliography.
Soloviev, Sergei M. *History of Russia: The Reign of Ivan III the Great*. Edited and translated by John D. Windhausen. Gulf Breeze, Fla.: Academic International Press, 1979. A very important study of Ivan's reign by a great, "classic" Russian historian. Soloviev discusses Ivan's campaigns against Novgorod the Great, the acquisition of the various Russian prin-

cipalities, his wars with the Eastern khanates, and Sophia and her influence in Russia.

_____. *History of Russia: Russian Society in the Age of Ivan III.* Translated and edited by John D. Windhausen. Gulf Breeze, Fla.: Academic International Press, 1979. A continuation of the previous work. Includes chapters on Ivan's wars with Lithuania and Livonia and a discussion of Russian society under Ivan.

Vernadsky, George. *Russia at the Dawn of the Modern Age.* New Haven, Conn.: Yale University Press, 1959. The most complete account and interpretation of Ivan's reign by an expert on the history of Russia. Vernadsky argues that Sophia had little influence in the court or upon Ivan. Contains an extensive bibliography of Russian works.

James J. Farsolas

IVAN THE TERRIBLE

Born: August 25, 1530; Moscow, Russia
Died: March 18, 1584; Moscow, Russia
Areas of Achievement: Politics and government
Contribution: Of all the Russian czars, Ivan contributed the most in giving shape to Russian autocracy as it would exist until the end of serfdom in 1861. He also conquered Kazan and Astrakhan, significantly reducing the Tatar threat and securing the important trade routes in the Volga region, and took the first steps toward the incorporation of Siberia.

Early Life

Ivan the Terrible was born in the Kremlin Palace in Moscow on August 25, 1530. His father, Vasily III, had married Ivan's mother, Princess Elena Glinskaya, when his first wife failed to provide him an heir. Vasily died in 1533, leaving the three-year-old Ivan to be reared in the world of Kremlin politics marked by violence, intrigues, and unashamed struggles for power among the hereditary nobles (boyar) and princely families. In order to forestall any threat to Ivan's succession, especially from his two uncles, Ivan was immediately declared as the next ruler. Under Muscovite law and custom, it was his mother who now exercised power as the regent. Although the next five years, until Elena's death in 1538, were normal years for Ivan, the Kremlin politics were far from normal. Elena faced threats from her husband's two brothers, forcing her to order their arrest and imprisonment. Even her own uncle, Mikhail Glinsky, on whom she had relied in the beginning, appeared too ambitious; he suffered the same fate as the others.

Elena's death in 1538 opened a new chapter in young Ivan's life. Within a week of his mother's death, his nanny, Agrafena Chelyadina, who had provided him with loving care and affection, was taken away. The Kremlin now reverberated with the intrigues and counterintrigues, especially of two princely families, the Shuiskys and the Belskys. Power changed hands more than once. The first round went to the Shuiskys. Of the two brothers, Vasily and Ivan Shuisky, who exercised power through the boyar Duma in succession, the latter made a special point of neglecting and insulting Ivan and his brother. Ivan later recalled that Ivan Shuisky once "sat on a bench, leaning with his elbows on our father's bed and with his legs upon a chair, and he did not even incline his head towards us . . . nor was there any element of deference to be found in his attitude toward us." Then, when power had passed to the Belskys and Ivan Shuisky was trying to regain it, Ivan had the horrifying experience of Shuisky's men breaking into his bedchamber in the night in search of the metropolitan. Ivan thus developed deep hatred for the boyars, especially for the Shuiskys, who now once again controlled power. Andrey Shuisky, who became the leader of this group after Ivan

Shuisky's illness, imposed a reign of increased corruption and terror. Ivan, in a bold move in 1543, when he was only thirteen years old, ordered Prince Andrey to be arrested and brutally killed.

During these early years, Ivan not only witnessed cruel acts perpetrated around him that implanted fear and suspicion of boyars in his young heart but also engaged in such acts himself for fun and pleasure. Torturing all kinds of animals, riding through the Moscow streets knocking down the young and the old, including women and children, and engaging in orgies became his pastime.

Ivan, especially under the guidance of Metropolitan Makary, also read the Scriptures and became the first really literate Russian ruler. Some scholars have cast doubt on this, challenging the authenticity of his correspondence with Prince Andrey Kurbsky after the defection of his once-trusted adviser to Lithuania, but most evidence suggests that Ivan became a well-read person. In Makary, Ivan also found support for his belief in his role as an absolute ruler whose power was derived from God.

Toward the end of 1546, when he was still sixteen, Ivan decided to have himself crowned as czar. He also decided to search for a bride from his own realm. Although his grandfather, Ivan III, had used the title of the czar, Ivan IV was the first to be so crowned in a glittering ceremony in Moscow on January 16, 1547. On February 3, he was married to Anastasia Romanovna Zakharina, of a boyar family. She was to provide him fourteen years of happy married life and to serve as a calming influence on his impulsive personality.

Life's Work

The first part of Ivan's rule as Russia's czar was marked by several important reforms. He hated the boyars but did not try to dismantle the boyar Duma at this time; instead, he created a chosen council consisting of some of his close advisers that included Metropolitan Makary, Archpriest Silvester, and Aleksey Adashev, a member of the service-gentry class. He also called the *zemskii sobor* (assembly of the land), representing the boyars and the service gentry as well as the townspeople, the clergy, and some state peasants.

A major drawback that adversely affected the fighting capacity of the Russian army was the system known as *mestnichestvo*, by which the appointments to top positions were based on the birth and rank of various boyars, not on their ability to command and fight. As he had done with the boyar Duma, Ivan did not end the system but provided for exceptions in case of special military campaigns. He also created regular infantry detachments known as the *streltsy*, to be paid by the state and to serve directly under the czar, and he regularized the terms and conditions under which a nobleman was expected to serve in the army. These steps greatly enhanced the army's fighting ability.

Some reforms in the system of local self-government were also undertaken in order to make it more efficient, especially for the purpose of tax collection. A collection and codification of laws resulted in the law code of 1550. A church council, the Hundred Chapters Council (for the hundred questions submitted to it), seriously undertook the question of reform in the Russian Orthodox church. Ivan, though not successful in secularizing church lands, was able to limit the church's power to acquire new lands which, in the future, could be done only with the czar's consent.

This early period of reform also saw the establishment of important trade links between Russia and England. In search of a northeastern passage to China, the English explorer Richard Chancellor found himself in the White Sea. Ivan warmly received him in Moscow and granted the English important trading privileges, hoping to acquire arms and support from the English against Ivan's European adversaries in his drive to find a foothold on the Baltic coast.

This earlier period of reforms was also marked by important successes in foreign policy. Although the long Mongolian domination over Russia had come to an end during the reign of Ivan's grandfather, Ivan III, the Mongolian khanates in the East and South still created problems. Their rulers undertook occasional raids against Moscow and the Muscovite territories. Ivan finally decided to undertake a military campaign to conquer the Kazan khanate in the upper Volga region. After some initial setbacks, he succeeded in capturing and annexing the whole khanate in 1557. While the Mongolian rule in Ivan III's time had ended without a major fight, the bloody battle at Kazan, with heavy casualties on both sides, came as a sweet revenge for the Russians. Ivan followed this by conquering Astrakhan in the south, thus acquiring the whole Volga region that now provided access to the Caspian Sea.

At this midpoint in his reign, Ivan experienced some unusual developments that reinforced his suspicion and hatred for the boyars. The result was the start of one of the bloodiest chapters in Russian history, during which thousands of people were tortured and executed. During his brief but serious illness in 1553, Ivan had asked various princes and boyars to take an oath of loyalty to his infant son, Dmitry. To his surprise and horror, he found that not everyone was ready to do so, including some of his closest advisers such as Silvester. Then, the dispute arose over Ivan's desire to engage in a war in the north to acquire territories on the Baltic coast from the Livonian Order of the German Knights. While Ivan decided to embark on the Livonian campaign in 1558, achieving some initial successes, the war was opposed by several members of the chosen council who noted the difficulties of fighting a two-front war. Finally, his beloved wife, Anastasia, died in 1560, removing a calming and restraining influence from his life.

Apparently deciding to destroy the power of the boyars, the hereditary aristocracy in Russia, Ivan undertook a reign of terror. Some, like Adashev, were thrown in prison, where they died of torture and hunger. Others, like Prince Kurbsky, fled the country and joined Ivan's enemies, further intensifying the czar's suspicions about their loyalty. Ivan, in a well-planned move in December, 1564, suddenly decided to leave Moscow in full daylight with his belongings and settled at nearby Alexandrovskaia Sloboda. In his message to the people of Moscow, he charged the boyars with disloyalty and treason but expressed faith in the ordinary people. As he had calculated, in asking him to return to Moscow, the people agreed to his condition that he should be allowed a free hand in punishing the boyars as well as in creating a separate state for himself that would be outside the jurisdiction of regular laws; this was to be known as *Oprichnina*. Ivan took immediate steps to assign vast tracts of land in the Moscow region and other parts of Russia to this autonomous state. As he did this, his objective seemed somewhat clearer. Much of the land belonged to the boyar families who were now forced to flee and seek land elsewhere. Ivan also selected a band of loyal guards, known as the *oprichniki*, whose number eventually rose to six thousand. They were assigned some of the newly vacated lands with the understanding that they would have the obligation to serve the czar. Thus, they became a part of the expanding service-gentry class.

While the aims of the *Oprichnina* seemed quite rational, what appeared incomprehensible was the excessive use of torture and murder by Ivan and his *oprichniki*. The job of the *oprichniki* was to clear the land of all possible traitors, but they themselves became a scourge of the land, killing and robbing innocent people. Anyone who criticized or opposed Ivan became his victim. Metropolitan Philip, who courageously castigated the czar for loosing these death squads on the Russian people, was thrown into a monastery and later strangled by one of Ivan's men. Ivan's cruelty, which bordered on insanity, was evident in the killings of thousands of innocent people that he personally undertook in Novgorod in 1570 on the suspicion that the territory was planning to defect to Lithuania.

In 1571, when the Crimean Tatars raided Moscow, the *oprichniki* failed to protect it. Instead, Moscow was saved when, in 1572, Russia's regular forces inflicted a crushing defeat on the Tatar army. Ivan then decided to disband *Oprichnina*. The Livonian War, however, did not go well for Ivan. After twenty-five years of fighting, Russia appeared exhausted. When the war ended in 1583, the country had lost all the gains it had made in the initial stages of the war. Indeed, Ivan had stretched himself too far. The end of the Livonian War also marked the end of his reign, as he died in 1584.

Summary

Ivan the Terrible's reign remains one of the most controversial eras in Russian history. There is no doubt that his achievements were many. The victory over Kazan, which Ivan memorialized in the construction of the magnificent St. Basil's Cathedral in Moscow, and the conquest of Astrakhan made available the whole Volga region for Russian trade and because of the exploits of the Cossack leader Yermak Timofey, started Russia on its march into Siberia. Ivan's reforms, undertaken painstakingly and thoughtfully in the earlier period of his reign, provided for a more efficient civil administration and a better fighting force. Without these reforms, his victory over Kazan would not have been possible.

Even his struggle against the hereditary boyars and the resulting expansion of the service-gentry class, essential elements in the strengthening of Russian autocracy, constituted a continuation of the process that had already existed. What makes this period so puzzling is the excessive amount of force, including the use of inhumane torture, freely used by Ivan in order to weaken the power of the boyars. Providing a pathological interpretation, some historians find Ivan a paranoid and his *Oprichnina* the work of a madman. Others, although acknowledging his excessive cruelty, see him not as a madman but as one who had lost his peace of mind and was haunted by an intense feeling of insecurity for himself and his family. Still others point to the fact that if Ivan used excessive force, it was not uncommon in a Europe dominated by the ideas of Niccolò Machiavelli. For them, Ivan, like some of his contemporaries, was a Renaissance prince. Whatever the final judgment may be, Ivan significantly expanded Russian frontiers and gave shape to a Russian autocracy that, in its essential contours, remained unchanged until the Great Reforms undertaken by Alexander II during the 1860's.

Bibliography

Cherniavsky, M. "Ivan the Terrible as Renaissance Prince." *Slavic Review* 27 (March, 1968): 195-211. This article argues that Ivan was no exception in using excessive force against his enemies in a Renaissance Europe dominated by Machiavellian ideas.

Grey, Ian. *Ivan the Terrible*. London: Hodder & Stoughton, 1964. A popular biography that presents an uncritical portrait of Ivan the Terrible. Blame for much of Ivan's cruelty is placed on his opponents. Contains a limited bibliography.

Keenan, Edward. *The Kurbskii-Groznyi Apocrypha*. Cambridge, Mass.: Harvard University Press, 1971. This book challenges the authenticity of Ivan's correspondence with Prince Kurbsky. Keenan's view remains controversial.

Kurbsky, A. M. *The Correspondence Between Prince A. M. Kurbsky and Tsar Ivan IV of Russia, 1564-1579*. Edited and translated by J. L. I. Fennell. Cambridge: Cambridge University Press, 1955. An excellent translation of a valuable but controversial historical source.

_____. *Prince A. M. Kurbsky's History of Ivan IV*. Edited and translated by J. L. I. Fennell. Cambridge: Cambridge University Press, 1965. Written by Prince Kurbsky after his defection, the book describes the events from 1533 to the early 1570's in a most critical manner. Though a valuable historical source, it is a highly partisan study of Ivan's reign.

Platonov, S. F. *Ivan the Terrible*. Edited and translated by Joseph L. Wieczynski. Gulf Breeze, Fla.: Academic International Press, 1974. An excellent translation of a work by a famous Russian historian of the old St. Petersburg school of Russian historiography, which emphasized facts in making historical interpretations. While Platonov does not accept the view of Ivan as paranoid, the book has an introductory part, "In Search of Ivan the Terrible," by Richard Hellie, that does.

Skrynnikov, Ruslan G. *Ivan the Terrible*. Edited and translated by Hugh F. Graham. Gulf Breeze, Fla.: Academic International Press, 1981. A serious and balanced study by a Soviet historian that presents Ivan and his *Oprichnina* in a nonideological framework. Contains a short bibliography of Russian-language books and articles.

Surendra K. Gupta

JACOPO DELLA QUERCIA

Born: c. 1374; probably Siena
Died: October 20, 1438; Siena
Area of Achievement: Art
Contribution: Heir to the late Gothic sculptural style of fourteenth century Italy and influenced by the spatial massing of form found in ancient classical art, Jacopo forged an independent, monumental style of great expressive power. Along with Lorenzo Ghiberti, Donatello, and Nanni di Banco, he is considered one of the most significant sculptors working in the early decades of the Italian Renaissance.

Early Life

While the sculptural commissions executed during Jacopo della Quercia's mature career are amply documented, very little is known about his early life. His father, Piero di Angelo, was a Sienese goldsmith and wood-carver who was married in 1370. Giorgio Vasari, a sixteenth century art historian, has left two versions of Jacopo's life. In the first version, written in 1550, he attributes to Jacopo an equestrian statue of the condotierre (mercenary military leader) Giovanni d'Arco that is now lost but was executed in 1391. To receive such a commission, Jacopo would have to have been at least nineteen years of age, placing his birthdate around 1371. Vasari's second version, written in 1568, claims that Jacopo was sixty-four years of age when he died in 1438, which calculates to a slightly later birthdate. What is known for certain is that by 1401, when Jacopo entered the famous competition for the Florentine baptistery doors commission, he must have been a master sculptor of some renown.

The meaning and origins of the name "della Quercia" is a mystery. He was identified by this name as early as the mid-fifteenth century, but early documents refer to him as "Jacopo di Maestro Piero," after his father, and even later he is occasionally called "Jacopo delle Fonte" in reference to his work on the Fonte Gaia in Siena. It is possible he either inherited the "della Quercia" from his grandfather, or that it refers to a district of Siena where he was born or lived. It is extremely doubtful that it indicates a birthplace outside Siena.

Jacopo's early career is the subject of scholarly conjecture. It is safe to assume that, in the tradition of the time, he received his initial training from his father, who worked as a wood-carver. Piero di Angelo did not carve in stone, however, nor was there much activity in that medium in Siena during the last years of the fourteenth century. It is generally accepted that during the 1490's Jacopo probably traveled to one of the Italian cities where major stone or marble sculptural programs were in progress. The possibilities include Bologna, Milan, or Venice, but theories concerning his activities in any of these cities are purely tentative.

The first firmly documented event in his life is his participation in the competition for the commission to create a set of bronze doors for the baptistery of the cathedral in Florence. Lorenzo Ghiberti won the competition, and Jacopo's bronze relief competition panel has not survived.

In 1403, Jacopo was in Ferrara, where he began an altar for the Silvestri family, completion of which occurred in 1408. A marble Madonna and Child created for this altar is the earliest extant work universally accepted by scholars as being an example of his style. (Earlier works have been attributed to him, but the attributions are controversial.) During these same years, he also traveled to Lucca to execute the sepulchral monument to Ilaria del Carretto-Guinigi, who died in 1405.

These two youthful works demonstrate a flexibility of expression which would mark his entire career. The *Silvestri Madonna* is boldly carved, forthright, and monumental. The Ilaria sepulcher, with its graceful effigy and sarcophagus base, presents a quieter, more romantic expression fitting to its subject. In both works one finds a classical, spatial massing of form coexisting with a rhythmic, elegant line derived from Gothic antecedents.

Life's Work

In 1408, Jacopo received a commission which would occupy him, on and off, until 1419. That was for the Fonte Gaia in Siena, a large fountain in the center of town, which would serve as a civic focal piece. Contemporary documents indicate that physical work on the fountain did not begin until 1414. The plan of the fountain ultimately included numerous figural and decorative reliefs and statues. The overall scheme, as well as the handling of the human figures and decorative motifs, were heavily influenced by antique classicism. In particular, the high reliefs depicting scenes from Genesis display, despite their badly weathered condition, an unusually well-developed sense of classically inspired physicality and of the potential for form to create emotional expression.

Concurrent with the Sienese project, Jacopo was executing commissions in Lucca. In 1412, Lorenzo Trenta, a wealthy Lucchese merchant, began building a family burial chapel in the Church of San Frediano. Jacopo was put in charge of the project, which was not totally finished until 1422. The archaic gothicisms which flavor the chapel's tomb markers and altar, especially surprising in the light of the contemporary Fonte Gaia, reflect Jacopo's willingness and ability to alter his style in the interests of harmonizing his work to the taste and style of its surroundings.

It is clear from the documentary sources that Jacopo was an ambitious sculptor who rarely refused an important commission. The result was delay and procrastination, as he attempted to juggle his various commitments. For example, while under contract for both the Fonte Gaia and the Trenta chapel, he accepted yet another assignment. In 1417, he was commissioned to make two bronze reliefs for the Siena baptistery font. By 1425, he still had not delivered the reliefs and the Opera del Duomo (cathedral works committee), which had already reassigned one panel to the Florentine sculptor Donatello, sued Jacopo for return of the money advanced. Not until 1430 would Jacopo be paid for completing his relief depicting the Annunciation to Zacchariah. Despite his procrastination, in 1427 he was placed in charge of the entire baptistery font program, perhaps in a bid to secure his attention.

In 1425, Jacopo began work on his most famous sculptural program, the main portal (porta magna) of the Church of San Petronio in Bologna. From then until his death in 1438, he would maintain two workshops, one in Bologna and one in Siena. The Sienese would try to keep him at home with commissions (the Vari-Bentivoglio monument and the Casini altar), fines, and finally, in 1435, an appointment as architect-in-chief of the cathedral works. Despite these demands, Jacopo would make one of his greatest artistic statements in the San Petronio sculpture, where the low relief Old Testament scenes display simplified, monumental compositions and classically rendered human nudes. The *Madonna and Child* for the project is admired for its handling of spatial massing, and all the sculpture is marked by a rippling, mobile line.

A fairly complete picture of Jacopo the sculptor emerges from the historical and physical evidence of his professional career. He personally traveled to marble quarries to choose the raw material for his projects but had little compunction about leaving major programs in the hands of assistants when other commitments required his absence. The work secured to his hand displays an ability to infuse classical forms with a high level of emotion. His compositions are marked by rhythms of line and form which imbue them with an unmistakable sense of movement. Rarely in sculpture does one find works in which line and mass coexist on such equal footing.

Jacopo is considered an independent artist, partly because his career took place outside of Florence, the major Italian center for sculpture in the early fifteenth century. He was well aware of the achievements of the Florentine artists, but forged a different, almost idiosyncratic, style connected to theirs but, at the same time, separate. The Florentine achievements in pictorial space, for example, never really concerned Jacopo. His emphasis was always on the heroically scaled foreground figures. Backgrounds and details were reduced to a minimum. His insistent, rippling line, at times poetic and at other times nervous and expressive, defined outlines and contours and had no equivalent among his major contemporaries.

The picture of Jacopo the man is less complete. Little is known about his private life. An impending marriage is recorded in 1424, but there is no evidence that it took place and neither a wife nor children were mentioned in his will. In 1413, he was involved in an affair with the wife of a wealthy

Lucchese merchant, and that year he and one of his assistants were accused of theft, rape, and sodomy. The assistant spent several years in prison, but Jacopo escaped Lucca, only returning upon receipt of safe conduct in 1416. This event did not seem to affect either his professional or social position. In 1418 and 1435, he was elected to the Sienese City Council, and in 1420, he was chosen to serve as the prior of his district in Siena. His inimitable style seems to have secured for him a fair degree of wealth, position, and protection. It certainly secured for him a prominent place in the history of art.

Summary

Although Jacopo della Quercia exerted some stylistic influence during his career and immediately after his death, full appreciation of his legacy did not develop until one hundred years later. In the late fifteenth century, another sculptor, also an independent and also fascinated by the expressive possibilities of form and heroic physicality, would be greatly impressed by exposure to Jacopo's work. That sculptor was Michelangelo. That Michelangelo studied Jacopo's sculpture is proved not only by historical documentation but also by the frequent quotations of Jacopo's San Petronio reliefs in Michelangelo's Sistine Chapel paintings. In Jacopo, Michelangelo found a stylistic ancestor. In Michelangelo, Jacopo's experiments in heroic form found their fulfillment.

A study of Jacopo's sculpture forces the viewer to confront the complexities of artistic style at the dawn of the Italian Renaissance. The Gothic style had not disappeared overnight. The forms and techniques of ancient classical art were not revived indiscriminately. The two traditions had been influencing Italian sculptors since the mid-thirteenth century, and they continued to coexist in Jacopo's work. Jacopo's responses to these traditions, however, were personal and independent. Gothic line and classical form were reinterpreted to ends that were expressive without being expressionistic and were classical without being revivalistic.

Bibliography

Hanson, Anne Coffin. *Jacopo della Quercia's Fonte Gaia.* Oxford: Clarendon Press, 1965. A monograph on one of Jacopo's most important commissions, giving special emphasis to the fountain's iconographic program and its joint civic and religious function.

Pope-Hennessy, John. *Italian Gothic Sculpture.* London: Phaidon, 1972. The chapter on Jacopo places him at the end of the development of late Gothic Italian sculpture. Comparative photographs support the often-neglected stylistic ties of Jacopo to this older tradition. Includes critical analysis, biographical and bibliographical summaries, an index, and photographs of major works with accompanying catalog entries.

Seymour, Charles. *Jacopo della Quercia: Sculptor.* New Haven: Yale University Press, 1973. The standard monograph in English. Discusses the documentary evidence of the major works and includes insightful critical commentary. Ample photographic reproductions including many details. Includes a chronological compendium of the documents, as well as the actual text of major contracts (not translated). Includes an index and a selected bibliography.

_____. *Sculpture in Italy, 1400-1500*. Harmondsworth, England: Penguin Books, 1966. The chapter on Jacopo provides an excellent summary of the artist's career and places him within the context of the early Italian Renaissance. Includes photographs, an index, a biographical summary, and a brief bibliography.

Vasari, Giorgio. *Lives of the Most Eminent Painters, Sculptors, and Architects*. Translated by Gaston du C. de Vere. Vol. 3. New York: Macmillan, 1912-1914. A translation of the 1568 edition of Vasari's biographies. An expanded biography of Jacopo, based most likely upon oral tradition.

Madeline Cirillo Archer

JAMĀL AL-DĪN AL-AFGHĀNĪ

Born: 1838-1839; Asadābād, Iran
Died: March 9, 1897; Istanbul, Ottoman Empire
Areas of Achievement: Philosophy and politics
Contribution: Afghānī was the Pan-Islamist politician and teacher whose intense hatred of, and opposition to, British colonial policies focused the energies of Middle Eastern, Central Asian, and Indian Muslim intellectuals on the plight of the masses. His untiring quest for Muslim solidarity influenced Egypt's nationalist movement and Iran's constitutional and Islamic revolutions.

Early Life
Jamāl al-Dīn al-Afghānī as-Sayyid Muhammad Ibn-i Safdar al-Husain was born into a family of sayyids in the village of Asadābād, near Hamadan, Iran. He claimed, however, that he was born in the village of As'adābād, near Kabul, Afghanistan. Only a sketchy account of Afghānī's childhood can be pieced together from the information provided by his biographer, Mīrzā Lutfullāh Asadābādī. Contrary to his own assertion that he grew up in Afghanistan, Afghānī was educated at home in Asadābād until age ten. He then attended school in Qazvīn and Tehran. During his teens, he studied theology and Islamic philosophy in Karbalā and An Najaf, centers of Shi'ite learning in Iraq.

In 1855, around the age of seventeen, Afghānī traveled to Būshehr, on the Persian Gulf, and from there to India. In India, he observed British imperialism at work. Indian Muslims were openly discriminated against in government appointments, religious institutions, and education. The Muslims' struggle against British tyranny left an indelible impression on the young Afghānī. He agreed with the Indians that the British intended to undermine and discredit Islam. From India, Afghānī journeyed to Mecca and then returned to the Shi'ite centers of learning in Iraq, where he had studied earlier. He remained in that area until 1865, when he traveled to Iran and, the following year, to Afghanistan.

Documented reports of Afghānī's early years date to 1866, when he was part of the entourage of Muhammad A'zam Khān, the military ruler of Qandahār under Dōst Muhammad Khān. When Dōst Muhammad died in 1863, his three sons fought among themselves for the rulership. Amīr Shīr 'Alī Khān, Dōst Muhammad's third son, assumed power in Kabul, pledging to modernize the nation. Shīr 'Alī's brothers, however, rebelled in Quandahār and ousted him in 1866. A'zam became king, and Afghānī entered Afghan politics with him as his close confidant. Afghānī reportedly drew up a national recovery plan that included provisions for a network of schools, a national newspaper, a centralized government, and a well-regulated communications system. In politics, he advised the king to ally himself with Russia against the British in neighboring India. A'zam's rule was short-lived. Shīr 'Alī returned in 1868, deposing Muhammad A'zam and expelling Afghānī—a foreigner who spoke Farsi with an Iranian accent. Afghānī's modernizing reforms, however, were retained.

Life's Work

Afghānī was a mullah with a strong constitution. He had a magnetic personality and a dogged determination, both of which he used competently to penetrate exclusive circles and promote his cause. He cherished secrecy at the expense of social norms. He wore a white turban, while calling himself a sayyid, and adamantly refused any association with women. He was quick-tempered, quick of action, and quick to envisage a British plot at every turn.

Afghanistan afforded Afghānī a worthy education by supplementing his understanding of the dynamics of struggle against imperialism with a possible response. He came to realize that the Shi'i and Persian rational philosophy that had inspired him in India could rid the Muslim masses of ignorance and poverty, if it were enhanced with armed struggle and savage confrontation. If Afghans with bare hands could defeat Great Britain in the First Afghan War, he imagined what the impact of an Islamic army under a charismatic leader would be. Afghānī decided to inject himself into the growing confrontation between the Muslim East and the Christian West in Afghanistan.

The Muslim ruler charismatic enough to realize Afghānī's secret aspiration was Abdülaziz, an Ottoman sultan. In 1869, Afghānī traveled to Istanbul by way of Bombay and Cairo, expecting to be named confidant to the sultan. Turkish officials, busy with the *Tanzīmāt* reforms, appointed him instead to a lesser position on the Council of Education. While serving in this office, Afghānī began a series of inspiring lectures on reform. These lectures, tinged with anti-imperialist allusions and modernist tendencies, and imbued with Shi'ite rational philosophy, raised the ire of the Sunnī ulema (holy men) in Istanbul, who found the lectures heretical. The powerful ulema waited for an opportunity to embarrass Afghānī publicly. This opportunity came when Afghānī compared the ulema with a human craft. The ulema brought their wrath down upon him, the sultan, and the *Tanzīmāt*. To save the *Tanzīmāt*, Abdülaziz was forced to expel Afghānī from Turkey.

With hopes dashed, Afghānī accepted Riyadh Pasha's invitation and, in 1871, went to Egypt. There he continued to teach and to pursue his dream of a Pan-Islamic nation free from imperialist domination. In a series of provocative lectures, he grafted the example of Egypt's economic strangulation by European banks to medieval Islamic philosophy in order to foment revolt against Western exploitation. He also formed and led a Masonic lodge in Cairo, among whose members were counted such promising young leaders as Muhammad 'Abduh, a future leader of the Pan-Islamic movement. Afghānī's activities in Egypt brought him in direct confrontation with Khedive Isma'il of Egypt and his suzerain, Sultan Abdülhamid II, as well as with European, particularly British, powers. Afghānī had placed Khedive Ismā'īl in a difficult position by openly condemning his financial misman-agement as the cause of Egypt's capitulation to European bankers. To ward off Afghānī's allegations, Ismā'īl blamed the foreign bankers, who, in turn, pressured the sultan to depose the Khedive, which the sultan did in 1879. Muhammed Tawfīq Pasha, Ismā'īl's son, expelled Afghānī from Egypt that same year. From Egypt, Afghānī traveled to Hyderabad, south of India, where, for two years, he offered seminars, gave public lectures, and wrote. "The Refutation of the Materialists" (1881) was written at this time. This essay affords a glimpse of Afghānī's growing interest in social conscious-ness, modernism, and rational thinking.

Writing within the Utopian tradition, Afghānī described his vision of the "Virtuous City," as a hierarchically structured society that functions on the principles of shame, trustworthiness, and truthfulness, and aspires to the ideals of intelligence, pride, and justice. Higher intelligence, Afghānī ar-gued, leads to new capabilities and advanced civilizations; pride leads to competition and progress; and justice leads to global peace and harmony among nations. Naturalists (*neicherīs*), Afghānī argued, intended to destroy the solidarity of the Virtuous City through division and sectarianism.

From Hyderabad, Afghānī traveled to London and, shortly thereafter, to Paris, where he engaged the French philosopher Ernest Renan in a debate on the position of scientific discovery in Islam. Then, in 1844, Afghānī began his most consequential activity—his collaboration with Muhammad 'Abduh on editing a revolutionary journal in Arabic, *al-'Urwat al-Wuthqā* (the firmest bond). This publication established Afghānī as the champion of Pan-Islamism, the movement rooted in the bitter memory of Abdülhamid's 1877 defeat in the Russo-Turkish War—whereby the *Tanzīmāt* reforms had been proved ineffective—and in the 1882 occupation of Egypt by Great Britain. *Al-'Urwat al-wuthqā* published articles by Afghānī and 'Abduh on diverse topics. The sultan was not impressed. Disappointed, Afghānī left for Russia. Waiting at Büshehr to collect his books, Afghānī received an invitation from Nāser od-Dīn Shāh, the sovereign in Tehran, who had read a translation of an essay from *al-'Urwat al-wuthqā*. When this brief interview did not go well, Afghānī resumed his trip.

In Russia, Afghānī continued his anti-British activities. He argued that, with his mobilization of Indian and Central Asian Muslims, Russians would easily drive the British out of the subcontinent. The Russians humored him, delaying his departure to irk the British. Afghānī's two-year visit in Russia gained for him a second royal invitation to Tehran. Iran of the 1890's was much like Egypt of the 1870's. It was plagued with financial mismanagement and hounded by foreign investors, who sought concessions on every resource. The shah, however, unlike the Khedive, ruled under the protection of divine right. He could sell Iran to whomever he pleased.

Afghānī arrived in Iran from St. Petersburg at a time when Iranians were growing increasingly alarmed by Nāser od-Dīn's doling out their country's resources. Afghānī himself had distributed leaflets condemning these concessions. Afghānī was not received by his host, who also denied Afghānī's claim that he had been commissioned in Munich to go to St. Petersburg and make amends on Iran's behalf. Worse yet, Afghānī was clandestinely informed of orders for his arrest. To save himself from the shah's wrath, he took sanctuary (*bast*) in the shrine of Shāh Abdul 'Azīm, south of Tehran. From there, using clandestine methods and superb oratorical techniques, Afghānī attracted Iranians in droves to his fiery attacks on the shah's past antireformist actions, especially the murder of Mīrzā Taqī Khān, Amīr Kabīr.

Afghānī predicted that Iran would capitulate to British might, as Egypt had in 1882. He demanded that Iranian revenues be spent on the construction of a railroad, on education and hospitals, and on a viable army to thwart imperialism, rather than on the shah's pleasure trips to Europe. Iranians, he said, must be given the right to express their opinions in publications independent of the government. Iran must have a constitution, a parliament, and a house of justice. Above all, he emphasized, Iranians deserved a just king.

Nāser od-Dīn was approaching his fiftieth year of rule. Since Afghānī had been instrumental in the shah's recent humiliation as the first shah to revoke his own writ—the tobacco concession—and since this action had precipitated Iran's first foreign debt, the shah ordered the unruly mullah to be expelled. Ignoring the rules of sanctuary, the shah's guards invaded the holy shrine in 1892, placed Afghānī, half naked and in the middle of winter, on the bare back of a mule, and deported him. Afghānī went to London, where he reestablished ties with his lodge members and then traveled to Turkey at the invitation of the sultan. Rather than becoming the sultan's confidant and Pan-Islamist consultant as Afghānī had hoped, he became the sultan's prisoner.

From Turkey, Afghānī continued to foment revolt in Iran, using his devotees to carry out his behests. One such devotee was Mīrzā Rezā Kermānī, who, in 1896, was commissioned to murder Nāser od-Dīn. Mīrzā Rezā carried out his mission on the anniversary of the shah's fiftieth year of reign in the very sanctuary in which Afghānī had been humiliated a few years before. Afghānī died of cancer of the chin at the age of about sixty and was buried in a secret grave. In 1944, the government of Afghanistan claimed him as a citizen, and his supposed remains were transferred to and buried on the grounds of the University of Kabul under a respectful shrine.

Summary

  Jamāl al-Dīn al-Afghānī was an Iranian by birth. His activities and the corpus of his writings reflect that. When visiting Europe, he affiliated himself with Afghanistan; when in Afghanistan, he associated himself with Ottoman Turkey and called himself "Istanbūlī," to gain the confidence of Sunnī rulers and evade Iranian officials. There are several reasons that Afghānī failed in materializing his dream. First, he put too much trust in the goodwill of Muslim rulers and too little in the people of the Middle East. In ignoring the grass roots support for his Pan-Islamism, he violated the rules of his own Virtuous City, a violation that he regretfully acknowledged in a letter he wrote from prison before his death. Second, he used religion to achieve political aims, and, assuming that world rulers acted independently of one another, secretly groomed all for the same office—that of caliph. This policy backfired on him many times, finally costing him his life. Third, he annoyed rulers by lecturing them. Nāser od-Dīn dismissed him when Afghānī blatantly offered himself as a sword with which the shah could cripple the imperialists. The sultan was more gracious. Finally, Afghānī failed to distinguish between policy and personal disposition. He sought Queen Victoria's assistance against Nāser od-Dīn within a short time of the tobacco boycott against British interests in Iran, a boycott that he himself had helped bring to fruition.

Bibliography
Ahmad, Aziz. "Sayyid Ahmad Khān, Jamāl al-Dīn al-Afghānī and Muslim India." *Studia Islamica* 13 (1960): 55-78. An important source of information on Afghānī's involvement in Indian Muslim affairs. Compares Afghānī's advocacy of *jihad* and *khilāfat* to Sayyid Ahmad Khān's policy of capitulation to British rule. Ahmad believes that Afghānī and Sayyid Ahmad Khān differed only in political matters.
Algar, Hamid. *Religion and State in Iran, 1785-1906.* Los Angeles: University of California Press, 1969. Provides the larger picture. Examines the life and works of Afghānī's colleagues and assesses Afghānī's contribution in the light of past philosophical and doctrinal efforts.
Hodgson, Marshall G. *The Venture of Islam.* Vol. 3, *The Gunpowder Empire and Modern Times.* Chicago: University of Chicago Press, 1974. Hodgson examines Afghānī's efforts in the context of an alliance among the Shi'i ulema, the *bazaaris*, and the intellectuals. Afghānī emerges as an opportunist in his calls for reform, emphasizing the political, religious, or social aspects depending on the weight each carried in a particular situation.
Keddie, Nikki R. *An Islamic Response to Imperialism: Political and Religious Writings of Sayyid Jamāl al-Dīn "al-Afghānī."* Berkeley: University of California Press, 1968. A comprehensive study of Afghānī's life. Includes sample translations of his works as well as analytical notes on his worldview. Also includes a bibliography and a good index.

Kedourie, Elie. *Afghani and 'Abduh: An Essay on Religious Unbelief and Political Activism in Modern Islam.* London: Frank Cass, 1966. Kedourie discusses Afghānī's teachings from the point of view of his disciple, 'Abduh, and of circumstances that influenced those teachings. Kedourie's discussion of Mahdīsm, as expounded by both Afghānī and Muhammad Ahmad of Sudan, is noteworthy.

Kramer, Martin. *Islam Assembled: The Advent of the Muslim Congresses.* New York: Columbia University Press, 1985. The first two chapters deal with the genesis of the Pan-Islamic ideal and its challenge to authority. The contributions of Afghānī are discussed in the context of a rising tide of discontent among Muslims from Indonesia, Sumatra, and Central Asia to Daghistan and the Crimea, as these are reflected at the court of the Ottoman sultans.

Iraj Bashiri

CORNELIUS OTTO JANSEN

Born: November 3, 1585; Accoi, Holland
Died: May 6, 1638; Ypres, Spanish Netherlands
Areas of Achievement: Church reform and religion
Contribution: Jansen created a new and challenging interpretation of the theology of Saint Augustine for the Catholic Reformation. Out of the controversy over his book *Augustinus* emerged Jansenism, a powerful church reform movement bearing his name.

Early Life

Cornelius Otto Jansen was born in Accoi, a village near Leerdam in southern Holland. Although the district was Calvinist, Jansen's family was Roman Catholic. After an elementary education at Culemborg, he attended the Latin school of Saint Jerome in Utrecht. In 1602, he entered the University of Louvain, where he resided in the Falcon College. An assiduous and intelligent student, he earned first honors among his colleagues in the liberal arts. In 1604, he began theological studies under the direction of Jacobus Jansonius, a fellow Dutchman from Amsterdam, who introduced him to the Augustinian views of Michael Baius, a controversial sixteenth century Flemish theologian, who had been condemned by Rome in 1567. At Louvain, Jansen also became familiar with the debate caused by the treatise of the Jesuit Luis de Molina on divine grace and free will. As a student, Jansen had adopted Augustinian in contrast to Jesuit positions on the points at issue. Nevertheless, while criticizing the theology and ecclesiastical privileges of the Society of Jesus, he learned to appreciate its religious spirit, zeal for the Church, and scholarly attainments.

After receiving the bachelor's degree in theology in 1609, Jansen left Louvain for Paris. This change of place was most likely the result of his growing desire to devote himself to the study of the Bible and the writings of the Fathers of the Church rather than to dogmatic theology. In Paris, while studying Greek, he met Jean Du Vergier de Hauranne, later Abbé de Saint-Cyran. Thus began a most influential friendship. Sharing a common love for the basic sources of theology, the two men continued their studies together at the estate of Du Vergier's mother, near Bayonne in southern France. Ordained priest in Mechelen in 1614, Jansen returned to France for two more years until obliged to return to the Low Countries, following his father's death. Chosen to lead a newly organized college for Dutch ecclesiastical students at Louvain, he earned a doctor's degree in theology at the university in October, 1617. He became a professor of theology in May of that year.

Life's Work

In 1623, Jansen began an extensive, systematic treatment of Saint Augustine's views on the subject of divine grace. This project, the principal occupation of his life, was soon interrupted. He was called upon by the university to represent its interests at the Spanish court in Madrid. Resigning his post as head of the Dutch college, he traveled to Spain in 1624 and again in 1626 to protect the university's monopoly on instruction from attempts by Jesuits to offer courses in Louvain. In those years, he was also drawn into controversies with Calvinists. From 1624 to 1626, and occasionally thereafter, Jansen disputed the Calvinists' theological positions as laid down in the decrees of the Synod of Dordrecht.

In 1628, he returned to his work on Saint Augustine with a celebrated sermon on the spiritual life based on Augustinian principles. Two years later, appointed regius professor of Holy Scripture, he undertook heavy instructional as well as administrative duties. The lectures that he prepared for his classes were published posthumously as commentaries on the books of the Bible. Based on patristic writings, his commentaries explain the literal meaning of the text and avoid excessive use of allegory. These commentaries were well received because of their author's clarity and sound erudition.

Jansen continued to pursue his scholarly goals despite distractions caused by the progress of the Thirty Years' War in the Low Countries. Alarmed by the invasion of his country by French and Dutch forces, he helped organize the defense of Louvain in 1635. In that same year, he also composed *Mars gallicus* (1636), an attack on Cardinal de Richelieu's policy of seeking Protestant allies in France's war against Spain. Translated into Spanish and French, the tract angered Richelieu and set off a polemic, which Jansen left to his friends to continue.

Nominated bishop of Ypres by the Spanish government in October, 1635, Jansen was consecrated the next year. A zealous pastor, he improved the administration of the diocese and cultivated good relations with the Society of Jesus. Neither the dignity nor the burdens of his new office, however, could draw him from his study of Saint Augustine. By this time, he had composed his thoughts in a large manuscript, entitled *Augustinus* (1640), which was known only to Du Vergier and a few other close friends. The great project was brought to a conclusion at the same time that Jansen was struck by the plague and died in 1638. *Augustinus* was published at Jansen's request in Louvain in 1640 by two friends, Calenus and Froidment, who had witnessed the treatise's development over many years.

Augustinus is a serious, logically constructed treatise, whose arguments are well buttressed with references to sources and by the author's own explanatory notes. It is written in a classicist Latin that reflects Jansen's intimate familiarity with the fourth century idiom of Saint Augustine. Jansen organized the treatise in three parts. In the first part, he describes Saint Augustine's critique of the positions taken by Pelagian and semi-Pelagian theologians on the relationship between divine grace and free will. In his introduction to the second part, Jansen examines the relationship between philosophy and theology. Rejecting the excessively rationalistic methods of Scholastic schools of theology, he declares that he intends to follow Saint Augustine on the doctrine of grace. The bulk of the second part is devoted to an examination of the effects of original sin on mankind and the fallen angels. These creatures have been completely alienated from their creator; their wills tend without fail toward evil. Even the most estimable achievements of unredeemed human nature are morally tainted at their root. Denying the concept of a state of pure nature to which Jesuit theologians argued that man had been originally called, Jansen contended that, by creation, man was called to a supernatural level of existence.

The third and most important part of the treatise explains Saint Augustine's concept of Christ's restoration of human nature by his redeeming grace. Although Christ's action heals the evil effects of sin and restores true human freedom, his grace remains continually necessary for any human work to be pleasing to God. Even when redeemed, man remains powerless to reconcile himself with God. Salvation, according to Jansen's reading of Saint Augustine, is profoundly paradoxical, for man's free will is neither forced nor compromised, although God's saving grace is irresistible and unfailingly effective. Human freedom consists in a voluntary compliance with the will of God.

Perhaps the most characteristic of the concepts that Jansen develops in this part of the treatise is his view that human existence is dominated by two conflicting delights or desires. *Delectatio coelestis*, or heavenly desire, is a product of divine grace working in a person, leading him or her to love God and to do good works. *Delectatio terrena*, in contrast, is a product of fallen human nature, inclining a person to love of the world and to sin. The inclination that prevails in a person's life is called by Jansen *delectatio victrix*, or the victorious desire.

Although Jansen focused the body of *Augustinus* on the doctrimes of the great Father of the Church rather than on contemporary theological controversies, he appended to the treatise an epilogue, attributing to Molina and other Jesuits the Pelagian and semi-Pelagian doctrines condemned by Saint Augustine. Even without this polemical appendix, the *Augustinus* was certain to provoke powerful opposition from the Jesuits, since it implicitly claimed the enormous authority of Saint Augustine in support of contemporary teaching on grace and free will that the Jesuits assiduously opposed. Jansen anticipated that the Jesuits would resort to any means to suppress his treatise, so he made elaborate arrangements to have it printed secretly. His unexpected death delayed, but did not prevent, Calenus and Froidment from having the treatise printed and widely distributed.

Summary
Cornelius Otto Jansen was an outstanding representative of the Reforma-

tion of the Roman Catholic church that took place in the Spanish Netherlands at the beginning of the seventeenth century. A devout priest of austere character, he worked loyally for the improvement of the Church as teacher, university rector, and bishop. As a scholar, he adhered to the best contemporary standards, attempting to reach truth in complex theological issues that aroused intense religious passions.

The historical impact of his treatise, *Augustinus*, was enormous. It was received favorably by persons who identified themselves with the Augustinian theological tradition. Jesuits and their allies, however, accused Jansen of falling into heresy. *Augustinus*, they contended, virtually denied human free will and repeated other errors taught by John Calvin and Baius, which the Church had already condemned. Prodded by Jansen's critics, Pope Urban VIII condemned *Augustinus* in 1643.

Conflict over the treatise spread from the Spanish Netherlands to France soon after its publication. Jansen's bitter enemy, Richelieu, died in 1642, but his hostility to Jansen and his work lived on in Jules Mazarin, who assumed control of the royal government. Jansen's friend Du Vergier nevertheless won support for *Augustinus*. In 1649, anti-Jansenists at the University of Paris drew several propositions, allegedly from the treatise, and demanded that they be condemned. A confusing debate ensued in which *Augustinus* was effectively defended by Antoine Arnauld. The disputed propositions were eventually limited to five that Pope Innocent X condemned in 1653.

The controversy over Jansen's work generated a movement, Jansenism, that waged war against his critics and enemies over a broad range of issues. Arnauld charged the Jesuits with laxity in regard to the proper disposition for reception of the sacraments, while Pascal ridiculed Jesuit casuistry. Although Jansenism's antiauthoritarian implications led Mazarin to seek its condemnation by Rome, its followers won support among magistrates in the high courts of law. Jansenist concepts of church reform, based on principles of Christian Humanism and the decrees of the Council of Trent, also proved attractive to some religious orders.

The growth of Jansenism provoked King Louis XIV to adopt a policy of ruthless extermination. From 1661 to 1667, the clergy of the kingdom were required to sign a condemnation of the five propositions. The resistance of Jansenists to this persecution led Pope Clement IX to acknowledge tacitly that the condemned propositions were not in fact representative of Jansen's views. By the end of the seventeenth century, Jansenism had developed a life of its own, pursuing causes other than the vindication of Jansen and his *Augustinus*.

Bibliography
Cognet, Louis, et al. *The Church in the Age of Absolutism and Enlightenment.* In *History of the Church*, edited by Hubert Jedin and John P. Dolan,

vol. 6. Translated by Gunther J. Holst. New York: Crossroad, 1981. This volume contains several chapters describing Jansenism, especially in France in the seventeenth century, by Cognet, the foremost authority on the topic. Jansen's background and his work at Louvain are briefly explained.

Delumeau, Jean. *Catholicism Between Luther and Voltaire: A New View of the Counter-Reformation*. Philadelphia: Westminster Press, 1977. Includes a chapter on Jansenism. The author discusses recent interpretations of Jansenism. He also treats briefly the issues raised by Jansen in his principal work, *Augustinus*, as well as the conflicts arising from its publication.

Gonzalez, Justo L. *A History of Christian Thought*. Vol. 3, *From Protestant Reformation to the Twentieth Century*. Nashville: Abingdon Press, 1975. A brief but clear analysis of Jansen's theological concepts. Gonzalez points out that, according to Jansen, the methods of philosophy and theology are radically different: Only the latter method can attain knowledge that is certain. The author also describes the course of Jansenism up to the French Revolution.

Hargreaves, Kevin John. *Cornelius Jansenius and the Origins of Jansenism*. Ann Arbor, Mich.: University Microfilms, 1974. A thorough investigation of the contributions that Jansen made to the movement that bears his name and to theology. A doctoral dissertation from Brandeis University, this book is the most extensive study of Jansenism available in English. The neglected sources examined by the author include Jansen's treatise on theological method, his introduction to the *Augustinus*, and his works on spirituality. Jansen's theological concepts are analyzed and placed in the context of the history of religious ideas from Saint Augustine to Calvin. Hargreaves contends that Jansen's theology represents an extreme critique of the rational, Scholastic tradition of theology.

Mosse, George L. "Changes in Religious Thought." In *Cambridge Modern History*, vol. 4. Cambridge: Cambridge University Press, 1970. Places Jansen and Jansenism in a general historical context. Mosse regards Jansenism as a challenge to orthodoxy within Catholicism analogous to Puritanism within Protestantism. He also attributes to Jansen a role in the beginning of modern rationalism.

Charles H. O'Brien

FRANCISCO JIMÉNEZ DE CISNEROS

Born: 1436; Torrelaguna, Province of Madrid, Spain
Died: November 8, 1517; Roa, Spain
Areas of Achievement: Government, politics, religion, and education
Contribution: Jiménez worked to maintain a united Spain at the beginning of
the sixteenth century. He founded the University of Alcalá de Henares and
sponsored the famous Polyglot Bible.

Early Life

Gonzalo Jiménez de Cisneros, the baptismal name of the future Regent of
Spain, was the first son of a family of esteemed lineage and humble means.
His father, Alonso Jiménez de Cisneros, was trained in the law and made a
modest living as collector and administrator of the papal tithe in the town of
Torrelaguna. Young Gonzalo received his earliest training in Latin and reading at the household of an uncle, Alvaro, a priest in Roa. He then traveled to
Alcalá and continued his studies of Latin and humanities in a school operated by the Franciscan Order. He entered Spain's prestigious University of
Salamanca in 1450 and remained there until he completed a degree in canon
and civil law. He also became well versed in the philosophical currents of
the day, showing particular affinity for biblical scholarship. Jiménez then
traveled to Rome in search of more promising opportunities. In Italy, Jiménez made a living as a lawyer, representing cases before consistorial
courts. He left Rome in 1465 and returned to his birthplace to care for his
recently widowed mother.

Life's Work

Aside from his ordination and legal experience, Jiménez's most promising
professional prospect upon his return was the hope of fulfilling the terms of a
letrae expectativae, a promisory papal letter appointing its possessor to any
expected vacancy in a particular diocese. Jiménez had to wait years for a
suitable opportunity. He lived in Torrelaguna until he received news of a
vacancy in Úceda, in the diocese of Toledo. The Archpriest of Úceda had
recently died, and Jiménez made a claim to that benefice in 1473. His ambitions were frustrated, however, when the powerful Archbishop of Toledo
Alfonso Carrillo blocked his candidacy. Jiménez's stubborn refusal to relinquish his right to Úceda so enraged Carrillo that he had Jiménez imprisoned.
Jiménez was jailed for six years and was released in 1479, when influential
relatives pleaded on his behalf. Once out of prison, Jiménez took possession
of the Úceda post.

By now in his forties, Jiménez would soon enter the most productive and
important stage of his career. He had the good fortune to come under the
protection of the Archbishop of Seville Cardinal Pedro de Mendoza, and

under his tutelage Jiménez moved to the chaplaincy of the Cathedral of Sigüenza in the archdiocese of Seville. Mendoza, an enemy and rival of Carrillo, was the scion of one of Spain's most influential and accomplished families and a political ally and confidant of Queen Isabella I of Castile. Jiménez's advancement was now assured.

Mendoza promoted Jiménez once again, to the post of General Vicar of Sigüenza, and even greater opportunities opened up when Mendoza succeeded Carrillo to the see of Toledo in 1483. Jiménez, however, opted for a different path. After his mother's death in 1486, he decided to set aside secular concerns and enter the Franciscan Order. He took vows in 1486, changed his name from Gonzalo to Francisco—in honor of the order's founder—and began a new life devoted to prayer, fasting, and contemplation. The physical descriptions and portraits of Jiménez that have survived depict his slight build, weather-beaten skin, sharp profile, and thin body, features believed to have resulted from his rigid adherence to the physical rigors of monastic life.

Jiménez played a central role in the events that shaped the last quarter of the fifteenth century. His belated and somewhat surprising rise as a public figure began when, at the recommendation of Mendoza, he was invited to the royal court to serve as Isabella's confessor. Isabella became devoted to her confessor. In the fall of 1495, in a bold move, she selected Jiménez to the archbishopric of Toledo. Mendoza had died earlier that year, and Isabella secured papal approval to appoint Jiménez to preside over Spain's wealthiest and most important ecclesiastical see. She had to defend and impose her will over her husband, who wanted the prestigious post reserved for his illegitimate son. Jiménez accepted this great honor without hesitation and proceeded to reorganize the archiepiscopal see to reflect his religious convictions, tastes, and predilections.

A story associated with this period of Jiménez's career merits repetition. When Jiménez moved into his new quarters at the archiepiscopal palace in Toledo, the story goes, he ordered his staff to live, dress, and eat with the simplicity and austerity of Franciscan monks. Believing that such external signs of humility would undermine the prestige of the see, members of his staff appealed to the pope, asking him to help persuade Jiménez to reconsider. It seems that Jiménez heeded papal advice rather well. The Toledean ecclesiastical palace became once again the model of elegance and splendor it had always been. Jiménez undertook a series of building projects such as the reconstruction of the main altar of the cathedral, contracting for that purpose the most accomplished architects, sculptors, and artists of the period. He also commissioned plans for the construction of his proudest achievement, the new University at Alcalá de Henares, which he foresaw as a center for humanistic learning. He entrusted the project to Pedro Gumiel, after receiving approval in a papal bull issued in April, 1499. The plans would come to fruition when several of the university's many colleges opened in 1508.

A related project was Jiménez's wish to prepare the world's first edition of a Polyglot Bible, intended to contain parallel, annotated Hebrew, Aramaic, Greek, and Latin versions of the Old Testament, and a Greek and Latin version of the New Testament. Jiménez gathered lexicographers and biblical scholars at Alcalá and purchased and borrowed an impressive number of biblical manuscripts from libraries throughout Europe for his scholars to consult and compare. The resulting six-volume work, known as the Alcalá or Complutensian Polyglot Bible, was printed in 1517 and distributed for the first time three years later.

Jiménez's interest in learning, evident during his years at Salamanca and in his sponsorship of the university and important works of scholarship, contrasts with his harsh treatment of the Muslim population of Granada. According to the terms of surrender of 1492, Spain's new subjects were assured freedom of religion. Ferdinand II and Isabella I hoped, however, that all Spanish Muslims would eventually renounce their faith and adopt Christianity. Isabella had appointed her own confessor Hernando de Talavera to oversee this transition. In 1499, impatient with the pace of Talavera's methods, Jiménez traveled to Granada to inject fervor and zeal into the process. When the Muslim majority protested his intrusion, Jiménez retaliated by ordering all Arabic books, sacred and secular, burned in public squares. He spared three hundred medical works, a collection destined for the bookshelves at Alcalá de Henares.

Jiménez's harsh methods backfired and caused a number of serious and violent uprisings. He is held responsible for the unnecessary chaos, bloodshed, and distrust that ensued and for the wanton destruction of precious and irreplaceable Muslim books and manuscripts. This entire episode served to tarnish his image as a Humanist and lover of learning, although it did not affect his relationship with his patron, Isabella. He remained her trusted and respected adviser until her death in 1504.

Isabella's death produced a political crisis in Spain by jeopardizing the partnership of the two crowns, Castile and Aragon, that comprised the nation. The union between the two had come about through marriage and personal agreement, and the death of one of the partners threatened this fragile arrangement. The question of inheritance was, then, crucial.

Isabella's choice of heir for the crown of Castile was her third daughter, Joan, who in 1496 had married Philip of Habsburg—Archduke of Austria and son of Emperor Maximilian of the Holy Roman Empire. The couple lived in Flanders. Isabella, recognizing her daughter's incapacity to rule— Joan was emotionally unstable and is known as "the Mad"—intended for the couple to rule jointly and to be succeeded by their first son, Charles. Isabella had also appointed her husband Ferdinand regent; he was expected to govern the country until Joan and Philip made their way to Spain. Rivalry between Philip and Ferdinand soon developed, however, and each side tried to recruit supporters from the always quarrelsome Castilian nobility.

Joan and Philip arrived in Castile in 1505, but their rule was a brief one; Philip died mysteriously in the fall of 1506, and Joan's mental state took a turn for the worse. Jiménez, in the absence of Ferdinand, who had removed himself to Aragon and then to Italy, assumed the regency until Ferdinand's return in 1507. As regent, he acted to protect the interests of Castile, while keeping in check the ambitions of a number of restless courtiers. That same year, Jiménez was elevated to cardinal by the Holy See, and Ferdinand conferred on him the title of Inquisitor General of Castile.

Jiménez the statesman and clergyman was also, for a brief time, a soldier. Using the rich rents of his archbishopric of Toledo, he persuaded Ferdinand to order a military campaign against the North African port of Oran, a favorite refuge of pirates who raided Spanish ships and ports. Jiménez planned and executed the military campaign that captured the city in 1509. Oran was to remain in Spanish hands until the eighteenth century.

After his military triumph, Jiménez returned to Alcalá de Henares to oversee the opening of the university and to attempt to recoup funds spent on the campaign. He remained in close contact with Ferdinand and might have been instrumental in persuading the king to cede the crowns of Aragon and Navarre (annexed by Ferdinand in 1512) to his grandchild Charles, as Isabella had done with Castile. Ferdinand's original choice had been his second grandchild and namesake who, unlike Charles, had been reared in Spain.

When Ferdinand died in 1516, Jiménez assumed the regency of Castile for a second time, in anticipation of the arrival and majority of Charles, who had remained in Flanders after his parents' return to Spain. Charles arrived on September 19, 1517, and was poised to claim the throne of a strong and united state composed of Castile, Aragon, and Navarre. The young king had intended to dismiss Jiménez, but Jiménez died on November 8, 1517, before receiving official notification of his dismissal. He was buried in the College of Saint Ildefonso at the University of Alcalá de Henares, and a magnificent marble monument was built over his grave two years later. The college fell into ill repair after the university moved to Madrid in 1836, and in 1857, the cardinal's remains were transferred to the Church of San Justo y Pastor in the city of Alcalá.

Summary

Francisco Jiménez de Cisneros was, in many ways, the quintessential Spaniard of the Renaissance, embodying all the conflicts and contradictions of the period. Personally and intellectually devoted to rigid Christian observance, he nevertheless displayed great interest in scholarship and learning. He at once persecuted Muslims and collected their medical works. As inquisitor general, he investigated and intimidated some Jewish converts to Christianity, while employing others in his biblical project. A Franciscan by choice and training, he was committed to a life of austerity; yet his personal disregard for material comforts did not interfere with his sense of duty and the demands of the high office he occupied. As Archbishop of Toledo, he was known to wear the coarse Franciscan hair shirt under the splendid robes of the office. Eager to devote himself to a life of contemplation, he led armies into battle more effectively than he led his own Franciscan monks to accept reform.

Jiménez's greatest achievement, however, might very well be his years of loyal service to Isabella and, after her death, to Ferdinand and the couple's heirs. As a statesman, he was dutiful and loyal, placing the interests of his patrons above his own and leading a life above reproach. While he did not introduce any significant new policies, through his patient and devoted service he made possible the continued union of Castile and Aragon, which made Charles the most powerful king of his age.

Bibliography

Lyell, James P. R. *Cardinal Ximenes*. London: Grafton, 1917. A brief account of the cardinal's career, which attributes to Jiménez a greater degree of cunning and deception than most of his other biographers.

Lynch, John. *Spain Under the Habsburgs*. Vol. 1, *Empire and Absolutism, 1516-1598*. New York: Oxford University Press, 1964. A serious and academic treatment of the first century of rule by the house of Austria; an excellent survey of all aspects of Spanish society during the 1500's.

Mariéjol, Jean Hippolyte. *The Spain of Ferdinand and Isabella*. Edited and translated by Benjamin Keen. New Brunswick, N.J.: Rutgers University Press, 1961. A favorable account of the role of Jiménez in the reign of the Catholic monarchs. The author praises Jiménez for undertaking the publication of the Polyglot Bible yet criticizes him for not requiring a more critical approach toward the material on the part of those who participated in the project.

Merton, Reginald. *Cardinal Ximenes and the Making of Spain*. London: Kegan Paul, Trench, Trubner, 1934. A fairly detailed biography of Jiménez. Merton believes that King Ferdinand and Jiménez were essentially rivals. In this account, Jiménez emerges as a paragon of virtue and statesmanship.

Prescott, William H. *History of the Reign of Ferdinand and Isabella, the Catholic*. 3 vols. 15th ed. Boston: Phillips, Sampson, 1859. The third and last volume of this classic work is devoted to a detailed narrative account of the final period of the reign of the Catholic monarchs. Prescott, a liberal thinker, is critical of Jiménez's dogmatism and of his religious bigotry, assigning part of the blame to the society and period in which Jiménez lived.

Starkie, Walter. *Grand Inquisitor*. London: Hodder & Stoughton, 1940. The author, whose interest in Spain is wide-ranging, approaches Jiménez as a cultural figure who embodies certain qualities associated with the national character, such as faith and the tragic sense of life.

Clara Estow

JOHN III SOBIESKI

Born: August 17, 1629; Olesko, Poland
Died: June 17, 1696; Castle Wilanów, near Warsaw, Poland
Areas of Achievement: The military, monarchy, government, and politics
Contribution: In lifting the Turkish siege of Vienna, Sobieski halted the Ottoman conquest of Europe, preserving Western culture and Christendom. The status of women, in particular, differs so profoundly in Christian societies from that in Islamic societies that the debt of Western women to Sobieski's generalship can hardly be overstated.

Early Life

John III Sobieski was born in Olesko Castle, near Zolkiew, then in southeastern Poland. During the first thirty years of his life, Poland was involved in two wars with Sweden, two with Russia, and virtually continuous strife in the Ukraine. Two reigning kings died and two replacements were elected by the uniquely Polish system that was in 1674 to crown Sobieski himself.

Sobieski's reputation as the most cultivated of all Poland's seventeenth century kings, and its greatest military hero, is in the tradition of his family, which descended from Poland's first ruler, Piast. Sobieski's highly educated father, Jakób, was the descendant of Dinarian country squires and prosperous Lechite nobles. He had become castellan of Kraków, Poland's highest ranking secular senator, before Sobieski was twenty. Governing and fighting, especially Turks, were Sobieski's predictable spheres.

Sobieski's intellect was appropriate to his remarkably large head. By middle age, his belly had expanded to match this head, which, taken with his surprisingly tiny feet, gave him rather an oval shape. The French ambassador wrote that he looked from a distance like a gigantic egg. Closer, he granted Sobieski an aquiline nose and a pleasant voice. Because of the rigors of his final campaign, Sobieski was in ill health for the last five years of his life, but for the preceding sixty-two his immense vitality had informed his every aspect. His mental capacities, his physical appetites, his capacity for rage and for sweetness, for thoughtful and for impulsive behavior, all were exaggerated.

Through the death of an elder brother, Sobieski inherited a great estate. Like most young Renaissance Poles of his class, he concluded his studies (at the University of Kraków) by touring Western Europe (1646-1647). He then joined the Polish army, fighting a Cossack uprising in the Ukraine, an area that was to be a grief and trouble to him throughout his life.

Life's Work

In 1569, the Ukraine was transferred from Lithuania to Poland. Lithuania had been unable to protect the Ukranians from the Tatar troops that regularly plundered them, taking so many captives to Crimean ports for sale as slaves to the Muslims that the Ukraine had become seriously underpopulated. This underpopulation had brought refugees from Polish Lithuanian feudalism, people willing to defend themselves from Tatars for the sake of freedom from taxes and serfdom. These Cossacks evolved into a distinct people, farmers and soldiers, resistant to Polish authority. Their military ventures into Moldavia (part of modern Romania), the Crimea, and Turkey, were blamed on the Polish Crown, which sometimes tried to subdue them and other times employed them against foreign enemies. Between Sobieski's birth and his first military service, the Polish army had marched against the Cossacks five times.

In 1648, Poland's king died. The Polish nobility elected Jan Kasimir Vasa, a Swede with a French wife (Marie Louise), to replace him. Sobieski's early military career was to benefit from Marie Louise's patronage, and he was to marry a woman from her court.

Like Sobieski when he became king, Marie Louise tried and failed to reform Poland's laws of succession. Poland's magnates enjoyed immense power, which they guarded so jealously as to keep their king too weak to pursue Poland's interests. Reasoning that a living king could influence the choice of his successor in favor of a son or close relative, which risked development of a despotic hereditary monarchy, the magnates would not designate a king's successor during his lifetime. Every reign ended with a dangerous interregnum. The result was that the Vatican and Poland's neighbors competed through bribery and intrigue to choose Poland's kings, each of whom was then his foreign patron's tool. Even so strong a character as Sobieski, who, like John II Casimir Vasa, began his reign with the backing of Louis XIV of France but who developed a foreign policy independent of French interests, was in the end unequal to the combination of domestic intransigence and foreign intrigue.

Casimir proved unable to achieve a compromise between the Ukranians and Poland's magnates, and in 1654 the Cossacks sought Russian help. Czar Alexis declared the Ukraine a Russian protectorate and sent troops against the Polish army there. Taking advantage of this, Sweden invaded Poland in 1655. Increased Swedish power on the Baltic was such a threat to the czar that he signed an armistice with Poland and directed his army against the Swedes. Sobieski continued fighting the Russians by joining the Swedish army.

The Protestant Swedes intended to destroy Catholicism in Poland. The wanton destruction, pillage, and massacres united the fractious Poles against them. In 1656, Sobieski rejoined the Polish army and took a leading part in fighting the Swedes. By the Peace of Oliwa in 1660, Sweden acquired Poland's last Baltic territories but otherwise withdrew. Poland was in ruins and again at war with the Russians and Cossacks in the Ukraine.

In 1665, Sobieski married the ambitious French widow Marie Casimire de la Grange d'Arquien, who at once began maneuvering to make Sobieski Casimir's successor. Marysieńka, as the Poles called her, was beautiful, brilliant, devoted to Sobieski, and one of history's most avaricious women. Influenced by her, Sobieski in the latter half of his reign sold every possible office, amassing an awesome fortune. This cupidity, plus her foreign birth, made Marysieńka unpopular in Poland, contributing to the Sobieskis' failure to secure Poland's crown for their eldest son.

In 1665, through the favor of Queen Marie Louise, Sobieski was made grand marshall, rising to field commander the following year. The Cossacks, having found Russian aid against the Poles insufficient, turned to the Tatars and Turkey. The threat of Turkish intervention in the Ukraine so alarmed the czar that he made a truce with Poland (Andruszów, January, 1667). Only Sobieski recognized in time that the Tatars marching into the Ukraine that summer meant to fight Poles, not Cossacks. With an army funded almost entirely by himself, he turned back Tatar troops numbering ten times his own at Podhajce in October, 1667. In 1668, he became grand hetman. Efforts by Marie Louise to reform the crippling features of Poland's constitution ended upon her death in 1667, and her discouraged widower abdicated. The Habsburgs' influence prevailed in the consequent election, and Michal Wiśniowiecki was crowned in 1669.

Sobieski's victories against the Cossacks continued, but the Seym (parliament) did not take his advice about the Turkish threat, and when Turkey invaded, Poland was forced to sign the Peace of Buczacz (1672), losing territory and, most galling, promising annual tribute. When Michal's death (1673) nearly coincided with Sobieski's tremendous victory over the Turks at Khotin, Sobieski became too popular in Poland for the Habsburgs' next candidate; in 1674, with lukewarm French support, he was elected king.

Louis XIV, almost continuously at war with the Holy Roman Empire (hence Turkey's ally), hoped to use Poland in this connection. By the secret Treaty of Jaworów (1675), he promised Sobieski to mediate a peace between Poland and Turkey to Poland's advantage and to subsidize a Polish campaign to recover Prussia from the elector of Brandenburg, a subsidy which would double if Poland fought Austria. The Prussian venture attracted Sobieski not only because of Poland's interest in the Baltic but also because he wanted the Prussian throne for his eldest son, Jakób. Yet the vaunted settlement with Turkey (signed at Zórawno, 1676) left half of the Ukraine a Turkish protectorate, and Sobieski's Baltic hopes were also disappointed. Turkey remained Poland's greatest enemy, making Austria rather than France her natural ally. Sobieski's initial rapport with France was also strained by Louis' unwillingness to do as much as Marysieńka expected for her immediate and extended family. In 1683, Sobieski signed a treaty with Austria whereby either would come to the aid of the other's capital should it be besieged by Turkey. That summer, Turkey marched 115,000 men on Vienna. Sobieski, as ranking officer, commanded the several armies which cooperated to lift the siege with half the Turks' manpower in one of the most brilliant and important battles of European history (Battle of Kahlenburg, September 12, 1683).

Sobieski's subsequent campaigns against the Turks, in Hungary and Moldavia, were unsuccessful. He dreamed of a "Holy League" of Christian nations to drive Turkey out of Europe, and in 1686 signed the Moscow Treaty whereby Poland ceded Kiev to Russia in return for Russia's less tangible agreement to join this league. His sons competed to succeed him, while Poland's magnates continued to be adamantly and successfully opposed to all three. The satisfactory marriage of his only daughter, Kunegunda, to the elector of Bavaria (1694) alleviated the disappointments of his final years. He died in the most lavish of his castles, the last great King of Poland.

Summary

John III Sobieski's aims as king were to strengthen Poland's government, especially by making the monarchy hereditary; to regain Polish territories lost in various wars; and, through his Holy League, to free Europe from Islam. Poland's kings, who could not tax or raise armies, were further weakened in 1652 by the magnates' successful assertion of the right of any single one of them to dissolve any session of the Seym upon demand. Moreover, when a magnate exercised this right (the *liberum veto*), all business conducted by the Seym up to that point was obviated. Foreign governments paid enormous sums for the timely exercise of the *liberum veto*. Of the Seym's forty-four sessions during the latter half of the seventeenth century, fifteen were dissolved by the *liberum veto*.

Constitutional reform was doomed by the narrow self-interest of Poland's magnates and by the vast sums Poland's neighbors made available to any of them who would block such reforms. Poland's inability to pacify the Ukraine, either militarily or by granting and securing justice to its inhabitants, was again chiefly a result of its weak central government. Sobieski perceived the lack and foresaw the consequences, making his administrative failures bitter. His dream of restoring Poland's Baltic power was similarly doomed. The great accomplishment of Sobieski's life was the deliverance of Poland from Tatar and Turk.

Bibliography
Battaglia, O. Forst de. "Jan Sobieski, 1674-1696." In *The Cambridge History of Poland*, edited by W. F. Reddaway, J. H. Penson, O. Halecki, and R. Dyboski, vol. 1. Cambridge: Cambridge University Press, 1950. Details the facts of Sobieski's administration, its background, and its significance. Recommended for a thorough study, as is the whole volume. Many photographic illustrations, two useful maps, and an index.

Dyboski, Roman. *Outlines of Polish History*. 2d ed. London: George Allen & Unwin, 1931. The history and ruin of old Poland, and twentieth century Poland's political resurrection prior to World War II. Concise. Bibliography helpfully confined to English-language texts. Contains an index.

Gronowicz, Antoni. *The Piasts of Poland*. Translated by Joseph Vetter. New York: Charles Scribner's Sons, 1945. A brief history of the Polish struggle for independence. Modern portions are subjective. Contains maps, interesting photographs, and an index.

Halecki, Oskar. *A History of Poland*. Translated by M. M. Gardner and Mary Corbridge-Patkaniowska. Chicago: Henry Regnery, 1966. A revised, enlarged edition of the author's 1933 survey of Polish history. Chapter 16, "John Sobieski," is a clear, worthwhile treatment. Contains an index.

Michener, James A. *Poland*. New York: Random House, 1983. A perfunctory fictional thread is woven through this clear, vivid history of Poland from Genghis Khan to Lech Walesa. Chapter 5 deals with Sobieski's administration, especially the rescue of Vienna. Contains endpaper maps and a useful introduction.

Martha Bennett Stiles

SAINT JOHN OF THE CROSS
Juan de Yepes y Álvarez

Born: June 24, 1542; Fontiveros, Spain
Died: December 14, 1591; Úbeda, Spain
Areas of Achievement: Church reform and religion
Contribution: Saint John of the Cross contributed to the renewal of monastic life and to the development of mystical theology during the golden age of the Catholic Reformation. His most lasting contribution has been to Western mysticism.

Early Life

Juan de Yepes y Álvarez (Saint John of the Cross) was born on June 24, 1542, in Fontiveros, Spain, a town of five thousand inhabitants situated on the Castilian tableland. His father, Gonzalo de Yepes, was the son of a prosperous local silk merchant. Gonzalo was disinherited for marrying Catalina Álvarez, an impoverished and orphaned Toledan, apprenticed to a weaver in Fontiveros. John was the third son born to this union. The death of his father following a prolonged illness when John was only two left John, his mother, and his siblings in dire poverty. Seeking help, Catalina left Fontiveros, going initially to the province of Toledo but later settling in Medina del Campo, a city of thirty thousand. In Medina, there was a doctrine, or catechism, school. As much an orphanage as an educational institution for the poor, this school received John as a student. Children were fed, clothed, catechized, and given a rudimentary education. Apprenticeship in various trades was also part of the program of the doctrine school. Little is known of the four trades that John tried, except that his efforts were unsuccessful. Since in later life John was fond of painting and carving, his failure, perhaps, was one of premature exposure rather than of aptitude. John was next attached to the Hospital de la Concepción, where he worked as a male nurse, begged alms for the poor, and continued his studies. Academic success caused him to be enrolled at the Jesuit College, situated barely two hundred yards from the hospital. Founded in 1551, this school enrolled forty students at the time John was in attendance, probably from 1559 to 1563. John's teachers recalled his passionate enthusiasm for books. With a good education in the humanities, John in 1563 found his life's vocation, taking the dark brown habit and white cloak of the Carmelites.

Life's Work

At the age of twenty-one, John entered the small community of the Carmelite brothers in Medina, then a fellowship of perhaps six members. The Order of Our Lady of Mount Carmel had been founded four centuries earlier, in 1156, in Palestine by Saint Berthold as one of extreme asceticism and of great devotion to Mary. By the sixteenth century, it admitted female as well as male members. The so-called Original or Primitive Rule of 1209 had been relaxed, the order following a Mitigated Observance. Why John selected this order is not known. Perhaps it was his love of contemplation, his devotion to the Virgin, or his practice of extreme asceticism that attracted him to the Carmelites. John of Yepes now took the name Fray Juan de Santo Matia (Brother John of Saint Mathias), though, five years later, when, on November 28, 1568, he professed the Carmelite Primitive Rule, he would change his name to Fray Juan de la Cruz (Brother John of the Cross). As a monastic reformer, John was to make a lasting contribution to Christianity.

Following his profession as a Carmelite, John continued his education at the College of San Andres, a school for sixteen years attached to the famed University of Salamanca. A good Latinist and an excellent grammarian, John took classes in the college of arts at Salamanca from 1564 to 1567. Perhaps seven thousand students were matriculated at the University of Salamanca at that time. Taught by a faculty known throughout Spain and the Habsburg lands, the young monk next turned his attention to theology, attending lectures in divinity in 1567-1568. At Salamanca, John was taught a clear-cut Thomism and was deeply immersed in the philosophy of Aristotle and the theology of Saint Thomas Aquinas. Concurrently, John was a master of students at San Andres.

Following his ordination as a priest in 1567, John met Saint Teresa de Jesús of Ávila. Daughter of a noble Spanish family, Teresa had entered the Carmelite Convent of the Incarnation (Mitigated Observance) at Ávila in 1535. Teresa had become persuaded that discipline was too relaxed and that there ought to be a return to the Primitive Rule of the Carmelites. Her followers were called Discalced Carmelites, in opposition to the Calced Carmelites, who continued to follow the Mitigated rather than the Primitive Rule. Within a year of his meeting with the remarkable Mother Teresa, John was committed to the so-called Teresian Reforms of the Carmelite Order. For that reason, in November, 1568, John was made professor of the Primitive Rule of the Carmelites at Duruelo. Resolving "to separate himself from the world and hide himself in God," John sought a strictly contemplative life. That wish was never granted, for John was often sought as a counselor and confessor (for the laity and the religious) and as a popular and persuasive preacher.

Soon John became subprior, then novice master, and finally rector of a new house of studies founded at Alcalá. This was a creative time for John, who was able to integrate the intellectual and the spiritual life and who could combine contemplation with active service, including becoming Teresa's confessor after 1571. John found "the delights which God lets souls taste in contemplation," but he was advised by Teresa that "a great storm of trials" was on the horizon.

Disputes between the Carmelites who followed the Primitive Rule and those who held to the Mitigated Observance caused John to become a focus of attention. Following an initial imprisonment in 1576, John was seized on December 2, 1577, by some of the Calced Carmelites and taken to Toledo, where he was commanded by superiors to repent of his reforms. This was yet another step in the antireformist policies that had prevailed in the Carmelite Order since a general chapter meeting in 1575. Because John refused to renounce the reforms, he was imprisoned for some nine months in a small cell. There was only one small opening for light and air. John's jailers were motivated by "vindictiveness . . . mingled with religious zeal," for they believed that his reforms of the order were a very great crime and revealed a stubborn pride and insubordination. John accepted his imprisonment, with its insults, slanders, calumnies, physical sufferings, and agonies of soul as a further labor by God to purify and refine his faith.

In August, 1578, John escaped from his captors and fled to southern Spain. The separation of the two branches of the Carmelite Order, the Calced and the Discalced, occurred in 1579-1580. John became the rector of a Discalced Carmelite college in Baeza in Andalusia, serving also as an administrator in the Reformed Carmelite Order, being Prior of Granada in 1582 and of Segovia in 1588. Vicar provincial of his order's southern region, by 1588 John was major definitor and was a member of the governing body of the society.

John's contemporary, Eliseo de los Martires, described him as "a man in body of medium size" and one of "grave and venerable countenance." His complexion was "wheaty," or "somewhat swarthy," and his face was filled with "good features." Normally John wore a mustache and was often fully bearded. Dressed in "an old, narrow, short, rough habit," one so rough it was said that "the cloak seemed to be made of goat-hair," John reminded many of a latter-day John the Baptist. John impressed those he met with his purity of character, his intensity of spirit, his austerity of life, his profound humility, his fondness for simplicity, and his honesty and directness in speech. Contemporary biographers also recalled his sense of humor, noting that he delighted in making his friars laugh, often sprinkling his spiritual conversation with amusing stories.

Perhaps John's greatest legacy to the world community is his writing about the interior life. During his trials, tribulations, and travels, John wrote of his encounters with God. These extensive treatises on the mystical life are a unique combination of his poems and his commentaries on those poems. *Cántico espiritual* (1581; *A Spiritual Canticle of the Soul*, 1862), part of which was said to have been composed while John was on his knees in prayer, is such a synthesis of poetry and commentary. That poetry is both didactic and symbolic, practical and devotional. The ancient threefold route of the soul to God is described in *A Spiritual Canticle of the Soul*. One moves from purgation (or confession of sin, the emptying of the self) to illumination (or instruction, revelation of God, filling with the divine) and then to union or perfection (going beyond a sense of separation to one of complete integration with God). This ongoing colloquy of Christ and the soul draws on the rich imagery of courtship and love, starting with the soul's search for the Beloved, continuing to an initial meeting, then describing the perfect union, and concluding with a discussion of the poignant desire for an everlasting intimacy with the Eternal, a longing that can only be fulfilled in eternity. *La subida del Monte Carmelo* (1578; *The Ascent of Mount Carmel*, 1862) is also a discussion of how the soul can attain mystical union with God. The journey to God contains a "Dark Night" because the spirit must quite literally mortify, or put to death, sensory experience and sensible knowledge and then maintain itself by pure faith. Following such purgations, as well as those that come from the faith experience itself, the soul enters into a transforming union with God. This is truly a passion, for it combines both intense suffering and ecstatic pleasure, the two components of overwhelming love. In *Llama de amor viva* (1581; *Living Flame of Love*, 1862), the spiritual marriage, or divine union, is further described.

Though he longed only for contemplation, John once more was caught up in controversy. In 1591, he found himself banished to Andalusia. After some time in solitary life, John became extremely ill, going to Úbeda for medical attention. Following extreme pain, John died at Úbeda on December 14, 1591. In his dying moments, John requested the reading of the "Canticle of Canticles," the moving love poem of the Old Testament. Interpreting it as an allegory of the soul's romance of God, John commented, "What precious pearls."

Summary

While controversial during his lifetime, Saint John of the Cross was commended by the Catholic church, following his death, as both a saint and teacher. Beatified by Pope Clement X in 1675, John was canonized in 1726 by Benedict XIII. In 1926, Pius XI declared him a doctor of the Church, one of perhaps thirty Catholics deemed a theologian of both outstanding intellectual merit and personal sanctity and to be received universally with appreciation.

John surely was a mighty doctor of the Church, embodying the profound spirituality of the Catholic Reformation in Spain, drawing on the same religious energies that inspired Teresa, Ignatius of Loyola, the founder of the Society of Jesus, and Francis Xavier, a missionary-evangelist of Asia. He will forever be one of the treasures of the Roman Catholic tradition.

As reformer, master, saint, doctor, poet, and seer, John transcended the limits of either one country or creed. His significance is greater even than that of enriching the piety of Roman Catholicism and of enhancing the literature of his native Spain. John's profound mysticism causes him to be ranked alongside the great religious seekers of all human history—with the saints of Hinduism, the sages of Buddhism, the Sufis of Islam, the seekers of Taoism, the teachers of Confucianism, the visionaries of Protestantism, and the holy men and women of Orthodoxy and Oriental Christianity. As such, John of the Cross is one of the major figures of world religion, combining intellectual rigor with a vigorous work ethic, wrapping both in a profound and appealing spirituality.

Bibliography

Bruno de Jesus-Marie. *St. John of the Cross*. Edited by Benedict Zimmerman, with an introduction by Jacques Maritain. London: Sheed & Ward, 1936. This extensively documented 495-page study by a Roman Catholic priest attempts to do justice to John as a reformer, theologian, and mystic, drawing on the insights of philosophy, history, and biography. The central thesis is that John was not simply a "Quietistic Mystic" who had mastered the interior life, but that he was also an "Activistic Churchman" who had a powerful impact on the external world of sixteenth century Catholicism.

Crisógono de Jesús. *The Life of St. John of the Cross*. Translated by Kathleen Pond. New York: Harper and Brothers, 1958. A thoroughly documented biography of John both as a person and as a monk. Illustrations, charts, notes, and references make this a useful starting point for further research.

Cugno, Alain. *Saint John of the Cross: Reflections on Mystical Experience*. Translated by Barbara Wall. New York: Seabury Press, 1979. This concise study in 153 pages contends that John was perhaps the greatest mystic produced by Christianity. Originally written for the University of Tours, this text attempts to understand John from a philosophical rather than a theological or mystical viewpoint. In six succinct and tightly written chapters, it explores such major themes in the philosophy of religion as the absence of God, the meaning of mysticism, the role of desire in religion, and the doctrine of the Kingdom of God.

Frost, Bede. *Saint John of the Cross, 1542-1591, Doctor of Divine Love: An Introduction to His Philosophy, Theology, and Spirituality*. London: Hodder & Stoughton, 1937. This classic study of John's thought attempts to do justice to the complexity and variety of the saint's writings. The author admits the inherent twofold difficulty of exploring John's thinking: mystical experiences in and of themselves are incommunicable and language proves inadequate to the description of such experiences, without the compounded problem of translation from Spanish to English.

John of the Cross, Saint. *The Ascent of Mount Carmel*. Translated by David Lewis, with a preface by Benedict Zimmerman. London: Thomas Baker, 1928. This indexed edition of John's major mystical work is useful as an introduction to a primary source for his thought. Indexed both by topic and by Scriptural references, the volume facilitates both the study of selected topics in John's piety and the identification of biblical sources for his themes.

Maio, Eugene A. *St. John of the Cross: The Imagery of Eros*. Madrid, Spain: Playor, 1973. In brief compass, the author introduces the reader to the mystical tradition of love, a theme central to John's life and thought. Chapters relate John to the poetic and mystical traditions of Spain, examine the role of Neoplatonism in Christian thought, and then explore the dynamics of John's spirituality. Contains an extensive bibliography.

Sencourt, Robert. *Carmelite and Poet: A Framed Portrait of St. John of the Cross, with His Poems in Spanish*. New York: Macmillan, 1944. This illustrated biography in 253 pages, with an appended anthology of John's verse in Spanish, examines the man from the standpoint of literature, providing the reader with "both the soul of poetry and the poetry of the soul." Extensive annotations compensate for the lack of a bibliography.

C. George Fry

JOSEPH II

Born: March 13, 1741; Vienna, Austria
Died: February 20, 1790; Vienna, Austria
Area of Achievement: Monarchy
Contribution: Joseph II contributed to the enlightened reform of the Habsburg monarchy at the end of the eighteenth century, which enabled it to survive as a great power until the end of World War I.

Early Life

Joseph was born while the far-flung and relatively backward Habsburg monarchy was in deep crisis, its northern province, Silesia, invaded by Frederick II of Prussia, and its other borders threatened by hostile neighboring states. His father was Francis Stephen, Duke of Lorraine, until 1736, when he became Grand Duke of Tuscany. Joseph's mother was Maria Theresa, daughter of Charles VI, Holy Roman emperor, from whom she inherited, in 1740, the Habsburg dynastic lands if not the imperial title. Joseph grew to maturity while his mother was trying to unify the monarchy in order to repel the invaders and to recover Silesia.

The first male child, Archduke Joseph was expected to succeed his mother as ruler and was accordingly prepared for the task. Much of his early instruction was too pedantic to arouse a love of learning. He became fluent, however, in Italian, Czech, and French. The study that most significantly touched him was natural law, as expounded by the noted Austrian jurist, Karl Anton von Martini, whose disciple, Christian Beck, tutored the young archduke. Joseph adopted their enlightened idea that a ruler, the first servant of the state, should be governed by considerations of social utility. Martini and Beck also inclined Joseph toward religious toleration as well as toward the reform of the monarchy's ecclesiastical institutions. Although the pious Maria Theresa insisted that Joseph receive rigorous instruction and training in the Roman Catholic religion, she neither alienated him from the Church nor turned him into a zealot. Joseph remained throughout his life a convinced, practicing Catholic.

To increase Austrian influence in Italy, Maria Theresa had her son marry Isabella of Parma in 1760. The marriage nevertheless became a love match. A slim, good-looking young man with remarkably blue eyes, Joseph was immediately attracted to the beautiful, intelligent, and well-educated young princess. Her early death after less than two years left Joseph despondent. The death of their young daughter and a second, brief marriage with a Bavarian princess whom he detested further dulled his affections. Henceforth, he remained cool and aloof toward people, reserving his emotional energies for the affairs of state.

Active, restless, and headstrong, Joseph learned the art of governing more through travel and practical experience in public affairs than through reading or academic training. In 1761, he began attending meetings of the state council. Crowned King of the Romans in 1764, he ascended the imperial throne the following year upon the death of Francis Stephen. Joseph's new imperial responsibility was largely honorific, but it prompted Maria Theresa to give him the office of coregent and a share of her power.

Life's Work

As coregent, Joseph was not permitted to carry out the radical, sweeping reform that he wished. Mistrusting her son's judgment, Maria Theresa retained control of the government. Since he was expected to sign all state documents, however, he could sometimes insist successfully that his views be adopted. Convinced that the oppression of peasants by their lords was depriving the state of productive subjects, Joseph agitated with some success for reforms. In Bohemia, where the evils of serfdom brought the peasantry to the point of insurrection, Joseph was responsible for the law of 1775 reducing the peasants' forced labor to a maximum of three days per week.

During the last several years of the coregency, tension between Maria Theresa and Joseph was aggravated by the issue of religious toleration. Although the Austrian Habsburgs had vigorously restored Catholicism in their dynastic lands during the Counter-Reformation, they had failed to eradicate Protestantism. In the kingdom of Hungary, Protestants formed a strong, legalized minority. Moreover, in Bohemia and Moravia thousands of crypto-Protestants were drawn out into the open during the peasant unrest of the 1770's. Joseph's opposition to his mother's decision to force these dissenters back into the Catholic church caused an impasse that remained unresolved, until he became the sole ruler of the monarchy.

In military and foreign affairs, Joseph was active but usually unsuccessful. His model, as well as his chief opponent, was Frederick II of Prussia. Endowed with modest military talents, Joseph attempted to Prussianize the Austrian army. His improvements, however, fell far short of giving Austria an advantage over Prussia. When Joseph's scheme to annex Bavaria provoked a brief war with Prussia in 1788, his army was unable to prevent the Prussians from occupying much of Bohemia. Pushing Joseph aside, Maria Theresa negotiated peace with Frederick in 1779, thereby restoring the prewar boundaries except for a small part of Bavarian territory that was given to Austria.

Maria Theresa's death, on November 29, 1780, meant that Joseph became the sole ruler of the Habsburg monarchy. He began his administration with uncharacteristic patience and good sense. He retained her chancellor, Wenzel Anton von Kaunitz, to advise him on key foreign and domestic issues. He also kept his mother's system of government virtually intact, but he tried to make it work more efficiently.

During his first year in charge, he issued the Edict of Toleration, one of the most lasting reforms of his reign. Lutherans, Calvinists, and Greek Orthodox were allowed to form congregations, worship together, own property, enter the professions, and hold public office. About 150,000 persons in Bohemia, Moravia, and Austria declared themselves Protestant, many more than expected, prompting strong protests from the Catholic hierarchy. Convinced that Catholicism should continue as the state's religion, Joseph, in 1783, made leaving the Catholic church more difficult. He also denied recognition to radical Protestant sects. The expressed purpose of the edict was to enable non-Catholics to become more useful subjects. A similar pragmatic concern moved him to extend toleration to the Jews. Crafts and trades, including the army, were opened to them, and many obstacles to their assimilation into Austrian society were removed.

It seemed clear to Joseph's utilitarian mind that the monastic system was grossly inefficient. Closing about a third of the convents and monasteries, he reduced the number of nuns and monks from sixty thousand to forty thousand. With the money realized from the sale of confiscated monastic property, he greatly improved the parish ministry of secular priests by reforming seminary education, building new churches where needed, and assigning the parish clergy a significant role in enlightening the people. He also carried out a rational realignment of diocesan boundaries. Although these reforms provoked protests from some members of the Catholic hierarchy and prompted Pope Pius VI to travel to Vienna, the emperor continued to bring the Church securely under the control of the state and to make it an effective instrument of social improvement.

As sole ruler, he quickly attempted to free the peasantry from bondage and oppression and to make them productive citizens of the state. In 1781, he decreed the abolition of serfdom in Bohemia, Moravia, and the Austrian duchies. He devised a new system of taxation of land, based on Physiocratic principles, that would shift the heaviest burden from the peasants to landowners, who could afford to bear it. Joseph's scheme included commuting the peasantry's forced labor into cash payments. These remarkable measures, however, were frustrated by the privileged classes and by financial pressures of war at the end of his reign.

Often thwarted by concerted domestic opposition, Joseph undermined his reform program by several unsuccessful ventures into European power politics. In 1784, he tried in vain to force the Dutch to lift the blockade that had closed the port of Antwerp in the Austrian Netherlands. The next year, his plan to exchange the Austrian Netherlands for Bavaria was frustrated by the coalition of German princes organized by Frederick. These failures further alienated the population of the Austrian Netherlands, who were already disturbed by Joseph's ecclesiastical and administrative reforms. Joseph nevertheless joined Catherine II of Russia in a plan to dismember the Ottoman

Empire. The war that broke out in August of 1787 went badly for Austria at first. Joseph, who personally commanded the army, was blamed for its humiliating defeat.

During the last two years of his reign, Joseph had to acknowledge the failure of much of his program of reform. The revolt in the Austrian Netherlands ended his rule there. The Hungarian nobility forced him to revoke all the reforms except the abolition of serfdom and the Edict of Toleration. Ravaged by tuberculosis, Joseph died disillusioned and alone, his life's work apparently in ruins.

Summary

Joseph II is generally regarded as the enlightened despot who most consistently attempted to apply reason and humanity to the administration of a major European state. His reforms were so sweeping as to be justly considered a revolution from above. They might have failed in any case, since he underestimated the resistance of the vested interests that they upset. He also lacked the well-trained, disciplined bureaucracy that was needed to carry out the reforms. Their failure was assured by the breakdown of Joseph's health and by the severe economic repercussions of the unfortunate war with the Turks.

Not all was lost. Begun by his mother and extended by Joseph, the public educational system survived. Moreover, his eclectic economic policies contributed to the rapid growth of industry in Austria and Bohemia. His religious toleration led to the establishment of two Protestant denominations in the western parts of the monarchy and the gradual assimilation of a large Jewish minority. As limited as it was, Joseph's toleration was remarkably enlightened by contemporary standards. While some of his reforms of the Catholic church, such as the state-controlled seminaries, were revoked, the improved parish ministry survived. In time, as the shortcomings of the man receded from public consciousness, a mythical Joseph II, "The People's Emperor," took hold in the popular imagination and influenced the growth of Liberalism in Austrian politics in the nineteenth century.

Bibliography
Beales, Derek. *Joseph II*. Vol. 1, *In the Shadow of Maria Theresa, 1741-1780*. Cambridge: Cambridge University Press, 1987. General study of Joseph's life and work up to 1780. A second volume in preparation will complete the study. A serious scholarly work, it is the first major interpretation of Joseph to appear in English. Contains a bibliographical essay, abundant footnotes discussing documentary sources and secondary literature, and a bibliography listing Beales's archival and printed sources. Beales's aim is to redraw the conventional picture of the coregency.
Bernard, Paul P. *Joseph II*. New York: Twayne, 1968. Brief but dependable

survey of the monarch's life. He is represented as an autocrat whose primary concern was to centralize the state and make it run more efficiently. Contains a short selected bibliography.

Blanning, T. C. W. *Joseph II and Enlightened Despotism.* New York: Longman, 1970. Would be useful in a classroom. Contains an analysis of the monarch's reign, a representative selection of documentary material, and a comprehensive bibliography. Presents Joseph as a pragmatic despot who was Catholic as well as enlightened.

O'Brien, Charles H. *Ideas of Religious Toleration at the Time of Joseph II: A Study of the Enlightenment Among Catholics in Austria.* Philadelphia: American Philosophical Society, 1969. Devoted to the sources and the principal features of Joseph's policy of religious toleration. Contends that Joseph viewed the Edict of Toleration as a genuine reform of the Catholic church as well as a measure making Protestants more useful to the state. Analyzes Joseph's policies toward Jews and radical Protestant sects.

Padover, Saul K. *The Revolutionary Emperor: Joseph II of Austria.* London: Jonathan Cape, 1934, reprint 1967. The most popular biography of the monarch in English, it has strongly influenced subsequent biographies. The main point is that Joseph is an outstanding product of the Enlightenment. Draws evidence and illustrations uncritically from the numerous contemporary fables about Joseph.

Temperley, Harold. *Frederic the Great and Kaiser Joseph: An Episode of War and Diplomacy in the Eighteenth Century.* 2d ed. London: Frank Cass, 1968. Valuable study contrasting the personalities, the achievements, and the significance of the two German monarchs. Focuses particularly on their conflicts over Bavaria. There are bibliographical notes.

Wangermann, Ernst. *The Austrian Achievement, 1700-1800.* New York: Harcourt Brace Jovanovich, 1973. An excellent brief description of Josephism, the concept of government, which was embodied in the monarch's reforms, especially those dealing with the relationship between church and state. Pays particular attention to social and economic forces that influenced political changes in the monarchy.

Charles H. O'Brien

BENITO JUÁREZ

Born: March 21, 1806; San Pablo Guelatao, Oaxaca, Mexico
Died: July 19, 1872; Mexico City, Mexico
Areas of Achievement: Government and politics
Contribution: The dominant figure of mid-nineteenth century Mexican politics, Juárez embodied a liberal vision of a democratic republican form of
government, economic development and modernization, virulent anticlericalism, and mandatory public education. Although he was prevented from
fully implementing his ambitious agenda by years of warfare against foreign intervention and his policies were anathema to many entrenched
conservative elements in Mexico, especially the Catholic church, Juárez's
reform program laid the groundwork for a modern Mexican nation.

Early Life

Benito Juárez was born in the small mountain hamlet of San Pablo Gue-
letao in the state of Oaxaca in southern Mexico in 1806. He was orphaned
when his parents died before he reached the age of four. Reared by his uncle until the age of twelve in a remote Zapotec Indian community, Juárez's
beginnings could not have been more humble. In 1818, he walked forty-one
miles to the state capital, Oaxaca City, and found work and shelter in the
home of a Franciscan lay brother who was a part-time bookbinder. Juárez
worked in the bindery and helped with chores, and in return was given
school tuition. Since he excelled in school, he was encouraged to enter the
seminary. Juárez later changed his mind, however, and in 1829 chose a career in law, entering the Oaxaca Institute of Arts and Sciences. Two years
later, he earned his lawyer's certificate, and that professional degree proved
to be his passport to politics. The same year he was graduated from law
school, he became an alderman in the city council and subsequently served
as state legislator. His improved social and economic standing was reflected
by his marriage in 1843 to Margarita Maza, the daughter of a prominent
Oaxacan family.

Even as a successful young lawyer, Juárez always remembered his roots
and did *pro bono publico* work for groups of impoverished peasant villagers.
Convinced that major structural change was needed to make Mexico a more
just society, Juárez decided to forgo his law practice and dedicate his career
to public service.

When war erupted between Mexico and the United States in 1846, Juárez,
who at the time was a deputy in the Mexican national congress, was recalled
to his home in 1847 to serve an abbreviated term as interim governor. A year
later, he was elected to a full term. Juárez proved to be a capable and honest
governor, overseeing the construction of fifty rural schools, encouraging
female attendance in the classroom, trimming the bloated state bureaucracy,

facilitating economic development through the revitalization of an abandoned Pacific port, and making regular payments on the state debt. Moreover, the idealistic governor raised eyebrows around Mexico when he refused to offer his state as sanctuary to General Antonio López de Santa Anna, the powerful dictator (caudillo) who would serve as president on eleven separate occasions during the first thirty chaotic years of Mexican nationhood. Santa Anna never forgave Juárez for this slight, and, when he became president for the final time in 1853, he arrested Juárez, imprisoned him for several months, and then exiled him aboard a ship destined for New Orleans.

Life's Work

In New Orleans, Juárez made contact with a burgeoning expatriate community who represented the best and brightest of a new generation of young, idealistic Mexicans. These liberals, who called themselves *puros*, were committed to wholesale changes in the political system, to modernizing the nation's stagnant economy, and to creating a more equitable society for all Mexicans. These *puros* knew that Mexico had been racked by political instability, that Mexico had suffered a humiliating defeat at the hands of the United States, that corporate institutions such as the military and the Church had a viselike grip on Mexican society, and that a small politically powerful and economically wealthy elite dominated thousands of impoverished Indians and mestizos. Influenced by nineteenth century European liberal thought and enamored of the North American republican experiment, the *puros* composed a statement of principles in exile and secured arms and ammunition for regional caudillos in Mexico who opposed Santa Anna. Juárez was smuggled into Mexico and served as an aide to Juan Alvarez, the caudillo who spearheaded the Ayutla Rebellion. In 1855, the rebels drove Santa Anna from power for the last time.

When the new government was formed, Juárez was named secretary of justice. Juárez's cohorts were determined to see Mexico erase the vestiges of the past and emerge from chaos and anarchy. The *puros* focused on the Catholic church as being the single most regressive institution in Mexican society and sought to curtail its pervasive influence. The secretary of justice was intimately involved with the first of a series of reform laws that attacked corporate interests. There came a series of reform laws—which gave the era its name, *La Reforma*—and which systematically dismantled the power of the Catholic church in Mexico. The *Ley Lerdo* prohibited corporate institutions from owning or administering property not used in their daily operations. The Church, local and state governments, and corporate Indian villages could retain their churches, monasteries, meeting halls, jails, and schools, but other property had to be put up for sale at public auction, with the proceeds destined for federal coffers. In the first six months following the implementation of the law, twenty-three million pesos worth of property was auctioned, twenty million of which had belonged to the Church.

The reform laws were incorporated in a new constitution (1857). This document gave Mexico its first bill of rights, abolished slavery and titles of nobility, and created a unicameral congress to diminish executive power. Conservatives, especially the Church, unleashed a torrent of invective against the liberal document. Priests who did not publicly disavow the constitution were suspended by the hierarchy. While bureaucrats who refused to take the oath of allegiance lost their jobs, soldiers who did take the oath were not treated in Catholic hospitals and were denied the last rites.

The War of the Reform broke out in 1858, when conservatives attacked and captured Mexico City, dissolved the congress, and arrested Juárez, who had recently been elected chief justice of the supreme court—a position that placed him next in line for the presidency. When President Ignacio Comonfort proved unequal to the task of reconciliation, he resigned. Juárez then managed to escape from conservative hands and was promptly named president by his liberal supporters. For three years, the war raged as Juárez made his temporary headquarters in the port city of Veracruz.

After a bitter and protracted struggle, the liberals persevered and in 1861 Juárez entered Mexico City triumphant. The president decided to treat his enemies leniently and tendered a generous amnesty. More pressing problems faced Juárez, since he inherited a depleted treasury and a destitute army that had not been paid. Moreover, Mexico owed a considerable amount of money to European creditors, who now demanded repayment. Juárez, in an act of fiscal desperation, ordered a two-year suspension of payments on the foreign debt. Spain, England, and France, in an effort to prod Mexican repayment, agreed jointly to seize ports along the Mexican coast to collect their claims.

Napoleon III viewed the joint occupation of the port of Veracruz as a vehicle to further his expansionistic aims. Hoping to re-create the empire of his great-uncle, Napoleon I, and to take advantage of a debilitated United States engaged in its own civil war, Napoleon III ordered his army to leave the port of Veracruz and march on Mexico City. (When the Spanish and English learned of Napoleon's true intentions, they withdrew their forces.) After a stiff fight, the French army reached Mexico City, only to find that Juárez had already evacuated the capital and had taken his government with him, constantly moving across the desert of northern Mexico to escape capture.

Napoleon III attempted to legitimate his imperialistic actions when he persuaded a Habsburg archduke, Ferdinand Maximilian, to leave Austria and bcome the Emperor of Mexico (with the backing of the French army). Conservatives and the Church, which had just been defeated in the War of Reform, were delighted and welcomed Maximilian. Maximilian, with his wife Carlota, arrived in Mexico in 1864 and quickly found that Juárez's liberals were still a force to contend with and that the French had not successfully pacified the country.

Portraying the conflict as a nationalistic struggle to oust the foreign usurper, the president inspired his forces to conduct a guerrilla campaign against the French. Juárez also asked and received war matériel from the United States, especially after the defeat of the Confederacy in 1865. Secretary of State William Seward sent threatening messages to the French king, protesting that the occupation was a violation of the Monroe Doctrine and demanding that the French withdraw from the Western Hemisphere. In addition, the French troops grew weary of the Mexican campaign, and Napoleon appeared to have lost interest as well. Concerned with Otto von Bismarck's aggressive foreign policy closer to home, Napoleon ordered his troops home in the spring of 1866. Soon thereafter, Maximilian's forces surrendered.

Maximilian was tried by court-martial, and the state asked for the death penalty. Despite intense pressure from the international community, Juárez stood by the sentence. After a devastating loss of territory to the United States and a nightmarish foreign interlude that cost more than fifty thousand Mexican lives, Juárez believed that Mexico had to make it clear that it would not countenance any more intervention. Maximilian was tried, convicted, and shot in 1867.

Most historians mark 1867 as the beginning of the modern Mexican nation. Juárez called for presidential elections and announced that he would run for an unprecedented third term. Since the first two terms were spent at war, most Mexicans believed that, under these extraordinary circumstances, the president was justified in seeking reelection. Moreover, given his back-to-back victories against the conservatives and Maximilian, Juárez's popularity was cresting.

His third term (1867-1871) was the first time the president had an opportunity to implement his liberal program in a peaceful atmosphere. The first order of business was to reconstruct Mexico's economy, which had been ravaged by nine years of war. To encourage foreigners to invest in Mexico, the president had to change the nation's image abroad. A rural police force was expanded to safeguard silver shipments and to protect highways from bandits. Mexico's first railroad from Mexico City to its chief port, Veracruz, was finally completed in 1872 by a British company with subsidies from Juárez's administration. Juárez also revised Mexico's antiquated tax and tarriff structures and sought to revitalize the mining sector to stimulate foreign investment further. Finally, Juárez appointed a commission to overhaul the national educational system. All of these policies collectively represented Juárez's vision for Mexico's future, and, although many were never fully implemented by his administration, they did put Mexico on the road to modernization.

One major problem that persisted throughout his third term was political unrest, especially at the regional and local level. Juárez spent much of his energies quieting one local uprising after another and found it necessary repeatedly to ask the congress to grant him extraordinary powers (martial law). Juárez's opponents believed that he had abused the constitutional principles he had fought so ardently to defend and that his rule was growing increasingly arbitrary and heavy-handed with time.

Despite the fact that his popularity had been falling for some time, Juárez decided to run for a fourth term in 1871. Two candidates, Sebastián Lerdo de Tejada (the brother of the author of the *Ley Lerdo*) and Porfirio Díaz, opposed him in the election. When no candidate received the requisite majority, according to the 1857 constitution, the congress would decide the outcome. The legislature, dominated by Juárez's supporters, elected him for a fourth term. Although Díaz revolted, federal forces quelled the rebellion. Soon after Díaz's defeat, however, Juárez suffered a coronary seizure and died on July 19, 1872.

Summary

Benito Juárez defined Mexican politics from 1855 to 1872. The fact that a full-blooded Zapotec Indian could become president of the nation demonstrated that Mexico had broken with its aristocratic past. The leader of an ambitious group of idealistic liberals, Juárez knew that the power of the Catholic church, the caudillos, and the army had to be diminished. Notwithstanding his more autocratic rule during his last years, especially his controversial decision to run for a fourth term, he remained true to his democratic principles.

Although Juárez is best known for his defeat of Maximilian and his anticlericalism, his greatest political legacy was his ambitious third term, which set the agenda for future presidential administrations. Juárez's successors, Lerdo de Tejada (1872-1876) and Díaz (1876-1911), faithfully followed his policies and programs. While some economic policies proved successful, the breaking up of village lands led to the expansion of the great estates or haciendas, and the destruction of semiautonomous Indian villages. Although Juárez's democratic principles were abused by Díaz during his long dictatorship, Díaz's policies and strategies for modernization bore the indelible stamp of Benito Juárez.

Bibliography

Bazant, Jan. *Alienation of Church Wealth in Mexico: Social and Economic Aspects of the Liberal Revolution, 1856-1857*. Cambridge: Cambridge University Press, 1971. A thorough analysis of the implications of the *Ley Lerdo* and its effects on church wealth in Mexico.

Berry, Charles R. *The Reform in Oaxaca, 1856-1876: A Microhistory of the Liberal Revolution*. Lincoln: University of Nebraska Press, 1981. A critical examination of how liberal policies were implemented in Juárez's home region, Oaxaca. Berry dispels certain myths about the land reform, arguing that it was not as thoroughgoing and disruptive as previously believed.

Hanna, Alfred J., and Kathryn A. Hanna. *Napoleon III and Mexico: American Triumph over Monarchy*. Chapel Hill: University of North Carolina Press, 1971. A fascinating account of the role of the United States in dislodging the French from Mexico. Utilizing Seward's diplomatic correspondence and other North American sources, the authors also investigate the moral and material help the American government gave Juárez against Maximilian and the French.

Meyer, Michael C., and William L. Sherman. *The Course of Mexican History*. 3d ed. New York: Oxford University Press, 1987. The best single-volume text on Mexican history. The material on Juárez is concise, thorough, and up-to-date.

Perry, Laurens B. *Juárez and Díaz: Machine Politics in Mexico*. De Kalb: Northern Illinois University Press, 1978. The only critical account of Juárez's arbitrary rule during his third term. Perry treats not only Juárez's administration but also the succeeding presidencies of Lerdo and Díaz.

Roeder, Ralph. *Juárez and His Mexico*. 2 vols. New York: Viking Press, 1947. A biography in English of Juárez, this massive, dated work details in narrative fashion his life and work.

Allen Wells

JULIUS II
Giuliano della Rovere

Born: December 5, 1443; Albisola, Republic of Genoa
Died: February 21, 1513; Rome
Areas of Achievement: Religion, the military, and patronage of the arts
Contribution: Julius II, the Warrior Pope, was the first and only pontiff personally to command and lead a papal army into battle. His military exploits regained large amounts of territory lost to the Papal States in wars with France and small Italian republics. Besides his attempts to strengthen church administration and reduce nepotism, he was also a patron to Michelangelo, Raphael, and Donato Bramante.

Early Life
Giuliano della Rovere was born in the small town of Albisola, Italy, in 1443. When his father's brother, Francesco della Rovere, became head of the Franciscan Order, Giuliano was educated under the direction of the Franciscans; soon after his studies were completed, he was ordained a priest. When his uncle became pope and took the name Sixtus IV in 1471, Giuliano was made a cardinal in the same year. Over the next few years, Cardinal della Rovere held eight bishoprics, controlled many more abbeys and benefices, and assumed the title of Archbishop of Avignon.

From 1480 to 1482, della Rovere served as legate to France. In this capacity, he showed great diplomatic skill in reconciling the differences between Louis XI of France and Maximilian of Austria. He returned to Rome when Sixtus IV died in 1484 and bribed many cardinals into electing Batista Cibo as Pope Innocent VIII. Innocent was controlled rather easily; indeed, his policies were to a large extent determined and implemented by della Rovere.

Because of his strong influence over Innocent, della Rovere was opposed by Cardinal Rodrigo Borgia; in a short time, the two men became bitter rivals. Their disagreements escalated to such an extent that, when Innocent died in 1492 and Cardinal Borgia was elected Pope Alexander VI, della Rovere was forced to flee to France in order to save his life.

Della Rovere tried to convince King Charles VIII of France that church reforms in Italy could only be achieved with his personal support. In fact, della Rovere was seeking help in removing Alexander from the Papacy. When Charles VIII decided to invade Italy, della Rovere accompanied him and attempted to win his backing for the convocation of a council to depose the pope on the grounds of his having won the election of 1492 through bribery. Unfortunately for della Rovere, Charles negotiated and signed a conciliatory treaty with Alexander in 1495—all della Rovere's efforts to get rid of his enemy were frustrated.

In 1498, della Rovere was reconciled with Alexander when his diplomatic skills helped to arrange the marriage of Charlotte d'Albret, sister of the King of Navarre, to Cesare Borgia, a relative of the pope. When Borgia attacked the dukedom of Urbino, however, where della Rovere's nephew stood next in line to succeed the duke, the peace was over. Once again, della Rovere had to flee far from Rome. Only the death of Alexander in August of 1503 made it possible for the cardinal to return to Rome.

Believing that the way was now clear for him to become pope, della Rovere did everything in his power to assure the outcome of the election. Yet the Italian cardinals were divided as to which candidate to support and della Rovere, although he received a majority of the votes, fell two short of the required two-thirds. Realizing that he was not going to be elected to the Papacy, he threw his support to the Cardinal of Siena, Francesco Piccolomini, who took the name Pius III. Yet della Rovere knew that the new pope's age and ill health meant a short tenure in office. When Pius died after only twenty-six days, della Rovere prepared for one last chance to wear the tiara.

Life's Work

By extensive promises to his opponents, and by resorting to bribery when necessary, della Rovere was unanimously elected pope on November 1, 1503, in the shortest conclave ever recorded, less than twenty-four hours. A proud and egotistical man, he changed two syllables of his given name, Giuliano, to come up with his papal name, Julius II. Extremely confident, impetuous, hot-tempered, and impatient, Julius soon gained the reputation of an activist pope, unable to listen to advice. He insisted on doing everything himself and was almost impossible to consult; when faced with a contrary opinion, he would stop the speaker with a little bell kept near him at all times. Although he was sixty years old at the time of his election to the Papacy and suffering from gout and kidney ailments, his spirit was indefatigable. He was a large man with a tight mouth and dark eyes; the word most often used by Italians in describing him was *terribilitá*, or "awesomeness."

Julius immediately began to repair the damage wrought on the Church by Alexander VI. He reorganized papal administration, planned to achieve financial solvency for the Church, promised to eliminate simony, and began to reduce nepotism. He established order in Rome by implementing harsh measures against bandits and hired assassins who had run rampant under Alexander; to serve as a bulwark against any foreign or domestic threat to himself, he hired mercenary Swiss guards as protectors of the Vatican.

Believing that the authority of the Papacy could be enhanced by the exercise of temporal power, Julius implemented a strategy of territorial conquest, expedient diplomacy, and the show of external pomp and glory. Accordingly, his first major decision as supreme pontiff was to recover the territories lost to the Papal States under the administration of and following the death of Alexander.

In the first year of his pontificate, Julius set out to regain the cities that Venice had seized from the Holy See and later occupied. Initially, he used diplomatic measures to isolate and pressure the Venetian republic to release its holdings. Venice did give back some of the land but continued to hold the cities of Rimini and Faenza. Frustrated by Venice's intransigence, the pope turned his attention to the recovery of Bologna and Perugia, two of the most important cities within the Papal States whose leaders ignored the authority of Rome. Impatient and reckless in his desire to recapture the land, Julius ignored the objections of many cardinals and shocked all of Europe when he personally rode at the head of his army to conquer the cities in 1506. Shortly afterward, when the papal fief Ferrara turned against him, the white-bearded pope donned helmet, mail, and sword, and led his troops in an attack through a breach in the fortress wall. During these years of violent disputes, Julius was continually on horseback, encouraging his soldiers, directing their deployment, and making certain that they used the armaments of modern warfare correctly.

Still unable to subdue Venice, Julius sought the help of the Holy Roman Emperor Maximilian and Louis XII of France. Julius convinced the two men to declare war on the republic and, with the added participation of Spain and Swiss mercenaries, formed the League of Cambrai to execute his plan. Julius also issued a bull of excommunication and interdict for the entire population of the city. When the Venetians were finally defeated at the Battle of Agnadello in May of 1509, one of the bloodiest conflicts in the history of warfare, the pope's troops reclaimed Rimini, Faenza, and other territories previously held by the republic.

Only one year later, Julius received a formal confirmation of ecclesiastical rights and authority in the Venetian territory; with this reconciliation, he lifted the ban of excommunication. Yet neither Louis XII nor Maximilian was ready to make peace and leave Italy; the expansion of their empires now dominated their strategy. Julius quickly recognized that there could be no consolidation of the Papal States as long as the French and the emperor remained in Italy. Convinced of the growing danger that foreign troops in Italy now posed, Julius made a complete about-face and formed an alliance in 1510 with Venice and Spain, along with Swiss mercenaries, against France. This new combination was called the Holy League, and Julius' new battle cry was, "Out with the barbarians!"

King Louis XII's resentment and animosity ran so deep as to label the war against himself illegal and convene, with the support of Emperor Maximilian and prominent French cardinals, a synod at Tours intended to depose Julius from the Papacy; in 1511, at the instigation of the French king, the rebel cardinals established their own antipapal council at Pisa. At the time, Julius was again waging war in person, on this occasion against the Duke of Ferrara, who supported the French. When he received news of the attempts to remove him from office, however, the pope reacted swiftly: He excommunicated Louis and the rebellious cardinals, convinced England to join the Holy League, and convened the Fifth Lateran Council in 1512 to oppose the schismatic meeting at Pisa and reassert his own papal authority.

After a number of setbacks, Julius and the Holy League finally defeated the French at the Battle of Ravenna and drove them across the Alps. With a few concessions to Maximilian, the pope's campaign to oust foreign troops from Italy came to a successful conclusion. Yet, even though Julius had regained large tracts of land for the Papal States, the nature of Italian politics and diplomacy frustrated him in providing definite and long-lasting resolutions to many territorial problems.

Weary with war and in ill health, Julius turned his attention to the Lateran Council and church reform. Initially, the council was preoccupied with problems surrounding the French presence in Italy and with the illegitimate council at Pisa. With the defeat of the French and the dissolution of the assembly at Pisa, Julius pushed for needed reforms and the Lateran council responded. One of the most important of Julius' papal bulls confirmed by the council voided any papal election tainted with simony; any offender would suffer the loss of his office and endure large financial penalties. The council also confirmed Julius' renewal of a bull by Pius II which prohibited switching an ecclesiastical appeal from a pope to a council.

One of Julius' last acts as pope, and one of the most far-reaching, was to grant a dispensation to Prince Henry of England, later King Henry VIII, enabling him to marry Catherine of Aragon. Julius II died on February 21, 1513, in Rome, but the Fifth Lateran Council he had convened remained in session for another four years.

Summary

The goal of consolidating the Papal States, Julius II believed, could only be attained by keeping France and the Holy Roman Empire out of Italy. This strategy was achieved in three stages: the regaining of lost territories, the expelling of all so-called foreigners from the Italian peninsula, and the assuring of papal authority in Rome and throughout the Papal States. For these reasons, Julius is regarded by many historians as one of the earliest and most important proponents of Italian unification.

Yet since the great powers returned to plague Italian politics after the pope's death, it is arguable that Julius' more significant and lasting contribution to the Papacy involved his patronage of the arts. He beautified Rome and initiated a large amount of new construction, including new and rebuilt churches, such as Santa Maria del Popolo and Santa Maria della Pace, and he helped establish the Vatican Library. He commissioned Raphael to paint new frescoes for the papal apartments. Michelangelo, against his will, was browbeaten by the pope into painting the ceiling for the Sistine Chapel; working alone on a scaffold for almost four years, Michelangelo allowed no one but Julius to view his work.

Bramante was one of the pope's favorite artists; Julius assigned Bramante the task of designing and building the courts of the Belvedere, where he started a collection of ancient sculpture. The monument to Julius' papacy was also given to Bramante to execute—the demolition of the old Basilica of St. Peter's and the construction of a new one. The cost of replacing the older building with a grander edifice significantly exceeded existing papal revenues and led Julius to implement a practice of dire consequence, the public sale of indulgences in Papal States. When the next pope extended the practice to Germany, it precipitated a revolt by a disillusioned and angry young cleric named Martin Luther.

Bibliography
Chambers, D. S. *Cardinal Bainbridge in the Court of Rome, 1509 to 1514*. London: Methuen, 1965. An account of one cardinal's tenure in Rome and his eyewitness observations of the persons and events surrounding the Papacy during Julius' reign. Particularly good in relating the machinations involved in ecclesiastical politics.
Erasmus, Desiderius. *Julius Exclusus*. Translated by Paul Pascal. Bloomington: Indiana University Press, 1968. This work was completed after the pope's death. Julius is characterized as the embodiment of war and all its accompanying evils. An extremely hostile polemic against Julius. Not until the twentieth century was Erasmus' authorship verified.
Gilbert, Felix. *The Pope, His Banker, and Venice*. Cambridge, Mass.: Harvard University Press, 1980. A detailed examination of Julius' involvement in the League of Cambrai and his war against the republic of Venice. Stresses the financial arrangements made by both the pope and the Venetian republic to carry out the extended conflict. An excellent insight into the diplomatic and financial policies at work in the Papacy. Notes at the end of the book shed light on some of the more elusive historical problems during Julius' pontificate.
O'Malley, John W. "Fulfillment of the Christian Golden Age Under Pope Julius II: Text of a Discourse of Giles of Veterbo, 1507." *Traditio* 25 (1969): 265-338. A contemporary interpretation of Julius' policy that temporal power gives authority and prestige to the Church. Focuses on the interaction between secular and spiritual pursuits in war, diplomacy, and art.
Tuchman, Barbara. *The March of Folly: From Troy to Vietnam*. New York: Alfred A. Knopf, 1984. A general overview of how the late Renaissance popes set the stage for Martin Luther's Reformation movement. More

specifically, a character study of Julius II that raises questions about the propriety of his decision to lead an army into battle.

Thomas Derdak

ENGELBERT KÄMPFER

Born: September 16, 1651; Lemgo, Duchy of Lippe
Died: November 2, 1716; Lemgo, Duchy of Lippe
Areas of Achievement: Literature, medicine, and botany
Contribution: Based on his own travels, Kämpfer wrote detailed and highly
   accurate accounts of Japan and other areas of Asia, the Middle East, and
   Russia. In addition, he wrote on Asian natural history, diseases, and med-
   ical practices.

Early Life
   Born the son of Johannes Kämpfer, a teacher and minister, Engelbert
Kämpfer was provided ample opportunity to study. As a youth, Kämpfer
studied the sciences and the humanities at a number of Swedish, Polish,
German, and Dutch schools and universities. Enrolled at Danzig in 1672, he
wrote a thesis on the politics of monarchy; the following year, he earned a
degree in philosophy from Kraków. He then studied medicine and natural
history at Königsberg. While his early education included the study of medicine, he did not take a formal medical degree until some twenty years later.
   Throughout his early education, Kämpfer was an avid student of foreign
languages. He learned French, Greek, and Latin, the primary languages of
intellectual discourse in his day, and also English, Swedish, Portuguese,
Spanish, Aramaic, Russian, and Polish. In his later medical and scientific
investigations, he often had occasion to draw on his multilingual background.
   By 1681, Kämpfer had traveled to Uppsala, Sweden, to study medicine
and anatomy with the famous physician, Olof Rudbeck. His excellent scholarship and ties to Rudbeck and other professors presented him with the
chance to travel to Persia, an opportunity which ultimately led him to journey to the Southeast Asian lands of Java and Siam (modern Thailand) en
route to Japan.

Life's Work
   At the age of thirty-two, Kämpfer joined a Swedish embassy to Persia.
Departing in 1683, he began a series of travels throughout the Middle East
and Asia that continued for ten years. Serious illness during this time did not
deter him from energetic investigation of the exotic lands he explored.
   Throughout his travels, he wrote detailed diaries which proved useful
sources of information for contemporary adventurers and later scholars alike.
Prior to his travels through Russia and Persia, Kämpfer's notebooks contained largely personal memorabilia—greetings from friends and relatives,
fellow students, and famous people he had met. Beginning with his entry
into Russia in 1683, Kämpfer's diaries reveal a boundless curiosity about
the lands and cultures through which he now passed.

Russian officials stalled the Swedish embassy because the Russian diplomatic ego was bruised by the fact that the embassy's itinerary listed Persia before Russia. It took two months for Swedish officials to resolve the dispute. During this time, Kämpfer absorbed all the new information he could acquire. His diaries include descriptions of a meeting with the young man who became Czar Peter the Great, reports of conditions in Siberia, and copies of letters to Czarina Sophia.

In January, 1684, the embassy finally reached Persia. Although the official business of the embassy was delayed for several months while permission for an audience with the shah (king) was arranged, Kämpfer found plenty to occupy his time. At Baku, on the Caspian Sea, he collected specimens representative of the flora and fauna of the area, explored the local geographic wonders, and practiced medicine.

The embassy's business was completed in a relatively short time, but when it returned to Sweden in 1685, Kämpfer decided to stay. He remained in Persia for three more years, working as an employee of the Dutch East India Company. While traveling to ports on the Strait of Hormuz, Kämpfer was stricken by serious illness—high fever, malaria, and dropsy. For a while, his life was clearly in danger, but he managed to recover by leaving the humid lowlands for the healthier climate of the hills.

Finally, in 1688, Kämpfer boarded ship for Southeast Asia. Traveling along the coast of Arabia, he crossed the Indian Ocean to Malabar, Ceylon, Bengal, and, ultimately, Sumatra. Throughout his voyage, he wrote a number of medical treatises. Among them, his essay on perical, the swollen foot ulcers unique to the inhabitants of Malabar, was the first to describe this ailment. In 1689, he arrived in Batavia (modern Jakarta). Staying there only a few months, he departed for Siam and Japan in May, 1690. He arrived in Japan that fall, on September 26, to spend a year as the resident physician to the Dutch trading community in Nagasaki.

At this time, opportunities for Europeans to travel to Japan were rare. After a major rebellion in which the Portuguese were implicated, Japan limited Western visits to Dutch traders in 1639—even the Dutch could enter and leave only on specified days of the year, regardless of weather conditions. Their business activity in Japan was restricted as well, and they could only establish an office (factory) on a small island (called Deshima) in Nagasaki harbor in southern Japan. While the Dutch were allowed to trade with Japan, suspicion of them remained high, and it was difficult for the Dutch traders to become intimate with any Japanese.

At the time of Kämpfer's arrival, Japan was enjoying a period of cultural expansion and economic prosperity. One hundred years of peace had given birth to bustling cities which supported an unprecedented array of poets, artists, bibliophiles, and theatrical troupes. Wealthy merchants as well as members of the ruling samurai (warrior) class supported the arts and demonstrated a high degree of intellectual curiosity.

Soon after his arrival, Kämpfer resolutely set about the task of overcoming Japanese reserve toward foreigners and began to explore the excitement of end-of-the-century Japan. Liberally dispensing European remedies to Japanese interpreters and their acquaintances, and treating them to large quantities of liquor, he gained their confidence. Through these people and in the course of his travels, he learned much about the natural history of Japan and its customs.

Kämpfer finally departed Japan in November, 1692. When he left, he brought with him a wide variety of suspiciously acquired Japanese memorabilia, in addition to his extensive notes. During his stay, he had managed to obtain a substantial number of Japanese books and other materials, despite the fact that such purchases were flatly illegal. These treasures included maps of Japan—maps that foreigners were not permitted to have because they provided information which the Japanese believed compromised their national security.

Upon his arrival in Europe, Kämpfer resumed his medical studies. In April, 1694, he received a doctorate in medicine from Leiden. His doctoral thesis was composed of ten essays based on his studies during his travels in Asia. Returning to his home near Lemgo, he engaged in the practice of medicine as physician to the Prince of Lippe. His medical responsibilities made it impossible for him to prepare his journals for publication. Only one collection of essays was published before he died, *Amoenitatum exoticarum*, which appeared in 1712.

Kämpfer did not marry until he was fifty-one. The marriage appears to have been little more than an attempt to acquire his bride's estate. He hoped that her wealth would provide him with the financial wherewithal to escape some of the burdens of his medical practice and free him to devote more time to his writing. His marriage to a woman thirty-five years his junior proved to be an unhappy one, and even Kämpfer's financial expectations were disappointed when his bride's estate was considerably smaller than he had thought. The tragedy of his marriage was compounded by the deaths in infancy of each of his three children.

In 1716, at the age of sixty-five, Kämpfer died at Lemgo. His dreams of publishing the findings of his world travels remained unfulfilled. All of his books, artworks, maps, and notes were left with a nephew, Johann Herman Kämpfer, with whom they remained for almost a decade.

Summary

Engelbert Kämpfer died an unhappy man. His life's ambitions in many respects were unfulfilled. True, he ranked as one of the seventeenth century's great explorers, but he had never had the opportunity to publish accounts of his travels and explorations in the depth and to the extent that he desired. Nevertheless, these pessimistic self-evaluations should not obscure the direct impact his travels, writings, and collections of Asiatica had in stimulating European curiosity about the Far East and the incisive understanding of Japan that he conveyed to his fellow naturalists and explorers. Unfortunately, much of the evidence of this success followed Kämpfer's death. The spread of Kämpfer's work and the preservation of his collections was almost accidental.

Kämpfer's collections might have remained at Lemgo and his most famous work, *The History of Japan,* might never have been translated and published were it not for the efforts of Sir Hans Sloane. Sloane never met Kämpfer but knew of him through his one publication, *Amoenitatum exoticarum.* Seven years after Kämpfer's death, Sloane negotiated with Johann Kämpfer for the purchase of the Kämpfer manuscripts, artworks, maps, books, and botanical specimens. Shortly thereafter, Sloane used his influence in the Royal Society of London to arrange for the translation of Kämpfer's manuscripts on Japan into English. The work was first published in two volumes in 1727. Ultimately, the Kämpfer collection, plus others gathered by Sloane, became part of the founding collection of the British Museum in 1759.

The most accessible of Kämpfer's work, *The History of Japan,* is much more than a survey of Japanese history and mythology. In addition, it includes an extensive, detailed account of Japan's geography and climate, Kämpfer's travels in Japan, and his experiences during audiences with the shogun, the most powerful man in the land. An appendix includes Kämpfer's argument in favor of Japan's policy of limiting contact with the West. When copies of *The History of Japan* entered Japan some years after it was published, it was translated into Japanese and used to bolster the arguments of political conservatives who wished to limit severely Japan's relations with Western nations.

Bibliography

Bowers, John Z. *Western Medical Pioneers in Feudal Japan.* Baltimore: Johns Hopkins University Press, 1970. Chapter 2, "The Early Years at Deshima: Willem Ten Rhijne and Engelbert Kämpfer," presents a lively but largely descriptive account of Kämpfer's life and travels. He credits Kämpfer with being the first great German explorer and the scientific discoverer of Japan. He presents a brief description of the Kämpfer collection in the British Museum and Kämpfer's travels in Japan. Bowers is strongest in his assessment of Kämpfer's impact on Europe as opposed to Japan.

Boxer, C. R. *Jan Compaigne in Japan, 1600-1817: An Essay on the Cultural, Artistic, and Scientific Influence Exercised by the Hollanders in Japan from the Seventeenth to Nineteenth Centuries.* The Hague: Martinus

Nijhoff, 1936, 2d rev. ed. 1950. Boxer's book is a general treatment of Dutch activities and influence in Japan. He presents little material that concentrates directly on Kämpfer and his activities in Japan, but his work is useful background for understanding the impact made on Japan by Europeans such as Kämpfer.

Gardner, K. B. "Engelbert Kämpfer's Japanese Library." *Asia Major* 7 (December, 1959): 74-78. Gardner identifies the specific parts of the British Museum collections which were the result of Kämpfer's efforts and discusses the unique characteristics of these materials. This work is helpful in gaining an understanding of Kämpfer's interests and the kinds of Japanese materials he introduced to Europe.

Goodman, Grant K. *Japan: The Dutch Experience*. Atlantic Highlands, N.J.: Humanities Press, 1985. Goodman's description of the Dutch factory in Japan is excellent, and, while he devotes little space to Kämpfer's activities, he provides a good account of the Dutch scientific and medical impact on Japan. Since Goodman draws rather heavily on Kämpfer's descriptions of Japan, this book itself is a good example of the impact that Kämpfer had on Western understanding of late seventeenth century Japan.

Kämpfer, Engelbert. *The History of Japan*. Reprint. Translated by J. G. Scheuchzer. 3 vols. Reprint. Glasgow, Scotland: J. MacLehose, 1906. Originally published in 1727-1728, multiple reprints of this work are widely available. Kämpfer's history is a remarkably accurate compendium of information on Japan and the most widely quoted source on seventeenth century Japan. Includes numerous illustrations, and extensive appendices contain discussions of the history of tea in Japan, medical practices, and other interesting aspects of Japanese life and customs. The introductory material includes a biography of Kämpfer.

Philip C. Brown

K'ANG-HSI

Born: May 4, 1654; Peking, China
Died: December 20, 1722; Peking, China
Areas of Achievement: Government and politics
Contribution: K'ang-hsi was the fourth emperor of the Ch'ing Dynasty that ruled China from 1644 to 1912. Blending knowledge and action in his leadership, he consolidated Manchu power and legitimated the Manchus' rule in China.

Early Life

K'ang-hsi, the third son of the Emperor Shun-chih, was born on May 4, 1654, in Peking, the capital city of the Manchu (Ch'ing) Empire. The Manchus, a branch of the nomadic Jurched tribe, arose in the twelfth century in Manchuria, where they subsisted by hunting and fishing. By the sixteenth century, they had absorbed so many Chinese cultural, economic, and technological influences that their nomadic existence had been thoroughly transformed. By the early seventeenth century, the Chinese Ming Dynasty (1368-1644) had fallen into steep decline. This allowed the Manchus, who had established powerful armies, to defeat the Ming and establish a new dynasty in Peking in 1644.

Although K'ang-hsi eventually became the fourth Manchu emperor of China, he was less than half Manchu ethnically, since his parents were of mixed Mongol, Chinese, and Manchu ancestry. K'ang-hsi was conscious of his multiple ethnic heritage and worked throughout his life to create a government representing all the diverse nationalities. As a youth, K'ang-hsi probably had as little experience of a happy, shared family life as any imperial prince of his time. His father took little interest in him; his daily care was entrusted to wet nurses; and palace eunuchs attended him in nearly all of his activities. It was impossible for him to be alone, and he rarely saw his mother and father. K'ang-hsi survived smallpox, one of the most dreaded diseases of the time, as a youngster, and this virtually ensured that he would lead a long life. This may have been the main reason for his being named the heir apparent. When his father died in 1661, K'ang-hsi assumed the throne at age seven.

A four-man regency, headed by the powerful Manchu general Oboi, ruled in his stead for the next eight years. Oboi used his position to secure a nearly impregnable hold on the court. K'ang-hsi's tutors, meanwhile, used these years to prepare him for ruling the empire. A voracious reader from the age of four, he eventually committed large sections of the Confucian classics to memory. He studied calligraphy, composed poetry, and later experimented with Western science and music. Two court controversies in the late 1660's offered K'ang-hsi the opportunity to wrest control of the throne from Oboi and the other regents. The first involved the making of the dynastic calendar. To the Chinese, a correct calendar was more than a method of reckoning time; it was a powerful symbol of imperial authority. An appropriate one would help to legitimate Manchu authority in the eyes of the Chinese. Early in the dynasty, the Manchus employed a German Jesuit missionary, Adam Schall, to prepare an official calendar. Schall created an astronomically correct document, but in doing so he relied on Western methods and unwittingly violated certain key elements of court etiquette. This exposed him to attacks by court factions opposed to Western influence.

Oboi took advantage of the calendar controversy to embarrass the Jesuits and solidify his own position. K'ang-hsi recognized Oboi's strategy, however, and conducted his own investigation of the matter. In time, he vindicated the Jesuits, who thereafter served as important advisers to him. Oboi's critics welcomed K'ang-hsi's independent actions and began to attack Oboi openly. K'ang-hsi, in turn, used the anti-Oboi factions to reshape the balance of power in the court to the point where, on June 14, 1669, he was able to arrest Oboi and take personal control of the government. Oboi died in prison shortly thereafter, and K'ang-hsi remained the uncontested ruler of China until his death in 1722.

Life's Work

K'ang-hsi's long reign of sixty-one years was characterized by courage, sagacity, and decisiveness. Under him, the Manchu state stabilized, the people prospered, and the empire expanded to unprecedented geographic and administrative limits. Militarily, K'ang-hsi completed the conquests begun by his Manchu predecessors and laid the foundations of the largest empire China had known, save for the Mongols. To consolidate Manchu control of China, he had to overcome threats from both the south and the north.

In the south, he was confronted by three Chinese generals who had helped the Manchus to conquer China and then were rewarded with virtually independent control over the Yunnan, Kwangtung, and Fukien provinces. Together, these vast domains were known as the Three Feudatories (*San-Fan*). Emperor Shun-chih had tolerated the autonomy of the Feudatories because he felt too weak to risk a civil war. K'ang-hsi, however, was determined to put an end to their independence. Consequently, he maneuvered them into open rebellion, and in 1681, after long and bitter campaigning, he narrowly defeated the three princes. Also plaguing the Manchus in the south was a Ming loyalist movement under the control of Cheng Ch'eng-kung and his son, Cheng Ching. After fighting against the Ch'ing in central China for many years, the Cheng forces retired to Taiwan, where they eliminated Portuguese claims to the island and continued their resistance to the Manchus until 1683, when Ch'ing armies finally vanquished them and turned Taiwan into a prefecture of the neighboring Fukien Province. This completed the Ch'ing conquest of the south and allowed K'ang-hsi to turn his attention to the north.

He confronted two threats there: the Olod Mongols in the northwest and the Russians in the northeast. Both of these powers had expanded their control after the 1640's, Russian settlers moving into Siberia and the Amur regions of northern Manchuria, and the Olod expanding into Eastern Turkestan and Outer Mongolia. It appeared possible that the Olod and the Russians might form an alliance against the Ch'ing. To prevent this, K'ang-hsi pursued a divide-and-conquer policy. He campaigned first against the Russians, defeating them at their advance base of Albazin and then offering them a generous settlement, the Treaty of Nerchinsk (1689). This first modern treaty between China and a Western nation established the frontiers of the Amur region and permitted the Russians to trade with Peking. This assured Russian neutrality between the Olod and the Ch'ing. K'ang-hsi thereupon turned his attention to the Olod, who had expanded across Outer Mongolia as far as the Kerulen River. After many years of desultory fighting, he finally defeated them in 1696. Thereafter, he extended Ch'ing rule to Outer Mongolia and as far west as Hami. After his death, his successors continued the westward expansion, eventually conquering Chinese Turkestan in the 1750's.

Within China, K'ang-hsi's administration was marked by extraordinary energy, diligence, and wisdom. Most Chinese believe that he possessed the characteristics of the ideal emperor. He was, above all, a capable administrator who provided just and benevolent rule for all of his subjects. Unlike many later Ch'ing emperors, K'ang-hsi repeatedly toured his far-flung empire, assessing for himself the needs of the people and ensuring that his officials met those needs. These excursions acquainted him with local conditions and solidified the presence of the central government in even the remotest parts of the empire. He broadened the ethnic base of his government by encouraging Chinese to take the civil service examinations and by appointing them to key bureaucratic posts. He named his own Chinese bondservants to high positions and used them as sources of information independent of normal bureaucratic channels. To ensure the support of the masses, he reduced the land and grain taxes numerous times, set customary rates of taxation, cleaned up government corruption, built water-conservancy works, and reversed the policy which had allowed the Manchus to take good Chinese farms in exchange for inferior Manchu lands. All this and more he accomplished by dint of extraordinary labor. He typically arose at four o'clock in the morning and usually did not retire before midnight. Few of his advisers could match his prodigious energy and capacity for hard work.

Contemporaries described K'ang-hsi as above average height, with large ears, a sculpted mouth, and a long, aquiline nose. He had a stentorian voice, and his face was handsome, though heavily pockmarked by smallpox. His unusually bright eyes gave his features great vivacity. Physically active even in his old age, he kept himself fit by a daily regimen of exercises and by vigorous riding and hunting trips. K'ang-hsi was also extraordinarily cultured and learned. Well versed in the Confucian classics, he also patronized other branches of Chinese learning. As a result of his patronage, scholars wrote the history of the preceding Ming Dynasty, compiled authoritative editions of the works of the great Neo-Confucian scholar Chu Hsi, and composed several landmark dictionaries and encyclopedias. His personal interests included painting, calligraphy, and Western learning. He studied Western music, geography, science, and mathematics with Jesuit missionaries at his court. While there is doubt that he mastered these subjects, his openness to them is one measure of the remarkable breadth of his intellectual interests.

Summary

K'ang-hsi was a conscientious ruler with extraordinarily broad interests. He created an integrated Manchu-Chinese government, broke down ethnic barriers, ended the civil war in the south, protected China's northern frontiers, opened China to Western scientific knowledge, and laid the foundations for a century of peace in East Asia. Under K'ang-hsi, Manchu rule in China became a settled fact. K'ang-hsi was keenly aware of the richness and variety of the China he ruled. He claimed to have traveled seven hundred miles in each direction from Peking, hunting, collecting flora and fauna, preparing his troops for combat by shooting, enduring camp life, and practicing formation riding. Ultimately, he traveled so that he could personally gather information about his realm. He was always reluctant to credit secondhand intelligence.

K'ang-hsi took seriously his rule over his 150 million subjects. His empire was the largest in the world at that time, and he was aware that his decisions often dictated the fate of countless millions. The immense suffering caused by his war against the Three Feudatories made him aware of how fateful his decisions could be. His concern for individual justice led him to review every sentence of death in the entire empire every year. In an attempt to gather accurate information from his government, he invented the palace memorial system, through which his ministers and officials wrote directly to him, thus circumventing possible censoring by other officials. He possessed an inquiring mind which was remarkably responsive to new intellectual phenomena. Although he was not profoundly philosophical, he had an irrepressible curiosity. This is demonstrated by his patronage of the Jesuits, who brought Western learning to his court, and his demand that the writing of the Ming Dynasty history conform as much as possible to the facts, even if they damaged the reputations of his Manchu ancestors.

K'ang-hsi, despite his admirable personal characteristics, could not escape the intrigues and tragedies of court politics. In the early decades of his reign, he could postpone problems caused by the misbehavior of his sons and the machinations of the pretenders to his throne. Yet he could not escape these difficulties as he grew old. As he became aware of the limitations of his heirs and as court factions jockeyed for position in the succession struggle, K'ang-hsi's judgment faltered and he sometimes behaved in hysterical and cruel ways. These tragedies, however, do not detract from the fact that K'ang-hsi was one of China's greatest emperors. He was at once a scholarly man of reflection and a man of action. He protected his subjects' livelihood and provided competent, predictable government in the largest empire in the world at that time. It is appropriate that he is often compared with Louis XIV and that he is remembered not only as a great conqueror but also as a conscientious, enlightened monarch.

Bibliography

Kessler, Lawrence D. *K'ang-hsi and the Consolidation of Ch'ing Rule, 1661-1684*. Chicago: University of Chicago Press, 1976. This thin, scholarly volume deals with the rise of K'ang-hsi to the throne and his subsequent consolidation of power. His dealings with Oboi are clearly explained, as is his vanquishing of his internal and external enemies. Eminently readable.

Lee, Robert H. G. *The Manchurian Frontier in Ch'ing History*. Cambridge, Mass.: Harvard University Press, 1970. Lee's book explains the problems the Manchus had with their northeastern frontier. In particular, Lee describes how the Ch'ing coped with the Russians.

Oxnam, Robert B. *Ruling from Horseback: Manchu Politics in the Oboi Regency, 1661-1669*. Chicago: University of Chicago Press, 1974. A detailed study of the period between K'ang-hsi's accession to the throne and his taking over of the government. Discusses such issues as the calendar controversy and the elimination of Oboi's regency.

Spence, Jonathan D. *Emperor of China: Self-Portrait of K'ang Hsi*. New York: Alfred A. Knopf, 1974. This beautifully written and illustrated book makes K'ang-hsi come alive as a man, not simply a grand historic figure. Spence presents K'ang-hsi in his own words, describing his methods of ruling and his relationship to his sons, among other topics.

_____. "The Seven Ages of K'ang-hsi (1654-1722)." *The Journal of Asian Studies* 2 (February, 1967): 205-211. This brief article describes the stages through which K'ang-hsi's life moved. Encapsulates the evolution of K'ang-hsi as a man and as a ruler.

_____. *Ts'ao Yin and the K'ang-hsi Emperor: Bondservant and Master*. New Haven, Conn.: Yale University Press, 1966. Spence here describes the way K'ang-hsi used his Chinese bondservants as his own eyes and ears within the government bureaucracy. Reveals much about the inner workings of K'ang-hsi's government.

Wakeman, Frederic E., Jr. *The Great Enterprise: The Manchu Reconstruc-*

tion of Imperial Order in Seventeenth-Century China. 2 vols. Berkeley: University of California Press, 1985. This massive work is indispensable for a detailed reconstruction of K'ang-hsi's reign. Extremely detailed and offers keen insights into the ways K'ang-hsi and others conceived and practiced their control of China.

Loren W. Crabtree

IMMANUEL KANT

Born: April 22, 1724; Königsberg, Prussia
Died: February 12, 1804; Königsberg, Prussia
Area of Achievement: Philosophy
Contribution: Kant vindicated the authority of science while preserving the autonomy of morals by means of a new system of thought called critical or transcendental philosophy.

Early Life

Immanuel Kant was the son of a harness maker and the grandson of a Scottish emigrant. As a child, Kant was especially close to his mother, a serene woman who possessed an incisive curiosity about the natural world and a great native intelligence. As one of nine children in a devout Lutheran Pietist family, Kant was reared to respect inner tranquillity, industry, truthfulness, godliness, and order as the highest goods in human life. Kant's mother died when he was thirteen, but he remembered her throughout his life with deep devotion; he told his friends that she had planted and nurtured the first seed of good in him and that her teachings had both opened his mind and provided a healing influence on his life.

Perhaps the most remarkable feature of Kant's life, especially in the light of his profound and pervasive influence on the history of Western thought, is his provinciality. Kant never left the environs of the town of Königsberg in which he was born. He was educated in the local high school, the Collegium Freidericianum, and later at the University of Königsberg. After completing his baccalaureate studies in 1746, he worked as a tutor for a number of local families. He was able to maintain his studies while working as a tutor and so was able to take his master's degree at Königsberg in 1755. That same year, he was appointed to the post of *privatdocent* (private lecturer) in the university. He gave regular courses of lectures, which continued through his 1770 appointment to the professorship of logic and metaphysics. Kant's early lectures and writings covered diverse topics, including physical geography, anthropology, mathematics, and theoretical physics, as well as logic, metaphysics, and moral philosophy.

Life's Work

Kant did his most original and important work quite late in his life. His project of critical philosophy began with *Kritik der reinen Vernunft* (1781; *The Critique of Pure Reason*, 1838), on which he worked between 1775 and 1781. This work aimed to resolve the disputes of all contemporary and traditional metaphysics by reinterpreting the conditions for human knowledge. Kant viewed the whole history of metaphysical inquiry as a series of failures to establish conclusive truths of first principles concerning God, human freedom, and immortality. In particular, he observed that rational cosmology (that is, metaphysical speculation concerning the nature of the world and its origin) was prone toward generating conflicting demonstrations which appeared to be equally valid. Kant named these conflicting arguments "antinomies," and he found them to be in a sense inherent in reason itself. In Kant's view, the preponderance of antinomies in the history of thought cast doubt on the whole enterprise of metaphysics.

Juxtaposed to his preoccupation with the self-contradictory nature and uncertainty of metaphysics were Kant's deep convictions about the value and trustworthiness of Isaac Newton's mathematical science. Mathematics and natural science yielded genuine knowledge. Kant took this as a clue to the sort of reformation that was called for in metaphysics. By inquiring into what made mathematical science possible, Kant hoped to uncover the conditions under which true metaphysical knowledge is possible.

Here is Kant's seminal discovery: What makes knowledge possible in mathematics or physics is man's possession of necessarily true propositions which are universally recognized as correct without any reference to experience. An example of such a proposition in mathematics is, "The sum of the angles in a triangle are equal to two right angles." The possession of such truths proves that man's cognition of the world is not necessarily a product of experience or the functioning of his senses. From one's senses one obtains raw intuitions, but these intuitions do not constitute authentic cognitions. Raw intuitions become substantive cognitions only when they are processed actively by the mind. The mind organizes and synthesizes the raw intuitions according to innate rules. Without the raw intuitions given by the senses a person could not be aware of any object, but without the active participation of the mind that person could form no conception of any object.

Kant reasoned that the certainty of science rested on the purity of its truths, that is, their independence of sensation. Nothing that was given to sense experience from the outside could be guaranteed even by science, for an additional observation might reveal an alternate sequence which would prove the scientist's first conclusion to be neither always nor inevitably true—neither universal nor necessary. If observational science was to be certain, it must proceed from propositions that were pure of sensation, that were a priori, or "present from the very first."

From this discovery, Kant devolved a new, chastened metaphysics, free of the liabilities of all previous metaphysical inquiry. He had determined that the mind actively supplied certain concepts to intuition or sensation before that raw material was perceived and subsequently cognized, prior to its being registered as experience at all. Accordingly, it was also clear that humans are not immediately in touch with things as they are in themselves. It is as if one views the world through a particular set of rose-colored glasses, glasses that one can never remove. Thus, according to Kant, previous metaphysicians had been misguided in their aspirations to know about the ultimate nature of things. What one can know, or make certain claims about, is one's experience of things (the appearances of things), not things in themselves. Kant said that one must take for granted that "things-in-themselves" are real per se, but that they are not directly known to man. Rather, one knows appearances of these things, as mediated through one's mind's perceptual and cognitive apparatus. What one has no experience of, including the nature and existence of God and the fate of the soul, one can access only by faith, not speculative knowledge. Thus, the new Kantian metaphysics confined itself to determining the necessary features of all objects of possible experience and to determining the structures of the mind which themselves impart to all objects of possible experience the features that they of necessity have.

This strict limitation on objects of knowledge, this restriction on the valid application of pure human reason, did not end in pure skepticism for Kant. Kant claimed that he found it necessary to deny knowledge in order to make room for faith. With the elimination of dogmatic metaphysics, he had silenced those who made knowledge claims or arguments on either side of speculative metaphysical issues. It was of no use, for example, to argue for or against God's existence, or to try to prove that men have or do not have free will. Such issues were beyond the ken of human understanding. Objections to morality and religion therefore carried no weight, since they mistook what was beyond the limits of human experience to be legitimate objects of human understanding. This engendered the other substantial phase of the Kantian philosophy, the writings on ethics and religion.

Although Kant set limits on speculative reason, he granted a practical employment of reason that articulated postulates, articles of faith, in matters where discursive knowledge was impossible. Kant saw that humans as a matter of fact made moral commitments and acted as if they had free will. This did not involve an illegitimate metaphysical knowledge claim but rather a postulate born of practical necessity. Kant's *Grundlegung zur Metaphysik der Sitten* (1785; *Foundations of the Metaphysics of Morals*, 1950) and his *Kritik der praktischen Vernunft* (1788; *The Critique of Practical Reason*, 1873) were devoted to working out such rational principles of morality.

Kant's analysis of morality revealed that an agent's goodness was not some quality of his behavior, nor a quality of his desire to cause some particular state of affairs. Goodness involved doing one's duty solely for the sake of so doing. Duty was what conformed with the moral law that Kant called the "categorical imperative." This stipulated that an action was moral if and only if one could will that it should become a universal law. The categorical imperative thus enunciated a purely formal, logical criterion for morality whose hallmark was a demand for complete impartiality.

The next ten years of Kant's life were spent in vigorous productivity. Among the twenty or so books and treatises composed during this time were enormously influential works on aesthetics, *Kritik der Urteilskraft* (1790; *The Critique of Judgment*, 1892), on rational theology and ethics; *Die Religion innerhalb der Grenzen der blossen Vernunft* (1793; *Religion Within the Boundaries of Pure Reason*, 1838); and the famous essay on political theory, *Zum ewigen Frieden* (1795; *Perpetual Peace*, 1796), in which Kant proposed the creation of a federation or league of nations as an antidote to international conflict resolution. Kant's powers began to fail in his last years. He gave up lecturing in 1799, and as he lost his eyesight and intellectual clarity, he slowly faded away. Almost all of Königsberg and many persons from all over Germany attended his funeral.

Summary

Immanuel Kant said that his project could be codified in the following three questions: What can I know? What ought I to do? For what may I hope? These are the questions that have occupied every philosopher in the history of Western thought, but Kant's answers to them dramatically altered how they were approached by all of his successors. No one before Kant had regarded human minds as actively operative organisms which drew their material from the senses while shaping this material autonomously, according to their own laws. His discovery that the mind forms its cognitions itself supplanted all previous epistemological theories and quickly became a philosophical commonplace. Since Kant, no one has been able to neglect the transforming and intrusive influence of the observer's cognizing process upon the object of observation. This insight spawned the whole twentieth century analytic movement in philosophy, which emphasizes logic and theory of knowledge and rejects metaphysics. It also gave rise to anti-Kantian theories of human experience offered by G. W. F. Hegel, Edmond Husserl, John Dewey, and Alfred North Whitehead.

The influence of Kant's deontological, antinaturalistic moral views was also very strong, especially among later ethical intuitionists. Yet it is a mistake to separate Kant's ethical thought from his overall system. The richest meaning of the moral doctrines emerges when they are seen as the central focus of his overall systematic approach to philosophy. The whole system yields a doctrine of wisdom concerning the human condition: What humans can know is extremely limited, but this fact need not be regarded as regrettable or disappointing, for it testifies to the wise adaptation of man's cognitive faculties to his practical vocation. If we had a clearer vision of the true natures of things, we would always do what we ought, but then we would not be acting out of a pure motive to do our duty. We would be acting rather out of fear or hope of reward. Thus we would lose the opportunity to manifest goodwill, which Kant called the only thing in the world (or even out of this world) which can be taken as good without qualification.

Bibliography

Broad, C. D. *Kant: An Introduction.* New York: Cambridge University Press, 1978. Broad, a distinguished philosopher in his own right, provides a close textual commentary of Kant's three critiques. The book's fifteen-page general introduction is most helpful for newcomers to Kantian philosophy; the rest of the book is an invaluable companion for one attempting to read Kantian texts for the first time.

Cassirer, Ernst. *Kant's Life and Thought.* Translated by James Hayden. New Haven, Conn.: Yale University Press, 1981. Cassirer was an influential neo-Kantian and offers here an eminently readable intellectual biography of Kant. This substantial work is well indexed.

Hartnack, Justus. *Immanuel Kant: An Explanation of His Theory of Knowledge and Moral Philosophy.* Atlantic Highlands, N.J.: Humanities Press, 1974. A concise exposition of these two main aspects of Kant's thought.

Hendel, Charles W., ed. *The Philosophy of Kant and Our Modern World.* New York: Liberal Arts Press, 1957. This is a series of lectures given at Yale University, which focus on the twentieth century legacy of Kantian thought. Contains a helpful bibliography of Kantian scholarship, including many classical sources.

Kemp, John. *The Philosophy of Kant.* New York: Oxford University Press, 1968. This book offers an exposition of Kant's epistemology, practical philosophy, and aesthetics in less than one hundred pages. It is very well indexed, and contains an annotated bibliography.

Körner, Stephan. *Kant.* Baltimore: Penguin Books, 1955. This overview of Kant's thought is concise, though quite technical. It would serve to help an advanced student interpret some of the nuances of Kant's system. It is well indexed and includes a short bibliography.

Patricia Cook

ANGELICA KAUFFMANN

Born: October 30, 1741; Coire, Swiss Confederation
Died: November 5, 1807; Rome
Area of Achievement: Art
Contribution: Refusing to accept the traditional role for the woman artist as a painter of portraits or still lifes, Kauffmann determined to become a history painter. An early exponent of neoclassicism, she produced some of the finest works done in this style, which helped greatly to popularize the movement throughout Europe and in England.

Early Life

Angelica Kauffmann was born in a small village in Switzerland in 1741, the daughter of a minor portraitist and painter of religious murals. She was a child prodigy who received her first commission at age eleven for a portrait of the Bishop of Como. Recognizing their daughter's talents, her parents made certain that she received a sound education in poetry, history, religion, languages, and the visual arts. She was also an accomplished musician, with a remarkably good voice; indeed, while still very young, she was faced with a choice between a career in opera or one in art. Later, Kauffmann reiterated the importance of this difficult decision in a painting entitled *The Artist Hesitating Between the Arts of Music and Painting* (1794), in which she appears between two allegorical female figures representing Music and Painting. Using gesture to indicate her choice, she looks with longing and regret at Music and squeezes her hand in farewell while making an open-handed sign of acceptance toward Painting.

Johann Kauffmann took his family to Milan in 1754, to further Angelica's artistic training in the city's many excellent galleries. There, she encountered for the first time the prejudice against women in the art world. Generally, women were allowed to work in the galleries only under the patronage of some important man. Legend has it that Kauffmann, lacking such a sponsor, copied in the galleries disguised in boy's clothing until her work attracted the attention of the Duke of Modena, who gave her several portrait commissions and introduced her into Milanese society. Early in her career, Kauffmann thus realized the necessity of acquiring important patrons. Later, in the Florentine galleries, she obtained studio space by using letters of introduction from her Milanese patrons to circumvent opposition from male students who resented her presence there.

After Kauffmann's mother died in 1757, she and her father traveled through northern Italy—where she studied the works of Correggio, the Carracci, and Guido Reni—arriving finally in Florence in 1762. It was there that she first encountered the newly emerging style of neoclassicism, primarily in the works of the young American painter Benjamin West. Going on to Rome the following year, she found herself in the center of the new style and became part of a sophisticated circle, which included Johann Joachim Winckelmann, the principal theoretician of neoclassicism, as well as artists such as Gavin Hamilton, Raphael Mengs, Pompeo Batoni, and Nathaniel Dance.

This was a busy, productive period for Kauffmann, as she involved herself in studies of ancient classical art and literature, architecture, and perspective. Acknowledgment of her success came in 1765, when she was elected to membership in the prestigious Roman Academy of St. Luke. Also during this period, the first of her neoclassical subjects appeared.

Life's Work

In October of 1765, the Kauffmanns went to Venice, where Angelica studied the great colorists Titian, Tintoretto, and Paolo Veronese, combining what she learned from them with the exalted language of the neoclassicists and the sensuality of Correggio. She was well on her way to formulating her own style of neoclassicism, which was witty, sophisticated, and elegant.

In Venice, Kauffmann met Lady Wentworth, wife of the British ambassador, and was invited to return with her to London as her house guest. Tempted by promises of commissions and fees exceeding what she could hope to get in Italy, Kauffmann accepted, but—as the invitation had been extended to her alone—she found herself separated from her father for the first time in her life.

Arriving in London in 1766, Kauffmann was reunited with her friends West and Dance. There, she met Sir Joshua Reynolds, the principal exponent of painting in the grand manner, who was so impressed with her work that he asked to exchange portraits with her. The friendship and patronage of people such as Lady Wentworth and Reynolds undoubtedly launched Kauffmann into a wealthy and aristocratic London society, but it was entirely through her own efforts that she succeeded there. Realizing that appearances were important in this society, she soon transformed herself into a fashionable lady and took a small apartment in a suitable neighborhood where she could receive her clients. Kauffmann was an attractive woman of great personal charm. Friends described her as talented, unpretentious, thoughtful, and modest, yet ambitious and industrious. A year after her arrival in London, she had saved enough money to send for her father and to acquire a comfortable house.

Kauffmann's studio became one of the most popular salons of the day, frequented by serious patrons drawn there by her work, as well as many fashionable young men and women who came to socialize. Although Kauffmann had many suitors, including the artists Henri Fuseli and Nathaniel Dance, it was not until 1767 that she made a brief and unfortunate marriage of which she soon repented.

When the Royal Academy was formed in London in 1768, Kauffmann was among the forty original members. The only other woman in this group was the popular English still-life painter, Mary Moser. It is unexpected to find two women included as founders of the Royal Academy and still more remarkable that Kauffmann had attained a position of such prominence after having been in the country for only two years.

Although it was her Romantic portrait style which first attracted the British, she had now introduced neoclassicism into the country and it was becoming the fashion. In the Royal Academy's first annual exhibition, she showed four paintings with subjects drawn from classical antiquity, one of which, *The Parting of Hector and Andromache*, was praised as having been among the most original and popular works in the exhibition. It is interesting to note that only Kauffmann and West sent history pictures—even Reynolds exhibited portraits.

Kauffmann continued to paint classical subjects throughout her London years, but she and others, such as West and Fuseli, who wanted to raise history painting to the prominence it had in France, never fully succeeded in winning the British audience away from its first love, portraiture. Thus, Kauffmann's subject pictures were always more highly regarded in Europe. Since Kauffmann earned most of her income in London with portraiture, she looked for ways to bring it closer to history painting. Primarily, she accomplished that by painting portraits as allegories; for example, the Marchioness Townshend and her son appeared as Venus and Cupid, Sir John and Lady Webb and their children staged *An Offering to Ceres*, and Frances Hoare offered sacrifice to a statue of Minerva. Kauffmann also worked with some of the most fashionable architects in England, decorating the interiors of neoclassical homes. She also contributed four allegorical paintings for the lecture-hall ceiling in the new quarters of the Royal Academy.

Her London period ended in 1781, when she married the painter Antonio Zucci and returned to Europe. In Venice, Kauffmann met the Grand Duke Paul of Russia, the first of the large numbers of European nobility who gave her their patronage in the next years. Then, during a brief stay in Naples, she was offered the position of royal painter to King Ferdinand, which she declined. In 1782, Kauffmann and Zucci settled permanently in Rome, where, during the next fifteen years, she produced some of her finest works. Many of these were sent to England, where she was still highly esteemed. In Rome, she was honored as the most famous and successful living painter, with her home and studio attracting many distinguished visitors. She worked at a slower pace after Zucci's death in 1795, although she continued to be at the center of artistic and literary circles and was considered the head of the Roman school of painting. When she died in 1807, at age sixty-six, her funeral procession was lavish, in the manner of Renaissance masters such as Raphael, and included all the Academicians of St. Luke as well as representatives from academies throughout Europe.

Summary

Angelica Kauffmann's neoclassical style was witty, sophisticated, and painterly. Her compositions were elegant. As a colorist, she was the equal of any
painter of her day. She also had a greater influence upon her contemporaries
than was understood by earlier writers. Artists such as Gavin Hamilton emu-
lated her, and many landscape painters of the later nineteenth century were
influenced by her interpretations of the English light and countryside. Even
Reynolds, from whom she learned much, gained a broader range of color
and emotion from her examples.

Kauffmann was a talented and serious artist who paid a high price for her
success—the loss of her privacy and the impugning of her moral character.
That happened to some extent to most successful women artists in the eighteenth and nineteenth centuries, but, in Kauffmann's case, the slander was
particularly vicious, vindictive, and totally absurd. It all began with her
arrival in London, thus coinciding with her first successes as a history
painter. Some of the attempts to defame her resulted from simple envy and
jealousy. Beyond that, in the art world of Kauffmann's day, a woman might
be tolerated if she contented herself with a career as a still-life painter or
minor portraitist. Any woman who aspired to go beyond those limits, as
Kauffmann did, was leaving herself open to personal as well as professional
criticism. Her private life became public property, and, if she happened to be
young and pretty, she would almost certainly be accused of using her femi-
nine charms to further her career. Kauffmann was ambitious, but she also
had the talent to succeed without resorting to tactics of that kind. It is very
much to her credit that, having the courage of her own artistic convictions,
she refused to allow anything to deter her from the goals she had set for
herself and for her art.

Bibliography

Clement, Clara Erskine. *Women in the Fine Arts, from the Seventh Century
B.C. to the Twentieth Century A.D.* New York: Hacker, 1974. Originally
published in 1904, this was an early attempt to assess the contributions
made by women artists throughout history. Arranged alphabetically, the
biographies are brief but fairly accurate in terms of basic facts. Affords
the reader a handy and reliable way to compare and contrast the career of
a particular artist with those of her peers.
Greer, Germaine. *The Obstacle Race: The Fortunes of Women Painters and
Their Work.* New York: Farrar, Straus & Giroux, 1979. A perceptive
and often witty analysis of the struggles and achievements of women artists in general. Contains a lengthy discussion of Kauffmann's personality
and works, with a much-deserved indictment of those writers who, while
largely ignoring her contributions, have perpetuated "the foolish prattle
about her love life."

1214 *Great Lives from History*

Harris, Ann Sutherland, and Linda Nochlin. *Women Artists, 1550-1950.* Los Angeles: Los Angeles County Museum of Art, 1976. The catalog of one of the first exhibitions to concentrate solely on women artists. Contains an essay which summarizes the complicated and varied highlights of Kauffmann's career, emphasizing her major achievements and contributions. Also analyzes several of her most significant neoclassical compositions.

Manners, Victoria, and G. C. Williamson. *Angelica Kauffmann, R. A.: Her Life and Her Works.* New York: Hacker, 1976. A reprint of a biography first published in 1924, which was based on a manuscript discovered in London's Royal Academy Library. Also includes listings of Kauffmann's works, arranged alphabetically by owners, by country, and by sale at auction. Contains a catalog of the engravings made after her works, with the names of the engravers.

Mayer, Dorothy. *Angelica Kauffmann, R. A., 1741-1807.* Gerrards Cross, England: Colin Smythe, 1972. This biography of Kauffmann updates the material found in Manners and Williamson. Also discusses the fluctuation of her reputation in the art world since her own time, pointing out that her work has regained some of its original prominence as a result of a revival of interest in the neoclassical era.

LouAnn Faris Culley

JOHANNES KEPLER

Born: December 27, 1571; Weil der Stadt, Swabia
Died: November 15, 1630; Regensburg, Bavaria
Areas of Achievement: Astronomy and physics
Contribution: Through the application of his exceptional intellect, faith, and
tenacity, Kepler created the science of modern astronomy and provided
the solid foundation upon which Isaac Newton built his laws of universal
gravitation.

Early Life

Johannes Kepler was born prematurely on the afternoon of December 27,
1571, at Weil der Stadt, Swabia, the first child of Heinrich and Katharine
Kepler. His childhood was exceptionally difficult. He was a small, sickly
child with thin limbs and a large, pasty face surrounded by dark hair. It is
one of the ironies of history that the child who would one day revolutionize
astronomy had poor eyesight. His mother was a small, quarrelsome woman
with a nasty disposition; his father appears to have had no established trade
and, in 1574, simply left the family to fight for the Catholic Duke of Alva in
the Netherlands. His mother followed a year later, leaving Kepler in the care
of his grandparents, who treated him badly. In 1576, his parents returned,
but this provided only a dubious improvement in his family life.

Under such circumstances, it is not surprising that Kepler's self-image as
a child was terrible; he described himself once as a "mangy dog." Possibly
in response to the instability in his life, Kepler developed a pronounced
religious disposition at a young age. Indeed, of all his childhood memories
only two stood out as pleasant. When he was six, Kepler's mother took him
to a hill to see a comet, and at age nine his parents took him outside to
observe an eclipse of the moon. The seeds were planted that would influence
the direction of his life.

Yet it was obvious even to his parents that Kepler was a bright child, and
school provided a way for him to divert himself from the suffering of family
life while building his self-assurance and developing his intellect. Kepler
was fortunate that the Lutheran Dukes of Württemberg provided generous
educational scholarships for the intelligent sons of poor parents.

Kepler began his schooling at age seven at the Latin school in Leonberg.
He completed the curriculum at age twelve, and his intellect, poor health,
and pious nature preordained him to a clerical career. After passing a competitive exam on October 16, 1584, Kepler continued his studies at the
higher seminary at Maulbronn. On September 17, 1589, he entered the University of Tübingen, where he was particularly influenced by his professor of
astronomy, Michael Mästlin. Mästlin was unique in that he believed that
Nicolaus Copernicus' heliocentric theory was essentially true. Influenced by

this exceptional teacher, Kepler accepted the Copernican view of the universe—an act that would have a profound impact on his life and the future of scientific thought.

At the age of twenty, Kepler was matriculated at the Tübingen Theological School. His career path seemed assured, but circumstances fatefully intervened. In 1593, the mathematician of the Lutheran high school of Graz died, and the school requested Tübingen to recommend a replacement. Kepler was nominated and agreed to accept the position.

His job was to teach mathematics and to publish the annual calendar of astrological forecasts. Kepler was lucky with his first calendar, correctly predicting a cold spell and a Turkish invasion. Kepler would be involved with astrology all of his professional life, but he did it primarily to supplement his income. Still, while he considered popular astrological forecasts a "dreadful" superstition, Kepler believed that astrology could become an exact empirical science, and with that aim in mind, he would write several treatises on the subject.

Kepler was a terrible teacher. He was often unintelligible, launching into obscure digressions whenever a thought occurred to him. Yet it was during one of these lectures that the event happened that set Kepler on the path that would ultimately lead him to reinterpret the prevailing view of the universe.

Life's Work

Kepler found his first year at Graz very trying. To escape its frustrations, he turned to the astronomical studies he had experimented with at Tübingen. The more he contemplated the Copernican system, the more he became convinced of its truth, but he was also aware that it was not the final, definitive explanation of the operation of the universe. Already in 1595, Kepler was beginning to ask the questions that would determine that course of his scientific inquiry. Why are there only six planets? What determines their distances from the sun? Why do the planets move more slowly the farther away they are from the sun? These and other queries had been coursing through his mind, when on July 19, 1595, as Kepler was teaching, an incredible thought struck him. On the blackboard, he had drawn a figure showing an outer circle circumscribing a triangle, which enclosed an inner circle. As Kepler looked at the two circles, he was suddenly dumbfounded by the realization that the ratios of the two circles were the same as those of the orbits of Saturn and Jupiter. Could it be that there were only six planets because planetary orbits were related to the five regular solids—the tetrahedron, cube, octahedron, dodecahedron, and icosahedron—of Euclid's geometry?

This revelation was the basis of Kepler's first major work, in 1596, *Prodromus dissertationum mathematicarum continens mysterium cosmographicum* (cosmographic mystery). His thesis was that one of the five regular solids fit between each of the invisible spheres that carried the six planets. The key insight of this book, however, revolved around his search for a mathematical relationship between a planet's distance from the sun and the time necessary for it to complete its orbit. Kepler concluded that there must be a force emanating from the sun that swept the planets around their orbits. The outer planets moved more slowly because this force diminished in a ratio to distance just as light did. Here is found the first hint of celestial mechanics, the joining of physics and astronomy, that would lead to the laws of planetary motion.

Kepler sent copies of the work to a number of scientists in Europe, including Tycho Brahe, who had spent several years making painstakingly accurate observations of planetary orbits and who would shortly become the Imperial Mathematician of the Holy Roman Empire. While he did not agree with the Copernican underpinning of Kepler's work, Brahe was impressed by Kepler's knowledge of mathematics and astronomy, and he invited Kepler to join his staff in the observatory at Benatek, just outside Prague. Kepler was flattered by the invitation, but he had just been married and was too poor to afford the trip. The deteriorating religious situation in Graz, in which Protestants were being forced either to convert to Catholicism or emigrate, compelled Kepler to make a decision. In 1600, Kepler joined Brahe in Prague, where he would remain until 1612. This period would be the most productive of his life.

Kepler's first publication after arriving at Prague, *De fundamentis astrologiae certioribus* (1601; the more reliable bases of astrology), while rejecting the belief that celestial bodies direct people's lives, supported the mystical view that there is a harmony between the universe and the individual. In 1606, after observing a supernova, Kepler published *De stella nova in pede serpentarii* (the new star in the foot of the serpent bearer), which argued that the universe of fixed stars was not pure and changeless, as had been believed. In 1604, Kepler authored a major work on optics, *Ad Vitellionem paralipomena, quibus astronomiae pars optica traditur* (supplement to Witelo, expounding the optical part of astronomy). The main subject was the atmospheric refraction, or bending, of light as it enters Earth's atmosphere from space. An understanding of this phenomenon was vital if Kepler was to make optimum use of Brahe's observational data. In this work, Kepler for the first time explained the fundamental structure and function of the human eye. Although he was unsuccessful in developing the law of refraction, he was able to create an improved table of refraction.

In 1610, Kepler concluded his work in optics with *Dioptrice* (1611), which not only restated his concept of refraction but also covered such subjects as reflections, images, magnification, and the optical principles of the astronomical telescope. These two works have justifiably established Kepler as the father of modern optics. That same year, Kepler wrote the *Dissertatio cum nuncio sidereo* (1610; *Kepler's Conversation with Galileo's Sidereal Messenger*, 1965), placing his then-considerable scientific prestige in support of Galileo's astronomical discoveries. Kepler's great magnum opus, published in 1609 after years of painstaking effort, was the *Astronomia nova* (new astronomy).

When Kepler first arrived at Prague in 1600, Brahe immediately assigned him to investigate the orbit of Mars, which Brahe and his assistant, Longomontanus, had been unable to determine. The selection of Mars was particularly fortuitous because of all the planets, Mars has the most elliptical orbit and, therefore, provided the best opportunity for discovering the secrets of planetary motion. Once Kepler had full use of Brahe's observational data following Brahe's death in 1601—for now Kepler was the Imperial Mathematician—he became completely immersed in this project.

As he began the study of Mars, Kepler had a thoroughly Copernican concept of planetary motion. Each planet revolved around the sun at a uniform speed in a perfectly circular orbit, considered the perfect geometrical shape. Accordingly, Kepler first tried to show that the Martian orbit was circular. After three years of intense, repetitive calculations, Kepler believed that he had proved Mars had a circular orbit, only to discover that two of Brahe's innumerable observations of the planet differed from Kepler's orbit by only 8 minutes of arc. (The width of a pinhead held at arm's length approximately equals 8 minutes of arc.) Previous scientists would have made the evidence fit the theory, but Kepler would not. Believing that God would not create anything imperfect, Kepler knew that he could not ignore those 8 minutes of arc. The orbit of Mars could not be circular but had to be some other geometrical curve.

Kepler now had to redetermine the Martian orbit, but first he had to recalculate the orbit of Earth. Earth was his observatory, and if there were any misconceptions regarding its motion, then all conclusions regarding other planetary motion would be in error. He discovered that Earth did not revolve around the sun at a uniform speed, but rather moved faster or slower depending upon its distance from the sun. Obviously, the Platonic and Copernican concept of uniform motion was incorrect. Kepler, however, discovered a new type of uniform motion: With the sun as its focus, the planet, while revolving along the periphery of its orbit, will sweep out, in equal intervals of time, equal areas of the orbit, and unequal arcs along the periphery of the orbit.

The second law determined the variations of the planet's speed along its orbit but not the shape of the orbit itself. For two more years, Kepler worked on that problem before coming upon the solution: an ellipse. This led to his first law (discovered after his second law): A planet moves in an ellipse with the sun at one of the two foci.

Kepler's third law was not published until 1619 in the *Harmonices mundi* (partial translation as *Harmonies of the World*, 1952). Here Kepler states that the squares of the planetary periods (the time it takes a planet to complete its orbit) are proportional to the cubes of their average distance from the sun (the 3/2 ratio). The farther from the sun an object is, the slower it moves.

These two works, the *Astronomia nova* and *Harmonies of the World*, completed Kepler's work on planetary motion and provided the basis for Isaac Newton's explanation of universal gravitation, which affects every material object in the universe.

In the meantime, Kepler's life underwent much upheaval. In 1610, his wife died, and the next year his patron, Rudolph II, slipped into insanity and was deposed by his brother, Matthias. Although he was reappointed Imperial Mathematician, Kepler left Prague and moved to Linz, Austria. In 1623, he was married to Susanna Reuttinger, who although several years younger than Kepler and of lower social status, proved to be one of the few joys of his later life.

While in Linz, Kepler published his *Epitome astronomiae Copernicanae* (1618-1621; partial translation as *Epitome of Copernican Astronomy*, 1939). This relatively unknown and underrated work is highly significant, ranking next to Ptolemy's *Almagest* and Copernicus' *Revolutiones* as the first systematic elaboration of the concept of celestial mechanics established by Kepler. In it, he not only conclusively proved the validity of the Copernican view of the universe but also revealed all the knowledge he had uncovered during his many years of research.

As he worked on *Epitome of Copernican Astronomy*, Kepler heard that his mother was going to be tried as a witch, a capital offense. Self-interest as well as familial devotion led him to conduct a successful defense. Had she been convicted, his status as Imperial Mathematician could have been imperiled.

Kepler also planned to publish *Tabulae Rudolphinae* (Rudolphine tables), named in honor of Rudolph II, in Linz, but a peasants' rebellion and religious unrest forced Kepler to move to Ulm, where the work was published in 1627. Based on Brahe's observations, *Tabulae Rudolphinae* is a book on practical astronomy. It became an indispensable astronomical tool for more than a century, and Kepler considered it the crowning achievement of his life.

The last three years of Kepler's life were a struggle. Albrecht von Wallenstein, the famous mercenary general of the Thirty Years' War, promised to meet Kepler's financial needs, but the general was unreliable. In 1628, Kepler moved to Żagań, Silesia, and late in 1630 he left for Austria to collect some funds which he was owed. He stopped at Regensburg, where the Imperial Diet was meeting, fell ill, and died on November 15, 1630. Scientists throughout Europe mourned his death.

Summary
   Johannes Kepler's impact on the development of astronomy and general science was enormous. By the sheer force of his intellect and the tenacity of his spirit, he forged further ahead in the understanding of the cosmos than any of his contemporaries. Kepler not only provided the mathematical proof of the Copernican system but also went far beyond it, creating the science of modern astronomy, in which physics, the concept of physical force, and astronomy were fused together. He discovered the famous three laws, created the science of optics, and came very close to discovering gravity. His determination that the theory must fit the facts and not vice versa established the standard for future scientific inquiry. Without Kepler, there would not have been Newton's laws of universal gravitation.
   Kepler also had a more abstract impact on Western society. A society's perception of the cosmos is reflected in the way it views itself. By demonstrating conclusively for the first time that the universe operates according to fixed, natural laws, Kepler assisted Western society in freeing itself from the shackles of superstition and ignorance.
   Basic to Kepler's success was his Christian faith. Although his belief in the harmony of the worlds led him into many mystical conjectures, Kepler's firm belief that God would only have created a harmonious universe, where there had to be a predetermined reason for the occurrence of certain events, provided the proper attitude for discerning the existence of natural laws. Indeed, Kepler's faith, rather than being a hindrance, was a creative force pushing him ever forward.

Bibliography
Armitage, Agnus. *John Kepler.* London: Faber & Faber, 1966. While not as detailed as other biographies of Kepler, this is a very good introduction to Kepler and his work. It is lucid, includes excellent illustrations, and provides clear explanations of Kepler's calculations. Contains a helpful glossary and an index.
Bishop, Philip W., and George Schwartz, eds. *Moments of Discovery.* Vol. 1, *The Origins of Science.* New York: Basic Books, 1958. Pages 265-277 contain an excerpt from *Astronomia nova* of Kepler's explanation of his first law. Helpful in providing the reader with the flavor of Kepler's writing.
Caspar, Max. *Kepler.* New York: Abelard-Schuman, 1959. This is a translation of the 1947 German edition and is the definitive work on Kepler. Every aspect of his life and work is thoroughly investigated. Well written and lucid, this work is a must for any study of Kepler. Contains an index and an outstanding bibliography.
Koestler, Arthur. *The Watershed: A Biography of Johannes Kepler.* Garden City, N.Y.: Anchor Books, 1960. This Science Study series volume is a

fine introduction to Kepler and his work. The discussion on Kepler and Galileo is excellent, showing that Kepler had a much greater impact on the development of astronomy and physics than did Galileo. Contains chapter notes and an index.

Small, Robert. *An Account of the Astronomical Discoveries of Kepler.* London: J. Mawman, 1804. Reprint. Madison: University of Wisconsin Press, 1963. This book is considered by many a classic in the field, and until the translation of Caspar, it was the best work on Kepler in English. For those interested in the mathematical details of Kepler's theories, this work is still the best in English. Contains an index, chapter notes, and reproductions of many of Kepler's geometric figures.

Ronald F. Smith

SØREN KIERKEGAARD

Born: May 5, 1813; Copenhagen, Denmark
Died: November 11, 1855; Copenhagen, Denmark
Areas of Achievement: Philosophy and religion
Contribution: Kierkegaard's challenge to neat systems of philosophical
thought, such as that propounded by Georg Wilhelm Friedrich Hegel, has
highlighted his philosophical influence. His predominant assumption, that
existence is too multiform to be systematized, created the fabric around
which existentialism, and indeed much of Continental philosophy, have
been woven.

Early Life

Søren Aabye Kierkegaard was the last of seven children born to Michael
Pedersen Kierkegaard and his second wife, Ane Sørensdatter (Lund); she
had been the maid of Michael's first wife, who died childless after two years
of marriage. The elder Kierkegaard, an affluent businessman, had himself
been born in poverty and virtual servitude, rising by dint of hard work and
good fortune to the comfortable status the family enjoyed at Søren's birth.

Despite such prosperity, the Kierkegaard household was haunted by early
death. Two of Søren's siblings died before he was nine; his mother and three
more siblings died in a span of less than three years before his twenty-first
birthday. Michael was never able to overcome the belief that these deaths
were punishment for the unpardonable sin he committed when, as a boy of
eleven, tending sheep and bitter at his lot, he cursed God.

The influence of the somber elder Kierkegaard upon his gifted son is
certain, but the extent to which it permeated Kierkegaard's character and
influenced his writings throughout his life is difficult to estimate. A key
passage from Kierkegaard's journals suggests that his father's inadvertent
revelation of some past misdeeds permanently altered their relationship:

> An affair between the father and son where the son finds everything out, and yet
> dare not admit it to himself. The father is a respectable man, God-fearing and
> strict; only once, when he is tipsy, he lets fall some words which arouse the most
> dreadful suspicions. Otherwise the son is never told of it and never dares to ask his
> father or anybody else.

Regarding this incident, Frederick Sontag says that it thrust Kierkegaard into
a "period of dissipation and despair," causing him for a time to neglect
completely his theological studies at the university.

In addition to his father's influence, Kierkegaard was indelibly marked by
his engagement to Regina Olsen. He met her for the first time at a party,
when she was fourteen. She was captivated by his intellectual sagacity; he
later admitted that that had been his design. They both endured a difficult
period of waiting until she was nearly eighteen before they became engaged.

Yet, having endured such a lengthy period of waiting, within days after the engagement had been effected Kierkegaard was convinced that it was a mistake. Some years after he had broken the engagement, he wrote in his journal:

> I said to her that in every generation there were certain individuals who were destined to be sacrificed for the others. She hardly understood what I was talking about. . . . But just this spontaneous youthful happiness of hers, set alongside my terrible melancholy, and in such a relationship, must teach me to understand myself. For how melancholy I was I had never before surmised; I possessed no measure for conceiving how happy a human being can be.

In 1841, not long after breaking his engagement, Kierkegaard successfully defended his doctoral thesis and departed for Berlin, where he stayed for several months attending lectures. Within two years, he published his first books, the product of an intense period of creativity, and his career was fully launched.

Life's Work

Kierkegaard was a powerful and prolific writer. The bulk of his corpus was produced within a period of about seven years, spanning 1843-1850. Appreciative readers of Kierkegaard's writings can be thankful for the voluminous groundswell of production which came in his early thirties, for he died a young man of forty-two. During the course of his writing career, he pursued several recurring themes; it would be misleading, however, to treat his work as though he had systematically moved from one arena to another in a planned, orderly fashion.

Indeed, Kierkegaard's decided distrust of the systematizing of Hegel had pushed him in the direction of an existential methodology which would be expressive of his whole personality. Rather than creating a system for the whole of reality which was necessarily linked by chains of reasoning, Kierkegaard created in his writings psychological experiments centered on persons confronting life situations. By so doing, he avoided both the strict rationalism and the Idealism so characteristic of analytic philosophers, and pulled his readers into existential consideration of life's dilemmas.

Kierkegaard considered his life and cojointly his works as an effort to fulfill a divinely appointed task. This conviction had led to his breakup with Regina because of what he called his destiny "to be sacrificed for the others." It also led him to the realization that his vocation was to confront his contemporaries with the ideal Christian life. He saw that as his purpose in life and consequently chose to lay aside every weight that would hinder him from "willing that one thing."

Denmark had appropriated Hegelianism as the proper mode of informed thinking. Indeed, Kierkegaard's countrymen had even allowed Christianity to be absorbed into the Hegelian system. Hence, the Christian ideal of individuals choosing Christ was lost: Every person in Denmark was nominally a Christian. When applied to the Church, the totalizing attempt prefigured in Hegel made everyone a Christian by birth. It was within this context, and for the purpose of confronting this attitude, that Kierkegaard arose to do battle in print. He described himself as a "midwife," helping to bring forth authentic individuals. His goal was nothing short of arousing his age from its complacence. Whereas Hegelianism might encourage rigors of thought, it made things easy through its promise of certainty. Kierkegaard, on the other hand, made things difficult by thrusting the individual into the fray, thereby teaching him what it truly means "to become a Christian."

An important aspect of many of Kierkegaard's works had to do with his method. For his philosophical works, he used a variety of often-flamboyant pseudonyms, such as Victor Eremita, Constantine Constantius, Virgilius Haufniensis, Johannes Climacus, and Anti-Climacus. At the same time, under his own name, he produced a number of devotional works and religious meditations. Kierkegaard's indirect communication has caused not a little bewilderment. He himself addressed what he referred to as his "polynymity" rather than "pseudonymity" in an appendix to *Afsluttende uvidenskabelig Efterskrift til de Philosophiske Smuler: Mimisk-pathetisk-dialektisk Sammenskrift, existentielt Indlæg* (1846; *Concluding Unscientific Postscript*, 1941, 1968). Given his consistent and unwavering emphasis upon "choice," it is reasonable to assume that Kierkegaard believed that this method of presentation enhanced his ability to confront the reader. As long as pseudonyms were used, his readers were not free to see what "Kierkegaard the authority" had to say about the issues. The reader would thus be thrown back upon himself, having to choose an interpretive stance for himself.

Since Kierkegaard was a difficult writer, ahead of his time, he received little income from his writings, depending largely on his substantial inheritance. Moreover, as a brilliant, acerbic, and uncompromising critic of his society, he was frequently embroiled in controversy; in his later years, he worked in great isolation. Near the end of his life, Kierkegaard wrote several books which dealt explicitly with Christianity. *Til Selvprøvelse* (1857; *For Self-Examination*, 1940) challenged his readers to view themselves in the light of New Testament descriptions of Christianity rather than simplistically accepting the terms which the established church was propounding. His final book, *Hvad Christus dømmer om officiel Christendom* (1855; *What Christ's Judgment Is About Official Christianity*, 1944), views the relationship between the state and Christianity. He shows that the official Christianity of which every Dane partook was far from New Testament Christianity.

On October 2, 1855, Kierkegaard collapsed while walking in the street. The nature of his final illness is not certain. He was hospitalized, accepting his fate with tranquillity. He died on November 11, 1855.

Summary

At the time of his death, and for a long period thereafter, Søren Kierkegaard's works were little known outside Denmark. Both his striking originality and the fact that he wrote in Danish delayed recognition of his achievement. By the early twentieth century, however, a wide diversity of thinkers reflected his influence, which has continued to grow since that time; he is often hailed as "the father of existentialism."

Even Kierkegaard's most explicitly philosophical writings, it should be noted, bear an undeniable theological character. In *Philosophiske Smuler: Eller, En Smule Philosophi* (1844; *Philosophical Fragments: Or, A Fragment of Philosophy*, 1936, 1962), he plumbs the epistemological depths of how a historical consciousness can confront an eternal consciousness and come away with what one might call "knowledge." In other words, to what degree can eternal truth be learned within the categories of time or space? In *Concluding Unscientific Postscript*, he confronts the objective problem of the truth of Christianity. The issue involved here is often referred to as "Lessing's ditch." Gotthold Ephraim Lessing believed that there exists an intellectually impossible leap from the contingent truths of history to the necessary truths of divine revelation. Kierkegaard looked at this problem and concluded that "a leap of faith" was required for the individual bound by finiteness and historical necessity to encounter eternal truth. This assertion has caused most to claim that Kierkegaard equated truth with subjectivity.

Bibliography

Blackham, H. J. "Søren Kierkegaard." In *Six Existentialist Thinkers*. New York: Macmillan, 1952. A brief but incisive treatment of Kierkegaard's championing of individuality and inwardness as opposed to Hegel's notion of abstract system building. Emphasizes Kierkegaard's claim that any true philosophy confronts the intellectual, the aesthetic, and the ethical arenas in terms of the existing individual's life situations. Further alludes that faith is a fourth category, not to be confused with any of the others.

Duncan, Elmer H. *Søren Kierkegaard*. Waco, Tex.: Word Books, 1976. Surveys Kierkegaard's thought for the stated purpose of "making him more accessible to all of us." Ties the theme of Kierkegaard's corpus to traditional problems of philosophy. Emphasizes Kierkegaard's lasting contribution of categories, such as "absolute paradox," "absurdity," and "angst," which have been used by the main voices of existentialism, as well as the key figures of contemporary theology.

Evans, C. Stephen. *Kierkegaard's "Fragments" and "Postscript": The Religious Philosophy of Johannes Climacus*. Atlantic Highlands, N.J.: Humanities Press, 1983. Provides a thorough and serious conceptual look at Kierkegaard's writings through the two books that he pseudonymously attributed to Johannes Climacus. Its intent is that of a "companion" to the two works. Provides as much elucidation as would a good commentary.

Lowrie, Walter. *Kierkegaard.* 2 vols. Gloucester, Mass.: Peter Smith, 1970. This is the definitive biography of Kierkegaard, written by one of the most prominent translators of his writings. Follow Kierkegaard's life chronologically, providing a list of dates for major events and publications. Also includes a helpful fifteen-page synopsis of Kierkegaard's works.

Sontag, Frederick. *A Kierkegaard Handbook.* Atlanta: John Knox Press, 1979. Sontag provides for Kierkegaard's works what Kierkegaard himself conscientiously avoided: a systematic approach. Sontag intended this dialectical study of key concepts as a companion reader for the student of Kierkegaard's corpus.

Stephen M. Ashby

HEINRICH VON KLEIST

Born: October 18, 1777; Frankfurt an der Oder, Prussia
Died: November 21, 1811; Wannsee bei Potsdam, Prussia
Areas of Achievement: Literature and drama
Contribution: Kleist was one of the most important literary figures in the development of the German *Novellen* of poetic realism. Although he is better known in Germany than in English-speaking countries, he is usually acknowledged to have been ahead of his time, a forerunner of the modern literature of the grotesque, usually associated with Franz Kafka a century later.

Early Life

Heinrich Wilhelm von Kleist was born on October 18, 1777, in Frankfurt an der Oder, the first son of a Prussian officer, Joachim Friedrich von Kleist, and his second wife, Juliane Ulrike Pannwitz. By the time he was fifteen, both of his parents had died and he, without much enthusiasm, had become a soldier. Although little is known about his childhood, what evidence there is available from letters and other sources indicates that he was bored and unhappy with his life as a soldier; although he was promoted to lieutenant, he resigned from the army in 1799 to enter the University of Frankfurt. While there for three semesters, Kleist threw himself wholeheartedly into his studies of mathematics, physics, and philosophy.

Also while at the university, Kleist met and became engaged to Wilhelmine von Zenge, the daughter of an army officer. His letters from this period suggest that he was an extremely serious young man, introspective and concerned with finding fulfillment in his life by means of intellectual pursuits. Even his love affair with Wilhelmine was characterized by his efforts to make her into a kind of idealized soul mate, an embodiment of intellectual and moral beauty. In letters to his sister and his fiancée, he talks of his "life plan," a rational pursuit that would prevent him from being merely a puppet at the mercy of fate.

Yet Kleist's hopes for a purely rational plan of life were crushed in 1801 by what his biographers refer to as his "Kantian crisis." In a letter to Wilhelmine, he declared that as a result of reading Immanuel Kant all of his faith in rationality as a basis for leading a purposeful life had been destroyed, and his anguish at facing a life governed by chance, fate, and meaninglessness had become almost unbearable. In what some have called an attempt to escape his intellectual torment, Kleist left Frankfurt and began traveling, first to Paris and then to Switzerland, where he became fascinated with ideas learned from Jean-Jacques Rousseau about leading the "natural life." Because his fiancée refused to go along with his new enthusiasm to lead the simple life of a peasant, their engagement was broken the following year. It was while living in Switzerland that Kleist began writing and thus launched his short-lived career.

Life's Work

Some of his biographers suggest that Kleist's literary career began because he was attempting to compensate for his failure to achieve his intellectual goals by succeeding immediately as a writer. While living on a small island on the Lake of Thun in Switzerland, he completed his drama *Die Familie Schroffenstein* (1803; *The Schroffenstein Family*, 1916) and began work on *Der zerbrochene Krug* (1808; *The Broken Jug*, 1930) and *Robert Guiskard* (1808; English translation, 1962). Although he began two of his best-known short fictions at this time, "Die Verlobung in St. Domingo" (1811; "The Engagement in Santo Domingo," 1960) and "Das Erdbeben in Chili" (1807; "The Earthquake in Chile," 1946), he had been greatly encouraged to continue his work on *Robert Guiskard* by the high praise for an early fragment of the play received from Christopher Martin Wieland, one of the most respected literary figures in Germany at the time.

For reasons known only to the tormented mind of Kleist, when he returned to Paris he burned the fragment of *Robert Guiskard*, which Wieland had said was worthy of Sophocles and William Shakespeare. Stung by his own self-imposed sense of failure, he joined Napoleon I's forces, which were ready for an invasion of England, perhaps hoping, as some biographers suggest, that death in battle would redeem his failure in a glorious way. Shortly thereafter, however, he was sent back to Germany and hospitalized for a nervous breakdown.

After recovering, Kleist obtained a post with the government in the Ministry of Finance. During this time, he continued to write, finishing *The Broken Jug*, drafting both plays *Amphitryon* (1807; English translation, 1962) and *Penthesilea* (1808; English translation, 1959), and beginning his best-known fiction, *Die Marquise von O . . .* (1810; *The Marquise of O . . .*, 1960). He suffered, however, from both depression and physical ailments that made it necessary for him to take an indefinite leave from his government job.

While on a trip to Dresden with two friends in January, 1807, Kleist was arrested by French authorities in Berlin on suspicion of being a spy and sent to prison in France. For several months during his imprisonment, he continued to work on his plays, especially *Penthesilea*. After being cleared and released, Kleist returned to Dresden to enjoy literary success as the author of *Amphitryon*, which had been published during his incarceration.

His newly raised hopes for a successful literary career seemed dashed when *The Broken Jug* was poorly received by drama critics and when a literary journal he had begun to edit had to be sold for lack of sufficient subscribers. At first seemingly undeterred by these setbacks, Kleist continued his writing, reconstructing the destroyed *Robert Guiskard* fragment, finishing *The Marquise of O . . .* , and beginning another great novella, *Michael Kohlhaas* (1810; English translation, 1844).

Kleist traveled to Austria in 1809 and attempted to start a patriotic journal in support of Germany's efforts against Napoleon; however, that too failed, and during this time he once again suffered depression and physical illness. There were even rumors that he had died. Nevertheless, he returned to Dresden, in good health, although penniless, in 1810. His play *Das Käthchen von Heilbronn: Oder, Die Feuerprobe* (1810; *Cathy of Heilbronn: Or, The Trial by Fire*, 1927) was staged in Vienna to an approving audience, and he now was making plans to stage *Prinz Friedrich von Homburg* (1821; *The Prince of Homburg*, 1875), which he had completed during his travels to Austria. Yet a planned performance of the play in the private theater at the palace of Prince Radziwill was canceled; the publisher of *Cathy of Heilbronn* refused to honor his promise to publish the work; and the director of the Prussian National Theater refused to allow the play to be staged. Again, Kleist's hopes for a literary career seemed dashed.

Kleist's next effort to support himself in the literary world was to become editor of the *Berliner Abendblätter*, the first daily newspaper to be published in Germany. Although the newspaper was popular with the public, it was somewhat too daring in its political editorials for the Prussian government censors. Although Kleist made strong pleas for freedom of the press, even to Prince Wilhelm, he was ignored. Despite the fact that the newspaper was forbidden from publishing what the government considered radical political ideas, it did publish Kleist's famous essay on the marionette theater, as well as some of his short fictions. Also during 1810, a second volume of his short fiction was published. The newspaper, however, was doomed to failure; the last issue of the *Berliner Abendblätter* was published on March 31, 1811.

At this time, Kleist was alone and without means of support; a request for a position with the government was ignored; his family, in a reunion at Frankfurt in October, was reluctant to support him. During this period, he met the young wife of a government official, Henrietta Vogel, who, biographers suggest, was suffering from an incurable illness. Together they made a suicide pact, and on November 21, 1811, near Berlin, Kleist shot Henrietta Vogel and then himself.

Summary

Heinrich von Kleist remains a mysterious figure in the history of literature. Relatively little is known about his tragic life, and his art and ideas have not been discussed in the United States or Great Britain to the extent that they have in Germany. The major focus of the criticism of Kleist's work has been on its philosophical content, although some studies (mostly in German) have been made on his narrative technique. Despite the fact that critical attention on Kleist has shifted to structural and textual analyses of his

Novellen and plays, the primary emphasis is still on the mysterious tension in his work between the nature of consciousness and the nature of external reality.

Kleist is an important German Romantic writer, who represents the significant intellectual shift in the early nineteenth century from an earlier dependence on rational, intellectual assumptions and structures to a new approach to reality based on the individual's own perception. He is often referred to as a precursor to twentieth century existential thought in his emphasis on the tension between the individual's desire for meaning and unity and the cold and unresponsive external world.

Bibliography

Ellis, John M. *Heinrich von Kleist: Studies in the Character and Meaning of His Writings*. Chapel Hill: University of North Carolina Press, 1979. Contains detailed analyses of Kleist's most mature works. Based on these discussions, Ellis provides a summary chapter on the general nature of Kleist's fiction, primarily its typical themes.

Gearey, John. *Heinrich von Kleist: A Study of Tragedy and Anxiety*. Philadelphia: University of Pennsylvania Press, 1968. A helpful and readable general study of the major short fictions and the plays. According to Geary, the basic tension in Kleist's works is not simply between rationality and emotion or even self-consciousness and the external world. More basically, his works focus on the general nature of opposition itself.

Heibling, Robert E. *The Major Works of Heinrich von Kleist*. New York: New Directions, 1975. A general introduction which surveys previous Kleist criticism, provides a brief biographical sketch, and then argues that Kleist's vision is tragic, not pathological. The predominant theme of Kleist's works is the conflict between the individual consciousness and the unresponsive external world.

Maass, Joachim. *Kleist: A Biography*. Translated by Ralph Manheim. New York: Farrar, Straus & Giroux, 1983. Maass's workmanlike biography, the first full-length account of Kleist's life available in English, was first published in German in 1957 and was reissued in a revised version in 1977, the basis for the English translation. Includes brief discussions of Kleist's major works. Illustrated, with indexes but no notes or bibliography.

McGlathery, James M. *Desire's Sway: The Plays and Stories of Heinrich von Kleist*. Detroit: Wayne State University Press, 1983. The primary focus of this relatively brief and highly documented critical study is the tension in Kleist's characters between their devotion to lofty ideas and their outbursts of passion—a tension which McGlathery says is typical of comedy.

March, Richard. *Heinrich von Kleist*. New Haven, Conn.: Yale University Press, 1954. Perhaps the best introduction to Kleist's life and art. Although this is only a brief (fifty pages) pamphlet, it provides a concise biographical sketch as well as an informed introduction to the basic themes in Kleist's work.

Charles E. May

ROBERT KOCH

Born: December 11, 1843; Clausthal, Prussia
Died: May 27, 1910; Baden-Baden, Germany
Areas of Achievement: Bacteriology and medicine
Contribution: Koch was a pioneer bacteriologist and the first to prove definitively that specific microorganisms cause specific diseases. He identified the bacterium that caused cholera, enabling the virtual elimination of that disease in the Western world. He isolated the causative agent of tuberculosis, eventually leading to the containment of that once-deadly scourge, and he discovered the reproductive cycle of anthrax, providing for the successful combating of that disease.

Early Life

Robert Koch was born in the mining country of the Harz Mountains in central Germany and was one of thirteen children of Hermann Koch and his wife, Mathilde Biewend. Hermann was a mining official and reasonably well off, although provision for a large family taxed his resources. A timely promotion assisted him in educating Robert, a precocious child drawn to the study of nature, who was able to excel at the local *Gymnasium*, or academic preparatory school. He went on to study at the nearby University of Göttingen. After a year of science and math, young Koch abandoned the idea of a teaching career and in 1863 transferred to the medical school at Göttingen, hoping that that field would allow him to pursue his love of science and travel. Koch's greatest scientific mentor was Jacob Henle, an anatomy professor who had published on disease causation and who speculated that infection might be transmitted by living organisms. At that time, however, no medical school in the world offered courses in bacteriology.

In 1866, at age twenty-three, Koch received his M.D. degree, passed his medical examination, and went to Berlin, where for a few months he attended lectures by the famous Rudolf Virchow, author of the notion that disease is the result of disturbance of cell function in the body tissues. Koch, from the very beginning of his career, was no mere medical practitioner concerned with diagnosis and treatment of disease but was a scientist interested in its very causes.

After a few months internship at Hamburg General Hospital, where he learned about cholera at first hand, he returned home and in July, 1867, married Emmy Fraatz, a daughter of the mining superintendent of Clausthal. Koch and his wife then lived for about a year at Langenhagen, Hanover, where he served at a hospital for mentally handicapped children while he practiced medicine privately in the community. By the time the couple's only child, Gertrud, was born in September of the following year, they were living at Niemegk, near Berlin. The young doctor's practice did not flourish there, and Koch moved his family to Rakwitz, near Posen, where he became a successful country doctor.

During the Franco-Prussian War, Koch entered the Prussian Army Medical Corps and served in 1870 and 1871 in France, working both with the wounded and with soldiers afflicted with typhoid. He left the army and returned briefly to his patients at Rakwitz, but in 1872 he secured appointment as district physician for Wollstein, another small town in the province of Posen. It was from that area of lakes, woods, and fields that Koch moved into national and international acclaim. A ruralist would have called the setting idyllic; Koch's later friend and admirer Élie Metchnikoff, a city-dweller, referred to Wollstein as "a God-forsaken hole in Posen." Nevertheless, it was the very rurality of Wollstein that provided Koch with his first great opportunity.

Life's Work

Koch had become a mature physician with a lengthy and varied record of civilian and military experience. A smallish man with a bristling beard and round spectacles, he was the stereotypical Germanic scientist, and he longed to do more actual research than he could perform by examining algae and lesions with a hand glass. A good microscope would have enabled him to peer more deeply into diseased tissue, but he believed that he could not afford such an instrument. His wife, Emmy, however, saved coins in a beer mug and surprised Koch with the money: The right man and the right research tool had come together at last. Like all men of genius, however, Koch was a driven man and made a poor companion. Emmy was neglected while her husband devoted most of his spare time to his laboratory, where he began by investigating the cause of anthrax—a very rural disease, a malady of grazing animals, primarily, but sometimes an ailment that could infect humans.

In the 1860's, the French physician-researcher Casimir-Joseph Davaine had discovered that a bacterium was the cause of anthrax. He called the rodlike microorganism "bactéridie" (later known to science as *Bacillus anthracis*), but he was not able to ascertain how the disease was transmitted or how the bacteria, which did not seem to be very long-lived, managed to survive between hosts.

Koch first verified Davaine's work by using sterilized wood splinters to inject anthrax bacilli into the tails of mice which he kept in cages in his laboratory. When the first mouse died, a drop of its blood was injected into a second mouse, and so on, until after eight mice the conclusion had to be reached that the poison was a living, self-perpetuating entity. A chemical poison would eventually have become so attenuated as to lose its potency. To grow his anthrax bacilli without contamination from other bacteria, Koch invented the hanging-drop technique. He ground out a depression in a thick glass slide, put a drop of blood containing anthrax microbes on a thin glass coverslip, put sealant around the edges of both sterile slides, placed the thick one over the thin one, and quickly inverted the pair, causing the drop to hang suspended over the depression. As a culture medium for the bacilli, he used liquid from the interior of the eye.

Only about one hundred miles from Wollstein was the large university city of Breslau in Silesia, and there the renowned botanist Ferdinand Julius Cohn had been working with bacteria. He had predicted that anthrax bacilli might form small eggs or spores. Koch clearly observed the spores, as he had been keeping his slides at body temperature, thus allowing the bacteria to develop through their life cycle though outside a host. Koch noted that, in the inert or spore stage, anthrax bacilli, normally quick to perish when not in a warm host, could survive for years and only be destroyed by burning. He found that the spores formed only when the host died but was still warm.

Koch wrote to Cohn at Breslau in 1876 and arranged to demonstrate his techniques and findings. Koch packed his equipment and animals and treated Cohn and other scientists to a history-making exhibition, during which the pathologist Julius Cohnheim was said to have rushed from the room in great excitement to summon his students to see the masterful work being demonstrated. Though self-taught, Koch handled his equipment like a master scientist, and his three-day re-creation of his experiments left no room for doubt that he had discovered the true etiology of anthrax. He was the first to prove that a microscopic one-celled organism caused a disease.

Cohn and Cohnheim became Koch's champions in the academic community. Cohn, in his biology journal, published Koch's paper on anthrax, and Koch's fame began to spread. While the Breslau scientists tried to find government support for Koch, he had to continue his researches in his tiny laboratory—a laboratory that Koch could hardly suspect would one day be turned into a museum. Koch, meanwhile, was making a definitive record of his observations by purchasing a special camera that he fitted to his microscope—a pioneer technique on which he wrote in 1877 in another article in Cohn's journal of biology. In the same article, he touted the use of the still fairly new aniline dyes for staining bacterial cultures on slides to make organisms contrast with the background. He had not been the first to employ the technique, but he was one of the earliest to advocate it.

By that time, the news of Koch's work had spread not only around Germany but also over all the world. Even the hidebound German bureaucracy began to pay attention. In 1879, Koch was given a post at Breslau, but it had an insufficient salary so the Koch family returned to Wollstein. Finally, the following year, Cohnheim succeeded in having Koch named as government counselor to the Imperial Bureau of Health in Berlin. A country doctor no more, Koch was given a laboratory, two assistants, and financial support.

It was after moving into his new laboratory in the capital city that Koch innocently made a rather rural discovery: He saw bacterial colonies growing on a slice of leftover boiled potato. Several different kinds were on the slice, and it struck Koch that a solid medium would provide an excellent way to keep separate the bacteria he was culturing. After a while, he abandoned cooked potato slices and employed a mixture of gelatin and beef broth, which he allowed to set in petri dishes. Louis Pasteur, who always cultured microorganisms in a souplike mixture, had a difficult time separating the desired microbes.

In Berlin, Koch concentrated on finding the agent causing tuberculosis, a slow but usually fatal endemic disease that was at its height in the late nineteenth century. Tubercle bacilli are much smaller and harder to grow than those of anthrax, but Koch persisted and produced a special blood-serum jelly to culture tuberculosis outside the body. Although he did prove that the tubercle bacillus caused the disease, Koch's vaunted tuberculin, a serum designed to cure tuberculosis in nonterminal patients, proved ineffective. Nevertheless, tuberculin can be used to diagnose the disease and is thus quite valuable.

Koch's greatest success story was the discovery of the cause of cholera— a horrible and usually fatal disease whose deadly epidemics were the terror of nineteenth century Europe and America. In 1883, cholera spread into Egypt and threatened to cross into Europe. To prevent this, the governments of France and Germany sent their best scientists to Alexandria: a French team consisting of Pasteur's top men and a German squad led by Koch himself. They searched for a microbe guilty of causing the feared cholera, and Koch was rather sure that he had located it. Then the epidemic left Egypt as mysteriously as it had come, and Europe was temporarily safe, but no one knew why. Back in Berlin, Koch asked the government to send him to Calcutta, eastern India, to find the disease in its permanent home. There, Koch and his assistants in early 1884 positively identified the vibrio bacillus as the cause and found that it was transmitted by water and other substances polluted with fecal matter. When the German scientists arrived home in May, they were greeted as conquering heroes. With lavish ceremony, the German Emperor William I personally decorated Koch with the Order of the Crown, with Star, while the Reichstag voted the scientist a large monetary gift.

Summary

Robert Koch shares with Pasteur the honor of founding modern medical bacteriology, but, in employment of solid culture media, discovery of improved sterilization by steam, use of staining techniques, and other innovations, he built the modern bacteriological laboratory. Koch's name is permanently associated with the conquest or taming of anthrax, cholera, and tuberculosis, but he did much other work. He always had a yearning to travel, frustrated in earlier years by family responsibilities. Leaving his perennial and only partially successful work on tuberculosis, Koch worked on malaria in Italy, rinderpest in South Africa, sleeping sickness and tick fever in German East Africa, and bubonic plague in northern India. He identified the rat and its flea as vectors of the plague, but it remained for Koch's Japanese disciple Shibasaburo Kitasato to isolate the actual microbe.

Koch scandalized Victorian mores in 1892 when, his marriage failing, he divorced his first wife and married a young actress, Hedwig Freiburg. Many of his biographers deliberately omitted any mention of the occurrence, as they themselves were scandalized—a comment on the strict middle-class morality of the late nineteenth century. Koch was awarded the Nobel Prize in Physiology or Medicine in 1905, primarily for his work on tuberculosis. It was an ultimate vindication for great efforts that bore fruit in many different ways that he was given such recognition for a disease that he had not managed to kill.

Bibliography

De Kruif, Paul. *Microbe Hunters*. New York: Harcourt, Brace, 1950. This readable yet detailed account has a lengthy chapter on "Koch: The Death Fighter." De Kruif's entertaining style makes the sometimes arcane world of microbiology accessible to the general reader.

Dubos, René. *The Unseen World*. New York: Rockefeller Institute Press, 1962. This work has a large section on Koch's life and contributions, including several interesting photographs. The book is an excellent and easily understandable introduction to microbiology and gives great credit to Koch as a founder of the science.

Fox, Ruth. *Great Men of Medicine*. New York: Random House, 1947. This book has a lengthy, thorough, and entertaining chapter on Koch. Fox concentrates on the early and middle portions of the pathologist's career.

Metchnikoff, Élie. *The Founders of Modern Medicine*. New York: Walden, 1939. This outstanding volume by a man who was himself a famous medical scientist and who knew Koch personally provides a rare and valuable look at Koch's scientific and personal lives.

Riedman, Sarah R., and Elton T. Gustafson. *Portraits of Nobel Laureates in Medicine and Physiology*. New York: Abelard-Schuman, 1963. Contains an excellent chapter on Koch plus a considerable amount of discussion of him in other chapters relating to researchers who were indebted to or in contact with him.

Stevenson, Lloyd G. *Nobel Prize Winners in Medicine and Physiology, 1901-1950*. New York: Henry Schuman, 1953. This volume concentrates on and gives a very good account of Koch's work on tuberculosis, as Koch's labor in this area was what won for him the Nobel Prize.

Allan D. Charles

ALFRED KRUPP

Born: April 26, 1812; Essen, Grand Duchy of Berg
Died: July 14, 1887; Essen, Germany
Areas of Achievement: Business, industry, and technology
Contribution: During the period of Germany's unification into one of the most powerful nations in Europe, Krupp expanded his family's steel-making concern into one of the most powerful industrial enterprises of the nineteenth century.

Early Life

The son of Friedrich Krupp, the founder of the family steel-making business, Alfred Krupp was born in the Ruhr River valley town of Essen only five months after Friedrich had founded the firm in 1812. When Alfred was fourteen, his father died and Alfred, along with his widowed mother, Therese, was left in charge of the business. Alfred had already been removed from school, largely because of his father's inability to make enough money to pay for his eldest son's education. As Krupp was to say in later life, his education came at an anvil, not a school desk.

As befitting a boy who had the responsibility of both a family and factory thrust upon him, Krupp became consumed with work. His family and friends at the time described him as tall, slim, and delicate-looking, but at the same time stoic and resolute. When Krupp inherited the family concern, the factory was almost bankrupt. Only seven men remained on the payroll, and wages had not been paid for several weeks. Moreover, few orders for steel products—the firm specialized in cutlery—were placed during the next several years. As Krupp later acknowledged, his mother held the family together during those lean times by sheer industriousness, a trait in himself which Krupp attributed to his mother's influence. From 1826 until he reached full adulthood, Krupp devoted every waking hour to the firm—helping either on the foundry floor or in the bookkeeper's office. Instead of playing with the other boys his age, young Krupp became obsessed with making steel.

Life's Work

For the next twenty years, Krupp endured a perpetual grind of hard work and impending financial collapse. The chief problem lay in competing with foreign producers. As late as 1848, steel from England still dominated the Prussian market. What little profit Krupp made during this time he put back into the firm, constantly attempting to expand and improve the foundry works. He was not above telling potential customers outright lies to gain a contract, nor was he reluctant to steal useful ideas from competitors. Finally, in 1834 Krupp steel was united with a force which was to transform the company as well as the map of Europe. This force was the kingdom of Prussia. Three years after the 1815 peace eliminated Napoleon I and restored the balance and power of Europe, the Prussian government abolished all hindrances to trade among its scattered provinces. On January 1, 1834, other German states joined Prussia in an economic union, the *Zollverein*, which extended to cover most of German-speaking Europe, with the exception of Austria and Hanover. Krupp was among the first businessmen to exploit this new advantage. By the end of 1834, he had traveled to all parts of the customs union and increased his orders for steel threefold. A year later, he again doubled his production, was employing seventy workmen, and had purchased a steam engine to power his foundry tools.

In 1847, the Krupp firm cast its first steel cannon, a small three-pound field gun, which attracted interest, but few orders. The foundry still specialized in the production of fine steel suitable for dies and machine tools. The big break came in 1851, however, at the London Exhibition. Krupp was determined to gain international renown for his firm by taking to London the best example of steel casting ever produced. The result, a flawless two-ton steel ingot, representing a giant step forward in metallurgy, caused a sensation and advertised Krupp's skill as no other demonstration could have. Following the London Exhibition, orders flowed in from around the world. The next step in the Krupp concern's development centered on mass production. By the late 1850's, Krupp had fully converted to the new production system. With his adoption of two new methods for steel manufacturing, which both lowered costs and increased production—the Bessemer and Siemens-Martin processes—Krupp was able to achieve such innovations as the seamless railroad wheel. This wheel revolutionized the railroad industry and made a fortune for Krupp; three interlocking wheels were chosen as the company emblem.

In 1858, large-scale armaments orders from the Prussian government began to dominate the firm's business. Krupp steel cannons became world-renowned after they helped Prussia defeat both Austria and France between 1866 and 1871. As a result, Krupp became a close associate of both Kaiser William I, who dubbed Krupp the "Cannon King," and German Chancellor Otto von Bismarck.

By 1871, Krupp employed sixteen thousand men in numerous foundries and workshops. Ever the paternalistic proprietor, Krupp furnished an elaborate social-welfare program for his workers, including low-cost housing, free medical care, pensions, and consumer cooperatives. Workers' unions, however, were vigorously opposed, and Krupp deemed any flirtation with unions a personal affront to him. Krupp became a leader of the other Ruhr industrialists in opposing workers' organizations, and he helped finance strident antiunion and antisocialist campaigns. Most of the Krupp employees remained loyal to the firm, however, and the majority enjoyed referring to themselves as "Kruppianer."

In the 1860's, Krupp pioneered the development of vertically integrated industry by his acquisition of coal mines and railroads. By the 1870's, Krupp had amassed one of the largest fortunes in Europe. The associated Krupp steel and coal companies employed more than twenty thousand men. The German elite, including the royal family, were frequent guests at Krupp's colossal mansion in Essen, the Villa Huegel, a Renaissance-style house built entirely of stone and Krupp steel. On July 14, 1887, Krupp died at Villa Huegel, attended by his family and mourned by the kaiser. Krupp's eldest son, Friedrich Alfred, continued the Krupp family's sole control over its steel empire until his death, when the firm became a corporation.

Summary

With the death of his father, the founder of the Krupp steel-making dynasty, Alfred Krupp saved the firm from near collapse and built it into an industrial giant by making use of the newest metallurgical techniques, by instilling tough discipline, and by obsessive hard work. Krupp began by making machine tools, coin dies, and steel cutlery, but his fame emerged with his production of steel cannons for the Prussian army in the 1860's and 1870's. By 1887, the name Krupp was world famous for the manufacture of quality steel, especially steel cannons for the Prussian army, which became the standard for comparison throughout the world. As an industrial empire builder, Krupp pioneered vertical integration by acquiring a variety of mining, power, and transportation concerns. An avowed opponent of socialism and labor unions, Krupp nevertheless was one of the first modern industrialists to provide full welfare services, including health insurance, pension benefits, and low-cost housing for his workers. Krupp served as a model for the nineteenth century aggressive, innovative, and paternalistic industrialist.

Bibliography

Batty, Peter. *The House of Krupp*. New York: Stein & Day, 1967. Batty's survey of the Krupp dynasty from its founding to the post-World War II period is less ambitious than Manchester's, but it provides the most readable and concise study. Batty thoroughly investigates Krupp's youth, and the author is especially adroit at displaying the youthful factors which later played a role in Krupp's direction of the firm.

Henderson, William Otto. *The Rise of German Industrial Power, 1834-1914*. Berkeley: University of California Press, 1975. The author concentrates on the role of unification in the rise of Germany as an industrial power. Krupp and the development of the Krupp firm from near bankruptcy to world acclaim is placed in the context of Germany's overall economic growth in the nineteenth century.

Kitchen, Martin. *The Political Economy of Germany, 1815-1914*. London: Croom Helm, 1978. The book addresses the relationship between the growth of German industry and the creation of an industrialist class. While the discussion centers largely on the political debate over tariffs and taxes, the Krupp dominance of German armaments is given partial credit for the direction of nineteenth century German foreign policy.

Manchester, William. *The Arms of Krupp, 1587-1968*. Boston: Little, Brown, 1968. The standard popular biography of the Krupp dynasty. A major section of the work concerns Krupp and his career as proprietor of the firm. Of special interest is Manchester's investigation of Krupp's private life and eccentricities, including the construction of the Villa Huegel. The work is careless in some of the details of the Krupp family saga.

Showalter, Dennis E. *Railroads and Rifles: Soldiers, Technology, and the Unification of Germany*. Hamden, Conn.: Archon Books, 1975. This work provides a close study of Krupp's role in the unification of Germany. The author focuses on Krupp's early years of business and his successful association with the Prussian government through the acquisition of government contracts. Especially well covered are Krupp's armaments contracts during the critical period of German unification in the 1860's and 1870's.

William G. Ratliff

JEAN DE LA FONTAINE

Born: July 8, 1621; Château-Thierry, Champagne, France
Died: April 13, 1695; Paris, France
Area of Achievement: Literature
Contribution: La Fontaine is recognized as one of the major writers of the French classical period. He wrote drama, ballet, popular tales, and various forms of poetry, but he is best known in France and abroad for his verse fables, a genre he developed to perfection.

Early Life

Jean de La Fontaine was born in Château-Thierry, a small farming town in Champagne located about fifty miles east of Paris. His father, Charles de La Fontaine, was a local administrator of forests and waters. His mother, Françoise Pidoux, belonged to a respected middle-class family from Poitiers. The widow of a wealthy merchant, she had one daughter when she married Charles in 1617.

Although little is known about La Fontaine's early years, most scholars believe he attended school in Château-Thierry before going to college in Paris. During his school years, he learned Latin rhetoric and grammar and was introduced to ancient works that would provide subjects for his later creative endeavors. He was most likely a sensitive student who liked to daydream and who perhaps found his teachers boring and authoritative. Several uncomplimentary references to schoolboys and schoolmasters in his fables suggest that his school years were not entirely pleasant.

On April 27, 1641, La Fontaine entered the Oratory, a religious seminary in Paris. By October, his teachers had discovered his preference for popular love stories and wrote that he should be strongly urged to study theology. After eighteen months, La Fontaine withdrew from the seminary and returned to Château-Thierry to read and daydream. Although many writers refer disparagingly to this idle period, La Fontaine was becoming familiar with ancient and modern authors, especially the poets François de Malherbe and Vincent Voiture, François Rabelais, and the Latin writers Horace, Vergil, and Terence.

From 1645 to 1647, La Fontaine studied law in Paris, spending much of his time, however, with aspiring young writers (François Maucroix, Paul Pellisson, and Antoine Furetière) who would influence and support him throughout his career. In this formative period, La Fontaine continued to increase his knowledge of ancient and modern literature.

In 1647, at the age of twenty-six, La Fontaine was married to Marie Héricart, who was fourteen and a half years of age, and who brought him a dowry of thirty thousand livres, a considerable sum. Although amiable at first, the couple drifted apart. Absorbed for weeks in his reading, La Fontaine ignored both his family and his duties as forest warden, a position he obtained in 1652. Although he appeared idle and absentminded, the extent of his voracious reading and keen observation would become evident in his later works.

Life's Work

During the classical period, which flourished in France from 1660 to about 1685, writers were expected to imitate and to adapt works of ancient authors, not by radically changing the originals but by presenting them in new styles to please contemporary audiences. As his first major work, La Fontaine tried to adapt a racy Latin comedy by Terence to the refined tastes of Parisian high society, but the necessary changes destroyed the flavor and unity of the original. Although *L'Eunuque* (1654; the eunuch) was never produced, its lively dialogue demonstrates his narrative skills.

For the next few years, La Fontaine was occupied by family affairs. The income from his administrative position and similar positions inherited from his father in 1658 was insufficient to pay family debts, forcing La Fontaine to annul his marriage in order to sell property held jointly with his wife. From this time on, he lived mostly apart from his family, relying on wealthy patrons to support his life's work.

His first patron was Nicolas Fouquet, a wealthy and ambitious minister of finance, whose estate at Vaux-le-Vicomte was being built as a showplace of the arts, and whose eighteen thousand employees included the leading artists, architects, gardeners, musicians, and writers. In addition to occasional verse to entertain the society at Vaux, La Fontaine wrote *Adonis* (1658), a six-hundred-line love story in rhymed couplets, which merges three distinct genres (heroic, idyllic, and elegiac) in a creative synthesis of earlier sources. La Fontaine was also working on *Le Songe de Vaux* (1659; the dream of Vaux), a mixture of poetry and prose in which the muses of painting, gardening, architecture, and poetry describe the wonders of Fouquet's magnificent estate, then under construction. The work reveals La Fontaine's remarkable ability to communicate visual imagery in verse.

When the young Louis XIV had Fouquet imprisoned for plundering the treasury, La Fontaine demonstrated his uncompromising loyalty to the finance minister in a short poem circulated anonymously among Fouquet's supporters, deploring the minister's downfall and asking the nymphs of Vaux to make the king merciful. A year later, in "Ode au Roi" (1663; ode to the king), La Fontaine urged Louis XIV to pardon his disgraced minister.

Forty years of age, without a patron and in disfavor with the young monarch who had taken Fouquet's role as patron of the arts, La Fontaine traveled to Limoges with his wife's uncle, Jacques Jannart, who had been exiled for supporting Fouquet. La Fontaine describes this trip, the longest he ever took, in six letters later published as *Relation d'un voyage en Limousin* (1663;

account of a trip to Limoges). Returning to Paris after a few months, La Fontaine found protection with the Duke and Duchess of Bouillon, perhaps discovering an appreciative audience for his licentious tales inspired by Giovanni Boccaccio, Ludovico Ariosto, and other writers.

Accepting an undemanding post as gentleman servant to the Duchess of Orléans in 1664, La Fontaine began his most productive period. His licentious *Contes et nouvelles en vers* (1664; *Tales and Short Stories in Verse*, 1735) became immediately popular among sophisticated society, accomplishing his chief goal: to entertain his readers. He published several more collections of tales.

La Fontaine's method of shaping new works from old sources, artfully departing from established rules of versification to create a studied negligence, and carrying on a dialogue with the reader worked even better in his fables. His first edition of *Fables choisies, mises en vers* (1688, 1678, 1694; *Fables Written in Verse*, 1735), a collection of 124 fables in six books, was an immediate success. In the introduction, La Fontaine declared that his fables presented important truths in amusing stories, adding that they were "portraits in which all of us are depicted."

In the fables, La Fontaine drew upon all of his previous reading and experience to present an overview of French society that included kings and nobles, lawyers and judges, students and teachers, doctors and philosophers, and the lowliest laborers. His goal, even when his characters were animals or plants, was to portray human nature and, like his friend Molière, to hold vices up to ridicule.

When the Duchess of Orléans died in 1672, La Fontaine was taken in by the intelligent and witty Madame de La Sablière, who introduced him to scientists, philosophers, and other intellectuals. Under her influence, La Fontaine published five more books of fables, widening his sources to include fables by the Indian sage Pilpay. He also treated philosophical questions in the 237-line *Discours à Mme de La Sablière* (1679), refuting René Descartes' claim that animals were a kind of machine.

Unable to limit himself to a single genre, La Fontaine experimented with a variety of hybrid works. *Les Amours de Psyché et de Cupidon* (1669; *The Loves of Cupid and Psyche*, 1744) was a fairy tale in prose and poetry related to three friends during a visit to Versailles. The four friends, traditionally identified as Molière, Jean Racine, Nicolas Boileau, and La Fontaine (because they were constantly together when the piece was composed around 1664), are now considered composite characters reflecting views discussed at length by La Fontaine and his many friends. Although the work was not popular, it inspired a successful play with music and ballet by Molière, Pierre Corneille, and Jean-Baptiste Lully in 1671.

Other works include a religious poem about the temptation of Saint Malc, a scientific epic about the fashionable drug quinine, an opera rejected by the composer Lully, a ballet with only two acts, a comedy that was performed only four times, and the opera *L'Astrée* (1692), which ran for six performances.

In 1683, La Fontaine was elected to the prestigious Académie Française, but Louis XIV refused to accept the vote until Boileau was elected in 1684 and La Fontaine had promised to write no more works such as *Tales and Short Stories in Verse*. As a member of the Académie, La Fontaine entered the Quarrel of the Ancients and Moderns with his *Épître à Huet* (1687; letter to Huet), which praised both ancient and modern writers while discouraging a slavish imitation of earlier works.

With the publication of his last collection of fables in 1694, La Fontaine completed his life's work. In his last years, he experienced a religious conversion, disavowed *Tales and Short Stories in Verse*, and destroyed a play he had been writing. La Fontaine died April 13, 1695, in Paris at the age of seventy-three.

Summary

Although he tried his hand at many literary forms, Jean de La Fontaine is remembered for his fables, which have survived translation into many languages. Except for *Tales and Short Stories in Verse*, his other works are relatively unknown outside his own country, even to students of French literature. One exception, his poem *Adonis*, has received much scholarly attention since its brilliant analysis by the French poet Paul Valéry in 1921.

A careful writer even when trying to appear casual, La Fontaine was totally dedicated to his craft, despite a reputation for idleness and an eagerness to please the audience of his day. Forced to seek patrons to support his work, he firmly but diplomatically maintained his independence as a writer, rejecting suggestions to write the fables in prose or to follow his sources more closely. His fables are a synthesis of his extensive reading, keen observation, and years of poetic experimentation. With his unerring ear for dialogue, his insight into human nature, and his skill as a poet and storyteller, La Fontaine carried the classic art of imitation to its highest extreme by molding the fable into a new poetic genre. More than three centuries later, his accomplishment remains unsurpassed.

Bibliography

Guiton, Margaret. *La Fontaine: Poet and Counterpoet*. New Brunswick, N.J.: Rutgers University Press, 1961. Examines La Fontaine's competing visions of comedy and imaginative poetry. French passages translated. Contains chronological table of La Fontaine's life and works.

La Fontaine, Jean de. *The Complete Fables of Jean de La Fontaine*. Edited and translated by Norman B. Spector. Evanston, Ill.: Northwestern University Press, 1988. A bilingual edition in clear, crisp rhymed verse.

Closer to the original language and imagery than many other versions.

_____. *The Fables of La Fontaine*. Translated by Marianne Moore. New York: Viking Press, 1954. A verse translation by the famed poet. Captures the flavor of the original fables but exercises more poetic license than other versions.

Lapp, John C. *The Esthetics of Negligence: La Fontaine's "Contes."* Cambridge: Cambridge University Press, 1971. Refutes previous disparaging studies by demonstrating how La Fontaine's wit, eroticism, lyricism, and charm make the *Tales and Short Stories in Verse* superior to their sources.

Mackay, Agnes Ethel. *La Fontaine and His Friends: A Biography*. London: Garnstone Press, 1972. Examination of La Fontaine's relationship with intimate friends and influential patrons. French passages translated in chapter endnotes.

Sweetser, Marie-Odile. *La Fontaine*. Boston: Twayne, 1987. A good place to begin a study of La Fontaine. Excellent review of La Fontaine's life, description of his major works, and concise summary of important studies. Lists selected critical articles, many in English.

Wadsworth, Philip A. *Young La Fontaine*. Evanston, Ill.: Northwestern University Press, 1952. A detailed study of La Fontaine's growth as a poet up to publication of his first fables in 1668. Good discussion of influences that shaped his early works.

Richard M. Shaw

JOSEPH-LOUIS LAGRANGE

Born: January 25, 1736; Turin, Sardinia
Died: April 10, 1813; Paris, France
Area of Achievement: Mathematics
Contribution: One of the most brilliant mathematicians of the mid- and late eighteenth century, Lagrange accomplished astonishing syntheses of the mathematical innovations of his predecessors, especially in the systems underlying classic physics. Almost as remarkable for his winning personality as his incisive intellect, Lagrange created the mathematical basis of modern mechanics.

Early Life
Born in what was then the kingdom of Sardinia of mixed French and Italian, though predominantly French descent, Joseph-Louis Lagrange was the first son in an influential and wealthy family. His father, however, once a highly placed cabinet official, burned with the speculative fevers of the early eighteenth century and ended by losing everything. Typically, Lagrange took that in stride, remarking later that losing his inheritance forced him to find a profession; he chose wisely. Although early in his formal education he found mathematics boring, probably because it began with geometry, at age fourteen he chanced on an essay by the astronomer Edmond Halley, which changed his mind, and his life. In this essay, Halley, one of Isaac Newton's disciples, proclaimed the superiority of the new analytical methods of calculus to the old synthetic geometry. From that moment, Lagrange devoted as much time as he could to the new science, becoming a professor of mathematics at the Royal Artillery School in Turin before the age of eighteen.

From the beginning, Lagrange specialized in analysis, starting the trend toward specialization that has characterized the study of mathematics ever since. His concentration on analytical methods also liberated the discipline for the first time from its dependence on Greek geometry. In fact, of his major work, *Mécanique analytique* (analytical mechanics), first conceived when he was nineteen but not published until 1788, he boasted that it contained not a single diagram. He then stated offhandedly that in the future the physics of mechanics might be approached as a geometry of four dimensions, the three familar Cartesian coordinates combined with a time coordinate; in such a system, a moving particle could be defined in time and space simultaneously. This system of analyzing mechanics reemerged in 1916, when Albert Einstein employed it to explain his general theory of relativity.

From the ages of nineteen to twenty-three, Lagrange continued as a professor at Turin, producing a number of revolutionary studies in the calculus of variations, analysis of mechanics, theory of sound, celestial mechanics, and probability theory, for which he won a number of international prizes and honors. In 1766, he succeeded Leonhard Euler as court mathematician to Frederick the Great in the Berlin Academy, the most prestigious position of the time. There, freed from lecturing duties, he continued to produce epochal studies in celestial mechanics, number theory, Diophantine analysis, and numerical and literal equations. He also found it possible to marry a younger cousin; the marriage was successful, and Lagrange was later devastated when his wife died of a wasting disease. Characteristically, he tried to overcome his grief by losing himself in his work.

Life's Work

For most of Lagrange's life, overwork was a habit. Yet it enabled him to achieve much at an early age. At twenty-three, Lagrange wrote an article on the calculus of variations, in which he foreshadowed his later unifying theory on the whole of mechanics, both solids and fluids. This integrated general mechanics in much the same way that Newton's law of gravitation unified celestial motion. Lagrange's theory proceeds from the disarmingly simple observation that all physical force is identical, whether operating in the solid or liquid state, whether aural, visual, or mechanical. It thus integrates a diverse array of physical phenomena, simplifying their study. In the same work, Lagrange applied differential calculus to the theory of probability. He also surpassed Newton by absorbing the mathematical theory of sound into the theory of elastic physical particles, becoming the first to understand sound transmission as straight-line projection through adjacent particles. Furthermore, he put to rest a controversy over the proper mathematical description of a vibrating string, laying the basis of the more general theory of vibrations as a whole. At this early age, Lagrange already ranked with the giants of his age, Euler and the Bernoulli family.

The next problems Lagrange attacked at Turin were those involved in the libration of the moon in celestial mechanics: Why does the moon present the same surface to the earth at every point in its revolution? He deduced the answer to this special instance of the three-body problem, a classic in mechanics, from Newton's law of universal gravitation. For solving this problem, Lagrange won the Grand Prix of the French Academy in 1764. The Academy followed by proposing a four-body problem; Lagrange solved this, winning the prize again in 1766. The Academy then proposed a six-body problem involving calculating the relative position of the sun, Jupiter, and its four then-known satellites. This problem was not completely solvable by modern methods before the development of computers. Nevertheless, Lagrange developed methods of approximation that were superseded only in the twentieth century. After his move to Berlin, for further work on similar problems—the general three-body problem, the motion of the moon, and cometary disturbances—Lagrange won further awards.

His career in Berlin lasted twenty years; during it, he distinguished himself by unfailing courtesy, generosity to other mathematicians, and diplomacy in difficult situations—he was a stranger in a strange court, but he thrived. In addition to working on celestial mechanics there, he diverted himself by investigations into number theory, the humble matter of what his age considered higher arithmetic. Quadratic forms and Diophantine analysis—exponential equations—particularly interested him: He first solved the problem of determining for which square numbers x^2, $nx^2 + 1$ is also a square, when n is a nonsquare, for example, $n = 3$, $x = 4$. This problem was an ancient one; Lagrange's paper is a classic, couched in his elegant language and supported by his equally elegant reasoning. He followed this by offering the first successful proofs of some of Pierre de Fermat's theorems and the one of John Wilson which states that only prime numbers are factors of the sum of the factorial series of the next lowest number plus one—that is, p divides $(p-1)(p-2)\cdots 3 \cdot 2 \cdot 1 + 1$ only if it is prime. His most famous proof in number theory shows that every position integer can be represented as a sum of four integral squares—a theorem that has had extensive applications in many scientific fields. He later did great work—which proved preliminary—on quadratic equations in two unknowns.

Perhaps the most important work of the Berlin period, however, relates to Lagrange's work in modern algebra. In a memoir of 1767 and in later sequels, he investigated the theoretical bases for solving various algebraic equations. Though once again he fell short of providing definitive answers, his work became an invaluable source for the nineteenth century algebraists who succeeded in finding them. The essential principles—that both necessary and sufficient conditions be established before solution—eluded him, but his work contained the clue.

Eventually, Lagrange's propensity for work broke both his body and his spirit. By 1783, he had sunk into a profound depression, in the grip of which he found further work in mathematics impossible. When Frederick died in 1786 and Lagrange fell out of favor in Berlin, he willingly accepted a position with the French Academy. Still, a change of scene brought no renewal of his interest in mathematics. When his monumental *Mécanique analytique* was published in 1788, Lagrange took no notice of it, leaving a copy unopened on his desk for more than two years. Instead, he turned his attention to various other sciences and humanities.

It took the French Revolution to reawaken Lagrange's interest in mathematics. Although he could have fled, as many aristocratic scholars did, he did not. The atrocities of the Terror appalled Lagrange, and he had little sympathy with the destructive practices of revolutionary zealots. Yet when appointed to the faculties of the new schools—the École Normale and the École Polytechnique—intended to replace the abolished universities and academies, Lagrange took up his professional duties enthusiastically. Because he became aware of the difficulties his basically unprepared students had with the theoretical bases of calculus, he reformulated the theory to make it independent of concepts of infinitesimals and limits. His attempt was unsuccessful, but he prepared the foundation on which modern theories are built.

Part of his duties at the École Polytechnique required Lagrange to supervise the development of the metric system of weights and measures. Fortunately, he insisted that the base 10 be adopted. Radical reformers lobbied for base 12, alleging superior factorability; it is still occasionally proposed as more "rational," and for centuries it played an infernal role in the British monetary system. To suppress the reformers, Lagrange argued ironically for the advantages of a system with base 11, or any prime, since then all fractions would have the same denominator. A small amount of practice convinced the radicals that 10 was more functional.

Teaching and supervision alone, however, did not suffice to relieve Lagrange's besetting melancholy. He was saved from despair at the age of fifty-six, by the intervention of a young woman, the daughter of his friend the astronomer Pierre-Charles Lemonnier. She insisted on marrying him despite their disparity in age, and, contrary to all expectations, the marriage proved a brilliant success. For the following twenty years, Lagrange could not bear to have her out of his sight, and she proved to be a faithful companion, adept at drawing him out of his shell. At the end of his life, he worked on a second edition of his masterpiece, *Mécanique analytique*, adding many profound insights. He was still improving it when death came, gradually and almost imperceptibly, on April 10, 1813.

Summary

Joseph-Louis Lagrange ranks with the outstanding mathematicians of all time; in his prime, he was widely recognized as the greatest living mathematician, and he is certainly the most significant figure between Euler and Carl Friedrich Gauss. Beyond the quality of his work, he was noted equally for the brilliance of his demonstrations and for his accessibility and personal charm. He is particularly celebrated as one of the classic stylists of mathematical writing, almost the incarnation of mathematical elegance. His composition combines exceptional clarity of description and development with remarkable beauty of phrasing. His language is supple, never stilted or contorted; he somehow seems to ease the effort of strenuous thought. Lagrange once remarked that chemistry was as easy as algebra; in his writing, he is able to make things seem transparent, especially those which seemed particularly dense before reading him.

Perhaps because of this ease of expression, Lagrange is more important for the stimulus he provided for others than for his own original work. Time after time, his contemporaries and descendants found inspiration in him. He made his foundations so complete that others were able to apply them to other cases. In some instances, he was simply ahead of his time; his ideas have had to wait for the ground to be prepared. At any rate, Lagrange's work proved to be extraordinarily rich for those who labored after him.

Lagrange's most important contributions lie in mechanics and the calculus of variations. In fact, the latter is the centerpiece on which all of his achievements depend, the insight which he used to integrate the theory of mechanics. This calculus derives from the ancient principle of least action or least time, which concerns the determination of the path a beam of light will follow when passing through or refracting off layers of varying densities. Hero of Alexandria began the inquiry by determining that a beam reflected from a series of mirrors reaches its object by following the shortest possible route; that is, it is the minimum of a function. René Descartes elaborated on the theory by experimenting with the effects of various lenses on a ray of light, showing that refraction also produced minima. Lagrange then proceeded to demonstrate that the general postulates for matter and motion established by Newton, which did not seem to harmonize, also fit this scheme of minima. Thus, he used a principle of economy in nature—that physical mechanics also tended to minimal extremes—to unify the principles of particles in motion. This not only was revolutionary in his time but also gave rise to the further integrating work of William Rowan Hamilton and James Clerk Maxwell, and eventually blossomed in Einstein's general theory of relativity.

Bibliography
Bell, Eric T. *Men of Mathematics*. New York: Simon & Schuster, 1937. Bell's work is famous for three features: readability, accessibility to the general reader, and general historical background. These qualities continue; this is the preferred reference work, though Bell does not provide the technical detail of other sources.
Burton, David M. *The History of Mathematics: An Introduction*. Newton, Mass.: Allyn & Bacon, 1985. Burton's book has some very attractive features, especially the examples and practical exercises in real mathematics. Users of his work should, however, be aware that his focus is on major developments and broad concepts, so that his treatment of Lagrange, in one sense admirably concise, is somewhat cursory.
Kline, Morris. *Mathematical Thought from Ancient to Modern Times*. New York: Oxford University Press, 1972. Kline offers a more thorough and more rigorously theoretical treatment than Burton, but he requires considerable mathematical sophistication. Still, the book is not aimed at specialists, and Kline explains thoroughly, emphasizing the coherent evolution of mathematical thought. He highlights Lagrange's consistency admirably.
Porter, Thomas Isaac. "A History of the Classical Isoperimetric Problem." In *University of Chicago Contributions to the Calculus of Variations*,

vol. 3. Chicago: University of Chicago Press, 1933. Porter's article is a study for professionals and scholars, with much detail and requiring advanced mathematics. It does, however, contain the most extensive account of Lagrange's most important work in the calculus of variations, with incidental reference to his other achievements.

Smith, David Eugene. *A Source Book in Mathematics*. Reprint. Mineola, N.Y.: Dover, 1959. Smith's work is for historians of mathematics, but his selections of extracts from Lagrange's works are representative and reveal the master's clarity of exposition and are thus quite accessible.

Struik, D. J., ed. *A Source Book in Mathematics, 1200-1800*. Cambridge, Mass.: Harvard University Press, 1969. This is an anthology of extracts from the original works, such as Smith's, but it is more extensive and representative of the entire body of Lagrange's work. The introductions and notes are useful and thorough, particularly good in helping the reader reach an appreciation of Lagrange's accomplishments.

James Livingston

PIERRE-SIMON LAPLACE

Born: March 23, 1749; Beaumont-en-Auge, Normandy, France
Died: March 5, 1827; Paris, France
Areas of Achievement: Astronomy, mathematics, and physics
Contribution: Laplace made groundbreaking mathematical contributions to
  probability theory and statistical analysis. Using Isaac Newton's theory of
  gravitation, he also performed very detailed mathematical analyses of the
  shape of Earth and the orbits of comets, planets, and their moons.

Early Life
  Pierre-Simon Laplace was born into a well-established and prosperous
family of farmers and merchants in southern Normandy. An ecclesiastical
career in the Church was originally planned for Laplace by his father, and he
attended the Benedictine secondary school in Beaumont-en-Auge between
the ages of seven and sixteen. His interest in mathematics blossomed during
two years at the University of Caen, beginning in 1766. In 1768, he went to
Paris to pursue a career in mathematics; he remained a permanent resident of
Paris or its immediate vicinity for the rest of his life. Soon after his arrival in
Paris, he sought and won the patronage of Jean Le Rond d'Alembert, a
mathematician, physicist, and philosopher with great influence among
French intellectuals. D'Alembert found Laplace employment teaching mathematics to military cadets at the École Militaire, and it was in this position
that Laplace wrote his first memoirs in mathematics and astronomy. In 1773,
Laplace was elected to the Academy of Sciences as a mathematician. This
achievement, at the relatively young age of twenty-four, was based upon the
merits of thirteen memoirs he had presented to academy committees for
review. Some of Laplace's earliest mathematical interests involved the calculation of odds in games of chance. At a time when there was not yet a field
of mathematics devoted to the systematic study of probability, Laplace
played a major role in carrying the early development of this topic beyond
the rules of thumb of gambling and the preliminary conclusions of earlier
mathematicians. In addition, Laplace emphasized the relevance of probability to the analysis of statistics. He believed that, since all experimental
data are imprecise to some extent, it is important to be able to calculate an
appropriate average or mean value from a collection of observations. Furthermore, this mean value should be calculated in such a way as to minimize
its difference from the actual value of the quantity being measured.
  Statistical problems of this type inspired Laplace's initial interest in astronomy. He became intrigued by the process through which new astronomical data should be incorporated into calculations of probabilities for future
observations. In particular, he concentrated on the application of Sir Isaac
Newton's law of gravitation to the motions of the comets and planets.

Laplace's interest in physics thus had a very mathematical orientation. Throughout his career, he retained his early concentration on the solution of problems suggested by the mathematical implications of physical laws; he never devoted himself to extensive experimental investigation of new phenomena. Laplace's primary motivation was a deep conviction that, even if human limitations prevent an exact knowledge of natural laws and experimental conditions, it is still possible progressively to eliminate error through increasingly accurate approximations.

Very little is known about Laplace's personal life during these early years. He does not seem to have stimulated strong friendship or animosity. In 1788, he married Marie-Charlotte de Courty de Romanges, who was twenty years younger than himself, and they had two children. Laplace established and maintained comfortable but disciplined living habits, and he retained an undiminished mental clarity to the moment of his death.

Life's Work

Although a brief summary of Laplace's life's work requires some classification by topics and an emphasis on final results rather than chronology, the highly integrated and developmental nature of his research should not be forgotten. For example, mathematical techniques that he invented for the solution of problems in probability theory often were immediately applied to similar problems in physics or astronomy. Since Laplace was particularly interested in approximate or probable solutions and the analysis of error, he repeatedly revised his mathematical techniques to accommodate new data.

Laplace's contributions to probability theory were both technical and philosophical. This twofold concern is expressed in the titles of the influential volumes in which he summarized his work, *Théorie analytique des probabilités* (1812; analytic theory of probability) and *Essai philosophique sur les probabilités* (1814; *A Philosophical Essay on Probabilities*, 1902). The *Théorie analytique des probabilités* was the first comprehensive treatise devoted entirely to the subject of probability. Laplace provided a groundbreaking, although necessarily imperfect, characterization of the techniques, subject matter, and practical applications of the new field. He relied on the traditional problems generated by games of chance, such as lotteries, to motivate his mathematical innovations, but he pointed toward the future by generalizing these methods and applying them to many other topics. For example, since the calculation of odds in games of chance so often requires the summation of long series of fractions in which each term in the series differs from the others according to a regular pattern, Laplace began by reviewing some of the methods he had discovered to approximate the sums of such series, particularly when very large numbers are involved. He then proceeded to state what has since come to be called Bayes's theorem, after an early predecessor of Laplace. This theorem states how to use partial or incomplete information to calculate the conditional probability of an event in terms of its absolute or unconditional probability and the conditional probability of its cause. Laplace was one of the first to make extensive use of this theorem; it was particularly important to him because of its relevance to how calculations of probability should change in response to new knowledge.

The *Théorie analytique des probabilités* includes Laplace's applications of his mathematical techniques to problems generated by the analysis of data from such diverse topics as census figures, insurance rates, instrumentation error, astronomy, geodesy, election prognostication, and jury selection. In particular, he gave an important statement of what has since been called the least square law for the calculation of a mean value for a set of data in such a way that the resulting error from the true value is minimized.

A Philosophical Essay on Probabilities has been one of Laplace's most widely read works; it includes the conceptual basis upon which Laplace constructed his mathematical techniques. Most important, Laplace stated and relied upon a definition of probability that has been a source of considerable philosophical debate. Given a situation in which specific equally possible cases are the results of various processes (such as rolling dice) and correspond to favorable or unfavorable events, Laplace defined the probability of an event as the fraction formed by dividing the number of cases that correspond to or cause that event by the total number of possible cases. When the cases in question are not equally possible (as when dice are loaded), the calculation must be altered in an attempt to include this information. Laplace's definition thus calls attention to his treatment of probability as an application of mathematics made necessary only by human ignorance. In one of the most famous passages in *A Philosophical Essay on Probabilities*, Laplace expresses this view by describing a supreme intelligence with a complete knowledge of the universe and its laws at any specific moment; for such an intelligence, Laplace believed that probability calculations would be unnecessary since the future and past could be calculated simply through an application of the laws of nature to the given perfectly stipulated set of conditions. Since knowledge of natural laws and the state of the world is always limited, probability is an essential feature of all human affairs. Nevertheless, Laplace's emphasis was not on the negative aspect of this conclusion but on the mathematical regularities to which even seemingly arbitrary sequences of events conform.

The domain in which Laplace saw the closest human approach to the knowledge of his hypothetical supreme intelligence was the application of Newton's theory of gravitation to the solar system. Since Newton's publication of his theory in 1686, mathematicians and physicists had reformulated his results using increasingly sophisticated mathematics. By Laplace's time, Newton's theory could be stated in a type of mathematics known as partial differential equations. Laplace made major contributions to the solution of equations of this type, including the famous technique of "Laplace transforms" and the use of a "potential" function to characterize a field of force.

Laplace made remarkably detailed applications of Newton's results to the orbits of the planets, moons, and comets. Some of his most famous calculations involve his demonstration of the very long-term periodic variations in the orbits of Jupiter and Saturn. Laplace thus contributed to an increasing knowledge of the stability and internal motions of the solar system. He also applied gravitation theory to the tides, the shape of Earth, and the rings of Saturn. His hypothesis that the solar system was formed through the condensation of a diffuse solar atmosphere became a starting point for more detailed subsequent theories.

Newtonian gravitation theory became Laplace's model for precision and clarity in all other branches of physics. He encouraged his colleagues to attempt similar analyses in optics, heat, electricity, and magnetism. His influence was particularly strong among French physicists between 1805 and 1815. By his death in 1827, however, this attempt to base all physics upon short-range forces had achieved only limited success; aside from the mathematical methods he developed, Laplace's conceptual contributions to physics were not as long-lasting as his more fundamental insights in probability theory.

Summary

Pierre-Simon Laplace's cultural influence extended far beyond the relatively small circle of mathematicians who could appreciate the brilliant technical detail in his work. In several ways he has become a symbol of some important aspects of the rapid scientific progress that took place during his career as a result of his role in institutional changes in the scientific profession and the implications that have been drawn from his conclusions and methods.

Laplace was very active within the highly centralized French scientific community. As a member of the French Academy of Sciences, he served on numerous research or evaluative committees that were commissioned by the French government. For example, following the French Revolution in 1789, he was an influential designer and advocate of the metric system, which has become the most widely used international system of scientific units. The academy was disbanded during the radical phase of the Revolution in 1793, but in 1796 Laplace became the president of the scientific class of the new Institute of France. Highly publicized institute prizes were regularly offered for essays in physics and mathematics, and Laplace exerted a powerful influence on French physics through the attention he devoted to choice of topic and support for his preferred candidates. He also played an important part in the early organization of the École Polytechnique, the prestigious school of engineering founded in 1795. Although Laplace lived through turbulent political changes, he remained in positions of high scientific status through the Napoleonic era and into the Bourbon Restoration, when he was raised to the nobility as a marquis. Laplace seems to have held few strong political views, and he thus is sometimes cited as an example of a powerful scientist indifferent to social or political conditions.

Aside from his work in probability and statistics, which has quite direct impact on modern societies, other aspects of Laplace's work have contributed to general perceptions of the goals, limitations, and methods of science. With Newton's theory of gravitation as his paradigmatic example, Laplace was convinced that, although human knowledge of nature is always limited, there are inevitable regularities that can be expressed approximately with ever-increasing accuracy. Laplace thus has become a symbol of nineteenth century scientific determinism, the view that the uncertainty of the future is only the result of human ignorance of the natural laws that determine it in every detail. When Napoleon I asked Laplace why God did not play a role in Laplace's analysis of the stability of the solar system, Laplace replied that he had had no need for such a hypothesis. Laplace thus contributed to a growing association of the scientific tradition with atheism and materialism. Finally, Laplace's style of mathematical physics has become a primary example of a reductionistic research strategy. Just as the gravitational effect of a large mass is determined by the sum of the forces exerted by all of its parts, Laplace expected all phenomena to reduce to collections of individual interactions. His success in implementing this method contributed to widespread perceptions that this is a necessary component of scientific investigation.

Bibliography

Arago, François. "Laplace." In *Biographies of Distinguished Scientific Men*. New York: Ticknor & Fields, 1859. Arago was a student and colleague of Laplace for many years. His essay discusses only Laplace's work in astronomy and concentrates on his study of the stability of the solar system.

Fox, Robert. "The Rise and Fall of Laplacian Physics." *Historical Studies in the Physical Sciences* 4 (1974): 89-136. This is an excellent summary of Laplace's efforts to direct French physics according to a research program based upon short-range forces.

Gillispie, Charles Coulston, Robert Fox, and Ivor Gratton-Guiness. "Pierre-Simon Marquis de Laplace." In *Dictionary of Scientific Biography*, vol. 15. New York: Charles Scribner's Sons, 1978. This chronological survey of Laplace's scientific career combines discussion of significant concepts with summaries of important mathematical derivations.

Hahn, Roger. *Laplace as a Newtonian Scientist*. Los Angeles: Williams Andrew Clark Memorial Library, 1967. This short essay describes the philosophical debate concerning the status of laws of nature that occurred during Laplace's formative period at the University of Caen and his early years in Paris. Laplace's convictions about the law-governed structure of the universe are traced to his reading of d'Alembert and Marquis de Condorcet.

Todhunter, Isaac. *A History of the Mathematical Theory of Probability from the Time of Pascal to that of Laplace.* New York: Chelsea, 1965. Chapter 10 provides a quite technical chronological account of the chief results and some of the derivations found in Laplace's publications on probability theory.

James R. Hofmann

BARTOLOMÉ DE LAS CASAS

Born: August, 1474; Seville, Spain
Died: July 31, 1566; Madrid, Spain
Areas of Achievement: Religion, colonial administration, and social reform
Contribution: Las Casas wrote a history of the early Spanish conquests in the New World and participated in the Spanish conquest of the Caribbean. Concerned with the plight of the Indians, he spent more than fifty years attempting to free the Indians from the oppression of their European conquerors, working to destroy the *encomienda* system and finding new ways of converting the Indians to Christianity.

Early Life

Bartolomé de Las Casas was born in Seville in 1474 into the family of a not very successful merchant, Pedro de Las Casas, who sailed with Christopher Columbus on his second voyage to the New World. Las Casas had witnessed the triumph of Columbus' return to Seville from his first voyage (March, 1493). He saw service in the militia against Moors in the Granada Rebellion (1497), studied Latin and theology at the cathedral academy in Seville, and became a lay teacher of Christian doctrine.

He accompanied Nicolás de Ovando, the designated governor, to Española (1502). There, he participated in putting down Indian uprisings, for which he was rewarded with a royal grant of lands and Indians (*encomienda*). He was successful as a planter, and he began to evangelize the Indians in his role as lay catechist. In 1506, he gave up his lands, going to Rome, where he took vows in the Order of Preachers (Dominicans). On his return to Española, in 1512, he was ordained a priest—probably the first in America to receive Holy Orders. He was made chaplain with the forces that were engaged in the conquest of Cuba (begun in 1511 by Diego Velázquez de Cuéllar, although Las Casas was there only in the last year, 1513), for which he again received a grant of Indians and lands.

Life's Work

Perhaps it has his experiences and observations in the Cuban conquest (including the massacre of Caonao) and other military expeditions in Española, or the harsh realities of treatment of the Indians in the mining and agricultural projects throughout the Spanish Antilles, where the number of natives was rapidly being depleted, or perhaps it was his position as priest and land grantee that led Las Casas to begin, at age forty, what would become his life's work. He attributes change of life-style to his meditations on chapter 34 of Ecclesiastes. In any case, he gave his *encomienda* holdings to Diego Columbus and began to preach against the oppression of the Indians, calling for an end to the system of expropriating their land and enslaving them. He returned to Spain to lobby in behalf of the Indians in 1515. The Cardinal Archbishop of Toledo, Francisco Jiménez de Cisneros, supported him in this crusade, naming him priest-procurator of the Indies and appointing him to a commission to investigate the status of the Indians (1516).

Las Casas developed a plan for peaceful colonization and returned to Spain in July, 1517, to recruit farmers and obtain land for the experiment. The Holy Roman Emperor and King of Spain Charles I gave him permission to colonize an estate in Curmaná, Venezuela (1510-1521). He later retracted a suggestion that slaves be imported for labor from West Africa. With an expression of shame, he regretted that he came so late to the realization that the natives from Africa had the same human rights as the Indians of the New World. The settlement was a failure, and Las Casas retired from public life to the Dominican monastery at Santo Domingo. It was during this time that he wrote the first draft of *Historia de las Indias* (wr. 1527-1561, pb. 1875-1876; partial translation as *History of the Indies*, 1971).

Las Casas was active in defense of the Indians in Mexico (1532) and in Nicaragua (1535-1536). During these years, he also visited and worked in defense of the Indians in Peru, Puerto Rico, and other settlements in the Spanish New World colonies. After Pope Paul III proclaimed the Indians' rationality and equality with other men to receive instructions and the faith (June 2, 1537), Las Casas renewed his activity to colonize and Christianize the Indians peacefully. His most notable success was in Guatemala.

In 1539, Las Casas returned to Spain. He continued his writings in defense of the Indians. His *Brevísima relación de la destruyción de las Indias occidentales* (1552; partial translation as *A Relation of the First Voyages and Discoveries Made by the Spaniards in America*, 1699) was written during this time although not published until many years later. In this treatise, he placed the desire for gold and material wealth at the center of motivation for all the injustice toward the Indians. Las Casas attributed the continued injustice to the greed of those in power. Because of this greed, those in power did not support just laws; rather, they opposed them in order to continue the system and institutions that would further their material gain.

Las Casas also began his struggle for the passage of the so-called New Laws (1542). These laws reorganized the Council of the Indies and prohibited the oppression of, exploitation of, and cruelty toward the Indians, against which Las Casas had long crusaded. These laws also prohibited the continuation of slavery for Indians of the second generation. Las Casas found support for his position in Spain at court, in the Church, and in the Council of the Indies. In the colonies, however, the New Laws were received with great opposition and were largely unenforced. They were revoked in part, but later the key elements were reinstated.

Las Casas was named Bishop of Chiapas in Guatemala and left Spain in July, 1544, with forty-four Dominicans to establish missions there for the peaceful Christianization of the Indians. He arrived in Guatemala after many interim stops in March, 1545. He proceeded with zeal rather than with practicality to enforce the New Laws, which led to protests and demonstrations against him in the colony. He was forced to return to Spain in 1547.

At the age of seventy-five, Las Casas renounced his bishopric and continued his life of tireless lobbying and protest in the cause of the Indians. He defended the equality and dignity of the Indians against all who were bent on their enslavement and oppression. In 1550 at Valladolid, he engaged in public debate with the Jesuit Juan Ginés de Sepúlveda, who had maintained that the Indians were inferior to the Spaniards. The controversy, which continued through the next year, has been debated anew through the centuries since. Las Casas organized missions to be staffed by learned and religious mendicants, who would Christianize and educate the Indians.

Las Casas continued to write. He also came to be an influential adviser to the Council of the Indies and at court on the many problems related to the colonies of the New World. He was a frequent witness at trials to free Indians, and much of his writing was directed to this end. He died in his early nineties in the Dominican convent of Nuestra Señora de Atocha in Madrid. The King of Spain, Phillip II, had all the works of Las Casas (published and unpublished) collected and preserved.

Summary

Bartolomé de Las Casas lived in the transitional period from the medieval to the modern age. He was traditional in his adherence to doctrine. His writings were based on the Gospel and teachings of the Church. Yet, he had an understanding of and sensitivity to the changing world about him. He was a Christian intellectual who became a prophet in the political and economic climate of his times; his society, however, was not ready and not eager to hear his message. He anticipated many of the principles enunciated in the Charter of the United Nations (1945) and proclaimed by Vatican Council II (1963). His preaching, his planning, his colonial enterprises, and his writings were concerned with reforming the colonial practices of his day, with preaching the Gospel by peaceful persuasion, with abhorrence of violence and oppression, and with individual liberty and self-determination as the right of all peoples. He meant his *History of the Indies* to be a call to social and political change. He clearly inveighed against the injustice and immorality of the colonial system and institutions of the fifteenth and sixteenth centuries. Through his writings, he inspired the nineteenth century revolutionary, Simón Bolívar, and the leaders of the Mexican Revolution in which the independence of that people was won from Spain.

Las Casas' most important writings among the vast works he produced were *Del único modo* (wr. 1539, pb. 1942), which was on the theory of evangelization, *Apologética historia de las Indias* (wr. 1527-1560, pb.

1909), which was an analysis of the Indians' abilities, and his two histories of the Indies. The last of these, according to his instructions, was not to be published for forty years after his death, although the prologue was published in 1562. Nevertheless, a manuscript was circulated even before the publication by the Academy of Madrid, 1875-1876.

His writings, while they exaggerate the plight of the Indians and the cruelty of the Europeans, have fueled the claims about the "Black Legend" of Spanish cruelty in the New World promulgated by Spain's enemies and, in the twentieth century, taken up by nationalists and anticolonialists. His teachings concerning all peoples of the earth (the Indians were not inferior to the Spaniards), all peoples' right to determine their own destiny (self-determination), and all peoples' right to have their basic needs (human rights) satisfied were his most important legacy and have caused his writings to be debated throughout the world for more than four hundred years.

Bibliography

Freide, Juan, and Benjamin Keen, eds. *Bartolomé de Las Casas in History: Toward an Understanding of the Man and His Work.* De Kalb: Northern Illinois University Press, 1971. This is a series of analytical essays on the life and ideology of Las Casas, on his activities and his impact on America and history, and on his writings. The essays are written by authors of different nationalities and ideologies, thus bringing a variety of perspectives to bear on their subject. The text vindicates Las Casas and his ideals in the course that history has taken since his death.

Hanke, Lewis. *Bartolomé de Las Casas: An Interpretation of His Life and Writings.* Philadelphia: University of Pennsylvania Press, 1959. Hanke's scholarly study is a sound biography of the life of Las Casas.

Helps, Arthur. *The Life of Las Casas: The Apostle of the Indies.* New York: Gordon Press, 1976. Helps writes a standard biography.

Las Casas, Bartolomé de. *History of the Indies.* Edited and translated by Andrée M. Collard. New York: Harper & Row, 1971. Collard's introduction provides helpful analysis of Las Casas the man, the thinker, and the writer. Collard also answers criticisms of Las Casas.

MacNutt, Francis A. *Bartholomew de Las Casas: His Life, His Apostolate, and His Writings.* New York: G. P. Putnam's Sons, 1909. This was the standard biography in English of Las Casas, but it has been superseded by the works of Lewis Hanke.

Wagner, Henry Raup, and Helen Rand Parish. *The Life and Writings of Bartolomé de Las Casas.* Albuquerque: University of New Mexico Press, 1967. This is a critical and detailed documented study of Las Casas. Wagner found much to identify with and to admire in his subject. He presents Las Casas as a prolific writer and, equally, as a man of action. Las Casas emerges with tremendous stature even among the giants of the sixteenth century. Wagner includes a narrative and critical catalog of Las Casas' writings.

Barbara Ann Barbato

FERDINAND LASSALLE

Born: April 11, 1825; Breslau, Prussia
Died: August 31, 1864; Geneva, Switzerland
Areas of Achievement: Political science and economics
Contribution: Lassalle was one of the founders of the German labor movement and the most important advocate of scientific socialism in Germany after the Revolution of 1848. His theory of evolutionary socialism eventually triumphed within the German Social Democratic Party.

Early Life

Ferdinand Lassalle was born on April 11, 1825, in Breslau, Prussia, the modern Polish city of Wrocław. He was the only son of Heymann Lassal, or Loslauer, a well-to-do Jewish silk merchant. Although admitted to the synagogue at thirteen, the young Lassalle never took his ancestral faith seriously. Lassalle lived at home until he was fifteen. Much of his time as a teenager was spent playing cards or billiards for spending money. Not a particularly bright student, Lassalle was expelled from the classical high school (*Gymnasium*) for forging his parents' signatures to his grade reports, an offense he committed repeatedly.

In May, 1840, Lassalle's father enrolled him in the Commercial Institute in Leipzig. His father had hopes that his son would eventually take over the family business, but Ferdinand was not willing. He announced his intention to study history, "the greatest subject in the world. The subject bound up with the holiest interests of mankind. . . ." After having passed his examinations in 1843, he was enrolled at the University of Breslau.

At the university, Lassalle studied history, archaeology, philology, and philosophy. It was while an undergraduate at Breslau that he was introduced to the works of the German philosopher Georg Wilhelm Friedrich Hegel. Hegel's dialectic soon became the cornerstone of Lassalle's worldview. This dialectic was for him, as it was also for Karl Marx, the key to understanding and interpreting the flow of human history. Like Marx, Lassalle came to believe that the future new order in society would be an inevitable product of the historical dialectic. Unlike Marx, who held to the necessity of revolution to move the dialectic forward, Lassalle came to understand it as a peaceful, evolutionary process.

In 1844, Lassalle entered the University of Berlin, where he continued studying philosophy. Although his interests extended to other philosophers such as Ludwig Feuerbach and the French Utopian thinkers, Hegel remained his primary influence. He would often rise at four in the morning to begin the day with readings from Hegel's works. He also began work on his doctoral thesis, a Hegelian interpretation of the Greek philosopher Heracleitus. From 1845 to 1847, Lassalle lived in Paris, where he met and was influenced by the French socialist and anarchist philosopher Pierre-Joseph Proudhon and the German poet Heinrich Heine. It was also during his stay in Paris that he changed the spelling of his last name from "Lassal" to "Lassalle."

In 1846, Lassalle met the Countess Sophie von Hatzfeldt, who was seeking a divorce from her husband, one of the wealthiest and most influential noblemen in northwestern Germany. Although not a lawyer, Lassalle took up her cause. Between 1846 and 1854, he conducted thirty-five lawsuits on behalf of the countess before eventually winning her case. The countess rewarded Lassalle with a lifelong pension that made him financially independent. It was also the beginning of a lifelong relationship that both positively and negatively affected his political career.

Life's Work

Lassalle's career as a labor organizer and political agitator began in earnest during the Revolution of 1848. He was living in Düsseldorf, an emerging industrial center in the Prussian-ruled Rhineland. In November, 1848, Lassalle was arrested for making an incendiary speech, calling upon the populace and the militia to rise up in armed revolt. The occasion for the speech was a meeting called by Friedrich Engels, Marx's chief collaborator. Lassalle's relationship with Marx was not a smooth one. When they first met during the Revolutions of 1848, Lassalle had not yet read *Manifest der Kommunistischen (The Communist Manifesto*, 1850), first published in 1848. Many scholars believe that many of Lassalle's theoretical assumptions, which were later harshly criticized by Karl Marx, were in fact borrowed from Marx's early writings, and may be found in *The Communist Manifesto*.

When the Revolutions of 1848 collapsed, most of the revolutionary leaders fled the Continent. Marx settled in London. After his release from prison in July, 1849, Lassalle chose to remain in Germany. It was a choice that no doubt helped him in his subsequent bid for leadership of the German labor movement.

During the 1850's, and until their final estrangement in 1862, Marx and Lassalle remained hospitable toward each other, at least publicly. Marx looked to Lassalle for help in getting his books and articles published in Germany. He also called upon Lassalle for financial support. Yet as Marx's own thought matured over the years, he became increasingly critical of Lassalle's writings and obviously jealous of Lassalle's emergence as the leader of the German working class.

The tension between Marx and Lassalle was the result in large part of the differing historical roles to which each was called. Marx was basically an intellectual, addressing a small international audience of highly educated intellectuals like himself. He was a theorist, constructing the guiding principles of a future society. Lassalle, on the other hand, was a man of action. He was addressing the uneducated, illiterate, and backward German working class. He was attempting to shake them out of their political lethargy and mold them into a major political force. For Lassalle, unlike Marx, the future new order in society was immediately obtainable.

Toward the end of 1861, Lassalle made two speeches in which he called upon the working class to form its own political party. He believed that once the workers became a formidable political force, it would have the effect of altering the power relationships in the state. Since he believed that the written constitution of necessity reflects the true power-ratio in society, Lassalle called upon the workers to organize and agitate for universal direct suffrage in all the German states.

In December of 1862, Lassalle was approached by the executive committee of the Central Committee to Convoke a General Congress of German Workers. They asked him to draw up a program for the congress. Lassalle's affirmative response marked the beginning of the final and most important phase in his life's work. Lassalle's response took the form of a pamphlet entitled *Offnes Antwortschreiben an das Central-Comité zur Berufung eines Allgemeinen Deutschen Arbeitercongresses zu Leipzig* (*Lassalle's Open Letter to the National Labor Association of Germany*, 1879), published in March, 1863. It contained his advice on what policies should be adopted by the working-class movement. Marx criticized the pamphlet as a vulgarization of his own ideas, but Lassalle's clarion call to action was well received by the workers. It led directly to the founding of the General German Workers' Association (Allgemeiner Deutscher Arbeiterverein) in Leipzig on May 23, 1863. Its chief goal, as stated in its bylaws, was to achieve justice for the German working class "through establishment of universal, equal, and direct suffrage."

Although Lassalle was a socialist, he was also a Prussian nationalist. He also felt the intellectual's usual frustration with the sluggishness of the working class. His attitude toward the workers was aristocratic and paternalistic, and his administrative style was authoritarian. He saw to it that the president of the association, the office he held, possessed dictatorial powers. "Otherwise," he said, "nothing will get done."

Being a nationalist, Lassalle did not find it necessary for the state to wither, as Marx did. In a letter to the Prussian prime minister Otto von Bismarck, in which he enclosed a copy of the association's bylaws, Lassalle said that the working class was instinctively inclined toward a dictatorship. He believed that the workers would prefer a monarchy, if only the king would look after their interests. Lassalle's willingness to consider the idea of a monarchical welfare state provided a common ground for his discussions and correspondence with Bismarck during late 1863 and early 1864. At that time, the prime minister was searching for allies in his struggle with the liberals in the Prussian parliament. The Bismarck-Lassalle talks came to nothing, however, in part because of Lassalle's presumptuousness and in part because of Bismarck's growing preoccupation with the unification of Germany.

By late spring, 1864, Lassalle was disappointed with the association's failure to increase its membership as rapidly as he had expected. He was also physically exhausted. His exhaustion was in part the result of his having contracted syphilis in 1847, when he was twenty-two. By the early 1860's, the disease was in the secondary stage, and the bones in one of his legs were deteriorating. In July, 1864, he decided to go to Switzerland for a rest.

In Geneva, Lassalle acted out the final chapter in his life as a romantic revolutionary. He had always pursued the conquest of women with the same enthusiasm as politics. He met and began courting passionately Helene von Dönniges. When he proposed marriage, he encountered opposition from her father and from her former fiancé, Yanko von Racowitza. In response to a challenge from Lassalle, a duel between Lassalle and Racowitza was fought on August 28, in a forest outside Geneva. Lassalle was mortally wounded and died three days later on August 31, 1864.

Summary

After Ferdinand Lassalle's death, Karl Marx and Friedrich Engels praised his memory in public, while continuing to criticize him in their correspondence with each other. Engels admitted that Lassalle had been politically "the most important fellow in Germany." In a letter to the Countess Hatzfeldt, Marx noted Lassalle's abilities, then added, "I personally loved him." He went on to lament the fact that they had drifted apart.

The General German Workers' Association continued to grow. By the late 1860's, it had split into two factions: the orthodox Marxists, who in 1869 founded the Social Democratic Labor Party (Sozialdemokratische Arbeiterpartei), and the Lassalleans, who were viewed by the former as reformist heretics. The two factions united in 1875 to form the Socialist Labor Party of Germany (Sozialistische Arbeiterpartei Deutschlands). The new party's program was largely based on theories and slogans associated with Lassalle.

In 1891, the party changed its name to the Social Democratic Party of Germany (Sozialdemokratische Partei Deutschlands), or SPD. The SPD was Marxist in theory, rather than Lassallean, but in practice it was becoming a mass parliamentary and reformist party, which is what Lassalle had advocated. The SPD became the largest and most influential socialist party in Europe prior to World War I. It was not until 1959, however, that the SPD formally abandoned all its Marxist ideology.

Much of what Lassalle had called for was later enacted by the German state under Bismarck's leadership. Perhaps, as some believe, Bismarck was only trying to win the workers away from socialism. In any case, speaking before the Reichstag in 1878, Bismarck said of Lassalle: "He was one of the most intelligent and likeable men I had ever come across. He was very ambitious and by no means a republican. He was very much a nationalist and a monarchist. His ideal was the German Empire, and here was our point of contact."

In 1866, Bismarck granted universal suffrage in elections to the Reichstag. In 1881, he began enacting a comprehensive social security program that included accident, health, and old age insurance. Bismarck's brand of "state socialism" may have been influenced by his earlier conversations with Lassalle. In any event, the German welfare program, inspired by Lassalle and initiated by Bismarck, served as a model for all other Western nations.

Bibliography

Bernstein, Edward. *Ferdinand Lassalle as a Social Reformer.* New York: Charles Scribner's Sons, 1893. Reprint. New York: Greenwood Press, 1969. A sympathetic but critical study by the father of revisionism in German social democracy. Bernstein was the most important figure in the SPD from Lassalle to the Nazi seizure of power in 1933. Bernstein also edited the party's official publication of Lassalle's collected works.

Footman, David. *Ferdinand Lassalle: Romantic Revolutionary.* New Haven, Conn.: Yale University Press, 1947. A very well-written and highly readable biography. It is the best book on Lassalle in English, and the place to begin a more detailed study. Footman believes that Lassalle's romantic nature is important for understanding his role in the birth of the German labor movement.

Gay, Peter. *The Dilemma of Democratic Socialism: Edward Bernstein's Challenge to Marx.* New York: Collier Books, 1962. Chapters 1 and 4 discuss Lassalle's influence on Bernstein and thus establish his place in the revision of Marxism that resulted in the modern SPD.

Meredith, George. *The Tragic Comedians: A Study in a Well-Known Study.* Rev. ed. New York: Charles Scribner's Sons, 1906. Lassalle's final days in Geneva, including his courtship of Dönniges, is the subject of this romantic novel. The story is based largely on Dönniges' own account. It is considered to be a creditable attempt at making history come alive.

Wilson, Edmund. *To the Finland Station: A Study in the Writing and Acting of History.* Garden City, N.Y.: Doubleday, 1940. A popular study of the revolutionary tradition in European history from the beginning of the nineteenth century to the triumph of the Communist Revolution in Russia. Chapter 13, "Historical Actors: Lassalle," provides a brief account of Lassalle's life and thought, and tries to define his contributions to the rise of socialism in Europe.

Paul R. Waibel

ANTOINE-LAURENT LAVOISIER

Born: August 26, 1743; Paris, France
Died: May 8, 1794; Paris, France
Areas of Achievement: Chemistry, cartography, and economics
Contribution: Besides important contributions to eighteenth century geology, physics, cartography, and economic reforms, particularly in agriculture and manufacturing, Lavoisier, through his discrediting of the phlogiston theory and his proof of the law of the conservation of matter, is best known as the father of modern chemistry.

Early Life

Antoine-Laurent Lavoisier was born on August 26, 1743, into an eminent bourgeois family. Over the preceding century, his family had risen gradually from humble origins. His father, who had inherited considerable wealth from an uncle as well as his position as attorney to the Paris Parliament, was a lawyer. Émilie Punctis, Antoine's mother, was equally well positioned socially, being the daughter of a parliamentary advocate. The Lavoisiers lived in Paris, and Antoine remained in his parents' home until he married.

Lavoisier's schooling, which probably began in 1754, seems principally to have been in Paris' small, but exclusive Collège Mazarin, where he won prizes for an industriousness that persisted throughout his life. Guided by tradition, he studied law, receiving his bachelor's degree in 1763 and his licentiate the following year. Not really engaged by his profession, Lavoisier began scientific studies with four of France's most eminent scientists: Abbé Nicolas-Louis de Lacaille, an astronomer and mathematician; Bernard de Jussieu, a botanist; Jean-Étienne Guettard, a geologist and mineralogist; and Guillaume Rouelle, a chemist. Each of these men was a cynosure of Parisian intellectual circles who closely interacted with leading figures in Europe's scientific communities: men exceptional in an eighteenth century context for the breadth of their curiosities.

Three such superficially unrelated curiosities marked Lavoisier's earliest research: First, his inquiries into the properties of minerals, gypsum in particular, led to his invention in 1764 of plaster of Paris, a feat that produced his first published work by the Academy of Sciences. In 1765, he was encouraged by an academy-sponsored prize competition for development of the best night lighting for large towns. He won both the prize and a medal awarded by the king. Concomitantly, pursuing geological and cartological work with France's premier geologist, Lavoisier collaborated in the production of an official geological atlas of France. Reward was swift: Considered for nomination as an academician in 1766, he was elected in 1768, a vacancy having opened with the death of a renowned chemist, Théodore Baron. Remarkable vigor characterized his academy work, which ranged over hundreds of projects, such as the adulteration of cider, theories of color, and mesmerism.

Life's Work

Lavoisier's scientific milieu, as had been true for two millennia, essentially accepted that all natural phenomena were the result of various mutations of earth, air, fire, and water. The general belief was that these "elements" were inexplicable, hence the long-standing interest in alchemy—the transformation of something base into something precious or valuable to the prolongation of life, invariably accompanied by often indecipherable language explaining alchemists' experimentation. Some alchemical philosophizing had been eroded by several of Lavoisier's predecessors, such as Robert Boyle, and contemporaries such as Joseph Priestley. Boyle, for example, had demonstrated that combustion (fire) cannot occur in an airless vessel, nor could many other processes, including life. In the mid-1600's, however, German chemists, notably Johann Joachim Becher and Georg Ernst Stahl, contrived a theory that combustion required no air, only an "oily earth" dubbed phlogiston. Armed with this dictum, followers of the phlogiston theory could also explain numerous other chemical processes.

Anxieties about the purity of Parisians' water supply brought Lavoisier into conflict with such traditional assumptions and methods. No standards existed then to ascertain water's purity; indeed, common scientific opinions held that evaporating water was transformed into earth. Lavoisier, having reviewed the endeavors of his predecessors, went directly to the fundamentals of the water problem; namely, whether matter was transmutable. After a series of exquisite experiments, he demonstrated that the earth produced in distilling and evaporating water, in fact, came from abrasive actions of water on the glass. Thus, two thousand years of belief in the transmutability of matter was refuted.

Both Lavoisier's public responsibilities and his science were made less burdensome by his happy marriage in 1771 to Marie Paulze, a woman of wealth and important family connections, but, more significant, a person intellectually drawn to her husband's work. She not only translated scientific materials for him but also aided him in the niceties of his experiments and made excellent scientific sketches.

Air and fire preoccupied Lavoisier during the late 1760's and the early 1770's, that is, he was absorbed by the phlogiston question. During the 1760's, Priestley experimented with the properties of gases and discovered new ones, such as ammonia and sulfur dioxide. Heating the calx of mercury (a compound resulting from heating a substance below its melting point), Priestley produced a special "air," one in which candles burned vigorously and mice lived longer than in ordinary air. Yet Priestley, a believer in phlogiston, simply described this as dephlogistonated air.

Lavoisier launched an intricate series of experiments on combustion: Was the destruction of a diamond by heating merely an evaporation, or was it combustion? Was the same true of phosphorus, or of sulfur? By 1774, his answers appeared in his *Opuscules physiques et chymiques* (*Essays, Physical and Chemical*, 1776). Burning sulfur or phosphorus, instead of expelling something, actually absorbed air. Further reduction of the calx of lead unleashed air (now known as carbon dioxide) that sustained neither combustion nor life; in sum, reduction of the calx of metals expelled rather than absorbed something. By 1778 and 1779, continuing such investigations, Lavoisier reported that air consisted of two distinct gases: The first, which he named oxygen, sustained life and combustion and made up one-quarter volume, and the other, not respirable, made up the other three-quarters volume and is now identified as nitrogen. The phlogiston theory had been overthrown, and the foundations of modern chemistry emplaced with his publication in 1786 of *Réflexions sur la phlogistique* (*Reflections on Phlogiston*, 1788). Lavoisier in 1787 then published his *Méthode de nomenclature chimique* (*Method of Chemical Nomenclature*, 1788), identifying a table of thirty-one chemical elements, adding heat and light as materials without mass. In full vigor, he proceeded conclusively to expound his oxygen theory, his new chemical nomenclature, and his statement of the law of the conservation of matter with publication in 1789 of a work rivaling any in the history of science entitled *Traité élémentaire de chimie* (*Elements of Chemistry, in a New Systematic Order, Containing all the Modern Discoveries*, 1790).

Genuine goodness and breadth of mind characterized both Lavoisier and his wife. Fine featured, delicate, and keenly intellectual, they look to each other lovingly, but with a hint of amused embarrassment, in a Jacques-Louis David portrait. Both an original experimenter and a superb scientific synthesizer, Lavoisier, aside from his establishment of modern chemistry, made immense contributions as a responsible, innovative public official. Though independently wealthy, Lavoisier had become a tax farmer to ensure his fortune. As a tax farmer, he relieved Jews from payment of the outrageous "cloven-hoof" tax; he sought relief for the poor from unjust taxation and instituted waste-cutting administrative reforms; he tried to protect honest Parisian merchants from smugglers who slipped by the *octrois* (a local import tax); he reformed the system and improved the quality of France's gunpowder production and generated a number of studies on the manufacture of saltpeter; he, like his brilliant successor, Alexis de Tocqueville, sought the reformation of France's penal system; and his elaborate calculations of French agricultural conditions entitle him to front rank as a political economist. These are only partial indications of Lavoisier's genius beyond the bounds of chemistry.

As is so often the case, he died for his mistakes and for misinterpretations of his intentions. During the Reign of Terror during the French Revolution, he was imprisoned, charged with counterrevolutionary conspiracy against France, and executed in Paris on May 8, 1794. One French notable remarked to another in respect of Lavoisier: "Only a moment to cut off a head and a hundred years may not give us another like it." The remark, like Lavoisier's achievements, remains a tribute to eighteenth century French culture.

Summary

Antoine-Laurent Lavoisier, though a man of many talents that would have qualified him for eminence in half a dozen scientific disciplines or fields of public service, was the founder of modern chemistry not only in an abstract or theoretical dimension but also in immediately practical ways. His intellections and experimentation banished the phlogiston theory that had led and entranced many fine minds for centuries. In the Linnaean tradition, he sought only the facts then classified them as they were verifiable through critical experimentation; he identified thirty-six chemical elements, not the least oxygen, and defined their characteristics and roles. He wrote the first precise texts, from which subsequent chemistry sprang, destined to be of incalculable benefit to humankind. Some of his work was entirely original; some was derivative; and, inevitably for great minds, some was magnificently synthetic. His official services to France ran a gamut that was encyclopedic and generally pragmatic, practical, and useful. He was preeminently the son of what then was Europe's greatest nation-state as well as its greatest center of mischief, intellection, and high culture.

Bibliography

French, Sidney J. *Torch and Crucible: The Life and Death of Antoine Lavoisier.* Princeton, N.J.: Princeton University Press, 1931. A readable and adequate survey of Lavoisier's life. The general context within which Lavoisier worked and the specifics of his experiments are not fully treated. There are a small number of illustrations and only a modest bibliography, which, through no fault of the author, needs updating.

Hall, Alfred R. *The Scientific Revolution, 1500-1800: The Formation of the Modern Scientific Attitude.* 2d ed. Boston: Beacon Press, 1966. This now classic work, written for general readers, does an outstanding job of placing Lavoisier and his work in context. The study is amply footnoted and has three appendices and brief but excellent bibliographical notes for each chapter at the end.

McKie, Douglas. *Antoine Lavoisier: Scientist, Economist, Social Reformer.* New York: Henry Schuman, 1952. The most expert and best-written coverage of Lavoisier's life and work, this book is essential reading. It covers, with the simplicity that only a skilled scholar can manage, an amazing array of Lavoisier's activities. Includes many helpful illustrations, a select but good bibliography, and a minimal index.

Meldrum, A. N. "Lavoisier's Early Work in Science." *Isis* 19/20 (1933/1934): 330-363, 398-425. An expert, detailed analysis.

Westfall, Richard S. *The Construction of Modern Science: Mechanisms and Mechanics*. New York: John Wiley & Sons, 1971. This scholarly work is chiefly about seventeenth century science, but chapter 11 is essential background for an understanding of Lavoisier. While authoritative, this work is for university undergraduates. Contains many illuminating illustrations, a fine critical bibliography, and a solid double-columned index.

Clifton K. Yearley

NICOLAS LEBLANC

Born: December 6, 1742; Ivoy-le-Pré, France
Died: January 16, 1806; Saint-Denis, France
Area of Achievement: Chemistry
Contribution: Leblanc, an amateur chemist, developed a process that now bears his name for making soda (sodium carbonate) from salt (sodium chloride). His use of limestone (calcium carbonate) to cause this conversion was at the core of his process, which played a fundamental role in creating the modern chemical industry.

Early Life

Tragedy haunted Nicolas Leblanc's life, but scholars do not agree about whether his numerous misfortunes were self-generated or the result of historical circumstances. His troubles began when his mother died not long after his birth in 1742 at Ivoy-le-Pré, a small town about 125 miles south of Paris. His father, an official in an ironworks, died in 1751, and Nicolas, a nine-year-old orphan, was sent to Bourges, about twenty miles northeast of his hometown, where he came under the care and influence of his father's good friend, Dr. Bien. From him, Nicolas absorbed an interest in medicine, and, when his guardian died in 1759, Nicolas went to Paris to study medicine at the École de Chirugie. While studying to become a doctor, Leblanc became very interested in chemistry and began attending the lectures of prominent chemists and befriending them.

After obtaining his master's degree in surgery, Leblanc began to practice medicine, but he continued to be interested in chemistry. After attending the popular lectures of the chemist Jean Darcet, Leblanc became a pupil of Darcet and through him met such chemists as Claude-Louis Berthollet, Louis-Nicolas Vauquelin, Antoine-François de Fourcroy, and Réné-Just Haüy.

Leblanc married in 1775, and his first child was born in 1779. His education had consumed the money left to him by his father, and his family responsibilities necessitated a greater income than he was obtaining from the fees paid by his patients. Consequently, in 1780 he became the private physician of Louis-Philippe-Joseph, the future Duke of Orléans. The patronage of the Orléans family also gave Leblanc the opportunity for chemical research. The duke was interested in chemistry, and he encouraged Leblanc's work.

Life's Work

Since his means were limited, Leblanc initially chose to study crystallization, a subject that required few supplies. The work that he did on crystal growth so impressed the French Academy of Sciences that a reviewing committee recommended the academy's support for a project in which Leblanc would study methods of obtaining complete crystals of a wide variety of substances. Yet before their recommendation could become a reality, the French Revolution resulted in the academy's dissolution, and it was not until 1802 that Leblanc was able to publish his work on crystallization.

Through his contact with the academy, Leblanc became aware of a prize that Louis XVI had established for a practical process for making soda from common salt. During the late eighteenth century, the shortage of soda was becoming an acute problem. Much of French soda was manufactured from barilla, a plant growing along the coast of Spain. This meant that France was forced to pay large amounts of money annually to the Spaniards, and during times of war, which were frequent in the eighteenth century, soda supplies would become scarce and expensive. A need clearly existed for a locally produced artificial soda. While working for the Duke of Orléans, Leblanc became interested in applying chemistry to industrial problems. Most of his time was devoted to the synthesis of soda—a goal which, as he knew, other researchers were also pursuing.

According to his patent application, Leblanc began research on soda in 1784, but some scholars are skeptical of this early date because of the lack of specific records. Leblanc once stated that he got the idea for his process by reading Jean Claude Delamétherie's account of his visit to England and Scotland in 1788 to study British industry. In Delamétherie's account, an erroneous soda-producing process is discussed directly after a section on iron industry, and some scholars believe that this juxtaposition gave Leblanc the crucial idea for his discovery: the use of limestone in helping to transform common salt into soda.

Leblanc's method was straightforward. He first treated common salt with sulfuric acid to produce "salt-cake" (sodium sulfate), which he then mixed with coal and ground limestone. He heated this mixture in a furnace, and the resulting black ash was leached to obtain the soda. Leblanc probably prepared soda crystals by this process in the latter half of 1789, for he and his assistant J. J. Dizé went to England in October, 1789, to confer with the duke about the commercial development of the process. The duke, Leblanc, Dizé, and Henri Shée (the duke's agent) then signed an agreement on February 12, 1790, the major provisions of which were that Leblanc would patent his process for making soda and the duke would furnish 200,000 livres to enable Leblanc and Dizé to carry out its commercial exploitation. In another agreement, signed about a year later, the duke, Leblanc, Dizé, and Shée stated the shares of future profits that each would receive.

The French Revolution delayed the implementation of these agreements. During this period, the duke abandoned his title, changed his name to Philippe Égalité, turned republican, and voted for the death of the king. These actions did not erase the Republic's difficulties with the duke's aristocratic background, but they permitted Leblanc to obtain a secret patent on September 25, 1791, which meant that he did not have to make a public disclosure of his method and that he obtained the exclusive right to exploit his process in whatever way he saw fit for a period of fifteen years. Between 1791 and 1793, with capital provided by Égalité, Leblanc oversaw the construction of a small factory at Saint-Denis, a town four miles north of Paris. This plant began to make soda.

Because of France's war with Spain, the price of barilla rose dramatically, and the shareholders of the Saint-Denis factory reaped huge profits from their manufacture of artificial soda. Unfortunately, the initial success of the plant was short-lived, and in July, 1793, the impossibility of obtaining sulfuric acid forced Leblanc to close the plant. He was unable to resume operations so long as stocks of sulfur and saltpeter were needed by the munitions industry.

The reopening of the plant was complicated further when Égalité, its principal owner, was tried and guillotined in November, 1793. Leblanc was compelled to leave the idle factory in Shée's care and return to Paris, where he took a post in the Gunpowder Agency and became involved in various political activities. On January 28, 1794, the plant and its associated property were formally confiscated by the Republic. The political authorities, in their revolutionary exuberance, believed that they could use the plant to enhance the industrial power of the Republic. On the very day that local authorities placed the Saint-Denis plant under sequestration, the Committee of Public Safety adopted a decree on the manufacture of artificial soda and appointed Darcet and other scientists to collect and publish all available information on the process. The committee hoped that the free flow of information would help resolve the shortage of soda. Perhaps through patriotism, perhaps through fear, Leblanc divulged the secrets of his process to the Committee of Public Safety. Some scholars see the committee's action as a great injustice to Leblanc, whereas others think that the committee showed Leblanc unusual consideration.

In either event, the publication of the Leblanc process did the war effort little good, and the report of Darcet's group, which was published in June, 1794, concluded that Malherbe's procedure for making soda was more economical than Leblanc's. At the time that the Saint-Denis plant was nationalized, Leblanc had not yet been able to show the superiority of his method over all others. Nevertheless, he had expected to be employed by the Republic to direct the soda works for the good of the people. Instead, he was notified that his government salary would end after April 1, 1794.

Within a short time, Leblanc's life was in disorder. Instead of running a profitable business, he found himself without a salary to support his ailing wife and their four children and severed from the discovery and factory on which he had planned his future. From this time until his death, his life became a dispiriting struggle against poverty.

Following the Reign of Terror, authorities sought to revive industrial enterprises, especially mining, and in June, 1795, the Committee of Public Safety sent Leblanc on a mission to the departments of Tarn and Aveyron in the south of France. His job was to resurrect the manufacture of alum, a substance widely used by dyers, papermakers, goldsmiths, and doctors. His salary and expenses were supposed to be paid by some of the people he was helping, but he received nothing; after thirteen months, he returned to Paris more impoverished and embittered than before. His proclivity for blaming his troubles on the authorities deepened.

Throughout these years of frustration, Leblanc continued the vain struggle to secure recompense for his soda process. His despair deepened when one of his young daughters died suddenly. Leblanc's luck seemed to change in 1801, however, when the Minister of Finance finally ordered the works at Saint-Denis to be given to Leblanc and his associates, although the state continued to own a substantial portion of the enterprise. The remnant of Leblanc's family returned to their former house on the factory grounds, and Leblanc tried to resume the production of soda but encountered insuperable difficulties. The plant had been abandoned for seven years, and both the government and vandals had removed much of the best equipment and supplies. Leblanc also found himself competing with manufacturers whose plants had not suffered the misfortunes of Saint-Denis. He tried in vain to attract investors and to diversify his factory's products, but each of these ventures consumed more of his time, energy, and money without enhancing his position.

Finally, on November 8, 1805, some of his claims, which had been in the courts for years, were recognized, and a board of arbitrators decided that, though most of Égalité's business belonged to the state, Leblanc's share was worth a sum equal to about ten thousand dollars. When even this inadequate sum was never paid, Leblanc became despondent. He had no income, his plant had failed, he was deeply in debt, and his wife was ill. His fortunes had reached bottom, and he increasingly withdrew into himself. Broken in spirit, he shot himself in the head on January 16, 1806.

Some scholars have suggested that Leblanc hoped that his suicide would shock the authorities into granting his family what they had previously denied him, but this did not happen. His death attracted little attention. In 1855, his achievements received belated recognition when Napoleon III made Leblanc's heirs a payment in lieu of the prize for his discovery of the soda process. In 1887, a monument was erected in his honor in Paris that depicts him as a somber man with downcast eyes: His clean-shaven face and classical head would have been appropriate on the shoulders of an ancient tragic hero.

Summary

Nineteenth century industrial chemistry is largely the story of the rise and fall of the soda-making process of Nicolas Leblanc. In the middle of the century, the great English chemical manufacturer James Muspratt wrote that the Leblanc process had a greater impact on social life, commerce, and chemical technology than any other discovery. Though most twentieth century historians would not go as far as Muspratt, they too recognize the great importance of Leblanc's method of producing soda in initiating the large-scale chemical industry. It is difficult to find an industry that was not influenced by the Leblanc process. For example, since the first step in the process depended on sulfuric acid, the expansion of Leblanc soda works was directly responsible for the growth of the sulfuric acid industry.

Unfortunately, Leblanc did not live to see the triumph of his method. Although he introduced his process in 1791, it did not become a significant producer of soda until two decades into the nineteenth century. By the time of Leblanc's discovery, scientists knew more than a dozen processes for converting salt into soda, at least seven of which had been tested on a large scale; five establishments were actually manufacturing artificial soda, mostly in association with more profitable chemical products. None of these processes, however, could compete with natural soda, which France continued to import from Spain. Though Leblanc's process was not completely novel, it was superior to these other methods, and it eventually came to be generally adopted. Leblanc himself did not really understand the detailed chemistry of the process he had discovered. In fact, the reactions of the Leblanc process were not precisely understood until the end of the nineteenth century, when the process itself began to go out of use.

During the 1820's, the Leblanc process began its triumphant spread to other countries. James Muspratt built his first major soda plant in Liverpool in 1823. A few years later, Charles Tennant built a soda factory in Glasgow, and it quickly became the largest in Europe, covering a hundred acres and employing more than a thousand workers. As these and other factories prospered, they encountered problems, because the Leblanc process, besides producing soda, produced poisonous fumes and large quantities of solid toxic wastes. Despite its obvious drawbacks, the Leblanc process dominated the industrial production of soda for nearly a century. It did not have a serious competitor until the end of the nineteenth century, when the process of a Belgian chemist, Ernest Solvay, proved its superiority. The Leblanc process continued to hold onto a significant proportion of the soda market until World War I, but its inevitable end came in 1923, when the last Leblanc soda works was scrapped.

The discovery, development, and decline of the Leblanc process are now part of the history of technology. Despite his deficiencies as a scientist and entrepreneur, Leblanc showed how soda, so vital to the glass, soap, dye, and textile industries, could be made cheaply from common salt. His process also led to the foundation of the first chemical industries to be operated on a massive scale, which forced technicians to develop new mechanical equipment to handle large amounts of material more efficiently. The disadvantages connected with the process also forced scientists to find ways to use or control the harmful by-products produced by the process. In this way the Leblanc process became the paradigm of not only nineteenth century chemical industry but also its twentieth century counterparts. Thus, Leblanc, a man who considered his life a dismal failure, became a posthumous success.

Bibliography
Clark, Ronald W. *Works of Man: A History of Invention and Engineering from the Pyramids to the Space Shuttle*. New York: Viking Press, 1985. Clark offers an anecdotal history of technology from the invention of the wheel to the miniaturization of the electronic computer. His theme is mankind's exploitation of the laws of nature for its own purposes. Briefly discusses Leblanc's work in connection with the development of man-made materials in the eighteenth and nineteenth centuries. Intended for general audiences and profusely illustrated with color and black-and-white photographs.

Daumas, Maurice, ed. *A History of Technology and Invention: Progress Through the Ages*. Vol. 2, *The First Stages of Mechanization*. New York: Crown, 1969. This volume has chapters written by distinguished experts and represents original work rather than a synthesis of secondary sources. Lavishly illustrated with hundreds of photographs, drawings, and diagrams, this book provides a chronicle of industrial civilization told largely through the creative technical ideas of such inventors as Leblanc.

Gillispie, Charles C. "The Discovery of the Leblanc Process." *Isis* 48 (1957): 152-170. Offers a revisionist view of Leblanc and his discovery. Attacks the so-called legend of Leblanc—the chemist whose discovery of the artificial soda process should have garnered for him rewards but instead made him a victim of the Revolution. Gillispie believes that this legend rests on very shaky information, almost all of which comes from a memoir published in 1884 by Leblanc's grandson, and that Leblanc was more the victim of his own difficult personality than of the accidents of history.

Haber, L. F. *The Chemical Industry During the Nineteenth Century: A Study of the Economic Aspect of Applied Chemistry in Europe and North America*. Oxford, England: Clarendon Press, 1958. This history of chemical technology, with an emphasis on economics, centers on the inorganic chemical industries and especially on four materials that governed the rate of expansion in the industry as a whole: sulfuric acid, soda ash, caustic soda, and bleaching powder. The changing role of the Leblanc process is studied in some detail. The technical and economic factors causing the rise and decline of Leblanc soda works in different countries and at different times form a major theme of this book.

Oesper, Ralph E. "Nicolas Leblanc (1742-1806)." *Journal of Chemical Education* 19/20 (1942/1943): 567-572, 11-20. A major source of Leblanc's life and work in English. Presents a fairly detailed account of Leblanc's life, the genesis of his process, his efforts to obtain recompense for his discovery, and his tragic end. In contrast to the Gillispie article above, Oesper blames circumstances rather than Leblanc for Leblanc's misfortunes.

Partington, J. R. *A History of Chemistry.* Vol. 3. New York: Macmillan, 1962. Contains much material of interest to social, economic, and science historians, notably an account of the beginnings of some important chemical industries. Leblanc's work is treated in chemical detail. Partington bases his text almost entirely on original sources, and he gives many quotations from these sources. The approach is encyclopedic rather than analytic, but this is a reliable source for those without the time or language skills to prospect through the original material.

Robert J. Paradowski

ANTONI VAN LEEUWENHOEK

Born: October 24, 1632; Delft, the Netherlands
Died: August 26, 1723; Delft, the Netherlands
Area of Achievement: Biology
Contribution: Leeuwenhoek took the microscope when it was a new and undeveloped instrument and made it a significant tool for scientific research. He built the best microscopes anyone was to have for another two centuries, and he discovered a new world of living organisms, never before seen by human eyes.

Early Life

Antoni van Leeuwenhoek was the son of a basket-maker, Philips Antonyszoon van Leeuwenhoek, and his wife, Margaretha. Antoni's father died when the boy was about seven, and about two years later his mother remarried. About that time, young Leeuwenhoek was sent to school at Warmond, just north of Leiden. Subsequently he lived with an uncle, a lawyer who served as town clerk of Benthuizen. Leeuwenhoek's early education must have provided a good foundation in geometry, trigonometry, and natural science, but his later writings show that he had received no instruction in Latin or modern foreign languages, and thus he had never been intended for the university.

At the age of sixteen, Leeuwenhoek was sent to the great city of Amsterdam to learn the cloth trade. It was as a draper that he returned to Delft after some six years, and he never resided anywhere else. In 1660, he was named chamberlain of the city hall. It was a well-paying sinecure, leaving him with a fair income, even after hiring the personnel and supplies necessary to clean, heat, and light the building.

Testifying to his mathematical ability, he was made municipal surveyor in 1677, and in 1679 he was named inspector of weights and measures. Eventually, as a result of his microscopy, he would become an institution in Delft, and the city would award him a special pension. As time went on, Leeuwenhoek spent fewer hours selling cloth out of the ground-floor shop in his house and more time in what today would be called his laboratory.

Leeuwenhoek was married twice, the first time to Barbara de Mey, a draper's daughter, in 1654. They had five children, but only one survived, Maria, who kept house for her father in later years. Barbara died in 1666, and Leeuwenhoek married a clergyman's daughter, Cornelia van der Swalm, in 1671. Cornelia may have borne him a child who failed to survive, but in 1694 she herself died, leaving Leeuwenhoek with no new children.

Numerous writers have agreed that Leeuwenhoek grew interested in lenses because drapers used magnifying glasses to check the weave and to count the number of threads per inch in cloth. Yet a later researcher, Brian J. Ford, credits Leeuwenhoek's acquaintance with *Micrographia* (1665; small drawings), by the English scientist Robert Hooke as the inspiration for Leeuwenhoek's move into microscopy. Leeuwenhoek apparently studied the illustrations and had sections of the book translated for him by friends.

The ingenious and meticulous Leeuwenhoek was self-taught. He seems to have done virtually everything on his own and owed little except his mathematical and drapery training to anyone else. Even his Dutch, his only language, was colloquial and nonliterary. The learned world would have paid no attention to such a man, unless his work was undeniably brilliant.

Life's Work

Leeuwenhoek was a proper, middle-class Dutch burgher. He wore respectable clothing and a wig, had the delicate hands of a craftsman, and possessed the keen eyesight and patience needed for detailed observation through the microscope. He was a man of presence, with a broad face and a large nose, and must have possessed an excellent constitution, for he lived to be almost ninety-one years of age.

It was apparently a Delft research physician and friend who enabled Leeuwenhoek to make connection with the Royal Society, a newly formed scientific organization in England. Leeuwenhoek had begun experimenting with microscopes in the late 1660's, and by 1673 he had made enough startling observations that it was time for him to be discovered. He wrote his findings in lengthy, rambling letters that for the remaining fifty years of his life were regularly published in the *Philosophical Transactions* of the Royal Society.

Thus the scientific world became aware of the work of the amazing Dutchman. He had not invented the microscope—indeed, microscopes had been used for at least half a century—but Leeuwenhoek's skill at lens grinding, along with his patient and insightful mind, made him the father of modern microscopy.

In his first letter to the Royal Society, Leeuwenhoek anonymously criticized famous scientist and society member Hooke for accepting the idea of spontaneous generation of life. Leeuwenhoek had already seen that life comes from life and that maggots in meat, for example, do not simply appear but are produced from eggs laid by adult flies. He later extended his research debunking spontaneous generation by work on fleas, weevils, shellfish, and eels.

In 1680 the then secretary of the Royal Society, Robert Hooke, proposed Leeuwenhoek for actual society membership, and he was unanimously elected. Cognizant of the honor, Leeuwenhoek remained devoted to the English organization and to no other for the rest of his life.

Leeuwenhoek's countryman Christiaan Huygens, the greatest educated scientist whom the Netherlands produced in the seventeenth century, spent many years in France and translated many of Leeuwenhoek's early letters into French for publication. Leeuwenhoek himself, however, dealt only with the English.

Hooke's microscopic work dealt primarily with insects and plant and animal tissue, and he is mainly famous for using his low-power microscope to discern and name the cells in cork. Later, under Leeuwenhoek's influence, he built a microscope of Leeuwenhoek's description and did additional work. Neither he, however, Huygens, nor any other "regular" scientist of that century or the next was both able and willing to grind the lenses and stare through them for the uncounted hours necessary to discern what was really happening in the microscopic world.

Leeuwenhoek was very accurate at estimating the relative and absolute sizes of the things he observed. The great Italian microscopist Marcello Malpighi had demonstrated in 1660 the existence of blood capillaries, but he could not see red blood cells clearly. Leeuwenhoek not only gave the world's first accurate description of red corpuscles but also correctly calculated the diameter of the red blood cell at one three-thousandth of an inch— amazingly close to the modern value.

The instrument which Leeuwenhoek employed was the simple microscope, one with a single, beadlike lens mounted in a hole between two small metal plates riveted together. An arrangement of three screws moved the object to the proper position in front of the lens, and the entire apparatus, no bigger than the palm of one's hand, was held to the eye for viewing. There were no tubes and no compound lenses. Hooke, with a compound lens, could only achieve a magnification of around fifty diameters, but Leeuwenhoek's instruments have been calculated to have attained some 266 power. It has been estimated that some of his microscopes no longer in existence must have attained about five hundred power magnification in order for him to have discerned the detail that he described.

Leeuwenhoek's microscopes were so simple that he made more than five hundred, of which there are about nine known survivors. Rather than disturb an interesting specimen that was properly mounted, he would often construct another microscope. His lenses were ground, never blown, and were convex on both sides. Leeuwenhoek kept his best observation technique secret, but it has been surmised from an obscure comment in one letter that he used dark field illumination for contrast. He did not employ any staining method.

Leeuwenhoek devoted much time to scrutinizing plant and animal tissue, but his best efforts were made observing microbes. He watched the movements of every kind of "animalcule," as he termed the tiny creatures that danced, darted, floated, and vibrated under his lens. He saw protozoa, smaller organisms called bacteria, and human spermatozoa, and he studied algae, yeasts, and molds.

He found these organisms everywhere—in his rainbarrel, in his mouth, in nearby ponds and canals, and in the soil. He was better at verbal than at artistic description, and so he retained the services of draftsmen to produce pictures of what he saw. In this effort, it is possible that his early work was assisted by his friend and neighbor Jan Vermeer, one of the best and most precise artists of all time.

The homegrown scientist not only studied how animalcules and insects reproduced but also experimented with what would kill them. He found that pepperwater would kill many microbes, that nutmeg would kill mites, and that sulfur dioxide would kill moths. He never seems to have suspected, however, that some of these tiny animals would be able to kill him. Leeuwenhoek was even visited by Hermann Boerhaave of nearby Leiden University, and the august personage gravely peered through the microscopes. Professor of medicine, botany, and chemistry, and a co-fellow of the Royal Society with Leeuwenhoek, Boerhaave had turned Leiden into Europe's best-known medical center of the time. Thus, as he drew no medical conclusions from observing the animalcules, Leeuwenhoek can certainly be forgiven for not doing so. That microbes were the source of many human diseases remained virtually unknown for another two centuries.

Asking himself how microbes came to inhabit a previously sterile medium, Leeuwenhoek concluded that they were borne on the very dust motes of the air. In fact there were few questions that Leeuwenhoek did not ask, but as a solitary and untutored investigator ahead of his time, the miracle is that Leeuwenhoek did what he did in the first place.

Summary

Antoni van Leeuwenhoek is recognized as having founded the disciplines of bacteriology and protozoology. Strangely, however, he established no school of followers. He had no disciples, and he refused to train younger men to succeed him. Even though Leeuwenhoek did not train others and establish a tradition of excellent microscopy, posterity does know what he did in his half-century of research, as he wrote some two hundred lengthy and illustrated letters to the Royal Society, letters which were published in English translation. The Royal Society also received twenty-six microscopes bequeathed in Leeuwenhoek's will—the only instruments he ever relinquished so far as is known. The society treasured them for years but eventually lost them. Luckily, the original letters were preserved.

Some of Leeuwenhoek's best work was done in his seventies and early eighties, mainly dealing with nonparasitical protozoa living in water. By that time, Leeuwenhoek was an international institution, a phenomenon to whom all paid tribute. The University of Louvain sent Leeuwenhoek a silver medal in 1716 to honor him for his work, and he was visited by numerous potentates and crowned heads of state.

Several editions of Leeuwenhoek's collected letters appeared in Dutch and in Latin while he was still alive. He was not a man who was forgotten until he had been long dead. He had looked deeper and longer into the microscopic universe than had any other person of his time, and his world honored him. He was largely overlooked by the next several generations, until he was rediscovered in the nineteenth century, an enigmatic precursor of a science regarded as absolutely fundamental to an understanding of nature.

Bibliography
Bender, George A., and Robert A. Thom. *Great Moments in Medicine: A History of Medicine in Pictures*. Detroit: Northwood Institute Press, 1966. This book contains an excellent chapter on Leeuwenhoek, giving accounts of his life and work. There is an excellent illustration of the microscopist and his workshop based on the four life portraits that were actually made of Leeuwenhoek and on other surviving artifacts and information.
De Kruif, Paul. *Microbe Hunters*. London: Jonathan Cape, 1926. Reprint. New York: Pocket Books, 1950. Originally published in 1926, this excitingly written volume has a long chapter on Leeuwenhoek, whom de Kruif justifiably labels "first of the microbe hunters." De Kruif conveys the excitement Leeuwenhoek must have felt at making mankind's first forays into the subvisible world.
Dobell, Clifford. *Antoni van Leeuwenhoek and His "Little Animals": Being Some Account of the Father of Protozoology and Bacteriology and His Multifarious Discoveries in These Disciplines*. London: Bale and Danielsson, 1932. Reprint. New York: Russell & Russell, 1958. The standard biography of Leeuwenhoek in English. Dobell, himself a microscopist as well as an excellent linguist and scholar, researched old Dutch records to uncover everything that could be found on Leeuwenhoek. He quotes and comments on Leeuwenhoek's letters and provides ample footnotes to explain sources and methods. Contains special sections devoted to different aspects of Leeuwenhoek's life and work.
Ford, Brian J. *Single Lens: The Story of the Simple Microscope*. New York: Harper & Row, 1985. This book gives the history of the development and use of the simple microscope from before Leeuwenhoek through the nineteenth century. More than half of the book is devoted to Leeuwenhoek, and Ford, also a microscopist, performed research which netted him some improvements over Dobell's detailed study.
Schierbeek, Abraham. *Measuring the Invisible World: The Life and Works of Antoni van Leeuwenhoek*. London: Abelard-Schuman, 1959. This book is an abridged translation of a two-volume biography in Dutch. Containing a biographical chapter written by Maria Rooseboom, the book gives a good overview of Leeuwenhoek's life and work.

Allan D. Charles

GOTTFRIED WILHELM LEIBNIZ

Born: July 1, 1646; Leipzig, Saxony
Died: November 14, 1716; Hanover
Areas of Achievement: Philosophy and mathematics
Contribution: Though never employed as an academic philosopher, Leibniz was one of the greatest intellectuals of his day: He was a metaphysician, theologian, philologist, historian, genealogist, poet, inventor, scientist, mathematician, logician, lawyer, and diplomat. He contributed to the development of rationalist philosophy, and he also corresponded with or personally knew virtually every major European thinker in every field of inquiry.

Early Life

Gottfried Wilhelm Leibniz was born into an academic family; his mother's father was a professor, as was his own father (who died when Leibniz was six). Leibniz was intellectually gifted; he taught himself Latin and read profusely in the classics at an early age. When he was an adolescent, Leibniz began to entertain the notion of constructing an alphabet of human thought from which he could generate a universal, logically precise language. He regarded this language as consisting of primitive simple words expressing primitive simple concepts which are then combined into larger language complexes expressing complex thoughts. His obsession with this project played an important role throughout his life.

Leibniz was formally educated at the University of Leipzig, where he received his bachelor's and master's degrees for theses on jurisprudence, and at the University of Altdorf, where he received the doctorate in law in 1666. He declined a professorship at Altdorf and entered employment as secretary of the Rosicrucian Society. Eventually he was employed as a legal counsel by Johann Philipp von Schönborn, a governing official of Mainz.

Life's Work

Leibniz's philosophy was rationalist. According to this theory, human knowledge has its origins in the fundamental laws of thought instead of in human experience of the world as in the doctrine of empiricism. In fact, Leibniz argued that the laws of science could be deduced from fundamental metaphysical principles and that observation and empirical work were not necessary for arriving at knowledge of the world. What was needed instead was a proper method of calculating or demonstrating everything contained in certain fundamental tenets. For example, he believed that he could deduce the fundamental laws of motion from more basic metaphysical principles. In this general conception, he followed in the intellectual footsteps of René Descartes. The great problem with interpreting Leibniz's contribution to this tradition of thought is that he published only one major book during his lifetime, and it does not contain a systematic account of his full philosophy. Accordingly, it is necessary to reconstruct his system from the short articles and the more than fifteen thousand letters which he wrote.

Leibniz's youthful dreams of constructing a perfect language quickly evolved into a theory of necessary and contingent propositions. He claimed that in every true affirmation the predicate is contained in the subject. This idea evolved from his conception of a perfect language which (in all of its true, complex statements) would perfectly reflect the universe. The true propositions of this language are necessarily true, and all necessary propositions are, according to Leibniz, ultimately reducible to identity statements. Such a conception was more plausible in the case of purely mathematical statements since, for example, "$4 = 2 + 2$" can be equated with "$4 = 4$." Yet this conception seemed impossible in the case of contingent statements; for example, in "the house is blue." Leibniz avoided this problem by arguing that the necessity in what appears as contingent truths can be revealed (or resolved) only through an infinite analysis and therefore can be carried out in full only by God. It follows that, for humans, all contingent truths are only more or less probably true. Such truths are guaranteed by the principle of sufficient reason, which states that there must be some reason for whatever is the case. Necessary truths, or truths of reason, on the other hand, are guaranteed by the principle of contradiction, which states that the denial of such a truth is a contradiction (though this can be known only by God). A logical principle closely related to the principle of sufficient reason is the notion of the "identity of indiscernibles," now known as Leibniz's law. This principle states that it is impossible for two things to differ only numerically, that is, to be distinct yet have no properties that differ; if two things are distinct, there must be some reason for their distinctness.

Leibniz had elaborated the rudiments of his metaphysical system while at Mainz, but it was during his sojourn in Paris that his philosophy matured. In 1672, he was sent to Paris on a diplomatic mission for the German princes to persuade Louis XIV to cease military activities in Europe and send forces to the Middle East. Leibniz remained in Paris for four years, and, though he failed to even gain an audience with the monarch, he met frequently with the greatest minds of the day, such as Christiaan Huygens, Nicolas de Malebranche, Antoine Arnauld, and Simon Foucher. He also carried out studies of the mathematics of Blaise Pascal and René Descartes and actually built one of the first computers—a calculating machine able to multiply very large numbers. While residing in Paris, he also made a brief trip to England, where he met with Robert Boyle and visited the Royal Society, to which he was elected.

When he returned to Hanover, he accepted a post as director of the library to John Frederick, the Duke of Brunswick, where he remained for the next ten years. It was only after working with Huygens in Paris on the nature of motion that Leibniz finally came to grips with the problem of the continuum. On his return trip from Paris, during which he visited Baruch Spinoza in Holland, he composed "Pacidius Philalethi" (1676), an extended analysis of this subject. This issue is traced back to the ancient Greeks and concerns the problem of resolving the motion of an object into its motions over discrete parts of space. If the body must pass through each successive parcel of space between two points, then it can never get from one point to another, since there are an infinity of such discrete parcels between any two points. It was in the context of this problem of motion and the continuum that Leibniz developed, in 1676, the differential calculus, publishing his results in 1684. Sir Isaac Newton had already discovered the calculus but did not publish his results until 1693, several years after Leibniz published his discoveries. Priority of discovery is accorded to Newton though the consensus now is that they arrived at the calculus independently.

Leibniz argued that Cartesian physics renders motion ultimately inexplicable on the basis of fundamental concepts, since it is grounded in the notion of matter as extension and does not accommodate dynamic properties. For Leibniz, the fundamental tenet is that activity is essential to substance. Substantial being is what is simple—what can be conceived by itself and what causes itself. The term "monad" was adopted by Leibniz to refer to this fundamental unit of existence. Monads are metaphysical entities that are not extended and are not of a material nature but are units of psychic activity. All entities are monadic, from God, the supreme monad who has created all the other grades of monads, to the lowest grade of being. The universe of monads is divided into two realms on the scale of perfection, that of nature and that of grace. Because monadic substances are psychic rather than material, Leibniz's philosophy has been labeled "panpsychistic idealism." On the level of phenomena, Leibniz retained a mechanical model: Matter in the phenomenal realm is "secondary matter," composed of monadic substances and having mass. Yet, according to Leibniz, substances and monads do not interact with each other. The universe consists of an infinity of such monadic substances, individuated by the principle of indiscernability and each of which undergoes changes. This change in the monad occurs entirely because of its own nature, according to a logically necessary law and not because of effects coming to it from outside. All of these changes in the monads have been harmonized by God into what appears as a causal order. Leibniz referred to this as the "way of preestablished harmony" and likened it to the synchronized sounding of two clocks. Since each monad/substance is completely independent of all the others, Leibniz said (in his later writings) that they are "windowless"; that is, they do not look out on the world. Though this conception may appear to be rather unusual, it does account for the plurality of existents in the universe, since the substances are infinite and independent of one another.

The changes of a monad are changes in the degree to which it expresses the universe. This expression or "perception" occurs on all levels of being; all individuals express the rest of the universe through the changes that occur in it. Since each individual represents all individuals, metaphysical accommodation is made of the unity of the universe in the diversity of an infinity of monads. An exhaustive specification of the nature of one substance/monad would give an exhaustive specification of the natures of all other substances/monads (from a particular point of view). Since such a specification would be logically necessary (in any true assertion the predicate is contained in the subject), the complete description of the universe is a tautology, though this could only be fully known by God.

The characteristics of the monad, activity and perception, are analogous to the features of the mental lives of human beings. In connection with the notion of perception, Leibniz later introduced the notion of "apperception." In *Principes de la nature et de la grâce, fondés en raison* (1714; *The Principles of Nature and Grace*, 1890), he distinguished between perceiving the outer world and apperceiving the inner state of the monad (which is self-consciousness in a human being). In fact, differences between monads relate to their degree of clarity of perception and the presence of perception of perception or apperception. At the bottom of the hierarchy of being are monads with confused perception and unself-conscious appetition. Leibniz's theory of human understanding is developed in his *Nouveaux Essais sur l'entendement humain* (1765; *New Essays Concerning Human Understanding*, 1896), written in response to John Locke but not published in his lifetime. The perceptions of the human soul are expressions of the perceptions occurring in the body and are confused and unclear. Since all changes occur according to internal principles, all the ideas of the human mind are innate.

Leibniz was the first thinker to employ explicitly the notion of the unconscious, which he did in connection with the distinction between apperception and perception—not all perceptions are apperceived. These perceptions he refers to as "petites perceptions" and gives as his favored example the sound of a wave crashing on the beach; the sound is composed of tiny perceptions of droplets hitting the beach, of which one is unaware though one is perceiving them.

During his years in Hanover, Leibniz grew very close to Sophia, the wife of his patron Ernest Augustus, First Elector of Hanover, and to Sophia's daughter Sophia Charlotte, who became the first queen of Prussia. Leibniz discussed many philosophical ideas with them, and from these conversations arose his only published book, *Essais de théodicée sur la bonté de Dieu, la liberté de l'homme, et l'origine du mal* (1710; *Theodicy*, 1951). In this text, Leibniz argued along Augustinian lines that evil exists in the world because the world could not be as good as it actually is without the evil that it contains. In fact, out of all the possible universes, Leibniz believed, this universe contains the greatest amount of good. This conception earned for Leibniz's theories the appellation a "philosophy of optimism."

Toward the end of his life, Leibniz became embroiled in an intellectual dispute with Samuel Clarke, a disciple of Newton. Leibniz claimed that Newtonian physics had contributed to a general decline of religion in England. Clarke defended Newtonian physics against this charge, while Leibniz attacked Newton's conceptions on philosophical grounds in a series of letters. Leibniz asserted that the notions of absolute space and absolute time violated the principle of sufficient reason and that the concept of gravity introduced the incomprehensible notion of action at a distance. Leibniz had earlier argued that space and time have no substantive existence and are only the ordered relations between coexistent entities and the ordering of successively existent entities, respectively. The death of Leibniz ended the debate with Clarke, who immediately published the correspondence. In spite of his extensive contacts with savants throughout Europe, Leibniz's death on November 14, 1716, was relatively unnoticed.

Summary

Gottfried Wilhelm Leibniz remained in the humble employ of royal patrons his whole life, though at one point he was offered the position of head librarian at the Vatican, which he declined to accept. In 1700, the Berlin Society of Sciences was founded, and Leibniz was elected president for life. Throughout his life, Leibniz speculated about grandiose social-intellectual projects. He advocated the Christian conquest of the pagan lands, the compilation of a universal encyclopedia of human knowledge, the reuniting of the Protestant and Catholic churches, and the restoration of peace in Europe under the Holy Roman Empire. In a true Enlightenment spirit, Leibniz also advocated the establishment of scientific academies throughout the world and actually corresponded with Peter the Great concerning such an academy for Russia. In spite of such visionary plans, Leibniz was very conservative politically; he did not criticize existing institutions and was opposed to innovation in moral and religious matters. Yet he was a man friendly to all, avid of learning of the world from everyone he encountered.

Leibniz had a tremendous influence on his contemporaries. Virtually all philosophers in Germany were Leibnizian during the years after his death. One early Leibnizian who proved to be equally influential in Germany was Christian von Wolff. Wolff had corresponded with Leibniz from 1704 to 1716 on mathematical and philosophical topics. Wolff taught the Leibnizian system to Martin Knutzen, who in turn taught it to Immanuel Kant, who long remained a Leibnizian. One of Kant's early essays in metaphysics was on the principle of sufficient reason and its relation to the logical principles of identity and contradiction. Writing in the light of the Lisbon earthquake of

1756, Voltaire bitterly satirized the philosophical optimism of Leibniz (along with Alexander Pope) in his work *Candide: Ou, L'Optimisme* (1759; *Candide: Or, All for the Best*, 1759). Leibniz's philosophical influence is still evident to this day. His law concerning the identity of indiscernibles is the starting point of much of the work done in the twentieth century on semantics, and his notions of necessity and possibility are the ancestors of work by contemporary modal logicians on the nature of necessity.

Bibliography
Broad, C. D. *Leibniz: An Introduction*. Cambridge, England: Cambridge University Press, 1975. A compilation of the lecture notes used by Broad, published after his death. A primarily expository but good analytic reconstruction of the whole of Leibniz's philosophy.
Hostler, John. *Leibniz's Moral Philosophy*. New York: Barnes & Noble Books, 1975. A full study of the metaethical dimensions of Leibniz's metaphysics. Argues that the metaphysics is worked out in the framework of his systematic moral ideas.
Jolley, Nicholas. *Leibniz and Locke: A Study of the New Essays on Human Understanding*. New York: Oxford University Press, 1984. A study of Leibniz's response to Locke. Attempts to substantiate the notion that the guiding motive of Leibniz in writing his study was to refute Locke's materialism.
Leibniz, Gottfried Wilhelm. *The Monadology and Other Philosophical Writings*. Translated with an introduction and notes by Robert Latta. Oxford, England: Clarendon Press, 1898. Contains a two-hundred-page introductory essay on the whole philosophy of Leibniz. Extensive discussion of the influences of Leibniz in the development of psychology in Germany in the latter part of the nineteenth century.
MacDonald, Ross G. *Leibniz*. New York: Oxford University Press, 1984. Claims that Leibniz hoped to create a synthesis of all knowledge traditions and did not simply construct an a priori rationalistic metaphysics. Part of the Past Masters series of books, it is very introductory.
McRae, Robert. *Leibniz: Perception, Apperception, and Thought*. Toronto: University of Toronto Press, 1976. Focuses on Leibniz's theory of knowledge and attempts to explain how perception and apperception combine to give thought.
Mates, Benson. *The Philosophy of Leibniz: Metaphysical Underpinnings*. London: Oxford University Press, 1986. This is an excellent introductory secondary work on Leibniz. Covers all aspects of his general metaphysics. Written by a contemporary logician.
Rescher, Nicholas. *Leibniz: An Introduction to His Philosophy*. Totowa, N.J.: Rowman and Littlefield, 1979. Argues that Leibniz's unorthodox metaphysical system is ultimately aimed at providing a foundation for

utterly orthodox views in ethics and religion.

Russell, Bertrand. *A Critical Exposition of the Philosophy of Leibniz*. Cambridge, England: Cambridge University Press, 1900. An important work on Leibniz by one of the most important philosophers of the twentieth century. Argues that Leibniz's philosophy can be understood in terms of five fundamental principles that are ultimately inconsistent.

Mark Pestana

ÉTIENNE LENOIR

Born: January 12, 1822; Mussy-la-Ville, Belgium
Died: August 4, 1900; La Varenne-Saint-Hilaire, France
Areas of Achievement: Invention and technology
Contribution: Lenoir invented a number of useful processes and devices, the most famous being an internal-combustion engine. The quality and significance of his engine are still matters of controversy, but there is little doubt that it stimulated the efforts of the other pioneers of internal-combustion-engine design.

Early Life

Although born in the French-speaking region of Belgium, Étienne Lenoir spent all of his productive life in France. He went to his adopted country at the age of sixteen in 1838 to begin work as a metal enameler. Within a few years, he had several inventions to his credit. In 1847, he patented an enameling process, in 1851 an electroforming process, in 1853 an electric-railway brake, and in 1865 an automatic telegraph that printed messages on a ribbon of paper. This telegraph was thus a forerunner of the ticker-tape machine. On January 24, 1860, he received a patent for his most famous invention—an internal-combustion engine.

Interest in internal-combustion engines was as old as the discovery of atmospheric pressure in the seventeenth century. Experiments and demonstrations that showed the power of atmospheric pressure working against or into a vacuum inspired a number of people to imagine an engine that could be powered by having atmospheric pressure drive a piston into a vacuum chamber. The difficulty in creating such an engine was in producing the vacuum—not once, but in rapid succession, since the piston must have continuous up-and-down motion. An obvious solution was to use gunpowder to burn the air in a chamber and to create a vacuum by allowing the resulting gas to cool. Christiaan Huygens actually constructed such engines, but they were impractical because of the incompleteness of the vacuum. The solution was the steam engine, as steam could drive the air from a chamber without an explosion and then be reduced to only one seventeen-hundredth of its original volume when converted to water.

There were suggestions for engines' employing heated air rather than steam in the late eighteenth century, and some were in use by the end of the century. The real impetus for an internal-combustion engine came, however, from the work of Sadi Carnot in the 1820's. Among the ideas about thermodynamics that Carnot established was the concept of a heat engine. He demonstrated that a steam engine was basically inefficient, because little of the heat produced to power it was actually used. He believed that an air engine would be much more efficient because more heat could be utilized.

By the time Lenoir appeared in Paris, the idea of an internal-combustion engine was widespread and a number had been built, but none proved practical enough to be offered commercially. In addition to the familiarity of the idea, the stage was further set for Lenoir by the ready availability of natural gas for the gas lighting that was becoming common in Paris.

Life's Work

Lenoir's gas engine was the first internal-combustion engine practical enough to be offered for sale in significant numbers. It ran on the natural gas piped into factories and businesses for lighting purposes or distillates of petroleum similar to modern gasoline. In 1897, Lenoir claimed in *France Automobile* that he used the engine to power a vehicle of some sort—probably a farm cart—for several trips between Joinville-le-Pont and Paris in 1863. The Automobile Club of France conducted an investigation in 1900 and concluded that he had made the world's first automobile trip in May, 1862, between Paris and Vincennes. It has been observed that the discrepancy in dates is rather suspicious. These claims came at a time when there was controversy about who had invented the automobile, involving French and German inventors as well as their champions. Even if one assumes that Lenoir powered a vehicle with an internal-combustion engine in 1862 or 1863, it was hardly more than a publicity stunt similar to the motorboat trips made on the Seine using his engine. He did nothing to develop a practical horseless carriage for his own use or for sale.

Although his engine was sold commercially and, in that sense, may be regarded as a success, there have been questions about the importance of his accomplishment. The most telling criticism of his work is that he did not understand the fundamental requirement for a truly successful internal-combustion engine, namely that the gas must be compressed before firing. A further complaint is that he thought of his engine as nothing more than an advanced steam engine. In his patent application he stated:

> My engine cannot be classed among gas engines. Indeed, the functions of the gas I employ do not consist in detonating or exploding it, thereby impelling the piston, as this has heretofore been done or suggested, but in the use of gas as a fuel that can be instantaneously and regularly ignited, and without producing any shock, for the purpose of heating the air that is mixed with it. The air thus dilated or expanded will act on the piston in the same manner as steam would in ordinary steam engines.

Despite his patent claims to have produced a gas engine unlike others, a company advertising brochure of 1864 pointed out that his engine was closely linked to those of previous inventors. It was stated that the Lenoir engine used Robert Street's piston with Philippe Lebon's double action, an ignition like that of Isaac de Rivas, and a cooling system similar to Samuel

Brown's. Perhaps these claims and denials, as well as the similarity in appearance of the engine to stationary steam engines, were meant to reassure a buying public dubious about the idea of gas explosions.

Whether owing to the conservative buying habits of potential customers, design inadequacies, or both, the engine was not a commercial success. Lenoir had done engineering work for Gautier and Company of Paris and apparently convinced its proprietors of the merits of his design. This company backed him in forming the Société des Moteurs Lenoir in 1859. Some four thousand stocks were issued in the new company but no dividends appear ever to have been paid. The Parisian Gas Company took control of the engine in 1863 and paid Lenoir a pension in his old age.

Most of the engines were built under license from Lenoir's company. The Reading Iron Works in England built about one hundred. Two German companies built some, and the Lenoir Gas Engine Company of New York sold some at a cost of five hundred dollars for the half horsepower model and fifteen hundred dollars for the four horsepower version. The Marinoni and Lefebvre companies of Paris produced more than any of the foreign manufacturers, but, all told, fewer than five hundred were made.

The Lenoir engine resembled a stationary, double-acting, horizontal steam engine. With power being produced on each side of the piston, it was, in effect, the equivalent of a two-cylinder engine. Sliding valves connected to the crankshaft by rods that covered and uncovered ports to admit fuel and exhaust-spent fumes. The ignition system was electric. A battery provided power to an induction coil with a vibrating contact to provide a primary spark, and a sliding distributor alternated delivery of current between the two spark plugs. The electrical system was changed at least twice, as it never worked satisfactorily. The final version used a rotary distributor with the rotor driven by the crankshaft. An unusual feature by comparison with later engines was that air and gas were admitted to the combustion chamber separately. This was the basis of Lenoir's claim that he had not produced an ordinary gas engine. He believed that the air should remain separate from the gas, at least in part, to provide a cushion between the explosion of gas and the piston head. Unfortunately, the exhaust ports opened before the expansion was complete, and much of the heat produced was lost to the cooling water in violation of Carnot's principles. The loss of heat also meant that there were problems with overheating and that a huge radiator was necessary. The company suggested a radiator capacity of one hundred gallons for the half horsepower model.

The engine was uneconomical for industrial applications. It consumed about one hundred feet of gas per hour in the half horsepower model, and it had maintenance problems. Overheating caused the valves to stick, there was no self-contained means of recharging the batteries, and the spark plugs required frequent cleaning. Later versions of this type of engine, such as that of Pierre Hugon, provided for the injection of a spray of water into the cylinder to help in cooling, but the improvement was not enough to rescue the design. A steam engine of comparable size was as economical to operate and much less troublesome.

Carnot had observed that the most obvious way to produce a great change of temperature, as required in an efficient engine, was to compress the air used in the engine. Since compression was the key to success, Lenoir's noncompressing engine was out of production by the late 1860's, but he tried again in the 1880's with a four-cycle compression engine. It had poppet valves and other advances over his earlier model, including a 300 percent improvement in fuel consumption rates. This engine was produced for a while by the Mignon and Rouart Company.

Lenoir made no substantial profits from any of his inventions, but he did receive several honors. For his engine, he received a prize at the London Exposition of 1862 and several French prizes including that of the Marquis d'Argenteuil, which brought him twelve thousand francs, in 1886. His most prestigious award was the Legion of Honor, which he received in 1881 for the invention of the teletype machine in 1865. He died in relative obscurity and poverty in 1900.

Summary

Even if Étienne Lenoir had not built an engine, his teletype machine and other inventions would have gained for him a respectable place in the story of modern technological development. It is, however, his production of the first commercial engine and, especially, his connection with the automobile, that has brought him more attention than the other engine designers who were his contemporaries. He was not the first to build an internal-combustion engine. In fact, by his own admission, his design depended almost entirely on the work of predecessors. Several hundred of his engines were built and sold, but, by all accounts, they were not very suitable. It is on the automobile connection that his fame primarily rests.

Assessment of Lenoir's achievements is made difficult by the controversies surrounding the invention of the automobile. As indicated, national pride and the championing of personal favorites has made this a hotly debated subject. Moreover, the difficulty in defining exactly what constitutes the first automobile probably means that there will never be a clear ranking of its inventors.

The claims and counterclaims in France and Germany as to who invented the automobile brought some attention to Lenoir at the end of his life, but it was the Selden Patent Case that did the most to bring him to the attention of the English-speaking world. George Baldwin Selden obtained a United States patent on automobiles in 1895. Although he never built any automobiles, the Association of Licensed Automobile Manufacturers was formed to exploit the patent by selling the right to manufacture to other companies. Henry Ford challenged the patent, and in the subsequent trials, which lasted from 1903 to 1911, the Ford Company maintained that Selden's patent was invalid because practical automobiles predated the patent by a number of years. A significant part of the Ford case was the claim that Lenoir had constructed an automobile in 1860. The Ford lawyers cited an article describing a self-propelled vehicle built by Lenoir that appeared in the June 16, 1860, edition of *Le Monde illustré*. There is no other evidence that this vehicle was ever built. Even Lenoir never claimed that he had built an automobile as early as 1860. The claims made for and by him in the late 1890's were also placed into evidence. When the Selden attorneys imported British experts to deny that an automobile could be powered by a non-compressing engine, the Ford Company actually built a copy of Lenoir's engine and used it to drive a Ford automobile. The attention drawn to Lenoir's name in this case has done much to establish him in the list of automobile pioneers.

Whatever one's opinion about Lenoir's importance as an inventor of the automobile, his engine stimulated the production of better engines and, ultimately, automobiles. All the pioneers of automobile design studied his engine. Those uninterested in automobiles were encouraged to build better stationary engines for industrial use, and Lenoir played a significant role in the transition from the age of steam to the age of oil.

Bibliography
Bishop, Charles W. *La France et l'automobile*. Paris: Librairies-Techniques, 1971. Gives considerable space to advocating Lenoir's importance and priority in developing engines and automobiles. The author carefully explains the invalidity of all complaints made against Lenoir or his engine. He is convinced that Lenoir invented the automobile and that others, such as Carl Benz and Gottlieb Daimler, were inspired by his inventions.
Cardwell, D. S. L. *From Watt to Clausius: The Rise of Thermodynamics in the Early Industrial Revolution*. Ithaca, N.Y.: Cornell University Press, 1971. Gives the early history of the effort to develop an efficient heat engine.
Cummins, C. Lyle, Jr. *Internal Fire: The Internal Combustion Engine*. Lake Oswego, Oreg.: Carnot Press, 1976. This is a history of the internal-combustion engine. Although Lenoir's work is covered only in a portion of one chapter, it is one of the best accounts of his activities in English. Contains technical details, graphs, and illustrations of the engine.
Field, D. C. "Internal Combustion Engines." In *A History of Technology*, edited by Charles Singer et al., vol. 5. New York: Oxford University Press, 1958. Details the general development of the internal-combustion engine and dismisses the value of Lenoir's engine except for the observa-

tion that its limited commercial appeal encouraged others to attempt improvements.

Mott-Smith, Morton. *The Concept of Energy Simply Explained.* Mineola, N.Y.: Dover, 1964. Presents the concepts of heat engines as well as major scientists who have dealt with the subject and their theories. Contains very little mathematics, and the author does a good job of explaining theories simply without being simplistic.

Philip Dwight Jones

ANDRÉ LE NÔTRE

Born: March 12, 1613; Paris, France
Died: September 15, 1700; Paris, France
Area of Achievement: Landscape architecture
Contribution: Le Nôtre's designs for great public gardens complement the architecture of many of the most important buildings in seventeenth century France. He virtually created the French formal garden, which subordinated nature to reason and order while maintaining a fascination with and awareness of nature's beauty and delight.

Early Life
André Le Nôtre was born on March 12, 1613, in his father's home, adjoining the Tuileries Gardens. Jean Le Nôtre, royal master gardener, served the king, as had his father, and was in charge of a specific part of the royal gardens. Like all tradesmen of the time, gardeners were a close-knit group, handing their jobs from father to son for generations. Le Nôtre's christening records substantiate that, for his godmother was the wife of Claude Mollet, a member of another third-generation gardening family which was then better known than the Le Nôtres.

Growing up amid this coterie of amateur and professional landscape architects and gardeners, the young Le Nôtre was undoubtedly influenced by their standards. Probably they even discussed his training and education. A prominent author, Jacques Boyceau de la Barauderie, had set forth the qualifications needed by gardeners: literacy, mathematical training, and drawing skill. Drawing was necessary in order to reproduce embroidery patterns on the ground to serve as designs for flower beds. Geometry was necessary to measure paths and flower beds. If he wished, a gardener might study architecture to enable him to design structures for his garden. This theoretical training would be accompanied by the more practical study of seeds, soils, transplanting, and weather prediction.

Apparently the youthful Le Nôtre showed such skill in drawing that his family arranged for him to study with Simon Vouet, the chief painter to Louis XIII. This natural skill is apparent in Le Nôtre's carefully executed and delicately colored garden plans, which exhibit draftsmanship and proportion characteristic of an artist. It is generally accepted that he must also have studied architecture, either with Jacques Lemercier or François Mansart. Judging by his later life, this education in painting and architecture must have been of a highly academic quality, accompanied by extensive reading in subjects such as optics, Turkish art, and Italian garden design.

After two years of architectural study, Le Nôtre began training as a gardener, serving as an apprentice to his father, who applied to Louis XIII to have his position descend to his son. The younger Le Nôtre went to work in the Tuileries, receiving his appointment, with a salary and a lodging in the park, in 1637. He remained in charge of these gardens all of his life, arranging for his nephews to inherit this responsibility after his death.

Even though Le Nôtre was a dashing and vivacious young man and lived in a notoriously amoral court atmosphere, no scandal was ever attached to his name. In 1640, he married Françoise Langlois, and his energies thereafter seem always to have been directed to his own family and to his work. He conducted both with discipline and humility. Their married life was happy as well as prosperous, although not untouched by sadness. Apparently neither their son nor their two daughters survived infancy. With no children of their own, Le Nôtre and Françoise cared for their nephews and nieces and a godchild. They also provided a home for his mother after Jean Le Nôtre's death. In their later years, both Le Nôtres inherited property and land from their parents. As Le Nôtre's reputation grew, he prospered, and ultimately he and his wife were wealthy, with an annual income equivalent to thirty-five thousand dollars.

Life's Work

Le Nôtre's work was known and admired by royalty, nobles, and his contemporaries as early as the 1640's. When only in his early thirties, he conceived a witty and original plan for an episcopal garden at Meaux in the shape of a bishop's miter. He had worked in the Luxembourg Gardens for Gaston, duc d'Orléans. His position as designer in ordinary of the king's gardens continued unchanged after the death of Louis XIII and the ascension of Louis XIV. It is generally accepted, however, that real fame came to him as the designer of the gardens at Vaux-le-Vicomte for Nicolas Fouquet.

Fouquet, superintendent of finance for the queen mother, had amassed a huge fortune, which he spent on a château designed to be the most magnificent that money could achieve. He seems to have been anxious to overawe the young Louis XIV and commissioned Louis Le Vau as architect, Charles Le Brun as designer of furnishings, and Le Nôtre as designer of the gardens. They created a masterpiece. The palace stood amid one thousand acres of gardens and park. During its construction, three small villages disappeared, rivers were diverted, and a whole forest was transplanted. In August of 1661, Fouquet invited six thousand people, including the king and the whole court, to a grand party. There were fireworks, illuminations, fountains arching into the sky, and a play performed in the gardens, written and directed by Molière. Although Fouquet was arrested and imprisoned twenty days later, Le Nôtre's triumph was undiminished. Furthermore, Louis XIV was apparently determined to build an even more magnificent palace at Versailles and to have the same three masters of art and architecture construct and design to their best ability, again with no regard for expense.

Ultimately, Louis XIII's unremarkable hunting lodge at Versailles was transformed into the Louis XIV's palace, the most extravagant and influential building and garden in European history. From its probable beginning date of 1662 throughout the rest of the king's life, the expansion of the buildings, parks, and gardens of Versailles became symbolic of the aggrandizement of France under his rule. The growth of his power can be charted in the growing acreage added to the gardens and parks. The king himself was active in designing his new city. The axis of the gardens and avenues designed by Le Nôtre at Versailles—eventually eight miles of them—literally converged in the king's apartment. The primary theme of the gardens and the sculptures therein is the mythology of Apollo, the original *roi de soleil* (Louis XIV was often called the Sun King). Additionally, the four rivers of France appear as ancient water gods. The four seasons, the four parts of the day, the continents, the four elements, and the various gods of nature and mythology relate to the garden. The image of the Sun King's supremacy was eventually translated into stone and marble, fabulous water displays, *bosquets*, and grottoes, in a symbolism that was complex and unified in its focus.

At Versailles, Le Nôtre followed an essentially orderly geometrical formula from which he rarely deviated throughout his career. The gardens and the buildings they surrounded were an architectural unit. The château was the focal point in a plan beginning with a central axis which bisected the structure and stretched westward to the horizon. Although actually on several different levels, at Versailles this long vista seemed to stretch to its vanishing point, past fountains, secondary canals, and ultimately the mile-long, sixty-foot-wide Grand Canal. Poets of the day said that this vista formed a pathway to the heavens so that the sun god could descend to his earthly domain. To the architects of the palace and garden, this grand view expressed the limitless power of the king, the personification of France. At right angles across the axis were laid other vistas, geometrically balanced and equally perfect on a smaller scale.

The park at Versailles had three vistas: the main one which extended to the west, and the lesser ones north and south. Each began at a parterre directly in front of the palace or its wings. These flower beds were planted to resemble embroidered fabric and were edged with low-growing shrubs. Rectangular green panels provided open spaces and led the eye to the many pools. Higher elements of relief, such as trees, were kept at a distance so as not to clutter the vista. The trees served to define the borders within the garden and to provide green walls for a series of cozy, intimate outdoor "rooms," the *bosquets*, which often served as outdoor ballrooms, theaters, or concert halls.

To the south of the château was a second series of terraces that contained the orangerie, which was designed by Le Nôtre and built by Mansart. From there, tubs holding trees laden with oranges, pomegranates, flowering jasmine, and oleanders were wheeled out in spring to form part of the planned garden. The man-made lake visible from the upper terrace was Le Nôtre's last work at Versailles, completed when he was seventy-four years old. North of the château, where the ground sloped sharply, was the third vista. Le Nôtre there showed his mastery of perspective, for he made the flower beds wedge shaped, with distant ones shorter and smaller and near ones larger, and with the longest sides of the triangles facing the château. Steps of rose-colored marble descended through a steep avenue, past two rows of fountains, through a wood, to reflecting pools, from which water rose in great spouts. This part of the garden also demonstrated the diversity of optical illusions of which Le Nôtre was capable, for when viewed from its farthest points the angle of ascent along the main axis was exaggerated by the luminous waters, the constant refraction of light, and the dazzling play of color in the greens of the woods, the sky-reflecting pools, and the gilded sculptures. All were planned and executed in a perfect harmony of proportion to be viewed from any point.

Le Nôtre's distinguished career was marked by many honors. He became a member of the French Academy of Architecture in 1681. The king honored him with the Order of Saint-Michel, a great mark of distinction. Following Le Nôtre's own whim, Louis XIV bestowed on him a coat of arms consisting of a gold chevron and three silver snails. Other architects and designers lost favor, but until his death Le Nôtre remained the honored friend of the king. The man, as the king himself recognized, was like his gardens: honest, straightforward, balanced, and without pettiness. One painting of Le Nôtre in middle age shows a successful, bewigged man with a strong face, intelligent expression, and large dark eyes that seem about to smile. When he died at the age of eighty-seven, his obituary noted that "he was esteemed by all the sovereigns in Europe and there are few who have not requested the design of a garden from him."

Summary

André Le Nôtre did not invent the formal garden, but he did carry its pattern to a level of artistic grandeur that set a pattern for the rest of Europe. He advanced the architectural design of the Renaissance garden, which had been evolving in Italy for two hundred years, to its ultimate form. His imagination, coupled with his artistic perception and the mathematical clarity of his vision, created gardens which epitomized seventeenth century neoclassicism. He had traveled to Italy and conferred with the pope. He had laid out gardens in England for Charles II and William of Orange. Besides his masterpiece at Versailles, the gardens at Hampton Court, Clagny, Triauon, Sceaux, and Pont Chavtrain further testify to his greatness. He left no personal literary record of his ideas, but his students were influential in France as well as in the rest of Europe for many years. Many of his gardens no longer exist in original form, but those which are unchanged show his brilliance. It was partly in reaction to his highly developed formality that the so-called romantic or English garden became popular in the more emotional eighteenth and nineteenth centuries.

Bibliography

Adams, William Howard. *The French Garden, 1500-1800*. New York: George Braziller, 1979. Based on careful examination of documents and manuscripts of the period, as well as actual explorations of surviving sites. An extensive chapter tells of Le Nôtre's life and of his architectural and landscaping innovations. Every chapter features contemporary architectural drawings and plans, which the author considers more accurate than later photographs.

Amherst, Alicia. *A History of Gardening in England*. 2d ed. London: Quaritch, 1896. Reprint. Detroit: Singing Tree Press, 1969. Helpful for its consideration of Le Nôtre's place in the development of landscape architecture and for its considerations of his formal garden designs in England. Amherst does not resolve whether Le Nôtre ever actually went to England (a point upon which authorities disagree), but her study of his gardens is thorough.

Fox, Helen. *André Le Nôtre: Garden Architect to Kings*. New York: Crown, 1962. A highly readable biography which presents Le Nôtre as a symbol of seventeenth century classicism. Fox includes a historical overview as well as separate chapters on Le Nôtre's great gardens. Also included are color reproductions of Le Nôtre's garden plans, sketches, and engravings of garden scenes, and some photographs, including one of Le Nôtre's portrait.

Hadfield, Miles. *Pioneers in Gardening*. London: Routledge & Kegan Paul, 1955. Examines the evolution of gardening as different from horticulture or botany. The chapters are arranged in a loose chronological sequence according to garden type, rather than by individuals. The chapter on the formal garden is almost totally devoted to Le Nôtre. Useful for placing him in historical context.

Hazlehurst, F. Hamilton. *Gardens of Illusion: The Genius of André Le Nostre*. Nashville, Tenn.: Vanderbilt University Press, 1980. A scholarly and complete study of the work of Le Nôtre, whom Hazlehurst calls "Le Nostre," consistent with seventeenth century spelling. This study examines major authenicated Le Nôtre garden sites in fourteen separate chapters, summarizing his life and accomplishments in accompanying chapters. Especially remarkable are the illustrations: contemporary engravings, artists' views, and several plan and elevation drawings done to scale by a modern architect.

Jellicoe, Sir Geoffrey, Patrick Goode, Michael Lancaster, and Susan Jellicoe, eds. *The Oxford Companion to Gardens*. New York: Oxford University Press, 1986. A comprehensive quick-reference volume containing condensed biographies of Le Nôtre and of his major contemporaries. Especially important for its definitions of the many specialized terms associated with gardening, past and present. One finds an explanation of treillage and bosquet, for example, in this comprehensive source.

Patricia A. Finch

LEO X
Giovanni de' Medici

Born: December 11, 1475; Florence
Died: December 1, 1521; Rome
Areas of Achievement: Government, politics, religion, and patronage of the arts
Contribution: As a patron of the arts, Leo X turned Rome into the cultural center of the Western world. As pope, he engaged in secular politics and presided over the period in church history that witnessed the outbreak of the Protestant Reformation.

Early Life

Pope Leo X was born Giovanni de' Medici, the second son of Lorenzo (the Magnificent) and his wife, Clarice Orsini. Though brought up in the lap of Renaissance luxury, he was groomed for a career in the Church from an early age. Tonsured at age seven, he was appointed a cardinal at age thirteen, although he did not receive the insignia and the privileges of that office until 1492. As a youth, he was tutored by the famous Humanists Marsilio Ficino, Angelo Poliziano, and Giovanni Pico della Mirandola, who imparted to him a love of literature and the arts, which characterized his entire life. From 1489 until 1491, Giovanni studied theology and canon law at the University of Pisa. Then, in 1492, he moved to Rome and assumed the responsibilities of a cardinal. He served on the conclave, which in that year elected Pope Alexander VI, although Giovanni did not vote for him.

After the death of his father in 1492, Giovanni returned to Florence, where he lived with his elder brother Pietro until the Medici family was exiled from their native city in 1494 during Girolamo Savonarola's "Reign of Virtue." For the next six years, Giovanni traveled in France, the Netherlands, and Germany, and then returned in May of 1500 to Rome, where, for the next several years, he immersed himself in literature, music, and particularly the theater, interests that were the great loves of his life, taking precedence even over hunting, of which he was extremely fond.

When his elder brother died in 1503, Giovanni became the head of the Medici family, and much of his energy and his revenues from his many church benefices was expended in the ensuing years in his efforts to restore his family to prominence in Florence. After a bloodless revolution in that city in September of 1512, the Medicis were allowed to return, and Giovanni became the de facto ruler of Florence, although the nominal ruler would be his younger brother Giuliano. Then, when Pope Julius II died in February of 1513, the seven-day conclave that followed elected Giovanni his successor. Giovanni was crowned Pope Leo X on March 19.

Life's Work

The portrait of Leo by Raphael, which hangs in the Pitti Palace in Florence, depicts the pope as an unattractive man, with a fat, shiny, effeminate countenance and weak, bulging eyes. Yet, according to contemporaries, his kind smile, well-modulated voice, kingly bearing, and sincere friendliness ingratiated him with everyone he met. While his manner of life was worldly, he was unfeignedly religious and strictly fulfilled his spiritual duties—he knew how to enjoy life but not at the expense of piety. He heard Mass and read his Breviary every day and fasted three times a week. Contemporaries report that there was scarcely a work of Christian charity that he did not support, as he contributed more than six thousand ducats per month to worthy causes. He enjoyed banquets and spent lavishly on them but never overindulged himself. Though his personal morality was impeccable, he sometimes attended scandalous theatrical presentations and seemed to enjoy the absurd and vulgar jokes of buffoons. Even during the very troubled period of 1520-1521, he amused himself during the Roman carnivals with masques, music, and theatrical performances.

Since Leo's love of literature and the arts was well known, soon after his elevation to the papacy Rome was flooded with Humanists, poets, musicians, painters, sculptors, and other talented men seeking the pope's patronage. The greatest among them, as well as many of the lesser, were not disappointed. Beneficiaries of his largess as patron were the Humanists Pietro Bembo and Jacopo Sadoleto, the artists Raphael and Michelangelo, the architect Donato Bramante, and hundreds of others. Leo collected books, manuscripts, and gems without regard to price. The construction of St. Peter's Basilica was greatly accelerated. So splendid was the cultural life of Rome during this period that it has been called the Leonine Age, for its patron. Leo is said to have spent 4.5 million ducats during his reign, leaving the papal treasury a debt of 400,000 ducats.

Although Leo showed little interest in theological matters, he did reconvene the Fifth Lateran Council, which had first opened its doors under Julius II but had adjourned without accomplishment. Its objectives were to promote peace within the Christian world, proclaim a Crusade against the Turks, and reform the Church. The council was poorly attended, and most of the councillors were Italians so that it was not representative of Christendom as a whole. At its conclusion in March, 1517, the council issued decrees calling for stricter regulation of the conduct of cardinals and other members of the Curia and denouncing abuses such as pluralism and absenteeism; these decrees would largely be ignored in practice, however, even by Leo himself. Leo did preach a Crusade against the Turks in 1518, but the monarchs of Europe showed little interest.

As secular ruler of the Papal States and protector of the Medici interests in Florence, Leo found it necessary to engage in the balance-of-power politics characteristic of the age; it is for his political role that he is most severely criticized by modern writers. In this political capacity, he was frequently guilty of treachery and duplicity. For example, when he began his pontificate, he was part of an alliance aimed at thwarting the French king's territorial ambitions in Italy. After Francis I's smashing victory at Marignano (September, 1515), however, Leo secretly deserted his allies, met with Francis, and negotiated the Concordat of Bologna, whereby, in return for guarantees of the integrity of Leo's territory in Italy, Francis was granted the right to nominate all the bishops, abbots, and priors within his realm, a right French kings would retain until the French Revolution.

Leo's capriciousness in political affairs was again demonstrated when Holy Roman Emperor Maximilian I died in January of 1519. The two leading contenders for this position were Francis and Charles I, King of Spain. Leo at first supported Francis, since he feared the territorial ambitions of Charles in both northern and southern Italy; since Francis had similar claims in Italy, however, Leo attempted to persuade Frederick the Wise of Saxony to be a candidate. When Frederick refused, Leo reverted to his support of Francis. When Charles was eventually elected in June of 1519, Leo moved quickly to establish a papal alliance with him. In May of 1521, Leo secretly concluded a treaty with Charles, in which the pope agreed to join Charles in a renewed effort to drive the French from Milan, in return for which Charles promised to close the meeting of the Imperial Diet at Worms with the outlawing of the excommunicate Martin Luther.

Like most Renaissance popes, Leo was guilty of nepotism. In order to provide his nephew Lorenzo with a title, Leo, in 1516, declared the duke of the small papal state of Urbino deposed and conferred the duchy on his nephew. To carry out the deposition, Leo had to raise an army and commit it to an arduous winter campaign against the former ruler. Leo then supported Lorenzo, Duke of Urbino, as the unofficial ruler of Florence. Among Leo's several relatives who enjoyed church appointments under that pontiff was his cousin, Giulio, whom Leo made a cardinal almost as soon as he himself had mounted the papal throne. Giulio would later be elevated to the papacy as Clement VII.

Despite Leo's irenic disposition, he made enemies, and he did not shrink from retaliation against those who threatened him. In 1517, when a conspiracy aimed at poisoning the pope was uncovered, one of the leaders, Cardinal Petrucci, was executed, several other cardinals were imprisoned and heavily fined, and Leo appointed thirty-one new cardinals in rapid succession so that the pope would have a college in which the majority of cardinals would be loyal to him.

The greatest crisis that Leo faced as pope came toward the end of his pontificate, and he died without really understanding its severity. Leo's predecessor, Julius II, had promulgated a plenary Jubilee indulgence in an effort to raise money for the building of St. Peter's Basilica in Rome. The indulgence had not sold well, and its sale was discontinued until its revival by Leo in March of 1515. Arrangements had been made with Albrecht of Brandenburg for the sale of the indulgence in his archdioceses of Mainz and Magdeburg. When the sale of these indulgences by the Dominican Friar Johann Tetzel began in 1517, it was not long before the matter came to the attention of a young German monk, Martin Luther, who lodged a protest. Pope Leo did not realize the seriousness of the protest and was preoccupied with the preparation for the upcoming imperial election and with his other worldly pursuits, and so the situation was allowed to deteriorate. In June of 1520, Leo issued the bull *Exsurge Domine*, in which Luther was accused of forty-one counts of heresy and ordered to recant on pain of excommunication. Luther's refusal to recant, together with his public burning of the bull, led to his formal excommunication on January 3, 1521. Within a short time after these events, Lutheranism had begun to win adherents among some of the northern German princes as well as in Denmark. Before the extent of the schism could be appreciated, Leo died, on December 1, 1521, from bronchitis.

Summary

In early accounts of Leo X's reign, he was alleged to have remarked at the time of his coronation: "Let us enjoy the Papacy since God has given it to us." While there is strong evidence that Leo never actually said this, this remark does seem to reflect his attitude toward his high office. Within two years in office, Leo had exhausted the full treasury left him by Julius II, and, despite the additional revenues generated by the sale of church offices and papal favors as well as indulgences, Leo's extravagance bequeathed a debt of 400,000 ducats to his successor. While Roman cultural life had never been so splendid as it was during his pontificate, Leo's devil-may-care attitude and his capricious political activities, coupled with his failure to understand the religious intensity of men such as Luther or to respond to it, help to explain Protestantism's early success.

Leo's accession to the papal throne was accompanied by much celebration. Of his passing, a contemporary observed: "Never died Pope in worse repute." While it is no longer contended that he was the victim of poisoning, the circumstances of his burial were severe. The candles used in his obsequies were those left over from another funeral, and no monument was erected to his memory until the time of Paul III. With Leo's death, the age of the Renaissance popes was nearly at an end.

Bibliography
Creighton, Mandell. *A History of the Papacy from the Great Schism to the Sack of Rome*. 6 vols. London: Longmans, Green, 1897. Provides a com-

prehensive survey of the pontificate of Leo. While Creighton gives recognition to Leo's importance as a patron of the arts, he is critical of Leo's reckless spending and his indifference toward spiritual matters. Concludes that Leo left a bitter heritage for his successors. A rather opinionated account.

Mee, Charles L. *White Robe, Black Robe*. New York: G. P. Putnam's Sons, 1972. Presents an account of the early Reformation period through an examination of the lives, careers, and ideas of Leo and Luther, vividly contrasting the two protagonists. While it presents little new information on either figure, the work skillfully blends discussion of the political background to the Reformation with that of its theological significance. Contains a useful bibliography.

Pastor, Ludwig. *The History of the Popes from the Close of the Middle Ages*. Vol. 8, *Leo X (1513-1521)*. London: Kegan Paul, Trench, Trubner, 1924-1953. The entirety of this volume of this classic, monumental study of the modern Papacy is devoted to the pontificate of Leo. Provides an extensive treatment of the cultural life of Rome under Leo's patronage. Includes footnotes and English translations of many previously unpublished documents in the appendices.

Roscoe, William. *The Life and Pontificate of Pope Leo the Tenth*. 5th ed. 2 vols. London: Henry G. Bohn, 1846. An excellent general history of the period of Leo's pontificate. Includes extensive notes and English translations of numerous documents relevant to the text. While mainly sympathetic to Leo, Roscoe maintains that criticism of Leo by contemporary and later writers is largely the result of Leo's duplicity and treacherousness as a political figure.

Schevill, Ferdinand. *The Medici*. New York: Harcourt, Brace, 1949. The chapter on Leo emphasizes how strongly he was motivated in most of his policies by his desire to advance the fortunes of the Medici family, both in Florence and in Italy as a whole. Schevill is critical of the artistic patronage of Leo, believing that he made poor use of the many talented men in the papal employ.

Vaughan, Herbert M. *The Medici Popes*. New York: G. P. Putnam's Sons, 1908. This work is primarily devoted to an examination of the personal character and the strengths and weaknesses of Leo. The work's attention to unimportant details to the exclusion of the political realities faced by Leo necessitates consulting other works on the pontiff.

Paul E. Gill

LEO XIII
Vincenzo Gioacchino Pecci

Born: March 2, 1810; Carpineto Romano, Italy
Died: July 20, 1903; Rome, Italy
Areas of Achievement: Religion and church reform
Contribution: Leo XIII, considered to be one of the greatest leaders of the
  Roman Catholic church during a period of crisis, tried to maintain the
  strength and power of the Church in a world changing through industry,
  colonization, and governmental upheaval. The fact that he was not always
  successful is not as significant as the fact that he was a pioneer, aware of
  the needs of the modern Roman Catholic church.

Early Life

Leo XIII was born Vincenzo Gioacchino Pecci in the hills south of Rome
in Carpineto Romano, in central Italy. His parents, Colonel Ludovico Pecci
and Anna Prosperi Buzi, were patrician, but neither wealthy nor of great
nobility. The sixth in a family of seven children, Pecci began his education
in Viterbo at the Jesuit college from 1818 to 1824. He was a brilliant student, with what became lifelong scholarly achievement in Latin. He continued his studies in Rome from 1824 to 1832 at the Roman College and in
1832 was admitted to the Academy of the Noble Ecclesiastics. He completed
his religious studies at the University of the Sapienza between 1832 and
1837, concentrating in theology and civil and canon law. He was ordained in
1837.

In the same year, he was appointed a domestic prelate, and in 1838 he was
named governor or apostolic delegate of Benevento by Pope Gregory XVI,
who had praised Pecci's courageous service during the cholera epidemic of
1837. His success in this position, especially in reducing banditry and eliminating the inroads being made by liberals, led to his appointment in 1841 to
the same position in Perugia. While this area had similar problems to solve,
Pecci went beyond his previous successes and improved the economy by
building roads, establishing a farmers' savings bank, and gaining great popularity among the residents.

With these achievements, Pecci was sent to Belgium as nuncio, the pope's
representative, in January, 1843, after having been consecrated titular Archbishop of Damietta. Pecci spent three difficult years in Belgium, which
finally ended when King Leopold requested of the pope that Pecci be recalled. The king and his Prime Minister Nothomb had been seeking to confer
the right to name members of the university juries to the government. In this
matter, crucial to the educational system of Belgium, Pecci sided with the
bishops and Catholic politicians in opposition to the king. Even though the
Catholic side won, the victory was empty for Pecci. While this period ap-

pears to have been a failure, Pecci gained experience that helped form his future conservatism. During this time, his only extended observation of the more industrialized, liberal areas of Europe, he saw the behavior of a liberal political regime toward Catholics and learned to oppose it. As he fought against unionism, the compromise and agreement between Catholics and moderate liberals in Belgium, he came to be wary of liberal hands extended in compromise.

Life's Work

When Pecci left Belgium, he returned to Perugia, where he served as archbishop until 1878 and further solidified many of the ideologies which would serve him during his pontificate. Along with his brother Joseph, a Jesuit seminary professor, he worked to increase the numbers of clerics; modernize the curriculum at the seminaries; revive Thomism, the medieval Scholasticism based on the Aristotelianism of Thomas Aquinas; and establish the Academy of Saint Thomas in 1859. As a result of these activities, Pecci was named a cardinal in 1853.

During the period that he was archbishop in Perugia, Pecci was politically prudent and reserved. He protested the annexation of Perugia by the kingdom of Sardinia in 1860; on the other hand, he would not join Cardinal Giacomo Antonelli, the Secretary of State to Pope Pius IX, in his methods of government and involvement in conflicts. Consequently, Antonelli considered Pecci an enemy and kept him from Rome. Following his moderate views as a Catholic, Pecci wrote his pastoral letters of 1874-1877, recommending that the Catholic church make conciliatory gestures toward contemporary society. Self-evident as it may seem, he recognized that the Church did not exist in a void, but rather in the quickly changing world of the late nineteenth century. These letters, in addition to his other achievements, gained for him the respect of Pius, and, when Antonelli died in 1877, Pecci was summoned to serve as camerlengo in the Roman curia, the chamberlain who oversees the Church when the pope dies.

When Pius died in 1878, Pecci was in a good position to be elected pope. Since this was the first conclave since the Holy See had lost its temporal power, Pecci's role as the leading moderate was important. He was indeed elected on the third ballot with forty-four of the sixty-one votes, after having received a plurality on the first ballot of nineteen votes, thirteen more than the second most favored candidate.

When he became Pope Leo XIII, Pecci was sixty-eight years old and in fragile health. These facts, combined with his delicate appearance, all indicated that his would be, at best, a brief transitional appointment. Yet he was popular. Because the Italian government feared demonstrations in his support in St. Peter's Square and all over Rome, his crowning took place in private on March 3 in the Sistine Chapel so that he would not appear publicly on the loggia to bless the people as he wished to do.

His acts on the evening of his coronation, however, foreshadowed the theme of Leo's reign: He wrote letters to the German emperor, the Swiss president, and the Russian czar announcing his election and offering hope that the Church might come to better accord with their governments. While doctrinally conservative, he sought to maintain a strong role for the Church in the modern world.

In the course of his papacy, Leo wrote numerous encyclicals on subjects ranging from traditional piety to social issues. He wrote eleven encyclicals to the Blessed Virgin Mary and the Rosary, two each to the Eucharist and the redemptive work of Christ, and one to the renewal of the Franciscan Third Order. In the Jubilee Year of 1900, he consecrated the entire human race to the Sacred Heart of Jesus, an initiative begun by Pius, and in 1893 instituted a feast of the Holy Family. Becoming more conservative in the final few years of his life, he published new norms for censorship in 1897 and a new Index in 1900, and he set up a permanent Biblical Commission in 1902 after writing the encyclical to Bible study, *Providentissimus Deus* (1893; *On the Study of the Scriptures*, 1894).

That Leo was able to align such conservative piety to a new recognition of modern states is quite remarkable. It was accomplished, however, not with statements of accord with government, but rather, with statements only of recognition. In 1878, the year of his coronation, Leo attacked socialism, communism, and nihilism in *Quod apostolici muneris* (*Concerning Modern Errors, Socialism, Communism, Nihilism*, 1895), and, in 1884, he wrote similarly on Freemasonry. He also acted to increase centralization within the Church, much to the disappointment of progressives. At the same time, however, he wrote encyclicals to the relationship of the Church to sociopolitical order: *Diuturnum illud* (1881; *On Civil Government*, 1942) recognized the existence of democracy in God's world; *Immortale Dei* (1885; *On the Christian Constitution of States*, 1885) defined the spiritual and temporal spheres of power; and *Libertas praestantissimum* (1888; *Human Liberty*, 1895) viewed the Church as the true source of liberty. Most important was *Rerum novarum* (1891; *The Condition of Labor*, 1891), which advocated private property rights, fair wages, workers' rights, and trade unionism, while, predictably, condemning socialism and economic liberalism. Because of the positions presented in this encyclical, Leo came to be known as "the workers' pope."

In addition to these, Leo wrote encyclicals to social and intellectual issues. *Arcanum divinae sapientia* (1880; *On Christian Marriage*, 1880) is a highly conservative statement on marriage, identical in tone and thought to writings of his predecessors. On intellectual matters, however, he was more open to new ideas than the revival of old ones. Following his lifelong respect for and study of Thomism, he encouraged Catholics to incorporate fully

Thomist metaphysics into Catholic philosophy in *Aeterni patris* (1879; *Scholastic Philosophy*, 1879). Leo also bridged the gap between Catholicism and the natural sciences by encouraging Catholics to study astronomy and the other natural sciences. He urged complete objectivity in all areas of scholarship done by Catholics; in an unprecedented ecumenical spirit, he opened the Vatican libraries to scholars of all faiths in 1883. This was begun in 1879, when he allowed the German historian Ludwig Pastor access to the secret archives of the Vatican.

In many ways, Leo was a far more political pope than was his successor, yet while he and his four secretaries of state had many diplomatic successes, he failed in matters closest to home, such as the achievement of accord with the Italian government. By 1887, Leo was willing to accept a compromise in which Italy would be entirely unified under the House of Savoy; the Papal States, a sixteen-thousand-square-mile area in central Italy, would be given to Italy; and an indemnification or compensation therefore, offered under the Law of Guarantee, would be received from Italy. The Italian government, however, wanted the abdication of the pope's sovereignty, which would lead inevitably to limited freedom for Leo himself and future popes. He made a counterrequest for a repeal of the anticlerical laws and restoration of papal rule for Rome, but it was denied. Thus, Leo was unable to achieve any resolution of conflict with the Italian government. None, indeed, was attained until the Lateran Treaty of 1929.

France, too, presented problems for the pope. With its republican government, France sought the separation of church and state and secular, social, and educational systems. Catholics within France were not enthusiastic in their support for the Church against their government. Soon, government recognition of all religious groups was required or the groups were to be disbanded. In 1880, the Jesuits were dissolved, followed in 1900 by the Congregation of the Assumptionists. Teaching orders went into exile, and the pope was unable to turn the tide, which became a crisis for his successor, Pius X.

Relations with England remained unchanged. At the beginning of his reign, Leo initiated a study seeking possible reconciliation with the Anglican church. When such a unification proved impossible, he issued an apostolic letter in 1896, discouraging any move in this direction; yet he was responsible for the cardinalship of John Henry Newman in 1878.

Leo actively sought a reunion with the Oriental and Slavic Catholic churches, going so far as to praise the work of Saint Cyril and Saint Methodius in the encyclical *Grande munus* (1880) and to discuss rites and reunion in the apostolic letter of 1894. Again, he was unable to make concrete advances in this direction.

More satisfactory were Leo's efforts in Belgium, Germany, and Russia. He negotiated agreements with Belgium in 1884 and with Russia in 1894. In

1886-1887, he successfully achieved the repeal of the anticlerical laws in Germany (the Kulturkampf) and, in his sole diplomatic success, he mediated in Germany's dispute with Spain over the possession of the Caroline Islands in the Pacific Ocean in 1885. He was, however, unsuccessful in his attempt to keep Germany and Austria from joining Italy in the Triple Alliance in 1887. Nor was he invited to the Hague Peace Conference of 1899, because of the intransigence of the Italian government.

In other areas of the world Leo recognized the importance of colonialism to Christian evangelism, and he approved 248 sees, forty-eight vicarates or prefectures, and two patriarchates in Scotland, North Africa, India, Japan, and the United States. Although he criticized "Americanism," which would have attempted to modernize Catholicism, in a letter of 1899, he named the first apostolic delegate to the United States in 1892.

The twenty-five years of Leo's reign ended in 1903 with his death at the age of ninety-three. He far exceeded expectations in the longevity, the social concern, and the intellectual strength of his service to the Church.

Summary

It was fortunate for the Catholic church that Leo XIII became the pope when the Western World was experiencing great turmoil. A brilliant man, he was able to steer the Church into a role in society which at once showed an awareness of the modern world but did not stray far from traditional church doctrine. The English writer Thomas Carlyle called him a great "reconciler of differences." Leo's was a strong voice against the growing popularity of socialism in Europe; yet he accepted democracy and advocated the rights of workers in the growing industrialized world. Within his own church, he was able to create a clear role of spiritual leadership for the pope to replace the recently lost temporal powers of the Papacy. While some scholars consider his learning antiquated, restricted, and perhaps obsessively concerned with Thomism, his intellectual breadth, strength of character, and devotion to service have brought him great praise. Even with his many failures, he is generally considered the greatest pope in three hundred years. Leo said of himself, "I want to set the church so far forward that my successor will not be able to turn back." As a pioneer whose ideas shone even more brightly after his death, he clearly achieved this goal.

Bibliography
Bokenkotter, Thomas. "Social Catholicism and Christian Democracy." In *A Concise History of the Catholic Church*. Garden City, N.Y.: Doubleday, 1927. A scholarly and detailed narrative of the political world into which Leo was thrust at his ordination. Leo's charitable piety is shown as it affected the changing governments and economies of the entire Western world.

Gargan, Edward T., ed. *Leo XIII and the Modern World*. New York: Sheed & Ward, 1961. A series of nine essays by various scholars preceded by an introductory essay and followed by an extensive bibliography on Leo and his period in history. The essays stress Leo's theological contributions, especially as a Thomist, and his impact on the European and American political worlds of the late nineteenth century.

McCabe, Joseph. "Leo XIII." In *Crises in the History of the Papacy*. New York: G. P. Putnam's Sons, 1916. An objective appraisal of the life and accomplishments of Leo, which assesses him as the best pope in three hundred years but a failure in gaining influence upon the thoughts or actions of Western society.

Miller, J. Martin. *The Life of Pope Leo XIII*. Philadelphia: National Publishing, 1903. A five-hundred-page biography written in praise of Leo that was begun before his death, containing several drawings and photographs. The author writes conversationally and quaintly, quoting letters and relating anecdotes in dialogue. His purpose is the veneration of Leo and nearly one-third of the book is devoted to a detailed description of Leo's final illness and death.

Wallace, Lillian Parker. *Leo XIII and the Rise of Socialism*. Durham, N.C.: Duke University Press, 1966. A presentation of the juxtaposition of two major antagonistic ideologies of the nineteenth century, held on the one side by Leo and his church and on the other by Karl Marx and his followers. This 464-page volume shows Leo's power as he stems the tide of Marxism in Europe with his intellectual and compassionate approach to the social problems of the industrial world.

Vicki Robinson

LEONARDO DA VINCI

Born: April 15, 1452; Vinci, near Florence
Died: May 2, 1519; Cloux Château, near Amboise, France
Area of Achievement: Art
Contribution: Leonardo da Vinci was the most outstanding painter of the Italian Renaissance; some authorities consider him the best painter and draftsman of all time. In addition, he made a number of discoveries in botany, anatomy, mechanical engineering, and medicine which were unprecedented and unparalleled until the twentieth century.

Early Life

Leonardo da Vinci was born on April 15, 1452, the illegitimate son of Piero da Vinci, descendant of a long line of Florentine minor officials, and a local woman known only as Caterina. Nevertheless, he was reared as a member of his father's household, first in Vinci and then in Florence; a notarized attestation of his birth by his grandfather signifies his family's recognition of him and of its responsibilities toward him. Still, there are few documented facts about his early life. Further, since the first biography of him—by the historian Giorgio Vasari—appeared only some thirty years after his death, conjectural reconstructions have flourished.

Leonardo himself recorded only one event from his childhood, recalled years later, when he was compiling notes on the flight of birds in his notebooks. He simply comments that he was probably fated to write about the flight of kites "because in the earliest memory of my childhood it seemed to me that as I lay in my cradle a kite came down to me and opened my mouth with its tail and struck me with its tail many times between the lips." As open to Freudian reconstruction as this seems to be, it may only document Leonardo's memory of the closeness of the physical environment natural to an upbringing in a Tuscan hill village. This is more likely, since his fascination with horses also seems to date from this period. Both interests continued throughout his life.

There is no evidence earlier than Vasari's biography that Leonardo served an apprenticeship under Andrea del Verrocchio, but legend, as well as some internal evidence, seems to make this likely. Under Verrocchio, Leonardo would have worked with fellow apprentices Perugino, later the teacher of Raphael, and Lorenzo di Credi, both to become masters in their own right.

Of Leonardo's work at this early period little survives, other than some sketches in his notebooks. One page of these, consisting of a series of portraits of the same head—a head which also appears in some of his earlier paintings—seems to record various impressions of himself. If they are self-portraits, they correspond to early reminiscences on the part of his contemporaries of his remarkable beauty and grace; the delicacy of his profile coincides with memories of fluid, dancer-like movement, of a luminous presence and carriage, of an unusually sweet singing voice, of considerable ability as a lutenist, together with quite unexpected physical strength. One early account credits him with contributing the head of an angel to Verrocchio's painting *The Baptism of Christ* (c. 1474-1475), and one head is clearly by a hand subtler and more delicate than Verrocchio's; Vasari reports improbably that Verrochio was so dismayed by the contrast that he refused to paint thereafter, confining himself to sculpture.

A final event from this period deserves mention. While staying at the house of Verrocchio—long after his apprenticeship had come to an end— Leonardo was twice accused of having visited the house of a notorious boy prostitute, which was tantamount to being accused of sodomy, a crime punishable at best by exile, at worst by being burned at the stake. In neither case was the evidence necessary for conviction brought forth, but the incident suggests something about Leonardo's sexual orientation and foreshadows his failure to develop a deep relationship with a woman.

Life's Work

Leonardo remains best known for his painting, even though it is now nearly impossible to restore his works to their original splendor. Yet his qualities announce themselves almost immediately in his first Florentine period (1472-1482). In *The Baptism of Christ* of Verrocchio, for example, his hand can be seen not only in the angel's head long attributed to him but also in the delicate treatment of the watercourse in the foreground and in the fantastic mountain landscape to the rear. Two similar paintings, both called *The Annunciation*—one in the Louvre, one in the Uffizi, both c. 1475— display advances in structure, delicacy of detail, and a personal iconography unlike that of any previous painter.

Among other masterpieces from this period are a portrait of Ginevra de' Benci (c.1474), *Head of a Woman* (c. 1475), and the *Madonna Benois* (c. 1478). Here the distinctive element is sensitivity of character, so that the figures rendered seem to take on a life of their own, almost as if establishing eye contact through the pictorial plane. Great as these are, the *Adoration of the Magi* (1481) completely transcends them. This unfinished painting occupied Leonardo's attention for the remainder of his stay in Florence, yet he completed only the preliminary underdrawing. Nevertheless, it displays an absolutely unprecedented sense of fantasy and imagination, all accomplished within the norms of accurate Albertian perspective. With this painting, Leonardo broke free from the confines of traditional Nativity iconography, relegating the ruined stable to the background and replacing it with the powerful symbol of the broken arch. He also regrouped the figures of the traditional scene so that they could appear both as individuals with distinct motives and as participants in a communal activity. Leonardo gives a theological doctrine a real psychological dimension.

Following this stay in Florence, Leonardo resided in Milan for nearly twenty years. Although he apparently hoped to be taken into the service of Duke Ludovico Sforza as military engineer, his principal activities were artistic. His first major work was the *Madonna of the Rocks*, two versions of which survive, one in the Louvre and one in the National Gallery in London, both c. 1485. This work was commissioned by the Convent of the Conception in Milan, and, although the doctrine of the Immaculate Conception had not yet been officially adopted, Leonardo chose to depict it in his painting.

The Last Supper (1495-1497), a fresco, is a true masterwork and a ruin. To get the effects he wanted, Leonardo invented new methods of applying color to wet plaster. At first he seemed to have succeeded, but by 1517 the work had already begun to deteriorate, and by 1566 Vasari pronounced it a jumble of blots. Only in the late twentieth century has restoration recovered the core of the original. What is there is astonishing in itself, but what is lost is irreplaceable. The work at first seems firmly rooted in tradition; the framing derives directly from previous treatments of the subject by Andrea del Castagno and Ghirlandajo. Where they focused on the moment when Christ confronted Judas, Leonardo chose to treat the instant when He revealed the presence of a traitor in the midst of the faithful. Leonardo thus transfixed the immediate response as with a candid lens; all the apostles save one act out their unique forms of the question, "Is it I, Lord?" In this way he reveals their responses both as individuals and as members of a communion. To get the expressions he wanted, he walked the streets for hours, sketching memorable faces on his portable pad, then fitting expression to individual character and working at the combinations until he got the exact effect he wanted. The unveiling of this fresco must have been explosive, for the moment catches the apostles' regrouping after the shock wave has passed. Few spectators would have noted that Leonardo had here also transcended the laws of Albertian perspective.

In 1500, Leonardo left Milan. Thereafter, except for a return lasting from 1508 to 1513, he was a transient. At first this did not keep him from painting. In Florence in 1501, he displayed a preliminary drawing for a *Virgin and Child with Saint Anne and the Infant Saint John*, though he did not complete the painting. The cartoon itself is marvelous in the integrity of the grouping, the revelation of movement in a fixed moment, and the combination of the casual with the intense. An equally celebrated and similar contemporary cartoon for the painting of *Virgin and Child with Saint Anne* (1508-1513) reveals how much has been lost, for this work again shows Leonardo's carrying his ideas one step further. In this painting, he places his subjects against a barren and forbidding backdrop and concentrates on the physical and theological fecundity of the Virgin, who is shown rocking in the lap of her mother while trying to contain her Child, who is evading her to clasp the lamb—the emblem of his sacrifice. Their expressions are joyful, serene, and supernally oblivious to the implications: Leonardo presents a quiet portrait of a family doomed to be ripped asunder to bring life to the world.

This painting, along with a late *Saint John the Baptist*, was among the three works taken by Leonardo when he moved to France in 1515. The third was the *Mona Lisa* (1503), easily the most celebrated and most identifiable painting in the world as well as one of the most controversial. Historians cannot even agree on the subject of the work, so that its proper title is still questioned; critics argue about whether the painting was finished, about the meaning of the famous smile, and about the significance of the background. Yet several points are indisputable. One is that Leonardo created a pose that would dominate portrait painting for the next three centuries. Another is that he made the depiction of arms and hands an indispensable element in the disclosure of character. A third is that the effect of the painting has much to do with the contrast between the savage, uninhabitable background of crag and moor and the ineffable tranquillity of the woman's face. This woman is ascendant over the barren land. That apparently meant everything to the artist as he aged.

For the last ten years of his life Leonardo did little painting, though he was much sought after; instead, he occupied himself with problems in mathematics, botany, optics, anatomy, and mechanics. He left unfinished his last commission, a battle piece for the Palazzo Vecchio in Florence, in which he was in direct competition with Michelangelo. At sixty-three, out of touch with the monumental achievements of his successors Michelangelo and Raphael, he accepted an appointment with the King of France to settle at the château of Cloux, near Amboise, where his only duty was to converse with the king. There he died, still pursuing his research, on May 2, 1519.

Summary

Leonardo da Vinci's achievement was nothing less than the foundation of the High Renaissance in painting, drawing, sculpture, and architecture, in theory or practice or both. His equally significant accomplishments in establishing the groundwork for the scientific study of botany, anatomy, physiology, and medicine fall short only because he did not publish his theories and observations and because his secretive manner of recording kept them from discovery until long after most of them had been superseded. His career presents a unique paradox. He is unique in having accomplished so much during his lifetime—he seems to be a compendium of several men, all of them geniuses. Yet he is also unique in having left so little behind and in having disguised or obscured much of that; some of his legacy was still being rediscovered in the middle of the twentieth century, and much of it will never be restored.

Leonardo's discoveries ranged across the boundaries of art and science, because for him there were no boundaries to the inquiring intellect. The key to opening up these realms of inquiry was the eye, for Leonardo the principal instrument of observation, with which discovery began. In both art and science, Leonardo held that observation had to take precedence over both established authority and established method. What was true to the eye was the supreme truth; the eye alone opened the window to the intellect and to the soul.

Bibliography

Clark, Kenneth. *Leonardo da Vinci: An Account of His Development as an Artist.* Rev. ed. Baltimore: Penguin Books, 1967. One of the best overall treatments of the technical and compositional qualities of Leonardo's work. Contains excellent plates and good illustrations. Makes fine connections between Leonardo's innovations in optics and anatomy and their effects on his painting techniques.

Goldscheider, Ludwig. *Leonardo da Vinci.* 6th ed. London: Phaidon Press, 1959. Presents a thorough survey of the life and accomplishments of Leonardo, with outstanding plates. Also presents a clear account of Leonardo's relations with other artists and with his patrons.

Hartt, Frederick. *History of Italian Renaissance Art: Painting, Sculpture, Architecture.* 3d ed. New York: Harry N. Abrams, 1987. Certainly the best-written overall account of its subject, with clear technical exposition, sumptuous illustration, and finely tuned tracing of the cultural complex. Written by an expert in the iconography of the period.

Heydenreich, Ludwig H. *Leonardo da Vinci.* 2 vols. New York: Macmillan, 1954. This standard scholarly biography abounds in illuminating detail about Leonardo's life, accomplishments, and environment.

Kemp, Martin. *Leonardo da Vinci: The Marvelous Works of Nature and of Man.* Cambridge, Mass.: Harvard University Press, 1981. Kemp concentrates on the revelations in the published notebooks and in other writings of Leonardo, reproducing the illustrations brilliantly and bringing them to bear on Leonardo's paintings. Kemp also pieces together Leonardo's detached observations into a coherent philosophical system, focusing on the priority of the eye.

Leonardo da Vinci. *Selections from the Notebooks of Leonardo da Vinci.* Edited by Irma Richter. London: Oxford University Press, 1952. The best succinct introduction to the wealth of material contained in Leonardo's notebooks, deciphered and fully published only in the twentieth century. Richter selects the material intelligently and provides the right amount of explanation.

Payne, Robert. *Leonardo.* Garden City, N.Y.: Doubleday, 1978. Payne provides an extremely readable and nicely detailed discussion of Leonardo's life and work, avoiding technical jargon and guiding clearly through obscure and confusing material. Some of his judgments are idiosyncratic, but he defends them bravely.

Pedretti, Carlo. *Leonardo: A Study in Chronology and Style.* London: Thames and Hudson, 1973. The most accessible book of the many on Leonardo by the foremost modern authority. Pedretti is full of insights and useful knowledge, particularly on the relation between the artist's writings and his work.

Wasserman, Jack. *Leonardo da Vinci.* New York: Harry N. Abrams, 1975. A solid art historian's approach to the life, reflections, and art of Leonardo, this book is more readable than most and provides solid background material as well as illuminating discussion of the paintings. Particularly good on the relationship between written material and art.

James Livingston

LEOPOLD I

Born: June 9, 1640; Vienna, Austria
Died: May 5, 1705; Vienna, Austria
Area of Achievement: Monarchy
Contribution: Leopold I presided over the revival of imperial and Habsburg influence after the defeats of the Thirty Years' War. He consolidated imperial authority in Germany, recovered Hungary from the Turks, and resisted the efforts of Louis XIV of France to achieve European hegemony.

Early Life

Born during the last years of the Thirty Years' War as a younger son of Emperor Ferdinand III and Maria Anna of Spain, the Archduke Leopold Ignatius was originally intended for a career in the Church. The education that Leopold received from the Jesuits at the Austrian and Spanish courts, intended to prepare him for the ecclesiastical career for which he was temperamentally so well suited, remained one of the most formative influences on his subsequent development.

This formation was a blend of the traditions of the house of Habsburg with the militant and authoritarian Counter-Reformation. The Austrian monarchy, more than any other European power, was the creation of its ruling dynasty, often the sole force holding together its disparate provinces. The imperial crown was seen as the patron and defender of the Church, continuing the traditions of the Crusades and the Spanish Reconquista, exemplified in Leopold's reign by the wars against the Turks. The Counter-Reformation, embodied in the Jesuits, represented an unbending aversion to all that was contained in the Protestant movement, exemplified in the harsh treatment of the Protestant inhabitants of Hungary and in Leopold's reluctance, despite pressing reasons of state, to ally with William of Orange.

With a German Habsburg father and a Spanish Habsburg mother, Leopold possessed all the family physical traits in an extreme form: the long, narrow face, the large and somewhat tired looking eyes, the slightly hooked nose, and above all the famous "Habsburg lip"—a protruding lower lip with a long, pointed chin. Quiet, withdrawn, and lacking self-confidence, Leopold was at ease only in the family circle. Despite his unprepossessing appearance and manner, however, Leopold was neither stupid nor devoid of personal resources, sharing with most members of his dynasty a great love of the arts, especially music, and possessing a high sense of duty and a tenacity of purpose which would characterize his policies.

With the death of his elder brother in 1654, this fourteen-year-old prince became the heir to one of the major thrones of Europe. He succeeded his father in the Habsburg lands in 1657 and was elected as Holy Roman Emperor of the German nation, despite French opposition, on July 18, 1658.

Life's Work

The patrimony that Leopold I inherited, consisting of the Austrian lands, the lands of the Bohemian crown, and the fragments of the Kingdom of Hungary independent of the Turks, each with its own character and institutions, was exhausted from the destructive warfare of the earlier seventeenth century. The administration, defense, and augmentation of this patrimony would be Leopold's life's work.

Located in Central Europe, with few natural boundaries, the Habsburg monarchy was vulnerable to enemies from all directions. During the first portion of the seventeenth century, the Habsburg emperors had attempted to strengthen the imperial power assisted by their Spanish cousins and the Jesuits but had been frustrated by the victorious forces of international Protestantism personified in King Gustavus II Adolphus of Sweden, assisted by the revived Bourbon monarchy in France.

Because the greatness of France under Louis XIV rested on her alliance with the Protestant powers to defeat the Habsburgs of Spain and the empire in the Thirty Years' War, Leopold identified the interests of Catholicism and of his imperial office with dynastic interests. At Leopold's accession, his greatest danger still appeared to come from the Protestant challenge, as King Charles X of Sweden threatened not only to seize control of Poland but also, in alliance with Prince George of Transylvania, to partition the Habsburg possessions, taking Bohemia for himself and placing George on the Hungarian throne. Immediately after his imperial coronation, Leopold sent an army under his leading military officer, Raimundo Montecuccoli, to bring the Swedish threat under control. By the time of the Peace of Oliva in 1660, Austria had successfully asserted her integrity and her leading role in Central Europe, saving not only Bohemia but also Poland. This success, however, was more than offset by the rise of a more dangerous power to the East in the revived Turkish Empire.

As the reinvigorated Turkish forces drove toward Vienna in the year 1664, the Ottoman power posed a threat not to Leopold alone. Crete, Poland, and Transylvania were similarly threatened by the renewal of the age-old struggle between Islam and Christendom. Consequently, Leopold's appeal for help received a widespread response, culminating in Montecuccoli's victory at Szentgotthárd on August 1. Leopold failed to follow up this victory with vigorous action. French successes in Lorraine and constant anxiety about the Spanish succession diverted his attention to the West. Hence, in the Treaty of Vasvár, Leopold obtained only a twenty-year truce, leaving important Hungarian strongpoints in Turkish hands.

Leopold's failure to profit from the victory of Szentgotthárd was a result of his involvement in dynastic considerations and the divided counsel received from his advisers. During the period of the 1660's and 1670's, the Habsburg dynasty was in danger of extinction. This is well known as it applies to the Spanish branch of the family, but it is often forgotten that between 1649 and 1678, no healthy male children were born to the Austrian Habsburgs, so that Leopold was constantly faced with the prospect of being the last of his line. Hence, dynastic considerations, meaning coordination with the court of Madrid, often took precedence with Leopold over the interests of his own lands. Obsessed with these concerns but lacking self-confidence, Leopold relied heavily on the advice of his Privy Council. That body was divided between a Spanish, or western faction, which was primarily concerned with keeping the goodwill of Spain while checking the expansion of France, and an eastern faction, which saw the greatest threat to the monarchy in the revived Turkish danger and the greatest opportunities in the recovery of Hungary. With a divided council, Leopold pursued his own overriding interest, turning his attention away from Hungary as soon as the immediate danger was passed and concentrating on the French menace.

This neglect of Hungarian affairs was greatly resented by the Magyars, leading to a conspiracy led by Peter Zrínyi and others, encouraged by France. The conspirators bungled their attempts and did not obtain the expected assistance from either France or the Turks. By 1671, the leaders were executed, and royal Hungary lay prostrate at the emperor's feet. The Privy Council proposed the complete centralization of authority in Vienna, as had been done with Bohemia after the victory at White Mountain in 1620, while utilizing the opportunity to re-Catholicize the realm completely. Although Leopold regarded the Hungarians as a burden rather than an asset and, like most statesmen of the age, looked upon religious dissent as actual or potential treason in league with foreign powers, he was not prepared to accept the sweeping proposals of his advisers. He rejected complete abolition of Hungarian autonomy as contrary to his coronation oath as Hungarian king. His intolerance is seen in the harsh measures taken against Hungarian Protestants, but his humanity appears in his commutation to fines and imprisonment of the many death sentences imposed by the courts. These measures left Hungary seething with discontent, so that Leopold was never able to concentrate fully on his goals to the West.

Two factors led to a revival of imperial prestige during the middle years of Leopold's reign. In the West, the aggressive policies of Louis XIV, exemplified in the capture of Strasbourg in 1681, began to win for Leopold the position of champion of German rights, culminating in the outbreak of the War of the League of Augsburg in 1689, in which Leopold figured as the leader of all Germany, Catholic and Protestant, against the ambitions of France. In the East, the equally aggressive ambitions of the Turks under the Grand Vizier Kara Mustapha Paşa resulted in the violation of the truce between the two empires and the Siege of Vienna in 1683. Once again, Leopold stood forth as the champion of Christendom. Europe held its breath while the western forces under the emperor's brother-in-law, Charles of Lorraine, and the Polish king, John III Sobieski, assembled for the relief of the beleaguered Austrian capital. The great victory at Kahlenberg in September, 1683, was the beginning of the recovery of Hungary for the West.

Although the campaign in the east would eventually result in the defeat of the Hungarian Protestants, who had joined with the Turks, and Prince Eugene's splended victory at Santa in 1697, resulting in the recovery of Hungary by the Treaty of Carlowitz in 1699, it also tied down a large portion of the resources at Leopold's disposal for sixteen years, preventing him from vigorously prosecuting the war with France and leaving him exhausted when the question of the Spanish succession came to a head at the turn of the century. Moreover, Leopold was uneasy in his conscience about his alliance with William of Orange, who had overthrown the Catholic James II of England. That unease appeared justified when his English and Dutch allies signed treaties with Louis XIV, partitioning the Spanish Empire.

Leopold believed that the Habsburg dynasty had the best claim to the Spanish throne, grooming his younger son Charles for that dignity, thus exhibiting a grasp of the European balance of power and of the shift of strength from Spain to Austria within the dynasty. When Charles II of Spain died in November, 1700, Leopold stood alone against the Bourbon hegemony represented by the succession of Philip of Anjou. Before Leopold's death a few years later, however, his brilliant general Prince Eugene had presented him with impressive victories in Italy and Bavaria, and the empire, the Dutch, and the English were once again allies of the house of Habsburg.

Internally, under constant pressure of war in East and West, the army developed into a powerful force for unity, but those same pressures prevented the formation of other organs of administration for the entire monarchy. Nevertheless, through his administrative reforms and support of mercantilist policies, Leopold left the Habsburg lands in significantly better condition than he found them in 1657 and prepared the way for the role Austria would play as the leading Central European power in the eighteenth century.

Leopold continued the long Habsburg tradition of patronage of the arts, especially of music, in which field he had the strongest personal interest, leaving behind an impressive corpus of his own compositions. After the Siege of Vienna, Leopold's patronage began the creation of the Baroque Vienna that would be the cultural focus of Central Europe for two centuries.

Summary

Leopold I reigned during a critical period for the Habsburg monarchy and for Central Europe. He found that power weakened and threatened with dissolution by its defeats in the Thirty Years' War, the ambitions of its neighbors, and the revived strength of the Ottoman Empire. A man without genius, but with integrity, a highly developed sense of responsibility, and tenacity, Leopold provided sound foundations for both the political and cultural development of his state in the next century, resisting without overcoming centrifugal forces while making Austria into an essential element in the continental balance of power. Faced with dangers to the East and West, he consistently preferred to meet the French challenge, believing that Providence would guarantee his success as the defender of Christendom against the Turks. Nevertheless, he failed to recover Alsace from France or to preserve the Spanish throne in the Habsburg dynasty. In the East, he recovered Hungary, confirmed its association with the dynasty, and presided over the beginnings of the eclipse of the Ottoman Empire as a major world power. Leopold is more significant for the forces that he embodied than for his personal contributions to their success or failure.

Bibliography
Barker, Thomas M. *Double Eagle and Crescent: Vienna's Second Turkish Siege and Its Historical Setting.* Albany: State University of New York Press, 1967. A detailed account of the Siege of Vienna in 1683, well written and presenting an account of not only the military but also the diplomatic and political aspects of the siege.
Coxe, William. *History of the House of Austria, from the Foundation of the Monarchy by Rhodolph of Hapsburgh, to the Death of Leopold the Second, 1218 to 1792.* London: T. Cadell & W. Davies, 1807. Despite its age, this standard work contains significant value for those interested in Austrian history. Propounds both thought-provoking analyses and interesting detail of court and personal life.
Evans, R. J. W. *The Making of the Habsburg Monarchy, 1500-1700.* New York: Oxford University Press, 1979. A detailed study, drawing on many sources unavailable in English for the formative forces underlying the Habsburg monarchy. Especially good on the influence of the Counter-Reformation.
McGuigan, Dorothy Gies. *The Habsburgs.* Garden City, N.Y.: Doubleday, 1966. A more popular work, containing excellent character sketches of the emperor and his family.
Spielman, John P. *Leopold I of Austria.* New Brunswick, N.J.: Rutgers University Press, 1977. The only full-length biography of the emperor in English, giving a balanced but generally favorable account of Leopold and the people around him.
Tapie, Victor-Louis. *The Rise and Fall of the Habsburg Monarchy.* New York: Praeger, 1971. This general history of the monarchy has good sections on the period of Leopold's reign, including cultural as well as political history.
Wandruszka, Adam. *The House of Habsburg.* Garden City, N.Y.: Doubleday, 1964. An excellent overview of the role of the Habsburg dynasty in

European affairs, containing good character sketches of the members. Particularly helpful on the shift of power from Madrid to Vienna during the reign of Leopold.

William C. Schrader

MIKHAIL LERMONTOV

Born: October 15, 1814; Moscow, Russia
Died: July 27, 1841; Pyatigorsk, Russia
Area of Achievement: Literature
Contribution: Lermontov left an impressive legacy as a poet during the Russian Romantic period, writing both lyric and narrative verse of lasting significance. He was also a dramatist and a novelist whose major work, *A Hero of Our Time*, presaged the great realistic pyschological novels of Leo Tolstoy and Fyodor Dostoevski.

Early Life

Mikhail Yuryevich Lermontov's father was a poor army officer, the descendant of a Scottish mercenary who had come to Russia in the early seventeenth century. He claimed relation to the twelfth century Scottish bard known as Thomas the Rhymer. A major success in his life was his marriage to seventeen-year-old Marya Arsenieva, the only daughter of the widowed Elizaveta Arsenieva, a member of the rich and powerful Stolypin family and the owner of a large estate, Tarkhany, in central Russia.

The death of Marya Lermontova in 1817, when the future poet was only three years of age, caused a one-sided power struggle for his custody between his grandmother and his father. Elizaveta Arsenieva desperately wanted to keep her young grandson in her household. She threatened to disinherit the child should he be removed from her and promised his disfavored father both money and the forgiveness of a previous debt if he would leave young Mikhail with her. Yury Lermontov therefore surrendered his son's custody and had only sporadic or indirect contact with him thereafter.

Lermontov's grandmother showered attention on the precocious boy. She hired foreign tutors, who taught him French and gave him the rudiments of Greek and Latin. He was given music lessons so that he was later able to compose tunes to accompany his own lyrics and was able to impress his contemporaries with his ability on the piano and on the violin. He was encouraged to draw and to paint, taking lessons from the artists A. S. Solonitsky and P. E. Zabolotsky, and his talent was so developed that his graphic oeuvre, consisting of more than four hundred oil paintings, aquarelles, sketches, and caricatures, is roundly praised by modern critics. It was Lermontov's early love of poetry, however, that was most thoroughly indulged. Having read Vasily Zhukovsky's translations of George Gordon, Lord Byron's verse, he desired to learn English so that he could read Byron's work in the original. Thus, when Lermontov was in his teens, a special tutor was engaged to impart this knowledge to him.

In addition to a remarkable home education, young Mikhail Lermontov received the benefit of three exciting journeys, made at ages three, five, and ten, to the Caucasus Mountains in the extreme south of Russia. The reasons for these journeys were both to avoid imminent visits at the Tarkhany estate by his father and to bolster his precarious health. Rheumatic fever and measles left him very frail, and he developed a stoop-shouldered posture and sickly pallor, which later caused him considerable ridicule from his schoolmates, who nicknamed him "the frog."

The spectacular scenery and the unsubjugated tribes of the Caucasus Mountains made a lasting impression on Lermontov, an impression of adventure and romance in an exotic locale which found its way into many of his later works, both poetry and prose. He gained there an appreciation for freedom as an ideal apart from that of civilization, which he came to regard as corrupt.

In 1827, Arsenieva moved with Mikhail to Moscow. The next year, she enrolled him in an elite preparatory school attached to Moscow State University, the Nobles' Pensionate, which employed a number of prominent university professors as faculty. There, Lermontov read and discussed the works of such contemporary Russian poets as Zhukovsky, Konstantin Batyushkov, and especially Alexander Pushkin, whose work Lermontov zealously admired. During this period, Lermontov began his own literary activity, having one of his poems accepted for publication by the journal *Atheneum* in 1830. Thereafter, he wrote almost continually, entering into his notebooks epigrams, commentary, drafts of a drama, and a number of lyrics on nature, death, and love.

Life's Work

In 1830, Lermontov enrolled in Moscow University's department of ethics and politics, from which he soon transferred to the department of literature. His classmates in the university included a constellation of later luminaries of Russian social and political dissidence: Vissarion Belinsky, the social literary critic; Aleksandr Herzen, the seminal socialist thinker and editor of radical émigré publications; Nikolai Stankevich, the social philosopher and organizer of radical salons; and Ivan Goncharov, the prominent novelist. Lermontov, however, held himself aloof from these future stars, regarding himself as superior not only to them but to the faculty as well. He took part in one major scandal, in which an unpopular professor was driven out of the classroom, and he quarreled with one of his examination committees severely enough that, in 1832, he left the university, intending to move to the capital and to enroll at St. Petersburg University. The paperwork required by such a transfer was more than Lermontov's patience could endure, however, and he instead enlisted in the army—a move unpleasantly surprising to his grandmother, who used her influence to have him enrolled in the School of Ensigns of the Guards and Cavalry Cadets.

The literary production of Lermontov's university years is highlighted by the remarkable poem "Angel," which evokes the blissful prenatal memories of an earthbound soul. Prominent also is "Parus" ("The Sail"), in which Lermontov gives a symbolic portrait of a revolutionary. It is at this time too that Lermontov began his ten years of work on the romantic narrative poem "Demon," which remained unpublished in his lifetime as the result of censorship. A fallen angel's love for a mortal woman is related amid sparkling descriptions of Caucasian natural splendor. The university years also produced a cycle of poems connected with Lermontov's unreturned love for a young woman.

In the army, Lermontov tried to find acceptance among his fellow cadets by posturing as a daredevil and a womanizer. The highly affected social life of St. Petersburg increased his cynicism and his bitterness at his intellectual estrangement from his compatriots. He did pen some ribald songs and some bawdy verse but for the most part turned his attention to drama and prose. The best of his five plays, *Maskarad* (1842; *Masquerade*, 1973), reflects, through his moody villain Arbenin, his disillusionment with St. Petersburg society. Influenced by the popular prose of Sir Walter Scott, he explored the genre of historical novel by beginning the unfinished *Vadim* (1832-1834; English translation, 1982), a contorted tale of unrequited love intertwined with the historical events of Russia's Pugachov Rebellion of 1773-1774. This work signaled the beginnings of Lermontov's work in prose, which continued through the unfinished society novel *Knyaginya Ligovskaya* (1836; *Princess Ligovskaya*, 1965) to the maturity of his masterpiece, *Geroy nashego vremeni* (1840; *A Hero of Our Time*, 1854). Before he was commissioned an officer in Czar Nicholas I's Life Guard Hussars in 1834, Lermontov began a lifelong attachment to Varvara Lophukhina, the attractive daughter of family friends. Although Lermontov never married, his attachment to Lophukhina survived even her marriage to a man much her senior, of whom Lermontov disapproved. The relationship with her caused him considerable despair, which infused his verse thereafter with a note of brooding melancholy over the impossibility of love and happiness.

Lermontov's poetic response to the death by duel of Pushkin in 1837 earned for him instant fame. His poem "Smert poeta" ("The Death of a Poet") was circulated throughout the St. Petersburg literary salons. It blamed the capital society and its authorities for inciting Pushkin to the duel which caused his death. Largely as a result of this poem, Lermontov was arrested, tried, and sentenced to serve among the frontline troops fighting wild tribesmen in the Caucasus. The intercession of his grandmother and the publication of his patriotic poem about the victory over Napoleon I at Borodino softened the czar's attitude, however, and he was allowed to return to the capital.

The years 1838-1841 found Lermontov at the height of his popularity. His verse frequently appeared in the leading literary journals. It was during this

time that his poems "Kazachia kolybelnaia pesnia" ("Cossack Lullaby")
and "Vykhozhu odin ya na dorogu . . ." ("I Walk Out Alone onto the
Road . . .") were published, providing the lyrics to well-known Russian
songs. His Byronesque narrative poem "Mtsyri" ("The Novice") extolls the
freedom experienced just before death by a native child pledged as a novice
monk by his captors.

In 1840, *A Hero of Our Time* was published in book form. The protagonist, Pechorin, epitomizes the emotional isolation and intellectual frustration
of his generation. Pechorin is the archetypical superfluous man later to be
found in many Russian literary portrayals. His intellect tells him that he
brings others only hardship and tragedy, but he lacks the moral certitude to
change his ways. There is much autobiography in Lermontov's depiction of
Pechorin, and it is a depiction in which every succeeding generation has
found relevance.

A duel with the son of the French ambassador, in which only Lermontov
was lightly wounded, caused him to be reassigned by the czar to front-line
duty in the Caucasus. Lermontov so distinguished himself in battle that he
was recommended for citation. He wrote a poem about the Battle of Valerik.
On a self-granted furlough to the spa city of Pyatigorsk, he tormented a
former cadet schoolmate, Nikolai Martynov, who challenged him to a duel.
Outside the city, at the foot of Mount Mashuk, the duel took place. Martynov shot first, killing Lermontov outright. Thus, before the age of twenty-
seven, Lermontov had inherited both Pushkin's literary fame and his personal fate.

Summary

Western evaluations of Mikhail Lermontov's impact on world literature
are often confined to discussing the influence of *A Hero of Our Time* on
subsequent novels by Ivan Turgenev, Dostoevski, and Tolstoy, and on the
stories of Anton Chekhov and Maxim Gorky, authors whose own influence is
better established and more familiar. This discussion focuses on the addition
of psychological examination, an inner dialogue of thought, to the realistic
portrayal of the characters' actions. Questions of good and evil are left
unresolved, at least in surface interpretations, much as Lermontov left unresolved in the minds of his readers the question of whether his main protagonist, Pechorin, is to be positively or negatively regarded, that is, is he
seriously, or only ironically, to be considered a hero of our time? In literature
of the previous Romantic period, good characters and evil characters were
clearly delineated. In this, Lermontov's work is transitional and therefore
important.

Russian evaluators of Lermontov's significance invariably foreground his
contributions as a poet. His verse is well woven into the fabric of Russian
society. Mothers sing his lullaby to their children. Children sing the words of

his patriotic "Borodino" to Modest Mussorgsky's music in school. In a nation of poetry lovers, Lermontov's popularity is unmatched by any poet except Pushkin. Subsequent poets, such as Boris Pasternak, have dedicated works to Lermontov as if he were still alive. The permanence of his poetic legacy stems from the musicality of his verse—the sound of which so pleases the ear that memorization is effortless—and its direct appeal to primary emotions, feelings of love, freedom, and patriotism.

In sum, Lermontov was a person with severe problems relating to others. Early bereft of his parents, spoiled by his guardian, failed in academic credentials, restricted and hampered by authorities, he died before he was truly mature. Yet his desire to find a soul mate, a confidante, became literary in method and, in the power and excellence of his still-developing talent, resulted in lasting achievement.

Bibliography

Eikhenbaum, Boris M. *Lermontov.* Translated by Ray Parrot and Harry Weber. Ann Arbor, Mich.: Ardis, 1981. A seminal study by the renowned Soviet scholar on Lermontov's poetic method, focusing on the literary precedents of his figures of speech. Includes a multitude of citations of poetry from Lermontov's Russian predecessors and contemporaries. A last chapter is included which examines Lermontov's prose in the light of the development of Russian as a literary language.

Kelly, Laurence. *Lermontov: Tragedy in the Caucasus.* New York: George Braziller, 1977. A biography of Lermontov which delves thoroughly into the influence on Lermontov's work of his time spent in the Caucasus Mountains. Both the childhood trips and the adult military sojourns are well treated. Appendices include treatments of the relationship of Byron and Lermontov, an essay on Lermontov's poetry, and "The Official Report on the Death of Lieutenant Lermontov."

L'Ami, C. E., and Alexander Welikotny. *Michael Lermontov: Biography and Translation.* Winnipeg, Canada: University of Manitoba Press, 1967. An older-style biography, replete with the reminiscences of Lermontov's contemporaries as to his character. A general outline of Russian history forms a significant part of this treatment. The second part of the book contains more than one hundred of Lermontov's poems in rhymed English translation as well as a small sample of prose.

Lavrin, Janko. *Lermontov.* London: Bowes and Bowes, 1959. The first widely available biographical treatment of Lermontov in English, introducing the reader not only to the personage of Lermontov but also to Russian history and Russian society of the early nineteenth century. Lermontov is seen as a key link in the historical development of Russian literature between the imitative eighteenth century and the world-leading literature of Russia's nineteenth century. Alexander Pushkin's influence is thoroughly treated.

Lermontov, Mikhail. *Major Poetical Works*. Translated with a biographical sketch, commentary, and an introduction by Anatoly Liberman. Minneapolis: University of Minnesota Press, 1983. A thorough detailing of Lermontov's life which takes good advantage of the previous works together with translations of more than one hundred of Lermontov's poems, not all of which have appeared in English previously. The translations have won much professional praise for their surprising poeticality which does not compromise accuracy. The text includes more than fifty illustrations and is wonderfully annotated and indexed.

Mersereau, John, Jr. *Mikhail Lermontov*. Carbondale: Southern Illinois University Press, 1962. A very concise biography which manages to include much valuable detail. The focus is distinctly on Lermontov's development of a prose style, with more than half of the book devoted to an examination of *A Hero of Our Time*.

Lee B. Croft

PIERRE LESCOT

Born: 1510?; Paris, France
Died: September 10, 1578; Paris, France
Areas of Achievement: Architecture and art
Contribution: Lescot was long regarded as the first of France's great architects, chiefly because of his redesign and reconstruction of the original Louvre. Although modern scholarship modifies this estimate, he remains ranked among the premier French architects and designers of the sixteenth century.

Early Life
Biographical material on Pierre Lescot's early life is limited and often unverifiable. He was probably born in Paris in 1510 into a well-positioned seigneurial family. His father, for whom he was named, was Francis I's crown attorney, an attorney for one of the courts of relief, or assistance, as well as the leader of the Parisian merchant guilds. The elder Lescot held estates at Lissy near Brie, and among others, at Clagny close to the royal residences at Versailles. Originally, the Lescots came to France from Italy, where their connections with the Alessi family affected the younger Lescot's later career.

While a young man, Lescot inherited the paternal estate at Clagny. Favored by Francis and Henry II, Lescot served as their principal chaplain, as their honorary church canon, as an associate abbey at Clermont near Laval, and as a canon at Nôtre Dame in Paris. Advantaged by such royal associations and family position, the younger Lescot began displaying talents as a painter, while at the same time studying mathematics and architecture. Very likely while young, Lescot journeyed to Italy, where, under the auspices of old family friends, he absorbed decorative and architectural concepts later manifested in his work. Unquestionably, he studied Italian architectural writings and examined many of France's Roman ruins many years prior to his official visit to Rome in 1556.

Under absolutist monarchs who were forging France into Europe's first nation-state, Paris during Lescot's lifetime was also changing. Whether engaged in the monarchs' hodgepodge administrative structures or in the small manufactures producing luxuries for crown and court, most of the 250,000 inhabitants of Paris clustered around the Île de la Cité, the Seine River island which from time immemorial simultaneously offered the people their best opportunities for defense and the first ford-bridge linking both riverbanks. During Lescot's lifetime, royalty, its retainers, and courtiers began converting the Marais (swamp), the oldest district on the Seine's north bank, into an aristocratic enclave, where services of architects—builders and artists—were ineluctably drawn.

Life's Work

Lescot's architectural work commenced during a period of brilliance in French Renaissance architecture, translating into its own idiom characteristics of Italian styles, while subduing elements of its own Gothic traditions. Among his contemporaries and colleagues were the great French sculptor Jean Goujon and Philibert Delorme, an innovative engineer. Encouraged by relative domestic peace, the Crown, its court, and other aristocrats not only began new constructions but also planned to redesign buildings and residences that formerly functioned as fortified positions. New or remodeled, these structures were intended as the abodes of men enjoying the money and leisure to live more ostentatiously, surrounded by what they conceived to be the ultimate in style.

Francis' own building obsession, which included several châteaus, was epitomized in 1519 by his redesign of Chambord, initially a feudal strongpoint, which, upon completion, reflected Italian symmetries imposed upon a functionally banal fortress. Partly a consequence of French and Italian architects and artists crossing one another's borders more frequently, Chambord, as an exemplar, inspired further imaginative, eclectic, and sophisticated architectural design in France.

Francis then turned his attention to the three-hundred-year-old Louvre in Paris, whose pattern closely conformed to other thirteenth century castles, many then still built of wood. It was replete with a strong tower and a donjon, and was surrounded by sturdy masonry walls.

Because the Louvre's poor drainage and *odeurs* made its precincts unfashionable and its proximity to religious houses and the raucous studentry of the Left Bank undesirable, Francis decided in 1526 on the Louvre's modernization, though aside from removing the donjon, nothing was done until 1546. That year, Lescot was selected to construct a new stucture on the site of the old château's west wing—the Old Louvre—then lying outside the old city walls. Considering the restricted Parisian work space available, Lescot planned for two floors of detached buildings, with a central pavilion and its staircase. Each side was to be flanked by large public reception rooms. Within five years, however, these plans had been revised, providing for a grander gallery (*salle*) and shifting the staircase to the north wing: in all, requiring construction of two new pavilions at each end with a new staircase for one of them. Moreover, the façade was raised one floor so construction of the King's Pavilion to the southwest would not overpower these two new pavilions.

Monarchs, the times, and styles altered events even as Lescot's revisions were under way. Sometime between 1551 and Henry's death in 1559, Lescot was called upon by the Crown to develop more ambitious plans, which he did. His new plans called for building a court enclosed by blocks double the length of his original wing. The Louvre façade was visually unified with pilasters of the then-preferred Corinthian and Composite orders. Pediments over windows were alternated between triangular and rounded ones: a variety demanding attention. Each of his three pavilions divided into separate bays, differing from the wings uniting them. Ground-floor windows were set inside rounded arches; those windows of the second floor featured open pediments; and attic windows were capped by sculpted crossed torches. All three pavilions, devoid of horizontal lines, were designed to accentuate the vertical: Double columns, among other devices, carried eyes upward. Overall, Lescot (with Goujon) successfully blended classical and traditional French architecture into his own style of French classicism.

Lescot's interior work on the new wing was brilliantly enhanced by Goujon's caryatids—ornamentation unknown in France and rare even in Renaissance Italy—and by the four groups of sixteen richly decorated Doric columns separating—yet affording monumentality—to the southern end of the great gallery. Their genius combined, Lescot's and Goujon's interior collaborations were almost inseparable: Both added distinctions to an architectural masterwork.

Although his career was preempted for years by the Louvre, Lescot managed many other commissions. Again in collaboration with Goujon, he built the Hôtel Carnavalet in 1545, filling the space between the Hôtel de Ville and the Bastille, thereby luring more courtiers and aristocrats into the Marais district. His use at Carnavalet of a wide street flanked by stables and a kitchen in lieu of a plain wall shortly became the rage among wealthy Parisians. Lescot worked on these other projects with great craftsmen. When Henry tired of his bedroom ceiling, Lescot and the Italian woodcarver Scribec di Carpi produced a new ceiling that rivaled any other of the period, including the magnificent ceilings for which Venice was famous.

After Henry's death in 1559, Lescot's personal life disappears from the historical record. Francis, who previously extended him his first commissions, enthusiastically supported him, partially repaying him by designating him the canon of Paris' metropolitan church (with its many perquisites) and by making him the Abbey of Clermont and a royal councillor as well. Francis' successors reconfirmed these prerogatives for him, and throughout his career he maintained his Clagny estate. There is no other substantial knowledge of him, except that his death occurred on September 10, 1578, in Paris.

Summary

For some modern architectural historians, Pierre Lescot has been a source of debate: He was basically an amateur architect, and he was not a critical figure in the development of French architecture, particularly the distinctive Gallic version of Renaissance architecture—French classicism. In addition, many of Lescot's plans and constructions were flawed, and some believe that

as a mere overseer he assumed credit for the genius of men such as Jean
Goujon. Whatever modicum of credibility may be accorded these views, in
the light of the overall evidence available, they fail to diminish significantly
his contribution to his singularly imaginative plans and designs combining
Italianate Renaissance elements with traditional French elements that produced a uniquely French architectural style. This was no more pronouncedly
evident than in the original reconstruction of the Louvre and in the designs
and plans that substantially determined the shape of that magnificent structure's future. Moreover, the design and embellishment of this and other of
his original work represents a rare conjunction of architectural, engineering,
and sculpting genius—that is, the collaboration of Lescot, Goujon, and Scribec di Carpi. In addition to all of their other accomplishments, they produced
a nucleus around which, architecturally, one of the world's most visual and
magnificent urban cultural centers would develop to the wonderment of many
subsequent generations.

Bibliography
Blunt, Anthony. *Art and Architecture in France, 1500-1700.* London: Pen-
    guin Books, 1953. Excellently and authoritatively written for laymen by a
    distinguished art critic and historian. Descriptions of Lescot's work on the
    Louvre are clear and detailed. Contains notes for each chapter and many
    illustrations and plates.
Gardner, Helen. *Gardner's Art Through the Ages.* 6th ed. New York: Har-
    court Brace Jovanovich, 1975. Chapter 14 is especially pertinent to the
    work of Lescot and his colleagues. The book is beautifully illustrated in
    both color and black-and-white and includes plates and schematics. The
    text is well written for both novitiates and more sophisticated art lovers.
    Contains a glossary, a bibliography, and an index.
Hamlin, Talbot. *Architecture Through the Ages.* New York: G. P. Putnam's
    Sons, 1940. Chapter 16 bears particularly on the Renaissance in France
    and Italy, and hence on Lescot's work on the Louvre. Older and less
    critical than Blunt's book, it is still accurate and substantial in its major
    features. Contains many fine photographs and schematics and an excel-
    lent, double-columned index.
Janson, H. W. *History of Art: A Survey of the Major Visual Arts from the
    Dawn of History to the Present Day.* Rev. ed. New York: Harry N. Ab-
    rams, 1969. Clearly written, and authoritatively so, this is a large, lav-
    ishly illustrated work with splendid black-and-white and color photographs.
    Part 3 of the book deals specifically with the Renaissance and Chapter 5,
    the subject of which is the Renaissance in the North, has excellent mate-
    rials, including photographs of Lescot's old Louvre.
Ranum, Orest A. *Paris in the Age of Absolutism.* New York: John Wiley &
    Sons, 1968. A brief, scholarly work, but readily understandable by lay-

men, this extended essay is very important to an understanding of the general social, political, and intellectual climate prevalent in Lescot's day. Lescot is mentioned both in connection with the Louvre and other works. Contains prints of local scenes, a fine view of the Louvre front, and portraiture paintings. Includes an excellent select bibliography and an extensive, double-columned index.

Clifton K. Yearley

FERDINAND DE LESSEPS

Born: November 19, 1805; Versailles, France
Died: December 7, 1894; La Chênaie, France
Areas of Achievement: Diplomacy and entrepreneurship
Contribution: Having initiated his career in diplomacy, Lesseps, though never trained as an engineer, is best known for his entrepreneurial abilities that led to the construction of the Suez Canal and the commencement of the transisthmian Panama Canal.

Early Life

Ferdinand-Marie Vicomte de Lesseps was born into a family of diplomats on November 19, 1805, literally within a few meters of the great architectural expression of French monarchism, the Palaces of Versailles, France. For several generations, the men of the family had been distinguished by their cultivation, vigor, belief in progress, extravagant life-styles, and womanizing. Long before Ferdinand's birth, his granduncle, Dominique, had been ennobled for his public services, namely for his extraordinary around-the-world adventures which resulted in his presentation to Louis XVI as a national hero; Ferdinand's grandfather, Martin, had served as a diplomat at the Russian court of Catherine the Great; and his father, Mathieu, a friend of the great statesman Talleyrand, performed with distinction in Franco-Egyptian relations and, while posted to the United States, negotiated France's first commercial treaty with that country. Thus, there was a firm foundation for adventure, valor, and endurance in the family, all of which characterized Ferdinand's life and career.

Ferdinand's mother was the daughter of a prosperous French vintner who had settled in Spain, where she spent her life until her marriage, so that Ferdinand grew up speaking Spanish as well as French. He would later claim that his Spanish temperament led Panama to "seduce" him. Although his family reputedly was wealthy, in fact money was generally scarce. His mother's jewelry was often pawned and his father died bankrupt. Ferdinand himself, while later to marry well and affect the high life, never enjoyed real wealth either.

Against this family background, Lesseps moved naturally into a diplomatic career, and while he had studied some law he was apprenticed, when he was nineteen, to an uncle then serving as France's ambassador to Portugal. Subsequently, he refined his diplomatic apprenticeship, serving with his father until his death in 1832 in Tunis, after which appointments received were his own.

Life's Work

Lesseps' diplomatic career had come naturally, and he enjoyed it, as did his ravishing Parisian wife, Agnes, who not only bore him five sons (two lived to maturity) but also was a marvelous asset to the sociability expected of her diplomat husband. They were indeed a handsome couple, he well formed and dark eyed, with a memorable smile. The first seven years of his official work were spent in Egypt, then, variously, in Rotterdam, the Netherlands, Malaga, Spain, and finally as France's minister to Spain in 1843.

Lesseps' interest in Suez was not born of interests in engineering; he enjoyed no training whatever along that line. Rather, it emerged from his partial adherence to the philosophy of Comte de Saint-Simon, who believed that private property and nationalism ought to be abolished and the world made over by scientists, engineers, industrialists, and artists.

Lesseps had met a coterie of French Saint-Simonian engineers during his duty in Egypt in the 1830's. This group, led by Prosper Enfantin, hoped to abolish war, end poverty, and generally reorder the world by great public improvements—railways, highways, and both a Suez and a Panamanian canal. For four years, perhaps with some financial assistance from Lesseps, Enfantin and his group labored to dig the canal but were ultimately defeated; indeed, their ranks were decimated by cholera. While little had been accomplished, many Europeans continued to hope for a canal.

A career crisis diverted Lesseps once again from Suez. He was dispatched on a diplomatic mission to Italy. Lesseps was reprimanded for exceeding instructions and fired in 1848. By 1850, Napoleon III, by *coup d'état*, had made himself Emperor of the Second Empire, had married one of Lesseps' distant cousins, and, surrounded by Saint-Simonians, had again urged great projects upon France. Meanwhile, political upheaval in Egypt had brought a new viceroy into power, Mohammed Said, whom Lesseps had befriended when Said was a boy. His diplomatic career finished and with Agnes dead the previous year, in 1854 Lesseps left his home at La Chênaie to join his old friend. Said, hopeful of launching his regime with some great enterprise, asked for Lesseps' advice: It was to dig a Suez Canal.

Tirelessly, meticulously watching details, and above all incessantly scurrying about the world raising or borrowing funds (half the money came from Frenchmen, the rest from Said and his successor), he justified a reputation as one of the nineteenth century's greatest entrepreneurs: patient, untiring, an imaginative propagandist, at times deceptive, and very much a shrewd actor-diplomat. On November 17, 1869, amid lavish fanfare, the 160-kilometer, sea-level canal opened. While, at most stages of its construction, Lesseps could have sold his rights and garnered great wealth, he was uninterested in money: The Suez had been dug for the good of humanity.

While being richly honored, lionized, and feted, he married the stunning young daughter of a wealthy friend and instantly started two great projects: founding what became a family of six sons and six daughters and planning a number of grandiose undertakings: a railway linking Paris, Moscow, Bombay, and Peking and the flooding of vast areas of the Sahara, among them. Before the Parisian Geographical Society in 1875, he proposed elaboration of plans for an interoceanic isthmian canal. To that end, he helped form the Société Civile Internationale du Canal Interocéanique de Darien, the so-called Türr Syndicate. Both the syndicate as well as Lesseps' role in it would be, and remain, controversial. The intent of Parisian Geographical Society was a binational effort composed of leading international scientists, ensuring an objective analysis of sites and possible problems; however, the Türr Syndicate agreed to handle everything. It did indeed make several expeditions; by 1882, it had contracted with the Colombian government in detail for a ninety-nine-year lease, financing, land concessions, rights of the syndicate to transfer its holdings to other individuals (or syndicates) but not to foreign countries, and distribution of profits.

Meanwhile, an international congress for the study of the isthmian canal convened in Paris in May, 1879. After much disappointing information, some disinformation, and intelligent conjecture, without consensus, Lesseps, who initially had seemed ineffectual, won his audience by declaring that for all insurmountable obstacles there existed men of genius to master them. Later in the day, another genius, a great engineer and the head of France's famed Corps de Ponts et Chaussees (bridges and highways), the only person present who had experience with construction in tropical America, warned of the deadly menaces of endemic, epidemic disease and of the impossibility of the sea-level canal (one without locks) upon which Lesseps was determined. Lesseps ultimately carried the day. His victory in the congress would shortly cost tens of thousands of lives, the loss of millions by investors, ruin of the syndicate, scandals which historians have not yet entirely unraveled, judicial probes, and eventually the then-greatest real estate transaction in history when the United States bought the remnants of Lesseps' efforts under dubious circumstances.

Yet Lesseps was magnificent in pursuit of his great objective: a Panamanian canal. He bought out the Türr Syndicate; created his own company; mesmerized general publics throughout Europe and the United States; and raised funds from a vast range of sources. He visited the Panama site, declared, with aplomb, that there were no insurmountable difficulties; hired a remarkable team of French engineers, whose general repute had been singular for nearly two centuries; mustered the great excavators necessary to gnaw their way through the terrain; provided the best housing and medical facilities then known for the protection of his aides, engineers, and workers; and launched the great dig in 1881. Before disease and natural obstacles made obvious the impossibility of a sea-level canal, and before Americans undertook construction of a lock canal, Lesseps' crews had excavated nearly a third of the distance between Colon, on the Caribbean, and Panama City, on the Pacific: if not the most difficult portion, a sterling achievement nevertheless. Yet by 1889, Lesseps' losses in life and money were too great. His grand enterprise was failed, bankrupt. Old, under financial pressures, he remained only vaguely aware of the press and judicial trials with which irate investors were crushing members of his family and colleagues, unaware that "Panama" had become a term of national opprobrium. Through his wife's protective care, the great adventurer sat at home in a seaman's peacoat, with his smoking cap and with his knees blanketed, wasting away, oblivious to the storms raging around his devastated enterprise. He died on December 7, 1894, at La Chênaie, and was quietly buried in Paris' Pére Lachaise Cemetery.

Summary

Ferdinand de Lesseps was the complex scion of a distinguished family. A successful diplomat, he was shamelessly duped by the state he served, only to turn about and become the driving force behind two immensely important undertakings: the Suez and the Panama Canals. At one he succeeded, at one he failed. Yet his success at Suez, certainly in global economic terms, far outweighed the financial disaster, and perhaps even the thousands of lives lost in Panama. For all of his deceptions, he was a heroic romantic, an inspired entrepreneur, suffused with the Saint-Simonian urge to remodel the world. In no technical or scientific sense did he qualify as an expert, and in an age in which the engineer and scientist became the forces with which to reckon, he relied upon his own fixations, rhetoric, and manipulations to launch his great enterprises. It had been the wisdom of Lesseps' father that he forget his great Panama scheme and settle for the undying fame earned at Suez. Yet hubris and heroism are usually intertwined. It remains sufficient that his accomplishment, against great odds at Suez, matched his daring but partial failure at Panama—partial because it finally moved the Americans to complete that singularly remarkable construction.

Bibliography

Beatty, Charles. *Ferdinand de Lesseps: A Biographical Study*. New York: Harper & Brothers, 1956. An eminently readable, well-researched biography of genuine quality on one of the more vital personalities of the nineteenth century. Contains a fine bibliography, a chronology, and a very useful double-columned index.

Cameron, Ian. *The Impossible Dream: The Building of the Panama Canal*. New York: William Morrow, 1972. A competent study, which while focused chiefly on the American effort, deals with Lesseps and the initial French enterprise, though it is less generous than other works on the real difficulties and progress made by the French. Contains a select bibliography and an adequate index.

Farnie, D. A. *East and West of Suez: The Suez Canal in History, 1854-1956*.

Oxford, England: Clarendon Press, 1969. A large scholarly study which helps place the importance of Lesseps' work in perspective of the canal's subsequent history. Scholarly and well written, this work has several graphs, statistical tables, maps, a fine, extensive bibliography, and a superb index.

Fitzgerald, Percy. *The Great Canal at Suez*. Reprint. 2 vols. New York: AMS Press, 1978. Delightful reading, lending an ambience to the great event hard to find elsewhere. While documentation is inserted in the text, there are no notes, bibliography, illustrations, or index.

McCullough, David. *The Path Between the Seas: The Creation of the Panama Canal, 1870-1914*. New York: Simon & Schuster, 1977. While detailed treatment of Lesseps occupies only a portion of this marvelous work—winner of many prizes—it is easily the most readable and most thoroughly researched study of the wonder that is the canal. Contains great photographs, an extensive and first-rate bibliography of primary and secondary sources, and a useful index.

Schonfield, Hugh J. *The Suez Canal in Peace and War, 1869-1969*. Rev. ed. Coral Gables, Fla.: University of Miami Press, 1969. A readable, competent, and scholarly study, the first six chapters of which cover Lesseps' planning and work. Contains seven useful appendices. The index is full and useful.

Clifton K. Yearley

GOTTHOLD EPHRAIM LESSING

Born: January 22, 1729; Kamenz, Saxony
Died: February 15, 1781; Brunswick
Areas of Achievement: Literature, theater, drama, and philosophy
Contribution: Lessing contributed to literature through his work in the field
of literary criticism and drama, to philosophy in his efforts to bring the
ideas of the European Enlightenment to Germany, and to theology in his
founding of the philosophy of religion.

Early Life

Born the son of a Protestant minister, Gotthold Ephraim Lessing enrolled
as a student of theology at the University of Leipzig in 1746, but he was
soon attracted by literature and the theater. He wrote his first play, *Der junge
Gelehrte* (the young scholar), a comedy which was performed with great
success by the local company in 1748. Other comedies were to follow, and
soon it became apparent that Lessing had embarked on a literary rather than
a theological career. Lessing's early comedies were comparatively trivial,
following the model advocated by Johann Christoph Gottsched, who dominated literary life in Germany until approximately 1750. Although Lessing
followed Gottsched, he did write two problem plays, which show his departure from the Gottschedian model: *Die Juden* (wr. 1749, pb. 1754; *The Jews*,
1801) and *Die Freigeist* (wr. 1749, pb. 1755; *The Freethinker*, 1838). In the
first comedy, Lessing attacked anti-Semitic prejudices, while in the second,
he neither glorified nor criticized his protagonist but tried to provide his
character with a larger degree of realism. While *The Jews* is a forerunner of
Nathan der Weise (1779; *Nathan the Wise*, 1781) in terms of its topicality,
The Freethinker is an anticipation of contemporary realist comedy, as represented by Lessing's *Minna von Barnhelm: Oder, Das Soldatenglück* (1767;
Minna von Barnhelm: Or, The Soldier's Fortune, 1786).

In 1748, Lessing went to Berlin, where he stayed until 1755. Lessing was
one of the first free-lance writers in German literature, trying to live by the
work of his pen. He failed in the end and had to take a civil service position,
as did the majority of intellectuals in eighteenth century Germany, such as
Johann Wolfgang von Goethe and Friedrich Schiller; Lessing's endeavors,
nevertheless, were an inspiration to subsequent generations of writers. Beginning his career as a journalist, Lessing also published a number of scholarly articles and was active as translator, editor, and literary critic. In 1751-
1752, he briefly attended the University of Wittenberg to obtain a master's
degree but returned to Berlin in November, 1752.

One of the most important events of Lessing's life in Berlin was the
beginning of his lifelong friendship with Moses Mendelssohn. Mendelssohn
had made the transition from the protected existence within the Jewish com-

munity, which had lived in the physical and intellectual isolation of the ghettos since the Middle Ages, to participation in the surrounding German and European life of commerce and intellect. Mendelssohn met with much prejudice, but Lessing accepted him on equal terms. Indeed, Lessing's support of Mendelssohn paved the way for Jewish emancipation in Germany. The Lessing-Mendelssohn friendship was perceived as a symbol of a successful German-Jewish symbiosis. While this symbol was rendered totally invalid by the Holocaust of World War II, it was, nevertheless, true for the eighteenth century. Lessing modeled Nathan the Wise, the noble Jewish protagonist of his last drama, after Mendelssohn.

Lessing's first successful tragedy, *Miss Sara Sampson* (English translation, 1789), was written, performed, and published in 1755. Lessing introduced domestic, or bourgeois, tragedy to the German stage. The introduction of middle-class characters and their family problems into tragedy constituted his break with Gottsched, who had reserved tragedy for affairs of state and the fate of princes. Because of its sentimental appeal and audience identification with the protagonists, the performance was a great success. The middle-class audience saw characters of its class onstage and witnessed their struggle with ethical norms and their ensuing tragic failures.

In 1756, Lessing planned to embark on a three-year grand tour of Europe as traveling companion to a wealthy young man, but they had to abandon their travel plans when the Seven Years' War broke out in Europe. After a short stay in Leipzig, Lessing returned to Berlin in 1758. There, he edited and published, together with Mendelssohn and Christoph Friedrich Nicolai, *Briefe, die neueste Literatur betreffend* (1759-1760; letters on current literature), a journal which employed the fiction of letters, reporting on recent publications to a friend. The criteria developed by Lessing and his friends in their literary criticism provided new standards of excellence for German literature, which was still in its beginnings at this time. One of Lessing's most famous contributions was the seventeenth letter of February, 1759, attacking Gottsched and his hold on German literature and recommending William Shakespeare instead of the French classicists as a model for German drama. Lessing praised Shakespeare as a far greater tragic poet than Pierre Corneille and suggested the Faust theme as appropriate for German drama in the Shakespearean tradition.

Lessing's journeyman years were over when he became a secretary to the Prussian commanding general in Breslau, Silesia, in 1760. This interlude from 1760 to 1765 marks the transition from Lessing's early years to the major works of his life.

Life's Work

Lessing's treatise *Laokoon: Oder, Über die Grenzen der Mahlerei und Poesie* (*Laocoön: An Essay on the Limits of Painting and Poetry*, 1836) of 1766 and his comedy *Minna von Barnhelm* were the major results of the productive pause of his Breslau years. With his treatise *Laocoön*, Lessing settled a problem that had plagued writers for generations, namely, that literature should paint with words. Lessing showed that literature cannot be judged by the same criteria as painting and sculpture; the various arts proceed according to their differing materials and methods, and their subjects are presented according to these differences.

Minna von Barnhelm is the first modern German comedy. Against the backdrop of the Seven Years' War, the comedy confronts the problem of honor and love. Uniting subjects of former enemy states (Prussia and Saxony) in marriage injected an element of a new German national consciousness into the play. The new realism made *Minna von Barnhelm* one of Lessing's masterpieces.

After resigning from his position in Breslau in 1765, Lessing went for a short stay in Berlin. In 1767, he accepted the position as official critic of the German National Theater. As such, he was to write weekly commentaries on the current productions, reviewing the plays and analyzing the performance of the actors. When the project of a national theater at Hamburg was abandoned, Lessing lost his position. His reviews were published in book form under the title *Hamburgische Dramaturgie* (1767-1769; *Hamburg Dramaturgy*, 1889). In these weekly commentaries, Lessing developed his own theory of drama, based on a reinterpretation of Aristotle's poetics. Rejecting French classical drama, Lessing embraced Shakespearean tragedy, which did not follow Aristotle's rules yet always achieved, according to Lessing, the effects of tragedy. Lessing interpreted Aristotle's concept of catharsis as purification of the passions of pity and fear aroused in the spectators. The goal of tragedy was the "transformation of the passions into virtuous faculties."

After the collapse of the national theater enterprise in Hamburg, Lessing accepted a position as court librarian at the ducal library in Wolfenbüttel, where the Dukes of Braunschweig-Lüneburg had assembled one of Europe's largest libraries. During his years in Wolfenbüttel, Lessing was very productive as a scholar, playwright, and theologian. In 1772, he authored the tragedy *Emilia Galotti* (English translation, 1786). Its subject is a middle-class woman named Virginia who lacks the political elements of the Roman Virginia, who was killed by her father to protect her honor from a tyrannical ruler. This sacrifice caused a revolt that abolished the tyranny in Rome around 450 B.C. Lessing may have wanted his audience to draw its own conclusions, but it took more than ten years before the political content of his tragedy was realized.

As a scholar, Lessing made available in print excerpts from a manuscript of his late friend Hermann Samuel Reimarus, who had advocated Deism, a denial of revelation in Christian religion. Such views were so controversial in Germany that Lessing published these excerpts from 1774 to 1778 under the fictitious claim of anonymous manuscripts, *Fragmente . . . aus den Papieren eines Ungenannten* (fragments . . . from the papers of an unknown [author]), found in the Wolfenbüttel library. Even this fiction, however, did not protect Lessing from the attacks by the Protestant clergy. He had to defend himself in numerous pamphlets against his adversaries, but finally the Duke of Braunschweig-Lüneburg imposed strict censorship on Lessing's theological writings. Lessing then turned to the stage, since literature was not subject to censorship, and presented his theological thoughts in the form of a drama, *Nathan the Wise*. The place of action is Jerusalem, where representatives of the three revealed religions, Judaism, Christianity, and Islam, meet during the Crusades to engage in a controversy that may end in tragic death. The main representatives are Sultan Saladin, a historical figure; Nathan the Wise, a noble Jew; and a Christian Knight Templar. The drama poses the question: Which of the three great religions is the true one? Nathan answers by telling the parable of the three rings. The moral of the parable advises the three principal characters of the play that verification of the true religion is as impossible as the identification of the original ring in the parable. The revelations of the major religions must rely on faith and tradition. Their representatives are enjoined to exercise tolerance and to strive for ethical superiority.

While Lessing's treatise *Ernst und Falk: Gespräche für Freimaurer* (*Masonic Dialogues*, 1927) of 1778 is considered a statement of his political philosophy, his tract *Die Erziehung des Menschengeschlechts* (*The Education of the Human Race*, 1858) of 1780 is called his religious testament. Lessing regarded Freemasonry as a means to counterbalance the inevitable evils of the absolutist state. The goal of Freemasonry was to unite men regardless of nationality, religion, and class. Lessing did not advocate revolution but expected changes to bring about a republican form of government. In *The Education of the Human Race*, Lessing presented his religious convictions within the framework of a philosophy of history. He conceived history as the process of the immanent revelation of God, which leads mankind toward independence and self-determination. This work may be considered the seminal document of modern philosophy of religion.

Summary

Gotthold Ephraim Lessing has been declared "the founder of German literature" by H. B. Garland. In 1750, when Lessing began his career, German literature was provincial and practically unknown in Europe. By 1781, when Lessing died, German literature had achieved world acclaim. As a theologian, Lessing defended religion against mysticism as well as rationalism. He became the most prominent spokesman and practitioner of religious and racial tolerance of his age. As the founder of the philosophy of religion, Lessing's ideas contributed toward the concept of the death of God long before Friedrich Nietzsche.

The most characteristic elements of Lessing's personality were his independence of mind, common sense, and integrity. These qualities made him, according to Garland, "the most admirable figure in the history of German thought and literature between [Martin] Luther and Nietzsche."

Bibliography
Allison, Henry E. *Lessing and the Enlightenment: His Philosophy of Religion and Its Relation to Eighteenth-Century Thought.* Ann Arbor: University of Michigan Press, 1966. An intellectual history of the philosophies of John Locke, Pierre Bayle, Baruch Spinoza, and Gottfried Leibniz and their impact on Lessing. Includes notes and index.
Brown, F. Andrew. *Gotthold Ephraim Lessing.* New York: Twayne, 1971. This biography discusses Lessing's works with references to scholarly works. Includes a selected bibliography, with annotations for individual titles, and an index.
Garland, H. B. *Lessing: The Founder of German Literature.* 2d ed. London: Macmillan, 1962. Best summary before Brown's biography appeared. Includes a one-page bibliographical note and an index.
Lamport, F. J. *Lessing and the Drama.* Oxford, England: Clarendon Press, 1981. A study of Lessing's practice and theory of dramatic writing. Includes a bibliography and an index.
Lessing Yearbook. 1-19 (1969-1988). This yearbook, edited by the International Lessing Society, covers current Lessing research.
Metzger, Michael M. *Lessing and the Language of Comedy.* The Hague: Mouton, 1966. A study of Lessing's theory of comedy and discussion of individual works. Includes a bibliography of sources consulted and an index.
Robertson, J. G. *Lessing's Dramatic Theory: Being an Introduction to and Commentary on His "Hamburgische Dramaturgie."* Edited by Edna Purdie. Cambridge: Cambridge University Press, 1939. Exhaustive study of Lessing's predecessors and sources.
Ugrinsky, Alexej, ed. *Lessing and the Enlightenment.* New York: Greenwood Press, 1986. Scholarly essays on current trends in Lessing studies. Numerous bibliographical notes, including an index of names.

Ehrhard Bahr

LI HUNG-CHANG

Born: February 15, 1823; Ho-fei, Anhwei, China
Died: November 7, 1901; Tientsin, China
Areas of Achievement: Government and the military
Contribution: Li played a leading role in the Ch'ing Dynasty, instituting reforms based on a moderate policy of Westernization known as self-strengthening, while in foreign affairs he adopted a firm, but conciliatory attitude.

Early Life

Li Hung-chang came from a wealthy and successful literati family. His father, Li Wen-an, was the holder of the highest imperial degree and had achieved that great status in 1838, along with Tseng Kuo-fan. Li Wen-an sent his son to Peking to study with Tseng; in 1847, Li Hung-chang also acquired the highest degree. He began service in the Hanlin Academy and was being groomed as an important high official. Li's career underwent a dramatic shift in 1853, when he and his father returned home to raise a local militia to protect their region from the Taiping rebels. Through his connections with Tseng, Li entered into the top ranks of the anti-Taiping forces in Anhwei Province. He served with great success in Anhwei and Kiangsi provinces until 1861. During this period, however, he had difficulties with his superiors, including Tseng, all of whom he believed were too cautious in taking the offensive.

Li was an unusually tall man for his time, more than six feet in height. As a young man, he was powerful and courageous; photographs taken in his sixties show a dignified, alert, and energetic man dressed self-assuredly in his official robes and with a small white beard. Li acquired enormous wealth in official service; at his death, his estate was estimated to be worth at least 500,000 Chinese ounces of silver, or several hundred million dollars. He used his wealth to sustain his political and family power; personally, he lived a plain and temperate life. Li had five brothers and six sons who profited from his prominence, both politically and financially, but none was as capable as he.

Life's Work

From 1860 to 1870, Li emerged from the ranks of Tseng's lieutenants to become a key regional official in the Lower Yangtze River valley and commander of his own regional force, the Huai Army (so named after a region within Li's home province, Anhwei, from which the army was raised). When Tseng assumed overall command of the anti-Taiping forces in 1860, he gave Li and the Huai Army a key role. Li joined in the campaign coordinated by Tseng that destroyed the Taipings in 1864. Three years later, still under Tseng's leadership, Li and his Huai Army implemented the offensive that destroyed the Nien rebellions in Shantung.

During the defense of Shanghai in 1862, Li incorporated into his forces the foreign-led and armed "ever victorious army" and became an advocate of Western military technology. Cooperating with Tseng, Li played an important role in the establishment of small-arms factories in 1863-1864, the Kiangnan Shipyard in Shanghai in 1865, and the Nanking Arsenal in 1867. These early self-strengthening projects were arms factories operated as official state enterprises and thus incorporated the nepotism and inefficiency typical of the Ch'ing bureaucracy. All were headed by foreign technical experts, who were to train Chinese technicians while producing modern arms.

The production of these arsenals was available to Li's own regional forces, further increasing his power. Unlike Tseng, Li did not disband his provincial forces following the Taipings' defeat. He and a few others continued to command independent regional armies, a characteristic that gives a special feudal flavor to the late Ch'ing period (1860-1911), in which militarily strong officials such as Li are seen as the precursors of China's twentieth century warlords.

Li's early regional effort at military modernization is important because it was more effective than another program directed from Peking by Prince Kung, a brother of the Hsien-feng emperor. Kung understood the significance of Western military technology after the sacking of the Summer Palace at Peking by an Anglo-French force in 1860, but his modernization efforts encountered delays and setbacks. Then Kung's power declined after the death of his brother, the emperor. The Empress Dowager Tz'u-hsi consolidated her power behind the new child emperor T'ung-chih, and she viewed Kung as a rival. By the 1870's, Kung was no longer a significant figure in Ch'ing politics.

In 1870, when a crisis arose in Tientsin following a riot in which foreigners were killed, the dynasty turned to Tseng. Tseng's health was poor, so he recommended Li, who was then appointed Governor General of Chihli and Commissioner of the Northern Sea. Li quickly settled the Tientsin incident and proceeded during the next quarter century to wield enormous power from his posts at Tientsin, which combined control of military, trade, and diplomatic affairs for the whole of China north of Shanghai. Li also held several key positions in the central bureaucracy at Peking, such as grand secretary (1872-1901), which further magnified his power.

Li maintained his positions through a combination of ability and political guile. He had relied upon Tseng until Tseng's death in 1872. Li cultivated Kung in the 1860's, when the prince's star was ascendant in Peking. In 1875, he helped Tz'u-hsi ensure the enthronement of her infant nephew as the Kuang-hsu emperor, and he became an important supporter of her long domination of the dynasty's fortunes. Li's penchant for modernization put him at odds with more conservative officials, and his willingness to compromise in the face of foreign threats of force brought him into disrepute with hot-blooded young officials who hoped to best the foreigners in war. Thus, while enormously powerful, Li was both dependent upon a short-sighted and narrow empress dowager and open to challenge by other officials on a wide variety of grounds.

From 1870 to 1895, while based at Tientsin, Li followed a three-pronged foreign policy which combined moderate accommodation of foreign demands; construction of new Ch'ing military power, especially a modern navy; and extension of Ch'ing influence through the new diplomatic forms emerging in East Asia. Li assumed that the Ch'ing Empire, like other ruling dynasties before, would continue to dominate all states in the region, including Russia and Japan, as well as the new trading powers such as Great Britain, France, Germany and the United States. Although similar to European conceptions of a diplomacy based on a balance of power, Li's ideas derived from traditional Chinese notions of international politics, in which the foreigners' advantages are turned against themselves and China plays various foreign powers' ambitions against one another.

Li's diplomatic record from 1870 to 1895 is not distinguished by great successes. He was forced to accept extensions of Japanese power in the Ryukyu Islands and Taiwan, Russian power in the far western Ili valley, and the assertion of French power into Vietnam in the period from 1870 to 1885. Li was strongly criticized by more aggressive officials at the time for his role in these affairs as well as by later, nationalistic historians, who often cast Li as a venal traitor. Still, aside from the defeat in the Sino-French War in 1884-1885, a war Li knew the dynasty should have avoided, the Ch'ing did not suffer any major defeats during this period.

The Sino-French War destroyed much of the Ch'ing's military and naval modernization efforts south of Shanghai and had the effect of further increasing the weight of Li's Peiyang (Northern Sea) commissionership. Li undertook modernization programs in his region after 1870 that included the China Merchants' Steam Navigation Company, the K'ai-p'ing Coal Mines, textile factories, a telegraph system from Shanghai to Tientsin, new arsenals, a railroad at Tientsin, and a major naval base on the Liaotung peninsula. Some of these mark a continuation of his pre-1870 pattern of military modernization; others included new forms of transportation and communication with commercial, diplomatic, and military advantages. Li also approved innovative forms of industrial operation involving less state control, a more active role for merchants, and greater opportunities for personal wealth for both the Chinese entrepreneurs involved and the Chinese officials, including himself.

In the late 1880's, Li undertook a diplomatic offensive in response to Japanese interest in extending their power into Korea. The complex machinations among the Koreans, the Ch'ing Dynasty, and the Japanese unraveled in the fall of 1894 and produced the First Sino-Japanese War (1894-1895). In this war, Li's Northern Sea fleet was destroyed, his armies were disgraced, and Japan won a massive victory. Li's career never recovered from these defeats. Still, he was dispatched to Japan to negotiate a settlement and while there was wounded in an assassination attempt. Ashamed, the Japanese agreed to impose slightly less humiliating terms on the Ch'ing.

As the distasteful peace with Japan was being concluded, Li became involved in a remarkable diplomatic maneuver known as the Triple Intervention. Seeking to offset Japanese power in Manchuria, Li concluded an agreement with Russia, Germany, and France to intervene and force Japan to give up the special privileges it had won from China in the First Sino-Japanese War. Japan grudgingly conceded to the international pressure but then was incredulous as the Ch'ing Dynasty proceeded to bestow on Russia special privileges, including railway and naval-base rights, in Manchuria. Li conducted negotiations on some of these matters in Europe and is believed to have accepted bribes from the Russian government for his favor to their interests in Manchuria. This charge of personal venality, combined with his compromise of Ch'ing sovereignty in Manchuria, has sealed the unfavorable judgment of Li held by most historians of modern China. Li's late diplomacy in Manchuria began the rivalry between Japan and Russia over control of this region of China. That rivalry led to the Russo-Japanese War of 1905 and later produced the 1931 Japanese takeover of Manchuria, one of the critical steps on the way to World War II in the Pacific.

Li had no role in either the Reform movement of 1898 or the Boxer Uprising of 1900. He appeared on the dynasty's behalf in 1901 to negotiate the settlement of the Boxer incident. He had little leverage because foreign armies occupied Peking and the empress dowager and emperor were in self-imposed exile away from the court, while Li himself was known to be out of favor and devoid of real power. Li died before agreement was reached on the final terms.

Summary

The failure of Li Hung-chang's efforts and the disgrace of his policies was much more than a great personal defeat. Li represented the best possibility that the Ch'ing Dynasty had to accommodate itself to the rapidly changing world of the post-1850 era. He understood the need for China to adapt itself to an altered political and military situation in Asia and made some of the most enlightened efforts to encourage moderate modernization. These efforts were more successful than those of other Manchu and Chinese leaders but still fell far short of what was necessary.

Personally, Li was a decisive, innovative official, who learned to act with restraint. His accommodation of Tz'u-hsi can be interpreted either as a necessary compromise to the reality of court politics or as tragic misjudgment that doomed to failure all Li's carefully laid projects and plans. Whatever weaknesses that Li's stewardship contained, they remained largely unrecognized until the First Sino-Japanese War, when all of his authority and glory were swiftly destroyed by the force of Japanese arms. Li's conception of what would happen to the dynasty and to China after this war remains a mystery, as does the full motivation behind his diplomatic maneuvers after 1895. The collapse of Li's own career by 1897 reflects the true decline of the Ch'ing Dynasty's power and authority.

Bibliography
Bland, J. O. P. *Li Hung-chang*. Reprint. New York: Books for Libraries Press, 1971. A biography of Li. Bland was a reporter in China, and his account contains much of the foreign community's gossip about Li.

Folsom, Kenneth E. *Friends, Guests, and Colleagues: The Mu-fu System in the Late Ch'ing Period*. Berkeley: University of California Press, 1968. A rich and useful study of Li and his staff that contains many details about Li's life and career.

Hsu, Immanuel C. Y. *The Rise of Modern China*. 3d ed. New York: Oxford University Press, 1983. The author of this standard text is an authority on the self-strengthening period; the section entitled "Self-strengthening in an Age of Accelerated Foreign Imperialism" puts Li's career into context.

Liu, K. C. "Li Hung-chang in Chihli: The Emergence of a Policy, 1870-1875." In *Approaches to Modern Chinese History*, edited by Albert Feuerwerker et al. Berkeley: University of California Press, 1967. Liu, who is a leading authority on Li, outlines Li's policies during his first years as governor-general and Northern Sea commissioner at Tientsin.

Spector, Stanley. *Li Hung-chang and the Huai Army*. Seattle: University of Washington Press, 1964. An important study that emphasizes Li's role in creating the system of regionally based military power in China after 1860.

David D. Buck

JUSTUS VON LIEBIG

Born: May 12, 1803; Darmstadt
Died: April 18, 1873; Munich, Germany
Area of Achievement: Chemistry
Contribution: Liebig was one of the most important chemists of the nineteenth century. In addition to pioneering experimental research that transformed the basis of modern organic chemistry, his studies on agriculture led to the development of agricultural chemistry, and his systematic processes for training students became institutionalized within the German research university.

Early Life

Born the second of nine children to Johann Georg and Maria Karoline Moserin Liebig, Justus von Liebig, the son of a dealer in pharmaceuticals and paint supplies, developed an interest in chemistry and experimentation at an early age. As a young boy, Liebig was especially fascinated with the explosive properties of silver fulminate, and his experiments with this material resulted in an explosion that prematurely ended his career as an apothecary apprentice. After returning home for a short time, Liebig enrolled at the University of Bonn in 1820, where he studied under the chemist Wilhelm Gottlob Kastner. Later in life, Liebig was particularly critical of Kastner's inability to teach him chemical analysis and the lack of adequate laboratory equipment, but Liebig followed Kastner from Bonn to the University of Erlangen, where he received a doctorate in 1822. It was at Erlangen that Liebig became convinced of the need to study abroad, and he successfully persuaded the Grand Duke Louis I of Hesse to award him a grant to pursue his chemical education in Paris from 1822 to 1824.

In Paris, Liebig received the chemical training that proved to be decisive and pivotal in his professional career. He attended the lectures of Louis-Jacques Thénard, Pierre-Louis Dulong, and Joseph-Louis Gay-Lussac and also gained entrance into the latter's laboratory through the intervention of Alexander von Humboldt. Liebig would leave Paris thoroughly trained in critical thinking, in chemical analysis, and in the experimental methods necessary for making careful physical measurements, all hallmarks of the "new" chemistry first articulated by Antoine-Laurent Lavoisier at the close of the eighteenth century.

Life's Work

Liebig returned to Germany in 1824 as extraordinary professor of chemistry at the University of Giessen; his appointment was the result of Humboldt's successful efforts in convincing Louis I that the young chemist had exceptional promise. Although his laboratory initially consisted of only one room surrounded by benches along its walls with a coal stove at its center, Liebig would quickly rise from these humble beginnings to become Europe's most distinguished chemist, the consequence of his personal charisma, scientific skills, and technical ingenuity.

Until the time of Liebig, organic chemistry was for the most part an inexact descriptive science based upon a hodgepodge of conflicting observations and personal opinions. There existed no viable classificatory scheme for organic substances, and there was little consensus concerning the fundamental building block of these materials, the molecule. Further, it was generally thought that a vital force arising from life itself was necessary for the synthesis of an organic compound. These uncertainties and others related to organic chemistry were ultimately explained by Liebig and his students using data gained from chemical analyses derived from the use of his combustion apparatus. This simple glass triangle consisted of several bulbs filled with potash, and it enabled the chemist to determine the percentage of carbon in a compound with great accuracy, precision, and relative ease. The combustion apparatus proved to be at the heart of Liebig's success, revolutionizing both organic chemistry and nineteenth century chemical education.

The use of exact analysis did much to elucidate the nature of·chemical compounds such as alcohols, aldehydes, ethers, and ketones during the late 1820's and 1830's. In the Giessen laboratory, where much of this compound characterization was done, large numbers of students, admitted on their talents and attracted by the low cost, flocked to the charismatic Liebig. While their training encompassed both theoretical and practical chemistry, the combustion apparatus was an integral part of a systematic curriculum that enabled even the average worker to make valuable contributions. Typically, the beginning student first sat in on Liebig's lectures on introductory chemistry and then was initiated in laboratory practices by doing qualitative analysis in which one characterizes a series of unknown compounds. Subsequently, a varied set of quantitative analyses were performed, followed by exercises in preparative chemistry in which certain substances were synthesized. After successfully completing these stages, the student was permitted to pursue independent research, often using the combustion apparatus to explore the reactions and compositions of organic substances. Since Liebig was editor of his own journal, *Annalen der Chemie und Pharmacie*, his students often had no problem in rapidly publishing their findings to a scientific community that by the 1840's recognized Giessen as the Mecca of organic chemistry.

Without doubt, Liebig's scientific reputation resulted in the best and brightest students in chemistry coming to study with him at Giessen during the second quarter of the nineteenth century. Among his students were August Wilhelm von Hofmann, discoverer of aniline and the first director of the British Royal College of Chemistry; Friedrich August Kekule von Stradonitz, whose structural interpretation of benzene was crucial to development in structural organic chemistry; James Muspratt of England, who was a leader in the late nineteenth century British chemical industry; and Oliver Wolcott Gibbs, who was a key figure within the emerging chemical community of nineteenth century America. Indeed, Liebig's influence was truly international, as by the 1850's most important academic positions in Western Europe were filled by his former students.

Liebig's fame among his contemporaries and especially the public was perhaps not so much the result of his students and their work as the result of his opinions and writings on agricultural chemistry. In 1840, Liebig, weary after more than a decade of debate with the French chemist Jean-Baptiste André Dumas over the nature of organic molecules, gave a series of lectures on agricultural chemistry in Glasgow, Scotland, that subsequently would be the basis of *Die organische Chemie in ihrer Anivendung auf Agricultur und Physiologie* (1840; *Organic Chemistry in Its Applications to Agriculture and Physiology*, 1840). This work, which dealt with the uses of fertilizers, plant nutrition, and fermentation was seriously flawed in its analysis but was so popular that by 1848 it appeared in seventeen editions and in nine languages, proving to be a powerful stimulus to the agricultural station movement in Europe and the United States. In addition to his views on agriculture, Liebig also extended into the area of physiology and in 1842 expressed his views on nutrition and the chemical changes taking place within living organisms in *Die Thier-Chemie: Oder, Die organische Chemie in ihrer Anwendung auf Physiologie und Pathologie* (*Animal Chemistry: Or, Organic Chemistry in Its Applications to Physiology and Pathology*, 1842). Like his agricultural chemistry, Liebig's animal chemistry aroused criticism that ultimately was crucial to the late nineteenth century development of modern physiological chemistry.

In 1852, Liebig left Giessen for a modern, well-equipped laboratory in Munich, where he would continue to research and write on aspects of organic chemistry. Although the latter stages of his career were not as fruitful as those early years at Giessen, his legacy in terms of ideas and of followers was crucial to the shaping of modern civilization.

Summary

Justus von Liebig perhaps did more than any other nineteenth century chemist in creating the modern synthetic world of the twentieth century. His reliance upon exact knowledge based upon chemical analysis resulted in the emergence of the discipline of organic chemistry, a field that has provided modern society with myriad synthetic products, including polymeric materials such as polyvinyl chloride, polypropylene, and synthetic rubber. Yet Liebig did far more than influence the internal aspects of science, for his work on agricultural chemistry had enormous consequences in influencing what would become an ongoing agricultural revolution, and his speculations on physiology reoriented the course of medical research. Finally, his ideas on chemical education—ideas that continue to be practiced in universities today—mark perhaps his most lasting contribution, for most chemists trace their educational heritage to a small laboratory in Giessen and to its master, Justus von Liebig.

Bibliography

Beer, John J. *The Emergence of the German Dye Industry.* Urbana: University of Illinois Press, 1959. One important legacy of Liebig is in the creation of a modern synthetic world, the ultimate fruit of his many students working in industrial research laboratories during the last quarter of the nineteenth century. Beer's study carefully traces the emergence of the science-based dye industry and the role of Liebig's ideas in influencing its organizational development.

Ihde, Aaron J. *The Development of Modern Chemistry.* New York: Harper & Row, 1964. This survey work in the history of chemistry is excellent in characterizing the nature of organic chemistry during Liebig's lifetime. Discusses Liebig's contributions to organic, agricultural, and physiological chemistry as well as to the field of chemical education.

Lipmann, Timothy O. "Vitalism and Reductionism in Liebig's Physiological Thought." *Isis* 58 (1967): 167-185. A superb article that serves as a model for scholarship in the history of science. Lipmann demonstrates that while Liebig did not believe in the doctrine of vitalism as applied to organic compounds, he did adhere to the notion that a living force (*Lebenskraft*) was an essential part of physiological processes and necessary for the building up of organized structures in living bodies.

Morrell, J. B. "The Chemist Breeders: The Research Schools of Liebig and Thomas Thomson." *Ambix* 19 (1972): 1-47. A penetrating study that examines the pioneering contributions of Liebig in establishing the first modern scientific research school. Morrell analyzes Liebig's charismatic personality, the significance of the combustion apparatus, his ability to control the field of organic chemistry with *Annalen der Chemie und Pharmacie*, and his ability to secure financial and institutional resources.

Rossiter, Margaret W. *The Emergence of Agricultural Science: Justus Liebig and the Americans, 1840-1880.* New Haven, Conn.: Yale University Press, 1975. Traces the diffusion of Liebig's ideas on agriculture from Europe to the United States during the nineteenth century. By the conclusion of the Civil War, a powerful movement to establish agricultural experiment stations emerged and Rossiter particularly focuses on the influence of Liebig on those scientists working at the Connecticut Station.

John A. Heitmann

WILHELM LIEBKNECHT

Born: March 29, 1826; Giessen, Hesse-Darmstadt
Died: August 7, 1900; Berlin, Germany
Areas of Achievement: Government and politics
Contribution: Liebknecht was a founding member of the German Social Democratic Party and an extreme critic of authoritarian government in Germany. He was a delegate to the German Reichstag and editor of the Social Democratic Party newspaper *Vorwärts*. His most important contribution was an effort to promote the ideals of democracy in the nineteenth century European socialist movement.

Early Life

Wilhelm Liebknecht was born in Giessen, a small town near Marburg in Hesse-Darmstadt. Liebknecht's father was a government registrar, and the family was considered middle class by the standards of the early nineteenth century. One of three surviving children, Liebknecht benefited from his father's study of post-Napoleonic Enlightenment thought, and from an early age he was interested in social justice. By December, 1832, however, both of his parents were dead and the six-year-old orphan was reared by Karl Osswald, a theologian, who had been a close friend of the family. By the time Liebknecht had reached his tenth birthday, what was left of his father's estate had disappeared. Although the sudden deaths of his parents and the descent into poverty must have made a lasting impression on him, Liebknecht seldom wrote of his childhood. His only lasting memories were of his uncle, the Reverend Friedrich Ludwig Weidig, a liberal democrat and author of fiery revolutionary tracts. Repeatedly jailed for his antimonarchist writings, in February, 1837, Weidig was apparently murdered in prison in Darmstadt. Although Liebknecht rarely referred to his uncle's death, evidence suggests that at this time he began to identify the authoritarian state as the source of his own bereavement and the problems of society.

Although reduced in circumstances, Liebknecht was still able to attend school, and it was education rather than hardship which pushed him in the direction of radical politics. In the autumn of 1845, Liebknecht left for Berlin to enroll at the university. Berlin was already an industrial city with a population approaching half a million, and the condition of the city's industrial workers, who were forced to live in appalling slums and to suffer brutal working conditions, made an instant impression on the young student. Indeed, Liebknecht's course of study at the university perfectly complemented his introduction to working-class life. His major interests lay in philosophy and economics, and he read avidly in the works of the French socialist Claude Henri de Saint-Simon. As Liebknecht himself admitted, however, his real grounding in socialist thought began with his reading of

Friedrich Engels' *Die Lage der arbeitenden Klasse in England* (1848; *The Condition of the Working Class in England in 1844*, 1887). This work persuaded Liebknecht to join the struggle against capitalism, and he cut his education short to join the liberal-democratic Revolution of 1848. The collapse of the revolutionary movement in 1849 forced Liebknecht to flee Germany.

Life's Work

Liebknecht's post-1848 travels took him to Switzerland and then to Great Britain. During his migration, he became acquainted with both Karl Marx and Engels. In 1850, he joined the Union of Communists and became a dedicated exponent of socialist political and economic theory. A proclamation of amnesty permitted Liebknecht to return to Berlin in 1862. He worked as a correspondent for various democratically oriented German and foreign newspapers and became a founding member along with Ferdinand Lassalle of the General German Workers' Association, an organization which favored workers' cooperatives financially supported by the state, universal suffrage, and a program of social legislation regulating wages and hours. In 1869, however, Liebknecht helped to create a new workers' party, the German Social Democratic Labor Party, a more radical organization which emphasized the class struggle and which demanded the abolition of class privileges in Prussia.

In the late 1860's, the two rival groups became parliamentary parties and sent representatives to the assembly of the North German Confederation, which had been created following the Prussian defeat of Austria in 1866. Liebknecht served as a Social Democratic delegate from 1867 to 1870 and vigorously attacked the reactionary policies of the Prussian Junker class and denounced Prussian militarism. Along with August Bebel, Liebknecht opposed the Franco-Prussian War of 1870-1871, fought against the annexationist plans of the Prussian government, and appealed for working-class solidarity with the Paris Commune of 1871. For his opposition to Germany's annexation of Alsace and Lorraine, Liebknecht was brought to trial in 1872 for treason against the state and sentenced to two years' imprisonment.

The Franco-Prussian War, however, led to increased cooperation between the Social Democrats and Lassalle's Workers' Association. Many factional disputes disappeared with the unification of Germany and, by 1875, the two socialist parties resolved to join forces against capitalism and Prussian militarism. At the Socialist Congress at Gotha in May, 1875, a new German Social Democratic Labor Party was founded, and Liebknecht became one of the most influential party leaders, along with Lassalle and Bebel. The Gotha Program reflected Liebknecht's democratic tendencies and was far from a radical socialist agenda. The party program called for such socialist measures as the abolition of "wage slavery" through the establishment of state-supported workers' cooperatives, but it also advocated many commonly held liberal-democratic policies, including universal suffrage, the secret ballot, guaranteed civil liberties, free public education, freedom of speech and assembly, and government-mandated social legislation. The republican nature of the Gotha Program engendered criticism from more doctrinaire socialists, including Marx. In 1875, Marx published his *Randglossen zum Gothaer Partei Programm* (1875; *Critique of the Gotha Program*, 1938), a scathing ideological attack on the German Social Democrats. Nevertheless, Liebknecht repudiated Marx's denunciation, and the new party achieved impressive electoral gains in 1877. The party's moderate-democratic approach allowed it to increase its popular vote by 40 percent and helped it to capture twelve seats in the German Reichstag.

Following the Gotha meeting, however, German Chancellor Otto von Bismarck took steps to prevent any further growth of socialism in Germany. As a result of Liebknecht's and other socialist leaders' opposition to Prussian policies during the Franco-Prussian War, Bismarck was inclined to regard all Social Democrats as enemies of the state. Therefore, in 1878, Bismarck persuaded the Reichstag to pass a series of antisocialist laws which suppressed all political and economic associations of the German socialists. Technically the German Social Democratic Party was not illegal, but party effectiveness was practically destroyed by curtailments in electoral funding and the harassment of party leaders. Liebknecht retained his democratic philosophy during this period and helped to retain party unity until the antisocialist legislation lapsed in 1890.

In 1890, Liebknecht became editor in chief of *Vorwärts*, the central organ of the Social Democratic Party. During this period, and until his death in 1900, Liebknecht's socialist beliefs centered on the issue of the legitimacy of parliamentary activity in the context of the class struggle against capitalism and militarism. Liebknecht's position held that the workers' interests would be more effectively served by sending deputies to the Reichstag who would use the democratic system to achieve social, political, and economic reform. Liebknecht, Bebel, and other moderates helped mold the German Social Democratic movement into a responsible parliamentary party, defending workers' interests and political liberalism. Liebknecht was especially responsible for formulating specific policies aimed at promoting social legislation, reducing the military budget, and eliminating economic protectionism. By the late 1890's, however, Liebknecht's position as party leader had diminished, largely as a result of his inexpert handling of intraparty strife. On the morning of August 7, 1900, Liebknecht suffered a fatal stroke while working at his office in Berlin. His leadership of the German Social Democrats fell to Bebel, Karl Kautsky, and Eduard Bernstein, but Liebknecht was eulogized as one who had helped to elevate a struggling socialist faction into the world's largest and most effective socialist party.

Summary

Wilhelm Liebknecht's achievement was to help to establish the world's first mass-based Marxist political party. He was a nineteenth century social democrat whose political philosophy was formed in the nexus of liberal-democracy, Marxism, and nationalism. He was noted as being tolerant, humanitarian, and democratic. While he did not excel as a statesman or political revolutionary, he was a master at political organization. His advocacy of revolutionary change was tempered with his abjuration of violence. He encouraged open discussion within his party, and he defended the right to hold dissenting viewpoints. In reaching decisions, he preferred persuasion and open voting to intimidation and deference to an elite party leadership. He rejected any form of conspiratorial action by a minority and based his socialism on the basic premise of mass participation. Liebknecht argued that the basic tool of working-class revolution remained education. Voluntary and enlightened mass participation in the revolutionary process was Liebknecht's aim. For him, the manipulative dictatorship of the proletariat always remained an incongruous part of Marxism. While most nineteenth century socialist movements indulged in sectarian debates and self-defeating intra-party rivalries, the German Social Democrats, largely as a result of Liebknecht's efforts, crystallized the socialist movement and forestalled party schism until 1917. Overall, Liebknecht's leadership molded the German socialists into a respected and effective workers' party and ultimately inspired the creation of modern European social democracy.

Bibliography

Braunthal, Julius. *History of the International*. Translated by Henry Collins and Kenneth Mitchell. 2 vols. New York: Praeger, 1976. This standard work on the Socialist International includes a discussion of Liebknecht's efforts in attracting German workers' attention to the First International. Places Liebknecht in the context of the early days of European socialism.

Dominick, Raymond H., III. *Wilhelm Liebknecht and the Founding of the German Social Democratic Party*. Chapel Hill: University of North Carolina Press, 1982. Dominick provides the standard biography of Liebknecht. His focus is on the philosophical struggle inherent in the founding of the German Social Democratic Party. He attributes to Liebknecht the party's emphasis on participatory democracy. Liebknecht is given credit for retaining party unity in the face of Prussian repression and ideological disputes within European socialism.

Hall, Alex. *Scandal, Sensation, and Social Democracy: The SPD Press and Wilhelmine Germany, 1890-1914*. Cambridge: Cambridge University Press, 1977. The author examines in detail the workings of such major Social Democratic organs as *Vorwärts* and provides a detailed discussion of Liebknecht's direction of the paper during the 1890's. Liebknecht is given

credit for maintaining his democratic principles in the face of severe criticism from both the government and his own party's radical elements.
Lidtke, Vernon L. *The Outlawed Party: Social Democracy in Germany, 1878-1890*. Princeton, N.J.: Princeton University Press, 1966. This study is devoted largely to the struggle of the German Social Democratic Party during the period of Bismarck's antisocialist laws. Early chapters, however, deal in depth with Liebknecht's role in the founding of the party. The author emphasizes the impact of Liebknecht's liberalism in the formulation of party ideology.
Roth, Guenther. *The Social Democrats in Imperial Germany: A Study in Working-Class Isolation and National Integration*. Totowa, N.J.: Bedminster Press, 1963. This work is basically a sociological view of the integration of the German working class into German society. The author attacks party leaders, including Liebknecht, for denying strict Marxism in favor of watered-down liberalism. Credit is given, however, for Liebknecht's criticism of militarism and other evils of Prussian authoritarianism.

William G. Ratliff

LIN TSE-HSÜ

Born: August 30, 1785; Hou-kuan, Fukien, China
Died: November 22, 1850; Ch'ao-chou, Kwangtung, China
Areas of Achievement: Government and politics
Contribution: A respected scholar-official serving the Manchu Ch'ing Dynasty, Lin led the effort to eradicate the sale of opium by foreigners at Canton, a successful campaign that led to the Opium War (1839-1842) and the ignominious 1842 Treaty of Nanking.

Early Life

Lin Tse-hsü was the second child born in 1785 to Lin Pin-jih, a poor scholar. His father, hoping to emulate earlier family members by entering the government bureaucracy through the civil service exam system, could not rise beyond the initial *hsiu-ts'ai* (cultivated talent) degree and at forty-one gave up his quest for the provincial level *chü-ren* (recommended man) degree to run a private school to support his growing family (ultimately three sons and eight daughters). The young Lin Tse-hsü grew up in a loving but impoverished family environment. His education began at home under his father's tutelage, and he entered school at age four. During his youth, he helped sell his mother's embroidery to make ends meet. A bright student, he entered the local academy at nine and won the *hsiu-ts'ai* degree when fourteen. In an oral test to choose the best of the exam entrants, he bested a rival candidate many years his senior.

At twenty, he passed the *chü-ren* exams, which entitled him to go to Peking to take the capital tests, but he could not afford to do so. Instead, he entered the local yamen (government office) as a clerk-scribe. When a New Year's greeting he wrote caught the attention of Chang Shih-ch'eng, the Fukien provincial governor, Lin was summoned to neighboring Foochow to serve for three years on Chang's staff.

Seven years after achieving *chü-ren* status, Lin finally went to Peking to take the highest-level exams. He attained *chin-shih* (presented scholar) rank and entered the Hanlin Academy. His nine-year stay in Peking gained for him considerable experience in handling the myriad governmental concerns brought to the attention of the six ministries at the top of the Ch'ing bureaucracy. He also made valuable, lifelong contacts within the power structure, connections important for career advancement.

In 1819, Lin was sent to Yunnan in the southwest to be head examiner in the provincial exams. This was a stepping stone to his first major appointment as intendant of the administrative circuit (*tao*) in the Hangchow area. In 1822, Lin went to Peking and had an audience with the newly enthroned Tao-kuang emperor. The emperor praised Lin's work in the Hangchow region and permitted Lin to return there. In succession, he was given posts in

Kiangsu (intendant) and Chekiang (salt monopoly controller) provinces. In 1823, he became surveillance commissioner of Kiangsu. By cleaning up a backlog of judicial cases with great impartiality and reforming the penal system, he earned the epithet "Lin as Clear as the Heavens" (Lin Ch'ing T'ien). The following year, his mother died, requiring a return to his hometown for a custom-dictated three years of mourning. This period was interrupted twice, first to help in flood relief in Kiangsu along the Yellow River, and then to work in the salt monopoly administration. After a visit to Peking in 1827, he was assigned to Sian in Shensi; there he became familiar with military affairs as a result of a nearby Muslim rebellion being quashed by the Ch'ing military.

While Lin was serving as financial commissioner in Nanking, his father died enroute to joining him. This again necessitated a three-year absence from government service for official mourning in his native village. In 1830, Lin was back in the capital, awaiting a new assignment. During this stay, Lin renewed and made friendships with middle-echelon bureaucrats, men on the periphery of power yet close enough to the real problems to be concerned about the dynasty's ossifying rule. Lin was part of a coterie (often meeting socially as the Hsüan-nan Poetry Society) of younger degree-holders, inspired by their study of "modern text" (*chin-wen*) Confucian writings to seek practical solutions to problems of governing. When Lin received his next set of assignments, he left the capital, invigorated with ideas shared by a nascent group of intellectual-administrators devoted to practical statecraft.

In the next twenty months, Lin was given five different assignments: provincial administration commissioner, in turn, of Hupei, Hunan, and Chiangning, followed by that of water conservancy director-general in Shantung and Honan, and, in 1832, governor of Kiangsu. He stayed in the latter post for five years. His tenure in Kiangsu under his friend Governor-General T'ao Shu added to his reputation. A new problem he encountered was the outflow of local silver used to pay for opium distributed into the hinterland from foreign sources at Canton.

Life's Work

At age fifty-two, Lin was appointed governor-general of Hupei and Hunan. Increasingly, much of his time came to be concentrated on a matter that was by this time a major local and national concern—opium control. Trade between the Western powers and China, begun in the mid-1700's, originally was in China's favor, since European and American demand for tea leaves, raw silk, rhubarb, chinaware, and lacquer items far exceeded Chinese interest in Western woolens, tin, lead, furs, and linen. The anticommercial Manchu rulers only begrudgingly tolerated this trade, despite its profitability, and confined it to the southern port of Canton, where foreigners could not easily press on the dynasty their demands for diplomatic recognition.

The import of tea to England was lucrative to the Crown as a result of a 100 percent excise duty, but, since it could not be paid for only by the sale of Indian cotton to the Chinese, Britain had to bring in silver bullion from Mexico and Peru to pay its bills. A triangular trade among England, India, and China operated through the "Canton system" whereby foreign ships, stopping first at the Portuguese enclave Macao, would proceed with Chinese permission to Canton and sell their cargoes at a waterfront warehouse enclave through the *co-hong* trade guild run by Chinese merchants supervised by the *hoppo* (customs official).

The British and the other foreigners tolerated this inconvenient system because it was lucrative. The trade imbalance in China's favor began to change with the export by the East India Company of opium from Bengal to Canton, starting in the 1770's. Opium was originally used for its reputed medicinal and aphrodisiac qualities, and, even though the Chinese repeatedly had outlawed its use, it became a popular drug, inhaled by pipe. The East India Company, to protect itself legally, consigned the opium transport and sale to private traders not bound by the intricacies of the formalistic Canton system. In 1834, the company's China trade monopoly was ended by the British parliament's response to domestic demands for free trade. The resulting free-for-all among opium dealers dramatically increased sales to the Chinese, and by the late 1830's anywhere from two to ten million Chinese had become addicted. In addition, the outflow of Chinese silver and the worsening exchange ratio between silver and Chinese copper coins (a problem Lin had confronted earlier) created economic havoc.

In China, a debate raged between those wanting to legalize the opium trade in order to control it and those favoring an end to it. The Tao-kuang emperor sided with the officials who opposed legalization, and Governor-General Teng T'ing-chen cracked down on the Canton opium trade between 1836 and 1838. He was successful in dealing with the Chinese end of the problem but had difficulty with the foreign merchants. After the East India Company's monopoly ended, the Chinese, preferring to deal with a formal middleman rather than a host of competing foreign interests, asked the British to designate someone to be *taipan* (head merchant). The British, wanting official Chinese diplomatic recognition, sent, in 1833, Lord William John Napier, assisted militarily by Captain Charles Elliot.

In one stroke the British put a government official in a position formerly occupied by the East India Company, thus making trade, originally a private arrangement between the company and the *co-hong* merchants, the official concern of the Crown. Increasingly, questions of commercial interests and national honor coalesced as the British, using commerce as a wedge, continued to attempt to persuade the Chinese to recognize their representative on a government-to-government basis.

Teng's anti-opium campaign was very successful. To preclude Teng from carrying out his threat to end all trade, the foreigners eventually reluctantly cooperated in the opium-suppression efforts. Smuggling by illegal profiteers, however, continued in the waters surrounding Canton. In Peking, pressure increased for the complete eradication of opium. Lin, successful in curbing opium use in his jurisdiction, was among the hard-liners. The emperor consulted with him personally and was impressed by his opium-elimination measures in Hupei and Hunan. On December 31, 1838, Lin was appointed imperial commissioner to eradicate the opium trade.

Lin arrived in Canton on March 10, 1839. The foreign community took his arrival calmly, viewing his subsequent crackdown on Chinese opium sellers and users as a continuation of the government's toughened policy. Lin's tack in dealing with the foreigners was to try to establish jurisdiction by getting them to accept Chinese legal rights and to convince them of the immorality of their actions. With imperial permission, he drafted two letters addressed to Queen Victoria, appealing to her moral propriety and common sense. Pointing out that opium smoking was a crime in England, he asked why her government promoted its use in his land and urged her to control her subjects' actions. These letters were widely circulated, for effect, among the foreign residents. A ship captain agreed to take a copy to England, but the foreign office refused to accept it.

On March 18, Lin ordered the surrender, through the hong merchants, of all opium in the foreigners' possession and required all to sign a bond pledging, on penalty of death, no longer to engage in this trade. A token 1,036 chests were turned in. Dissatisfied, Lin attempted to coerce Lancelot Dent, a major opium supplier, to surrender himself to Chinese authority. Dent refused, and Elliot, fearing the worst, left Macao for Canton, arriving on the day before Lin enacted a total trade embargo and ordered all Chinese help out of the foreigners' compound, thus imposing a siege on the 350 foreigners trapped there. The standoff ended after six weeks on Elliot's promise to have the foreigners turn over all of their opium to Lin. This was readily done, since there no longer was a market and Elliot promised reimbursement. The forfeited 21,306 chests were emptied into a huge pit and the opium was dissolved in seawater and lime, ending up in the ocean. Lin was victorious; however, by making his demands of Elliot, he now was dealing directly with a representative of the British government.

On May 24, all the British evacuated Canton for Macao. News of their confinement had infuriated the British public, and foreign secretary Lord Palmerston was bombarded with traders' petitions to be compensated for their losses. The British refugees thought they were secure in Portuguese Macao. The killing of a Chinese peasant on July 12 by some drunken British sailors at Kowloon, however, led to Lin's demand that the perpetrators be turned over to Chinese jurisdiction. This was refused. Lin had supplies to Macao cut off and ordered troops to surround it. The Portuguese evicted the

British, who now sailed for Hong Kong. They were prevented from landing to replenish supplies. Elliot then ordered his ships to fire on some Chinese junks after being refused water and food.

By the fall of 1839 some British traders, aware that Americans were taking over their lucrative business in Canton, broke ranks with Elliot and decided to sign Lin's bond. On November 3, as some British traders were preparing to give in, a naval skirmish occurred at Ch'uan-pi. Losing several ships, the Chinese retreated. On December 6, Lin ordered the end of all trade with the British. Unaware of this last event and responding to earlier provocations, the British Parliament, after an acrimonious debate between Tories opposing a war to support opium smugglers and prowar politicians prodded by a strong China lobby with vested interests, voted by a narrow margin to retaliate.

A large British expeditionary force under Elliot's uncle arrived in Chinese waters in June, 1840. Anticipating this reaction, Lin fortified the Canton area. Coastal batteries at the Bogue were augmented with foreign-purchased guns, war-junks surrounded Canton waters, and chain blockades were put across the Pearl River. Peasant militia were mobilized in Kwangtung Province. Martial arts fighters and Taoist magicians were also mustered. Lin wrote to the emperor that the large British warships were incapable of sailing up the Pearl River, adding that foreign soldiers, inept at fighting with swords and fists, could easily be routed.

Lin patiently waited for the British attack, but the fleet under Elliot's command, after blockading Canton, proceeded northward to deliver written ultimatums from Henry John Temple, Viscount Palmerston, directly to the court. After being refused at several ports, which were then blockaded, the British arrived in late August at the Peiho River near the Taku forts, protecting the approach to Peking. The court was shocked that the local problem of Canton was now brought to its doorstep. Palmerston's letter of demands, putting most of the blame on Elliot's personal nemesis, Lin, was accepted. The emperor now saw Lin as a convenient scapegoat. On July 1, 1841, Lin was ordered into exile in remote I-li in Central Asia.

Lin's dismissal was merely an interlude in what became known as the Opium War. Diplomatic efforts to prevent further military action failed, and Elliot's military campaigns in the Canton delta eventually gave the British the upper hand. Sir Henry Pottinger, commanding a punitive naval force sent from India and England, followed up in 1841 with attacks on major Chinese ports. The Chinese reluctantly agreed on August 29, 1842, to the Treaty of Nanking, requiring the payments of a war indemnity and reparations for seized opium, the opening of five coastal cities to trade and diplomatic residence, the abolishment of the *co-hong* monopoly, and the ceding of Hong Kong.

Though in official disgrace, Lin was still a faithful servant to the dynasty.

On his way to exile he was asked to fight a break in the Yellow River dykes at Kaifeng. While banished in I-li, he directed irrigation projects which reclaimed much land for farming. In 1845, he was recalled to service as acting Governor-General of Shensi and Kansu, followed by posts in Shensi and Yunnan. His final task was imperial commissioner to fight the T'ai-p'ing rebels in the Kwangsi region. He died on November 22, 1850, en route to this last assignment.

Summary

Lin Tse-hsü was a victim of two cultures; his Confucian upbringing and fidelity to the Ch'ing required him to deal with the opium problem in an administrative and moralistic way that was outdated in the face of British might and the Western concept of foreign relations that denied China her self-assumed superiority. The Opium War, and Lin's role in it, marked a watershed in Chinese history. The "Middle Kingdom" would never recover from the burden of the "unequal treaties" begun at Nanking and the Western powers were not appeased by this first of many concessions to be extracted over the ensuing century. This happened despite Lin, not because of him.

Chinese Marxist historians use the Opium War as the beginning event in the history of modern China, the story of a collapsing feudal system ravished by foreign imperialism. Irrespective of ideology, Chinese everywhere respect Lin as a patriot who stood up to foreign aggression and the venal opium trade that symbolized it. His loyalty, though, was misplaced. It would take nationalism and revolution in the twentieth century to replace Lin's form of parochial dynastic allegiance before the Chinese would be able to reclaim their destiny for themselves.

Bibliography

Chang, Hsin-pao. *Commissioner Lin and the Opium War.* Cambridge, Mass.: Harvard University Press, 1964. The most thorough study of the events leading to the Opium War are examined in the context of Lin's role in them. Uses Chinese and Western sources to give a well-rounded account, analyzing, from respective perspectives, the positions of the English and the Chinese. Portrait of Lin faces the title page. Includes copious notes, a glossary, and a bibliography.

Compilation Group for the "History of Modern China" Series. *The Opium War.* Peking: Foreign Language Press, 1976. A booklet based on research by history professors at the University of Futan and Shanghai Teachers' University depicting Lin as one of "the capitulationists of the landlord class" who appeased Western imperialists in the Opium War; useful for understanding the Chinese Marxist historiographical approach.

Fairbank, John K., ed. *The Cambridge History of China.* Vol. 10, *Late Ch'ing, 1800-1911, Part 1.* Cambridge: Cambridge University Press,

1978. Includes "The Canton Trade and the Opium War" by Frederic Wakeman, Jr., concisely narrating and analyzing the events before and after the war, including Lin's participation.

Teng, Ssu-yü, and John K. Fairbank. *China's Response to the West: A Documentary Survey, 1839-1923*. Cambridge, Mass.: Harvard University Press, 1965. Lin's famous 1839 letter to Queen Victoria admonishing the British for their moral double-standard in opium dealing and a short 1842 letter to a friend concerning the military superiority of the West are given in translation.

Waley, Arthur. *The Opium War Through Chinese Eyes*. New York: Macmillan, 1958. Uses Chinese documentary sources, Lin's diaries, and other writings to present the Opium War from a Chinese point of view.

William M. Zanella

LINNAEUS
Carl von Linné

Born: May 23, 1707; Sodra Råshult, Sweden
Died: January 10, 1778; Uppsala, Sweden
Areas of Achievement: Botany and natural history
Contribution: Linnaeus created a new classification system for all nature, establishing in the process the binomial system of nomenclature for organisms.

Early Life

Carl von Linné's father adopted the name Linné (and the Latin form, Linnaeus) while studying for the ministry. Ordained in 1704 at the age of thirty, the minister married Christina Brodersonia, the daughter of the Vicar of Stenbrohult. In addition to his pastoral duties, Nils Linné was an enthusiastic gardener, who was particularly knowledgeable about herbs. Carl, his eldest son, was born May 23, 1707, and soon exhibited an avid interest in botany. As a young child, Carl enjoyed taking nature walks with his father and developed a firsthand knowledge and appreciation of plant and animal life.

School, however, was not enjoyable for the younger Linnaeus, and his only successes came in the physical-mathematical subjects. He had tremendous powers of observation, and in his four autobiographies often commented on his own "brown, quick, sharp eyes." His physics teacher, Johan Rothman, recognizing Linnaeus' penchant for empiricism, encouraged him by giving him Hermann Boerhaave's and Joseph Pitton de Tournefort's works to read. At Rothman's urging, Linnaeus' parents agreed to send Carl to medical school. In 1727, at the age of twenty, he went to southern Sweden and entered the University of Lund but transferred the following year to the University of Uppsala, which not only was nearer his home but also had a reputation for higher standards. His knowledge of botany and understanding of nature soon brought him to the attention of Olof Celsius, a theology professor and dean, who took him into his home.

While still an undergraduate, Linnaeus conducted research on the reproductive structures of plants, gave lectures on botany (attracting large audiences), and received travel grants to collect materials for research on both natural materials and human customs and habits. During one of these trips, he met his future wife, Sara Elisabeth Moraea, the daughter of the wealthy town physician of Falun. Linnaeus was granted permission to marry her (and thus have access to her father's wealth) on the condition that he go to the Netherlands to get the degree of doctor of medicine, a degree not then available in Sweden. Linnaeus went to the small and not-too-rigorous university in Harderwijk, where he took his doctor's degree in a few weeks. He then went to Amsterdam and Leiden, where he met a number of noted scientists, and through these contacts was able to secure the patronage necessary to continue his research. During the three years he spent in the Netherlands, he published the work for which he is best known, *Systema naturae* (1735; *A General System of Nature Through the Three Grand Kingdoms of Animals, Vegetables, and Minerals*, 1800-1801).

Linnaeus returned to Sweden, married Sara, tried to establish a medical practice in Stockholm, and became increasingly disillusioned with medicine as a career. Finally, in 1741, he was named professor of botany at Uppsala. His fame spread, and he attracted students from many countries to join him in identifying new species and classifying them. The period of the late 1740's to the 1750's was the apogee of his career.

Life's Work

Linnaeus was interested in a wide range of topics in natural history, but his primary interest was classification. His goal was to produce a system by which one could correctly identify organisms, and his method was to use the common Aristotelian technique of downward classification. This method involved taking a class of objects, dividing it into two groups (for example, the class of living organisms can be divided into animals and nonanimals), and continuing the process of dichotomous divisions until there was only the lowest set, the species, which could not be further divided. Such a system was highly artificial, since the basis for many of the divisions was arbitrary. Based on his philosophical and theological commitment to the argument from design, however, Linnaeus believed that if the correct character was chosen as the basis of division, natural relationships would be revealed. In his characteristically arrogant manner, he claimed to have discovered that trait and built his system around it. He called it his "sexual system."

He first presented his ideas in *A General System of Nature*. In its first edition, the book contained only about a dozen pages and presented what Linnaeus referred to as a natural system. His only taxonomic groupings at this stage were class, genus, and species. In this work, he accepted the ideas of earlier taxonomists that species, which he took as the starting point for his system, were immutable and that each one had been created at the beginning of time. Moreover, every species must be strictly intermediate between two other species in order to maintain the plenitude of the chain of being. Plants were assigned to a particular species based on the number and position of their reproductive parts (hence the term "sexual system"). Four elementary criteria were used to classify a plant: number, shape, proportion, and situation. Thus, to assign a plant to a particular species, one counted the number of stamens (the pollen-bearing male organs) and pistils (the female organs), examined them to see if they were separated or fused, compared relative size, determined their position vis-à-vis each other and the other flower parts, and found out whether both male and female elements were on the same flower. Species which had obvious similarities were brought together into a higher-level grouping labeled "genus"; then, similar genera were grouped into classes. Linnaeus believed that only the first two categories—species and genus—were natural ones, with higher division existing only as an artificial aid for the ordering of nature.

Since the primary purpose of a classification system, as far as Linnaeus was concerned, was to allow one to know the plants, that is, to be able to name them quickly and accurately, it did not matter if the system mixed natural and artificial categories. The value of the Linnaean system was that any botanist who learned a few parts of a flower and fruit could come to the same decision as to its name that Linnaeus did. This value was quickly recognized and greatly appreciated given the state of plant taxonomy at that time. It is estimated that in 1600, approximately six thousand plants had been recognized; by 1700, an additional twelve thousand had been discovered. It was therefore crucial to know what a plant was and to what group of plants it belonged. Linnaeus immediately became famous for the way in which he solved these problems. His victory was complete when Bernard de Jussieu, the leader of French botany, declared in 1739 that the Linnaean system was preferable to that of the Frenchman Tournefort.

Yet Linnaeus was not content with his first attempt. He published *Fundamenta botanica* (1736; foundation of botany) the following year and *Classes plantarum* (1738; classes of plants) two years later. Including *A General System of Nature*, which went through ten revisions by 1758, these works contain the basis of all the essential changes which Linnaeus would bring to systematics. By the tenth edition, which had grown to two volumes and 1,384 pages, Linnaeus had added the category "order," and he recognized twenty-four classes of plants. The number of pistils determined the order to which the plant was assigned, while the number of stamens determined the class. Moreover, he had begun to use the only two natural categories—genus and species—as the basis for naming plants.

The contribution for which he is best known, the binomial system of nomenclature, was first articulated in *Species plantarum* (1753; species of plants), in which Linnaeus himself classified more than eight thousand plants from all over the world. Yet Linnaeus viewed the binomial system as only a minor modification and outgrowth of his sexual system. Having assigned an organism to a particular genus and species as a result of the characteristics of the reproductive organs, he suggested using the Latinized names of the genus and species together to identify a specific plant. This reform is currently viewed as his most lasting contribution to biology, for it could be retained even when the specific Linnaean system of classification was rejected in favor of one acknowledging phylogenetic relationships.

During his later years, Linnaeus was increasingly plagued by poor health.

He suffered from migraine headaches, rheumatism, fevers, and bouts of depression. In 1761, he was ennobled and appointed a member of the Swedish House of Lords. In 1774, he suffered the first of a series of strokelike attacks, which he called his "message of death." A second one in 1778 left him totally incapacitated, and he died in the early winter of that year. A family quarrel between his widow and daughters, on one side, and his son, on the other, over possession of his library, herbarium, and papers was finally settled in favor of his son, who died shortly after the arrangements were completed. Linnaeus' widow then sold the collection to a London physician, J. E. Smith, who, along with two friends, founded the Linnean Society, the organization which would become famous for first receiving the papers of Alfred Russel Wallace and Charles Darwin on their theory of evolution by natural selection.

Summary

Peter J. Bowler described Linnaeus' goal for his work very well:

> If the species were created by God, one could assume that a rational Creator would have formed the world according to a meaningful order that man himself could hope to understand. Linnaeus believed that he had been privileged to see the outline of the Creator's plan and his efforts to represent it would become the basis of a new biology.

In fact, his "new biology" was more adapted to botany than to zoology. With his system, he was personally able to classify more than eighteen thousand species of plants. His attempts to classify animals, however, created duplications and confusion, primarily because he could not find a characteristic which would work for animals the way reproductive structures did for plants. His inclination to classify everything can also be seen in his attempts to classify diseases, humans, and even botanists.

Linnaeus should not be regarded as merely a taxonomist. His essays and lectures provide evidence that he was exploring ideas which would now be considered basic to ecology and biogeography. He sought to develop, within both a theological and biological context, a concept of the harmony of nature. Finally, he tried not to allow his philosophical or theological positions to blind him to his data. As a result of his evidence, he revised his views on fixity of species to allow for a kind of evolution—formation of new species by hybridization—below the genus level.

Bibliography

Bowler, Peter J. *Evolution: The History of an Idea*. Berkeley: University of California Press, 1984. Bowler traces the interactions of philosophy, natural history, and taxonomic systems to show their effects on the concepts of species and species change. He furnishes an excellent context for Linnaeus and shows the effect of his work on future evolutionary ideas.

Frängsmyr, Tore, ed. *Linnaeus: The Man and His Work*. Berkeley: University of California Press, 1983. This edited collection of works by Swedish scholars describes the personality of Linnaeus and examines his contributions to botany, geology, and human anthropology. It also looks at him as a Swedish national hero, trying to understand the difference between the man and his works, and the myth which has developed.

Gardner, Eldon J. *History of Biology*. 3d ed. Minneapolis: Burgess, 1972. The chapter "Systematizers of Plants and Animals" describes the various pre-Linnaean systems of classification, the contributions of Linnaeus (including a minimum amount of biographical material), as well as the post-Linnaean strategies with respect to taxonomy. There are helpful chronological and reference sections at the end of the chapter.

Gilbert, Bil. "The Obscure Fame of Carl Linnaeus." *Audubon* 86 (September, 1984): 102-114. This relatively short article gives personal glimpses of Linnaeus while discussing his many scientific contributions. It does not analyze the strengths and weaknesses of his works, but it does create a good introduction to his ideas and the intellectual environment in which he worked.

Hankins, Thomas. *Science and the Enlightenment*. New York: Cambridge University Press, 1985. The last third of chapter 5 is an excellent introduction to the philosophical commitments underlying eighteenth century taxonomy, showing how Linnaeus was both a product of his time and an innovator. The bibliography for the chapter provides the serious reader with several references dealing with specific issues concerning Linnaeus' system.

Mayr, Ernst. *The Growth of Biological Thought: Diversity, Evolution, and Inheritance*. Cambridge, Mass.: Harvard University Press, 1982. Mayr's treatment of Linnaeus places his work within the context of other naturalists, making clear the extent to which Linnaeus depended on other ideas and the degree to which his work was original.

Weinstock, John, ed. *Contemporary Perspectives on Linnaeus*. Lanham, Md.: University Press of America, 1985. This series of essays covers a number of aspects of Linnaeus' work: his relationship to Scholasticism; his impact on the development of evolutionary theory and the impact of evolutionary ideas on Linnaean taxonomy; the connection between Linnaeus' theology and his understanding of ecological relationships and the problem of extinction; his anthropology; and his status as a Swedish folk hero.

Sara Joan Miles

HANS LIPPERSHEY

Born: c. 1570; Wesel, Westphalia
Died: c. 1619; Middelburg, Zeeland, United Provinces
Areas of Achievement: Invention and technology
Contribution: Lippershey, a lens grinder and spectacle maker, generally receives credit for the invention of the telescope and binoculars in 1608.

Early Life

Hans Lippershey was born in Wesel, Westphalia, around the year 1570. Almost nothing is known about Lippershey's life, but it is apparent that between 1570 and 1608, Lippershey became a master lenscrafter and spectacle maker and established a shop in Middelburg, the capital of the province of Zeeland, in the United Provinces. In Lippershey's shop, many different kinds of glass lenses were ground and sold; spectacles, or eyeglasses, were also manufactured and sold there.

The idea of using lenses to make distant objects appear closer to the viewer was suggested by the Englishman Robert Grosseteste, Bishop of Lincoln, in the thirteenth century and was most likely considered even earlier. In the mid-sixteenth century, his fellow countryman and mathematician Leonard Digges appears to have devised a successful single-lens telescopic instrument. In 1585, another Englishman, William Bourne, described the use of a convex lens to magnify objects at a distance, although his device had the disadvantage of inverting the object's image in the lens. Bourne also hinted that a combination of a concave mirror with a convex lens might produce telescopic effects. Before 1589, Giambattista della Porta seems to have arranged one convex and one concave lens into a telescopic combination of perhaps 1 or 2 magnifications, as did Raffaelo Gualterotti in 1590. These lens combinations were used by Porta and Gualterotti only in spectacles to sharpen and correct short-range vision; they were ineffective when they were applied to viewing faraway objects. By the early seventeenth century, however, lensmakers had improved their ability to grind strong concave lenses; concave lenses with short focal lengths were also increasingly manufactured. Thus, the makings of the first telescope—a strong concave lens combined with a weak convex lens—were available in the spectacle makers' shops. Yet these improved lenses remained solely confined to use in eyeglasses.

Life's Work

Extant evidence remains insufficient to answer the question of who first arranged a combination of one strong concave with one weak convex lens that was of appreciable use in long-distance vision, that is, who invented the telescope. Historians still argue over assigning priority for the invention.

According to some accounts, of questionable validity, an early telescope was made in Italy in 1590 and was brought to the United Provinces in 1604. There is little doubt, however, that by 1608 the first working telescope—a convex objective lens combined with a concave eye lens to produce a sharp and upright image of a distant object—had been constructed. Historical records confirm that in October, 1608, three Dutchmen were in possession of such a device.

Lippershey is commonly awarded credit for inventing the telescope because he was the first to apply for a patent for such a device. The two other candidates for the title of inventor of the telescope are Zacharias Janssen and Jacob Metius. Janssen was another early seventeenth century Middelburg spectacle maker and peddler, of somewhat disreputable character. According to his son, a source many historians have discredited, Janssen constructed a telescope in 1604, after seeing an Italian model dated 1590. Metius, the son of engineer, mathematician, and burgomaster Adriaen Anthonisz, and the brother of mathematician Adriaen Metius, was a resident of Alkmaar. Historians supporting Metius' claim contend that Metius placed an order for some lenses to be ground at Lippershey's shop, and, while working with the lenses, Lippershey discovered his customer's intent. Metius' claim, however, rests more firmly on the fact that approximately two weeks after discussing Lippershey's application, the States-General (the representative assembly of the United Provinces) discussed the patent application for a telescope similar to, but not as well made as Lippershey's, which Metius had submitted.

Hieronymus Sirturi, in *Telescopium: sive ars perficiendi* (1618), first connected Lippershey with the invention of the instrument. In the seventeenth through the nineteenth centuries, opinion as to the device's inventor oscillated between Lippershey and Janssen. Modern historians consider Lippershey and Janssen as the two likely candidates for the title of inventor of the telescope, with Lippershey possessing the strongest claim.

Those who proclaim Lippershey the inventor of the telescope have related several stories describing the occasion of this invention, all with a common thread. According to the story, sometime in the summer of 1608 (or perhaps earlier) someone in Lippershey's spectacle shop looked through two lenses at once at a weather vane on a nearby church steeple and was surprised to find that the combination of lenses made the weather vane appear closer. The stories vary as to who made this discovery; two playing children, one of Lippershey's apprentices, and Lippershey himself have all been suggested. Lippershey then mounted two lenses in the same arrangement in a tube, thus constructing the first telescope. According to some sources, Lippershey's telescope was constructed using a double convex lens as the object glass and a double concave lens as the eyepiece and thus did not produce an inverted image. Other accounts describe it as a combination of two convex lenses, which did invert. This telescope probably was mounted in a paper tube about one and a half feet long, was about an inch and a half in aperture, and had no focusing mechanism. Both types fall into the general category of refracting telescopes.

Subsequent events in the history of the invention of the telescope are more clearly documented. After constructing his telescope, Lippershey wrote the provincial government of Zeeland about his invention. They referred him to Maurice of Nassau, Stadholder of the Dutch Republic, and to the republic's States-General. Lippershey contacted the States-General, requesting a thirty-year exclusive patent to the telescope's production and sale. According to its official records, on October 2, 1608, the States-General discussed Lippershey's petition, noting that he desired either an exclusive patent to the instrument or an annual pension, which would allow him to make telescopes solely for the use of his country. Lippershey's telescope was successfully tested by members of the States-General. On October 6, the government asked whether its manufacturer could improve the telescope so that the viewer might look through it with both eyes at once. Answering that he could, Lippershey set a price for the binocular of one thousand florins. Shortly thereafter, the spectacle maker furnished the States-General with a telescope, which a committee tested and agreed might be useful to the republic. The committee, reiterating their request for binoculars, reached an agreement with Lippershey for the price of nine hundred florins, three hundred of which they would pay in advance. On December 15, 1608, Lippershey presented the first binoculars to the States-General, received their approval and an order for two more, and requested a patent for the binoculars as well. Ultimately, however, the Dutch government concluded that, since other persons in addition to Lippershey were able to construct telescopes and binoculars, they could not grant him patents for the devices. Instead, they awarded him monetary prizes for the invention.

In 1612, Greek mathematician Joannes Dimisiani coined the word telescope, from the Greek "to see at a distance," for the new device, and after 1650 that gradually became its commonly accepted name. The type of instrument that many believe Lippershey constructed is often referred to as a Dutch telescope.

Summary

By the end of 1608, news of the telescope—or Dutch trunks, perspectives, or cylinders, as they were called—had spread to France, and the devices themselves could be purchased in the Holy Roman Empire. Early in 1609, telescopes could be bought in Paris. By May, 1609, the news of the invention had reached Milan, and before the end of the year, telescopes were being manufactured in England.

The significance of the telescope in military operations was recognized immediately upon its invention, and it was quickly put to use in warfare. Only in the eighteenth century, however, did the telescope become a common part of surveying and navigational instrumentation.

Eventually, the telescope exerted its greatest, although less tangible, impact upon the European intellectual world. The invention of the telescope was a key technological event that gave impetus to the scientific revolution. In May, 1609, Galileo, while visiting Venice, heard that a Dutchman had invented a device that made distant objects appear nearer and larger. Returning to Padua, Galileo immediately built his own, greatly improved telescope. Galileo turned his telescope to the skies and became the first person to view the sun and planets other than with the naked eye. His observations and discoveries dealt a crushing blow to the old geocentric astronomy and paved the way for the acceptance of the heliocentric system.

At first, the telescope was used only for qualitative astronomical observations. Within a few decades, however, the telescope was applied to quantitative observation of the heavens, and it greatly increased the level of accuracy obtainable. Still, the instrument itself, and its relative the microscope, remained novelties and did not become widely accepted scientific instruments until a generation after their invention. It was not until about 1660 that telescopes and microscopes were regularly manufactured, and not until after 1665 was observation of the heavens with the naked eye abandoned and the telescope deemed indispensable in astronomical observation. From this time until the early twentieth century, the telescope remained the primary astronomical instrument.

Bibliography
Doorman, G. *Patents for Inventions in the Netherlands During the 16th, 17th, and 18th Centuries with Notes on the Historical Development of Technics.* Translated by Johann Meijer. The Hague: Martinus Nijhoff, 1942. The best available English source of information on Lippershey's claim to the title of inventor of the telescope. Contains an essay on the telescope and a history of the patent applications for its invention. An important and detailed study.
King, Henry C. *The History of the Telescope.* New York: Sky, 1955. The standard monograph history of the telescope that should be read by everyone interested in its invention and development. Contains an excellent summary of the device's early history and what is known of Lippershey's work.
Maddison, Francis. "Early Astronomical and Mathematical Instruments: A Brief Survey of Sources and Modern Studies." *History of Science* 2 (1963): 17-50. This easily obtainable article contains an excellent, annotated bibliography of the literature available on the telescope and related instruments.

Moll, Gerard. "On the First Invention of Telescopes." *Journal of the Royal Institution* 1 (1831): 319-332, 483-496. Invaluable, though somewhat hard to find, as a source of information about the early history of the telescope. It discusses the patent applications made to the States-General of the United Provinces and provides excerpts from the official state records concerning Lippershey's and others' applications.

Singer, Charles. "Steps Leading to the Invention of the First Optical Apparatus." In *Studies in the History and Method of Science*, edited by Charles Singer, vol. 2. Oxford, England: Clarendon Press, 1921. This essay concisely and chronologically examines developments in optical theory and technology from antiquity through the construction of the first telescopes in the early seventeenth century. Excellently documented, the work includes references to and excerpts from the works of a wide range of scientists and inventors. Singer presents a discussion of the claims of Lippershey, Janssen, and Metius to the instrument's invention, but in this regard Singer has been superseded by Albert Van Helden's work.

Van Helden, Albert. "The Historical Problem of the Invention of the Telescope." *History of Science* 13 (1975): 251-263. An authoritative discussion of the debate over who should receive credit for the invention of the telescope. Discusses the claims of Lippershey, Janssen, and Metius, based on an examination of early historical documents and treatises on the history of the telescope. Contains references to numerous valuable foreign-language sources on the invention and history of the telescope.

Wolf, Abraham. *A History of Science, Technology, and Philosophy, in the 16th and 17th Centuries*. 2d ed. Vol. 1. Gloucester, Mass.: Peter Smith, 1968. An easily accessible work which gives a concise history of the invention of the telescope and its subsequent development by Galileo, Johannes Kepler, and others in the sixteenth and seventeenth centuries. The work shows the immediate and long-range consequences of the application of the telescope to astronomy and also discusses the telescope as one of several crucial technological developments of the period.

Martha Ellen Webb

FRANZ LISZT

Born: October 22, 1811; Raiding, Hungary
Died: July 31, 1886; Bayreuth, Germany
Area of Achievement: Music
Contribution: Liszt revolutionized the art of piano playing and thus established the vogue of the recitalist. As a composer, he attempted to reconcile the trends of French and German Romanticism, created the musical genre of the symphonic poem, founded new innovations in harmony and form, and in his late works anticipated many devices of twentieth century music.

Early Life

Franz Liszt was born in Raiding, near Sopron, in the province of Burgenland. His father, Ádám Liszt, was a clerk in the service of Prince Nikolaus Esterházy, the Hungarian noble family that had supported Joseph Haydn. An amateur cellist, Ádám Liszt had played in orchestras under Haydn and Ludwig van Beethoven and was his son's first teacher in piano.

Young Liszt showed phenomenal gifts for music as a child and began to study piano in his sixth year. His debut concerts in Sopron and Bratislava at the age of nine enabled him to acquire the support of several Hungarian nobles to finance his musical studies in Vienna under Karl Czerny and Antonio Salieri. Liszt soon acquired a reputation as a formidable sight reader. He published his first composition, a variation on a waltz by Anton Diabelli, in 1822, and in the following year made his debut in Vienna. The often-repeated story that Beethoven attended the concert and kissed the boy afterward cannot be proved, but it is certain that Liszt met Beethoven at his apartment and forever cherished the meeting.

Liszt continued his musical eduation in Paris. Denied admission to the Paris Conservatory because of his foreign citizenship, he studied privately with Anton Reicha and Ferdinando Paer. In 1824, he began his concert tours of England; until 1847, he was best known as a virtuoso pianist who revolutionized the art of playing that instrument and who was a pioneer in giving solo recitals performed from memory; he even invented the term "recital," to describe his solo programs in London in 1840.

The death of his father in 1826 and the rejection of his suit of Caroline de Saint-Cricq by her noble family brought about a period of depression when he contemplated entering the priesthood. In the early 1830's, he came under the influence of the Saint-Simonian movement and the liberal Catholicism of the Abbé Hughes-Félicité-Robert de Lamennais; both placed art in a central place in society. Liszt's first mature compositions, the *Apparitions* (1834), were written under Lamennais' influence, whereas his piano piece *Lyon* was influenced by a silk-weavers' strike there in 1834.

Life's Work

Liszt compensated for his lack of formal education by extensive reading and by seeking the company of writers. He was introduced to the Countess Marie d'Agoult, of German descent, who left her husband and children in 1835 to live with Liszt in Switzerland and Italy. The musical results of the sojourn were the first two volumes of the *Années de pèlerinage* (1835-1877; years of pilgrimage), featuring, in the first volume, nature scenes in Switzerland and, in the second, the art and literature of Italy. D'Agoult guided Liszt in his reading and interested him in the visual arts. They had three children. Blandine and Daniel died while in their twenties, but Cosima lived until 1930, to become the wife first of the pianist-conductor Hans von Bülow and then of the composer Richard Wagner.

Liszt's decision to return to concert playing in 1839 placed a strain on his relationship with d'Agoult, which ended in 1844 during a hectic period of concertizing all over Europe, performing as far afield as Portugal, Ireland, and Turkey, traveling under primitive conditions, and being subject to the kind of adulation given to modern rock stars. The main works of this period were his songs for voice and piano (highly expressive and unjustly neglected) and his opera paraphrases and transcriptions for the piano. The transcriptions are reproductions of the vocal music, but the paraphrases are virtual recompositions of the opera based on its main tunes; the most famous of these is the *Réminiscences de Don Juan* (1841), based on Wolfgang Amadeus Mozart's opera *Don Giovanni* (1787). During his tours of Hungary, he was able to hear authentic Gypsy music and re-created these sounds in his Hungarian Rhapsodies (1839-1847).

On his last concert tour in 1847, he met in Poland the Princess Carolyne de Sayn-Wittgenstein, with whom he began a lengthy relationship; because the Czar of Russia would not grant her a divorce, she could not marry Liszt but was able to flee Russia with most of her money. Liszt, in turn, accepted an offer to become musical director of the court at Weimar and was able to abandon his career as a touring piano virtuoso in 1847 to devote himself to musical composition. He and Carolyne moved there during the following year.

During Liszt's thirteen years in Weimar, he revised most of his earlier compositions for publication and embarked on many ambitious musical projects which he had sketched earlier, such as his two piano concerti. During these years, Liszt invented the symphonic poem, an extended programmatic work for orchestra. His first two works in this genre, the so-called Mountain Symphony (begun 1848) and *Tasso* (begun 1849-1854), required assistance from others as Liszt was learning how to write for orchestra, but the next work, *Les Préludes* (1854), his best-known symphonic poem, shows his complete mastery of both form and instrumentation. Among the best of the remaining nine are *Orpheus* (1853-1854) and *Hamlet* (1858). The culmination of his orchestral works is his monumental *A Faust Symphony* (1854-1861), composed of three movements, character portrayals of the three main personages in Johann Wolfgang von Goethe's drama: Faust, Gretchen, and Mephistopheles. The less conventional *A Symphony to Dante's "Divina Commedia"* (1855-1856) was originally intended to accompany a stage performance with dioramas and does not follow normal symphonic form. A work of "absolute music" without an overt program is the Sonata in B Minor (1852-1853) for piano, the culmination of Liszt's experiments in harmony, form, and the construction of a large-scale work from a few ideas which are extensively developed and transformed.

While in Weimar, Liszt continued his altruistic gestures that got the music of his contemporaries performed. Earlier he had played the large piano works of Robert Schumann and Frédéric Chopin when their composers were physically unable to do so, and widened the audience for Beethoven's symphonies and Schubert's songs by arranging them for the piano. Now he devoted his energies to organizing and conducting performances of the operas of Richard Wagner, who was in exile in Switzerland after his participation in the abortive revolt in Dresden in 1849. Though Liszt had abandoned concertizing except for benefits and charities, he had a large number of piano students whom he taught without charge, and a coterie of ardent musical disciples. Disappointed at the lack of support he was receiving in Weimar from the new grand duke, who preferred the theater to music, Liszt resigned as musical director in 1858 and made it effective after a music festival in 1861, when he moved to Rome to join Carolyne.

The wedding of Liszt and Carolyne was to have taken place on the composer's fiftieth birthday, but it was abruptly canceled; the reasons have yet to be revealed. Shortly thereafter, Liszt took the initial steps toward entering the priesthood; though he dressed in clerical clothes and was known as "Abbé Liszt," he did not complete the final stages of holy orders and thus could not say Mass or hear confessions. Not until 1865 was his entry into the religious life generally known. During this period, he wrote principally religious music, especially choral works such as the *Missa Choralis* (1865) and completing two large oratorios, *Die Legende von der heiligen Elisabeth* (1857-1862) and *Christus* (1855-1866) but also including the "Legends" for piano (1863) and the *Totentanz* (1849, revised 1853, 1859; dance of death) for piano and orchestra, a paraphrase of the *Dies Irae* (day of wrath) chant from the Requiem Mass.

In 1869, Liszt was reconciled with the Grand Duke of Weimar and began his *vie trifurquée* (three-pronged life) between Rome, Weimar, and Budapest. The third book of his *Années de pèlerinage* reflects his journeys, especially to Rome and Hungary. The best known of the works in this set is "The Fountains of the Villa d'Este" in Rome, where Liszt often stayed; this piece anticipates many of the impressionistic harmonic and coloristic effects of Claude Debussy and Maurice Ravel.

In Weimar and Budapest, Liszt held master classes in which he trained a new generation of pianists. His style of composition also changed to a very spare, attenuated style, avoiding extensive developments or repetitions and using often unusual harmonic sonorities which he treated in unconventional ways. Many of these last pieces are extremely short, beginning and ending abruptly, without the extensive introductions or closes of his Weimar works. Publishers rejected these compositions, nearly all of which were published long after Liszt's death. Best known of these late works are the short piano pieces, such as "Unstern" (evil star) and "Nuages gris" (gray clouds) from the 1880's, and the *Via Crucis* (1879; the way of the cross) for chorus and organ.

Liszt's death in 1886 came, after an extensive tour of Belgium and England, in Bayreuth, Germany, where he had attended a festival of operas by his son-in-law Richard Wagner. The cause of death was pneumonia; he had earlier suffered from edema.

Summary

Franz Liszt was a man of immense personal magnetism and charisma, as attested by the immense acclaim he received during his years as a virtuoso and reflected in later years during his charity concerts and appearances as a conductor. He attracted a devoted coterie of students, and though he failed to found a school of composition, he influenced virtually every composer of the second half of the nineteenth century and anticipated many of the devices and techniques of the twentieth.

A man of formidable energy, he composed about thirteen hundred works. He was one of the leading letter writers of the century, and, though he did not write the many books and essays attributed to him, he dictated their ideas, edited the text, and assumed responsibility for their final form. If one had to choose a single composer whose works sum up the nineteenth century's achievements, innovations, and also weaknesses, Liszt would be the most likely candidate.

Bibliography

Fay, Amy. *Music-Study in Germany*. Chicago: Jansen, McClurg, 1881. Reprint. New York: Dover, 1965. This engagingly written firsthand account of Liszt's teaching in Weimar was written by one of his few American pupils; her study also gives an incisive view of Germany shortly after unification.

Journal of the American Liszt Society. 1960-   . This journal, edited since 1987 by Michael Saffle, is principally devoted to articles dealing with Liszt's musical style. Also contains numerous investigations of Liszt's life, works, students, associates, and ambience.

László, Zsigmond, and Béla Mátéka. *Franz Liszt: A Biography in Pictures.* London: Barrie & Rockliff, 1968. This series of pictures and facsimiles of manuscripts and documents is arranged to provide a chronological account of Liszt's life, achievements, and circle of friends and students. An extensive commentary explains and connects the various illustrations.

Longyear, Rey M. "Ferenc (Franz) Liszt." In *Nineteenth-Century Romanticism in Music.* Englewood Cliffs, N.J.: Prentice-Hall, 1969, 3d ed. 1988. A brief survey of Liszt's musical style, emphasizing the Weimar and late works, which relates Liszt's music to that of the century as a whole. Liszt is also presented as a seminal composer for the twentieth century.

Merrick, Paul. *Revolution and Religion in the Music of Liszt.* Cambridge: Cambridge University Press, 1987. This interesting and controversial study emphasizes Liszt's music with religious import, particularly the choral works; the author tends to overstate his case in seeking hidden religious programs in some of the instrumental works.

Searle, Humphrey. *The Music of Liszt.* London: Williams & Norgate, 1954. A still-valuable survey of this prolific composer's works. Not too technically oriented for the person with limited musical background. Searle's book was a landmark in restoring Liszt's works to musical respectability after decades of neglect and disdain.

Searle, Humphrey, and Sharon Winklhofer. "Franz Liszt." In *The New Grove Early Romantic Masters I: Chopin, Schumann and Liszt,* edited by Nicholas Temperley. New York: W. W. Norton, 1985. A concise study, balanced between Liszt's life and his music, derived from Searle's article in *The New Grove* and revised by Sharon Winklhofer. The list of Liszt's approximately thirteen hundred compositions is particularly valuable.

Walker, Alan. *Franz Liszt.* Vol. 1, *The Virtuoso Years, 1811-1847.* Rev. ed. Ithaca, N.Y.: Cornell University Press, 1987.

——————. *Franz Liszt.* Vol. 2, *The Weimar Years, 1848-1861.* New York: Alfred A. Knopf, 1989. Walker's two-volume study is the most complete biography of Liszt. Though the focus is on his biography, some often insightful discussion is given to his music. Volume 2 provides the definitive account of his most productive years and shows Liszt not only as the musical director at Weimar but also as a composer, teacher, administrator, and writer on music.

Rey M. Longyear

NIKOLAY IVANOVICH LOBACHEVSKY

Born: December 1, 1792; Nizhny Novgorod, Russia
Died: February 24, 1856; Kazan, Russia
Area of Achievement: Mathematics
Contribution: Lobachevsky was the boldest and most consistent founder of a post-Euclidean theory of real space. His persistence in holding open his revolutionary line of inquiry into the reality of geometry helped to set the stage for the radical discoveries of twentieth century theoretical physics.

Early Life

Nikolay Ivanovich Lobachevsky, whose parents were a minor government clerk and an energetic woman of apparently no education, was a member of what most nearly corresponded to a middle class in preemancipation Russia. As a government-supported student, he was recorded in school as a *raznochinets* (person of miscellaneous rank—not a noble, a peasant, or a merchant). Despite the early marriage of his mother, Praskovya, to the collegiate registrar Ivan Maksimovich Lobachevsky, the evidence strongly suggests that Nikolay and his two brothers were the illegitimate sons of an army officer and land surveyor, S. S. Shebarshin. Ivan Maksimovich Lobachevsky died when Nikolay, the middle son, was only five years old. The widowed Praskovya left Nizhny Novgorod and moved eastward along the Volga to the provincial center of Kazan. She enrolled all three boys in the local *Gymnasium* (preparatory school). Nikolay attended the school between 1802 and 1807.

Lobachevsky's student years at Kazan University (1807 to 1811) were a time when Russia was eager to learn from the West and to give more than it had received. Lobachevsky was awarded Kazan's first master's degree for his thesis on elliptic movement of the heavenly bodies. He worked closely with Johann Martin Bartels, who had earlier discovered and taught Carl Friedrich Gauss, a great mathematician of the day.

Lobachevsky taught at Kazan University from 1811 until his mandated but most unwilling retirement in 1846. The tenure of Mikhail Magnitskii as curator from 1819 to 1826 was the school's most difficult period. A religious fanatic who attempted to give this particularly science-oriented university the atmosphere of a medieval monastery, Magnitskii was imprisoned in 1826 for his gross incompetence. He was particularly suspicious of the philosophy of Immanuel Kant. All the distinguished German professors left; for a time, the young Lobachevsky carried the burden of providing all the advanced lectures in mathematics, physics, and astronomy alone. His own development and integrity were only strengthened during this phase. It did Lobachevsky no harm that he too was anti-Kantian; he completely disagreed with Kant's view that Euclidean geometry was proof of the human mind's inborn sense of lines, planes, and space.

Life's Work

As a young professor in 1817, Lobachevsky was intrigued by the problem of Euclid's fifth postulate, which implies the possibility of infinitely parallel lines. More technically, one may draw a single line through a given point on a given plane that will never intersect another given line on the same plane. On the one hand, this is not a simple axiom that has no need of proof. On the other, it cannot be proved. Two thousand years of general satisfaction with Euclidean geometry had seen many vain attempts to prove the fifth postulate and thereby give this geometry its final perfection. Such attempts became particularly frenzied in the eighteenth century. A rare few thinkers began to entertain the idea that the postulate was wrong, but they denied it even to themselves.

From 1817 to 1822, Lobachevsky made repeated attempts to prove the fifth postulate, already resorting to non-Euclidean concepts such as an axiom of directionality. Once he perceived the hidden tautology of even his best attempts, he concluded that the postulate must be wrong and that geometry must be put on a new foundation.

In addition to the resistance of intellectual tradition, Lobachevsky could expect little support in a country whose ruling house saw itself as the very embodiment of stability and conservatism. The unsettling implications of losing true parallelism and rocking the foundations of classical geometry were as unwelcome in czarist Russia as they could possibly have been anywhere in the world. This resistance makes Lobachevsky's boldness all the more impressive. Simultaneously and independently, two leading mathematicians of the day—Gauss in Germany and János Bolyai in Hungary—were facing the same conclusion as Lobachevsky. Despite their secure reputations, both refrained from pursuing the implications of negating the fifth postulate, correctly assessing that the world was not ready for it.

To exacerbate the radicalism of his approach in a highly religious country, Lobachevsky, though not an atheist, was a materialist in a most fundamental and original sense of the word. In his mathematical syllabus for 1822, he made the extraordinary statement: "We apprehend in Nature only bodies alone; consequently, concepts of lines and planes are derived and not directly acquired concepts, and therefore should not be taken as the basis of mathematical science."

In 1823, Lobachevsky's full-length geometry textbook *Geometriya* was submitted to school district curator Magnitskii, who sent it to the St. Petersburg Academy of Sciences for review. The text was emphatically rejected, and Lobachevsky's difficulties with the academy began. A subsequent manuscript, "O nachalakh geometrii" (1829-1830; on the elements of geometry), was also submitted to the academy. Not only did the academy reject the manuscript but also an academician's flawed critique was fed to the popular press, which turned it into a lampoon of Lobachevsky.

The date February 7, 1826, marks the official debut of Lobachevskian geometry as an independent theory. On that day, Lobachevsky submitted to his department his paper entitled "Exposition succincte des principes de la géométrie avec une démonstration rigoureuse du théorème des parallèles." It was rejected for publication, as his colleagues ventured no opinion on it. Other major works continued to be largely ignored.

Nevertheless, the new school district curator who replaced Magnitskii, Count Mikhail Musin-Pushkin, was sufficiently impressed with Lobachevsky to make him rector of Kazan University in 1827. Thus began Lobachevsky's dual life as a brilliantly successful local administrator and a frustrated intellectual pioneer kept outside the pale of the St. Petersburg establishment. During his tenure as rector, Lobachevsky built Kazan University into an outstanding institution of high standards. He founded the scientific journal *Uchenye zapiski*, in which he published many of his works and which has flourished to the present day.

In 1846, Lobachevsky's life in the sphere of action fell apart, as he received a succession of blows: Musin-Pushkin was transferred to the St. Petersburg school district; the request to forestall Lobachevsky's mandatory retirement was denied; his eldest son, Aleksei, died of tuberculosis at nineteen; his wife became seriously ill; his wife's half brother, dispatched to handle the sale of two distant estates, gambled away both the Lobachevskys' money and all of his own; and Lobachevsky's eyesight began to deteriorate. In the last year of his life, he was virtually blind, yet he dictated his best and strongest work, *Pangéométrie* (1855-1856). His views had evolved from rejection of Euclidean parallelism into a vision of reality that anticipated theories of the curvature of space and was validated by Albert Einstein's general theory of relativity.

Summary

When Nikolay Ivanovich Lobachevsky's ideas first caught the imagination of a wide audience in the late nineteenth century, he was dubbed "the Copernicus of geometry," partly because of his Slavic origin (Nicolaus Copernicus was Polish), but far more because of the profound reorientation of thought that he set in motion. Lobachevsky forced the scale of earthly dimension as the measure of the universe off its pedestal, as Copernicus had earlier shattered the illusory status of Earth as the center of the solar system. This upheaval, which initially met with great resistance, forced the mind to focus on awesome phenomena that were not so much abstract as invisible to the human eye. Lobachevsky promoted bold and fruitful speculation about the nature of reality and space.

In *Pangéométrie*, his crowning work, Lobachevsky opens: "Instead of beginning geometry with the line and plane, as is usually done, I have preferred to begin with the sphere and the circle. . . ." For this geometry, there are no straight lines or flat planes, and all lines and planes must curve, however infinitesimally. Yet, while pointing to modern concepts of the curvature of space, Lobachevsky does not abolish Euclidean geometry. In some areas, his geometry and Euclid's coincide. Yet the latter is a limited case, whose relative certainties hold true on a merely earthly scale. In the conclusion to *Pangéométrie*, Lobachevsky correctly predicted that interstellar space would be the proving ground for his theory, which he saw not as an abstruse logical exercise but as the real geometry of the universe.

Bibliography
Bonola, Roberto. *Non-Euclidean Geometry: A Critical and Historical Study of Its Development*. Translated by H. S. Carslaw. Mineola, N.Y.: Dover, 1955. Very up-to-date for its time, and still relevant to the general reader. Focuses on a basic exposition of Lobachevsky's theories without the highly sophisticated applications thereof. Contains several relevant appendices.
Kagan, Veniamin Fedorovich. *N. Lobachevsky and His Contributions to Science*. Moscow: Foreign Languages, 1957. A solid, basic account by one of the chief Russian experts on Lobachevsky. Omits most of the human-interest material to be found in Kagan's 1944 biography. Includes a bibliography, necessarily of primarily Russian materials.
Kulczycki, Stefan. *Non-Euclidean Geometry*. Translated by Stanisław Knapowski. Elmsford, N.Y.: Pergamon Press, 1961. Another introduction for the general reader, which updates but does not supplant Bonola.
Shirokov, Pëtr Alekseevich. *A Sketch of the Fundamentals of Lobachevskian Geometry*. Edited by I. N. Bronshtein. Translated by Leo F. Boron and Ward D. Bouwsma. Groningen, the Netherlands: P. Noordhoff, 1964. Written in Russian in the 1940's, it appears to have been aimed at the secondary-school mathematics student.
Smogorzhevsky, A. S. *Lobachevskian Geometry*. Translated by V. Kisin. Moscow: Mir, 1982. Partly accessible to the general reader but of particular interest to the serious student of mathematics. Emphasizes specific mathematical applications of Lobachevsky's theories.
Vucinich, Alexander. "Nikolay Ivanovich Lobachevsky: The Man Behind the First Non-Euclidean Geometry." *Isis* 53 (December, 1962). A substantial, well-written article, abundantly annotated to point the reader in the direction of all the basic sources, which are primarily in Russian. Highlights some avenues not mentioned elsewhere, such as Lobachevsky's role in the mathematization of science. Includes a balanced account of Lobachevsky's life.

D. Gosselin Nakeeb

MIKHAIL VASILYEVICH LOMONOSOV

Born: November 19, 1711; near Kholmogory, Russia
Died: April 15, 1765; St. Petersburg, Russia
Areas of Achievement: Literature, chemistry, physics, and historiography
Contribution: Through his reform of the Russian literary language, his scientific investigations, and his reinterpretation of early Russian history, Lomonosov was at the beginning of modern Russian intellectual history and a founder of Russian nationalism.

Early Life

Mikhail Vasilyevich Lomonosov was born in 1711 the son of prosperous peasant parents near Kholmogory, Russia. His father was a fisherman. Lomonosov seems to have been a voracious reader at an early age, and gradually he came to outgrow the small village of his birth. In 1730, he went to Moscow on foot, pretending to be the son of a priest, to enroll in the Slavo-Greco-Latin academy of the Zaikonospassky monastery, where he studied Greek and Latin. From there, he continued to study at the St. Petersburg Imperial Academy of Sciences in 1736, but he soon secured a newly created traveling scholarship to study in Germany.

In 1736-1739, Lomonosov studied principally the humanities under the mathematician Christian von Wolff at the University of Marburg and in 1739-1741 changed to chemistry, mining, and metallurgy at the University of Freiburg in Saxony. He may have married a German woman in 1740, but, apparently to escape her, his own drunkenness and debts, and possible imprisonment for them, Lomonosov joined the Prussian army later in that same year. In 1741, he returned home to Russia to become a professor of chemistry at the new University of St. Petersburg Imperial Academy of Sciences and a member of the academy. It remained the base for his life's work.

Life's Work

In St. Petersburg, Lomonosov became Russia's first great scientist. By 1748, he had founded the first chemistry laboratory in the Russian Empire. He worked on the mechanical nature of heat and developed a kinetic theory of gases. In 1752, his investigations led to the initial discovery of the law of conservation of matter eighteen years before similar work of the French chemist Antoine Lavoisier was published and earned for him the lion's share of the credit in his own time and through history. Lomonosov also had an impact on the development of Russian geography and cartography. For example, he redrew and reconstructed an immense globe of 3.1 meters in diameter, which had been a gift from Duke Christian August of Schleswig-Holstein-Gottorf to Peter the Great at the end of the Great Northern War in 1721. Lomonosov and his team took almost seven years (1748-1754) to complete the work.

Under Empress Elizabeth, the Russian Empire was still somewhat too far out of the mainstream of Western civilization for achievements such as Lomonosov's to be fully noticed. Yet his work could not be denied. He published numerous scientific studies of importance, including *Slovo o pro-iskhozhdeni sveta* (1756; comments on the origin of light representing a new theory of color). For his accomplishments in the fields of chemistry, optics, metallurgy, geography, natural sciences, physics, and astronomy, Lomonosov was made a member of the Swedish Academy of Sciences in 1760 and the Bologna Academy of Sciences in 1764.

As important a scientist as Lomonosov was, his influence on the development of the arts in Russia, especially literature, was far greater. He revived the ancient art of mosaics in Russia and was a folklorist, poet, dramatist, historian, and philologist. In 1755, Lomonosov contributed to the founding of Moscow University, which today bears his name as Mikhail Lomonosov University.

While his poems and plays were very artificial, mechanical, and typically classicist (many being in honor of Elizabeth), Lomonosov's most important achievement was in the field of philology. In 1757, he published his monumental *Rossiyskaya grammatika* (Russian grammar), which initiated the reform of the Russian literary language. In opposition to the ideas of many of the leading Russian literary figures of the time, including Vasily Trediakovsky, Lomonosov adopted a syllabotonic versification system between Old Church Slavonic and vernacular Russian for the standard written Russian language. These linguistic changes, fostered by Lomonosov in the middle of the eighteenth century, formed the basis for the literary achievements of the golden age of Russian literature in the first half of the nineteenth century.

During his study of Old Church Slavonic, Lomonosov came to know the early Russian chronicle literature quite well. He wrote several works critiquing this genre, including *Kratkoy rossiyskoy letopisets* (1759; brief Russian chronicle). Gradually, his examinations of the chronicles led him into the field of historiography to challenge the Normanist interpretation of the founding of the first Russian state, the Kievan Rus, in the ninth and tenth centuries.

The Normanist view was the product of the serious scholarship of several prominent German historians who had been brought into Russia since the reign of Peter the Great to help staff the Russian Academy. Largely based on the evidence provided by the chronicle literature, the Normanist historians, including G. A. Bayer, G. F. Müller, and August Ludwig von Schlözer, attributed the establishment of the first Russian state to outside (primarily Norse and Germanic) influences. This interpretation was an affront to Lomonosov's nascent Russian nationalism, evident in his work in Russian philology and based on his critique of the chronicles. He sought to counter it and to combat the influence of the so-called German Party in the Russian

Academy. In so doing, he became, along with a fellow Russian historian, Vasily Nikitich Tatischev, a founder of the anti-Normanist interpretation of early Russian history and the nationalist or state school of Russian historiography. Lomonosov's final ideas on the subject appeared posthumously in 1766.

As an early Russian nationalist, Lomonosov came to admire Peter the Great for making the Russian Empire great. In part because of his praise for her and her father and because he shared her anti-German sentiments, Lomonosov was favored by the Empress Elizabeth but not so by her more Germanic-oriented successors, Peter III and Catherine the Great. Lomonosov died in St. Petersburg in 1765 probably of alcoholism.

Summary

Mikhail Vasilyevich Lomonosov was the unheralded founder of modern Russian science, literature, and culture. He was a protean intellect and a genius, rightfully compared to Benjamin Franklin, another universal thinker of the eighteenth century. Lomonosov laid the foundation for scientific investigation in Russia, and many times his own discoveries led to or even predated later accredited advancements in the West. He pointed the way to the greatness of Russian literature and historiography in the nineteenth and twentieth centuries.

In his Russian self-consciousness, Lomonosov mirrored and stimulated the early stirrings of nationalism that were beginning to manifest themselves among some of the more progressive members of Russia's elite. He not only felt them and reflected them in his linguistic, literary, and historical works but also began to provide these nationalist feelings with a sound intellectual matrix. In this respect, Lomonosov can be seen as an early advocate of what would become the early nineteenth century conservative Romantic nationalism of Russian Slavophilism. At the same time, his achievements became a source of pride, inspiration, and direction for the Russian nation and helped it to contribute to and to move closer to the mainstream of Western civilization.

Bibliography

Florinsky, Michael T., ed. *McGraw-Hill Encyclopedia of Russia and the Soviet Union*. New York: McGraw-Hill, 1961. This older standard reference work offers a rather lengthy and balanced listing on Lomonosov. His artistic and scientific achievements are generally treated equally.

Kudryavtsev, B. B. *The Life and Work of Mikhail Vasilyevich Lomonosov*. Moscow: Foreign Languages, 1954. A rare English translation of a Soviet biography. A thorough treatment, stressing his scientific achievements and offering the standard Stalinist-nationalist view of him.

Menshutkin, B. N. *Russia's Lomonosov: Chemist, Courtier, Physicist, Poet*.

Princeton, N.J.: Princeton University Press, 1952. An updated and edited translation of the czarist 1912 original. Still one of the best and most readable biographies of Lomonosov.

Mirsky, D. S. *A History of Russian Literature*. Rev. ed. New York: Alfred A. Knopf, 1964. This work goes well beyond placing Lomonosov in perspective with the development of modern Russian literature, lionizing him as the father of modern Russian civilization.

Rice, Tamara Talbot. *Elizabeth, Empress of Russia*. New York: Praeger, 1970. Chapter 8 of this cultural biography of the daughter of and successor to Peter the Great and her times is largely on Lomonosov and his literary achievements. Easy reading and well illustrated.

Rogger, Hans. *National Consciousness in Eighteenth Century Russia*. Cambridge, Mass.: Harvard University Press, 1960. Lomonosov is put into perspective with the development of Russian nationalism in the eighteenth century and the eighteenth century Russian intelligentsia. Includes essential background on Lomonosov and his Russia. Scholarly and well written.

Segel, Harold B., ed. *The Literature of Eighteenth Century Russia*. Vol. 1. New York: E. P. Dutton, 1967. This multivolume anthology includes several good examples of Lomonosov's more important literary works with rather extensive introductions to them.

Silbajoris, Frank R. "Mikhail Vasilievich Lomonosov." In *Handbook of Russian Literature*, edited by Victor Terras. New Haven, Conn.: Yale University Press, 1985. A capsulization of the more current interpretations of Lomonosov and his literary work. Deemphasizes his scientific contributions.

Stacy, Robert H. *Russian Literary Criticism: A Short History*. Syracuse, N.Y.: Syracuse University Press, 1974. This volume contains an informative chapter on Lomonosov's life and achievements.

Dennis Reinhartz

LOUIS XI

Born: July 3, 1423; Bourges, France
Died: August 30, 1483; Plessis-les-Tours, France
Areas of Achievement: Politics and government
Contribution: Louis XI rebuilt France from the Hundred Years' War, prevented renewed English invasion, demolished Burgundy as a great power within France, ended the era of feudal dominance, restored the extent and influence of the royal domain, and reorganized medieval France as a modern nation-state, with himself as the prototype of Renaissance despotism.

Early Life

When Louis de Valois was born in 1423 to Charles VII and Mary of Anjou, the misfortunes of the Hundred Years' War saw most of France controlled by the English or their Burgundian allies following the 1415 Battle of Agincourt. Louis was reared with middle-class companions at Castle Loches in Touraine and was educated on broad lines, while his father, disinherited by the 1420 Treaty of Troyes, dawdled at Bourges, essentially waiting on events. Joan of Arc's victories in 1429 and 1430 revived confidence in the Valois cause, and, following the Franco-Burgundian alliance of 1435 and the 1436 recapture of Paris, Charles VII felt secure enough to bring the dauphin, Louis, into public affairs.

In 1436, Louis entered an arranged political marriage to eleven-year-old Princess Margaret of Scotland, an unhappy and barren union. His soldiering also began in 1436, and by 1439 he held independent commands. As a general, Louis was energetic, courageous, and moderately successful. As king, he would prefer diplomacy to war from his personal experience that "battles are unpredictable."

From 1436 to 1445, Louis and his father agreed on broad royal policy, but not on specific men and measures, and in 1440 the dauphin was persuaded by powerful magnates to head a rebellion dubbed "the Praguerie." The revolt failed, and reconciliation followed. After his wife's death in 1445, the dauphin resumed his demand for new royal advisers, and in 1447 Charles sent his heir to semibanishment as governor of Dauphiné.

Louis reorganized the government in Dauphiné and took his own line in foreign policy, including his 1451 marriage to Charlotte of Savoy, which Charles refused to accept. The crucial father-and-son quarrel centered on the efforts of each to control or bribe the advisers of the other. In 1456, Charles sent his troops to Dauphiné to enforce his authority, and Louis fled to the court of Burgundy.

Louis spent five years in the Burgundian Netherlands as a guest of Duke Philip the Good and his son, the future Duke Charles the Bold. Louis could see that their wealth, army, and ambition were all organized toward making Burgundy an independent power in France and Europe. Charles VII died on July 22, 1461, and Louis at last came to the throne of France. He was thirty-eight years old.

Life's Work

As king, Louis initially replaced most of his father's advisers but continued basic royal policy. External defense and internal coordination were still the great national problems. Territorial feudalism still defied control by wreaking local havoc, but the feudal levy of lance-wielding knights could not defend France in wars of gunpowder and missiles. Yet the king's expensive, new standing army of middle-class professionals threatened the whole structure of feudal government, and the great magnates resisted in four separate rebellions against Louis.

In the first of these feudal revolts, audaciously advertised as "The League of the Public Weal," Charles led a concerted advance on Paris in 1465. The indecisive Battle at Montlhéry on July 16 left Paris saved by Louis but besieged by Charles and the magnates. To keep Paris, the king was forced to give the rebels territories later expensively regained. The Burgundian settlement was challenged by Charles after his 1467 accession, and Louis was then forced to make humiliating concessions at the Peronne Conference of 1468.

The 1468 marriage alliance of Charles and Margaret of York, sister of Edward IV of England, posed an open threat to Louis of invasion. His bold support of the Lancastrian restoration of 1470 seemed ill-judged when Edward resumed power in 1471. By the time Edward invaded France in June of 1475, however, Charles was preoccupied in a Rhineland siege. Louis came to terms with Edward in the August 29 Treaty of Picquigny, offering him money and a pension; the two monarchs exchanged sardonic compliments through an iron grill.

Charles, meanwhile, pursued his claims in other quarters. In 1476, the duke and his army advanced to Lake Neuchâtel and began a campaign in which he was thrice soundly beaten in unexpected attacks by Swiss infantry— at Grandson, Murten, and Nancy, where Charles died fighting in 1477. His heir was his nineteen-year-old daughter, Mary.

Louis gave the Swiss only money until they began to win and then moved decisively, bringing Nevers, ducal Burgundy, Charolais, Picardy, Artois, Boulogne, and Rethel under the control of France. Mary, to protect Franche-Comté, Luxembourg, and the remaining Burgundian Netherlands, married Maximilian of Habsburg. Louis broke the power of Burgundy in France by being ready and able to invade in the hour of Burgundian defeat.

By inheritance and pressure, Louis acquired Provence, Anjou, Maine, and Bar. The emerging geographic outline of modern France was accompanied by a strategic linkage of royal lands in the Loire and Seine river valleys. With the Duke of Alençon under control, the estates of Armagnac partitioned, the heir of Bourbon married to Louis' daughter Anne, and the elderly Duke of Brittany now harmlessly isolated, Louis was now the feudal master of France, which he had to be in order to change the feudal system.

Externally, Louis managed to gain Roussillon from the aged and wily John II of Aragon, but John's revenge was masterful. His son Ferdinand married Isabella of Castile in 1469, commencing an age of increasing Spanish unity, nationalism, and anti-French sentiment. In Burgundy, Spain, Italy, and elsewhere, the fear of French strength prepared the way for the future Habsburg-Valois wars.

Domestically, Louis replaced the military, administrative, police, tax, and judicial institutions of the territorial lords with agencies of the Crown. The nobles who had ruled fiefs became a privileged class of patriotic military and civilian servants sworn in loyalty to the king. The 1472 concordat with the pope gave Louis somewhat comparable powers in the appointment of new bishops. Significantly, the king's taxes, such as *taille*, *aides*, and *gabelle*, were now collected without representative consent, and the remaining parlements merely registered the king's laws.

Additionally, Louis invested in and promoted new industries such as silk production and modernized mining as well as many commercial enterprises. A royal messenger system became a sort of postal service, conveying not only government business and privileged letters but also the publications of the new printing industry which Louis helped to develop.

This rebuilding and modernization of French life depended on the safety of commerce and the tranquillity of a country no longer beset by ravaging armies. In the revised order of the new French state, the greatest economic benefit went to the bourgeoisie and the wealthiest peasants, but political power in France was concentrated in the hands of the king. On the whole, Louis governed wisely and well, but he institutionalized despotism.

Great in his accomplishments for France, Louis was not impressive in appearance, being short, fat, bald, and somewhat ugly. His dress and manners were informally bourgeois rather than royal. Louis was witty, garrulous, and even charming in conversation or letters, but he lacked the touch of dignity, heroism, generosity, or even understandable vice that would cause men to overlook the cruelties of which, like his contemporaries, he was sometimes capable.

Apoplexy crippled Louis as early as February, 1481, and eventually killed him. He died at Plessis on August 30, 1483, hopeful that his religious observances, his generosity to the Church, and his sincere faith would gain for him a fair judgment from God. His only son succeeded as Charles VIII with his sister Anne as regent. A younger daughter, Jeanne, became Duchess of Orléans.

Summary

When Louis XI ascended the throne in 1461, the postwar lives of Frenchmen were still dominated by territorial feudal lords whom the king could not control. When Louis died in 1483, a centralized nation-state monarchy was the new great fact for the future of France. The scattered royal domain lands of 1461 were increased in extent, geographic cohesiveness, and economic leadership. Most conspicuously, Louis' policy helped to shatter the Burgundian power which, in alliance with the external foes and internal rivals of the French Crown, had long constituted a threat to the survival of France itself as a nation of consequence.

The nation-state that Louis created gave the country more security, peace, and order, as well as better laws and justice; new industry, production, commerce; and a better life, especially in the towns, than feudal Europe had ever sustained. High taxes were the naturally unpopular price for the benefits. Louis' political system endured basically unchanged for three centuries, until the old regime was swept away in 1789.

Despite the greatness and importance of Louis' achievements, legend, fiction, and even some historians have distorted and diminished his reputation. Most scholars agree that he deserves a better place in public estimation. Apart from the problem of misrepresentation, however, the evidence at hand suggests that, while Louis XI was in his own time respected and feared, he did not, for whatever reason, capture great sympathy and affection.

Bibliography
Champion, Pierre. *Louis XI*. Translated by Winifred Stephens Whale. New York: Dodd, Mead, 1929. Once the standard biography on Louis XI, this work is weakened by its reliance on Philippe de Commynes, sparsity of detail, and lack of footnotes, but it is still a clear and enjoyable account.
Commynes, Philippe de. *The Memoirs of Philippe de Commynes*. Edited by Samuel Kinser. Translated by Isabelle Cazeaux. Columbia: University of South Carolina Press, 1969. These readable memoirs are the contemporary source most used by later biographers. The author, an adviser and confidant to Louis for eleven years, combines an intimate and generally favorable account of the king with his own reflections on politics.
Kendall, Paul Murray. *Louis XI*. New York: W. W. Norton, 1971. The most useful single volume to consult on Louis XI. Kendall's research is comprehensive. This book is scholarly, informative, and accurate, with an extensive bibliography and footnotes that give the reader the sources for everything consequential. Although it is well written, the complex story is not as easy to follow as in Champion.
Lewis, D. B. Wyndham. *King Spider*. New York: Coward, McCann, 1929. A popular work, now dated, but useful for the section translating a short selection of Louis' letters from the eleven-volume French edition. The

book's title comes from Charles the Bold's description of Louis XI as "the universal spider," a label that has lasted.

Mosher, Orville W., Jr. *Louis XI, King of France*. Toulouse, France: Édouard Privat, 1925. Many biographers complain of the distortion and legend surrounding Louis without adequate explanation. Mosher supplies this, although the work should be read with later works.

K. Fred Gillum

LOUIS XIII

Born: September 27, 1601; Fontainebleau, France
Died: May 14, 1643; Saint-Germain-en-Laye, France
Areas of Achievement: Government and the military
Contribution: Louis XIII governed France during an era of conflict. Over-
shadowed by his father and son, he increased the power of the Crown
with the help of Cardinal de Richelieu.

Early Life

France entered the seventeenth century with a royal wedding. The groom,
Henry of Navarre, mounted the throne of France on the death of his cousin,
Henry III, after civil war and conversion from his Huguenot faith. The bride
was Marie de Médicis, niece of Phillip III of Spain. She brought Catholic
stability and the hope of an heir for the new royal house. The newlyweds
met in December, 1600, and a healthy son was born the next September.

The early childhood of Louis XIII passed in the shelter of the royal nursery. He was attended by his own physician, indulged by an adored nurse,
and surrounded by a retinue of servants shared with his siblings and the
many royal bastards. Louis was a stubborn child with a violent temper and
was often beaten on his father's orders. Henry was an expansive, promis-
cuous, hot-tempered man, intelligent but manipulative. He alternately ignored and overwhelmed Louis. Henry looked for adult qualities in the small
son who both adored and feared him. He openly preferred his older bastards.
Louis was a timid child but overcame fears of loud noises and rough weather
to develop kingly courage. He also strove to conquer his temper and submit
to Henry in order to win his love. Marie was a shallow, cold woman with
little affection to share with her children. She largely ignored Louis during
his nursery days.

An intelligent and perceptive child with a retentive memory, Louis learned
early lessons in reserve and in secrecy from his courtiers. Rumored to be a
simpleton, he later said that he had not been taught to read or write. In fact,
he could do both before leaving the nursery in January, 1609. He used
rumors of disability as a protective cover, although he resented them. Books
did not appeal to him; he preferred military studies and hunting. Louis was
surrounded by older men, friends of his father who were skilled in military
arts. He excelled in falconry, was fond of dogs and horses, and showed
precocious skill with firearms. Scrupulous in Catholic observances, Louis
may have lacked deep Christian faith. He was passionately attuned to questions of rank and greatly resented his father's preference for his other children. In his features and physical makeup, Louis was a Habsburg like his
mother. He was intelligent like Henry but reserved and suspicious as a result
of a childhood spent among manipulative adults.

On May 14, 1610, Henry of Navarre was assassinated. He had been preparing to go to war against Spain. Louis became king, with his mother as regent. At first, Marie retained Henry's counselors, but she changed policies. She humbled France to Spain and Austria and arranged marriages for Louis and for her eldest daughter with the eldest children of the King of Spain. This policy angered many of France's most powerful nobles, who also resented the fact that she never learned to speak French well and surrounded herself with Italians. Her beloved foster sister, Leonora Galigai, and her husband, Concino Concini, were the courtiers most hated by the French. Led by Henry of Condé, the nobles rose in a series of revolts against the regent. Condé's first revolt ended in a lucrative agreement which gave large pensions to the rebels and demanded a meeting of the Estates-General, begun in October, 1614.

Louis had reached his official majority by this date, but he was still helpless. He resented the power of the Concinis and their following as well as his mother's extravagance. The Estates-General brought no great reforms but gave the young Bishop of Luçon (later known as Richelieu) the chance to flatter the regent in a closing speech. He became a favorite of the queen mother, devoted to her service for years, a role Louis XIII later found hard to forgive. In November of 1615, the royal court celebrated the weddings of Elizabeth of France with the future Phillip IV of Spain and of Louis XIII with the young infanta Anne of Austria. Condé led another uprising but was upstaged by the pageant of the royal weddings. Louis' marriage was not happy, owing to court intrigues, and the young couple did not establish regular conjugal relations for three years. Anne suffered a number of miscarriages, and Louis' younger brother Gaston remained the royal heir until the birth of the future Louix XIV in 1638.

Louis began his personal rule in April, 1617, with the murder of Concini and the exile of the regent, soon followed by the trial and execution of Marie's beloved Galigai. He reinstated several of his father's former ministers but continued his mother's pattern of rule by favorites in following the wishes of his hunting companion, Charles d'Albert, Duc de Luynes.

Life's Work

When Louis assumed control of the government, France was surrounded by Habsburg holdings in Austria, Germany, Italy, Spain, and the Netherlands. Europe was a hotbed of religious tension, with conflict between Catholics and Protestants. Henry's Edict of Nantes guaranteed Huguenots religious freedom and possession of certain free cities, but in May, 1621, the La Rochelle Assembly established a Protestant state within France. The free cities were fortified as if in preparation for war. Protestant England and Catholic Spain encouraged the rebels, even though the queens of both countries were sisters of Louis XIII.

Family and political life were mingled and were unlucky for Louis. Although reconciled with his mother after the death of Luynes, Louis suspected her of complicity in plots to replace him with his brother Gaston. Louis' trust in his queen had been compromised by the extravagant court paid her by George Villiers, Duke of Buckingham, the special envoy who arranged the marriage of Charles I of England to Henrietta of France. In 1626, a plot was discovered for the destruction of Richelieu and the removal of Louis in favor of Gaston. Anne's distant implication in the intrigue damaged relations even more. Richelieu was named a cardinal in 1622. By 1624, he joined the Royal Council. He gave Louis absolute fidelity coupled with a visionary focus on French national destiny. Both men shared a taste for military life.

It was almost a relief for Louis when open war broke out with the Huguenots of La Rochelle in 1627. Cardinal Richelieu prepared to lay siege to the rebellious port city by fortifying islands in the harbor. Buckingham countered in June with a fleet of English ships. Louis and the cardinal joined the French troops in October, and the king himself worked on the construction of a dike across the harbor. Buckingham was forced to retreat in November. Two more English fleets appeared and retreated, and the people of La Rochelle suffered a siege which reduced their number from twenty-five thousand to five thousand. On their surrender in November, 1628, Louis guaranteed their religious freedom and spared the lives of their leaders but razed the city walls.

No sooner was La Rochelle pacified than Louis and Richelieu plunged into another campaign over the succession of Mantua, in Italy. A French nobleman had fallen heir to the city-state, but his inheritance was contested by both Spain and Austria. The French army made a winter crossing of the Alps and enjoyed early successes in Italy, but worries over the continuing religious troubles in France and Louis' health forced a return to France. Louis was to enjoy more victories over his Huguenot subjects, but the stress of war and intrigue made him ill. By the fall of 1630, he lay near death and received last rites. At the same time, the Diet of Ratisbon was meeting in Germany to decide the affairs of the Holy Roman Empire.

As Richelieu grappled with the political maneuvers of the German meeting, which eventually allowed him to defuse the Mantuan situation, Louis was reconciled with his wife and mother. The two queens hated and feared Richelieu and demanded his removal. The situation culminated on November 10, 1630, the Day of the Dupes, when Marie's extravagant behavior completely estranged her from Louis. She was sent into exile, never to return, and died in Cologne in 1642. Richelieu was firmly established and his policies vindicated.

Although often at odds with his wife, Louis was a faithful husband and pursued his conjugal duties on a regular schedule, though with no great enthusiasm. Popular history attributes the birth of their first child to survive, the future Sun King, Louis XIV, to a snowstorm which forced Louis XIII to share the only royal bed in the Louvre in December of 1637. Great joy greeted the birth of a dauphin on September 5, 1638. The succession was secured when a second son was born in 1640.

Plagued by illness and unable to trust Anne of Austria, who was known to have pursued secret correspondence with Spain during wartime, Louis designed limits to be enforced on her regency in the case of his death. Richelieu died, after a long illness, on December 4, 1642. Louis spent the winter of 1642-1643 in preparation for a campaign against the Spanish governor of the Netherlands but fell ill and died on May 14, 1643, just before the great French victory over the Spanish at Rocroi (May 19). Anne immediately had his reservations set aside and entered into an unlimited regency for her four-year-old son.

Summary

In many ways, Louis XIII was an ordinary man caught in an extraordinary period in history. His father had been able to charm by flamboyant personality. His son enjoyed a long reign marked by personal absolutism. Louis was handicapped by the limits of his personality, his health, and the politics of his time. Intelligent, conscientious, and hardworking, he was lucky in the service of men such as Richelieu. He was able to consolidate and hold power for France and for the monarchy. He bequeathed his son a hunger for military victory and an empty treasury. Yet he reformed and strengthened the French navy and army. Although personally intolerant, he continued to protect Protestant worship after religious wars curtailed Huguenot political powers. The French Academy took wing under him. Despite a tendency toward resentment and suspicion, he gained a reputation for clemency and was known in his time as Louis the Just.

Bibliography

Belloc, Hilaire. *Richelieu*. Garden City, N.Y.: Garden City Publishing, 1929. The prolific biographer centers his study on the establishment of French nationalism, through the partnership of Richelieu and Louis XIII.
Boulenger, Jacques. *The Seventeenth Century*. New York: G. P. Putnam's Sons, 1920. This general history is written in a lively style and takes a sympathetic view of Louis. Chapters are followed by short bibliographies.
Burckhardt, Carl J. *Richelieu and His Age*. Translated by Edwin Muir and Willa Muir. New York: Harcourt, Brace & World, 1940. Burckhardt's three-volume work has a dual focus, illuminating with a wealth of detail the great cardinal and the king he served. The bibliography is arranged by chapter, and the last volume includes genealogical charts.
Marvick, Elizabeth Wirth. *Louis XIII: The Making of a King*. New Haven, Conn.: Yale University Press, 1986. Marvick has produced an unusual

book, based on the detailed journal kept by Louis' personal physician. Her perspective is Freudian. The material she marshals is fascinating and illuminates Louis' life and personality. Includes a substantial bibliography of primary and secondary sources.

Ranum, Orest A. *Richelieu and the Councillors of Louis XIII.* Oxford, England: Clarendon Press, 1963. Ranum studies the interplay of power and personality in the managerial policies of Louis XIII and Richelieu. Includes an appendix of documents and a bibliography.

Anne W. Sienkewicz

LOUIS XIV

Born: September 5, 1638; Saint-Germain-en-Laye, France
Died: September 1, 1715; Versailles, France
Areas of Achievement: Government and politics
Contribution: Known as *le Roi Soleil*, or "the Sun King," Louis XIV led
France to the pinnacle of power and prestige in seventeenth century Europe, and, more than any other monarch, embodied the principle of absolutism in royal authority. Dedicated to bringing glory to France, he sponsored magnificent cultural achievements but left his country bankrupt and weakened through a long series of costly wars.

Early Life

Louis XIV was born on September 5, 1638, the son of Louis XIII and Anne of Austria. At age four, he succeeded his father to the throne, under the regency of his mother. As a result, much of his character and outlook was shaped in a harrowing environment of court intrigue and conspiracy, as noble factions fought one another for power and influence. Though regarded by French law as a sacred person, he was frequently neglected. Once, he wandered into a pond and nearly drowned. When he was nine, many of the nobility, supported by the Parlement de Paris (a powerful law court), revolted against the prime minister, Cardinal Jules Mazarin. As the symbol of power, Louis was dragged about the country and often simply left in places supposedly safe from the rebels. One evening, some of them burst into his bedroom, and he barely escaped with his life.

After five years of civil war, known as the Fronde, Mazarin finally quelled the revolt and began rebuilding the central government and administration, as well as training Louis for the role of king. By age fourteen, when Louis reached his legal majority, he had acquired an education in horseback riding, dancing, hunting, and the uses of power. As a king, he would be expected to lead his armies, so he served his apprenticeship in the war which had erupted between France and Spain in 1635. This conflict was part of the Thirty Years' War, in which political leadership in Europe passed from the Habsburg rulers of Spain and the Holy Roman Empire to France.

As Louis matured, he developed an inveterate hatred for anyone who would seek to limit his authority. When Mazarin died in 1661, Louis astonished his royal council of ministers by announcing that no successor to Mazarin would be appointed—he, himself, would assume all power and responsibility for ruling the kingdom.

Life's Work

For the next fifty-four years, Louis dedicated his life to the task of ruling France. No detail of administration escaped his notice, and he tried to control every action of his government, from the system of administration to proper etiquette at court. In fact, he used the ceremony and protocol of the court to help him resolve the greatest long-standing threat to the authority of the French monarchy: the landed nobility.

Since the development of the feudal system in the Middle Ages, French kings had had to contend with the determination of the nobles to rule their territories independently of the Crown. Because the nobility formed the officer corps of the army, medieval French kings had often been at their mercy. An informal alliance between the kings and the rising middle classes, however, had gradually given the monarchy the tax income to create a professional army, and technological changes had made the mounted knight obsolete. This eliminated the feudal justification for the power of the nobility. The nobles were not to be humbled without a fight, and they had frequently revolted against the growing centralization of the royal government. The Fronde was the last of these revolts, proving that the nobility was still a force with which to be reckoned.

Louis accomplished this task by building a magnificent palace, the envy of Europe, at Versailles and luring the nobles to his court with high-sounding but meaningless titles and the opulence of court life. He kept them occupied with a constant round of entertainment, sponsoring playwrights such as Molière and Jean Racine and composers such as Jean-Baptiste Lully and fostering a complex web of competition and intrigue for his favor. The lord who could best master the intricate system of courtesies, ceremonies, and flattery might well be rewarded with a high-sounding but inconsequential position, while the real work of government was performed by Louis himself and a small circle of trusted ministers.

Among these ministers was Jean-Baptiste Colbert, a financial genius who attempted to revolutionize the French economy through the establishment of a mercantilist system. Under Louis' supervision, Colbert sought to make France self-sufficient through the construction of a merchant fleet and a navy to protect it. He awarded monopoly charters to royally subsidized companies to trade with French colonies and implemented a massive program of road, port, and canal construction. At the same time, Louis' minister of war, the Marquis de Louvois, modernized the French army by limiting the practice of purchasing officers' commissions, expanding its peacetime base to more than 100,000 men (and more than 400,000 in wartime) and developing an efficient procurement and supply system. Between them, Colbert and Louvois forged the state and the army into an effective instrument of royal policy.

Louis soon put this instrument to use. In 1648, the Treaty of Westphalia had ended the Thirty Years' War and established the "balance of power" as the fundamental principle of international relations within Europe. Even though Louis' Habsburg rivals had seen their fortunes decline in the war, they were still in control of the thrones of Austria, which possessed territories on the eastern border of France, and of Spain, which also ruled the portion of the Netherlands that became Belgium. Thus, Louis was surrounded on three sides by enemies. In 1667, he invaded the Spanish Netherlands, claiming that they were the rightful inheritance of his wife, the daughter of the Habsburg King of Spain. This inaugurated a half-century of wars, which eventually gained for France the provinces of Lorraine and the Franche-Comté to the east, and part of Flanders to the north.

Yet these rewards had a terrible price. Not only did Louis expend tremendous sums of money and large numbers of men but also he earned the enmity of nearly every other power in Europe. Then, he created hostility and fear within France itself by revoking the Edict of Nantes, which had guaranteed religious and political rights to the Huguenots, or French Protestants, since 1599. The revocation prompted a wave of persecution, forced conversions to Roman Catholicism, and drove thousands of refugee Huguenots into the arms of Louis' enemies. Since most of the Protestants were hardworking businessmen and skilled artisans, France was thus deprived of a great national resource. Many historians have dated the beginning of the decline of France's industrial development from this time.

In 1688, the English, the Dutch, and the Habsburgs united to break Louis' hegemony over Western Europe in a war that lasted until 1697 and forced Louis to return part of the territories he had won. Finally, in 1700, Charles II, the last Habsburg King of Spain, died, leaving his kingdom to Louis' grandson, Philip of Anjou. Louis had little choice but to accept the inheritance, since declining it would have meant Austrian control of Spain. The Holy Roman Emperor, Leopold I, immediately contested the award and began constructing another coalition against France. In the resulting War of the Spanish Succession, lasting from 1701 to 1714, Louis lost nearly all the territorial gains of previous wars, bankrupted his treasury, and gained only the hatred of his own people.

At the same time, he suffered untold personal grief, as his son, two grandsons, and a great-grandson died within the space of a few months. The new heir to the throne, Louis' sickly great-grandnephew, was only five years old. This nearly guaranteed that a domestic power struggle over the regency would ensue upon Louis' death. Louis attempted to avoid this by drawing up a will that gave the actual power of the regency to the Duc de Maine, his son by one of his mistresses. After Louis died, however, on September 1, 1715, the Parlement de Paris was convened to nullify the will. In so doing, the Parlement asserted a new political power: As the body charged with responsibility for registering royal edicts before they became law, the Parlement now claimed the right to approve or disapprove of edicts before they were registered. Without a strong king to suppress this power, the Parlement de Paris was able to defer royal reforms which might have prevented the French Revolution. Thus, ironically, the king who had brought royal power to its peak may also have been responsible for its ultimate destruction. As Louis' funeral cortege carried his body to the tomb of French kings in the basilica at Saint-Denis, his own people jeered and spat upon him.

Summary

The reign of Louis XIV lasted seventy-three years, the longest of any known monarch in history. So thoroughly did he stamp his imprint into the consciousness of Europe that historians refer to this period as the Age of Louis XIV. His brilliant court and the unparalleled splendor of Versailles were the envy of and model for all the other crowned heads of Europe, who vainly tried to copy French culture, manners, and power. Louis made French the international language of royalty and diplomacy. On the other hand, those same crowned heads feared Louis' ambition, regarding him as a bloodthirsty tyrant who sought to conquer them all.

Louis embodied both the principle of absolutist monarchy and the myth of the glory of France. In fact, Louis identified so completely with his role as king that it is virtually impossible to discern an individual personality lurking beneath the role. Louis was proud, courageous, highly self-disciplined, intolerant, and passionate in his love for beauty and order; yet all these qualities are reflected in his actions as king, rather than in his personal life. When asked what defined the French state, he is said to have replied, *"L'etat, c'est moi"* ("I am the state"). This was not an expression of arrogance but of his belief that God had entrusted him with the responsibility for the power and prosperity of France.

As is true for many other of the greatest figures in history, a balance sheet of Louis' reign reveals a roughly equal total of credits and debits. His support of Colbert's program brought France a colonial empire and encouraged industry and internal development, but his view that colonies existed solely as a royal preserve discouraged settlement. As a result, the more populated British colonies easily overwhelmed French North America only fifty years after Louis' death. While the new roads and canals Colbert created reduced internal trade barriers, Louis' persecution of the Huguenots precluded the maximum utilization of France's economic potential. Louis' destruction of the power of the nobles ended much of the anarchy of provincial administration, but it also centralized the government to the extent that it became removed and remote from the people of France and could no longer cope well with local problems. Louis preferred to think in grander terms, and he ignored grievances of the rural peasantry that would eventually fuel the French Revolution and destroy the monarchy. Louvois made the French army the largest, best-trained, and best-equipped in Europe, but Louis wasted it in ill-advised wars; yet, when he died, Louis left France more territorially secure and slightly larger than it had been. The king's patronage of the arts fostered a renaissance in French music, literature, drama, and painting, and his regal tastes became those of Europe.

His palaces, monuments, and court, however, came to be seen as an expensive irrelevance by a peasantry without bread and a middle class without status. These contrasts have made Louis' reign subject to much interpretation and furious debate. None could deny, however, that his impact and influence upon the course of European history was immense.

Bibliography

Ashley, Maurice. *Louis XIV and the Greatness of France*. London: English Universities Press, 1946. A brief introduction to Louis and his period. Though scrupulously balanced, Ashley's account rehabilitates the monarch's historical reputation and discusses how events subsequent to Louis' reign have tended to create a biased view. Includes an excellent annotated bibliography.

Bernier, Oliver. *Louis XIV: A Royal Life*. Garden City, N.Y.: Doubleday, 1987. Though intimate biographies of historical figures have gone out of fashion, Bernier has succeeded in crafting a history of Louis in the grand manner. Bernier suggests that, in the light of most recent research, many of the traditional criticisms of Louis are no longer valid. Well written and entertaining.

Church, William F. *Louis XIV in Historical Thought: From Voltaire to the Annales School*. New York: W. W. Norton, 1976. Though very brief, this is an essential work for anyone seeking to understand Louis' place and importance in history, as well as how history is crafted. Summarizes how and why historians have varied in their approaches to Louis' reign. Contains an outstanding bibliography.

Cronin, Vincent. *Louis XIV*. London: Collins, 1964. Of all the many biographies of Louis, Cronin's is by far the best for the general reader. Extremely well written, as well as thoroughly researched. Focuses sympathetically on Louis as both individual and monarch. Contains excellent illustrations and bibliography.

Erlanger, Philippe. *Louis XIV*. Translated by Stephen Cox. New York: Praeger, 1970. A standard biography by a well-known French expert. Takes a balanced, if somewhat melancholy, view of Louis' reign. Contains excellent illustrations.

Judge, H. G., ed. *Louis XIV*. New York: Longmans, Green, 1965. This is a compilation of brief selections from a variety of important documents created during Louis' reign. Especially relevant to the study of Louis' government. An excellent source for students, containing a fine bibliography.

Lewis, W. H. *The Splendid Century*. New York: William Sloane, 1954. An entertaining look at several aspects of French life during Louis' reign. Not only discusses important elements in French politics, such as the royal court, the Church, and the army, but also focuses on the peasantry and the rural nobility. Includes a brief biography of Louis, and chapters on seventeenth century French medicine, daily life, and the literary world. Extensive bibliography.

Moote, A. Lloyd. *The Revolt of the Judges: The Parlement of Paris and the Fronde, 1643-1652*. Princeton, N.J.: Princeton University Press, 1971. Though this is a specialist monograph, it is also an especially interesting study of the anarchy and conflicts within French society and government early in Louis' life and is essential reading for an understanding of Louis' attempts to centralize authority.

Mossiker, Frances. *The Affair of the Poisons: Louis XIV, Madame de Maintenon, and One of History's Great Unsolved Mysteries*. New York: Alfred A. Knopf, 1969. This is a fascinating account of a sordid scandal during the 1670's, in which Louis' wife, Madame de Maintenon, and many of the greatest nobles of France were charged with practicing witchcraft and the poisoning of many prominent people. Based on the trial documents and the notebooks of the head of the Paris Police Department.

Packard, Laurence Bradford. *The Age of Louis XIV*. New York: Henry Holt, 1929. A classic, brief introduction to the period. Summarizes developments in France and Europe generally and includes a thorough, annotated bibliography.

Rule, John C., ed. *Louis XIV and the Craft of Kingship*. Columbus: Ohio State University Press, 1969. A compendium of essays on many aspects of Louis' life and reign, his approach to power, and French and European society in his time. Much more interesting than many works of this type because of the high quality of the selections and expertise of their authors.

Thomas C. Schunk

MARQUIS DE LOUVOIS
François-Michel Le Tellier

Born: January 18, 1639; Paris, France
Died: July 16, 1691; Versailles, France
Area of Achievement: The military
Contribution: Louvois used his administrative genius and harsh discipline to create and maintain France's first military complex. He established unprecedented civilian control over the military and heavily influenced King Louis XIV's foreign policy.

Early Life
François-Michel Le Tellier, the Marquis de Louvois, was born in Paris, France, on January 18, 1639. His father, Michel Le Tellier, had a tremendous impact upon his son's life. Yet while the elder Le Tellier was gentle, modest, and intelligent, Louvois, who was equally intelligent, was often brusque, violent, and arrogant. Like his father, however, Louvois hated extravagance and inefficiency. Michel Le Tellier was an excellent administrator and passed his skills on to his son. He also taught his son how to survive and prosper as a minister in the king's council. Le Tellier, well versed in courtly intrigue, taught his son to use flattery and to bow with humble submission. Furthermore, he instructed that no act of servility was too great in satisfying the needs of the monarch.

Le Tellier, as secretary of state for war, perceived himself as rivaled in the king's eyes by one man only—Jean-Baptiste Colbert, the king's minister of finance. Le Tellier passed on this jealousy and animosity to his son. Under Colbert, France's economy and treasury had recovered from severe depression, and France was enjoying great prosperity. Louvois' intent was to rival Colbert for the king's confidence and eventually replace him by bringing him into disgrace. Eventually, Louvois would have more influence over the king than Colbert, but, for most of his life, many of Louvois' actions were motivated by this jealousy.

Louis, who became King of France at age four in 1643, was only a few years younger than Louvois. The two boys went to school at the same time, experienced similar problems of youth, and developed an unusual relationship. The king quickly recognized Louvois' talents; Louvois was energetic, ruthless, persistent, and an administrative genius. Louis knew that he could always depend upon Louvois to finish any project he began. Louis liked Louvois not only because of his abilities but also because he played to the king's vanity and pettiness.

In 1656, Louvois was guaranteed succession to his father's position, which Le Tellier had held since 1643. For five years, beginning in 1661, Louvois was an assistant in his father's office. In 1666, Louvois was given the title minister of war; however, Le Tellier did not relinquish complete control of the war ministry to his son at this time. Louvois was astute enough to recognize his father's brilliance and to capitalize upon it. He spent the first few decades of his career building upon his father's work. When Le Tellier became chancellor in 1677, Louvois was formally named secretary of state for war and became a member of the king's inner council.

Life's Work

Louvois knew that through military victory he could ingratiate himself to Louis and possibly undermine Colbert. Thus, in 1667, he devised his first military campaign with the Spanish Netherlands (particularly Flanders) as the target. Louis' wife, a Spanish princess, had renounced her claim to this land in exchange for payment of a dowry when she married Louis. Thus, even though Louis was attracted to the idea, he was hesitant. Quickly, Louvois found several lawyers and theologians who eased the king's conscience by citing the fact that the dowry had never been paid.

The greatest obstacles to Louvois' plans came from the minister of finance and from one of Louis' greatest generals. Colbert, whose economic policies depended upon the continuation of peace, told Louis that France could continue to prosper only if internal and external tranquillity were maintained. At the same time, General Henri de La Tour d'Auvergne, Vicomte de Turenne, warned that France's neighbors were already envious and that if France attempted any military action against Holland or Germany, it might cause the formation of a league of European nations against France. Louvois realized that Louis was heavily influenced by these two adversaries. Therefore, he played upon the king's intense interest in the military and his need for glory. Louvois brought Louis to one of the various encampments constructed to maintain military habits during peace. Louis, predictably, was totally captivated with the pomp and pageantry and immediately announced his military intentions. Louvois won his first victory over Colbert and Turenne, who now had to support their king's military effort.

Louvois' great administrative talents were demonstrated for the first time during this military campaign. With ease and brilliance, he transported several large forces. He developed an excellent system of storage places to provide food and supplies anywhere on the frontier. Louvois also enlisted Sébastien Le Prestre de Vauban, the chief engineer responsible for constructing fortifications. Louvois was often on the battlefield making certain that all of the troops' needs were met.

Thus, his first military action was an easy victory over a veteran army. In less than three months, France controlled a substantial number of fortifications as well as Flanders. Louis returned to Paris victorious and with an appetite for military conquest, which his minister of war would happily try to satisfy.

Even as negotiations for Flanders were being conducted, Louis was looking for yet another conquest. At the suggestion of Louvois, Louis asked his
cousin, Louis II de Bourbon, Prince de Condé (later known as The Great
Condé), to command an army against Franche-Comté. Louvois employed all
of his wiles in this war effort and established an ingenious precedent. He
began a war of corruption in the area before the advancement of troops. His
plan called for secret agents to bribe many of the magistrates. The area
would then split into factions, making it easy prey. The plan worked without
incident, and Condé led a military force into the region. Louvois preceded
him, undermining local control and maintaining the flow of supplies. Within
less than three weeks, all of Franche-Comté was invaded. Meanwhile, in
1668, Louvois became the superintendent general of the mail in France, and
he organized a "black chamber," which enabled him to observe foreign
correspondence. He always informed Louis of any questionable information.

By this time, the Triple Alliance of 1668 (England, Sweden, and the
United Provinces) formed and forced Louis into negotiations. Louis was
given Franche-Comté as a peace offering and hostilities ended. By the early
1670's, Louis was interested in conquering Holland, and Louvois encouraged him. Louvois began a campaign to develop apathy regarding Holland in
France's neighbors. He entered into negotiations with various rulers who
granted France two towns on the Dutch frontier as French depots. Thus, he
was able to move magazines and military stores far into the territory before
hostilities began. He sent agents in disguise to buy supplies and munitions
from the Dutch for the French army.

Louvois then recommended invasion. In the beginning of the Dutch War
(1672-1678), Condé and Turenne faced little resistance. As the army advanced, it systematically destroyed fortified cities. Louvois recommended
that these cities be spared. Playing on the king's vanity, Louvois suggested
that Louis keep the captured cities, thereby increasing his own power and
prestige. Again, Louis heeded Louvois' advice. Many of the troops were
used as occupation forces, however, and thus fewer could be used on the
battlefield.

By 1673, French troops were approaching Amsterdam. The Dutch government sent diplomats to meet with Louvois to discuss terms. When Louvois
finally opened negotiations, he treated the envoys rudely and made excessive
demands. The Dutch responded with greater resistance. Because the number
of battle-ready French troops was now reduced, France was unable to crush
the renewed resistance.

On August 30, 1673, the United Provinces, Spain, the Holy Roman Empire, and Lorraine composed the first important military coalition against
Louis XIV. By the end of 1673, the French army experienced severe military
reversals. Coalition forces took the offensive. Turenne needed reinforcements, which Louvois refused to send. Louvois, apprehensive about the

military reversals, drafted very specific battle plans, which he issued to the generals in the field. Insulted by this interference, Turenne and Condé blamed Louvois for the military failures. Le Tellier heard rumors of the plot to disgrace his son and successfully bribed Condé. When Turenne brought his charges against Louvois, Condé did not support these charges, and they were dropped. Louis forced Louvois and Turenne to reconcile, but the issue was never resolved. By this time, the French treasury was nearly exhausted, and Louvois was losing favor with the king. Louvois regained Louis' respect by uncovering a conspiracy to overthrow the king. Louvois named the conspirators and was instrumental in their arrest.

In 1675, Turenne was killed in battle and Condé retired. The war was not going well for France, but by 1678 Louis and Louvois managed to turn potential defeat into victory. After the fall of Ghent, the Treaty of Nijmegen (1678) was signed against Louvois' recommendation. The next year, French troops advanced toward Strasbourg. On September 30, 1681, the French army and Louvois captured the city in less than twenty-four hours. Again, Louvois had employed intrigue, bribery of local magistrates, and terrorism to facilitate the conquest of a city known for its defensive complement of nine hundred cannons.

By the 1680's, France was torn by religious conflict with the Huguenots. The Catholic church and Louvois urged Louis to take action against them. Louvois saw an opportunity to disgrace Colbert (who had always favored the Huguenots) by Colbert's association with the Reformers. By 1681, the Crown forced Colbert to issue a decree banning the Huguenots from certain business associations and Louvois obtained a decree that stated that all Huguenot children at age seven had to renounce their religion. Children not complying would be arrested and soldiers would be quartered in their parents' homes. Many Huguenot families fled France. As many of the Huguenots were artisans and sailors, the council issued a decree that made it illegal for these professionals to leave France. Many of the Huguenot ministers were persecuted, and places of worship were closed. The Huguenots were stripped of their noble rank, and certain professions were closed to them. Many of the Huguenot leaders were physically tortured and executed.

After the death of Colbert in 1683, Louvois dominated the royal council. He was named superintendent of buildings, arts, and manufacturing. By 1685, Louvois recommended that stronger measures be taken against the Huguenots. Places of worship were demolished, Huguenots were forced to renounce their religion or die, and the Edict of Nantes (1598), which guaranteed religious toleration, was revoked by the Edict of Fontainebleau. This last act proved disastrous for France, as a mass exodus of Huguenots occurred, and most of the Protestant nations of Europe united against Louis. Once again, the advice of Louvois did not serve the best interests of France.

On July 9, 1686, the Holy Roman Empire, Spain, and Sweden formed the

League of Augsburg as a defensive coalition to halt French expansion. In August, 1688, Louis invaded Germany, and in September, he invaded the Palatinate. England joined the coalition (now called the Grand Alliance), and the War of the Grand Alliance (1688-1697) began. In February, 1689, Louvois ordered the complete destruction of the Palatinate to interdict the league's means of supply, to save Lorraine and Alsace, and to prevent the potential invasion of France. The army advanced into the territory, warned the citizens to evacuate, and sacked, ravaged, and burned everything. Europe was shocked at the cruelty, and army officers were ashamed of their own actions. Consequently, they blamed Louvois, who had advised Louis strongly to take such action. Louvois did, however, make provisions for the refugees. They were invited to live in Alsace and Franche-Comté and were exempt from taxation for the next ten years.

By 1689, the treasury was practically empty, and France experienced a number of military defeats that caused Louvois' influence with Louis to diminish. Louvois managed one last great maneuver by capturing two major cities. The coalition was determined, however, and Louis was pessimistic about France's chance for victory. On July 16, 1691, while at a strategy session with the king in Versailles, Louvois collapsed. Within hours, the secretary of state for war was dead. Louvois' son, the Marquis de Barbesieux, inherited his father's position, but Louis assumed full responsibility for the war effort.

Summary

François-Michel Le Tellier, Marquis de Louvois, revolutionized the military system in France. He accomplished this feat by the creation, maintenance, training, and disciplining of a large force (more than 100,000 troops) in times of peace, which could be transformed easily into a force more than double its size in times of war. Louvois assembled Europe's first great standing army by actively recruiting troops from other countries such as England, Scotland, Ireland, Germany, Switzerland, and Italy. He devised a method for transporting the large force and organized a system by which he could supply this great army with munitions and other necessary supplies during war. Old fortifications were always well stocked, and new ones were inspected, redesigned, and rebuilt to Louvois' specifications. His knowledge of the army went beyond his desk, as he had been an apprentice to Turenne on the battlefield.

Upon assumption of his position, Louvois gradually began constructing a regular military administration. First, he divided control of the army into four sections: administration, inspection, munitions, and supplies. As there was no regimentation or discipline but much corruption and abuse of privilege, he devised France's first systematic ranking of officers, the order of seniority, which named the king as the highest ranking officer. Louvois also coordinated the various branches of service, grouped regiments into brigades, and gave permanence to companies. He introduced strict discipline by demanding it of the officers as well as of the men, a move that did not make him well liked among the noble officers. He also issued a military uniform, created specific insignia to distinguish units and ranks, and introduced the idea of marching in time. Louvois provided systematic training for artillerymen at schools located in Douai, Metz, and Strasbourg. He also appointed inspectors to maintain the high standards he had set forth. One such man was Inspector-General Jean Martinet, whose model regiment, the "King's Regiment," was known for its rigid militarism, and whose name became synonymous with strict discipline. These innovations and others helped Louis transform France into the leading military nation of Europe in the 1600's.

Bibliography
Bertrand, Louis. *Louis XIV*. Translated by Cleveland B. Chase. New York: Longmans, Green, 1928. While this work gives credit to Louvois for advising the king, it downplays the extent to which Louvois and not Louis was responsible for the cruelties as well as the accomplishments of Louis' reign. The work's 366 pages are primarily aimed at developing Louis' personality. Contains numerous illustrations and an index.

James, G. P. R. "Life of François Michel Le Tellier, Marquis de Louvois." In *Lives of Cardinal de Retz, Jean Baptiste Colbert, John de Witt, and the Marquis de Louvois*, vol. 2. Philadelphia: Carey, Lea and Blanchard, 1837. A two-volume work detailing the lives of several European personalities, one of whom is Louvois. Volume 2 contains a forty-seven-page chapter on Louvois, which presents his life from birth to death. The work is unfavorably biased against Louvois, often blaming him for Louis XIV's errors or cruelties.

Packard, Laurence Bradford. "Louvois and the First Great Standing Army." In *The Age of Louis XIV*. New York: Henry Holt, 1929. This 144-page work contains an eight-page section of a chapter on Louvois. The book concentrates on many aspects of France during Louis' reign and contains a bibliography. Emphasis on Louvois reflects upon his positive contributions to the development of the army.

Voltaire. *The Age of Louis XIV*. Translated by Martyn P. Pollack with a preface by F. C. Green. London: J. M. Dent & Sons, 1966. Originally published in 1751, this work contains language that is sometimes difficult to comprehend. It presents excellent background information about France under Louis. Emphasis is placed on Louvois' military campaigns and his persecution of the Huguenots. Contains an index and a select bibliography.

Wolf, John B. "The First World War: Louvois." In *Louis XIV*. New York: W. W. Norton, 1968. Provides excellent background information and objectively presents information on Louvois. The seventeen-page chapter emphasizes the relationship between Louvois and Louis and Louvois' role in their military exploits. Includes excellent illustrations and portraits, a map of Europe during Louis' reign, notes, and a bibliographical section.

Victoria Reynolds

SAINT IGNATIUS OF LOYOLA

Born: 1491; Loyola, Guipúzcoa Province, Spain
Died: July 31, 1556; Rome
Area of Achievement: Religion
Contribution: Founder of the Society of Jesus, better known as the Jesuits, Loyola was a dynamic religious leader whose life and writings strongly influenced his times. His religious order has been particularly notable in the field of education.

Early Life
The youngest son of a family known for its prowess in war, Ignatius was given as an infant into the care of a nearby farm woman. During his childhood and youth, Ignatius was thus divided between his father's house, Casa Torre, and his foster mother's home, giving him a view of life from two sides—that of the rulers and that of the ruled. Of Basque descent, the Loyola family shared the characteristics of being deeply religious as well as hot-tempered. Ignatius' father, Don Beltram, had close connections with the king for services rendered and, in return, received many privileges, both lay and clerical. He had justifiably high aspirations for all of his children.

Ignatius spent his early teens mostly at Casa Torre, taking school lessons from the village priest. At the age of sixteen, he was taken as a page into the house of Juan Velázquez de Cuéllar, a family relative who was treasurer of Castile and royal major domo at the court. In his service, Ignatius learned to sing, dance, and play musical instruments—skills he retained for the remainder of his life. For ten years, he lived as a courtier, traveling with his master and the royal court, visiting all the towns of Castile. Thoroughly trained in formal manners and caught up in court life, Ignatius spent much time reading romances, tales featuring ghosts, dragons, princesses, and heroes engaged in impossible adventures.

Upon the death of King Ferdinand in 1516, Juan Velázquez lost most of his estates and his position at court. He died in 1517, and a bereft Ignatius went to Pamplona, the capital of Navarre, to enlist in the viceroy's army, having decided to become a career soldier. From 1517 to 1521, a captain in the service of the Duke of Najera, Ignatius fought the French, who were attempting to seize all of Navarre by capturing the strategic city of Pamplona. In 1520, Ignatius participated in its defense, and, in a fierce battle lasting six hours, he was struck by a cannon ball, suffering a broken right leg. The victorious French treated him well, returning him to Casa Torre for recuperation.

During his convalescence, a bored Ignatius, lacking his usual romances, read a life of Christ and a book on the lives of the saints. He was attracted by the sanctity of Christ and His saints and wanted to imitate their virtues.

Meditating on his past and on the future, he felt a need to do penance, which would culminate in a pilgrimage to Jerusalem. Upon recovery, he set about carrying out this goal.

Life's Work

In the spring of 1522, Ignatius visited Montserrat, the site of a famous shrine to the Black Virgin. From there, he went to Manresa, where he stayed about a year, undertaking a program of prayer and penance. During this period, Ignatius first conceived the idea of founding a "spiritual militia" for the service of the Church. At Manresa, he began writing his *Ejercicios espirituales* (1548; *The Spiritual Exercises*, 1736), for the use of directors of spiritual retreats. This famous book gives methods of freeing the soul to seek and to find the will of God. The practitioner goes through stages of meditation, examination of conscience, and methods of prayer; the exercises require thirty days to be completed. These exercises remain a vital part of the life of Jesuits.

From Manresa, Ignatius went to Barcelona in 1523, a stopover before continuing on to Rome. While in Barcelona, he occupied himself in prayer and good works, visiting hospitals and prisons. In March of 1523, he left for Rome, where he received Pope Adrian VI's blessing on his pilgrimage to Jerusalem. Leaving Venice, he was delayed for two months before finally sailing for Palestine. Ignatius and his fellow pilgrims arrived at Jerusalem in September, 1523, to be guided by Franciscan Friars in their visits to the Holy Places. Although he wanted to stay permanently, converting the Muslims, Ignatius was refused permission by the Franciscan superiors. The pilgrims left Jerusalem and were back in Italy in October, 1523. Ignatius returned to Barcelona, arriving in March, 1524.

Wealthy friends paid for Ignatius' studies at the University of Barcelona, where he studied grammar. In 1526, he switched to Acalá University, studying logic, theology, and physics. Between classes, Ignatius begged alms for the poor and taught *The Spiritual Exercises* to any willing pupils. He gathered four like-minded companions about him and they went throughout the city teaching Christian doctrine. Thus were sown the seeds of the future Society of Jesus.

In 1528, leaving his companions to follow at a later date, Ignatius went to France to attend the University of Paris. Dominican professors at both Barcelona and Salamanca judged him not ready to be a valid preacher. Needing a good foundation in systematic learning, Ignatius spent the next years studying Latin grammar, classical texts, theology, and philosophy. He obtained his Licentiate in March, 1533, and his master's degree in 1534. In addition to his studies, Ignatius taught *The Spiritual Exercises* to fellow students. Among these was a roommate from Navarre, Francis Xavier, whom Ignatius eventually won to his way of life and who was destined to be the glory of Jesuit missionary work. By 1534, Ignatius had nine companions who agreed to unite in any needed spiritual enterprise.

The band of nine went to Rome in 1537, seeking the pope's approval of their new order. In 1539, Pope Paul III gave verbal approval to the society and in September, 1540, they were granted canonical approval. That June, Ignatius and seven of his companions were ordained priests. They settled in Rome, living on alms and preaching sermons, catechizing children, and attending the sick.

Ignatius intended his Society of Jesus to be at the service of the pope and, thereby, of the universal church. The Renaissance church was in need of reform, being secularized by the prevailing educational and cultural milieu. Ignatius' society took a vow to obey the pope in all things and to go where and when he indicated a need for their services. In 1540, the first Jesuits were sent to the foreign missions. Two of them were chosen to work in India, one being Francis Xavier. From Goa, Xavier traveled to Japan, arriving in 1549. Later, he attempted to work in China but died before that desire could be fulfilled (1553). Jesuits fanned out all over the globe, with a concentration in Europe.

Ignatius and his society focused on education as the chief tool for reform within the Church, establishing many secondary schools and universities. Educated laymen were needed to spread the Christian spirit. Martin Luther's teachings were widespread in Europe in the sixteenth century, and Ignatius' society was in the vanguard of the Church's Counter-Reformation.

In 1541, Ignatius was elected the first general of the Society of Jesus— head for life. He began drafting the *Constitutions* for the society, setting a solid foundation and structure on which his followers could build. The *Constitutions* set down the qualities needed for the Jesuit general, among them a holy life, prayerfulness, humility, charity, and circumspection. There were also rules for admitting or expelling members, for the examination or formation of novices, and regulations for prayers. With some adaptation, *The Spiritual Exercises* and *Constitutions* remain basic to Jesuit life.

In 1553, pressed by his friends, Ignatius began narrating his autobiography, completing it in early 1555. He spent the last year of his life overseeing the work of his far-flung order, which, by that time numbered about one thousand members. Ignatius died in 1556, confident that his society was fulfilling his hopes for it, revitalizing the spiritual life of the Church.

Summary

Although Saint Ignatius of Loyola did not found his society expressly to combat the Protestant Reformation, his Jesuits are credited by his contemporaries and by later historians with having stemmed its tide. They were instrumental in winning back many who had fallen away from the Church and in opening vast new territories to the Church (for example, the Indies, China,

Japan, South America, and North America). A contemporary of such giants as Sir Thomas More, Desiderius Erasmus, Niccolò Machiavelli, Ferdinand Magellan, Michelangelo, Martin Luther, and the Tudors, Ignatius helped train and form men who became formidable theologians, lawyers, scientists, and mathematicians and who would be at home in the courts of European and Asian princes as well as around the campfires of American Indians. The society's ultimate goal always remained the greater glory of God.

Because of strong criticism by opponents—chiefly within the Church— the Jesuit Order was suppressed in 1773 by Clement XIV. It dwindled in number but not in fervor and, upon formal restoration in 1814, under Pius VII, it quickly regained its former vitality. Friends and foes alike acknowledge the tremendous effect of the Society of Jesus upon the world, then and now. In 1622, the Catholic church gave its highest seal of approval to Ignatius Loyola, canonizing him a saint.

Bibliography

Loyola, Ignatius. *The Autobiography of Saint Ignatius Loyola*. Edited by John C. Olin. Translated by Joseph F. O'Callaghan. New York: Harper & Row, 1974. Contains an informative introduction. Sets the autobiography in the context of its time and gives a brief biography of Ignatius. The preface is by Father Luis Goncalves da Camara, to whom Ignatius narrated his life story. Contains reproductions of illustrations from a work published in Rome in 1609, footnotes expanding on the text, and appendices. Contains a short annotated bibliography.

Maynard, Theodore. *Saint Ignatius and the Jesuits*. New York: P. J. Kenedy and Sons, 1956. Examines the life of Ignatius in eight chapters, briefly, and gives the remaining seven to an analysis of the Jesuit Order and its experiences in the following centuries. Focuses on missionary activities, the suppression of the order, Jesuit education, and corporate achievement. Defends and admires the Society of Jesus. Contains a bibliography and an index.

Mitchell, David. *The Jesuits*. New York: Franklin Watts, 1981. A balanced, critical but respectful treatment of Ignatius and his Jesuits. Covers beginnings to the late 1970's. Contains several illustrations. Appendices include a list of the generals and general congregations, common words used with reference to Jesuits, and a list of popes. Contains an extensive bibliography and a detailed index.

Purcell, Mary. *The First Jesuit*. Westminister, Md.: Newman Press, 1957. Based on contemporary evidence: the writings of Saint Ignatius and records of the first companions and fathers of the first generation of the Society of Jesus. Contains three appendices, a source list, notes, and an index.

Ravier, André, S. J. *Ignatius Loyola and the Founding of the Society of*

Jesus. Translated by Joan Maura and Carson Daly. San Francisco: Ignatian Press, 1987. An interpretation of Ignatius and his society. Begins with a chronology of Ignatius and his followers' activities; ends with an analysis of the message and mission of Ignatius. Based on Ignatius' correspondence and his autobiography, letters of some of his close collaborators, and several volumes of the Monumenta Historica Societatis Jesus. Contains a bibliography (primarily French sources) and an index.

Richter, Friedrich. *Martin Luther and Ignatius Loyola, Spokesmen for Two Worlds of Belief.* Translated by Leonard F. Zwinger. Westminster, Md.: Newman Press, 1960. A comparison/contrast of the careers of Luther and Ignatius. Analysis of Protestant and Catholic thought and teachings. No bibliography, but contains a brief index.

Tylenda, Joseph N., ed. and trans. *A Pilgrim's Journey: The Autobiography of St. Ignatius of Loyola*. Wilmington, Del.: Michael Glazier, 1985. A brief biography of Ignatius in the introduction. Contains a commentary on each page to flesh out allusions in the text. Contains appendices, select bibliography, and notes for each chapter.

S. Carol Berg

ISAAC BEN SOLOMON LURIA

Born: 1534; Jerusalem
Died: August 5, 1572; Safed
Areas of Achievement: Philosophy and religion
Contribution: Luria was the culminating figure in the history of the Jewish
mystical tradition known as Cabala, which, originating in southern France
in the last quarter of the thirteenth century, reached its height in the
sixteenth century. Luria's revision of key Cabalist concepts and his theory
of a dynamic creation—catastrophically altered by sin but capable of re-
generation and final redemption—had a profound influence on subsequent
Jewish thought, including Hasidism, and on messianic movements in both
the Jewish and the Christian worlds.

Early Life

Isaac Luria, also known as ha-Ari (the acronym of the Ashkenazic Rabbi
Isaac), was born in Jerusalem in 1534. His father was an Ashkenazi who had
come from Germany or Poland, and his mother was of Sephardic stock. At
his father's death, his mother took him to Egypt, where he grew up in the
household of his wealthy uncle, a tax collector. Details of his life are sparse;
the principal source is the *Toledot ha-Ari* (life of the Ari), an account written
fifteen or twenty years after his death in which fact and legend are freely
mingled.

Luria was highly precocious, and his uncle provided him with able tutors,
including David ibn Ali Zimrah and Betsal'al Ashkenazi. He collaborated
with the latter in producing legal commentaries and wrote a study of the
Book of Concealment section of the *Zohar*, the central text of the Cabalist
tradition. In later life, he disdained to write, however, preferring personal
teaching and communication with his disciples; his mature thought is known
only through their accounts, particularly those of Chaim Vital (1543-1620),
who claimed to have recorded his master's thoughts verbatim.

Luria married at the age of fifteen and later went into commerce, in which
he was engaged to the end of his life. At the age of seventeen, he began an
intensive study of the Cabala, focusing on the *Zohar* and on the works of his
elder contemporary, Moses Cordovero (1522-1570), the leading figure of the
major Cabalist school at Safed in Palestine. In early 1570, he took up residence in Safed with his family and studied briefly with Cordovero himself,
who was said to have appointed him his spiritual successor.

Life's Work

At Cordovero's death, Luria became the head of a group known as the
Cubs (his own nickname of Ari meant "Holy Lion" in Hebrew), who formed
a core of devoted disciples about him. They lived as a community, with

quarters for themselves and their families. Luria lectured to them on the Sabbath, after they had donned ritual white garments and marched processionally into the neighboring fields. He also worked with them on an individual basis, imparting the techniques of mystical meditation and elucidating the spiritual ancestry of each in accordance with the Cabalist principle of transmigration.

The impact of Lurianic doctrine may be attributed not only to its intrinsic power as a revision of Cabalist tradition but also to the condition of Jewry in the aftermath of the Spanish expulsion of 1492 and the revived anti-Semitism of Reformation Europe. For Jews seeking a divine meaning in these calamities and thrown back anew upon the painful consciousness of their *Galut*, or exile, Luria's thought had both explicative and consolatory appeal.

Traditional Cabalism described the creation of the universe as a wholly positive event, emanating from God's benevolence and unfolding in orderly stages. Luria, in contrast, described this process as involving an act of privation, a contraction or concentration (*tzimtzum*) of the Godhead into itself to create a space outside itself (the *tehiru*, or void) in which the universe could be formed.

The divine light of creation was released into the void, but some of the forms or vessels (*sefirot*) created to receive it were overwhelmed by its force. This "breaking of the vessels" (the *shevirah*) caused a catastrophic scattering of light. The intact vessels constituted a perfected but incomplete upper realm, while the broken ones (including the highest, Adam Kadmon, or Primal Man, which consisted not only of Adam but of the souls of all of his progeny as well) produced a lower, fallen world, to which, however, many sparks of divine light still clung. The sin of Adam then produced further ruin, increasing the alienation of the fallen world from the Godhead.

Adam having failed, God turned to the people of Israel to accomplish the redemption (*tikkun*) of the fallen world and to liberate the divine sparks from their material prison. Each Jew could advance or retard this process by his ethical conduct; with each pious act, a spark was redeemed, but with each wicked or impious one, a spark of the sinner's own soul was lost to chaos. The individual thus not only sought personal salvation by his acts but also participated in the process of universal redemption.

The most esoteric part of Luria's doctrine concerned the divine motive for creating the world and its abortive realization. Luria suggested that there were elements of disunity within the Godhead itself, although the divine essence was seamless and could be conceptualized only as light. In the act of *tzimtzum*, God differentiated these elements (the *reshimu*), which cleaved to the "surface" of the *tehiru* in the manner of water clinging to a bucket. From this exteriorized residue, the vessels were to be composed, and this formed emptiness, penetrated by retained light from the Godhead. Thus, the creation of the universe was to accomplish the reintegration of the Godhead with itself. The world of evil resulted when the refractory vessels failed (or refused, since they were composed both of and by the *reshimu*) to contain the Godhead's light; yet even that world was penetrated by divine goodness in the form of the sparks.

Luria's explanation of the fallen world may be regarded as an abstract reconceptualization of the story of the rebel angels, filtered through Manichaean and Gnostic thought. His attempt, as with all theodicy, was to account for the presence of evil without imputing it directly to God. Despite its abstract nature, it presented a powerfully compelling picture of creation itself as the process of God's own self-exile and redemption, and the *tikkun* as Israel's opportunity to participate in the completion of His design for the universe. Israel's own exile, and the tribulations heaped on it by the forces of evil, could thus be seen as a mirror of the divine travail. The more closely the final victory of *tikkun* approached, the more violently evil resisted. Thus, the expulsion of the Spanish Jews and the general persecution of Israel were indications not of the weakness of the Jews in the face of their enemies but of their gathering strength against all opposition to the divine will.

Luria's brief ministry ended with his death in August, 1572, during an epidemic in Safed, but such was the force of his personality and doctrine that his teachings were rapidly propagated throughout the Jewish world, where they profoundly influenced both contemporary messianic movements and the theological, liturgical, and literary traditions of Judaism.

The Safed Cabalists believed that the moment of redemption was imminent. Luria may have conceived of himself as the Messiah ben-Joseph, the first of the two messiahs prophesied in Jewish tradition, whose fate was to be slain in the war of Gog and Magog; he was apparently so regarded by his admirers, and his sudden death did nothing to dispel the notion. Messianic expectation, nourished by Lurianic doctrine, flourished widely in the Jewish world for the next hundred years, culminating in an attempted mass migration to Palestine in 1665-1666 under Sabbatai Zevi. Christian chiliasts, who believed that the Jews' return to Palestine was the prelude to the Second Coming of Jesus, were deeply stirred by this ferment, and the Lurianist Menasseh ben Israel paid a state visit to England at the behest of Oliver Cromwell.

Summary

Isaac ben Solomon Luria was the culminating figure in the Cabalist movement, the major tradition of Jewish mysticism and speculative theology in the late medieval and early modern world. Menasseh ben Israel declared that "the wisdom of Rabbi Isaac Luria rises above the highest mountains," and a modern scholar, Joseph Dan, has called the concept of *tikkun* "the most powerful idea ever presented in Jewish thought." After 1620, almost all works of ethics in Hebrew used Lurianic symbolism, and, as Dan further comments, "Lurianism became a national theology for Judaism for several generations." Although Luria's influence reached its apogee in the seventeenth century, it remained important in the eighteenth and nineteenth centuries, and passed directly into Hasidism. Luria's emphasis on the world-altering significance of each believer's acts revitalized Jewish ethics and continued to animate it long after his arcane theology had become, for most, a historical curiosity. The critic Harold Bloom has tried to revive Lurianic Cabalism as a device of literary scholarship, and a current periodical of Jewish American thought calls itself *Tikkun*. Luria thus remains one of the most seminal figures in the past five hundred years of Judaism.

Bibliography
Bloom, Harold. *Kabbalah and Criticism*. New York: Seabury Press, 1975. A modern reinterpretation of Luria's Cabalism as a "psychology of belatedness" that anticipates Freudian doctrine, a philosophy of suffering that anticipates Friedrich Nietzsche, and a system of signs with affinities to Charles Sanders Peirce. Bloom also proposes Luria's thought as a paradigm for literary interpretation.
Fine, Lawrence. *Safed Spirituality: Rules of Mystical Piety, the Beginning of Wisdom*. Ramsey, N.J.: Paulist Press, 1984. Focuses on the customs and rituals practiced by Luria and his disciples.
Schechter, Solomon. "Safed in the Sixteenth Century: A City of Legists and Mystics." In his *Studies in Judaism*. Philadelphia: Jewish Publication Society, 1908. A classic essay, still valuable, on the Cabalists of Safed and especially Luria.
Scholem, Gershom. *Major Trends in Jewish Mysticism*. 3d ed. New York: Schocken, 1961. Scholem was the foremost twentieth century scholar of Jewish mysticism and the Cabala. His work has been so dominant that it has spawned a major literature of reinterpretation and revision, best summarized in Joseph Dan's *Gershom Scholem and the Mystical Dimension of Jewish History* (1987). Luria's system is treated in the eighth chapter of Scholem's book, which was first published in 1941. Includes an analysis of the textual issues in reconstructing the system from the writings of the disciples, with special emphasis on Joseph ben Tabul.
——————. *On the Kabbalah and Its Symbolism*. New York: Schocken, 1965. Another of Scholem's major works, indispensable for understanding the Cabalist tradition and containing a chapter on Luria. See also his book-length essay, "Kabbalah," in the *Encyclopedia Judaica* (Jerusalem: Keter Publishing House, 1971).
Tishby, Isaiah. *Torat ha-Ra veha-Kelipah be-Kabbalat ha-Ari*. Jerusalem: Magnes Press, 1983. This important book deals with the problem of

Luria's conception of evil and treats, as does Scholem, the textual problems of his system.

Robert Zaller

MARTIN LUTHER

Born: November 10, 1483; Eisleben, Saxony
Died: February 18, 1546; Eisleben, Saxony
Areas of Achievement: Theology, philosophy, religion, and church reform
Contribution: Out of his own personal struggle and his conflict with the
   Church, Luther developed a theology and a religious movement that re-
   juvenated the Christian faith and had a profound impact on the social,
   political, and religious thought of Western society.

Early Life

Martin Luther was born on November 10, 1483, at Eisleben, Saxony, to
Hans and Margarethe Luther. Soon after his birth, the family moved to
Mansfield, where his father worked in the copper mines, prospering sufficiently to become one of the town's councillors in 1491. Possessing a
strong, forceful character, Hans Luther had a great impact on his son. He
could be exceptionally stern; years later, Luther stated that his father gave
him a sense of inferiority that took years to overcome. Yet, recognizing that
his son had a promising intellect, his father sent Luther to Latin school at
Mansfield. At age twelve, he spent a year at a school in Magdeburg operated
by the Brethren for the Common Life and in 1498 attended a school at
Eisenach. In 1501, Luther entered the University of Erfurt, one of the best
universities in Germany, obtaining his bachelor's degree in 1502 and his
master's degree in 1505.

His father wanted Luther to pursue a legal career. Luther, however, was
suffering from depression, a lifelong chronic condition. On July 2, 1505, as
he was returning to Erfurt from Mansfield, a lightning bolt knocked him to
the ground. Fearful, facing eternity, Luther at that moment vowed to become
a monk. Without consulting his father, Luther immediately entered the Augustinian monastery in Erfurt. He was ordained in 1507 and was selected for
advanced theological studies, receiving his doctorate in theology from the
University of Wittenberg in 1512. Luther then succeeded his mentor, Johann
von Staupitz, to the chair of biblical theology at Wittenberg.

Beneath his successful exterior, however, all was not well with Luther.
Between 1505 and 1515, Luther underwent an acute personal crisis. Harboring terrible anxieties about sin and his own salvation, Luther believed that no
matter how irreproachably he lived, he was unable to satisfy God. Luther
was clearly headed for a breakdown. At this juncture, Staupitz interceded
and told Luther to abandon the concept of God as judge, to focus on Christ,
and simply to love God. This was a revelation for the young monk. While
studying Paul's Epistle to the Romans, Luther realized that mankind is saved
by faith and not by works. Thus, the essential theology of Protestantism
arose to a large extent from Luther's inner, personal struggle.

Life's Work

The issue that ignited Luther's conflict with the Church was the sale of indulgences in Germany by the Dominican friar Johann Tetzel. Indulgences were the remission for money of part of the temporal (priest-assigned) penalties for sin. They were granted on papal authority and sold by licensed agents. While the Church never maintained that divine forgiveness could be obtained through an indulgence, unscrupulous agents such as Tetzel employed such claims with great success. Luther, disturbed that ordinary people were having their salvation endangered by these false claims, authored ninety-five theses attacking indulgences and fastened them to the door of All Saints Church in Wittenberg on October 31, 1517. Contrary to Luther's wishes, the theses were widely circulated, striking a responsive chord among the Germans. What Luther had intended as a local, scholarly debate was becoming a public controversy.

The Archbishop of Mainz, who was profiting directly from the sale of indulgences, forwarded copies of the ninety-five theses to Rome, requesting that Luther be disciplined. Pope Leo X, viewing the dispute as an argument betwen the Augustinians and Dominicans, simply told the former to deal with Luther. At this point, the scope of the controversy suddenly widened. A colleague of Luther at Wittenberg, Bodenstein von Karlstadt, responding to criticisms of Luther's positions by Johann Eck, published 405 theses, some of which attacked Eck personally. Eck's order, the Dominicans, were outraged, and heresy proceedings against Luther began to move forward in Rome. Luther himself inflamed the situation by publishing a sermon on excommunication which clearly questioned papal authority.

Rome sent a summons for Luther to appear at Rome to Cardinal Thomas Cajetan, who was at Augsburg. For political reasons, however, the pope could not afford to antagonize Frederick II of Saxony, an elector of the Holy Roman Empire and Luther's protector. Luther was instead given a safe-conduct to have a personal interview with the conservative Cajetan.

History will always note the dramatic presentation of the ninety-five theses in 1517 and the even more significant confrontation at Worms in 1521, but the meeting at Augsburg in 1518 probably had more impact than either. In 1517, Luther was insulated by his anonymity; in 1521, he was famous, with possibly half of Germany supporting him. Yet in 1518 Luther was vulnerable, not yet famous and not certain how the Church would deal with him. The Church had an opportunity to silence Luther without suffering severe damage and failed to do so. Cajetan had no intention of hearing Luther's statements, and, although he promised to forward Luther's "explanations" to Rome, he demanded that Luther recant. Luther refused and, in fear for his life, fled Augsburg.

While he had been in Augsburg, Luther had met with Eck and had agreed to a debate at Leipzig in July, 1519. This dispute did not go well for Luther.

Eck was able to maneuver him into supporting some Hussite positions and into questioning papal authority as well as the authority of ecclesiastical councils. The Church responded on June 15, 1520, with a papal bill condemning many of Luther's teachings. The papal legate sent to circulate the bill among the German cities was shocked to discover German opinion solidly behind Luther. Luther's friends, aware of his dangerous position, tried to have him moderate his beliefs, but Luther had already moved beyond that point and in 1520 published three of his most famous treatises.

In January, 1521, the Church formally excommunicated Luther. At this juncture, Frederick obtained a promise from Emperor Charles V to provide Luther with an opportunity to defend himself before the Imperial Diet then meeting at Worms. At the meeting, it became clear that Luther had been summoned only to recant. Since his life could depend on his answer, Luther requested time to think. The next day, Luther made a skillful statement, and the Chancellor of Trier made an equally skillful reply from the papal perspective. He concluded with a demand that Luther give a simple answer to the question, "Do you recant, yes or no?" Luther responded with a reply that change the course of history. Unless he were proved wrong on the basis of the Scriptures and sound reason—for popes and councils had erred and might do so again—he was bound by his conscience to the Word of God. He concluded in German, "May God help me. Amen."

There was no doubt that Luther had won a great moral victory, but his enemies also gained something important: the Edict of Worms, which declared Luther an outlaw and proscribed his writings. This edict would dog him all of his days, but while it could restrict his freedom of movement, it could not restrict Luther's ideas. It did mean that his protector, Frederick, could not openly support Luther, so for political reasons and for Luther's own safety, Luther was "kidnapped" to the castle at the Wartburg. He found this enforced inaction tiresome and depressing, but he did use the time to begin the translation of the New Testament from Greek into German. Published in September, 1522, it was a historic work which would have a tremendous influence on German language, life, and religion. Luther remained informed about developments beyond the Wartburg, and when he left in March, 1522, he faced a situation that gravely concerned him.

Religious doctrine can easily have social and political ramifications, and Luther was very alarmed by the political and social unrest his theological cornerstones—justification by faith and the priesthood of all believers—had engendered. Luther, always a conservative, feared that the new radical teaching by Karlstadt and others would lead to revolution. In response, Luther in 1523 postulated the Two Realms theory. There is the spiritual realm, where man exists only in relation to God, and the temporal realm, where man exists as flesh, subject to sin and the needs of the flesh. Since both realms are divinely inspired, man has a duty to obey civil authority, and thus it is sinful to rebel against lawful authority. Freedom for Luther consisted of man's freedom to obey the Gospel. These views help explain Luther's strong condemnation of the Peasants' Revolt of 1524-1525.

The year 1525 was pivotal for Luther and the Protestant Reformation. Luther was married to Katherina von Bora, a former nun, who proved to be a wonderful wife, bringing much-needed stability into his life. Also that year, relations were severed between Luther and Desiderius Erasmus. Early in the Reformation, Erasmus had supported its goals, but he had counseled caution, peace, and change through a reforming council. He feared a catastrophic split in the Church. As Luther's theology evolved and it became clear that the Reformation was no longer a reformation but a religious revolution, Erasmus parted company with Luther and chose the Church.

By the end of 1525, the lines were clearly drawn. From this point, Luther was the leader of a great religious movement—a man of true accomplishment. He would have to deal with doctrinal problems, the more radical Protestant leaders such as John Calvin and Huldrych Zwingli, and, as he grew older, others, especially Philipp Melanchthon, would share the mantle of leadership with Luther. Early in 1546, Luther traveled to Eisleben to settle a quarrel between two young princes. The weather was awful and cold. On February 17, he suffered a heart attack and died the next day. When news of his death reached Wittenberg, Melanchthon announced to his class, "Alas, gone is the horseman and the chariots of Israel," citing the words spoken by Elisha when Elijah was taken to heaven.

Summary

Martin Luther rejuvenated and restored the Christian faith. Rather than canon law, it was now the Bible that was at the center, leading people to a life of faith, love, and good works. Jesus of Nazareth was once again considered to be a personal savior and not a distant, judgmental God approachable only through priestly mediation. The Church returned to being a community of believers and not a legalistic, bureaucratic institution. In accomplishing these reforms, Luther transformed the face of Europe as radically as Napoleon I or Otto von Bismarck and dramatically changed the course of Western civilization.

Luther himself is more difficult to summarize. He was clearly a man constrained by his love of God and the Scriptures. He was often depressed by the evil he found in the world but was ultimately confident of the salvation and glory that awaited after death. That this attitude gave Luther tremendous courage and confidence in the face of powerful opposition is seen in an incident that occurred early in the Reformation. While at the Wartburg, in hiding from his enemies under the ban of the empire, and with his own future far from certain, Luther wrote, "Our enemies threaten us with death. They would do better to threaten us with life."

Bibliography

Atkinson, James. *Martin Luther and the Birth of Protestantism*. Reprint. Atlanta: John Knox Press, 1981. This book is essentially a theological account of Luther that is engagingly written and very understandable. Luther comes alive on these pages as a theologian and as a historical figure. Includes a subject index, an index of biblical references, a select bibliography, and a chronological table. Highly recommended.

Boehmer, Heinrich. *Road to Reformation: Martin Luther to the Year 1521*. Translated by John W. Doberstein and Theodore G. Tappert. Philadelphia: Muhlenberg Press, 1946. Based thoroughly on primary sources, the book's detail and insight into Luther's life and thinking to the conclusion of the Diet of Worms are exceptional. Lucid and well written, this work is considered by many Luther scholars to be a classic in the field. Includes an index.

Ebeling, Gerhard. *Luther: An Introduction to His Thought*. Translated by R. A. Wilson. Philadelphia: Fortress Press, 1964. Although this work is not popular discussion of Luther's thought, it does not assume any special knowledge on the part of the reader. It concentrates on the dynamics of Luther's thought. The discussion of Luther's view of philosophy and theology is particularly insightful.

Schwiebert, Ernest G. *Luther and His Times*. St. Louis: Concordia, 1950. Schwiebert lays stress upon the philosophical, theological, and sociogeographical factors that contributed to the molding of Luther. The first three chapters give an excellent historical background to the Reformation. This highly impressive, scholarly, yet accessible book should be a standard in any Luther bibliography. Includes an index, chapter notes, bibliographical notes, numerous photographs, and illustrations.

Smith, Preserved. *The Life and Letters of Martin Luther*. Reprint. New York: Barnes & Noble Books, 1968. The author is considered one of the great Reformation scholars. This book is an excellent introduction to Luther's letters with comments by the author placing them in historical context. Includes an index, chronological tables, and a detailed bibliography.

Thompson, W. D. J. Cargill. *The Political Thought of Martin Luther*. New York: Barnes & Noble Books, 1948. Thompson was recognized as a leading authority of Luther's political thought. He places Luther's political views in the context of his complete theology. The discussion of the Two Realms theory is outstanding. Includes an index and a select bibliography of secondary sources.

Todd, John M. *Luther: A Life*. New York: Crossroad, 1982. Like all top biographers of Luther, Todd draws heavily from Luther's own writings. This historical and theological account of Luther is lucid, providing an excellent discussion of the historical currents and events that helped to shape the Reformation. Includes an index, an excellent appendix on indulgences, numerous illustrations, and a map of Germany.

Ronald F. Smith

JOAQUIM MARIA MACHADO DE ASSIS

Born: June 21, 1839; Rio de Janeiro, Brazil
Died: September 29, 1908; Rio de Janeiro, Brazil
Area of Achievement: Literature
Contribution: Because of his uniquely modern and boldly experimental contribution to narrative form and technique, as well as the universal appeal of his works, Machado is considered the greatest figure in nineteenth century Brazilian literature and a world master of the short story.

Early Life

Joaquim Maria Machado de Assis' father, Francisco José de Assis, was a native of Rio de Janeiro, the son of free mulattoes, and a housepainter by trade. His mother, Maria Leopoldina Machado da Câmara, was a Portuguese woman from the Island of São Miguel in the Azores. His mother could read and write, and similarities observed between her handwriting and that of her son indicate that she may have taught her son how to read and write as well.

Machado had a younger sister, Maria, who died of measles in 1845; his mother died of tuberculosis in 1849, when he was ten years of age. His father remarried Maria Ignez da Silva on June 18, 1854, but he died ten years later, on April 22, 1864. While the exact circumstances of the boy's early life as well as his relationship with his stepmother are matters of speculation among his biographers, it is believed that Machado did not get along with his stepmother or her family. Although one of his early poems is dedicated to a cousin, Henrique José Moreira, nothing else is known about this or any other relative.

It is believed that when he was ten years of age, Machado went to live with a priest who provided the boy with a primary education; Machado never attended secondary school. Largely self-taught, the young man was an avid reader, who educated himself by spending his free time at the Library of the Portuguese Cabinet of Reading. Nothing further is known of Machado until his fifteenth year, when one of his poems was published in the magazine *A Marmota*. Henceforth, his professional activities, at least, are well known. At the age of seventeen, he was a typesetter; at the age of nineteen, he was a proofreader; and at the age of twenty-one, he was on the editorial staff of the republican newspaper *Diário do Rio de Janeiro*.

By 1860, Machado had begun to gain recognition with theater criticism, articles, poems, and stories. At the age of twenty-five, he published a first volume of verse, *Chrisalides poesias* (1864). The young man continued writing poems, more or less successfully—columns of clever and insightful commentary on current events, translations from French and English, and drama—but soon realized that fiction was the genre in which he was most proficient.

Machado was short and slight; his facial features were strong, although he was not considered handsome, and he was pronouncedly nearsighted. He was extremely conscious of his appearance and suffered from a lifelong inferiority complex because of his racial heritage. He was á victim of epilepsy; the illness was particularly pronounced during his early years and the last four years of his life—after the death of his wife.

Machado married Carolina Augusta Novaes (sister of the Portuguese poet Faustino Xavier de Novaes) on November 12, 1869, and in the same year became the assistant director of *Diário do Rio de Janeiro*, a post which he held until 1874. Machado and his wife remained devoted to each other throughout their marriage. During his lifetime, Machado never even ventured more than a few miles beyond the city limits of his native Rio. From 1873, his meager income as a writer was augmented by a position at the Ministry of Agriculture, where he served until his death in 1908. An exemplary civil servant, Machado never missed a day at the office.

During the period of Machado's novelistic production—his career as a novelist began in 1872 with the publication of *Resurreicão* (resurrection)—romanticism was still flourishing, but the incursions of naturalism were soon apparent. In general, Brazilian Romanticism is characterized by lyric poetry, Indianism, poetry of the *mal du siècle*, and sociopolitical literature concerned with events such as abolition. The movement included the expansion of literary genres and was based on a veneration of nature and the observation and analysis of customs and characteristic types.

From the beginning of his novelistic career, Machado outlined an experimental literary form which contained some Romantic elements but was not strictly representative of the movement. While his earlier novels utilize some Romantic devices, they also demonstrate many of the features to be found in his later works. In breaking with the movement, Machado freed himself not only from the school of Sir Walter Scott but also from all literary schools. With the publication of the novel *Yayá Garcia* (1878; *Iaia Garcia*, 1977), Machado ended the first phase of his literary career.

Life's Work

When he was already forty-two, Machado published his first great novel *Memórias póstumas de Bráz Cubas* (1881; *The Posthumous Memoirs of Brás Cubas*, 1951; better known as *Epitaph of a Small Winner*, 1952). The appearance of this work marks the beginning of the second, more powerful phase of the author's career. In this period Machado violently attacked the naturalist movement, which he referred to as *realismo* (naturalism applied a scientific objectivity to the representation of reality). His advice to young writers in Portugal and Brazil was not to be lured into a movement which, despite its novelty, was already obsolete.

Machado took from the reigning schools, Romanticism and naturalism, only those elements which he chose to incorporate into his own aesthetic. In *Epitaph of a Small Winner,* he announced that he would make no concessions to popular literary fashion, despite the limited number of readers that the book would probably have. In that novel, Machado first introduced in his work archaic literary techniques of the eighteenth century. Yet his archaism is surprisingly modern in, among other things, its formal fragmentation, use of ellipsis, and irony.

In one sense, Machado's fiction can be seen as a continuation of the work of the Brazilian writer José de Alencar. Yet at a time when Alencar was still struggling to rid himself of Romantic attitudes and methods, Machado, quickly and with apparent ease, abandoned Romanticism, and Alencar, in the incredible maturity of *Epitaph of a Small Winner.* Whereas Alencar represented the clash and conflict of sharply delineated characters in concrete settings and in a series of well-staged confrontations, Machado developed the art of ambiguity and understatement. Instead of the social criticism that in Alencar bordered on satire, he chose irony. Machado's characters are always plagued by their own demons: They are caught in a web of their own fears and dreams, and their vision of reality is entirely subjective.

Machado was deeply indebted to such British writers as Laurence Sterne. In the major works of both writers, the story is never presented directly to the reader but always through a first-person narration by the protagonist. The narrator, who is usually the main actor as well as the storyteller, becomes an unreliable witness. He is also so often compelled to discuss his own version of the facts that the novels become exercises in a new type of self-reflexive fiction. The text itself ultimately emerges as the protagonist.

In this second phase of Machado's writing, in addition to the short stories collected in *Histórias sem data* (1884; timeless stories) and *Várias histórias* (1896; stories), he wrote other novels. In the next twenty years he would complete a kind of trilogy with *Epitaph of a Small Winner, Quincas Borba* (1891; *Philosopher or Dog?,* 1954), and *Dom Casmurro* (1899; English translation, 1953). Before his death, he completed two extremely subtle novels, *Esaú e Jacob* (1904; *Esau and Jacob,* 1965) and *Memorial de Ayres* (1908; *Counselor Ayres' Memorial,* 1973).

Machado died in his native city of Rio in 1908. The Chamber of Deputies, in a special session, voted to hold a state funeral with civil and military honors. This was the first time in the history of Brazil that a literary man of humble origins was buried like a hero. The author was eulogized throughout Brazil, and in France a memorial service was held in his honor at the Sorbonne, with Anatole France presiding.

Summary

A master of realistic and accurately detailed portrayal, Joaquim Maria Machado de Assis so subtly distorted the proud self-image of his generation that the brilliance of his critical eye was almost a century in being appreciated. In presenting the follies and foibles of his contemporaries, he was not only a faithful portraitist but also a judge. Yet, while Machado's writing reveals a bitter disillusionment with mankind, it exhibits the serenity of one who has learned to laugh at his own lost illusions and broken dreams.

Machado has achieved a unique place in Brazilian literature, above and beyond all artistic schools and cultural movements. Besides demonstrating insight, simplicity, and subtlety, his work reveals a spirit that animated the new generation of modernism. Yet his novels about life in Rio are realistic psychological studies set in a middle-class milieu. No writer in Latin America has embraced as much and as varied a terrain as has this Brazilian author.

Many honors in recognition of his writing were bestowed on him, the first by the emperor in 1867. Finally, when the Brazilian Academy of Letters was founded in 1897, he was elected its first president and perpetually was re-elected. Thus, although he was not widely known outside Brazil, his talents were appreciated and acknowledged during his lifetime. This acknowledgment has continued through the years.

Bibliography
Bettencourt Machado, José. *Machado of Brazil: The Life and Times of Machado de Assis, Brazil's Greatest Novelist.* New York: C. Frank, 1962. This rather sentimental study focuses primarily on the life of Machado and secondarily on his work. Since little factual information exists on Machado's early life, and since Bettencourt does not reveal the sources of his information, his interpretation is interesting, although largely a matter of speculation. Includes a bibliography of primary and secondary works.
Caldwell, Helen. *Machado de Assis: The Brazilian Master and His Novels.* Berkeley: University of California Press, 1970. In this well-written and informative work of literary analysis, Caldwell discusses, after an introductory chapter, Machado's first four novels. Then follows a chapter on *Epitaph of a Small Winner,* one on *Philosopher or Dog?* and *Dom Casmurro,* and a concluding chapter on the writer's last two novels. Contains extensive footnotes and a brief biographical epilogue.
Nist, John. *The Modernist Movement in Brazil.* Austin: University of Texas Press, 1966. In this work, Nist attempts to describe and illustrate the modern spirit in Brazilian poetry and fiction. In the section devoted to Machado, Nist discusses the author's antiromantic temperament and aesthetics in the context of the new social and political order in Brazil, assesses the writer's contribution to modernism, and praises the universality of his works. Nist's book contains a bibliography of general works on the Brazilian modernist movement.
Nunes, Maria Luisa. *The Craft of an Absolute Winner: Characterization and Narratology in the Novels of Machado de Assis.* Westport, Conn.: Green-

wood Press, 1983. This brief but insightful work maintains that the most important element of Machado's art was his exploration of character. It is also the first study in English to apply systematically a philosophical and aesthetic critical apparatus to the texts of Machado, specifically that of narratology. Includes a bibliography of primary and secondary works.

Putnam, Samuel. *Marvelous Journey: A Survey of Four Centuries of Brazilian Writing*. New York: Alfred A. Knopf, 1948. In this survey, Putnam's purpose is to acquaint English-speaking readers with the main figures and currents in Brazilian literature of the past four centuries. In a rather lengthy chapter devoted to a discussion of Machado's work, "Machado de Assis and the End-of-the-Century Realists," Putnam places Machado's writing in the literary and social context of nineteenth century Brazil, and highlights the rebelliousness, originality, and universality of the author's work. Contains extensive footnotes, a bibliography, chronological tables, and reading lists.

Genevieve Slomski

NICCOLÒ MACHIAVELLI

Born: May 3, 1469; Florence
Died: June 21, 1527; Florence
Areas of Achievement: Political science, historiography, and literature
Contribution: Machiavelli's posthumous reputation rests primarily on his having initiated a pragmatic mode of political discourse that is entirely independent of ethical considerations derived from traditional sources of moral authority, such as classical philosophy and Christian theology.

Early Life
The year 1469 has a dual significance in the historical annals of Florence, since it marks both the date of Lorenzo de' Medici's ascension to power and that of Niccolò Machiavelli's birth. The boy was reared in a household consisting of his parents, Bernardo and Bartolomea, along with two older sisters and a younger brother. Bernardo, a tax lawyer and petty landowner of modest means, was a man of pronounced scholarly proclivities with a genuine passion for Roman literature. Machiavelli's own schooling in the principles of Latin grammar and rhetoric began at the age of seven. The study of arithmetic, however, was deferred until several years later. Although the family was too poor to own many books, it did possess a copy of the first three decades of Livy's survey of ancient Roman history. This work must have been a favorite of both father and son, since it was eventually sent to the bindery when Niccolò was seventeen years of age. Little is known for certain about the next decade in Machiavelli's life. There is some evidence which indicates that he may have spent most of the years between 1487 and 1495 in Rome working for a prominent Florence banker.

The political climate in Florence had altered drastically in the years immediately preceding Machiavelli's return from Rome. Lorenzo de' Medici died in 1492 and had been succeeded by his eldest son, Piero, an inept youth barely twenty years of age. Piero was soon confronted with a major crisis when King Charles VIII of France invaded Italy in 1494 to lay claim to Naples, and Piero's feckless conduct vis-à-vis the French monarch met with such revulsion on the part of his fellow citizens that they resolved to banish the entire Medici clan from the city forever. Soon thereafter, control of the Florentine republic fell into the hands of an austere Dominican friar from Ferrara, Girolamo Savonarola.

While Savonarola made considerable headway in mitigating the dissolute moral conditions that pervaded Florence, he had considerably less success with his self-imposed mission to restore Christian virtue to the Roman Catholic church. His adversary in this struggle was the Spaniard Rodrigo Borgia, whose reign as Alexander VI is generally conceded to represent the moral nadir in the history of the Papacy during the Renaissance. Savonarola's

persistent challenges to papal authority led to his being formally excommunicated by the Roman pontiff; this event emboldened the friar's political adversaries into taking direct action to destroy him. The climax of this struggle
occurred on May 23, 1498, when Savonarola and his two closest confed-
erates in the Dominican Order were escorted to the main square in Florence
and hanged atop a pile of brush and logs that was thereupon promptly set
ablaze by the hangman. Several hours later, the charred remains of the three
men were tossed into the Arno River. Machiavelli witnessed Savonarola's
rise and fall at first hand and viewed the episode as an object lesson as to the
danger of being "an unarmed prophet."

Life's Work

Savonarola's demise turned out to be highly beneficial with respect to
Machiavelli's own personal fortune, for a few months thereafter he was
called upon to serve in the newly reconstituted municipal government in
several important posts. Its chief executive, Piero Soderini, appointed him
both head of the Second Chancery and secretary to the Council of Ten for
War. It remains unclear why an inexperienced young man of twenty-nine
from an impoverished family should have been elevated to these key offices.
Most likely, it was his keen intelligence which recommended him to Soderini, for each of the artists for whom Machiavelli chose to pose has fully
captured this character trait. In addition to the bemused cynicism manifested
in his facial expression, Machiavelli is depicted as a slender man with thin
lips and penetrating eyes. He was, in short, a man whose crafty countenance
must have caused others to be on their guard while conducting official business with him.

Despite his initial lack of diplomatic experience, Machiavelli was rou-
tinely commissioned to undertake sensitive missions to other Italian states as
well as to the courts of Louis XII in France and Maximilian I in Germany.
Diplomatic activities such as these played a vital role in Machiavelli's development as an uncompromising exponent of political pragmatism. Most
instructive of all in this context were his extensive contacts with Cesare
Borgia in Romagna during 1502-1503. It was this illegitimate son of Pope
Alexander VI who best exemplified the quality of manliness (*virtù*) that
Machiavelli most admired in a political and military leader. Cesare Borgia's
meteoric career was, however, terminated abruptly as a result of the death of
his father in 1503. The new pope, Julius II, was an inveterate enemy of the
entire Borgia clan and soon sent Borgia into exile, where he later died.

Julius was also responsible for terminating Machiavelli's career as a civil
servant. When Louis XII of France invaded Italy and succeeded in establishing control over the Duchy of Milan, Julius proceeded to form a political
coalition known as the Holy League, whose aim was to drive the invader
from Italian soil. Soderini, despite Machiavelli's advice, refused to permit

Florence to join the coalition and insisted on its maintaining strict neutrality throughout the entire conflict. After the expulsion of the French, Julius decided to punish the Florentine republic and compelled its citizenry to accept the return of the Medicis. Both Soderini and Machiavelli were immediately dismissed from office. On February 23, 1513, moreover, Machiavelli was falsely accused of being part of a conspiracy to reestablish the republic and put to torture on the rack. Though lack of evidence compelled the authorities to release him, he feared rearrest and decided to retire to his ancestral villa at Sant' Andrea, near Florence, together with his wife, Marietta Corsini, and their six children.

His premature retirement from public life at age forty-three enabled Machiavelli to study Roman literature and to compose many original works. His major political treatises are *Il principe* (wr. 1513, pb. 1532; *The Prince*, 1640) and *Discorsi sulla prima deca di Tito Livio* (wr. c. 1513-1517, pb. 1531; *Discourses on the First Ten Books of Titus Livius*, 1636). Since Machiavelli focuses upon issues pertaining to the governance of principalities in *The Prince* and of republics in the *Discourses*, these works constitute, in effect, a unified exposition of the author's political theories and should therefore be studied in conjunction with each other. The title of the *Discourses* is, however, misleading to the extent that this work is not really a commentary on Livy's history of ancient Rome. Machiavelli subscribed to a cyclical view of history based on the theories propounded by the Greek historian Polybius, and he used the *Discourses* to draw parallels between the events depicted by Livy and the political situation of his own time. He next tried his hand at writing comedies for a brief period. The most celebrated of his works in this genre is *La Mandragola* (c. 1519; *The Mandrake*, 1911), the other two being adaptations of plays by Terence. Foremost among the other books that Machiavelli wrote at Sant' Andrea are *Libro della arte guerra* (1521; *The Art of War*, 1560) and *Istorie fiorentine* (wr. 1520, pb. 1525; *The Florentine History* , 1595). In *The Art of War*, Machiavelli argues strongly in favor of the greater efficacy of native militias as opposed to mercenary armies, and in *The Florentine History* he chronicles the city's fortune from the fall of the Roman Empire to the death of Lorenzo the Magnificent.

Even though Machiavelli had been an ardent supporter of the republic headed by Soderini, he considered himself to be a professional civil servant above all else and burned with a desire to be of service to his native city. Machiavelli, in fact, wrote *The Prince* for the express purpose of getting the Medici family to recognize his political sagacity and offer him employment in the new regime. Within a few years, the responsibility of governing Florence passed into the lands of Lorenzo de' Medici, to whom Machiavelli decided to dedicate *The Prince*. Lorenzo, however, showed no interest in the treatise. Lorenzo died prematurely in 1519 at the age of twenty-seven and was succeeded by Cardinal Giulio de' Medici, under whose administration of the city's affairs Machiavelli's personal fortunes improved somewhat. He was entrusted with a few minor diplomatic missions on behalf of the Medicis. More important, it was Giulio who commissioned Machiavelli to write *The Florentine History.*

Giulio de' Medici became Pope Clement VII in 1521 when the immediate successor to Pope Leo died after a brief reign of twenty months. A series of diplomatic missteps on the part of Clement led to the horrendous sack of Rome in 1527 by mercenaries in the service of the German Emperor Charles V. The citizens of Florence took advantage of the occasion and expelled the Medicis from their own city for the sake of reestablishing the republic. Machiavelli expected to be reinstated in the posts that he had held under Soderini. The Florentines, however, took a dim view of Machiavelli's previous association with the Medicis and declined to entrust him with any posts in the new regime. Bitterly disappointed, Machiavelli died in Florence a scant few months after the city had regained its liberty. The eclipse of the Medicis turned out to be a short one since Pope Clement and Emperor Charles were quick to reconcile their differences. The Medicis returned to Florence in 1530, but this time they did so as a hereditary nobility. The city's days as an independent republic were thus ended forever.

Summary

Niccolò Machiavelli's political writings have elicited an unusual number of disparate reactions over the course of time. The negative viewpoint was initiated by the Roman Catholic church when it decided to ban open dissemination of Machiavelli's works by placing his entire oeuvre on its Index of Prohibited Books in 1559. Oddly enough, even though an English translation of *The Prince* did not appear until 1640, it was the frequent allusions to Machiavelli which occur in plays by Elizabethan dramatists such as Christopher Marlowe and William Shakespeare that did most to popularize his image as an evil counselor. It is generally assumed that the Elizabethan public had already derived a measure of familiarity with the contents of *The Prince* from earlier French translations of the work. Sir Francis Bacon, on the other hand, took a more favorable view of Machiavelli and hailed him as a fellow empiricist who described "what men do, and not what they ought to do." Jean-Jacques Rousseau went even further in vindicating Machiavelli by contending that the real purpose of *The Prince* was to expose the modus operandi of tyrants and thereby to advance the cause of democracy. In modern times, however, *The Prince* has frequently been called "a handbook for dictators."

Whatever may be said for and against Machiavelli's political doctrines, it is necessary to recognize that he himself was deeply committed to a republican form of government. Even after one concedes Machiavelli's genuine patriotism and his deeply held commitment to republican virtues, there are a number of disquieting elements in his political philosophy that cannot easily be dismissed. There is, for example, his excessive taste for violent and cruel solutions to political problems as reflected in his unabashed admiration for the bloody deeds of Cesare Borgia. Similarly, he held the view that morally reprehensible actions in terms of Christian standards are fully justifiable if perpetrated for what has come to be known as "reasons of state." For these and other reasons, Machiavelli continues to be a disturbing figure in the cultural pantheon of Western culture.

Bibliography
Bondanella, Peter E. *Machiavelli and the Art of Renaissance History*. Detroit: Wayne State University Press, 1973. This astute study constitutes a chronological survey of Machiavelli's development as a literary stylist. Focuses on the compositional techniques that he employed in depicting the character and conduct of heroic personages. Lacks a formal bibliography, but there are copious endnotes for each chapter.
Hale, John Rigby. *Machiavelli and Renaissance Italy*. New York: Macmillan, 1960. Hale's primary objective is to demonstrate the extent to which Machiavelli's writings are a reflection of the political events that were unfolding in Italy during his own lifetime. Generally viewed as the best introduction to the study of Machiavelli and his age. Contains two maps and a brief annotated bibliography.
Machiavelli, Niccolò. *Machiavelli: The Chief Works and Others*. Edited and translated by Allan Gilbert. 3 vols. Durham: Duke University Press, 1965. The most extensive collection of Machiavelli's writings currently available in English translation. Although textual annotations are dispensed with, there are succinct introductions to the individual selections as well as an outstanding index to the entire corpus.
Pitkin, Hanna Fenichel. *Fortune Is a Woman: Gender and Politics in the Thought of Niccolò Machiavelli*. Berkeley: University of California Press, 1984. This pioneering study of gender as a factor in political theory depicts Machiavelli as a misogynistic authoritarian. It is particularly useful in clarifying the manner in which Machiavelli employs the concepts of *fortuna* and *virtù*. The text is extensively annotated and supplemented by a highly detailed index and a useful bibliography of works cited.
Ridolfi, Roberto. *The Life of Niccolò Machiavelli*. Translated by Cecil Grayson. Chicago: University of Chicago Press, 1963. This biography is generally regarded as superior to the earlier efforts of Pasquale Villari and Oreste Tommassini by virtue of its focus on the course of Machiavelli's life rather than on his ideas or his cultural and historial milieu. Exhaustive documentation of sources.
Strauss, Leo. *Thoughts on Machiavelli*. Glencoe, Ill.: Free Press, 1958. The

author, one of the most renowned political scientists of the modern age, argues that Machiavelli was a teacher of wickedness. This work is especially helpful in evaluating the relationship between the ideological content of *The Prince* and the *Discourses*. Minimal index, but each chapter is accompanied by extensive endnotes.

Victor Anthony Rudowski

FERDINAND MAGELLAN

Born: 1480; northern province of Minho, Portugal
Died: April, 1521; Mactan Island, the Philippines
Area of Achievement: Exploration
Contribution: Magellan was the first person to command an expedition that circumnavigated the earth. While doing so, he discovered the southernmost point of South America (later called the Strait of Magellan), was the first to sail across the Pacific Ocean (which he named), and discovered the Philippine Islands. His feat also proved that the earth is indeed round.

Early Life

Ferdinand Magellan was born in the northern Portuguese province of Minho, the third child of Dom Roy and Donha Alda Magalahães. His father was high sheriff of the district and city of Aveiro, located south of the city of Pôrto on the Atlantic coast. Magellan grew up with his siblings—sister Isabel and brother Diogo—in the Torre de Magalhães, the family farmhouse, and had a pleasant childhood in this rustic setting. At the age of seven, he attended school in the nearby monastery of Vila Nova de Mura, where he learned basic arithmetic, Latin, and the importance of harboring a strong faith in the power of Christianity.

When he was twelve, Magellan, with his father's influence, was able to travel to Lisbon and attend Queen Leonora's School of Pages with his brother, Diogo. The King of Portugal, John II, was a great supporter of marine exploration, and the young pages were expected to master such subjects as celestial navigation, cartography, and astronomy as well as the regular court subjects such as court etiquette, hunting, jousting, and swordsmanship.

In March, 1505, Magellan, his brother Diogo, and his cousin, Francisco Serrano, sailed with the fleet of Francisco de Almeida to the Orient, the three young squires having signed for a three-year service with the fleet. Magellan would serve eight years in the Orient, leaving as an extra sea hand and returning as an accomplished captain. During his service in the East, he helped establish major ports from the East African coast all the way to the Malay Peninsula. He was also involved in major confrontations with Muslim and Indian forces and was wounded several times.

Magellan, stocky in height with dark, swarthy features and piercing yet sympathetic eyes, developed strong leadership qualities and a keen appetite for adventure during his years in the East. He was also known as a fair and just man, who many times risked his life for his fellow crewmen.. He was a soldier, one who could remain calm and decisive during a crisis, but one who preferred the excitement of discovery to the life of a military officer.

In July, 1511, Magellan captained a Portuguese caravel to a destination that remains unclear but was probably the Moluccas, or Spice Islands, in

Indonesia, the ultimate destination of all explorers. Pepper, which was used as a food preservative by all the major countries and was therefore nearly as valuable as gold, was exported largely from the Spice Islands. During his travels, Magellan became convinced that there was an alternate route to the Spice Islands and the Indies, one that could be attained by sailing west from Europe as Christopher Columbus had done. Unlike Columbus, Magellan had knowledge of a passage around the newly discovered South American continent, previously explored by a fellow navigator and friend, John of Lisbon. John had also informed Magellan that an unexplored ocean existed through the South American passage and that the Spice Islands could be reached in a few weeks time by sailing across this ocean.

When Magellan returned to Portugal in 1512, he was anxious to find backing for an expedition to discover the new sea route. He found no support from John II's successor, King Manuel I, who was much less receptive to new exploratory ventures. Rebuffed by Portugal, Magellan sailed to Spain in October, 1517, hoping to present his proposal to King Charles I. Magellan's chief contact in Spain was Diogo Barbosa, a former Portuguese navigator who had made a fortune in the spice trade and who was now the wealthy governor of the Castle of Seville. Magellan married Barbosa's daughter, Beatriz, in December, 1517. The marriage gave Magellan much pleasure, as well as a son, Rodrigo. On March 22, 1518, Magellan secured an audience with Charles. Charles was so impressed with Magellan and his proposal that he approved the expedition that same day. Preparations were then made for what would turn out to be the most epic voyage in the history of exploration.

Life's Work

During the year it took to prepare for the voyage, Magellan dealt with all details, from the rigging and loading of the ships to preventing riots and pilferage caused by spies sent from Portugal and Venice to sabotage the voyage. In the end, Magellan triumphed and finally set sail with 277 crewmen and five ships—the *Victoria*, the *Santiago*, the *Concepcion*, the *San Antonio*, and the *Trinidad*—on September 20, 1519, from San Luca, Spain, for westward passage to the Indies.

Soon after leaving Spain, Magellan's Spanish captains, led by second-in-command Juan de Cartagena, began ridiculing Magellan's authority, attempting to provoke him so that they could justify a mutiny and take command of the voyage. Magellan, however, refused to be provoked.

After suffering major storms along the African coast and disturbing doldrums near the Equator, the ships successfully crossed the Atlantic by early December, 1519. On December 8, the coast around Cape Roque in northern Brazil was sighted. Knowing that this area was under Portuguese domain, Magellan headed south into unclaimed territory and landed in what is modern Rio de Janeiro on December 13. There the crewmen secured provisions and indulged in friendly and amorous relations with the generous natives. Two weeks later, they set sail down the coast, looking for *el paso*, the pathway first revealed to Magellan by his friend John of Lisbon.

Three months later, when no trace of *el paso* had materialized, the crew was at its breaking point. Winter storms, the worst of the expedition, began battering the ships. Magellan gave the command to seek a harbor where the ships and crew would wait out the winter for five months. The Spanish captains thought that he was mad and urged him to sail eastward for Africa's Cape of Good Hope and follow the old route to the Indies. The crew wanted him to return to the idyllic harbor at Rio de Janeiro and spend the winter there. Magellan, however, held firm.

The armada anchored at San Julián in southern Argentina on March 31, 1520. The following evening, the Spanish captains mutined. Under the leadership of Juan de Cartagena, they quickly secured three of the five ships. During a confusing boat exchange of crewmen between mutinous ships, Magellan was able to capture one of the small boatloads of men, substitute his own men for the mutiny sympathizers, and send the boat back to one of the Spanish captains along with another boat load of Magellan's men. While the Spanish captain was dealing with the first boat load, one of Magellan's men suddenly pulled out a knife and stabbed the mutinous captain as the second boat load reached the ship and scrambled on deck, ready to do battle with the rebellious crew. The crew, shocked by the sudden turn of events, became sympathetic to Magellan once more. With three ships in his favor, Magellan surrounded the other two ships and forced the remaining captains to surrender.

A trial was held for the mutineers. Two men were beheaded, and their ringleader, Juan de Cartagena, was set adrift in a small boat, never to be seen again. Through the ordeal of the mutiny, in fact through every ordeal the expedition faced, Magellan remained strong and decisive. The fact that he never doubted his ability to succeed with his mission ultimately inspired his crew to follow him, even when conditions were unbearable.

The expedition spent a total of seven months waiting for the storms to subside, first at San Julián and then farther south at Puerto Santa Cruz, where the *Santiago* was smashed against the shoreline and lost. Finally, on October 18, they set sail once again in search of *el paso*. Three days later, they came to a narrow inlet protected on either side by jagged cliffs. The inlet seemed too dangerous to navigate, but Magellan, by now appearing nearly insane to his crew, ordered the *Concepcion* and the *San Antonio* to explore the inlet. The two ships had just entered the pathway when a storm suddenly rose and swept the ships through the inlet and out of sight, while forcing Magellan's *Trinidad* and the *Victoria* out to sea. For two days, Magellan fought the storm until he was able to return to the inlet where the *Concepcion* and the *San Antonio* had disappeared. Close to panic, fearing that the two ships had been destroyed, Magellan entered the treacherous pathway. The following morning, a cloud of smoke was sighted. Then, miraculously, the two lost ships sailed into view, flags and pennants waving and crewmen cheering excitedly. They had found *el paso*.

Navigation of the strait (which Magellan called the Strait of Desire, but which was later named for him) was not complete until mid-November. During that period, the *San Antonio* disappeared. Magellan searched for the missing ship until it became apparent that the *San Antonio* had deserted and returned to Spain. Because the *San Antonio* was the largest ship and carried the bulk of their provisions, the crew urged Magellan to turn back as well. Magellan, however, would not be deterred. After the three remaining ships had sailed out of the treacherous strait and into the surprisingly calm waters of a new ocean, Magellan spoke to his men: "We are about to stand into an ocean where no ship has ever sailed before. May the ocean be always as calm and benevolent as it is today. In this hope, I name it the Mar Pacifico [peaceful sea]."

No one encountering the Pacific Ocean for the first time could have anticipated its immensity. In the following three months, nearly half of the remaining men died of starvation and scurvy. Magellan was unfortunate in that his course across the Pacific Ocean led him away from all the major groups of islands that would have supplied him with necessary provisions. During the ghastly voyage across the Pacific Ocean, Magellan threw his maps overboard in anguish, knowing that they were uselessly inaccurate. Some of the men began to believe the old superstition that the ocean would lead them not to the other side of the world but to the end of the world. When the food rotted and the water turned to scum, the dying men began eating rats and sawdust. On March 4, 1531, all the food was gone. Two days later, after ninety-eight days and thirteen thousand miles across the mightiest ocean on the planet, they reached Guam and salvation.

Taking on provisions at Guam was made difficult by the weakened state of the men and the hostility of the natives. As quickly as he could, Magellan set sail and, on March 16, found the island of Samar in the Philippines. Magellan had now achieved his personal goal, having discovered a new chain of islands for Spain. Here the expedition rested and the sick were tended, Magellan personally nursing his emaciated men.

On March 28, during the start of Easter weekend, the crew held a pageant to which the natives were invited. Magellan had made friends with the local raja and began encouraging him and his followers to convert to Christianity, which they did by the thousands. Inspired by this enthusiastic acceptance of his religion, Magellan decided not only to claim the island chain for Spain but also to convert as many natives to Christanity as he could. His desire to reach the Spice Islands, always of secondary importance to him, faded as he became more determined to make the Philippines his ultimate destination.

One month later, after exploring more of the Philippines and being favorably accepted, Magellan attempted to force the powerful raja of the island of Mactan to honor Magellan's presence. When the raja refused, Magellan assembled a small army of volunteers and the next morning, on April 27, 1521, led an attack on the raja and his followers. Because of all the hardships he had encountered and conquered, and because his expedition had now taken on a divine mission, Magellan must have come to think of himself as invincible. Unfortunately, he realized too late that he was not.

Magellan quickly realized that he and his men were hopelessly outnumbered. When he ordered a retreat, a panic ensued in which his men scrambled to the shoreline and frantically rowed back to the ships, leaving Magellan and a handful of men stranded. For more than an hour, the men defended themselves as the rest of the crew watched from the ships, until finally Magellan was struck down and killed. Antonio Pigafetta, the chronicler of the voyage, was one of the men who fought beside Magellan when he was struck down. Pigafetta was able to escape during the frenzy that followed. Later he wrote: "And so they slew our mirror, our light, our comfort and our true and only guide."

Summary

On September 8, 1522, sixteen months after Ferdinand Magellan's death, a floating wreck of a ship with an emaciated crew of eighteen men sailed into the harbor of Seville, Spain. The ship was the *Victoria*. The men, led by Juan Sebastián de Elcano, a former mutineer, staggered out of the ship and marched barefoot through the streets to the shrine of Santa Maria de la Victoria, Our Lady of Victory, the favorite shrine of their fallen leader. They lit candles and said prayers for their dead comrades, then proceeded through the streets of Seville, shocking the citizens with their wasted appearance. The *Victoria* had returned laden with riches from the Spice Islands, which had indeed been reached on November 8, 1521. As for the fate of the remaining two ships, the *Concepcion* had been burned before reaching the Spice Islands and the *Trinidad* had been captured by the Portuguese, its fifty-two crewmen hanged.

Magellan's reputation was at first defiled and degraded by his contemporaries as they learned about his behavior from the crew of the *San Antonio*, the ship that had deserted in South America. Later, however, the magnitude of his accomplishments could not be denied. He had proved that the Indies could be reached by sailing west, had discovered a pathway around the southern tip of South America, had named and crossed the largest body of ocean on the planet, had discovered a new chain of islands, had accumulated a mountain of new information about navigation, geography, and exploration, and had commanded an expedition which, after three years and forty-two thousand miles, had circumnavigated the world.

Bibliography

Cameron, Ian. *Magellan and the First Circumnavigation of the World*. New York: Saturday Review Press, 1973. Generously illustrated with maps, woodcuts, and drawings, this biography of Magellan details his life and his voyage and uses generous quotes from other biographers as well as passages from the journal of Antonio Pigafetta. Includes a selected bibliography.

Humble, Richard. *The Explorers*. Alexandria, Va.: Time-Life Books, 1978. Contains an overview of the accomplishments of the four most significant Renaissance explorers: Bartolomeu Dias, Christopher Columbus, Vasco da Gama, and Magellan. Nearly a third of the book is devoted to Magellan. Includes excellent maps and charts plus an illustrated section on the ships and navigational instruments used by the explorers, as well as a detailed description of the *Victoria*. Includes a selected bibliography.

Parr, Charles McKew. *So Noble a Captain: The Life and Times of Ferdinand Magellan*. New York: Thomas Y. Crowell, 1953. The definitive biography of Magellan. Traces Magellan's ancestry, details the lives of all the principal men and women who affected or were affected by Magellan, vividly re-creates the time in which he lived, and chronicles his accomplishments in minute detail. Contains an extensive bibliography, including books on such related subjects as the history of Spain and Portugal, sailing-ship construction, navigation, and various locations visited by Magellan.

Pigafetta, Antonio. *Magellan's Voyage: A Narrative Account of the First Circumnavigation*. Translated by R. A. Skelton. New Haven, Conn.: Yale University Press, 1969. This is an English translation from a French text of Pigafetta's Italian journal. It is full of detailed descriptions of the events of the voyage, the lands discovered, the natives encountered and their habits and customs, and the tales told by the natives and examples of their vocabulary.

Sanderlin, George. *First Around the World: A Journal of Magellan's Voyage*. New York: Harper & Row, 1964. An interesting reconstruction of Magellan's life and voyage using letters and journals of Magellan's contemporaries. The early texts are linked by comments from the author. Most of the book is composed of excerpts from Pigafetta's journal. Illustrated, with a selected bibliography.

Zweig, Stefan. *Conqueror of the Seas: The Story of Magellan*. Translated by Eden Paul and Cedar Paul. New York: Viking Press, 1938. A full account of Magellan's life from the time of his first voyage in 1505 to his death, and the results of his epic voyage. Contains maps and illustrations of the principal events taken from early texts.

James Kline

MARCELLO MALPIGHI

Born: March 10, 1628; Crevalcore, near Bologna, Papal States
Died: November 29, 1694; Rome
Areas of Achievement: Botany, zoology, and physiology
Contribution: Malpighi's most noteworthy contributions are the discovery of
the blood capillaries and the demonstration of the fine structure of the
lungs, thus laying the foundation for knowledge of the physiology of
respiration. Other important studies were in embryology, plant anatomy,
and invertebrate zoology.

Early Life

Marcello Malpighi was born in Crevalcore in 1628, the year that William
Harvey's book on the circulation of blood was published. His parents were
farmers and financially independent. Not much is known of Malpighi's
childhood. As the eldest child in the family, he had the advantages of masters and schools. He began attending the University of Bologna on January 8, 1646, where he studied Aristotelian philosophy and met Bartolomeo
Massari, a professor of anatomy. Massari soon became aware of Malpighi's
genius in science, and the latter rose from being a pupil to become an
associate and close friend.

In 1649, both of Malpighi's parents and his paternal grandmother died
within a few days of each other. Since he was the eldest child, he had to
interrupt his studies to settle his father's affairs and look after his brothers
and sisters. His uncle, Alessandro Alfiere Malpighi, came to his aid, and he
was able to resume his studies. In 1651, Malpighi decided to study medicine
and soon became a candidate for doctoral degrees in both medicine and
philosophy. On April 26, 1653, both degrees were conferred. He began to
practice medicine, and, toward the end of the 1655-1656 academic year, he
was also a lecturer in logic at the University of Bologna.

Malpighi's brilliance soon became apparent, but some opposition to his
anti-Galenist, proexperimental ideas and his advanced views in medicine
delayed his advancement. In 1656, when the Senate of Bologna established a
professorship for him, he declined and accepted an appointment to the chair
of theoretical medicine at Pisa, where the Grand Duke of Tuscany had instituted a new university on a much more liberal scale. At Pisa, he became
acquainted with Giovanni Alfonso Borelli, who was then professor of mathematics with an interest in biology. This association developed into a lifelong,
mutually beneficial friendship.

Life's Work

Malpighi's true scientific career began at Pisa. By 1659, he returned again
to Bologna, for his health, where he was appointed an extraordinary lecturer

in theoretical medicine. He also applied himself assiduously to the investigation of microscopic anatomy. In 1662, upon Borelli's recommendation, he was invited to fill the primary chair in medicine at the University of Messina. Four years later, he returned to Bologna, where a professorship awaited him, to lecture in practical medicine. He held this position with honor for twenty-five years.

Malpighi's greatest contribution to science was his demonstration and description of the capillaries in the lungs. This was the first important discovery made with the aid of the microscope, and it completed William Harvey's work on the circulation of blood. These studies were described in two letters to Borelli, who published them as *De pulmonibus observationes anatomicae* (anatomical observations on lungs), in 1661. The lung was thought to be a fleshy organ in which blood and air freely mixed. Working at first on the lungs of dogs, Malpighi determined them to be an aggregate of membranous vesicles (alveoli) opening into the tracheobronchial tree surrounded by a capillary network. Subsequently, he investigated the lungs of frogs, which are more transparent, and demonstrated the capillary circulation as a connecting link between arteries and veins.

In his treatise *De cerebro* (1665; on the brain), Malpighi showed that the white matter of the central nervous system is composed of bundles of fibers, arranged in tracts connecting the brain with the spinal cord. His *De viscerum structura exercitatio anatomica* (1666; on the structure of viscera) contains his basic observations on microscopic mammalian anatomy. He described the histology of the liver and determined that it secreted the bile that passes through a duct to the gall bladder, which simply stores and releases it. In addition, he determined the structure and function of the kidneys.

On February 21, 1667, Malpighi married Francesca Massari, the fifty-seven-year-old sister of his former teacher Massari. In 1667, Malpighi received an invitation from Henry Oldenburg, Secretary of the Royal Society in London, to correspond with the society. He gracefully accepted and was honored the following year by being elected a Fellow of the society.

Malpighi's publication on the silkworm moth, *De bombyce* (1669), represents the first full account of the anatomy of an insect. With his microscopes and wonderful skill, he was the first to observe the spiracles and the system of air tubes associated with them, the multichambered heart, the ventral nerve cord with its ganglia, and the silk-forming apparatus. He showed that the method of gas exchange was through the system of air tubes or tracheae, communicating with the exterior through the spiracles. He anatomized all phases of the species, and he discovered the system of excretory tubules now known as Malpighian tubules.

In the field of embryology, Malpighi published two pioneer works, *Dissertatio epistolica de formatione pulli in ovo* (1673; on the formation of the chick in the egg) and *De ovo incubato* (1675; on the incubated egg). The subject was not quite a new one; Aristotle, Harvey, and others had preceded him. He, however, enjoyed one great advantage over his predecessors; he was able to use a microscope in his studies and proceeded to produce a masterpiece, one of the best studies of the subject ever made.

In addition to the extensive studies of animal anatomy, Malpighi made the structure of the plant the subject of detailed and systematic investigations. In 1675, he published the first part of his *Anatome plantarum* (plant anatomy) and the second part in 1679. This, one of his largest and best monographs, earned for him acclaim, along with Nehemiah Grew, as the founder of the study of plant anatomy. Malpighi used a variety of microscopes and was able to magnify objects up to 143 times. In his investigations of stems, he found tiny ducts that possessed a spiral structure. Because of their resemblance to the tracheae of insects, he incorrectly attributed a respiratory function to them. He discovered stomata on the leaves but was unable to determine their function. In his studies of plant anatomy, Malpighi anticipated, to a certain degree, the cell theory. He described plants as being composed of separate structural units, which he called utricles.

Malpighi devoted special attention to the study of gall formations in several plants. He believed, as did nearly all scientists of his era, that these growths were spontaneous productions. He demonstrated, however, that several galls contained insect larvae. These, in some instances, he traced to an egg and onward to an adult insect. Malpighi's description of the egg-laying apparatus (ovipositor) of the gallflies was so detailed and accurate that it enables modern entomologists to identify the species. His research on plant galls convinced him that they were produced by the action of insects. He also determined that the tubercles on the roots of leguminous plants, which were first described by him, were not caused by insects; he failed, however, to explain their origin.

On February 6, 1684, Malpighi's house caught fire during the night and burned, resulting in the loss of many microscopes, books, research notes, and observations. In subsequent years, he suffered from nephritic and articular pains, and his health continued to decline steadily. In 1691, Malpighi reluctantly accepted an invitation from Pope Innocent XII to become the pope's personal physician in Rome. On October 4 of that year, he left Bologna with his aged wife, a maid, and a servant and moved to Rome. Despite his new position and ill health, he continued his research. On August 11, 1694, his wife and loving companion for twenty-seven years died. Three months later, on November 29, an apoplectic stroke ended Malpighi's life. After his death in Rome, his body was returned to Bologna to be interred with great pomp and ceremony.

Summary

Marcello Malpighi was a physician, an anatomist, an embryologist, a botanist, and a naturalist. He was comparative in his approach and among the first to make use of the microscope. His work on the lungs and the discovery of capillaries explained a major step in the process of respiration. What William Harvey had made a logical necessity, Malpighi showed to be a reality. Malpighi made the first microscopic analyses of the structure of the spleen, the kidney, the liver, the tongue, the skin, and the brain. He introduced the use of stains and wax injections in his histological studies. His name has deservedly become an eponym of numerous anatomic structures. His monograph *De bombyce* is an original and important contribution to zoology. Malpighi's study of the embryology of the chick was the best that had yet been made. Although he had no deep interest in causal factors and thus contributed little in this area, his descriptive embryology was masterful. His monograph on plant anatomy was so important for botany that, with the exception of Nehemiah Grew's work, which readily admits Malpighi's priority in several areas, it was not surpassed by a single production during the next 120 years.

Malpighi's career at the University of Bologna is a contrast to that of the scholars who worked at Padua. Bologna was under the jurisdiction of the pope. Literature and ideas were censored, and the Inquisition was ready to investigate serious heresy. The forces of dogmatism were so powerful that anatomical demonstrations and microscopic proof were inadequate to enlighten these opponents of progress. Malpighi, as one who dared to combat the ancient ideas, was confronted with much hostility, yet he triumphed and was recognized as one of the greatest scientists of the seventeenth century.

Bibliography
Adelmann, Howard B. *Marcello Malpighi and the Evolution of Embryology.* 5 vols. Ithaca, N.Y.: Cornell University Press, 1966. A monumental and definitive work that highlights the major controversies and publications of Malpighi's career, and interprets Malpighi's role in the evolution of embryology. Contains an extensive literature-cited section and a comprehensive index.
Cole, F. J. *A History of Comparative Anatomy from Aristotle to the Eighteenth Century.* London: Macmillan, 1949. Reprint. New York: Dover, 1975. An excellent presentation of the works of notable comparative anatomists. Chapter 18 treats Malpighi. Includes an appendix containing biographical notes, a helpful bibliography, and an index.
Foster, Michael. *Lectures on the History of Physiology During the Sixteenth, Seventeenth, and Eighteenth Centuries.* Cambridge, England: Cambridge University Press, 1901. Nine lectures presenting specific highlights in the history of physiology. Lecture 5 is a superb presentation of Malpighi's life and work, with translations of some of his writings. Contains a comprehensive index.

Locy, William A. *The Growth of Biology.* New York: Henry Holt, 1925. A comprehensive work on the history of biology. Includes a well-balanced presentation on Malpighi. Sections on his personal qualities, education, university positions, honors at home and abroad, and his research are particularly valuable. Contains an extensive bibliography of primary and secondary sources and a good index.

Miall, L. C. *The Early Naturalists, Their Lives and Work, 1530-1789.* London: Macmillan, 1912. Contains much biographical information on naturalists of this period. Malpighi is well covered in a twenty-page account in section 5. Although all of his major contributions are described, his work on plant anatomy is given the most extensive coverage. Contains a useful index and valuable footnotes.

Nordenskiöld, Erik. *The History of Biology: A Survey.* Translated by Leonard Bucknall Eyre. New York: Tudor, 1928. The best one-volume history of the biological sciences with an emphasis on the philosophical and medical background. Contains a useful sources and literature section and a detailed index.

Singer, Charles. *A History of Biology to About the Year 1900.* New York: Abelard-Schuman, 1931. One of the best books on the history of biology. A brief but well-balanced account on Malpighi is given in part 2. Contains an excellent index.

Ralph Troll

ÉDOUARD MANET

Born: January 23, 1832; Paris, France
Died: April 30, 1883; Paris, France
Area of Achievement: Art
Contribution: In a relatively short career of just over twenty years, Manet challenged the conventions of European art by creating a body of paintings, drawings, and etchings manifesting novel approaches both to form and to content. His works and his career were the focal points of the struggle for artistic independence waged by a generation of French artists and writers in the mid-nineteenth century.

Early Life

Édouard Manet was born in Paris at 5 rue de Grands Augustins, a street bordering the Seine, not far from the Cathedral of Nôtre Dame. His father, Auguste Manet, was a high official in the Ministry of Justice. At the time of Édouard's birth, his mother, Eugénie-Désirée Manet, was twenty years old, fourteen years her husband's junior. The family was prosperous from the beginning, and in keeping with its social status Eugénie Manet held twice-weekly receptions for the influential associates of her husband; Auguste, nevertheless, preferred the company of scholars and ecclesiastics to that of his colleagues.

From the ages of six to eight, Édouard attended the Institut Poiloup in Vaugirard; in his twelfth year, he began studies at a boarding school, the Collège Rollin, where he befriended Antonin Proust, who later wrote about his childhood friend. During these school years, Manet and Proust frequently visited the Louvre, accompanied by the former's maternal uncle, Captain Édouard Fournier, who encouraged his nephew's interest in art by paying for drawing lessons. Though Édouard excelled at drawing and soon expressed his wish to follow an artistic career, Auguste Manet's ambition for his eldest son was that he become a lawyer (Édouard's brothers, Eugène and Gustave, born in 1833 and 1835, were to become civil servants). Since his teachers at the Collège Rollin had found him "distracted" and "slightly frivolous," in July, 1848, Auguste Manet proposed a compromise in which Édouard would apply to the École Navale, or naval school. Failing the entrance examination, he embarked on a training ship instead, sailing on December 8 for Rio de Janeiro, Brazil. He is reported to have found the cruise boring; after his return to France in June, 1849, having again failed the entrance examination, he was finally allowed to study for an artistic career. By January of 1850, he had registered as an art student to copy paintings in the Louvre, and in September he and Antonin Proust joined the studio of Thomas Couture, a noted painter of innovative, though not revolutionary, sympathies.

Soon after his return from the sea voyage, Édouard and his brother Eugène began to take piano lessons from a young Dutch woman, Suzanne Leenhoff. It seems clear that his association with Suzanne quickly blossomed into love, and when she became pregnant in the spring of 1851, Manet, who was still required to obtain his father's permission to go out at night, succeeded in keeping his liaison a secret from him. The child born to Suzanne Leenhoff was registered as the son of a probably fictitious Koëlla but was presented socially as Suzanne's younger brother, Léon. It was not until 1863, more than a year after the death of Auguste Manet, that Suzanne Leenhoff and Manet were married.

Living in his parents' home, and with their financial support for his study of art, Manet continued working at the studio of Couture during the early 1850's. His relationship with his teacher was frequently stormy, and Manet acquired a reputation as a rebellious pupil, but Couture was in many ways a good choice of teacher. He represented a middle ground between the academic side of French art, with its often-rigid adherence to tradition, and the experimental, individualistic tendencies of artists such as Honoré Daumier and Gustave Courbet. Manet was, by nature, a somewhat conservative personality—he was always well dressed, even fashionable, and he enjoyed the civil pleasures of bourgeois life—but as an artist he challenged from the outset many of the conventions of painting, even as he learned from the masters of the past.

Life's Work

After leaving Couture's studio in 1856, Manet occasionally brought his works to the master for criticism, a circumstance that must have been more than a polite gesture. Manet's interest in tradition was profound, but his studies of the past were undertaken to achieve a personal understanding of the old masters rather than to emulate their styles. Like many young Parisian artists, Manet often copied paintings in the Louvre and elsewhere. He was particularly attracted to Spanish masters such as Diego Velázquez but also copied works by Peter Paul Rubens and Eugène Delacroix, from whom he personally requested permission to copy *The Barque of Dante*. Equally important for his future as an artist, however, was Manet's devotion to recording the life of the Paris boulevards, where he daily observed the activities of all levels of society. Despite his comfortable family background, Manet had an instinctive appreciation for the urban poor, and in 1859 he submitted his painting *The Absinthe Drinker* to the Salon, a biennial exhibition of art which was judged by the established painters of the day. *The Absinthe Drinker* is based in part upon Manet's observation of a ragpicker named Collardet, part of a legion of characters who were increasingly visible as a result of the redevelopment of Paris begun in 1853 under the direction of Baron Eugène Hausmann. Although such a subject was considered appropriate for the popular press, it was thought too vulgar for the Salon, and

Manet's painting was rejected. In 1861, however, two of his works were accepted into the exhibition; one of them, *The Spanish Singer*, received an honorable mention.

At this time in his career, Manet's art had been noticed appreciatively by a few knowledgeable critics, but his audience was comparatively small. An event in 1863 changed not only Manet's relationship to the public but also that of a generation of French artists. This was the Salon des Refusés, an exhibition held by order of the Emperor Napoleon III, which was to include all of the work rejected by the jury from the regular Salon of 1863. The emperor's decree invited the public to be the final judge of the quality of the art rejected, and the public responded with tumultuous curiosity and derision. Manet's principal submission, *Déjeuner sur l'herbe* (luncheon on the grass), while appreciated by a discerning few, was taken by many visitors to the exhibition to be the flagship of artistic revolt. The work shows a nude woman with two fashionably dressed men in a modern parklike setting, and although the painting is based upon various historical prototypes, its broad, painterly technique and contemporary setting seem intended to challenge the public's artistic taste and its moral standards. *Déjeuner sur l'herbe* marks the beginning of a widespread but often-hostile interest in the dissident claims of modern art; the polarization of the art world into "academics" and the "avant-garde" had begun.

In Manet's paintings of the early 1860's, one sees the influence of his friend the poet Charles Baudelaire. In an essay written years earlier, Baudelaire had called for an art based upon "the heroism of modern life" which would show "how great and how poetic we are with our neckties and our varnished boots." Manet's emphasis on clothes, costume, fashion, and other aspects of everyday life, rather than giving a trivial view of society, shows urban life as a complex network of signs which require a skilled interpreter. The emergence of the city as the fulcrum of modern culture is one of the implicit themes of Manet's art, though this is seen more often in his graphic works than in his paintings.

Manet caused another public outcry at the Salon of 1865 with his *Olympia*, which depicts a nude courtesan, attended by a black servant and a cat, looking impudently toward the viewer. One critic advised that "women on the point of giving birth and proper young girls would be well-advised to flee this spectacle," and two guards were stationed by the painting, which had already been removed to an obscure and dishonorable location within the immense exhibition. The audacity of *Olympia* far outdistanced that of *Déjeuner sur l'herbe*, and in addition to suffering criticism on account of the theme, Manet came under attack for the structure and technique of the painting. Courbet said that it looked flat, like a playing card, and a newspaper critic accused Manet of "an almost childish ignorance of the fundamentals of drawing." It is clear that Manet, though not systematically courting the disfavor of the public, was willing to suffer incomprehension both of his treatment of subjects and of his style. He was fully capable of painting appealing subjects in a more traditional manner, but for complex reasons he ruled out forms of compromise which might have gained for him a higher level of public esteem. He subsequently painted popular pictures, such as *The Good Glass of Beer* (1873), and though he wished for broad acceptance of his art he was never inclined to pursue it.

In many of his works of the 1870's Manet sought an increasing naturalism by emphasizing lighter colors and more varied surfaces. In paintings made in 1874 at Argenteuil, a few miles northwest of Paris, Manet drew close to the group which became known that year as the Impressionists. He borrowed the light and color of his younger friends Claude Monet and Pierre-Auguste Renoir, but his canvases are more deliberately composed and are much less extraverted than theirs of the same period. Some critics who had been sympathetic to Manet's work, including the novelist Émile Zola, considered Manet's technical gifts unequal to his ambition of painting in the open air; others recognized that these works were, in part, the result of exacting formal experimentation. In a famous remark made in 1890, the painter Maurice Denis asserted that "a painting—before it is a battle horse, a nude woman, or some anecdote—is essentially a flat surface covered with colors assembled in a certain order." To a significant extent, Manet's work of the 1870's is a precocious fulfillment of this concept, particularly in a work such as *The Rue Mosnier with Pavers* (1878), which brings the spontaneous brushwork, subtle coloration, light, and movement of the Argenteuil paintings back to the streets of Paris. Manet had by this time developed fully a means of drawing with strokes of paint which both represents objects in space and unifies the painting as an assemblage of shapes and colors.

In late 1878, Manet began to have trouble with his leg, and by September of the following year he was seeking treatment for it. The precise nature of his ailment has never been specified, but it seems likely that he was suffering from the advanced stages of a syphilitic infection contracted in his youth. During his last three years, he was in pain, and small drawings and oil paintings began to take the place of larger works, reflecting his diminished mobility. There are a number of fine portraits and still lifes dating from 1880 through 1882, and there is also one major subject painting, *A Bar at the Folies-Bergère*. This work, which is about three feet high by four feet wide, is widely considered to be one of Manet's finest works. It shows a barmaid at the celebrated Paris "café-concert," standing behind a marble counter on which have been placed bottles of ale and champagne, a compote with mandarin oranges, and a glass holding two pale roses. Behind the melancholy and distracted young woman, a mirror reflects a brightly lit crowd which seems unaware of a trapeze artist whose green-slippered feet are whimsically shown in the upper left-hand corner of the painting. There are many subtle, calculated ambiguities concerning things viewed either directly or in reflection. Manet seems to have decided, at the end of an artistic career often criticized for a lack of psychological insight, to address the human element in one final, haunting but luminous canvas. In early April, 1883, as Manet's health precipitously declined, he briefly considered taking lessons in miniature painting from a friend, but by April 20 his condition required that his left leg be amputated, and on April 30 he died.

Summary
Édouard Manet has been celebrated as a rebellious artist who was rejected by his own time; however, such a stereotyping of his career ignores not only the complexities of his personality and artistic production but also the varieties of response which his work elicited from his contemporaries and from the generation that followed. For years, many critics and art historians fostered the notion of a noble, progressive lineage of art which was engaged in perpetual conflict with a defensive, static "establishment" art supported by reactionary social forces; Manet, quite understandably, was installed as the great progenitor of the progressive trend. As the discipline of art history established a broader foundation of fact and methodology during the first half of the twentieth century and the issues of mid- and late-nineteenth century art became both clearer and more intricate, the assessment of Manet's achievement in particular came to be seen more as a problem in defining the changing relationship of artists and audiences than of arriving at objectively valid, stabilized conclusions about his paintings.

Manet was somewhat conservative by temperament, but he was also creatively independent. Though many of his images involved adaptations of ideas and images borrowed from the past, and thus appealed to aspects of public taste, other elements of his work were vibrantly novel and challenged both the visual imagination and social consciousness of his contemporaries. These contrasting elements in Manet dictated that he could not rely on conventional taste to provide him with a constituency; his success was one that might be earned only by tremendous labor and courage. Finally, it was a largely posthumous success. In his later career, he frequently despaired at the inconsistency with which his work was received, believing, perhaps somewhat naïvely, that it should suffice for an artist to present sincere work. Like many of his contemporaries, he hoped that the public would be able to recognize and value sincerity and commitment and would reward it at least as strongly as virtuosity and predictability. In hoping for this kind of relationship with an ever-expanding mass audience, Manet presents to history a modernity of outlook in keeping with the adventurousness of his finest paintings.

Bibliography
Adler, Kathleen. *Manet*. Oxford, England: Phaidon Press, 1986. An excel-

lent source of collateral illustrations concerning Manet's life and times, as well as of his art and its sources. The text emphasizes the eclectic nature of the artist's work and provides an integrated view of modern scholarship concerned with Manet's place in nineteenth century art.

Bataille, Georges. *Manet.* New York: Rizzoli, 1983. Françoise Cachin, in her introduction to this reprinting of Bataille's 1955 essay, shows how the author's view of Manet was colored by his close association with the artistic trends of his own time. Nevertheless, she concedes, Bataille's essay has "unusual penetration and appeal."

Blunden, Maria, and Godfrey Blunden. *Impressionists and Impressionism.* New York: Rizzoli, 1977. Manet is accorded only his share of attention in this survey volume, but contemporary photographs and documents, many of which are seldom reproduced, vividly reveal the artist and his contemporaries. Text and images are presented in a loosely integrated but nevertheless effective manner.

Cachin, Françoise, Anne Coffin Hanson, et al. *Manet: 1832-1883.* New York: Metropolitan Museum of Art, 1983. This large, indispensable volume was issued in connection with a major international exhibition organized to commemorate the one hundredth anniversary of the painter's death. There are several fine essays, and the book is illustrated with hundreds of exemplary color and black-and-white plates, most of which are discussed in some detail by accompanying text.

Hamilton, George Heard. *Manet and His Critics.* New York: W. W. Norton, 1969. This book, originally published in 1954, is a chronological study of the criticism published about Manet and his art during his lifetime, with some mention of critical material appearing after his death. The mediocre illustrations are suitable only for reference.

Mauner, George. *Manet, Peintre-Philosophe: A Study of the Painter's Themes.* University Park: Pennsylvania State University Press, 1975. The author is one of many who have sought to provide a corrective to a once-prevalent view of Manet as a painter obsessed with structural matters and indifferent to meaning; his scholarly arguments are involved but clearly stated. The lack of color plates does not diminish the book's interest.

Rewald, John. *The History of Impressionism.* New York: Museum of Modern Art, 1946, rev. ed. 1973. This masterly chronological study of the Impressionists does full justice to nine artists in addition to Manet, but Manet's art is unquestionably the author's touchstone. There is an excellent annotated calendar covering the years 1855-1886, as well as an extensive bibliography and an index.

Schneider, Pierre. *The World of Manet, 1832-1883.* New York: Time-Life Books, 1968. The popular format of this book should not be allowed to obscure the fact that it contains a wealth of information. The quality and variety of its reproductions are matched by an intelligent, readable text.

Sloane, Joseph C. "Manet." In *French Painting Between the Past and the Present: Artists, Critics, and Traditions from 1848 to 1870.* Princeton, N.J.: Princeton University Press, 1973. The author's emphasis is upon the reaction of critics and the public to Manet's paintings of the 1860's, and he shows why the artist's innovations were met with resistance. The text as well as an excellent bibliography is unrevised from the original 1951 edition.

Wadley, Nicholas. *Manet.* London: Paul Hamlyn, 1967. This survey of the artist's paintings is valuable principally for its good color plates, which are briefly annotated. A modest essay is complemented by a chronology and extensive quotations from Manet and his contemporaries.

C. S. McConnell

FRANÇOIS MANSART

Born: January 23, 1598; Paris, France
Died: September 23, 1666; Paris, France
Area of Achievement: Architecture
Contribution: Mansart is generally recognized, along with Louis Le Vau, as one of the two greatest French architects of the seventeenth century and is credited with reviving classicism in French architecture while retaining enough vestiges of the prevailing Gothic to produce buildings that were truly unique.

Early Life

In François Mansart's day, people who wanted to be architects did not go to school to learn their profession. Rather, they apprenticed to people in the building trades, who were the designers of most new buildings. Mansart was born into a family of carpenters and masons. His father, Absalom Mansart, was the king's carpenter and his mother, Michelle Le Roy, was a sensitive woman of exquisite taste. Mansart began to learn carpentry from his father as soon as he was old enough. When Absalom Mansart died in 1610, the training of his twelve-year-old son fell to the boy's brother-in-law, Germain Gaultier, a sculptor and architect of some repute.

Someone interested in architecture and design could not have been born at a more challenging time. Henri IV, who reigned from 1589 to 1610, sought to enhance the royal revenues by curtailing the extravagant building of palaces that had been going on and by emphasizing building projects that would benefit the people both by employing them in the building trades and by revitalizing Paris.

Henri encouraged members of his court to build country houses, and this encouragement resulted in the emergence of an interesting domestic architecture, designed generally for economy, achieved by a new simplicity of design. On Henri's death, Louis XIII began a thirty-three-year reign that emphasized the building of churches and royal palaces. The Palace of Luxembourg in Paris was completed in 1615, following the design of Salomon de Brosse, with whom François may have served a brief apprenticeship as an adolescent.

Soon Mansart began to work with his mother's brother, Marcel Le Roy, a noted contractor. He presumably worked on site with Le Roy's contracting syndicate when it built a bridge across the River Garonne at Toulouse, and it is thought that Mansart, now around twenty-two, might have designed the bridge's triumphal arch. It is known that, in the same year, his uncle dispatched him to collect some money owed the contracting syndicate by the city of Toulouse.

During his early twenties, Mansart, thin and wiry with sharp features, a long pointed nose, and dark, animated eyes, again represented his uncle's construction syndicate, presenting to the city fathers of Rouen their proposals to build a bridge. Mansart clearly had sufficient aplomb and self-assurance to handle intensive questioning from these burghers, most of them more than twice his age. He obviously controlled enough technical information to explain to them intricate details of the proposed project and to respond effectively to their searching questions. He withstood the most rigorous tests of accountability and was soon widely recognized as someone who understood construction and design well enough to be entrusted with his own commissions.

Life's Work

Mansart received two of his own commissions around 1623. One was to design the façade of the Church of the Feillants, later destroyed, in Paris. The other was to remodel the Château de Berny, south of Paris, part of which survives. In that work, he was able to display one of his greatest talents, that of working from the original design of an extant building and, within the structural and physical limitations of that building, to create something unique. Mansart retained the two side pavilions and courtyard of the Château de Berny but added a towering central portion to the plan, linking it with colonnades to the side pavilions and adding a pavilion that contained a remarkably graceful staircase. A portion of one of the side pavilions has survived, but Mansart's plans are preserved in the National Archives in Paris.

In the nearly two decades between 1623 and 1642, Mansart was actively engaged in all sorts of architectural projects, civic, domestic, and ecclesiastical. His Château de Balleroy in Normandy, begun in 1626, survives and reflects the kind of design Mansart favored. Using the native yellow stone of the region as his base, he faced the walls of the château with thin squares of white ashlar, a stone that lends a serenity and dignity to the surface it creates. Like the Château de Berny, Balleroy has a high center structure, in this instance crowned with a cupola. It took more than a decade to complete Balleroy, and by that time Mansart had begun to imbibe the Baroque influence coming to France from Italy, so the central portion of Balleroy and its quadrant colonnades, reminiscent of Berny's, are more ornate.

Mansart provided designs for such ecclesiastical structures in Paris as the high altar in the Church of S. Martin des Champs (c. 1625), the Altar of the Virgin in the Cathedral of Nôtre Dame (1628), the Convent of the Visitation (c. 1633), and the Church of the Visitation (c. 1633). During the same period, however, Mansart also engaged in all sorts of secular projects, including such diverse construction or remodeling jobs as the Château de Plessis-Belleville (1628), the Hôtel de l'Aubespine (c. 1630) and the Hôtel de la Vrillière in Paris (c. 1637), an aqueduct for the Château de Limours (1638), and walls around the park of the Château de Chambord (1639). During this period, he was gaining great confidence in his ability to produce fine structures, and he enjoyed a reputation that made him known throughout France. He received more commissions than he could accept.

The self-assurance that had been an asset to Mansart in his twenties was turning into an arrogance that offended many people during this middle period of his life. Jean-Baptiste Colbert, as emissary of Louis XIII, commissioned Mansart to draw plans for an addition to the Louvre. Colbert, knowing that Mansart had a reputation for changing designs and demolishing already completed work to accommodate his changes, stipulated that Mansart could not make changes once his designs were in and construction was begun. Mansart refused the commission, viewing it as an inhibition to his artistic freedom.

Among those willing to tolerate Mansart's arrogance and changeability was René de Longueil, a wealthy merchant, for whom, between 1642 to 1651, Mansart designed and erected the Château de Maisons on the banks of the Seine. This building, which has survived, is one of Mansart's two greatest works, and the only one for which he received full credit. Mansart brilliantly adapted this château to its surroundings. Well into the project, Mansart revised his plans drastically, and all the construction that had been done was torn down so that he could begin again, instituting the new, more imaginative design he had devised. His patron's wealth was sufficient to permit this costly redirection, and apparently de Longueil was willing to bow to Mansart's superior architectural knowledge despite the inordinate cost and unseemly delay it occasioned.

Maisons deviated from Mansart's earlier practice of building a high central portion. The central part of this building and its two wings are of almost equal height except for a small tower and cupola in the central portion. The main building itself is starkly classical, its pilasters unadorned. Two courts in front of the building are surrounded by a dry moat, and a substantial terrace extends to the river front.

The pitch of the roofs and the chimney stacks are adaptations of the Gothic architecture that prevailed in France during the preceding century. The château is known for its gracefully dramatic staircase, a hallmark of Mansart's domestic architecture. As the early Greeks had done in the Parthenon, Mansart used optical illusion and slight distortion to create proportion in the eyes of those who beheld the building from ground level.

Mansart's other truly great project was the palace, convent, and church of the Val-de-Grâce in Paris, begun in 1644. The work was commissoned by the Queen Mother, Anne of Austria, widow of Louis XIII. Mansart's plans for this vast project were highly elaborate and imaginative. His concern was with the creation of beauty in its purest form. He viewed money merely as a necessary commodity to be provided by his patrons in whatever quantity his extravagant plans demanded.

The queen mother was a frugal woman, too timid to lock horns directly with Mansart, who was something of a bully, intolerant of artistic opinions save his own. After putting up with Mansart's antics for more than a year, the queen mother in 1646 replaced him quietly with Jacques Lemercier. By this time, the foundation was laid and considerable progress had been made toward completing the church. When Lemercier took over, he scrapped most of Mansart's plans, although the church definitely reflects Mansart's genius. The palace plans were completely redone; Lemercier's palace is a more pedestrian building than the church.

Mansart lived for another twenty years, his fortunes now in decline, largely because of his cantankerous personality. His reputation for artistic excellence remained unsullied, but commissions were scarce. He continued to work on projects, few of them executed, and those few were usually for remodeling jobs or for funerary monuments.

Summary

François Mansart was almost too large for life. He had colossal ideas that captured the imaginations of the rich. When he was able to capture the purses of the rich as well, he could bring these ideas to fruition spectacularly. When he could not do so, he was incapable of compromise and resorted to tactics that made people avoid him. Mansart is often credited with having invented a roof that bears a corruption of his surname, mansard. Actually, this type of roof, common in much modern domestic architecture, existed before Mansart's time. He employed variations of it in some of his châteaus, but he cannot be credited with its invention.

When the famed British architect Sir Christopher Wren visited France in 1665, the year before London's great fire, he visited Mansart and expressed his admiration for and appreciation of Mansart's contributions to classical French architecture. Techniques Mansart used in the Church of the Val-de-Grâce, particularly in the dome, show up in St. Paul's Cathedral in London, for which Wren was chief architect. Mansart's great-nephew, Jules Hardouin-Mansart, adopted Mansart's surname and went on to become a famous architect in the last half of the seventeenth century. His most famous design was the palace at Versailles.

Bibliography

Arts Council of Great Britain. *François Mansart, 1598-1666.* London: Author, 1970. This brief pamphlet offers highlights of Mansart's life and professional career and provides pictures of some of his buildings and copies of some of his architectural plans. Allan Braham and Peter Smith contribute biographical notes, and the chronology is useful.

Blunt, Anthony F. *Art and Architecture in France, 1500 to 1700.* Baltimore:

Penguin Books, 1953. Blunt makes pertinent comments about Mansart's contributions to French architecture, identifying him as one of the two greatest French architects of the first half of the seventeenth century. The section on Mansart, although only twenty pages long, is accurate and informative.

_____. *François Mansart and the Origins of French Classical Architecture*. London: Warburg Institute, 1941. This book presented the first full treatment in English of François Mansart. Rich in information, it examines Mansart against the larger backdrop of the development of classicism in the architecture of France. Blunt's book remains an authoritative source for the study of Mansart and his work.

Braham, Allan, and Peter Smith. *François Mansart*. London: A. Zwemmer, 1973. Braham and Smith present a full treatment of Mansart, replete with illustrations. A valuable adjunct to Blunt's earlier book. Presents full discussions of each of Mansart's major works and provides valuable information about the plans of those buildings that have not survived.

Watterson, Joseph. *Architecture: A Short History*. Rev. ed. New York: W. W. Norton, 1968. Although Watterson devotes only a few pages to Mansart, his comments are serviceable. Offers insights into Mansart's most important buildings and makes interesting comparisons. Also provides a social commentary that places Mansart in the political milieu in which he functioned professionally.

R. Baird Shuman

JULES HARDOUIN-MANSART

Born: c. April 16, 1646; Paris, France
Died: May 11, 1708; Marly-le-Roi, France
Area of Achievement: Architecture
Contribution: Hardouin-Mansart contributed extensively to French architecture and city planning in the reign of Louis XIV, especially in designing and in altering the huge complex of Versailles Palace and its environs. His further legacy included his training of other architects, sculptors, stonecutters, Gobelin tapestry weavers, porcelain specialists, and crystal cutters. From his architectural achievements, a more beautiful Paris and Versailles emerged.

Early Life

Jules Hardouin (he would take the name Mansart in 1668) was born in Paris into a family that produced architects, artisans, and artists for generations. He is often mistaken by the casual reader for his great-uncle François Mansart, a formidable architect whose building designs reflect classicism. Because Jules's early years were spent in François Mansart's household, he was taught architecture by his great-uncle and imbued with his bias. He was also trained in drawing by C. Poerson. François Mansart hosted famous statesmen and architects such as Jean Baptiste Colbert, a virtual dictator of the arts, as well as an important governmental figure, André Le Nôtre, Louis Le Vau, and Libéral Bruant. Hardouin was thus influenced by such men of distinction.

Hardouin was one of four children—the third child and the second of three sons. His father held the position of first painter in the cabinet of the king. The Mansarts descended from artisans in Italy (the Mensartos), who had gravitated to France at the beginning of the French Renaissance. In 1556 their name appeared as Hardouyn. By the time of François Mansart's death in 1666, Jules (then twenty years old) had been directly influenced in architecture by his great-uncle, but at the same time he developed his own métier. Hardouin inherited not only his great-uncle's drawings and papers but also his considerable fortune. Among the inherited papers were designs that had been commissioned by the king but not used, although the king technically was still privy to them. Two years later, Hardouin married Anne Bodin; the couple produced five children: three girls and two boys. His own sons became the fathers of architects. That year, Hardouin took his great-uncle's surname, Mansart.

Louis XIV, the Sun King, ascended the throne at age four in 1643 and had one of the longest reigns in French history. Mansart's professional life was inextricably associated with this monarch. The king presided over a virtual bureaucratic stronghold in business and also in all the arts. To survive, let alone to prosper, under Louis XIV, an aspirant needed to subscribe at least partly to his vagaries. The king's goal in the arts was to revive classic expression filtered through the French spirit. Scholars are in agreement that during Louis' reign the thrust of the arts was to compete with Periclean Athens and Augustan Rome. The arts did flourish, and dozens of brilliant people emerged in this era—Jean-Baptiste Colbert, Molière, Pierre Corneille, Claude Lorrain, Jean Racine, and Jean Lully, among many others. Mansart joined these luminaries in his eventual appointment as architect in chief to the court; Versailles is invariably linked with the name and the work of this architect.

At age twenty-four, Mansart assisted the work in progress on the Hôtel des Invalides, the modern tomb of Napoleon. By that time, he had already designed a number of buildings and the next year was at work in a limited position at Versailles. Four years later, Colbert, the minister and financier of the court, recognized the talents of Mansart and gave him the opportunity to design the Château de Clagny, in the forest of Saint Germain, belonging to Madame de Montespan, the king's favorite. This celebrated and headstrong beauty of royal blood, who was aggressive and ambitious, convinced the king of the importance of architecture as a metaphor of royal power. It is believed that because of her influence Louis arranged for royal commissions of extravagant and ornate designs, a practice that continued throughout much of his reign. Mansart's first royal commission to build the Château de Clagny was fortuitous for his career, but his architectural initiative was always to be narrowed by the demands of royal edict. This limitation consigned Mansart to following plans that interfered with a level of his creative development. Colbert continued to be closely affiliated with Mansart; at age twenty-nine, the architect was pressed by Colbert into membership in the Academy of Architecture, a highly conservative group. Soon afterward, Mansart was introduced to the king and given the remarkable commission of designing and building huge additions to Versailles, plans that were often structured by Louis XIV. Mansart was then only thirty years old.

Life's Work

Mansart is closely associated with the additions to Versailles, both interior and exterior, which became his main preoccupation from 1678 until his death. At his death, he was held to be the undisputed main architect of Louis' kingdom. His impact on the design and execution of Versailles' development is greater than any other architect's work. During his tenure there, significant and stunning designs were executed, including the great forecourt, the Hall of Mirrors, and the horseshoe-shaped stables (for approximately six hundred horses and equipage), which formed part of the entrance design. Numerous additions to the principal façade contributed to the splendor of Versailles: the central block of the garden façade, two sprawling wings that extended the main structure to 1,935 feet, and the Hall of Mirrors (which remains one of the favorite apartments of visitors). Specialists and tourists also delight in the orangerie. Mansart was also involved in the design of the Grand Trianon and the charming buffet d'eau fountain, as well as with the Parish Church of Versailles. Although built from his plans, the church was not completed until after Mansart's death.

Mansart, who was inundated with commissions while architect at Versailles, also designed the impressive châteaus at Saint Cyr and Marly-le-Roi. The aqueducts and waterworks of Marly-le-Roi are also the inspiration of Mansart. Paris is studded with his monuments, considered outstanding by architects the world over—the Place des Victoires (where only remnants are visible), the Dome des Invalides, and the Place Vendôme, which remains one of the most impressive squares in all Europe. What is notable about the Place Vendôme is the design, in which the interior angles are limited. The use of space hems in the square without distracting from the central axis. Art critic Anthony Blunt suggests that it is a Baroque concept with details of classicism.

Mansart garnered most of all the possible honors during his mature years. In 1683, he was ennobled; ten years later, he was made Comte de Sagonne; and at age fifty-three he was given the post of superintendant des bâtiments du roi. Unlike his great-uncle François Mansart, he worked within the limitations of the king's wishes, and he was rewarded with honors and money. By age fifty-nine he ranked as one of the most influential people in the court and held the post of cabinet minister.

Apart from his work on official monuments, buildings, and Parisian palaces, Mansart also worked on town houses. His designs altered the appearances of town houses to make them seem more informal, light, and cozy. He diversified the shaping of rooms, made frequent use of mirrors, and adopted a lightness and elegance of decorative line. With his design of the Hôtel de Noailles at Saint Germain, he developed a new horizontality. These same effects are noted in the Hôtel de Lorges, the Convent des Recollets, and in his own magnificent *maison* in the rue des Tournelles. The Palais Royale was redesigned, and, in conjunction with A. J. Gabriel, he made additions to the Pont Royal.

Having achieved eminence as a result of his architecture and his influence through the teaching and the training of many artisans, Mansart was the subject of many paintings and sculptures. In one engraving, Mansart is depicted with a strapping physique, his huge, curly periwig framing a large face with a dimpled chin and broad brows, his observant eyes staring with a calm assurance. His lips are full, almost sensual. After his death at age sixty-two, Mansart was interred in his own parish of Saint-Paul, with a Latin epitaph stating that he had influenced architects, sculptors, painters, and ornamentalists.

Summary

Jules Hardouin-Mansart is not definitely associated with any particular school of architecture. Certainly, he worked in the Palladian school (a revival classic style based on the works of Andrea Palladio). Accomplished at composition, adept at managing proportion and scale, Mansart designed the wondrous Hall of Mirrors at Versailles, the Grand Trianon, and the stables. The Place Vendôme near the Louvre remains the quintessential Parisian square. Typical of Mansart's period is the elevation in his structures, his capacity for good massing (like that of his great-uncle) reflected in the Dome des Invalides, which is freestanding. This monument is notable because of the Baroque energy of the lines, which virtually dance to the very top of the dome. Such an effect is characterized by some historians as a main sign of seventeenth century architecture.

Centuries after Mansart's death, much evaluation still needs to be done to determine his architectural niche. Because he was deluged with commissions, both royal and private, he catered to many of the preconceived ideas and styles of his monarch and his patrons. Often he was too pressed to be discriminating, and thus, according to some critics, elements of his work suffer because of an architectural eclecticism. He is denounced for ruining Le Vau's Ionic order on the principal story of Versailles, which looked "mean" when the pattern was repeated over the six hundred yards of the extended front.

Mansart's influence is far-reaching because of his training of architects and allied artisans, his work with city planning, and his reorganization of the Royal Academy. Even Thomas Jefferson's Monticello, some insist, bears the stamp of Mansart's inspiration. Some French writers and historians believe that Mansart has not received the recognition that he deserves; others deem that he has been overpraised. Still, Versailles clearly reflects his influence in the second stage of redesigning and rebuilding, and it is significant, indicating the unlimited resources of the architect. Paris, too, reveals the treasures of Mansart's work in architecture, gardening design, and the arts, a distinct contribution to the enrichment of Western civilization.

Bibliography

Blunt, Anthony. *Art and Architecture in France, 1500 to 1700*. Baltimore: Penguin Books, 1953. Gives a succinct yet detailed overview of the history, politics, and architecture during the life of Mansart, including the influence of the Cardinal de Richelieu, Jules Mazarin, and Colbert. Particular emphasis is placed on the work of Mansart at Versailles and on his other designs in Paris and throughout France.

Braham, Allan, and Peter Smith. *François Mansart*. London: A. Zwemmer, 1973. An exhaustive study of the great-uncle of Mansart. Examines his designs of town houses and drawings for the Louvre and his significant influence on his great-nephew. Provides important background for the life and times of Jules Hardouin-Mansart.

Cronin, Vincent. *Louis XIV*. London: Collins, 1964. Standard biographies of Mansart appear only in French. This biography of the Sun King provides a context for the life and work of Mansart. Material on Madame Athénaïs de Montespan and Colbert is informative and amusing.

Mitford, Nancy. *The Sun King: Louis XIV at Versailles*. New York: Harper & Row, 1966. A lively, well-illustrated book containing valuable detail and information on Louis and devoting ample attention to the genius and con-tributions of Mansart. Emphasizes the solid reputation of Mansart, after which he was given the challenge and responsibility of a major overhaul-ing and additional architectural design of Versailles.

Van Derpool, James Grote. *Jules Hardouin-Mansart*. New Haven: Connecti-cut Society of Civil Engineers, 1947. Gives an overview of Mansart, who, Van Derpool says, determined the character of French architecture during Louis XIV's reign. Provides a basic discussion of the techniques of archi-tecture and Mansart's contributions.

Julia B. Boken

ANDREA MANTEGNA

Born: c. 1431; Isola di Cartura, Republic of Venice
Died: September 13, 1506; Mantua
Area of Achievement: Art
Contribution: Mantegna contributed to the growth of Renaissance art in northern Italy while at the same time creating an individual style appreciated for its powers of invention, directness of presentation, illusionism, and detailed realism. His most important contributions were centered in his roles as transmitter of the Florentine Renaissance to his northern Italian contemporaries and as artistic interpreter of antiquity for his own and succeeding generations.

Early Life

Andrea Mantegna was born in Isola di Cartura, near Padua, in northern Italy. His probable birth date of 1431 is based on an inscription, preserved in early documents, from a lost altarpiece of 1448 executed for the Church of Santa Sofia in Padua. It lists his age as seventeen when the project reached completion. Little is known of Mantegna's life before he reached the age of ten. At that time his father, Biagio, a carpenter, gave him up for adoption to the painter Francesco Squarcione, who appears to have acted as adoptive father to several talented boys. In addition to his activities as a painter, collector, and dealer, Squarcione trained his young charges while providing them with a home and the necessities of life. Once their schooling was complete, the master contracted with wealthy patrons for the services of his young protégés.

Mantegna served his apprenticeship in the workshop of his adoptive father from 1442 to 1448. During the 1440's in Padua, Squarcione's *bottega* functioned as an exchange for ideas and methods among important artists and craftsmen. In this ambience, Mantegna was introduced to the best talents and the latest artistic developments of the time. The superior genius of Donatello, the Florentine sculptor, provided a focus for Paduan art from 1443 to 1453. Donatello's works must have been a major topic of conversation among artists and patrons who frequented Squarcione's workshop.

Other Florentine artists influenced Mantegna's development through the agency of Squarcione's *bottega*. In 1447, the master and his apprentices moved to Venice and resided there for several months. Paolo Uccello, Fra Filippo Lippi, and Andrea del Castagno had preceded them by the period of a decade or more, and at different times. These artists had all left the mark of the Florentine Renaissance on the city of canals and lagoons. It should also be noted that Lippi had executed in Padua works that Mantegna would already have seen. Elements peculiar to the individual styles of these artists were transmitted to Mantegna at that formative period in his career.

The atmosphere of Squarcione's shop, with its constant activity and opportunity for dialogue, provided Mantegna with all the conditions necessary for his accelerated development as a painter. Squarcione's own approach to painting appears to have had minimal impact on Mantegna. The importance, however, of Donatello and the new Florentine art in the formation of Mantegna's style is universally recognized and may be clearly distinguished in the young artist's paintings of the 1450's. In addition to providing Mantegna with an entrée into the contemporary art circles, Squarcione instilled in his adopted son a love of antiquity. The influence of classical art and literature appear constantly in Mantegna's earliest and latest work.

Mantegna's early training came to a close in 1448. In January, the young man sued Squarcione over the terms of his adoption and what he considered to be insufficient compensation for his six years as an apprentice. The two men reached a compromise that enabled Mantegna to declare his independence and to take control of his own finances. It seems extraordinary that Mantegna was able to do this at the tender age of seventeen, unless he had made significant contributions as a member of Squarcione's *bottega*, thereby establishing his reputation as a painter of great potential.

Life's Work

Mantegna received his first major independent commission in May, 1448. The plan for decoration of the Ovetari Chapel in the Church of the Eremitani in Padua included provisions for an altar and frescoes with scenes from the lives of Saints James and Christopher, who were patron saints of the church. At the outset, Mantegna shared this work with several other artists. For several reasons, including the death of two participants and withdrawal from the project by the others, Mantegna was left with a large number of scenes to finish by himself. The three standing figures of Saint Peter, Saint Paul, and Saint Christopher in the vault of the chapel's apse were probably the earliest frescoes that Mantegna completed. If this is true, they were done while Niccolò Pizzolo, a Paduan painter who initially shared Mantegna's half of the commission, was still alive. Modern scholarship supports the conclusion that Pizzolo may have had an even stronger influence on Mantegna's artistic formation than Squarcione. As Mantegna's older associate in the Ovetari venture, Pizzolo may have cemented the connection between the younger artist and the new Florentine art. Mantegna's three saints do not have the strong sculptural quality of Pizzolo's adjacent figures, but the draperies are carefully studied and the poses are harmonious and symmetrically balanced in the new manner.

Saint James Baptizing Hermogenes and *Saint James Before Herod Agrippa* are the first completely mature works by Mantegna in the Ovetari Chapel. The painter's thorough knowledge of Leon Battista Alberti's perspective system, published in *De pictura* (1435; *Of Painting*, 1726), is visible in the precisely measured perspective grid of each fresco as well as in the common vanishing point employed for these two adjacent scenes. The classical derivation of the architectural settings and the sculptural decorations in these works reveal Mantegna's growing love of the antique. Although there is no direct proof, the soldier standing in the right foreground of *Saint James Before Herod Agrippa* is often identified as a self-portrait. The sharp angular features and the distinct frown fit written descriptions of Mantegna's serious and often severe demeanor.

Two other scenes, *Saint James Led to Execution* and *Martyrdom of Saint James*, are impressive in their continued exploration of perspective and figural relationships. Their position on the wall places the lower edge of each composition approximately at eye level, making the figures and architecture appear to move down the picture plane as they recede in the picture space. Several of the figures in the foreground seem to violate the picture plane and project into the viewer's space. By this time, such effects were common in Florentine painting but still quite unusual in northern Italian art. The sculptural, stony quality of Mantegna's figures was very likely a result of his love of ancient sculpture and an appreciation for the work of Donatello. This sculpturesque quality combined with the northern Italian penchant for detailed realism are two of the major components of Mantegna's mature style. During the nine years the painter worked in the Ovetari Chapel, from 1448 to 1457, his formation as a major Renaissance artist occurred.

Between 1457 and 1459, Mantegna was occupied with the commission for a major altarpiece for the Church of San Zeno in Verona. The main part of this polyptych consists of three panels which depict a *Madonna Enthroned with Saints*. The carved and gilded wooden frame with its arched pediment and entablature form a temple format using the Corinthian order. Its design and the general placement of the figures in the painting are thought to reflect the original disposition, now much changed, of the principal elements in Donatello's altar for Sant'Antonio. Mantegna visually attached the columns of the frame to piers in the painting and continued the illusion by creating a square loggia that encompasses the Madonna, the Christ Child, and the saints, while defining the perspective space of the picture. A "classical" frieze of cherubs, clearly Mantegna's own invention, surrounds the level above the piers. The spatially conceived garland of fruit painted at the front of the picture, the crisp detail, and the bright colors show Mantegna at his best. The San Zeno altarpiece sets the tone for a whole group of works of this category in northern Italian art in the fifteenth and sixteenth centuries.

By 1459, Mantegna had accepted the invitation of the Marchese Ludovico Gonzaga, Lord of Mantua, to become his court painter. As one of the first Renaissance artists officially attached to a princely court, Mantegna found himself painting altarpieces, frescoing churches, decorating palaces, and even designing costumes and entertainments for lavish court pageants. The frescoes of the Camera degli Sposi (chamber of the bride and groom) in the Gonzaga Palace were painted between 1465 and 1474, and are considered to be major works in Mantegna's mature style. He covered the walls and ceiling of the square chamber with scenes from the life of the Gonzaga family. The left wall contains a depiction of the meeting between Ludovico Gonzaga and his son, Cardinal Francesco. The Gonzaga court is shown on the right wall, and the ceiling fresco takes the form of a circular architectural opening, the eye, or oculus, of a dome. The intermediate zone, which ties the lower scenes to the oculus, consists of illusionistically painted transverse arches that crisscross a flattened domical ceiling and encompass wreathed medallions containing the busts of Roman emperors. Although there is a wealth of classical allusion juxtaposed with scenes from the life of the Gonzaga family, the exact meaning and relationship of the parts have not yet been satisfactorily explained. The overall design and meticulous detail of the chamber reveal Mantegna's genius as a decorator and his skill with trompe l'oeil effects. The oculus in particular is a tour de force of perspective and foreshortening and, when viewed from the proper vantage point beneath, surprises and amuses the viewer with the artist's expertise and gentle sense of humor.

Mantegna continued in the service of the Gonzagas after Ludovico's death in 1478, first for Federico and then for Francesco. Francesco presented Mantegna to Pope Innocent VIII in June, 1488, and this trip to Rome gave Mantegna the opportunity to study the classical antiquities of the Eternal City. In addition, he was commissioned by the pope to paint a small chapel in the Vatican. Upon his return from Rome in 1491, a change occurred in Mantegna's style. The paintings of his late period, such as the *Madonna of the Victory* (1495), are almost overrefined. Linear elements increase in complexity and tend to rob figures and objects of their three-dimensional form. The brilliance of the earlier works is exchanged for softer tones. While still the works of a great painter, the later productions lack the force and vitality of his youth, and instead evoke an idyllic mood of quiet and gentleness.

The *Triumph of Caesar* (begun c. 1486) was the last great series created by Mantegna. These enormous canvases painted in tempera are 274 by 274 centimeters and represent a theme based on Petrarch's description of a triumphal procession. Clearly inspired by Mantegna's trip to Rome, these works are the masterpieces of his late style. They are carefully planned and executed to provide a continuity of atmosphere from one canvas to the next as the procession unfolds. They are also so precisely detailed that they present an unparalleled feeling of truth to nature. Yet, in all of their complexity of line, foreshortening, and changes in scale, designed to portray the noise and clamor of such an event, they exude the same curious quietness and serenity that mark many of Mantegna's late works.

A letter from Mantegna's son to Francesco Gonzaga tells of the artist's death at seven in the evening on Sunday, September 13, 1506. Although Mantegna suffered from recurring ill health and financial problems toward the end of his life, he remained an active and innovative figure in northern Italian art to the end.

Summary

Andrea Mantegna stands forth as a major figure in the history of Renaissance art. For his northern contemporaries, he functioned as an important interpreter of the new Florentine art. He was among the very few artists working in Padua, Venice, or the other princely states of the north who was intellectually prepared to understand and absorb the full meaning and potential of the art of Paolo Uccello, Filippo Lippi, Andrea del Castagno, and Donatello. Mantegna's coherent and consistent vision of the physical world, fostered by his Florentine contacts, became the standard to which his contemporaries conformed. His passion for perspective devices and foreshortening was also born of this connection. Mantegna combined his knowledge of the new Florentine experiments with the native northern Italian tradition of detailed realism and created a style that guided his own generation and the next into a full-fledged Renaissance.

Mantegna was also the principal interpreter of antiquity for his generation. His constant use of classical references, real or invented, resulted in the synthesis of ancient and contemporary forms and ideas central to any definition of the Italian Renaissance. Mantegna had the courage to use his artistic genius to the fullest, to give free rein to his intellectual curiosity about the distant past, and to use his talent to explore the latest contemporary developments in art. He was truly and completely a man of his time and deserves to be remembered as a major contributor to the northern Italian Renaissance.

Bibliography

Camesasca, Ettore. *Mantegna*. New York: Harper & Row, 1981. A well-illustrated survey that contains a discussion of all the major works of the artist and includes reference to the most recent primary evidence that sheds light on the artist's career and production. Presents summaries of many of the scholarly arguments relative to questions about Mantegna's work in an attempt to arrive at a consensus concerning perennial problems in the artist's oeuvre. Includes excellent color reproductions and a good general bibliography.

Fiocco, Giuseppe. *The Frescoes of Mantegna in the Eremitani Church, Padua*. Introduction by Terisio Pignatti. New York: Phaidon Press, 1978. This definitive study of the Ovetari frescoes was first published in 1947, after the destruction of the chapel by stray bombs during World War II. Updated by Pignatti to include all the more recent research, which includes new documentation that confirms Fiocco's original assertions about Mantegna's part in the frescoes and the influences at work on him.

Hartt, Frederick. *History of Italian Renaissance Art*. 3d ed. Englewood Cliffs, N.J.: Prentice-Hall, 1988. The most recent comprehensive survey of Italian Renaissance art, including painting, sculpture, and architecture. Written for the general reader and copiously illustrated with black-and-white and color illustrations.

Kristeller, Paul. *Andrea Mantegna*. London: Longmans, Green, 1901. The earliest definitive monograph on Mantegna, marked by a scholarly and thorough use of all available documentary evidence related to the life and work of the artist. This monograph is a valuable and comprehensive study that will reward the serious reader with many insights about Mantegna's contributions to Renaissance painting.

Mantegna, Andrea. *All the Paintings of Mantegna*. Text by Renata Cipriani. Translated by Paul Colacicchi. 2 vols. New York: Hawthorn Books, 1964. Illustrates in black-and-white all the known and attributed works of the artist. Contains a general essay on Mantegna's life and work, biographical notes and dates, a brief catalog of works, selected criticism, and a selected bibliography. Good as a quick reference.

John W. Myers

MANUEL I

Born: May 31, 1469; Alcochete, Portugal
Died: December 13, 1521; Lisbon, Portugal
Area of Achievement: Monarchy
Contribution: Manuel I, known as "the Fortunate," is considered one of
Portugal's most illustrious monarchs. His reign represents the zenith of
Portuguese imperial strength. Continuing the centralizing trends and over-
seas expansion policies of his predecessors, Manuel brought both to a
climax, while presiding over a court remarkable for its splendor.

Early Life

Manuel I of Portugal was born in the town of Alcochete on the east bank
of the Tagus River. He came from a prominent family, the youngest of nine
children of Prince Fernão, the Duke of Viseu. He was a grandson of King
Afonso V, a cousin to King John II, and the younger brother of John's queen
Leonor. Despite the prominence of his family, Manuel's upbringing was
filled with turmoil. Four of his elder brothers died before he reached adulthood. In 1484, in reaction to the growing threat of royal absolutism, his
brother, the Duke of Viseu, became involved, along with other members of
the nobility, in a plot against John. The plot was discovered and the duke
died by the king's own hand. Yet the intervention of his sister the queen
protected Manuel's interests. When John's only legitimate son, Afonso, died
in 1491, Leonor was able to block his attempts to have his illegitimate son,
Jorge, declared his heir. Instead John was forced to accept Manuel, Leonor's
last surviving brother, as the future king. When John died on October 25,
1495, Manuel, Duke of Beja and Master of the Order of Christ, ascended
the throne as the fifth monarch from the House of Avis. Historian H. V.
Livermore describes the twenty-six-year-old monarch as "fair, rather thin,
diligent, sparing in his food and drink, musical, vain, and fond of display." These personal traits would also be characteristic of Manuel's administration.

Life's Work

As king, Manuel continued the centralization of royal power begun by his
predecessors. Ironically, he benefited from the results of John's ruthless
policy of breaking the independent power of the nobility that had led to his
elder brother's death. There was now much greater acceptance of royal authority. Manuel was able to strengthen royal authority further in a number of
ways. The three military orders came under the control of the Crown, and
memberships were dispensed as rewards for royal service. A system of royal
allowances encouraged the nobility to reside at court, where their actions
could be more easily monitored while at the same time increasing their

financial dependency on the Crown. The system of justice was centralized and the laws codified by the compilation of the first modern legal code, called the Ordinances of King Manuel. Administrative power began to pass from the old privileged groups into the hands of an expanding royal bureaucracy, much of it consisting of university-trained legists dependent on the monarch for their livelihood. Manuel called the Cortes only four times in his twenty-six-year reign, reflecting the Crown's lessening dependence on it as a source of revenue. Weights and measures were standardized after 1499 to facilitate national trade. In the early sixteenth century, Manuel introduced Portugal's first postal system, which helped to link the countryside to Lisbon and the royal court.

The greatest achievements attributed to Manuel's tenure as king came in overseas expansion. After nearly a century of success in exploring and mapping the African coast, as Manuel took the throne, Portuguese navigators were poised to open an all-water trade route to India. Vasco da Gama's groundbreaking voyage (1497-1499) had been authorized and planned before John's death, and it was left to Manuel to implement his predecessor's plans. Following da Gama's triumphal return from India, the king obtained papal confirmation of the discoveries and assembled a huge fleet under Pedro Álvars Cabral to follow up on contacts. On this voyage, Cabral made contact with lands on the western side of the southern Atlantic, thus establishing Portugal's claim to Brazil. He then completed his voyage to India. Portuguese trade contacts in India and other lands bordering the Indian Ocean continued to expand during Manuel's reign. This trade, transacted at enormous profit, made Portugal the richest kingdom in Europe. Manuel maintained the Portuguese presence in North Africa and, during this same time, Portuguese explorers visited Greenland, Labrador, and Nova Scotia, failing to find the fabled Northwest Passage but in the process opening the bountiful waters off Newfoundland to Portuguese fishermen.

Manuel not only sought to enlarge the empire through further exploration but also hoped to increase his dominions by marriage alliances with other royal houses. Yet these dreams came to nothing in the end. Manuel hoped to join the crown of Portugal with those of Ferdinand II and Isabella of Aragon and Castile by producing a joint heir. As this coincided with Ferdinand's own dynastic designs, a marriage was arranged in 1497 between Manuel and their eldest daughter, Princess Isabella, the widow of John's son Afonso and second in the line of royal succession after her brother Juan. Following the death of Juan, Manuel and Isabella were proclaimed heirs of Castile (although not Aragon); Isabella died in childbirth, however, and their son died soon after. Manuel then married a younger daughter of Ferdinand and Isabella, Maria, who produced his heir in 1502.

One major aspect of Manuel's reign that brought him no glory was his vacillating policy toward the Jewish population of Portugal. Prior to Manuel's tenure, the small but significant Jewish community was generally tolerated and allowed to follow its religious and cultural traditions. In fact, many Spanish Jews were allowed to settle in Portugal following their 1492 expulsion from Spain. The Jewish community made important intellectual and economic contributions that served the Crown in a number of important ways in the fifteenth and sixteenth centuries. After continuing this liberal policy of toleration upon his succession, Manuel soon changed his mind. Manuel had wished to marry Isabella for reasons of dynastic union. Under Spanish pressure, as part of that marriage agreement, Manuel promised to expel all unconverted Jews. All were ordered out of the country by October, 1497, the month the marriage took place. This decree proved to have far-reaching economic consequences as large numbers of Jews prepared to liquidate their holdings and move their families out of the country. Faced with financial dislocations, the king settled on a controversial policy of forced conversion as a way to meet his obligations yet preserve for Portugal the Jewish community's financial assets. To soften the blow of forced conversion, Manuel embarked on a policy of gradual assimilation of the so-called New Christians. They were to be given a twenty-year grace period, during which their religious practices and social customs would not be scrutinized. Yet even converted Jews would not be allowed to leave, underscoring the essentially economic rather than religious motivation of this policy. This policy, tied to the trend toward royal centralization, created an atmosphere of resentment against the New Christians, many of whom continued to practice Judaism under the protection of the royal decrees. Only after serious rioting in Lisbon in 1506 and the massacre of thousands of New Christians did Manuel give in to their pleas and again grant permission to leave and reenter Portugal at will. Nevertheless, at the same time Manuel secretly requested from the pope the establishment of the Inquisition (a request only granted in the reign of Manuel's successor) apparently as a means of controlling Judaization among the population he had agreed to protect from such scrutiny.

The fabulous material wealth flooding in from Portugal's overseas trade (estimated at more than one million cruzados a year) created opulence at home. Manuel's court was known for splendor and ostentation. In 1513, for example, Manuel sent to Rome richly bejewelled vestments, an Eastern manuscript, and a selection of exotic animals that included a trained elephant as a gift to the newly elected Pope Leo X. Yet the money went for more than luxury and waste. The wealth pouring in from the empire not only supported a sumptuous court but also financed patronage for artists and intellectuals. The reign of Manuel saw the first blossoming of Humanism in Portugal, which would reach its rather modest peak in the reign of John III. Manuel provided patronage for Portuguese students abroad and undertook the reform of the University of Lisbon in the early sixteenth century. The wealth arriving from the Portuguese Indies provided commissions for buildings, decorative sculptures, and paintings. The buildings were often designed in the late Gothic style (marked by lavish decoration on a basic Gothic structure) called "Manueline" by art historians, although the style remained popular in Portugal long after Manuel's death. The reign of Manuel is also remarkable for the numerous paintings produced on royal commissions.

Manuel died in Lisbon on December 13, 1521. His son John inherited a prosperous kingdom, but one beginning to show the strains of rapid growth, which would lead to a noticeable decline in Portuguese fortunes by the end of John III's reign.

Summary

Manuel I, aptly called "the Fortunate," ruled Portugal at the high point of its imperial fortunes. His reign represents the culmination of several trends begun earlier in the fifteenth century by the Avis monarchs, most notably the growth of royal power and the search for a water route to India, which Manuel completed. His tenure marks the clear emergence of the Renaissance state in Portugal. He was an able administrator, who could build on John II's accomplishments to establish firmly the dominance of royal authority and complete the centralization of administration. Manuel's approach to government was practical. Even his inconsistencies with regard to the Jews are best understood in terms of administrative rather than religious imperatives. It was Manuel's good luck to ascend the throne at the precise moment in which the all-water trade route to India, proved by the voyage of Bartolomeu Dias, was about to be activated. The enormous profits accruing to the Crown ensured the funds to support Manuel's other policies. He is justly credited with generously patronizing intellectuals, artists, and architects and in so doing helping to usher in a golden age in Portugal. Yet his royal absolutism, harsh treatment of the economically important Jewish community, and lavish spending of the Indies wealth on ostentation blocked modern economic development and thus hastened the decline in Portugal's economic fortunes that would follow his reign.

Bibliography

Diffie, Bailey W., and George D. Winius. *Foundations of the Portuguese Empire, 1415-1580*. Minneapolis: University of Minnesota Press, 1977. The best summary in English of Manuel's involvement in the Portuguese overseas expansion in the late fifteenth and early sixteenth centuries. Voyages of discovery and the evolution of Portuguese policy are both addressed. Includes an extensive bibliography.

Greenlee, William Brooks. *The Voyage of Pedro Álvares Cabral to Brazil and India from Contemporary Documents and Narration*. London: Hakluyt Society, 1938. The extensive introduction to this volume of documents gives considerable information on Manuel's involvement in the voyages of discovery undertaken under his auspices. The work is also valuable for its translated documents, which include letters written to Manuel describing the discovery of Brazil and from Manuel to other monarchs concerning Cabral's voyage.

Livermore, H. V. *A New History of Portugal*. Cambridge: Cambridge University Press, 1966. Gives a chapter-long overview that covers the main aspects of Manuel's reign. While royal centralization, the Jewish question, and Manuel's dreams of dynastic union with Spain are all addressed, the greatest attention is given to Portugal's successes in overseas expansion.

Oliveira Marques, A. H. de. *History of Portugal*. 2 vols. New York: Columbia University Press, 1972. Presents a concise description of the development of the Renaissance state under kings John II, Manuel I, and John III. Useful in tracing institutional developments in Manuel's reign. This work covers intellectual and artistic achievements in addition to tracing political and religious change.

Payne, Stanley G. *A History of Spain and Portugal*. 2 vols. Madison: University of Wisconsin Press, 1973. Volume 1 contains an overview describing major political, economic, religious, and cultural aspects of Manuel's reign. Gives attention to fiscal and economic matters as well as social and demographic factors contributing to the rise and eventual decline of Portuguese power in the sixteenth century. Each volume has a bibliography, but most works cited are written in Portuguese or Spanish.

Yerushalmi, Yosef Hayim. *The Lisbon Massacre of 1506 and the Royal Image in the "Shebet Yehudah."* Cincinnati, Ohio: Hebrew Union College-Jewish Institute of Religion, 1976. A critical view of Manuel's relationship with the New Christian community in Portugal and his handling of the 1506 riot in Lisbon. It cites resentment of royal centralization as the real cause of the 1506 pogrom and the New Christians as the convenient targets for pent-up frustration. The notes provide a bibliography on the subject of the Jews in Portugal.

Victoria Hennessey Cummins

ALESSANDRO MANZONI

Born: March 7, 1785; Milan, Lombardy
Died: May 22, 1873; Milan, Italy
Area of Achievement: Literature
Contribution: Among his writings in various genres, Manzoni authored the great Romantic historical novel *The Betrothed*, an acknowledged world masterpiece and much-beloved expression of Italian culture that contributed to the unification of Italy and to the Italian language.

Early Life

Alessandro Manzoni was born into the aristocratic liberal circles of late eighteenth century Milan, which, influenced by the Enlightenment, was the leading political and intellectual center of preunification Italy. His maternal grandfather was Cesare Beccaria, an economist and jurist whose lectures anticipated the theories of Adam Smith and Thomas Malthus and whose influential work *Dei delitti e delle pene* (1764; *An Essay on Crimes and Punishments*, 1767) reformed thinking on penology. Beccaria introduced the modern view that punishments should be for the purpose of protecting society, not for taking vengeance on criminals. Among Beccaria's close friends were such writers as Giuseppe Parini and the brothers Pietro and Alessandro Verri. The young Manzoni idolized his grandfather and his grandfather's friends, who provided him with role models and a liberal outlook.

Young Manzoni seriously needed such role models, since his parents took little interest in his upbringing. His mother, Giulia Beccaria Manzoni, unfortunately resembled her mother, Teresa de' Blasco Beccaria, a lovely but scandalous lady who caused discord between Cesare Beccaria and his family and friends and who finally died of venereal disease. Young Giulia became involved in an affair with Giovanni Verri, the pleasure-seeking younger brother of Pietro and Alessandro Verri. In an attempt to end the affair, Pietro Verri arranged her marriage to Pietro Manzoni, a stolid middle-aged member of the Lecco landed gentry. The marriage was a disaster from the beginning, but then young Manzoni was born (no one is sure whether Pietro Manzoni or Giovanni Verri was his actual father). With no talent or taste for motherhood, Giulia farmed him out to a wet nurse, a peasant woman who cared for him in her home. Eventually, Giulia and Pietro Manzoni separated, and Giulia fled to London and then Paris with a rich Milanese banker, Carlo Imbonati.

Manzoni spent his childhood and youth in a series of boarding schools. From 1791 to 1798, he attended schools in Merate and Lugano run by the Somaschi friars, and from 1798 to 1801 he was at schools in Magenta and Milan run by the Barnabite fathers. A sensitive child, he longed for his mother (he and Pietro Manzoni never cared for each other), endured the bullying of headmasters and other students, and led a miserable existence. Besides reducing him to a shy, withdrawn individual prone to assorted life-long paranoias, one notable result of his religious schooling was to turn him into a youthful atheist. When he was sixteen, Manzoni's formal education ended, and he moved into a Milan townhouse with an aunt (a former nun), who introduced him to a life of dissipation, which included gambling and women. At the age of sixteen, Manzoni also wrote his first surviving verse, including the unpublished four-quarto poem "Il trionfo della Libertà" ("The Triumph of Liberty").

In 1805, his mother and Carlo Imbonati invited him to join them in Paris, but before Manzoni arrived, Imbonati died, leaving Manzoni's mother a fortune. While Manzoni consoled her, she introduced him to the literary salons of Paris. There Manzoni absorbed the brilliant conversations of writers, philosophers, and politicians that, combined with his avid reading of French literature, made him extremely fluent in French. He became friends with a number of French intellectuals, particularly the literary and historical scholar Claude-Charles Fauriel, who remained a lifetime friend and correspondent. Gradually, however, events began to occur that would draw Manzoni away from Paris. In 1807, Pietro Manzoni died, leaving Manzoni the family estate in Lecco. Then in 1808 Manzoni married Henriette Blondel (who changed her name to Enrichetta), a sixteen-year-old Swiss Calvinist, and in 1810 Enrichetta, Manzoni, and his mother all converted to Catholicism and returned to Italy.

Life's Work

Most commentators cite Manzoni's conversion as the turning point in his life, but a more propitious event might have been his marriage to Blondel, who probably influenced his conversion. Gentle, loving, and strong, she provided Manzoni with the family life and stability that he had never had before. With Manzoni's mother, they settled near Milan on the Brusuglio estate that his mother had inherited from Carlo Imbonati (in 1813 Manzoni also purchased a home in Milan and in 1818 sold the Lecco estate). They proceeded to have a houseful of children while Manzoni practiced agronomy and wrote.

Among the first fruits of his conversion were the *Inni sacri* (1812-1815; *The Sacred Hymns*, 1904), followed by an essay defending Catholicism, *Osservazioni sulla morale cattolica* (1819; *A Vindication of Catholic Morality*, 1836). Then, however, Manzoni turned to history for inspiration in writing two verse tragedies, *Il conte di Carmagnola* (1820; the count of Carmagnola) and *Adelchi* (1822), which, like most Romantic dramas, are hardly suited for the stage, although *Adelchi* was performed. He also wrote an ode on the death of Napoleon, "Il cinque maggio" (1821; "The Napoleonic Ode," 1904), and *Lettre à M.**** *sur l'unité de temps et de lieu dans la* *tragédie* (1823) defending Romantic drama. His next work was the first version of his masterpiece, the long historical novel *I promessi sposi* (1827, 1840-1842; *The Betrothed*, 1828, 1951). Manzoni then spent the next fifteen years rewriting, revising, and polishing *The Betrothed*.

Aside from his literary publication, Manzoni led a retiring and tranquil life on his farm among his family. He needed such a placid life, since he still suffered from phobias (for example, he reputedly weighed his clothes several times a day) and nervous disorders that occasionally left him incapacitated. The various portraits of Manzoni suggest his nervous disposition through his slimness and his long, thin nose that seemed to grow sharper with age. Otherwise, the portraits show a man with regular, almost handsome features whose dark hair and sideburns gradually turned white over the years.

Manzoni's tranquillity was disturbed only by a series of deaths in his family. One child died in 1811, another in 1823, and in 1833 the most shattering blow of all occurred, his beloved wife died. Before Manzoni could recover from her death, their eldest child, Giulia, died in 1834. Needing the supportive companionship of a wife, Manzoni in 1837 married a widow, Teresa Borri Stampa, who brought along stepchildren. The intermittent deaths of his many children continued, and Manzoni outlived all except two. These somber events may help account for Manzoni's turning away from poetry and fiction in his later life to take up the study of history, literary theory, and language. Manzoni published an account of the seventeenth century Milan plague, *Storia della colonna infame* (1842; *The Column of Infamy*, 1845), appended to the final version of *The Betrothed*. Later writings included *Del romanzo storico* (1845), which theorized about historical novels; *Dell'invenzione* (1850), a theoretical work concerning creativity; and *Dell'unita della lingua e dei mezzi di diffonderla* (1868), a report on the Italian language commissioned by the government.

As this last work indicates, Manzoni received much official recognition during his later years. In 1860, the newly unified Italy granted him a pension and made him a senator; he was visited by foreign government dignitaries and by other writers. Most satisfying, however, was the unofficial veneration heaped upon him by the Italian people. Few writers have lived to see such adoration. His death on May 22, 1873, was considered a national tragedy. Giuseppe Verdi's *Messa da requiem* (*Requiem Mass*) was composed and performed in Manzoni's honor the following year.

Summary

The writing of *The Betrothed* presented Alessandro Manzoni with a unique problem that most modern writers face only in translation. That is, at the time Manzoni wrote, not only was Italy divided into different states ruled by various rulers, but also Italians spoke provincial dialects. There was no unified or standard Italian language. Like other Italian writers at the time,

Manzoni briefly considered writing his novel in French, but patriotic sentiments prevailed: How could the great Italian novel be written other than in Italian? Manzoni wrote the first version of *The Betrothed* in his native Lombardy dialect, sometimes called Milanese, but he was dissatisfied with the first version as soon as it appeared. He decided to rewrite the whole novel in the Tuscan dialect, which Dante had used for his *La divina commedia* (c. 1320; *The Divine Comedy*), and which Manzoni considered the purest and most graceful Italian dialect. For purposes of learning the Tuscan dialect, Manzoni made several visits to Florence and grilled any Florentine visitors. Experts in the Italian language still find Lombardisms in *The Betrothed*, but the novel gained such immense popularity that, together with Dante's *The Divine Comedy*, it is credited with establishing the Tuscan dialect as standard Italian.

The unification of the Italian language only begins to account for Manzoni's achievements in *The Betrothed*. By balancing the good-hearted but shrewd Italian peasant against the disorder and tyranny of Spanish rule in seventeenth century Lombardy, *The Betrothed* fueled the nineteenth century Risorgimento movement which was still trying to throw off foreign rule and unify Italy. It is no wonder that when unification came about Manzoni was hailed as both poet and patriot. Religious readers also found cause for praise in Manzoni's theme of divine Providence working through history. Finally, a reader looking for a good story was bound to be enthralled by the novel's long, suspenseful plot, its memorable characters, and its climax during the Milan plague. When Manzoni gratefully acknowledged the influence of Sir Walter Scott on *The Betrothed*, Scott generously replied that it was by far the best novel Manzoni had ever written.

Bibliography
Barricelli, Gian Piero. *Alessandro Manzoni*. Boston: Twayne, 1976. A competent and useful source containing a brief biography followed by a critical survey of Manzoni's writings, concentrating on *The Betrothed*. Includes an annotated bibliography.
Caserta, Ernesto G. *Manzoni's Christian Realism*. Florence: Leo S. Olschki, 1977. Focuses on Manzoni as a Christian writer. Begins with an examination of his aesthetic theory, then traces his development as a Christian writer from the *Inni sacri* through *The Betrothed*.
Chandler, S. B. *Alessandro Manzoni: The Story of a Spiritual Quest*. Edinburgh: Edinburgh University Press, 1974. Another competent critical survey of Manzoni's writings, concentrating on *The Betrothed*. Includes a fairly extensive bibliography.
Colquhoun, Archibald. *Manzoni and His Times*. New York: E. P. Dutton, 1954. The best biography of Manzoni in English, written by the translator of the definitive English version of *The Betrothed*. Provides a context of

extensive social and family background and includes sixteen pages of photographs.

De Simone, Joseph Francis. *Alessandro Manzoni: Esthetics and Literary Criticism*. New York: S. F. Vanni, 1946. A dull but informative source, originally a Columbia University Ph.D. thesis. The first part traces Manzoni's aesthetics through three phases—classicism, Romanticism, and "negation of his poetic work"—while the second part surveys Manzoni's critical opinions of other writers, primarily French and Italian.

Ginzburg, Natalia. *The Manzoni Family.* Translated by Marie Evans. New York: Seaver Books, 1987. A translation of *La famiglia Manzoni* (1983). Using letters and other old documents, the author constructs a loose account of Manzoni's family from 1762 to 1907, concentrating on his mother, his two wives, his friend Claude Fauriel, and his children.

Matteo, Sante, and Larry H. Peer, eds. *The Reasonable Romantic: Essays on Alessandro Manzoni*. New York: Peter Lang, 1986. An anthology of seventeen original essays (a few using deconstruction techniques) written by new and established Manzoni scholars to introduce Manzoni. The first section is a general introduction, followed by sections on Manzoni and Romanticism, language, history, and religion.

Reynolds, Barbara. *The Linguistic Writings of Alessandro Manzoni: A Textual and Chronological Reconstruction*. Cambridge: W. Heffer and Sons, 1950. Originally a University of London Ph.D. thesis. A bit of scholarly detective work that uses Manzoni's published and unpublished writings to reconstruct his changing theories on language, particularly on how to achieve a standard Italian language.

Wall, Bernard. *Alessandro Manzoni*. New Haven, Conn.: Yale University Press, 1954. A short introduction to Manzoni's life and works, marred by its brevity and stereotypical thinking, but still useful.

Harold Branam

MARIA THERESA

Born: May 13, 1717; Vienna, Austria
Died: November 29, 1780; Vienna, Austria
Area of Achievement: Government
Contribution: Beset by adversity, Maria Theresa proved herself to be the greatest ruler produced by the house of Habsburg. She initiated the reforms which transformed her vast holdings into a unified state and created modern Austria.

Early Life

Born in Vienna on May 13, 1717, to Charles VI, Holy Roman Emperor, and his extraordinarily beautiful wife, Elizabeth Christina of Brunswick-Wolfenbuttel, the beautiful and graceful Archduchess Maria Theresa was considered just another daughter by her father. The emperor was obsessed with the hope of fathering a son who would succeed him and consequently neglected to educate his eldest surviving daughter in the affairs of state. Maria Theresa's only brother died in infancy, as did one of her sisters, but these tragedies did not deter her father in his quest for a male heir. He was convinced that he would outlive his empress, who was in frail health, and then he could marry a princess who would give him many sons. Yet the empress outlived her husband, who died unexpectedly on October 20, 1740, of a fever contracted on a hunting expedition. He was the last Habsburg in the direct male line.

Despite the fact that he really did not believe that Maria Theresa would succeed him, Charles had taken elaborate precautions to protect his empire and ensure its continued existence. The device by which he sought to accomplish the preservation of the state was the Pragmatic Sanction. To win the support of the various rulers of Europe for this scrap of paper, he made a number of concessions to friend and foe alike. While each in his turn solemnly swore to recognize the Archduchess Maria Theresa as her father's successor, not one of them intended to support the provisions of the Pragmatic Sanction beyond their own interests. The emperor was particularly concerned about the Elector of Bavaria, who was married to his niece, Maria Amelia. Charles had become emperor in 1711 after the death of his brother, Joseph I, who left two daughters, one of whom was the wife of Charles Albert of Bavaria. In the event of his death, Charles was determined that his daughter must be protected from her cousins and their claims on the Habsburg inheritance. He believed that the Pragmatic Sanction would provide that security.

If he could not produce a son of his own, Charles might at least hope for a grandson to whom he might leave his crown, and so in 1736 Maria Theresa was married to her cousin, Francis of Lorraine. Unfortunately, Francis arrived in Vienna almost a man without a country. At the insistence of France, the new archduke had to exchange his native Lorraine for Tuscany before the marriage could be sanctioned by the great powers, who seemed bent upon humiliating the emperor and his house. Maria Theresa, for her part, cared little for the jealousies of Austria's neighbors, for she was already hopelessly in love with her bridegroom. She was never blind to Francis' faults, but she adored him and defended him until his death in 1765. Then she spent the rest of her life mourning him. Unfortunately for her father's peace of mind, the three children born to Maria Theresa and Francis before 1740 were all girls, but the child she was carrying at the time of her father's death was the future Emperor Joseph II.

Life's Work

Maria Theresa inherited a realm near bankruptcy. There was no one to advise her during the first critical weeks of her reign; Archduke Francis had a head for finance but little else, and her counselors were ancient incompetents inherited from her father. Her army was at half strength, all of the primary sources of her imperial revenues were mortgaged, and there was a crushing national debt. Yet Maria Theresa did not hesitate to face these problems and the other burdens which threatened to crush her spirits. Then Frederick II of Prussia struck.

In the spring of 1740, Frederick William of Prussia died in Berlin, and his son succeeded him. The old king had always been loyal to the emperor, and it was assumed that his son would be the same. In December, 1740, Frederick II invaded Silesia. Austria was not prepared to withstand such a blow, but Maria Theresa would not surrender a scrap of territory without a struggle. Her refusal to follow the advice of her ally Great Britain to accommodate Prussia led to the War of the Austrian Succession, which lasted until 1748. Maria Theresa did not regain Silesia, but she proved her mettle and rallied the diverse peoples of the empire to her cause.

Often Maria Theresa had reason to despair in the years between Frederick's invasion and the signing of the Peace of Aix-la-Chapelle. In 1742, she had made peace with the Prussians at Berlin, only to have her old enemy reenter the war when he feared that he would not receive his fair share of the spoils. On January 24, 1742, Frederick engineered the election of Charles Albert of Bavaria as Holy Roman Emperor, with the title Charles VII. Maria Theresa was furious that her husband had been denied that honor by treachery, and she was determined that Charles VII would not enjoy his triumph. Harried from his capital of Munich, he became a mere pawn in the hands of the diplomats. On January 25, 1745, he died, and Maria Theresa immediately secured the election of her husband as Emperor Francis I. Only after his election in 1745 and his coronation in 1746 was Maria Theresa able to bear the title of empress; however, there was never any doubt in anyone's mind, including that of Francis, who really exercised the power.

Having prevented the dismemberment of her kingdom, Maria Theresa began to plan her revenge on Frederick II. Great Britain had to be discarded as an ally, because George II and his ministers had proved unreliable: They were more interested in preserving the Kingdom of Hanover than in fulfilling their obligations to the empress. During the eight years which separated the War of the Austrian Succession from the Seven Years' War, Austria and France effected a diplomatic revolution which left the traditional alignment of European nations in disarray. Sworn enemies for generations, Austria and France became allies, while Prussia was forced into an uneasy arrangement with Great Britain, her former adversary. The final seal on Maria Theresa's brilliant diplomatic coup would be the marriage of Marie Antoinette, her ninth child, to the Dauphin of France, the future Louis XVI.

During the brief years of peace, Maria Theresa was also able to devote her energies to reforming the antiquated institutions of her empire, while centralizing its government. Blessed with the rare talent for choosing able subordinates and then placing each in the area best suited to his talents, she slowly rebuilt her cabinet.

The great nobles of the empire had regularly ignored any directives from Vienna and ruled their holdings like independent rulers, while the provincial estates passed laws with little or no concern for the central government. Under Maria Theresa, these abuses ceased. Count Haugwitz had been the governor of a portion of Silesia when Frederick invaded that province, and he had observed at close range the reforms which the Prussians imposed on their new subjects. With the support of the empress, he then instituted similar reforms in all parts of the empire except Hungary, which was protected by special privileges.

For the first time, the nobility was forced to pay taxes. Increased revenues permitted Maria Theresa to create a centralized bureaucracy, a permanent standing army serviced by military academies, and a system of secondary education. In 1749, the administrative and judiciary functions of the government were separated, and a complete codification of the law was ordered. Begun in 1752, it was finally finished in 1811 during the reign of Maria Theresa's grandson.

Beginning in the forests of North America, the Seven Years' War soon involved most of the world. When the conflict ended in 1763, France was near bankruptcy, while Great Britain was without question the most powerful nation on earth. Austria did not capture Silesia, but it did regain much of its lost international prestige. Maria Theresa had the satisfaction of watching her archenemy brought to the brink of destruction. Only the accession of a new ruler in Russia and his own daring saved Frederick from disaster. With the war's completion, Maria Theresa resolved never again to commit her nation to battle save in self-defense.

Two years after peace was signed, Emperor Francis I died unexpectedly. Despite her loss, Maria Theresa sought to devote herself to the service of the state. Her children—there were sixteen of them—continued to bring her great joy and at times disappointment. Yet none of them was as difficult as her heir, Joseph II.

Burning with a zeal to reform Austria, the new emperor lacked both tact and caution. Only his mother's resolve kept his often ill-directed enthusiasm in check. Together they ruled the empire until Maria Theresa's death, but it was not always a cordial relationship. In 1772, Joseph outraged his mother's sense of decency by engaging in the first partition of Poland. Maria Theresa's prediction that no good would come of this despicable act, which was shared with Prussia and Russia, was ignored by Joseph. Mercifully, the empress did not live to see the final dismemberment of Poland. Maria Theresa died in Vienna on November 29, 1780, after a long and painful illness.

Summary

Against all odds, Maria Theresa succeeded in saving the ramshackled empire which she inherited from her father. She was the architect of modern Austria, and, thanks to her care, the empire survived into the early twentieth century. She had an uncanny talent for selecting subordinates and then placing them in positions which allowed them to employ their talents to the fullest. Even her own husband, Francis I, was assigned to that area of government he best understood, finance. With her advisers, she centralized the imperial government, putting an end to centuries of inefficiency and mismanagement. Only the Hungarians resisted the reforms, but Maria Theresa charmed the Magyars into submission and contained their fierce longing for independence. By her frugality, she restored the financial integrity of her nation, and with the profits of her labor she built Schönbrunn Palace, her favorite residence, and perhaps the finest example of the Austrian Baroque style.

When she effected a diplomatic revolution by making her country's ancient enemy, France, her firm ally, Maria Theresa sacrificed her daughter to seal the bargain, but she would not willingly countenance the cynical dismemberment of Poland. Her court was adorned with artists, writers, and musicians, such as Franz Joseph Haydn and Wolfgang Amadeus Mozart, but Maria Theresa never forgot that to the ordinary folk she was like a mother. Seeking to improve their lot, she initiated a number of reforms for which her successors were often given the credit. She was the greatest ruler of the Habsburg dynasty.

Bibliography
Anderson, M. S. *Europe in the Eighteenth Century, 1713-1783*. London: Longman, 1961, 3d ed. 1987. A solid treatment of the period. Well-

written and very easy to follow, it has an excellent annotated bibliography for further study.

Crankshaw, Edward. *The Habsburgs: Portrait of a Dynasty.* New York: Viking Press, 1971. A good introduction to the rather complicated story of Austria's development under the Habsburgs. The chapters on Maria Theresa are quite useful and contain a good outline of her life and reign. Excellent photographs.

_____. *Maria Theresa.* New York: Viking Press, 1969. Like the Hungarian nobility, Crankshaw has fallen under the spell of the beautiful empress, and therefore this work must be read with care. Yet it is a well-written biography and contains a very useful bibliography.

Gooch, G. P. *Maria Theresa and Other Studies.* Reprint. New York: Archon Books, 1965. The two essays which begin this work, "Maria Theresa and Joseph II" and "Maria Theresa and Marie Antoinette," are based on the correspondence between the empress and her children. The humanity of Maria Theresa, as well as her deep feelings for her son and daughter, is easily discernible in these two works.

Pick, Robert. *Empress Maria Theresa: The Earlier Years, 1717-1757.* New York: Harper & Row, 1966. A remarkably well-written work, it is meant for the scholar. Balanced, sensitive, and illuminating, it is perhaps the best biography of Maria Theresa in English.

Roider, Karl A., Jr., ed. *Maria Theresa.* Englewood Cliffs, N.J.: Prentice-Hall, 1973. This slender volume is a treasury of materials dealing with Maria Theresa. Part 1 contains letters and papers of the empress on a number of subjects. Part 2 contains views of Maria Theresa by her contemporaries. Part 3 contains eight brief statements by historians.

Wandruszka, Adam. *The House of Habsburg: Six Hundred Years of a European Dynasty.* Translated by Cathleen Epstein and Hans Epstein. Garden City, N.Y.: Doubleday, 1964. The portions of this work which deal with Maria Theresa are valuable, because they briefly analyze her approach to governing and to reform. The influence of the empress on the two sons who succeeded her is carefully considered. Good bibliography.

Clifton W. Potter, Jr.

KARL MARX

Born: May 5, 1818; Trier, Prussia
Died: March 14, 1883; London, England
Areas of Achievement: Economics and philosophy
Contribution: Marx's ideas concerning modes of economic distribution, social class, and the developmental patterns of history have profoundly influenced theories in philosophical and economic thought and have helped shape the political structure of the modern world.

Early Life

Karl Marx was born into a Jewish family in the city of Trier in the southern Rhineland area. When the Rhineland was rejoined, after the Napoleonic Wars, to Protestant Prussia in 1814, his father, a public lawyer, had converted to Christianity. In 1830, the young Marx entered the Trier secondary school and pursued the traditional humanities curriculum. In the fall of 1835, he entered the University of Bonn as a law student but left the following year to enroll at the University of Berlin. His studies were concentrated on law, history, and the works of the then-leading philosophers Johann Gottlieb Fichte and Georg Wilhelm Friedrich Hegel.

Marx was graduated in 1841, after writing his doctoral dissertation, and returned to Bonn, where he became involved with his friend Bruno Bauer in left-wing politics and in the study of the materialist philosophy of Ludwig Feuerbach. In April, 1842, he began writing radical articles for the *Rheinische Zeitung* (Rhenish gazette), and he assumed its editorship in Cologne that October. He married in June, 1843, and moved to Paris that October.

In August, 1844, Marx met Friedrich Engels in Paris, and the two began a productive collaboration. Marx's articles had angered the Prussian government, and in February, 1845, he moved to Brussels. In 1848, the year of revolutions in many European countries, Marx was ordered to leave Brussels; he returned to Paris and then to Cologne. He was again compelled to leave in 1849 and went to London, where he would remain for the rest of his life.

Life's Work

Marx's lifelong critique of capitalist economy began in part as an analysis of the then-dominant Hegelian system of philosophical Idealism. Influenced to a degree by Feuerbach's materialism, Marx rejected Hegel's metaphysical vision of a *Weltgeist*, or Absolute Spirit. It was not metaphysical Spirit that governed history but rather material existence that determined consciousness. The ways in which an individual was compelled to seek physical necessities such as food, shelter, and clothing within a society profoundly influenced the manner in which a person viewed himself and others. As Hegel (and others) suggested, the course of history was indeed a dialectical process of conflict and resolution, but for Marx this development was determined to a great extent by economic realities. Whereas Hegel saw dialectical process (thesis/antithesis/synthesis) as one of ideas, for Marx it was one of class struggle. Hence Marx's position is called dialectical materialism. He stood in staunch opposition to the prior philosophical tradition of German Idealism and thinkers such as Immanuel Kant, Fichte, and Hegel. German philosophy, he believed, was mired in insubstantial theoretical speculation when concrete and practical thought about the relationship between reality—especially economic and political realities—and consciousness was needed. In general, Marx was a synthetic thinker, and his views represent a mixture of German materialist philosophy such as that of Feuerbach; the French social doctrines of Charles Fourier, Comte de Saint-Simon, and Pierre-Joseph Proudhon; and British theories of political economy such as those of Adam Smith and David Ricardo.

Marx's philosophical position of a dialectical materialism suggests a comprehensive view of social organization—which is, broadly speaking, a dimension of human consciousness—in all its manifestations. The determinant of all societal forms is its economic base (*Basis*), that is, the means of production and the distribution of its produced wealth. All aspects of human social interaction, what Marx called the superstructure (*Überbau*), are influenced and shaped by the economic base and its consequent relationships of power among social classes. The superstructure ultimately involves a society's educational, legal, artistic, political, philosophical, and scientific systems. The nature of the economic base—above all the power relationships of the classes—tends to be reproduced in an overt or covert fashion in the various dimensions of the societal superstructure. The pedagogical curriculum of the school system, for example, might reproduce or reinforce in some unconscious manner the inequality of the social classes upon which the mode of production is based. Various aspects of the artistic or cultural dimensions of a society (a novel, for example) might also incorporate in symbolic expression the nature of the economic base. Thus Marx's economic theories provide an account for a wide variety of phenomena.

In capitalist political economy, the individual must sell his physical or intellectual labor, must sell himself as a commodity, in order to survive. Thus, Marx's early writings, such as *Ökonomische und philosophische Manuskripte* (1844; *Economic and Philosophic Manuscripts of 1844*, 1947), deal with the pivotal concept of alienation (*Entfremdung*) as a central aspect of the worker's experience in capitalism. Since the worker is reduced to an exploited commodity or object, this is above all a condition of dehumanization (*Entmenschlichung*). The individual is alienated or divorced from his full potential as a human being. Committed to long hours of labor in a factory, the worker—and this means man, woman, and child—has no time to develop other facets of the personality. In a capitalist society, individuals are estranged not only from aspects of their own selves but also from others in that the labor market is a competitive one, and workers must outdo one another in order to survive. In its crudest form, capitalist economy, Marx would assert, is a kind of Darwinian "survival of the fittest," in which the weak—those who cannot work—must perish.

In his *Die deutsche Ideologie* (1845-1846; *The German Ideology*, 1938), Marx discusses earlier forms of social organization, such as tribal or communal groups, in which the estrangement of the individual in industrialist society was not yet a crucial problem. His vision of an ideal socialist state would be one in which the individual might, for example, manufacture shoes in the morning, teach history in the afternoon, and play music in an orchestra in the evening. In other words, a person would be free to utilize or realize all dimensions of the self. This idealized notion of social organization in the writings of the young Marx indicates the utopian influence of romantic thought upon his initial critique of capitalist society.

In 1848, after the Paris revolts of that same year, Marx and Engels published *Manifest der Kommunistischen Partei* (*The Communist Manifesto*, 1850), a booklet that has become the best-known and most influential statement of Marxist ideology. It presents a brief historical sketch of bourgeois society and suggests that capitalism will eventually collapse because of its inherent pattern of cyclical economic crises and because of the worsening situation of the worker class, or the proletariat, in all capitalist nations. The proletariat has become, they argue, more conscious of its situation, and a worker revolution is inevitable. The international communist party presents a revolutionary platform in which the workers are the ruling class in charge of all capital production. Marx and Engels call for a worker revolt to overthrow the "chains" that bind them.

Marx wrote and published *Zur Kritik der politischen Ökonomie* (1859; *A Contribution to a Critique of Political Economy*, 1904), which became a preliminary study for the first volume of his and Engels' planned multivolume analysis of capitalist political economy, *Das Kapital* (1867, 1885, 1894; *Capital: A Critique of Political Economy*, 1886, 1907, 1909, better known as *Das Kapital*). Marx actually completed only the first volume; the second and third were edited from his notes by Engels, who was helped on the third by Karl Kautsky. This work is a more technical economic analysis of the capitalist mode of production with the intention of revealing "the economic law of motion" that underlies modern (industrial) society.

It would be beyond the scope of this study to provide a detailed summary of this complex work, but a few words of general explanation may be given. Marx discusses economic issues such as the labor theory of value and commodities, surplus value, capital production and accumulation, and the social relations and class struggles involved in capital production. Capital accumulation, the central goal and justification of the system, is beset by certain internal contradictions, such as periodic episodes of moderate to extreme market inflation and depression and a tendency toward monopoly. These inherent conditions usually have their most deleterious effects upon the wage laborer. Such cycles will eventually lead to economic collapse or revolutionary overthrow by the proletariat. In general, Marx's analyses were flawed—especially the labor theory of value upon which much of this work is based—and could not account for adaptive changes in the capitalist system.

In December, 1881, Marx's wife, Jenny, died, and his daughter died the following year. Marx himself, after a life of overwork and neglect of his health, died in 1883.

Summary

Karl Marx was a critical social and economic philosopher whose materialist analyses of bourgeois capitalist society initiated a revolution that has had profound effects on the development of human civilization. Despite some of the later ideological, and at times quasi-religious and fanatical, adaptations of his thought, the basic philosophical assumptions of Marx's approach remain humanistic and optimistic; they are based upon fundamental notions of the European Enlightenment, that is, that human reason can successfully alleviate the problems of life. Alienation is, for example, in Marx's view (as opposed to modern existential thought) a historical and societal phenomenon that can be overcome through a change in the social-economic order. Marxism has remained a vital intellectual position and therefore possesses much relevance to the modern world.

Subsequent developments of Marxist thought have resulted in Communist Party revolutions in a number of countries such as that led by the ideologue Vladimir Ilich Lenin (1870-1924) within czarist Russia in 1917 or that of the popular leader Mao Tse-tung (1893-1976) in the Republic of China in 1949. Unfortunately, these revolutions have involved pogroms and mass executions of certain segments of the population, usually elements of the landed bourgeoisie. This was the case under the rule of Joseph Stalin (1879-1953) in Soviet Russia. These socialist governments have become reified, for the most part, at the intermediate stage of a party dictatorship rather than the essentially free state of the people that Marx had ideally envisioned.

Marx's philosophy has led to fruitful thought in areas other than social and economic thought. The notion that the power relationships of the economic base effect in various ways the manifestations of the societal superstructure has produced an analytical mode called ideological criticism, in which the hidden dimensions of class ideology are revealed in their social expressions. This has been especially productive in the field of literature and the arts. Marxist analyses of literary texts have yielded new insights into the nature of literary production and its relationship to society at large. The Hungarian critic Georg Lukács (1885-1971), for example, wrote many excellent books and essays on the history of European literature, establishing a new model of Marxist interpretation and criticism.

Bibliography

Bottomore, Tom, ed. *Karl Marx*. Englewood Cliffs, N.J.: Prentice-Hall, 1973. An excellent collection of essays by prominent scholars on various aspects of Marx's thought. Contains a selected bibliography.

Henry, Michel. *Marx: A Philosophy of Human Reality*. Translated by Kathleen McLaughlin. Bloomington: Indiana University Press, 1983. An important critical work by a French scholar who gives close readings/interpretations of Marx's key texts.

McLellan, David. *Karl Marx: His Life and Thought*. New York: Harper & Row, 1973. An excellent critical biography of Marx by a prominent Marxist scholar. Contains a good bibliography.

—————. *Marx Before Marxism*. New York: Harper & Row, 1970. An excellent study of Marx's important early years as a student and the development of his initial ideas. Contains a selected bibliography.

Singer, Peter. *Marx*. New York: Oxford University Press, 1980. A brief but informative introduction to Marx's life and major ideas. Contains suggestions for further reading.

Suchting, W. A. *Marx: An Introduction*. New York: New York University Press, 1983. A good critical biography of Marx presented chronologically and by topic. Contains helpful guide for further reading.

Thomas F. Barry

MASACCIO
Tommaso di Giovanni di Simone Guidi

Born: December 21, 1401; Castel San Giovanni, Republic of Florence
Died: 1428?; Rome
Area of Achievement: Art
Contribution: During a brief career, Masaccio became one of the major creators of the new Renaissance style of painting. His innovations utilizing perspective created a standard of realism admired and imitated by subsequent generations of artists.

Early Life

In contrast to the lives of such prominent Renaissance artists as Leonardo da Vinci and Michelangelo, little is known concerning the life of the Florentine painter Masaccio, who managed during his brief life to revolutionize the world of painting. He was born Tommaso di Giovanni di Simone Guidi in the small Tuscan town of Castel San Giovanni, now known as San Giovanni Valdarno, on Saint Thomas' Day, December 21, 1401.

His grandfather had settled in San Giovanni in the 1380's and established himself as a successful furniture maker. Masaccio's parents, Giovanni di Mone Cassai and Monna Iacopa di Martinozzo, were only twenty and nineteen when their first son was born; they still lived with his grandfather. Masaccio was a nickname derived from Tommaso, meaning "hulking Tom," or "slovenly Tom." In 1406, his parents had another son, Giovanni, who also became an artist and was nicknamed "Lo Scheggia," meaning "the splinter," or "chip." In the same year, Masaccio's father died, and his mother soon remarried. Her second husband was an elderly pharmacist named Tedesco.

The next sixteen years of Masaccio's life are essentially a mystery. Coming from a prosperous family of artisans, he no doubt enjoyed a comfortable childhood. The first specific records of him after 1406 date from January, 1422, when he enrolled in the Florentine guild of physicians and apothecaries, which then included artists in its membership. It remains uncertain under whom he trained, the old theory that he studied under the artist Masolino having been convincingly disproved. He possibly learned some basics about painting from one of the artisans who decorated the painted chests produced in his grandfather's shop. It is also uncertain exactly when Masaccio left San Giovanni for the greater opportunities afforded by Florence. He may have studied there with the painter Mariotto di Cristofano, the husband of one of his stepsisters.

The Florence which became the adolescent Masaccio's new home was then one of the most vibrant and important cities in Europe, on the threshold of its greatest century. One of the chief ways the city fathers expressed their pride in Florence's increasing prominence was by commissioning paint-ers, sculptors, and architects to produce works of art for the city. Masaccio arrived in Florence at exactly the time when monumental artistic projects were making the city the leading artistic center of Europe.

Though the identity of Masaccio's teachers remains a mystery, his revolu-tionary style was undoubtedly influenced by three key individuals: Giotto, Florence's greatest painter of the previous century; Donatello, the contempo-rary master sculptor; and Filippo Brunelleschi, the inventive architect and artist. By his early twenties, Masaccio had absorbed the simple dignity of Giotto's composition and solid naturalism of Donatello's sculptures and ap-plied them to Brunelleschi's new laws of linear perspective, so that he was ready to produce some of the most influential paintings and frescoes of the century.

Life's Work

The young Florentine genius enjoyed an active career of less than a decade before his premature death. His earliest known work, a triptych discovered in the obscure Church of San Giovenale in the valley of the Valdarno in 1961, consisted of a Madonna and Child flanked by four saints, a very traditional subject. Already, however, Masaccio was showing signs of a new naturalism and inventiveness in this work. The Christ Child was originally completely nude and depicted eating grapes, an iconographical innovation referring to the Eucharist. The triptych's figures clearly mirrored those of Giotto a century earlier and showed a skilled use of foreshortening and light.

Another early work, dating from approximately 1423, was his *Madonna and Child with Saint Anne and Angels*, an altarpiece painted for the Church of Sant'Ambrogio in Florence. Evidently part of this work was painted by Masolino, although scholars disagree on the exact division of work between the two.

One of the few works of Masaccio that can be dated definitively is another altarpiece, a polyptych done for the Church of Santa Maria del Carmine in Pisa. The work was commissioned for a chapel, and Masaccio received eighty florins for his undertaking. The polyptych was dismantled in the eigh-teenth century and the various pieces scattered. Scholars have subsequently identified eleven of these, and they are now housed in museums in London, Berlin, Naples, Pisa, and Vienna. The only surviving description of the entire work is found in Giorgio Vasari's history. For his centerpiece of the Pisa polyptych, Masaccio again painted the *Madonna and Child*. Surround-ing them are four small angels, two of them playing lutes. Another key panel features a dramatic crucifixion scene notable for its rather bulky rendition of Christ and its moving Mary Magdalene. Surviving pieces from the work's predella include a visitation by the Magi and scenes from the lives of various saints.

Works such as the Pisa altarpiece undoubtedly added to the growing reputation of the young painter. Contemporary records reveal little about the details of his life in Florence during this period. The number of known works he produced demonstrates that he was rarely without work and thus reasonably secure financially. Tax returns from July, 1427, indicate that he was living in a house rented for ten florins a year. His younger brother and widowed mother were living with him. He also rented part of a workshop for an additional two florins a year. Donatello and Brunelleschi were among his close friends. Writing more than a century after Masaccio's death, Vasari characterized him as an affable, absent-minded individual unconcerned with worldly goods and careless about his dress.

By the mid-1420's, several key elements combined to produce Masaccio's distinctive style. In obvious rebellion against the delicacy of the International Gothic favored by such successful contemporary Florentine artists as Gentile da Fabriano, Masaccio emphasized solid, monumental figures accompanied by somber and simple backgrounds. His careful study of the human form and the effect of light produced works of revolutionary realism. Although color was not unimportant to him, Masaccio was more clearly dedicated to form. His figures emerged as unique individuals rather than faceless stereotypes. Instead of the elaborate brocades habitually used in International Gothic, Masaccio's biblical figures wore simple, heavy cloaks. Above all, the new laws of perspective enabled the young master to produce works that put his figures in believable space rather than having them float aimlessly against solid gold backgrounds.

The outstanding examples of Masaccio's style are found in his frescoes located in the Brancacci Chapel in the Florentine Church of Santa Maria del Carmine. The exact date of his work there remains unclear, as does the name of the patron, although it was undoubtedly a member of the influential mercantile Brancacci family. Some of the chapel's frescoes were the work of Masolino, who had earlier collaborated with the young artist on the altarpiece for the Church of Sant'Ambrogio. It remains uncertain whether the two worked together in the chapel or whether Masolino began the project and then abandoned it to Masaccio when he left for another commission in Hungary. The chapel remained unfinished at the time of Masaccio's death and was completed only in the 1480's by a third artist, Filippino Lippi.

Scholars generally attribute six of the major scenes and part of another to Masaccio. One of these includes *The Expulsion from Paradise*, a moving work showing Adam and Eve being driven from the Garden of Eden. The figures, depicted against a bleak landscape, almost resemble free-standing sculpture in the new tradition of Donatello. Masaccio's masterful use of atmospheric perspective and emotional expression infuses the scene with drama.

The majority of his Brancacci chapel frescoes, though, depict various scenes from the life of Saint Peter, a rare iconographical theme in Florence during this period. By far the most famous of these, and generally regarded as his masterpiece, is *The Tribute Money*. Inspired by the biblical story found in Matthew 17:24-27, the fresco is a simultaneous narrative in three parts. In the center section, a tax collector confronts Christ and his apostles and demands tribute. On the left, Saint Peter obeys Christ's injunction to cast forth his hook and take a coin out of the mouth of the first fish he catches; on the left, Saint Peter pays the tribute to the tax collector. This fresco was perhaps inspired by a new tax imposed by the Florentine government in 1427. Whatever the inspiration, the figures in *The Tribute Money*, as well as in Masaccio's other frescoes in the chapel, exhibit a convincing realism and individuality.

Masaccio's most unconventional fresco is located in the Church of Santa Maria Novella in Florence. The famous *Holy Trinity with the Virgin and Saint John*, most commonly dated to 1425, again shows his creative genius. It depicts the Trinity within an architectural framework inspired by Brunelleschi, expertly creating an illusion of depth through the barrel vaulted ceiling. To accompany the Trinity, Masaccio painted figures of Mary and John and below them full-size portraits of the donor and his wife. Their identities remain uncertain although it is possible that they were members of the Lenzi family. For the first time, the donors are portrayed on the same scale as the divine figures, a significant innovation. Long covered by a sixteenth century altar, *Holy Trinity with the Virgin and Saint John* was not rediscovered until 1861. When it was cleaned in 1952, restorers discovered a skeleton painted below the donors. Such memento mori were rare in Florence's artistic tradition.

In addition to the previously discussed works, Masaccio produced several others which have been destroyed. These included a "Consecration" fresco for the Carmine Cloisters in Pisa, a fresco of Saint Ives and his wards for Florence's Church of the Badia in 1627, and a Saint Paul fresco for that city's Church of the Carmine. Vasari mentions that Masaccio painted several portraits of eminent Florentines, but these remain lost or have not survived.

Sometime in 1428, the young artist abandoned work on the Brancacci Chapel and left Florence for Rome. The reason remains unclear, although it was possibly a response to a summons from his friend Masolino, who was then in the city. Before the end of the year, Masaccio died, so suddenly and unexpectedly that rumors spread that he had been poisoned. His friend Brunelleschi summarized the impact of the twenty-seven-year-old genius' demise when he remarked that the art world had suffered a most grievous loss.

Summary

The paintings of Masaccio had an influence upon the formation of the Renaissance style equal to the contemporary accomplishments in sculpture by Donatello and in architecture by Brunelleschi. The young Florentine was thus one of the three pivotal influences in establishing Florentine ascendancy in the art world during the fifteenth century, a most remarkable achievement considering the brevity of his career.

His handful of surviving frescoes inspired generations of painters who studied them for their masterful skill in making the human figure come alive. Such prominent artists as Fra Filippo Lippi, Sandro Botticelli, Andrea del Verrocchio, Leonardo da Vinci, Michelangelo, and Raphael all found inspiration for aspects of their style in the work of Masaccio. All made the pilgrimage to the tiny Brancacci Chapel to study his masterly modeling of the human figure.

Influenced by the earlier works of Giotto, as well as by classical sculpture, Masaccio created a brilliant new standard for painting that effectively abandoned medieval two-dimensionality and instead explored the possibilities for realism provided by atmospheric and linear perspective. Masaccio's figures emerged as real individuals, full of emotion and dignity. They symbolized the self-confidence of the Renaissance epoch dawning in Florence and served as models for countless later Renaissance works. The Brancacci Chapel frescoes established artistic standards that endured virtually unchallenged until the nineteenth century. Although the details of his life remain obscure and largely undocumented, Masaccio's importance in art history remains firmly entrenched. Few other painters, if any, have managed to transform the course of painting so decisively in such a short time.

Bibliography
Berti, Luciano. *Masaccio*. University Park: Pennsylvania State University Press, 1967. A lucid and lavishly illustrated biography, meticulously researched, with detailed explanatory footnotes. Contains a chronological bibliography of books and articles written about Masaccio between 1436 and 1964. Includes a catalog of Masaccio's known and lost works and of paintings that have generally been attributed to him.
Cole, Bruce. *Masaccio and the Art of Early Renaissance Florence*. Bloomington: Indiana University Press, 1980. This well-researched monograph contains three chapters on Masaccio, dealing respectively with his life, the Pisa Altarpiece, and his frescoes. The other four chapters discuss the nature of Florentine art in the decades immediately preceding and following his death. The bibliography contains more than sixty books and articles on Masaccio, as well as many others dealing with the period.
Hartt, Frederick. *History of Italian Renaissance Art: Painting, Sculpture, Architecture*. 2d ed. Englewood Cliffs, N.J.: Prentice-Hall, 1979. A standard survey of the major achievements of the era. Hartt's chapter on "Gothic and Renaissance in Florentine Painting" discusses Masaccio's life and works, especially relating them to Masolino. Contains useful introductions and a good bibliography.

Vasari, Giorgio. *The Lives of the Artists*. Edited by William Gaunt. 4 vols. London: J. M. Dent and Sons, 1963. First published in 1550 and substantially expanded in 1568, Vasari's collection of biographies of famous Renaissance architects, sculptors, and painters provides the earliest secondary information about the life and career of Masaccio. He established many historical traditions about Masaccio and described some of his works that have subsequently been destroyed or lost. Some of his statements have been disproved by modern art historians.

Venturi, Lionello, and Rosabianca Skira-Venturi. *Italian Painting: The Creators of the Renaissance*. Paris: Albert Skira, 1950. This volume deals with the thirteenth through the fifteenth century in Italian painting and includes a brief chapter on Masaccio. Contains large color reproductions of many of his major works and a useful chart on the Brancacci Chapel frescoes.

Tom L. Auffenberg

MATSUO BASHŌ

Born: 1644; Iga province, Ueno, Japan
Died: October 12, 1694; Osaka, Japan
Area of Achievement: Literature
Contribution: Bashō is considered one of Japan's greatest poets, especially
as master of the haiku. While the haiku was already established as a
poetry form prior to the Tokugawa era, Bashō is credited with reinvigorat-
ing the form at a time when it was in severe decline.

Early Life

Matsuo Bashō was born Matsuo Kinsaku in Ueno, in the province of Iga,
near Kyoto, on the island of Honshu in Japan. His father, Matsuo Yozaemon,
was a samurai of minor rank and a teacher of calligraphy. His mother was
also of samurai stock. He had an elder brother and four sisters. When Bashō
was a young boy, he became a page at Ueno Castle and was a companion to
the son of the lord of the castle, Tōdō Yoshitada. The two boys had a
common interest in poetry, and they no doubt influenced each other. During
this time, Bashō assumed a samurai's name, Matsuo Musafune. This relationship with Lord Yoshitada's son came to an untimely end when the young
lord died in 1666. Grief-stricken, Bashō left his service at Ueno Castle and
began to devote more of his time and commitment to his poetry. While the
later years of his youth are not well documented, it appears that Bashō spent
much of his time wandering about Kyoto and studying with masters of literature there. At some time during this period, he abdicated his samurai status.

In his late twenties, probably around 1672, Bashō left the Kyoto area and
settled in Edo. Why he moved is not clear, and he apparently had a difficult
time getting established. Around 1677, he began to gather around himself a
circle of pupils, many of whom would become his disciples and perpetuate
his style. During this period, Bashō gained some reputation as a master of
haiku, the brief seventeen-syllable verse form for which he is best known. In
1680, he was the recipient of a cottage which had banana trees planted on
the land, and soon he was known as the "banana tree man," hence the name
change to Bashō. Thought to have been a gift of Sampū, an admirer, the hut
was located near the Sumida River in an isolated area. Two years later, the
Bashō hut burned, to be replaced the following year. That same year, his
mother died in Ueno. Although some early biographers have suggested that
Bashō may have had a mistress and one or more children, such a relationship
cannot be clearly documented.

Life's Work

Bashō's life's work divides itself rather naturally into five stages, beginning with his earliest extant haiku written at age eighteen, in 1662, and
lasting about ten years. For some years, his work showed evidence of change

and maturity as he sought to master new techniques. In 1684, Bashō became a Buddhist priest and began a series of pilgrimages. His first important journey is recorded in *Nozarashi kikō* (1698; *The Records of a Weather-Exposed Skeleton*, 1959). Most of Bashō's finest haiku are written in his travel journals, and these diaries are themselves of high literary quality. Perhaps the best idea of his physical appearance is to be found in a wooden image, by an unknown carver; Bashō is in the dress of a Zen monk and has a typically Japanese expression of serenity and wisdom. Between the years 1686 and 1691 Bashō was at the peak of his career, producing five poetic diaries containing haiku: *Kashima kikō* (1687; *A Visit to the Kashima Shrine*, 1965), *Sarachina Kikō* (1704; *A Visit to Sarashina Village*, 1957), *Oku no hosomichi* (1694; *The Narrow Road to the Deep North*, 1933), *Saga nikki* (1691; the saga diary), and *Oi no kubumi* (1709; *Manuscript in My Knapsack*, 1962). In addition, he was overseer for an anthology of haiku poems, *Sarumino* (1691; *Monkey's Raincoat*, 1973).

Prolific output of poetry is not, in itself, a sign of quality; indeed, compared to other haiku poets, Bashō is far from being the most prolific. What was characteristic of the work during this peak period was the distinctive style that Bashō developed. While he would continue to borrow from and allude to classical Chinese literature, as poets before him had done, he would continue to refine techniques that he had established in his earlier writing. In much of the poetry of this period, however, the unique quality of *sabi*, or loneliness, appeared. Always at the heart of this "loneliness," is the recognition of the fragility and transience of some manifestation of life merging into the vastness of nature. As Makoto Ueda has noted, the haiku that use *sabi* by implication, if not more explicitly, centers on "the merging of the temporal into the eternal, of the mutable into the indestructible, of the tiny and finite into the vast and infinite, out of which emerges a primeval lonely feeling shared by all things in this world."

Bashō's haiku are inseparable from the frequent journeys that occasioned their composition. In perhaps the most relaxed, even carefree, period of Bashō's life, he traveled to Kashima, a small town some fifty miles to the east of Edo. Bashō's reason for the journey was to view the harvest moon. This journey provided the materials for *A Visit to the Kashima Shrine*. The first half of the journal describes the trip, and the latter half is a collection of poems by Bashō and others from the area of Kashima. This journal has as its primary motif the appreciation of the beauty of nature and the idea that through this appreciation one can have union with poets of the past. Objectivity perhaps best describes Bashō's eight haiku in this volume.

In 1687, Bashō undertook a long journey westward which resulted in *Manuscript in My Knapsack*. This volume records the first half of the journey that extended into 1688. In this, one of his longer journals, Bashō records his travel from Edo westward to his hometown of Ueno and thence to the coastal town of Akashi. The prose style resembles that of the earlier journal *A Visit to the Kashima Shrine* in using restrained language. The distinctive feature of *Manuscript in My Knapsack* is that in it Bashō makes a theoretical statement as an aesthetic primitivist, an advocate of a "return to nature." In this aspect, it is something of an extension of the earlier Kashima journal. While Bashō retains the modest tone characteristic of his writing, he nevertheless exhibits a clear sense of self-confidence.

During the same year, 1688, Bashō's shortest journal recorded his travel to Sarashina Village. The half of the journal devoted to poetry contains eleven haiku by Bashō. Although Bashō had presumably gone through a period of having nothing new to say, he apparently found in the fresh, undeveloped, natural beauty of Sarashina a source for poetry that he had not considered appropriate earlier. The Sarashina journal provides an opportunity to record a new stage in Bashō's development.

Struck with this new dimension of nature, Bashō's next journey was northward, to the least developed area of Japan. This 1694 volume, *The Narrow Road to the Deep North*, is the longest of the journals. What is particularly interesting about the diary is its metaphorical title: It is a record of a spiritual journey as well as a literal one. While it is a journey in quest of the best of nature, it is also a search for what Bashō believes man has lost in the contemporary world.

The 1691 journal *Saga nikki* is, in some ways, most like an ordinary diary in that each entry of an approximately two-week visit in Saga is dated. In other ways, it is clearly akin to the other travel journals, especially in the central theme of forgetting one's material poverty and enjoying a serene, leisurely life attuned to nature.

Early in the summer of 1691, at the peak of the Bashō-style haikai, Mukai Kyorai and Nozawa Bonchō, under Bashō's guidance, published an anthology of haikai, *Monkey's Raincoat*. The volume is especially significant because it lent credence to the haikai as a serious art form.

In 1692, the third Bashō hut was built, and the next year Bashō closed his gate and did not receive visitors for a time. In the summer of 1694, however, the poet began what was to have been a long journey, although one of his haiku documents his awareness of approaching death. He became increasingly ill, and, in early autumn, surrounded by some of his disciples and relatives, Bashō died in Osaka.

Summary

Matsuo Bashō is without question among the greatest, if not the greatest, of the haikai poets that Japan has produced. Hundreds of years after his death, his reputation remains secure. Many of his pupils perpetuated his style and passed on the tradition to others: In bringing to new life the artificial, steadily dying form of the earlier haikai, he raised the genre to a new height; indeed, he founded a new genre.

Bashō was a master in his use of season words; in his use of associations with historical places or situations, and with historical sources for materials; and in his parody of old poems. Especially noteworthy were his style of expression and his ability to evoke the quality of *sabi*. Bashō also excelled as a critic and is considered a major contributor to Japanese literary aesthetics.

Bibliography

Aitken, Robert. *A Zen Wave: Bashō's Haiku and Zen.* New York: Weatherhill, 1979. The introduction provides a concise sketch of Bashō's life and a discussion of the historical development of the haiku. The main body of the book is given to commentary on a number of Bashō's haiku, with some comparison of various English translations of a given poem.

Caws, Mary Ann, ed. *Textual Analysis: Some Readers Reading.* New York: Modern Language Association of America, 1986. Earl Miner's chapter on Bashō has as its main thesis that Bashō has not been known in the West as he would have wished to be known. The focus of his discussion is the fact that the Western concept of mimesis, what is real and what is fiction, differs from its Eastern counterpart, opening the way to misunderstanding.

Henderson, Harold G. *An Introduction to Haiku.* Garden City, N.Y.: Doubleday, 1958. Based on an earlier work, *The Bamboo Broom* (1934). The author makes an excellent translation of about seventy of Bashō's haiku. Strives to retain the original syllable pattern while avoiding distortion of English grammar in doing so.

Keene, Donald. *World Within Walls: Japanese Literature of the Pre-Modern Era, 1600-1867.* New York: Holt, Rinehart and Winston, 1976. In a chapter devoted to the haikai poetry of Bashō, Keene evaluates Bashō's reputation in his lifetime and then outlines Bashō's life, discussing haiku that are based on particular situations. The narrative explains, interprets, and comments on noteworthy examples of Bashō's work.

Ogata, Tsutomu. "Five Methods for Appreciating Bashō's Haiku." *Acta Asiatica: Bulletin of the Institute of Eastern Culture* 28 (1976): 42-61. An elucidation and identification of methods for appreciating Bashō's haiku.

Ueda, Makoto. *Matsuo Bashō.* New York: Twayne, 1970. In a biographical sketch of Bashō, the author traces five stages of development in Bashō's literary career, giving representative haiku from each period with commentary of each one. Excellent bibliography, but many of the works are in Japanese.

_____. *Zeami, Bashō, Yeats, Pound: A Study in Japanese and English Poetics.* The Hague: Mouton, 1965. Notes the influence of Zen on Bashō's haiku and their modernity. Discusses Bashō's poetic theory on such concepts as permanence and change.

Victoria Price

MATTHIAS I CORVINUS
Mátyás Hunyadi

Born: February 24, 1443; Kolozsvár, Transylvania
Died: April 6, 1490; Vienna, Austria
Areas of Achievement: Monarchy, government, politics, the military, and patronage of the arts
Contribution: Matthias I excelled as soldier, diplomat, and legal reformer. Most important, he moved Hungary from feudal particularism toward a more centralized state and through his lavish patronage promoted a remarkable Humanist literary and artistic achievement on the model of the Italian Renaissance.

Early Life

Matthias I Corvinus was the second son of János Hunyadi, a self-made man of the lesser Hungarian nobility. Hunyadi won great military renown fighting against the Ottoman Turks and in the process had become the largest single landowner in the kingdom, arousing the fear and resentment of the magnates, to Matthias' later detriment. Meanwhile, Matthias as a boy received under his father a rigorous military training. He polished his soldierly skills in battle and was knighted at the age of fourteen during a victorious engagement with the Turks at Belgrade. Matthias' father also provided him with a superior education through private tutors headed by János Vitéz, a man of strong Humanist sympathies. Matthias became fascinated with Italian Renaissance culture.

Upon the sudden death of his father in 1456, Matthias and his elder brother were seized by feudal enemies of the Hunyadi family, with the approval of the impressionable boy-king Ladislas V. Matthias' brother was executed, but Matthias was spared, apparently because of his youth. When Ladislas died without an heir in late 1457, the Diet of Hungarian nobles decided, with some qualms, to elect as king the fifteen-year-old Matthias, preferring him both for his native birth and for the heroic image left by his father. The candidates of assorted Polish, Saxon, and Austrian Habsburg dynasties were passed over. At his accession, Matthias was a blond-haired, vigorous, powerfully built youth. He had a charming manner that belied a sometimes-fiery temper.

The new king faced a desperate situation. The royal treasury was empty while hostile forces pressed from virtually all sides. As Czech marauders and Hungarian rebels plagued much of northern Hungary, Turkish armies to the south held all of Serbia and raided Hungarian territory continually. Meanwhile, to the west the Austrian Habsburg Emperor Frederick III, who coveted the Hungarian crown, plotted Matthias' overthrow with the help of an alienated faction of the Hungarian magnates. Finally, a crippling condition of Matthias' election was that he submit during the first five years of his reign to a regency government under his uncle and a council of state composed mainly of magnates. In meeting these challenges, Matthias soon demonstrated that Hungary had acquired no ordinary monarch.

Life's Work

Matthias I rejected from the outset the authority of the regency council. Within months he had deposed his uncle, the regent, and replaced the magnates on the council with his personal choices. The young king then drew upon his private resources to crush the northern rebellion and clear that region of its roving Czech military bands. By 1462, he had met temporarily the challenge of the Austrian emperor from the west through a skillfully negotiated treaty. That gave Matthias the breathing space to turn finally to the south, where Turkish forces had advanced from Serbian bases to overrun the neighboring Hungarian region of Wallachia. In a series of brilliant campaigns, Matthias recovered northern Serbia and most of Wallachia. He consolidated his gains with a chain of forts.

Matthias' impressive military and diplomatic successes were attributable largely to a complete restructuring of the Hungarian army accomplished during his first years in power. Believing the traditional feudal levy inadequate to his needs, the king recruited an army composed mostly of Czech and German mercenaries, professional soldiers who could be mobilized on short notice. These troops, supplemented by native feudal contingents, he personally trained and maintained with firm discipline and good pay. At its peak, the new standing army numbered some thirty thousand men, about two-thirds of them heavily armed cavalry. Known from their garb as the Black Army, these forces became the chief instrument in carrying out Matthias' foreign policy objectives.

To support his large military establishment, the king had to overhaul the tax system. A decree of 1467 become the cornerstone of a fiscal policy designed to produce the funds not only for the army but also for Matthias' extensive political and cultural projects. Previously inviolate tax exemptions for the magnates were drastically curtailed, while heavy new taxes were imposed on the free peasantry. Old taxes were given new names and expanded in scope. To handle the windfall of revenue, Matthias staffed his treasury office with specialists. Despite widespread protests and occasional tax rebellions, Matthias' fiscal reforms yielded a tenfold increase in royal income over that of his predecessor.

The king pursued other administrative and social reforms. Deeply suspicious of the feudal magnates, Matthias chose to run his government through a professionalized chancellery office staffed by men of humbler social background. He also won the gratitude of many towns through royal grants of autonomous status through the local feudal jurisdictions. To improve the administration of justice generally, Matthias revamped the court system. He installed a new appeals procedure that ran from local jurisdictions through an intermediate level to the royal court itself, at each stage conducted by judges knowledgeable in the law. Also, new laws were decreed that protected the rights of the free peasantry, softening the impact of his taxes by improving their status in relation to the magnates, while other legislation prohibited the tightening of bonds on serfs. Matthias' legal reforms culminated in a royal decree of 1486, in which he sought to provide a synthesis or codification of the best principles of Hungarian jurisprudence, both in criminal and in civil law.

Following his early military and diplomatic victories, Matthias determined to use the Black Army to unite the Czech and Austrian realms with Hungary. Although his long-range policy goals were never clearly stated, it is possible that he contemplated the building of a coalition of central European Christian states to deal decisively with the Muslim Turkish menace in the Balkans, something he felt unable to achieve alone. In any case, from 1468 onward, Matthias began to compete more aggressively for the crown of Bohemia. By 1478, after defeating a combined Czech, Polish, and Austrian force four times the size of the Black Army, Matthias had his prize. Under terms of the Peace of Olomouc, the Hungarian monarch took not only the title of King of Bohemia but also the associated lands of Moravia, Silesia, and Lusatia. Then, between 1477 and 1490, Matthias fought three wars against his old antagonist the Austrian Emperor Frederick III. By 1485, the Black Army had occupied the Habsburg capital of Vienna and most of southern Austria soon afterward. Matthias triumphantly took up residence in Vienna, but the imperial crown itself would elude him, as Frederick III refused to designate Matthias his heir.

The most enduring achievement in Matthias' reign would lie not in his political and military exploits but in the prodigious cultural energies he brought to focus in Hungary. Convinced that cultural distinction was essential to a prince of his eminence in the Renaissance era, Matthias determined early to create a court life that was at once enlightened, elegant, and cosmopolitan. To this end, he gathered Humanist scholars around him, mostly from Italy, and drew many of his officials from their ranks. Further, he subsidized with great generosity the work of painters, sculptors, architects, and goldsmiths. Himself highly educated, the king often was a participant in the lively philosophical and scientific discussions he encouraged at court. His marriage in 1476 to Beatrix, daughter of the King of Naples, only intensified the impact of the Italian Renaissance on Hungarian elite society.

Resident Italian historians such as Antonio Bonfini now wrote histories of Hungary in which Matthias, to his delight, was hailed as a "second Attila." The same flattering Humanist Bonfini also stretched Matthias' genealogy to include as forebear a distinguished ancient Roman consul whose family crest, a crow (*corvinus*), Matthias promptly made his own. Finally, the king imported art work from Italy and ordered the decoration of his various palaces with appropriate Renaissance paintings and statues.

Matthias' reputation as "friend of the muses" would rest above all on the splendid Corvina library he assembled in his Buda palace. The estimated twenty-five hundred manuscripts of the Corvina at its peak contained some six thousand distinct Greek and Latin works. These titles, by pagan and Christian alike, reflected the breadth of Matthias' interests. The books ranged in subject from military strategy and law through art and theology to Renaissance literature. Matthias also employed transcribers and book illuminators to copy and adorn selected works and emboss them with gems and precious metals. The Corvina would remain his greatest cultural legacy.

Matthias Corvinus died at age forty-seven in Vienna, the victim of a stroke that ended prematurely his grand scheme of a Hungarian empire embracing south-central Europe. He was interred near Budapest. He left only an illegitimate son who was quickly passed over by the Diet of magnates. They elected a Polish youth who seemed malleable enough and who, above all, was not of the house of Corvinus. In the grim generation that followed, the Black Army was disbanded, and Matthias' other major reforms were allowed to lapse. In 1526, an overwhelming Hungarian defeat at Mohács began two centuries of Turkish occupation.

Summary

Most of King Matthias' achievements proved fleeting because of the lack of capable successors. Yet the thirty-two years of his reign remain among the most remarkable in Hungarian history. Against heavy odds, Matthias I Corvinus managed to reverse several generations of feudal anarchy. He did so by remodeling the central government in ways similar to innovations then being ventured in the major Renaissance monarchies of the West. In particular, Matthias' administrative and legal reforms laid the foundations for a regime perceived as more stable and more just in its relations with its citizens generally. The renown of his judicial measures is reflected in the popular lament that followed his passing: "Matthias is dead; justice has fled." In addition to his judicial and economic reforms, Matthias created in the Black Army one of the earliest standing armies in Europe. It made Hungary for a time the major power of central Europe. Yet there is some validity to the criticism that Matthias became so obsessed with the conquest of the Habsburg lands and the imperial crown that he badly neglected the critical problem of the Turks.

Matthias is remembered not only as a warrior, statesman, and lawgiver, but also as an extremely generous patron of arts and letters. The Corvina library ranked with the Vatican and the Medici collections in Italy as the foremost in Europe.

Matthias I, the Renaissance King of Hungary, was inspired by a larger vision than most princes of his time regarding the distinctive values of a civilized society and how to achieve them. A generation of prosperity and promise for his people expired with the man himself.

Bibliography
Csapodi, Csaba. *The Corvinian Library: History and Stock.* Translated by Imre Gombos. Budapest: Akadémiai Kiadó, 1973. The definitive descriptive and historical account of Matthias' library. Provides valuable information on the scribes and illuminators of the books and where manuscripts are to be found. Provides an informed estimate that the Corvina originally contained at least twenty-five hundred manuscripts.
Kosáry, Dominic G. *A History of Hungary.* New York: Benjamin Franklin Bibliophile Society, 1941. Foreword by Julius Szekfü. An admiring but solid account of Matthias' chief policies and achievements. Kosáry argues that Matthias' efforts at erecting a central European empire of Austria and Bohemia, along with Hungary, was intended only as a prelude to ending decisively the Turkish threat in the south.
Kosztolynik, Zoltan J. "Some Hungarian Theologians in the Late Renaissance." *Church History* 57 (1988): 5-18. A good overview of an important segment of intellectual life in Matthias' Hungary, focused especially on the distinguished theologian Pelbart of Temesvar. Valuable for aspects of Matthias' relationship with the Hungarian church, particularly in substantiating the underlying resentment and hostility of leading Hungarian churchmen toward their Renaissance king.
Sinor, Denis. *History of Hungary.* New York: Praeger, 1959. The most balanced, scholarly, and informative account available in English. Provides a careful appraisal of the weaknesses as well as the strengths of Matthias' impressive reign. Sinor argues, contrary to Kosáry, that Matthias' pursuit of an elusive Hungarian empire that would include Austria and Bohemia was an end in itself, not directed toward building an anti-Turkish alliance.
Vámbéry, Arminius, with Louis Heilprin. *The Story of Hungary.* New York: G. P. Putnam's Sons, 1886. Lacking a good modern biography in English, this rather uncritical treatment remains useful for the vivid, extensive detail relating to Matthias himself, especially the earlier years, on which little is available elsewhere.
Varga, Domokos G. *Hungary in Greatness and Decline: The Fourteenth and Fifteenth Centuries.* Translated by Martha S. Liptaks. Budapest: Corvina Kiadó, 1982. The most extensive treatment available in English on the core period of Matthias' regime. The main value of this work lies in its extensive citations of original chronicle sources and its excellent illustrations.

Donald D. Sullivan

GUY DE MAUPASSANT

Born: August 5, 1850; Château de Miromesnil, near Dieppe, France
Died: July 6, 1893; Passy, France
Area of Achievement: Literature
Contribution: Maupassant was one of the major literary figures at the end of the nineteenth century to help move short fiction away from the primitive folktale form to the short story of psychological realism. His most significant contributions to the form may be found in such affecting realistic stories as "Boule de Suif" and such powerful tales of psychological obsession as "The Horla."

Early Life

Henri-René-Albert-Guy de Maupassant was born on August 5, 1850. He was the first son of Laure Le Poittevin and Gustave de Maupassant, both from prosperous bourgeois families. When Maupassant was eleven and his brother Hervé was five, his mother, an independent-minded woman, risked social disgrace to obtain a legal separation from her husband. With the father's absence, Maupassant's mother became the most influential figure in the young boy's life.

At age thirteen, he was sent to a small seminary near Rouen for classical studies, but he found the place unbearably dreary and yearned for home, finally getting himself expelled in his next-to-last year. He returned home to the influence of his mother, as well as her brilliant brother Alfred and his student and friend Gustave Flaubert. At age eighteen, Maupassant was enrolled at the Lycée de Rouen, and he began law studies soon afterward in Paris, only to have these studies interrupted by the Franco-Prussian War, for which he enlisted. After the war, he gained a position in the Naval Ministry, but under the tutelage of Flaubert he began to publish poetry and stories in various small journals. He also became part of a group of literary figures, including Alphonse Daudet, Émile Zola, and Ivan Turgenev, who met regularly at the home of Flaubert.

Life's Work

Maupassant's first published story, "La Main d'écorché" (1875; "The Skinned Hand," 1909), which was reworked in 1883 as simply "La Main" or "The Hand," belongs to a tradition of supernatural short fiction that is as old as legend itself; in reworking the story, however, Maupassant grounded it in the revenge-tale tradition popularized by his countryman Prosper Mérimée and at the same time managed to make the story an ironic comment on supernatural fictions.

With the publication of "Boule de Suif" (1880; English translation, 1903), a tale which Flaubert praised extravagantly, Maupassant ceased working for the government and devoted himself to a career as a writer, excelling especially in the genre of the *conte*, or short story, which was quite popular at the time in periodical magazines and newspapers. Before achieving this initial success, however, Maupassant contracted syphilis, which was to take his life after a relatively brief writing career of ten years.

After the success of "Boule de Suif," the touching story of the prostitute who reluctantly goes to bed with a Prussian officer in order to procure the release of her traveling companions, only to be scorned by them, Maupassant began to write anecdotal articles for two newspapers, the practice of which served as preparation for writing the short stories that were to make him famous.

His first full volume of short fiction appeared in 1881 under the title of his second important story, "La Maison Tellier" (1881; "Madame Tellier's Establishment," 1903), a comic piece about a group of prostitutes who attend a First Communion. After the success of this book, Maupassant published numerous stories in newspapers and periodicals. These stories were reprinted in volumes containing other Maupassant stories. Many of his stories created much controversy among the French critics of the time because he dared to focus on the experiences of so-called lowlife characters.

In addition to the realistic stories of the lower classes, Maupassant experimented with mystery tales, many of which are reminiscent of the stories of Edgar Allan Poe. Instead of depending on the supernatural, these stories focus on some mysterious dimension of reality which is justified rationally by the central character. As a result, the reader is never quite sure whether this realm exists in actuality or whether it is a product of the narrator's obsessions.

After having published as many as sixty of Maupassant's stories, the newspaper *Gil-Blas* began the serialization of his first novel, *Une Vie* (*A Woman's Life*, 1888), in February, 1883, which was published in book form two months later. The year 1884 also saw the publication of Maupassant's most famous short story and his most widely read novel. The story, "La Parure" (1884; "The Necklace," 1903), has become one of the most famous short stories in any language. Indeed, it has become so famous that it is the story which most commonly comes to mind when Maupassant's name is mentioned, despite the fact that most critics agree that Maupassant's creation of tone and character in such stories as "Boule de Suif" and "La Maison Tellier" is much more representative of his genius than this ironically plotted story about a woman who wasted her entire life working to pay back a lost necklace, only to discover that it was fake.

"Le Horla" (1887; "The Horla," 1890), a story almost as famous as "The Necklace," is often referred to as the first sign of the syphilis-caused madness that eventually led to Maupassant's death. As a story of psychological horror, however, it is actually the pinnacle of several stories of madness with which Maupassant had previously experimented. The story focuses on the central character's intuition of a reality which surrounds human life but remains imperceptible to the senses. Told by means of diary entries, the story charts the protagonist's growing awareness of his own madness as well as his lucid understanding of the process whereby the external world is displaced by psychic projections.

What makes "The Horla" distinctive is the increasing need of the narrator to account for his madness as the result of something external to himself. Such a desire is Maupassant's way of universalizing the story, for he well knew that human beings have always tried to embody their most basic desires and fears in some external but invisible presence. "The Horla" is a masterpiece of hallucinatory horror because it focuses so powerfully on that process of mistaking inner reality for outer reality—a process which is the very basis of hallucination. The story is too strongly controlled to be the work of a madman.

Moreover, those who argue that with the writing of "The Horla" Maupassant was already going mad cannot explain the fact that the following year he published the short novel *Pierre et Jean* (1888; *Pierre and Jean*, 1890), which is one of his best-conceived and best-executed works. This work was his last major contribution, however, for after its publication his intensive production of stories slowed almost to a halt, and he began to complain of migraine headaches, which made it impossible for him to write. His eyesight began to fail, his memory faded, and he began to suffer from delusions.

Just after the first of the year in 1892, Maupassant had to be taken to a sanatorium in a straitjacket after having slashed his own throat in a fit of what he himself called "an absolute case of madness." In the sanatorium, he disintegrated rapidly until he died on July 6, 1893.

Summary

Guy de Maupassant is one of those writers whose contribution to literature is often overshadowed by the tragic facts of his life and whose unique experimentation is often ignored in favor of his more popular innovations. Too often it is his promiscuity and profligate Parisian life-style that receive the most attention from the casual reader. As if to provide evidence for the payment Maupassant had to make for such a life-style, these readers then point to the supposed madness-inspired story "The Horla" as a fit ending for one who not only wrote about prostitutes but also paid for their dangerous favors with his life. Yet Maupassant's real place as a writer belongs with such innovators of the short-story form as Anton Chekhov, Ivan Turgenev, Ambrose Bierce, and O. Henry. Too often, whereas such writers as Turgenev and Chekhov are admired for their so-called lyricism and realistic vignettes, such writers as Bierce and O. Henry are scorned for their so-called cheap narrative tricks. Maupassant falls somewhere in between. On the one hand, he mastered the ability to create the tight, ironic story that depends, as all short stories do, on the impact of the ending. On the other hand, he had the ability, like Chekhov, to focus keenly on a limited number of characters in a luminous situation. The Soviet short-story writer Isaac Babel has perhaps paid the ultimate tribute to Maupassant in one of his stories by noting that Maupassant knew the power of a period placed in just the right place.

Maupassant had as much to do with the development of the short-story genre in the late nineteenth century as did Chekhov, although in somewhat different ways. Yet, because such stories as "The Necklace" seem so deceptively simple and trivial, his experiment with the form has often been ignored.

Bibliography
Ignotus, Paul. *The Paradox of Maupassant*. London: University of London Press, 1966. A biographical and critical study that focuses much more on the unsavory aspects of Maupassant's life than it does on the excellence of his fiction. Ignotus insists, with little evidence to support his arguments, that Maupassant was primarily driven by his sexual appetites, perversions, and immoralities.
Lerner, Michael G. *Maupassant*. New York: George Braziller, 1975. Primarily a biographical study, although discussion of the publication of Maupassant's work is often accompanied by some brief discussion of how his novels and stories are influenced by and in turn reflect his own social milieu.
Steegmuller, Francis. *A Lion in the Path*. New York: Random House, 1949. Not only the best biographical study of Maupassant but also one of the most perceptive critical estimates of Maupassant's works; it is the one indispensable book on Maupassant by an excellent biographer and critic who clearly understands the important role that Maupassant plays in the history of French literature.
Sullivan, Edward D. *Maupassant: The Short Stories*. Great Neck, N.Y.: Barron's, 1962. Although little more than a pamphlet-length introduction to some of Maupassant's basic themes and story types, this valuable study can serve to orient the reader to Maupassant's contribution to the short-story form. Particularly helpful is Sullivan's attempt to place Maupassant's short stories within their proper generic tradition.
_____. *Maupassant the Novelist*. Princeton, N.J.: Princeton University Press, 1954. A study of the basic themes and technique of Maupassant's novels, as well as an attempt to synthesize his aesthetic and critical ideas from his essays and newspaper articles. Sullivan admits that Maupassant was a "natural" short-story writer but argues that a study of his novels provides an opportunity to study Maupassant's creative process.
Wallace, A. H. *Guy de Maupassant*. New York: Twayne, 1973. A conven-

tional biographical and critical study that adds little to Steegmuller's earlier work. Wallace focuses on Maupassant's use of fictional themes and obsessions taken from his own life, primarily the cuckoldry of his father, the women in his life, and his madness.

Charles E. May

MAXIMILIAN I

Born: March 22, 1459; Wiener Neustadt, Austria
Died: January 12, 1519; Wels, Austria
Areas of Achievement: Government and politics
Contribution: Maximilian I revived and strengthened both the concept and the actual position of Holy Roman Emperor by a great reform movement. These accomplishments were short-lived, however, and his enduring contribution lies in the development of German and Austrian nationalism.

Early Life

Maximilian was the only son of the emperor Frederick III and Eleanor of Portugal. The varied genetic background of Maximilian (he was also the great-great-grandson of John of Gaunt and had Polish, Lithuanian, and Russian blood from his paternal grandmother) combined to produce a highly interesting character. He was energetic, vivacious, and restless; he was an adventurer, an avid hunter, and a mountaineer; he was friendly, gregarious, and popular because he inspired confidence; and he loved writing, music, and the study of different languages. He was filled with curiosity, a love of learning, and a desire to meet people.

With his dynamic personality, it is not surprising that even before he became emperor, on the death of his father in 1493, Maximilian could boast of an impressive string of accomplishments. On February 16, 1486, he was crowned king at Aix-la-Chapelle, becoming coruler with his father. In 1486, he was also granted the title King of the Romans. Frederick worked patiently with Maximilian to teach him the concepts of governing an empire, a sense of responsibility, and political ethics. Maximilian also gained from his father personal strength and dignity. These lessons would prove valuable when Maximilian assumed full control of the imperial office.

In 1477, with his career just beginning, Maximilian married the heiress of the Burgundian lands, Mary, daughter of Charles the Bold. Charles had just been killed in battle against the Swiss, who, along with the French, moved quickly to appropriate portions of his inheritance, which Charles had carefully and laboriously assembled in the hope of Burgundy's becoming a kingdom. Maximilian, often called "the last knight," arrived just in time to prevent the dismembering of Burgundy. By his marriage to Mary, he added her lands, consisting of the Netherlands, Luxembourg, Artois, and Picardy, to the Habsburg holdings. Maximilian also recovered Franche-Comté and lands in Austria and the Tyrol. By 1491, he had made claim to Hungary and Bohemia. Maximilian not only acquired lands but also emerged as a recognized leader in the field of European politics, giving rise to the power of the house of Habsburg. Thereafter, the Habsburgs retained control of the imperial office, and France was forced to pursue its expansionist policies in Italy.

Maximilian's relationship with Mary resembled a storybook romance. He loved her sincerely, spending much time with her at sporting activities, social events, and government functions. Together they had two children, Philip and Margaret. Mary was killed in 1482, however, as a result of a fall from a horse, causing Maximilian to have to face the resistance of stubborn Netherlanders who did not want to see Mary's children entrusted to his guardianship. In 1488, the citizens of Bruges even took him prisoner, although he was rescued by his father. All the events, however, successful and frustrating, of his involvement with Burgundian politics taught him valuable lessons in statecraft and gave him insights into ethnic characteristics of the Flemish people that he could use later.

Life's Work

Maximilian became Holy Roman Emperor in 1493 after the death of his father. His great popularity, untiring energy, and capacity for work aroused the concern of the electors, who did not want to see the imperial office regain real power. The leader of the opposition was his lifelong enemy, Prince Berthold, Elector of Mainz. Berthold attempted to increase opposition to the emperor and create an administrative machine which would weaken Maximilian's hand and require approval for his acts. Berthold proposed a regency council (*Reichsregiment*), which the emperor bitterly fought. It was adopted in 1500 but failed two years later. Had it continued, it would have represented a great victory for the Electors and the Estates of Germany. Maximilian, trying to sabotage the council, acted independently of it, gaining support from the young princes of Germany, with whom he was highly popular. He also took advantage of the quarrels and dissension among council members.

His need for money to deal with the threat of invasion by the Turks forced him into a meeting with the electors and princes in 1495. This assembly, the Diet of Worms, marked the real beginning of his reign. Maximilian showed his capability as a ruler by dealing with the demands of the jealous nobility through compromises in which he gained more than the nobility. One of the results was the Common Penny, a tax collected from subjects throughout the realm to provide funds for Maximilian's campaign against the Turks. In return, he allowed the Estates the opportunity to be included in his new bureaucratic offices. As a counterpoise to the proposed *Reichsregiment*, Maximilian established the Imperial Chamber (*Reichskammergericht*), a supreme court of justice with a president appointed by the emperor and sixteen justices appointed by the Estates. The chamber acted as a court of appeals in private cases and as a court to settle disputes among princes. It is important to note that the chamber implemented Roman law and served as a court of the empire rather than of the emperor. It also served as a rival to the regency council and gave the emperor considerable influence in judicial proceedings.

Perhaps the most significant accomplishment of the Diet of Worms was the peace (*Landfriede*), which effectively brought an end to personal warfare. With the decline of feudal power and the loss of feudal restraints, private vendettas were rife in Germany. This peace, to be eternal, meant that private disputes would now be settled in a court of law.

In another move to centralize power, Maximilian activated the six administrative circles originally planned by Emperor Albert II in 1438. In 1512, Maximilian added four circles. Each major district of the empire contained the organization for both war and peace as each circle had a military commander and an administrative director. In 1501, Maximilian created the Aulic Council, which had eight members appointed by the emperor. This council allowed the emperor to hear appeals and to exercise supreme jurisdiction, extending the emperor's authority even into Italy.

Maximilian also had a separate financial administration dependent on him alone and a modern chancery with judges whom he appointed. Within a few years, Maximilian was able to replace the old feudal power of the Electors and the Estates of Germany with a new, modern, centralized bureaucracy. By 1505, Berthold was dead, leaving Maximilian with no enemies. He had gained the support of the young leaders, and he had reached the apex of his power and influence. In 1508, Pope Julius II approved for him the title Roman Emperor Elect. Maximilian took very seriously his religious responsibilities, believing that he was born destined to be a new Constantine who would strengthen and extend the borders of Christ's kingdom. He also took quite seriously the concept that he was destined to perpetuate the ancient Roman Empire as a new Augustus.

As important as Maximilian's modernized bureaucracy was to the enhancement of Habsburg power, perhaps more important were the dynastic marriages he arranged. He promoted a double marriage between his son Philip and Joanna, the second daughter of Ferdinand and Isabella of Spain, and between his daughter Margaret and the Spanish prince John. The untimely deaths of the heirs to the Spanish throne placed Philip in a position to inherit the Spanish empire. He later arranged a marriage between his granddaughter and Louis II, son of Ladislas, the King of Hungary and Bohemia, and between his grandson Ferdinand and Louis' sister. These dynastic marriages extended Habsburg control to include an extensive empire.

Maximilian's apparent genius as a leader and his successes attracted the attention of the scholarly community of Europe, who looked to Maximilian to establish an enlightened Christian empire. Humanists, whose vision centered on classical antiquity and the days of imperial Rome, were drawn to the patronage of Maximilian's court. They sincerely believed that Maximilian was destined to restore glory to Germany; Maximilian felt keenly this sense of his own destiny to be the founder of a new world order. At the same time, he found the Humanists useful in spreading the good news of his glorious reign. Maximilian worked hard to upgrade learning in the empire; he turned the University of Vienna into one of the most significant universities in Europe. He also composed works of his own: the *Weisskunig*, an account of his life, *Freydal*, and *Theuerdank*.

The least successful of Maximilian's policies was his involvement in Italian affairs. Maximilian made an alliance with Ludovico, tyrant of Milan, sealing it by marrying Ludovico's niece, Bianca Maria Sforza, in 1494. His purpose was to counteract the growing French influence in Italy, caused to a large degree by Maximilian's expulsion of the French from Burgundian lands. In 1495, he joined the Holy League with the pope, Milan, England, and Aragon to stop the French in Italy. In 1508, he joined the Cambrai League against Venice, and then the new Holy League against the French in 1513. The league forced the French king Louis XII to withdraw, but the French returned later under Francis I. Maximilian's anti-French policy contributed to the protracted war between German and French forces in Italy, which escalated into a series of bloody conflicts over both politics and religion that did not end until 1648. Maximilian also struggled in vain against the Swiss. They fought his forces to a standstill in 1499 during the Swabian War, resulting in the de facto independence of the Swiss, recognized officially at the Peace of Westphalia in 1648. In his declining years, Maximilian spent his time preparing his young grandson Charles to assume the throne. (His son Philip had died in 1506, leaving Charles as heir to the entire Habsburg holdings.) Maximilian died on January 12, 1519, in Wels.

Summary

Maximilian I was able to restore the effectual authority of the emperor and the prestige and prominence of the Holy Roman Empire to its greatest degree of strength since the downfall of the Hohenstaufens. The empire had now at least the appearance of a united state. His own position as a Habsburg ruler was the strongest of any of his family, largely because of his timely dynastic marriages. He was responsible for a more cohesive Germany and for the cultivation of a spirit of national pride within the German people. His *Land-friede* program brought about peace and order, ending the tyranny of robber barons. Maximilian faced political realities and could conceive of modern alternatives to feudal traditions and institutions. He was not an original thinker, but he was able to take ideas from others and make them work, creating an effective political machine. He was an enlightened ruler who showed an interest in church reform and the advancement of learning. He showed a modern adroitness in political propaganda—a politician's skill in disarming his opponents—usually coming out on the winning side.

Maximilian's reform, however, was short-lived. Internally, his power was never more than an uneasy balance between imperial and feudal elements. Although the Aulic Council continued to the end of the empire, generally his efforts to create permanent centralized institutions failed. His efforts probably had more to do with the rising of Austrian and German national states than with the preservation of the empire. Some consider him to be the last ruler of the Holy Roman Empire. Certainly he is a transition figure from the old medieval empire to the modern national states. He had energy and a dedication to work, but he lacked clear objectives and persistence. The death of his wife was not only an emotional catastrophe for him but also a political one. His involvement in Burgundy drove the French to Italy, and his involvement in Italy resulted in war and great distress for Germany. Switzerland was lost to the empire; Burgundy became an area fought over by France and Germany for centuries.

The most important and lasting achievement of Maximilian was the cultivation and the institutionalizing of German nationalism. In years to come, the efforts of this "last knight"—who himself was the bridge to the modern world—contributed to the rise of the nineteenth and twentieth century political realizations of the German Reich.

Bibliography
Bryce, James. *The Holy Roman Empire*. Rev. ed. New York: Macmillan, 1904. Important for the discussion of the transfer of the imperial consciousness from Roman to German and the carrying forth of the concept that the one empire is eternal. Somewhat dated but thorough, especially in the discussion of the relationship of Germany to the Church.
Gilmore, Myron P. *The World of Humanism, 1453-1517*. New York: Harper & Row, 1952. Very valuable source for the study of Humanism, which provides the intellectual context for Maximilian's time. The chapter on dynastic consolidation is interesting, especially as it pertains to Germany. The discussion of Maximilian is highly informative.
Heer, Friedrich. *The Holy Roman Empire*. Translated by Janet Sondheimer. New York: Praeger, 1968. A most valuable source for students of medieval German history. Begins with the birth of the Roman Empire and traces the development of imperial consciousness. Excellent discussion of Maximilian and his relationship to the general picture. Good illustrations, an excellent index, and a bibliography.
Holborn, Hajo. *A History of Modern Germany*. Vol. 1, *The Reformation*. New York: Alfred A. Knopf, 1959. Begins with the German migrations and continues through the history of the empire to the sixteenth century. Very good for setting forth ideas and underlying causes; good analysis. Overview of Maximilian's life is good; main points delineated well.
Maehl, William H. *Germany in Western Civilization*. Tuscaloosa: University of Alabama Press, 1979. This critical and very comprehensive work begins with ancient times and follows the history of Germany to the post-World War II era. An excellent index, a bibliography, a glossary, and a

chronological list of German rulers. Especially good discussion of Maximilian's dedication to scholarship, his marriage alliances, and his Italian policy.

Stubbs, William. *Germany in the Later Middle Ages, 1200-1500*. Edited by Arthur Hassall. New York: Howard Fertig, 1969. First published 1908, this work consists of a series of lectures which the author delivered at the University of Oxford. Provides a detailed view of Germany in the thirteenth, fourteenth, and fifteenth centuries.

J. David Lawrence

JULES MAZARIN

Born: July 14, 1602; Pescina, Papal States
Died: March 9, 1661; Vincennes, France
Areas of Achievement: Government, politics, and patronage of the arts
Contribution: Mazarin played a central role in stabilizing the French monarchy and laying the political foundations for French absolutism in the critical period between 1643 and 1661. Mazarin's patronage of the arts and letters was extravagant, and he exercised profound influence in shaping the foundations of modern French art, music, and drama.

Early Life

Jules Mazarin was born on July 14, 1602, at Pescina in the Abbruzi region of central Italy. The oldest son of a minor government official, he received his early education from the Jesuits in Rome. From 1622 to 1624, he studied law at Alcalá in Spain. In 1624, Mazarin became a captain in a papal regiment. In 1626, he took up the position as secretary to G. F. Sacchetti, who received an appointment two years later as papal nuncio to the Spanish viceroy of Milan. Continuing his service in Milan under Sacchetti's successor, Cardinal Antonio Barberini, Mazarin undertook his first important mission as a diplomat in 1630, when he carried out negotiations with the French minister Cardinal de Richelieu at Lyons. In October, 1630, as the Spanish forces besieging the French at Casale prepared to attack, Mazarin boldly rode through the Spanish lines shouting "Peace!" as though hostilities had been suspended. In the resulting talks, he persuaded the Spanish to call off their attack.

Rewarded for his daring diplomacy with a canonry (a minor ecclesiatical office not requiring holy orders), Mazarin's star was clearly on the rise. From 1632 to 1634, Pope Urban VIII entrusted Mazarin with a series of special diplomatic missions and in 1634 named him special nuncio to France. Once in France, Mazarin took every opportunity to acquaint himself with the workings of the French government, and while he failed to prevent France from declaring war on Spain in 1635, his services were so valued that he was soon acting as France's unofficial ambassador in Rome. Mazarin received France's nomination for the cardinalate in 1636, but the Spanish faction in Rome blocked his hopes for the honor. Officially entering France's service in December, 1639, Mazarin began a career that would bring him to the heights of power and wealth in only a few short years.

Life's Work

Entering Richelieu's diplomatic entourage, Mazarin immediately became the French plenipotentiary at the peace talks with the Habsburgs. At that point in the Thirty Years' War, neither side saw any advantage to immediate peace and the talks came to nothing. After undertaking several additional diplomatic missions, he was created cardinal in December, 1641. A trusted adviser to Richelieu, Mazarin's scope of political activity expanded when he assisted in dealing with the conspiracy of *Cinq-Mars*. Strongly recommended to the king, Mazarin joined Louis XIII's council immediately after Richelieu's death in December, 1642. Following the king's own death six months later (May 18, 1643), Mazarin joined the regency council formed to govern in the name of the five-year-old Louis XIV. Within days, however, the Queen Mother, Anne of Austria, had disbanded the council, claimed the regency for herself, and named Mazarin her principal minister. From that point until Mazarin's death in 1661, Mazarin and Anne of Austria ruled France—in Louis' name until 1651, when he declared his majority, with the king's authority thereafter.

Historians have devoted much attention to the relationship between Mazarin and Anne of Austria, especially over the question of a secret marriage. Such a liaison was not inconceivable (Mazarin never took the vows of the priesthood) but if known would have proved problematic and extremely damaging. No known documents support the notion of the marriage, but to concentrate exclusively on such legal formalities is to miscast the historical questions concerning their relationship. They never lived as man and wife, but they shared an intimacy and a convergence of interests so close as to mark their union as extraordinarily personal. Moreover, Mazarin formed an extremely paternalistic bond with Louis, Anne's son. For his part, the young king clearly responded to Mazarin as a son would to a father.

Mazarin became Richelieu's successor as France's principal minister, but his tenure in that position was marked by circumstances dramatically different from those Richelieu had enjoyed. First, he served a regency government that had to defend itself from enemies among the highest nobility, several of whom enjoyed claims to the regency at least as strong as Anne's. Second, Mazarin's Italian birth and speech marked him as a foreigner, and he did nothing to diminish the French tendency toward xenophobia as he brought numerous members of his extended family to France to arrange marriages or place them in political offices. Indeed, Mazarin's nepotism and his persistence in pursuing advantageous marriages for his many nieces became legendary. Third, as the French involvement in the Thirty Years' War deepened and as the fighting dragged on year after year, the people of France became increasingly restive under the extraordinary tax burdens Mazarin and Anne imposed.

Following the first outbreak of opposition among the *parlementaires* (judges and lawyers of the Paris law court) and the Parisian bourgeoisie in mid-1648, Mazarin and Anne pressed the military commanders in the field to provide a quick resolution to the war. The Great Condé, a prince of the blood, provided that victory at Lens in August, 1648, and with Condé's victory all the major belligerents, except France and Spain, arrived at terms in a series of treaties that has come to be known as the Peace of Westphalia. Although the specifically French-Spanish conflict dragged on for another ten years, the peace of 1648 marked a reduction in hostilities that allowed Mazarin and Anne to turn their attention to subduing the *parlementaires*. Supported by Condé's troops, Mazarin and Anne instituted a reversal of earlier concessions to the Paris opposition. This move led to the first war of the Fronde (January to March, 1649), which pitted the City of Paris against a coalition headed by Mazarin, Anne, and Condé. Quickly victorious in quelling the Fronde of the *parlementaires*, Condé sought higher positions for himself and for his entourage.

Frictions with Anne and Mazarin finally led Condé to declare a second Fronde against them. This second prince's Fronde lasted from January, 1650, until February, 1651, only to be succeeded by the third Fronde (December, 1651, to February, 1653), once again led by Condé. In the second Fronde, the battle was for the regency over Louis XIV, and the basis for that war ended with Louis' premature declaration of his majority in September, 1651. With the third Fronde, Condé had lost any claim to legality for his actions and the fighting ended only with his military defeat and a formal charge of treason against him. From 1653, until the Treaty of the Pyrenees (1659) put an end to war (and gave reinstatement to his title and lands in France), Condé fought in Spain's service.

The three Fronde and Condé's treason pointed up the weakness of the French monarchy. Twice during the Fronde, Mazarin had been forced to flee into exile in the Germanies to escape not only the *frondeurs* but also the wrath of factions loyal to the monarchy. Following the Fronde, Mazarin devoted all of his energy to rebuilding the monarchy's political foundations. Among his more important acts, the reestablishment of the royal commissioners (intendants) in the provinces and his gathering together of supporting ministers proved to have the most enduring consequences. Later formalized under Louis XIV and Colbert, the system of intendants furnished the basic administrative mechanism for royal government until the Revolution. In that sense, Mazarin's reforms following the Fronde marked the end of the traditional feudal form of the French monarchy. The feudal nobility retained its titles and status, but following the establishment of the intendancies the monarchy moved quickly toward a centralized, bureaucratic administration.

In bringing together his own circle of advisers, Mazarin also selected and trained the ministers who were to dominate the first half of Louis' personal reign: François-Michel Le Tellier, Hugues de Lionne, Jean-Baptiste Colbert, and the ill-fated Nicolas Fouquet. Many have noted the brilliance of these ministers and have credited Mazarin with much of the success of Louis' early personal reign. Such a claim can have only limited value, but it is borne out to some degree through comparisons drawn between the successes of Le Tellier, Lionne, and Colbert and the lackluster performances common among Louis' later ministers. Certainly, Mazarin had a talent for selecting and preparing his favorites for political service.

During his last years, Mazarin was preoccupied with achieving an advantageous peace with Spain and arranging the king's marriage. He succeeded in both these tasks at the same time, making Louis' marriage to Philip IV's eldest daughter Marie-Thérèse one of the terms included in the Treaty of the Pyrenees. The marriage posed a serious obstacle to the negotiations, since Philip insisted on protecting the Spanish inheritance from the possibility of its falling into Bourbon hands. In what was perhaps his greatest diplomatic victory, Mazarin persuaded Philip to agree to an extraordinarily large dowry (500,000 gold ecus) as the price for Louis' renunciation of all claims to the Spanish crown. Mazarin saw clearly that Spain would never be able to make the payments on this astronomical sum, which was scheduled to be paid in installments. He thus laid the basis for later French claims (and ultimate Bourbon succession) to the Spanish throne.

Throughout his service to France, Mazarin proved himself to be an avid patron of the arts and letters. His most noteworthy accomplishments in this regard are found in his devotion to his library and his patronage of the Academy of Painting and Sculpture, which he founded in 1648. After his library had been broken up and sold by his enemies during the Fronde, he patiently reassembled the collection during the late 1650's. Following his death, his library formed the basis for the first of the great royal collections, and his endowments established the College of the Four Nations, an educational institution established for the king's non-French subjects. His *Hôtel* in Paris houses the Institut de France, and his library serves as the core of that institution's collections.

Mazarin died of cancer at the château of Vincennes on March 9, 1661. Popular hostility toward the cardinal minister had never abated. He was the continuing target of scurrilous lampoons and pamphlets that came to be known as *mazarinades*. Nevertheless, he enjoyed Louis' steadfast support to the end, and when Mazarin willed all of his earthly goods to the king, Louis returned them as a gift in order to demonstrate his confidence in the minister. Clearly, Louis held Mazarin in the very highest regard, and it is certain that so long as Mazarin lived he delayed implementing his plan to take personal responsibility for ruling France. At Mazarin's death, the king did announce that decision, and in that sense Mazarin's passing marked one of the most significant turning points in the history of France.

Summary

Jules Mazarin stands as the pivotal figure between Cardinal de Richelieu's first policies tending toward absolutism and Louis XIV's implementation of a full-scale, centralized monarchy. Acting as regent and principal minister,

Mazarin steered the monarchy through the perilous years of Louis' minority and early reign. Certainly, his foreign birth and his style of governing contributed to the antagonisms engendered in the Fronde, but any minister who sought to pursue Richelieu's vision of the state would have faced severe difficulties in the France of the 1640's. Given the circumstances he faced in 1643, Mazarin achieved remarkable successes: He pursued war with France's foreign enemies to successful conclusion; he broke the hold of the high nobility over the throne; he avoided financial collapse; and he exercised a guardianship over the young Louis XIV that must be counted as one of the most successful apprenticeships in statecraft ever achieved. Perhaps the best measure of his success is simply to compare the political, social, and economic condition of France at the moment of his rise to power (1643) against conditions at his death in 1661. There is no question that Mazarin deserves major credit for laying the foundation for Louis XIV's France.

Bibliography
Dent, Julian. *Crisis in Finance: Crown, Financiers, and Society in Seventeeth-Century France.* New York: St. Martin's Press, 1973. An important exposition of the financial workings of the seventeenth century French monarchy, this work explains the intricacies of the system Mazarin allowed to develop. Primarily aimed at explaining attempts at reform in the later seventeenth century, Dent's work nevertheless serves as an essential introduction to the realities of Mazarin's ministry.
Friedrich, Carl J. *The Age of the Baroque, 1610-1660.* Edited by William L. Langer. New York: Harper & Row, 1952. With an excellent chapter on France under Richelieu and Mazarin, this work, part of The Rise of Modern Europe series, offers important insights into the politics of absolutism. Friedrich characterizes the early seventeenth century with cultural definitions, and his work makes a strong case for dealing with historical context as the key to understanding Mazarin's political ideas.
Maland, David. *Culture and Society in Seventeenth-Century France.* New York: Charles Scribner's Sons, 1970. The best survey in English treating French high culture and political involvements with patronage. This work places Mazarin and his patronage against the larger backdrop of very rapid developments in art, drama, and literature. Especially valuable for its portrayal of the political implications of patronage.
Ogg, David. *Europe in the Seventeenth Century.* 8th ed. New York: Macmillan, 1960. A heavily political survey, Ogg's work is excellent for placing Mazarin's ministry in larger European perspective. This work is also particularly valuable for its straightforward treatments of the specifically French political chronology under Mazarin.
Ranum, Orest. *Paris in the Age of Absolutism.* New York: John Wiley & Sons, 1968. Ranum traces the cultural, social, and political histories of

Paris from the reign of Henry IV through the third quarter of the seventeenth century. Very good expositions of the history of the Fronde from the Parisian perspective.

Shennan, J. H. *The Parlement of Paris.* Ithaca, N.Y.: Cornell University Press, 1968. Although a survey running from the Middle Ages to the Revolution, the two chapters on the seventeenth century provide excellent material on the basic constitutional issues facing Richelieu and Mazarin. The material on the period of the Fronde is heavily weighted toward discussion of opposition to Mazarin.

Wolf, John B. *Louis XIV.* New York: W. W. Norton, 1968. Particularly valuable for insights into the personal relations between Mazarin, Anne of Austria, and Louis XIV. Wolf's scholarship is authoritative, and this work stands as one of the most widely respected treatments of Louis' reign. The material on Mazarin's policy objectives deserves special notice.

David S. Lux

GIUSEPPE MAZZINI

Born: June 22, 1805; Genoa, Ligurian Republic
Died: March 10, 1872; Pisa, Italy
Areas of Achievement: Philosophy, politics, and government
Contribution: Mazzini was the most influential leader of the Risorgimento—
the Italian national unification movement. His political activities and philosophy were carried beyond Italy and inspired fledgling nationalist and
democratic reform movements throughout the world.

Early Life

Giuseppe Mazzini was born in 1805, the son of a well-to-do Genoese
family. A sickly but precocious child, he could scarcely walk until the age of
six. His mother, Maria Drago, practiced the morally rigorous Catholic doctrine of Jansenism and provided the young Mazzini with Jansenist tutors. His
political education began at home under the influence of his father, Giacomo—a renowned physician and a professor at the University of Genoa.
Mazzini's father, like many educated Italians, had embraced the nationalist
and democratic ideas of the French Revolution. These ideas endured even
after the Napoleonic Wars, when authoritarian rule had been restored to the
various Italian states. Giacomo and other Italian patriots nurtured hopes for
democratic reform, independence from foreign rule, and ultimately a united
Italy.

As a young man, Mazzini was deeply moved by the suffering of others
and was recklessly generous in his charity. He tended to be melancholy,
always dressed in black—as if in mourning—and enjoyed long, solitary
walks. At the University of Genoa, he studied law, but his real interest was
in history and literature. He organized a student group to study censored
books and wrote provocative essays for several literary journals. The Italian
universities in the 1820's were a conduit for subversive political organizations. During his student years, Mazzini became involved with a secret revolutionary society—the Carbonari. The July Revolution of 1830 in France
inspired the Carbonari to plot insurrections in Piedmont and other Italian
states. Government officials uncovered the conspiracy and arrested hundreds
of suspects, including Mazzini. He defended himself successfully in court,
but the Piedmontese authorities forced him into exile. At the age of twenty-
six, he left Genoa for France.

Life's Work

The failure of the Carbonari insurrections during 1830-1831 led Mazzini
to organize his own secret society, Young Italy. Through this group, he
hoped to bring a youthful energy and idealism to the movement for Italian
independence and unification. His sincerity and the quiet strength of his

convictions won for him a devout following. His agents distributed the news-paper *Young Italy* and established affiliated societies throughout the Italian peninsula. In 1833, Mazzini joined with nationalists from other countries to found Young Europe. This organization embodied the aspirations of many European nationalities seeking to break free of the Austrian and Russian empires and to establish their own independent states with democratic in-stitutions. Mazzini's European network of secret societies made him a noto-rious figure. The Austrian government considered him an international ter-rorist, a threat to the entire European order. Yet to the peoples of Europe who chafed under authoritarian rule, he appeared as a symbol of liberty.

The insurrections organized in the 1830's by Mazzini and his followers failed to ignite a popular uprising in Italy. For his subversive activity, he received the death sentence in absentia from a Piedmontese court in 1833. His life in exile took him from France to Switzerland to Great Britain. He traveled like a fugitive—under the constant threat of arrest and imprison-ment. To survive these difficult years in exile, he relied on the loyalty of his followers and the generous financial support from his mother. Once in Lon-don, he devoted his time to writing for popular journals and to publishing his own newspaper. His most notable work during his years in exile was *Doveri dell'uomo* (1860; *The Duties of Man*, 1862). Through his many editorials, essays, commentaries, and correspondence, he shaped and refined his politi-cal philosophy. He became a celebrated figure among intellectuals and re-formers in Great Britain and the United States. At the same time, he gener-ated international sympathy for the Italian cause.

Mazzini based his philosophy on a profound belief in God, in human progress, and in the fundamental unity and cooperation of mankind. The banner of Young Italy best summarized his thought: "Liberty, Equality, Hu-manity, Unity." These words had universal application. For Mazzini, liberty meant the elimination of all despotism, from tyranny in Italy to slavery in the American South. His belief in equality extended to women as well as men, and for this he won the admiration and devotion of many women's rights advocates in Europe and the United States. His faith in humanity was expressed in the Latin epithet: *Vox populi, vox Dei* (the voice of the people is the voice of God). He believed that the Italian unity would be forged through a spontaneous, general uprising of the Italian people. Mazzini's call for unity transcended national boundaries. He envisioned no less than a brotherhood of nations, beginning with a new federation of European states— a United States of Europe—with the new Italy in the vanguard.

Mazzini's religious faith bordered on mysticism. Yet despite his religious convictions and his Catholic education, he had no room for the authority of the pope, either as civil ruler of the Papal States or as the spiritual leader of the Christian world. Although sympathetic to the plight of the working class, he rejected the materialist, atheistic character of socialist philosophy and avoided emphasizing class conflict as the Marxists would later do. Instead, he advocated worker-aid associations and a spirit of cooperation between labor and capital. He sought to extend the Christian ethic from the home to the workplace to the halls of government and spoke more of duties and responsibilities than of rights and privileges.

The popular revolts in Europe during 1848-1849 gave Mazzini the opportunity to return to Italian soil. He arrived in Milan in April, 1848, shortly after the city's heroic five-day uprising against Austrian rule. Despite the generous welcome extended to the exiled patriot, Mazzini represented only one of several political factions vying for leadership. He left Milan after a failed attempt to organize the city's defenses against the returning Austrian army.

His second opportunity to create a new Italy came in November, 1848, when the populace of Rome revolted, drove Pope Pius IX from the city, and established a republican government in the Papal States. Mazzini entered Rome as an elected leader and immediately implemented his reform program. Church lands were confiscated and redistributed to the peasants, church offices became shelters for the homeless, and public works provided labor for the unemployed. The new republic lasted only a few months. In response to the pope's plea for intervention, the French government dispatched an army to central Italy. The French occupied the Papal States and won control of Rome, despite a tenacious, monthlong defense of the city led by Giuseppe Garibaldi. Mazzini, devastated by the turn of events, left Rome and once again went into exile.

Mazzini's direct influence on Italian politics waned after the failed Revolutions of 1848. The work of Italian unification passed to the hands of the Piedmontese prime minister Count Cavour, who preferred international diplomacy to popular uprisings to achieve his goals. Mazzini maintained contacts with republican groups who attempted several unsuccessful, sometimes tragic, insurrections during the 1850's. These failures provoked public criticism even from his supporters. He made several secret trips to Italy and in one instance was arrested and imprisoned briefly near Naples.

Mazzini held stubbornly to his republican principles. Elected to the Italian parliament in 1865, he refused his seat because of the required oath of allegiance to the monarch. He also rejected the general amnesty offered to him by the king in 1871. He spent his last years in Pisa and lived to see Italy unified with Rome as its capital. His political legacy was continued by his followers, many of whom championed further democratic reforms in the parliamentary politics of postunification Italy.

Summary

Giuseppe Mazzini was the international spokesman for Italian unification and the Italian people. Ironically, he knew little of his own country. He spent much of his life in exile and, before 1848, had never traveled in central or southern Italy. Much of his knowledge of Italy came from history texts and secondhand reports from visitors, and he did not have many contacts with working-class Italians. His concept of "the people" was a middle-class intellectual's romanticized notion, far removed from the brutish existence of the Italian peasant.

Mazzini was not a profound philosopher; many of his writings are characterized by vagaries, inconsistencies, and temperamental ramblings. Despite these shortcomings, his life had a mythical, heroic quality, and his political philosophy had universal appeal. He personified the idealism, optimism, and faith in humanity that motivated many nineteenth century reformers in Europe and the United States. Even Indian and Chinese nationalists invoked Mazzini's name in their efforts to create new democratic nations. They all found inspiration in his life and in his thoughts on political freedom, social equality, economic cooperation, and the brotherhood of nations.

Many of Mazzini's ideas seemed unrealistic in his own time, but some had a prophetic ring, and others have become even more relevant in the twentieth century. His hopes for an Italian republic were finally realized in 1946. His proposals for worker associations and a reconciliation between labor and capital proved far more constructive than did Karl Marx's vision of unmitigated class conflict, and his dream of a United States of Europe anticipated the post-World War II movement toward a unified European community.

Bibliography

Griffith, Gwilym O. *Mazzini: Prophet of Modern Europe*. London: Hodder & Stoughton, 1932. The best written of the English biographies, this work offers an uncritical study with emphasis on Mazzini's theology.

Hales, Edward E. Y. *Mazzini and the Secret Societies*. New York: P. J. Kenedy & Sons, 1956. A critical study of Mazzini's early years. Hales highlights the climate of conspiracy to which the young Mazzini was drawn and describes the making of the Mazzini "myth." Contains a helpful annotated bibliography.

Hinkley, Edyth. *Mazzini: The Story of a Great Italian*. Reprint. Port Washington, N.Y.: Kennikat Press, 1970. First published in 1924, this sympathetic biography emphasizes Mazzini's profound religious convictions and the universal character of his philosophy.

King, Bolton. *Mazzini*. London: J. M. Dent, 1902. The first serious English study of Mazzini. King offers a very generous portrayal of Mazzini as a historical agent of political and moral progress. Includes an appendix containing several of Mazzini's letters and a bibliography listing many of Mazzini's writings published in English during the nineteenth century.

Lovett, Clara M. *The Democratic Movement in Italy, 1830-1876*. Cambridge, Mass.: Harvard University Press, 1982. Places Mazzini in the broader context of a complex and diverse democratic political movement.

Mazzini, Giuseppe. *Life and Writings of Joseph Mazzini*. 6 vols. London: Smith, Elder, 1890-1891. A comprehensive collection of Mazzini's writings available in English.

Salvemini, Gaetano. *Mazzini*. Translated by I. M. Rawson. Stanford, Calif.: Stanford University Press, 1956. An English translation of Salvemini's study, originally published in 1905 and revised in 1925. His commentary provides a good, critical introduction to Mazzini's thought and writings but contains very little biographical information.

Michael F. Hembree

LORENZO DE' MEDICI

Born: January 1, 1449; Florence
Died: April 8, 1492; Careggi, near Florence
Areas of Achievement: Banking, finance, government, politics, diplomacy, and literature
Contribution: Florence's Lorenzo de' Medici was the most important statesman in Italy during the latter part of the fifteenth century. Lorenzo was also a noted banker, poet, and patron of the arts. He epitomized the concept of the Renaissance man.

Early Life
Lorenzo de' Medici was born in Florence in 1449. His father, Piero, died at age fifty-three in 1469. Lorenzo's grandfather, Cosimo, building on the accomplishments of his father, Giovanni, had established himself as the most powerful individual in the Florentine Republic. Medici influence resulted in the wealth accumulated through banking activities. Financial abilities were joined to political talents and ambitions, which made them the most formidable nonroyal family in fifteenth century Europe.

The Medicis were not unique. By the 1400's, there were other influential families in Florence whose wealth and power also came from banking and commerce. Although a republic, Florence was not a democracy; political rights came from membership in the various guilds which had evolved in the later Middle Ages. At the apex were a small number of Florentines, and it was this wealthy oligarchy which controlled the government. All offices were constitutionally open to all guild members, but through various techniques it was possible to manipulate the system. In Renaissance Florence, however, life was more than simply wealth and power for their own sakes. Civic responsibilities went together with political ambition; one was expected to provide public buildings, sponsor schools, or be a patron of the arts. Participation in politics was also expected, as the Medicis well understood, and other Florentine families matched them in wealth and ambition.

In addition to his banking and political responsibilities, Piero, Lorenzo's father, was a patron of the sculptor Donatello and the painter Sandro Botticelli. Lorenzo's mother Lucrezia Tornabuoni, was a poet of note. Privately tutored, Lorenzo received a humanistic education through the Latin and Greek classics. Education was not merely intellectual: The body and spirit were equally important. He played the lyre, sang his own songs, and wrote his own verse. He rode well and was an accomplished athlete, and he enjoyed talking to both peasants and popes. Piero arranged for Lorenzo's marriage to Clarice Orsini, from an aristocratic Roman family; political and economic considerations were more important than love. Lorenzo was not handsome, with his dark complexion, irregular features, jutting chin, and misshapen nose which denied him a sense of smell. Yet he had a brilliant mind and a charismatic personality.

Life's Work

Lorenzo was only twenty when Piero died. Given his age, he was reluctant to assume the various political and economic responsibilities, but in fact it was impossible for him not to do so. As he himself noted, it did not bode well for someone of wealth to evade his civic obligations. The same techniques that the Medicis had used to gain influence at the expense of others could equally be used against them; if they wished to maintain their position, they had to participate in the political arena. Not only had Lorenzo been trained by scholars, but also he had been sent upon several diplomatic missions before Piero's death. At that time, modifications were made in the Florentine constitution which assured the continued primacy of the Medici party, both for Lorenzo and for those other oligarchs who had attached their ambitions to the Medici banner. Nevertheless, Florence remained officially a republic and Lorenzo, ostensibly a private citizen.

During Lorenzo's lifetime, the Medici banks continued to be influential throughout Europe, but less so than earlier. Lorenzo was not particularly interested in banking. Over time, the Medicis became relatively less powerful in banking matters as other cities and nations of Europe rose to positions of power. During Lorenzo's era, his resources were occasionally put under pressure and he was accused of manipulating the economy of Florence to the benefit of the Medicis. Lorenzo could argue that his position, unofficial as it was, benefited all Florentines and that he deserved to be recompensed. Given the nature of Florentine politics, it was perhaps impossible to separate Lorenzo's private needs from the republic's welfare.

Other Italian city-states and European nations were accustomed to dealing with the head of the Medici family directly instead of through the official Florentine government. Lorenzo's position of primacy was never officially avowed: He remained merely a citizen, although the most important citizen. While Lorenzo was the unquestioned leader of a banking and merchant oligarchy, he did not always enjoy absolute freedom to commit his city to a particular course of action, freedom such as the hereditary Dukes of Milan or the popes in Rome exercised.

The Medicis had a close relationship with the Kings of France: Louis XI had granted Piero the right to incorporate the three lilies of the French royal house of Valois onto the Medici arms. Lorenzo realized, however, that it was necessary to keep that large kingdom's military might out of Italy. The peninsula was divided by various ministates and their rivalries. To the south lay the Papal States and the Kingdom of Naples, and to the east, the Republic of Venice. To balance those powers, the Medicis relied upon an alliance with the Dukes of Milan.

In 1471, Francesco della Rovere ascended the papal throne as Pope Sixtus IV. Intitially, the relationship between Sixtus and Lorenzo was cordial, but within a few years it soured. The pope had a large family to support, and Lorenzo feared that those needs threatened the security of Florence and of the Medicis. For several decades, the Medicis has been the papal bankers, a connection which was beneficial to both parties, but when Sixtus requested a loan to purchase Imola for one of his nephews, a city which Lorenzo considered to be within the Florentine sphere of influence, Lorenzo refused. Sixtus ended the papal connection with the Medici bank and turned to another Florentine banking family, the Pazzis.

The Pazzis, though connected to the Medicis through marriage, were political and economic rivals. In addition to the Imola loan, other issues combined which led to a plot, known as the Pazzi conspiracy, to remove the Medicis from power. Sixtus stated that while he wished the Medicis to be gone, he did not want it accomplished by murder. It is doubtful, however, that Sixtus truly believed that such an end could be attained without violence. The other conspirators turned to assassination.

The conspirators struck on a Sunday in April, 1477, during the High Mass in the cathedral of Florence. They were partially successful: Giuliano, Lorenzo's brother, was stabbed to death. Lorenzo, however, though injured, survived. Florence rallied to Lorenzo. Most of the conspirators, including leading members of the Pazzi family, were quickly seized and brutally executed. Sixtus responded by accusing Lorenzo and Florence of murder. Lorenzo was excommunicated from the Church, and Florence was placed under an interdict. Because of the animosity toward Sixtus, however, the churches of Florence remained open.

Sixtus also declared war on Florence. As a result of the recent assassination of its duke, Galeazzo Maria Sforza, Milan was of no assistance to Florence, and with King Ferrante of Naples allied to the Papacy, with an economic downturn in part caused by the military situation, and with the onset of plague, life in Florence soon became very difficult. Finally, in an act of calculated courage, Lorenzo journeyed to Naples and placed himself in the hands of Ferrante. Although he had some indication that Naples might be willing to agree to a treaty with Florence, Lorenzo's action was still a gamble. A treaty was agreed to, and Lorenzo was returned to Florence as a hero.

Afterward, Lorenzo took an even greater interest in public affairs. His power in Florence increased, although constitutionally he was still only a private citizen. In 1484, Sixtus died, and his successor, Innocent VIII, developed a close relationship with Lorenzo, sealed with the marriage of one of Lorenzo's daughters to one of Innocent's sons. Lorenzo also concerned himself with the relations of the other Italian states, and until his death major conflict was avoided. To what degree his policies were responsible for peace is impossible to ascertain, but Lorenzo received the credit. As Scipio Ammirato noted, Florence

> remained free of all troubles, to the great reputation of Lorenzo. The Italian princes also enjoyed peace, so that, with everything quiet beyond her frontier and with no disturbances at home, Florence . . . gave herself up to the arts and pleasures of peace.

The arts and pleasures of peace were an integral part of Lorenzo's life and character. He arranged festivals and took part in jousts. He was a patron as well as a colleague of various writers and artists, including Michelangelo. He himself was a poet of considerable ability and a supporter of the Universities of Florence and Pisa. Suitably, on his deathbed, one of his last statements was to express regret that he was not going to live to assist in completing a friend's library.

Summary

Lorenzo de' Medici died in the spring of 1492 at Careggi, one of the family's villas outside Florence. Inheriting his father's medical maladies, Lorenzo in his last years suffered increasingly from gout and other illnesses. He was only forty-three. Shortly before his death, Lorenzo received Girolamo Savonarola, a Dominican monk who had recently become a notable figure in Florentine life for his vehement condemnations of Renaissance society in general and Lorenzo in particular. Within two years, Savonarola became the ruler of Florence. Lorenzo's son, Piero, had neither his father's abilities nor his luck, and the Medicis were forced into exile.

Yet Medici wealth and influence were not extinguished. Just before Lorenzo's death, one of his sons, Giovanni, age sixteen, had become a cardinal in the Catholic church. In 1512, the Medicis returned to Florence from exile, and in the following year Giovanni was elected pope as Leo X. He died in 1521, and after a brief hiatus his cousin, Giulio, the illegitimate son of Lorenzo's brother, ascended the papal throne as Clement VII. In 1533, Clement performed the marriage of Catherine de Médicis to the son of King Francis I of France. She became one of the most powerful women of the sixteenth century. In Florence, the Medicis became hereditary dukes. The republic was over.

Lorenzo was a controversial figure in his own era and has remained so ever since. His status is suggested by the epithet that frequently accompanies his name: Il Magnifico (the Magnificent). During his era that appellation was used as an honorary title for various Florentine officials; in time, however, it was applied only to Lorenzo. Fifteenth century Florence epitomizes the civilization of the Renaissance, and Lorenzo the Magnificent remains inseparable from the history of that civilization and that city. His reputation has fluctuated; he has been praised for qualities he perhaps did not possess, and he has been condemned for activities which were not within his responsibility. One of his critics was his fellow Florentine, the historian Francesco Guicciardini, an avid republican in ideology. Still, even Guicciardini had to admit that if Florence was not free under Lorenzo, "it would have been impossible for it to have had a better or more pleasing tyrant."

Bibliography

Ady, Cecilia M. *Lorenzo dei Medici and Renaissance Italy.* London: English Universities Press, 1955. There has been no major biography of Lorenzo in English in recent decades; Ady's work is the most satisfactory substitute.

Hale, J. R. *Florence and the Medici: The Pattern of Control.* London: Thames & Hudson, 1977. This study of the Medicis traces the family from its earliest days through its decline in the eighteenth century. Hale places Lorenzo within the overall context of Florentine politics.

Hibbert, Christopher. *The House of the Medici: Its Rise and Fall.* New York: William Morrow, 1975. The author is a prominent narrative historian who has written many works on English and Italian subjects. A well-written survey of the Medicis.

Rowdon, Maurice. *Lorenzo the Magnificent.* Chicago: Henry Regnery, 1974. This brief work traces the story of the Medicis through the fifteenth century to Lorenzo's death in 1492. The author tells the tale adequately and is especially helpful on the broad economic issues affecting the Medicis. Includes many illustrations.

Williamson, Hugh Ross. *Lorenzo the Magnificent.* New York: G. P. Putnam's Sons, 1974. This volume is similar to Rowdon's work although somewhat more extensive. Like Rowdon, Williamson recites the history of Lorenzo and his family. Includes illustrations.

Eugene S. Larson

1538

MEHMED II

Born: March 30, 1432; Adrianople, Ottoman Empire
Died: May 3, 1481; Hunkârçayırı, Ottoman Empire
Areas of Achievement: Government and the military
Contribution: As Sultan of the Ottoman Empire, Mehmed II commanded armies that captured Constantinople, and under his rule control of the Balkans and Anatolia in substantial portions was extended as the Ottoman state became one of the most important powers of early modern times.

Early Life
Although it is known that, as a prince of the Ottoman Empire, Mehmed was the son of Murad II, the sixth sultan, the identity of the boy's mother has not been established with certainty. It would appear that she was one of the sultan's slave girls, and she may have been from a non-Muslim family in the Balkans. Mehmed was born on March 30, 1432, in Adrianople, the Ottoman capital of that time. At about the age of two, he was sent to a special court at Amasya, in north central Anatolia; later, he was taken to Manisa, near Izmir, where he was educated by tutors who subsequently gained distinction in the academic profession or as government ministers.

For reasons that still remain obscure, and notwithstanding Ottoman reverses of this period during fighting in Europe, in August, 1444, Murad abdicated in favor of Mehmed. A coalition of Christian powers had been formed, under the leadership of Hungary's János Hunyadi, which was also promoted by the Byzantine Empire, the Papacy, and Venice, in an effort to present a common front against the Ottoman state. After attending to conflicts in Asia, and even with his son nominally ruler, Murad returned at the head of a large army, and a major defeat was inflicted upon their opponents at Varna, in Bulgaria, on November 10, 1444. While this major battle served notice to European governments that the Ottomans could not easily be dislodged from the Balkans, other engagements followed; though the position of George Branković, the despot of Serbia, remained problematical, the renowned Skanderbeg (George Kastrioti) of Albania had commenced resistance to the Ottomans. In May, 1446, Murad returned to the throne in the wake of a janissary revolt. Another important battle was fought in October, 1448, at Kosovo in Serbia; while Murad commanded Ottoman troops, Mehmed also took part in actual fighting as Hungarian and other armies were put to flight.

For Mehmed, family concerns arose at a relatively early age. His first son, who later was to become his successor as Bayezid II, was born to him by Gülbahar, a slave girl, in December, 1447, or January, 1448. In 1450, Mehmed's second and favorite son, Mustafa, was born, though the identity of the mother remains unclear. Subsequently a marriage with a woman from a suitable social station was arranged when Mehmed took Sitt Hatun, from a noted family of central Anatolia, as his wife. Mehmed also became the father of six other children, some of whom were born from liaisons or marriages that were concluded after he came to power. Although during Murad's second reign Mehmed may have continued to regard himself as the rightful sultan, a reconciliation of sorts would appear to have taken place; yet Murad died of apoplexy rather unexpectedly. On February 18, 1451, Mehmed ascended to the throne in Adrianople. While in the past Ottoman rulers, including Murad, had eliminated family members for political reasons, Mehmed had two of his brothers executed and sanctioned the practice of fratricide by which, for nearly two centuries, sultans summarily were to remove potential rivals from any struggle for supreme power.

Life's Work

At the outset of his second reign, Mehmed II attended to a flurry of unrest in Anatolia and stirrings of discontent among the janissaries before turning to military planning, which was centered upon a single consuming ambition. The Byzantine Empire had maintained a prolonged and precarious existence even though Constantinople was surrounded by territories under Ottoman control; by virtue of its double line of walled fortifications and its position at the edge of the Bosporus, the imperial city remained difficult of access to armies in the field. While the Byzantine emperor Constantine IX Palaeologus had threatened to support a different claimant to the Ottoman throne, a trade agreement with Venice had been renewed, at the request of Çandarlı Halil, the grand vizier, and a treaty was negotiated with Hungary; though Halil advised against precipitous action, it had become evident that the beleaguered city could expect little European assistance. Mehmed commenced preliminary operations with the construction of a major fortress north of Constantinople; a sympathetic Hungarian gunsmith known as Urban helped to cast cannon of a size larger than any that previously had been used. In the face of an Ottoman blockade, Byzantine forces received few reinforcements, apart from a Genoese contingent from Chios; some Venetian and Genoese fighting men already had been stationed nearby. The Ottomans possessed an immense numerical advantage, with possibly eighty thousand men under arms, as opposed to about nine thousand defenders.

The siege began on April 6, 1453, and, following repeated bombardments, Mehmed resolved finally to storm the city. On May 29, after some sharp fighting at many points, Ottoman troops entered Constantinople through a gate to the north and subdued their opponents in short order. Apparently Constantine died at this time. For his military prowess, Mehmed acquired the byname *Fatih,* or the Conqueror. The city was pillaged briefly, and some prominent men, including Çandarlı Halil, were executed; afterward, to encourage the restoration and development of the new Ottoman capital, which became known as Istanbul, the sultan allowed many original inhabitants to return to their homes. Further settlers, both Muslims and Christians, were recruited from Asia and Europe. As a mark of his toleration for religious communities within the Ottoman Empire, Mehmed recognized Gennadius II Scholarius, a churchman who had opposed union with the Catholics, as the Greek Orthodox patriarch; a Jewish grand rabbi and an Armenian patriarch also were accepted as representatives of their faiths in Mehmed's capital.

Subsequent military endeavors revealed the broad sweep of Mehmed's ambitions and the extent of Ottoman power on two continents. Although in 1456 Ottoman forces failed to take Belgrade after a siege of six weeks when Hunyadi's forces intervened successfully against them, the Hungarian commander died later that year, and shortly thereafter George Branković of Serbia also died. In 1459, the Ottomans annexed what remained of the southern Slavic area, while in 1463 most of Bosnia was occupied as well. During other expeditions, Ottoman forces captured Athens in 1456, and during the next four years much of the Morea was overrun. Some setbacks which were suffered by Mehmed's armies did not have lasting effects. A campaign into Wallachia to enforce a previous tributary relationship, against the infamous Vlad Țepeș (the Impaler, who was also the historical prototype for the famous horror figure Dracula), resulted in a grisly massacre of Ottoman soldiers. Yet, under pressure from Mehmed, Vlad was deposed in 1462, and when he returned to power much later he met with death in battle.

In Asia Minor, Ottoman forces secured the submission of Trebizond, the last Greek kingdom of the Byzantine era, in 1461. Subsequently a particularly dangerous threat arose when Uzun Hasan, of the Turkmen Ak Koyunlu state that had become established in western Iran, attempted to displace Mehmed's authority in central Anatolia. An entire Ottoman army was mobilized, and, when Mehmed led his troops in person, a convincing victory was obtained at Bashkent near Erzincan, on August 11, 1473. Ottoman control of the area northwest of the Euphrates River thus was consolidated; an important success for Ottoman policy on the northern coast of the Black Sea came in 1475, when the Tatar khanate of the Crimea acknowledged Mehmed's suzerainty. Political complications at several points in the Balkans had led to a prolonged war with Venice, between 1463 and 1479, and during much of his later reign Mehmed was also involved in undertakings of several sorts in Europe. Although the redoubtable Skanderbeg, who was allied with the Venetians, had resisted Ottoman incursions until shortly before his death in 1468, eventually the fortress of Krujë surrendered to Mehmed himself in 1478, and Ottoman forces held most of Albania. In the end, Venice was compelled to make peace on relatively harsh terms. Mehmed evidently was not entirely appeased, and in 1480 an Ottoman army obtained a foothold in Italy by capturing Otranto; a landing at Rhodes, in the eastern Mediterranean, was repelled, however, by the Knights of Saint John.

While Mehmed frequently accompanied his armies during their campaigns, his administrative work brought many reforms, some of which provoked an adverse reaction after his death. His conception of power was along strictly autocratic lines, and often he did not attend meetings of the Divan, or council of state; where he did delegate authority, he exercised some care in maintaining distinctions among offices which were subordinate to his. Mehmed also directed the codification of laws, which were promulgated on his authority and were meant to serve regulatory purposes alongside Koranic law. Fiscal policies were far-reaching but high-handed. Mehmed instituted the sale of private monopolies in essential goods to augment government revenues; some private estates and religious foundations were confiscated as state lands. Commercial relations with other countries were promoted even as Mehmed had customs duties increased. One of the most widely resented of Mehmed's measures, however, was the repeated reduction in the silver content of Ottoman coinage. In other respects, Mehmed has been regarded as having had an urbane and cosmopolitan outlook. He was a patron of literary men, including Persian poets, and he composed a collection of verse in his own right. In addition to supervising the conversion of Byzantium's most famous church into the Hagia Sophia mosque, he left further architectural monuments, of which the Fatih mosque in İstanbul was perhaps the most notable. He had an interest in the visual arts that overcame any religious objections to such forms of representation, and he supported the production of medals and paintings by which his appearance has become known. The most famous portraits of Mehmed, by Sinan Bey, a Turkish artist, and by Gentile Bellini, a Venetian master whom Mehmed commissioned to paint his likeness, show broad, angular features with the eyes set in a stern fixed gaze; a large curved nose was set above thin, taut lips and a small, slightly receding chin. A brown or reddish mustache and full beard suggested somewhat more of an imperious bearing. Sinan's work also depicts Mehmed as having some tendency toward corpulence, which reputedly affected the sultan during his later years. Indeed, when Mehmed died, on May 3, 1481, at a place about fifteen miles east of İstanbul, the effects of gout were cited as a cause; some suspicion has existed, however, that he was poisoned.

Summary

The interpretations that have generally been advanced of Mehmed II's character and aims are of several sorts; while his importance in the expansion of Ottoman power has invariably been acknowledged, some have maintained that he intended essentially to extend his authority over an area roughly corresponding to that of the Byzantine Empire from a much earlier period. It has further been contended, though with some notable exaggerations, that older Byzantine practices served as the model for some of the measures that were implemented during his reign. Other views have emphasized the Turkic elements in his methods of rule and have noted that continuity among Ottoman rulers was stressed in the official court historiography of Mehmed's period. It has been maintained as well that, because primacy with respect to other Islamic states was asserted in many of Mehmed's pronouncements, he regarded his efforts as the fulfillment of aspirations that were at once both religious and political. The conception of Mehmed as a Renaissance ruler who was at home in several cultural milieus, while alluring to certain writers, has been sharply criticized as neglecting the priority he typically assigned to military matters. On the other hand, the notion that Mehmed was unusually cruel and vindictive, or inordinately devoted to conquest as an end in itself, has been challenged by those who would argue, with some justice, that the Ottoman ruler was probably no more severe than other commanders of his age. In all, it would appear that, very much in the way that Ottoman traditions combined political and cultural elements from several sources, the achievements of Mehmed may have arisen from aims and ideas that reflected his various purposes.

Bibliography
Babinger, Franz Carl Heinrich. *Mehmed the Conqueror and His Time.* Edited by William C. Hickman. Translated by Ralph Manheim. Princeton, N.J.: Princeton University Press, 1978. This bulky and imposing work by an important modern scholar is by far the most significant Western study of Mehmed's statecraft. Although some specialists have found Babinger's interpretations idiosyncratic and biased, and the original German edition of 1953 appeared without notes or scholary apparatuses, the English translation provides updated references that summarize scholarly views and research findings.
Ducas. *Decline and Fall of Byzantium to the Ottoman Turks.* Translated by Harry J. Magoulias. Detroit: Wayne State University Press, 1975. A well-informed Greek writer produced this chronicle of which the most useful and detailed portions deal with events from the time of Murad until 1462. In spite of a tendency to criticize Mehmed harshly, the author provides some shrewd insights about political developments of this period.
Gueriguian, John L. "Amirdovlat, Mehmed II, and the Nascent Armenian Community of Constantinople." *Armenian Review* 39, no. 2 (1986): 27-48. Some interesting and little-known facts about one of Mehmed's personal physicians are presented here alongside speculation about Mehmed's physical and psychological condition.
Inalcik, Halil. "Mehmed the Conqueror (1432-1481) and His Time." *Speculum* 35 (1960): 408-427. Shortcomings and lacunae in the original edition

of Babinger's work are discussed in this acute, sometimes caustic, article.
_____. "The Policy of Mehmed II Toward the Greek Population of Istanbul and the Byzantine Buildings of the City." *Dumbarton Oaks Papers* 23/24 (1969/1970): 231-249. In a solid scholarly study, the author demonstrates the extent of Mehmed's efforts to promote recovery and urban development after the siege of 1453.

Kritoboulos. *History of Mehmed the Conqueror.* Translated by Charles T. Riggs. Princeton, N.J.: Princeton University Press, 1954. The divided sympathies of a Greek writer who became the Governor of Imbros under Mehmed are expressed in this narration of events from 1451 until 1467. The work was dedicated to Mehmed and praises him highly in places, but delivers lamentations for the fate of peoples in formerly Byzantine lands.

Michałowicz, Konstanty. *Memoirs of a Janissary.* Translated by Benjamin Stolz. Ann Arbor: Department of Slavic Languages and Literatures, University of Michigan, 1975. The experiences of a Southern Slav who was taken prisoner and accompanied Mehmed's armies were set down in this account, which is of particular value for the period between the fall of Constantinople and the Bosnian campaign of 1463. Text transcribed from a Czech manuscript, with the translation on facing pages.

Phrantzes, Georgios. *The Fall of the Byzantine Empire.* Translated by Marios Philippides. Amherst: University of Massachusetts Press, 1980. In this autobiographical chronicle by a well-placed Greek observer, who was captured briefly and suffered family losses after the siege of Constantinople, personal impressions are provided of events through 1477.

Raby, Julian. "Pride and Prejudice: Mehmed the Conqueror and the Italian Portrait Medal." *Studies in the History of Art* 21 (1987): 171-194. A noted art historian herein provides some interesting evidence, drawn partly from Venetian archives, about Mehmed's interest in portraiture during various stages of his career.

Runciman, Steven. *The Fall of Constantinople, 1453.* Cambridge: Cambridge University Press, 1965. This study, by a distinguished Byzantinist, is probably the standard work in English on the famous siege; attention to scholarly detail does not impede the retelling of enthralling and tragic episodes from the last days of the city's resistance to the Ottomans.

Tursun Beg. *The History of Mehmed the Conqueror.* Edited and translated by Halil Inalcik and Rhoads Murphey. Chicago: Bibliotheca Islamica, 1978. The work of an important Ottoman writer is presented here in a summary translation followed by a facsimile of an original Turkish manuscript. The author, who participated in a number of Mehmed's campaigns, comments in places on the harsher qualities of Mehmed's character in an account which was meant partly as instruction for Mehmed's successor.

J. R. Broadus

PHILIPP MELANCHTHON

Born: February 16, 1497; Bretten, Baden
Died: April 19, 1560; Wittenberg
Areas of Achievement: Religion, theology, and education
Contribution: Melanchthon was a German Humanist scholar who became a
close associate of Martin Luther in the Protestant Reformation. Known for
his warm evangelical piety and his irenic, ecumenical spirit, he was the
author of the Augsburg Confession of 1530, basically a summary of Luther's teachings, which remains as the fundamental confessional platform
of worldwide Lutheranism. Melanchthon also is credited with having established the German school system.

Early Life
Philipp Melanchthon was born in the village of Bretten in the German
Rhineland, some twenty miles south of Heidelberg, on February 16, 1497.
His real name was Philipp Schwartzerd; his father, Georg Schwartzerd, was
an armorer under the Palatinate princes. His mother, Barbara Reuter, was a
niece of the great Humanist and Hebrew scholar Johannes Reuchlin, whose
influence over Philipp can be seen not only in his early studies but also in his
Humanist leanings.

The eldest of five children, Philipp proved himself something of a child
prodigy under the direction of his great-uncle Reuchlin, at that time regarded
as the best Greek and Hebrew scholar in Germany. It was Reuchlin who first
recommended Johann Unger of Pforzheim as Philipp's private tutor and who
later caused him to enroll in the Pforzheim Latin school, one of the most
celebrated in the Palatinate. At Pforzheim, Philipp came under the influence
of Georg Simler and John Hiltebrant, both classicists and excellent scholars
of Latin, Hebrew, and Greek. It was there that Reuchlin, in recognition of
Philipp's accomplishments in the Greek classics, followed a contemporary
custom and declared that such a brilliant young man should no longer be
known by the humble name Schwartzerd (meaning "black earth") but should
henceforth be called by its Greek equivalent—"Melanchthon."

In October, 1509, Melanchthon followed the advice of Reuchlin and Simler and enrolled in the University of Heidelberg. During his years at Heidelberg, he seems to have pursued his studies for the most part by himself,
preferring the Greek classics, such as the orations of Cicero and Demos-
thenes, to the medieval Scholastic orientation of Heidelberg. There, he also
studied the writings of Rodolphus Agricola and the warm devotional sermons
of Johann Geiler von Kaysersberg.

In 1511, Melanchthon, not yet fifteen years of age, was awarded the
bachelor of arts degree from Heidelberg. Yet after another year of devoted
study of Scholastic philosophy, his application for the master of arts degree

was denied, primarily because of his youth and boyish appearance. Small for his age, Melanchthon had a somewhat shy and awkward manner about him and suffered from attacks of fever from time to time. Later portraits of him reveal a more serious demeanor, a thoughtful face marked by a very high forehead, penetrating eyes, and an aquiline, craggy nose. When lecturing on a topic of particular interest, he is said to have visibly changed in appearance, with his voice becoming clear and forceful, his actions animated, and his large blue eyes sparkling with delight and excitement.

In the fall of 1512, again at the advice of Reuchlin, Melanchthon left Heidelberg and moved south to Tübingen, Reuchlin's own university, where he would reside as a student and later as professor for the next six years. A much newer university than Heidelberg, Tübingen had been founded in 1477 and was less under the influence of medieval Scholastic philosophy. At Tübingen, Melanchthon heard lectures on Aristotle that fascinated him for years. There, he came under the influence of the great Desiderius Erasmus, as well as certain "reformers before the Reformation," such as John Wessel. He also began serious study of Hebrew and Latin. In 1514, he was awarded the master of arts degree, the first among eleven in his class. He then became a tutor at the university and, two years later, professor of rhetoric and history. During his Tübingen years, he published translations of Plutarch, Pythagoras, Agricola, and Terence Lucidas, as well as a Greek grammar and a handbook of general history, and began major works on Aristotle and Aratus. Melanchthon and his work were highly praised by Erasmus, and at Tübingen he became widely recognized as the finest humanistic scholar in Germany.

Life's Work

In the autumn of 1518, at the age of twenty-one, Melanchthon was called to become professor of Greek at the University of Wittenberg, once again largely as a result of the highest recommendation of his kinsman Reuchlin. At Wittenberg, he would spend the rest of his career; marry and rear a family; come under the powerful influence of Martin Luther, his closest friend for nearly thirty years; and become intimately involved in the Protestant Reformation and the education of Germany's youth. Only four days after he arrived in Wittenberg, on August 29, 1518, Melanchthon delivered a lecture on the improvement of studies, in which he called for fresh study not only of the Latin and Greek classics but also of Hebrew and the Bible. This was an indication of his early interest in education, which would bear fruit in later years.

Melanchthon began his own lectures in Wittenberg with Homer and the Epistle to Titus. Luther was so inspired by Melanchthon's lectures, some of which attracted as many as two thousand persons, including professors, ministers, and various dignitaries as well as students, that he made much more rapid progress in his translation of Scripture into German than he had made

before. Melanchthon assisted Luther in collating the various Greek versions
and revising some of his translations.

In November, 1520, Melanchthon married Katharine Krapp, daughter of
the Wittenberg burgomaster, apparently primarily because Luther had concluded that it was time for Melanchthon to take a wife. Four children were
born of this apparently happy union, which lasted thirty-seven years.

Melanchthon was first drawn into the Reformation controversies when he
accompanied Luther and others to Leipzig in June and July of 1519 for the
Leipzig Disputation between Luther and Andreas Carlstadt on one side and
Johann Eck of Ingolstadt on the other. Melanchthon attended as a spectator
but was shortly afterward attacked by Eck for aiding Luther and Carlstadt.
Melanchthon replied to Eck in a brief treatise, in which he supported Luther's argument on the supreme authority of Scripture and denied the authority of the Church Fathers on whom Eck had relied so heavily in Leipzig.
From that point onward, Melanchthon's die was cast with the Protestant
Reformers. Shortly thereafter, at Luther's insistence, Melanchthon was made
lecturer in theology in addition to his professorship in Greek. The degree
bachelor of divinity was conferred upon him; it was the only theological
degree he ever accepted.

In 1521, during Luther's confinement in Wartburg, Melanchthon became
the main leader of the Reformation in Wittenberg. At that time, he had
chosen Paul's Epistle to the Romans as the subject for his lectures and had
compiled from that letter a series of classified statements of scriptural truths
that were to become one of the most influential manuals of Protestant theology. He wrote them primarily for his own personal use and called these
statements "common places," or *Loci communes rerum theologicarum* (1521;
The Loci Communes, 1944), following a phrase of Cicero. At the encouragement of others, he allowed them to be published, and this document almost
immediately established him in the theological forefront of the Reformation.
Luther once even praised *The Loci Communes* as worthy of a place in the
canon of Scripture.

For most of the remainder of his career, Melanchthon was greatly occupied with theological controversy and debate, largely in defense of Luther
against charges brought by the Roman Catholics. He insisted that Luther was
accused of heresy not because of any departure from Scripture but because
he opposed the universities, the Fathers, and the councils of the Church in
their theological errors. During Luther's absence from Wittenberg in 1521
and 1522, a much more radical group of Reformers took control, primarily
under the leadership of Carlstadt. Ecclesiastical vestments were abolished;
persons were admitted to communion without confession or repentance; and
pastoral oversight was neglected, as were hospitals and prisons. Melanchthon, the scholar, opposed such radical changes but was powerless to check
them until Luther's return in March, 1522. After he had restored some sem-

blance of order to the Reformation in Wittenberg, Luther, with Melanchthon's encouragement, completed his translation of the entire Bible into German, in many· ways his own most important work and the one which introduced the Reformation to the masses.

After the First Diet of Speier in 1526, Melanchthon was one of those commissioned to visit the various reformed states and issue regulations for the churches. This resulted in the publication, in 1528, of his *Unterricht der Visitatorn* (visitation articles), which contained not only a statement of evangelical Protestant theology but also an outline of education for the elementary grades. This was shortly thereafter enacted into law, and, as a result, Germany had the first real Protestant public school system, one which was soon copied far and wide. Hundreds of teachers were also trained in Melanchthon's methods and thousands of students instructed by his textbooks. He encouraged the establishment of universities and revised dozens of schools' curricula. All of this earned for him the title "Preceptor of Germany." His influence on German education can hardly be overstated.

A man of moderation and peace, Melanchthon was also present at the Second Diet of Speier, when the protest, from which the name "Protestant" originated, was lodged against the Roman Catholic majority in 1529. He was the leading representative of Protestant theology at the Diet of Augsburg in 1530 and the author of the Augsburg Confession of 1530. This document remains the basic confessional statement of worldwide Lutheranism, which has influenced nearly every subsequent major Protestant creed. Melanchthon tried very hard to be conciliatory in the Augsburg Confession without sacrificing important convictions. He met with papal representatives amid frequent charges of collaboration in an effort to reconcile Protestant-Roman Catholic differences. Eventually, he wrote a spirited defense of the Augsburg Confession entitled *Apologie der Confession aus dem Latin verdeudschet* (1531), or the *Apology*, also generally recognized as one of the best writings of the Reformation.

Melanchthon staunchly held the middle ground between more radical Reformers and the Roman Catholic theologians. He defended the Reformation doctrines of justification by faith and the authority of the Scriptures; yet for the sake of unity he was willing to accept a modified form of the Papacy. After Luther's death in 1546, Melanchthon's later years were marked by poor physical health and major theological disputes, especially the so-called *Adiaphoristic* controversy and arguments concerning the role of humans in salvation.

Adiaphora, religious beliefs and practices of indifference, were areas where flexibility or compromise may be necessary. Melanchthon, however, was unfairly accused of including among the *Adiaphora* such essentials to the Protestant cause as justification by faith. He was, indeed, willing to recognize the necessity of good works for salvation, not as in any way meriting God's favor but as the inevitable fruits of faith. Melanchthon eventually also seems to have rejected the doctrine of predestination, which he earlier shared with Luther. In the *Apology* of 1531, he represented the mercy of God as extended to all; yet he insisted that God draws to Himself only those who are willing to turn to Him. Humans thus have an important role in the process of salvation, although a secondary one of response to God's initiative in the written and preached Word. Melanchthon was unjustly accused of the heresy of Pelagianism as a result of his theological views, and his influence declined during his lifetime. It is only in modern times that his contributions have come to be fully appreciated.

Summary

Philipp Melanchthon is a prominent example of an outstanding theologian and scholar whose works have been neglected. His was a melding of the twin influences of the Renaissance and the Reformation. His services to educational reform in Germany, as well as to classical scholarship and Humanism, were outstanding, but it was as a theologian that he excelled. Throughout his lifetime, he tried to be a reconciler, and his influence was consistently thrown on the side of moderation and peace. Yet he was misunderstood and unappreciated by many of those on both sides of the great theological controversies of his age.

Bibliography

Hildebrandt, Franz. *Melanchthon: Alien or Ally?* Cambridge: Cambridge University Press, 1946. An exploration of the complex relationship between Luther and Melanchthon, this volume is primarily an examination of the five main "concessions" said to have been made by Melanchthon to elements outside the inner circle of Protestant evangelicals. Particularly valuable in highlighting some of the most important doctrinal differences between Luther and Melanchthon.

Manschreck, Clyde L. *Melanchthon: The Quiet Reformer.* New York: Abingdon Press, 1958. One of the most important works on Melanchthon currently available in English. Basically a historical approach. Manschreck also gives a sympathetic and lively description of the doctrinal issues that preoccupied so much of Melanchthon's career. The volume is copiously documented and indexed, with a variety of interesting illustrations.

Melanchthon, Philipp. *Melanchthon on Christian Doctrine: Loci Communes, 1555.* Edited and translated by Clyde L. Manschreck. New York: Oxford University Press, 1965. The first translation into English of the 1555 (final) edition of *The Loci Communes*, this volume is translated and edited by the English-speaking world's foremost Melanchthon scholar. Contains a valuable preface by Manschreck and an introduction by Hans Engelland, a German Melanchthon scholar. Good bibliography and index.

Richard, James W. *Philip Melanchthon: The Protestant Preceptor of Germany, 1497-1560.* New York: G. P. Putnam's Sons, 1898. One of the best nineteenth century biographies of Melanchthon available in English. Richard includes many quotations from Melanchthon's letters and other writings in this volume. Carefully documented and includes a helpful index and many illustrations.

Vajta, Vilmos, ed. *Luther and Melanchthon in the History and Theology of the Reformation.* Philadelphia: Muhlenberg Press, 1961. A series of addresses on the relationship between Luther and Melanchthon delivered before the Luther Research Congress. Most are in German, but among the English contributions of particular interest are "Luther and Melanchthon" by Wilhelm Pauck, in which the inseparability of the two theologians' works is clearly demonstrated, and "Melanchthon in America" by Theodore G. Tappert, in which the revival of interest in Melanchthon during the first half of the nineteenth century in the United States is explored.

Wilson, George. *Philip Melanchthon: 1497-1560.* London: Religious Tract Society, 1897. Published after the death of its author, this brief biographical work is a more personal memoir than the volumes by Manschreck and Richard. Wilson had planned a much more complete work on Melanchthon than this but did not live to finish it.

C. Fitzhugh Spragins

GREGOR JOHANN MENDEL

Born: July 22, 1822; Heinzendorf, Austria
Died: January 6, 1884; Brno, Austria
Area of Achievement: Genetics
Contribution: Mendel demonstrated the rules governing genetic inheritance
with his statistical approach to experiments in plant hybridization.

Early Life

Gregor Johann Mendel's father, Anton, was a peasant and his mother the
daughter of a village gardener. They had five children. Two of Mendel's
sisters died, but Veronica, born in 1820, and Theresia, born in 1829, survived. The Mendel lineage included other professional gardeners. Fortunately for his future career, Mendel went to a village school where the
teacher taught the children about natural science. Mendel was exposed early
to the cultivation of fruit trees, at the school as well as at home, where he
helped his father with the family orchard. Mendel attended secondary school
in the year 1833 and then spent six years in the *Gymnasium* in Troppau,
where he did well overall.

His nervous physical reaction to stress, which partially determined Mendel's choices and possibilities in later life, became evident when he was a
student. Initially, when Mendel's father, unable to work because of serious
injuries, had to give his son-in-law control of the farm in 1838, Mendel gave
private lessons to make money. The stress affected him to such a degree that
he had to miss several months of his fifth year at the *Gymnasium* in order to
recover. He started a philosophy course at the Philosophical Institute at Ol-
mütz in 1840 but was unable to find tutoring jobs. He fell ill again and spent
a year with his parents. His sister Theresia offered to support him out of her
dowry so he could continue his studies. With her aid, Mendel completed the
two-year course in philosophy, physics, and mathematics, which would have
led to higher studies. He did well enough that one of his professors, who had
lived in an Augustinian monastery for nearly twenty years, recommended
Mendel to the same monastery.

Life's Work

Mendel entered the Augustinian monastery, taking the name Gregor, on
October 9, 1843, out of sheer financial necessity. It proved, however, to be a
fruitful decision. Though he felt no great vocation to be a monk, he found
himself in the environment most conducive to his studies; it was at the
monastery that Mendel was able to concentrate on those studies in meteorol-
ogy and, more significant, plant reproduction that made him a pioneer in
genetics.

The abbot of the monastery was actively involved in encouraging agricultural studies, so Mendel was surrounded by other scholars and researchers. The nervous disposition which had affected him as a student continued to plague him, for he would become ill when he visited invalids. Useless as a pastor, he was assigned instead to the *Gymnasium* in Znaim as a substitute teacher. In this capacity, Mendel was successful and was encouraged to become a teacher permanently, if he could pass the required examinations for a license.

Ironically, this careful researcher never made much headway in official academic circles, though his education was crucial to shaping the course of his experiments. He failed to pass all the examinations to become a permanent teacher and was sent to the University of Vienna to study natural science more thoroughly. From October, 1851, to August, 1853, Mendel was in the intellectually stimulating company of men such as Franz Unger, a professor of plant physiology, who asserted that the plant world was not fixed but had evolved gradually—a view that caused much controversy. From Christian Doppler and Andreas von Ettingshausen, both physicists, Mendel most likely acquired the technique of approaching physical problems with mathematical analysis. He served as a demonstrator at the Physical Institute in Vienna and became adept at the physicist's approach to a problem. In 1855, Mendel took the teachers' examination again but fared even worse; he became sick after writing the first answer and was apparently so ill subsequently that his father and uncle came a long way to visit him. Because he never tried the examinations again, Mendel remained a substitute teacher for sixteen years, kind, conscientious, and well-liked.

In 1856, he began his experiments with garden peas. It was known at the time that the first generation reproduced from hybrids tended to be uniform but that the second generation reverted to the characteristics of the two original plants that had been crossbred. Such facts were observable, but the explanations remained unsatisfactory. In *An Introduction to Genetic Analysis* (1976, 1981) the authors note that before Mendel, the concept of blending inheritance predominated; that is, it was assumed that offspring were typically similar to the parents because the essences of the parents were contained in the spermatozoon and the egg, and these were blended at conception to form the new offspring. Mendel's work with pea plants suggested another theory, that of particulate inheritance; this theory postulated that a gene passes from one generation to the next as a unit, without any blending.

As several historians of science have noted, Mendel approached this problem of heredity in hybrids as a physicist would, and this may account for some of the suspicion surrounding the success of Mendel's famous experiments with garden peas. Instead of making many observations of natural life and then looking for the general pattern, as was the conventional approach of biologists, Mendel determined the problem first, devised a solution to the problem, then undertook experiments to test the solution. Mendel prepared the groundwork for his experiments by testing thirty-four varieties of peas to find the most suitable varieties for research. From these, he picked twenty-two to examine for two different traits, color and texture. He was then able to trace the appearance of green and yellow seeds, as well as round and wrinkled ones, in several generations of offspring. By literally counting the results of his hybridization, he found the ratio of dominant genes to recessive ones: 3 to 1. In effect, he demonstrated that there was a rule governing inheritance.

When he finished his experiments with peas in 1863, Mendel was well aware that his conclusions were not what the scientific knowledge of the time would have predicted. To confirm his findings, he experimented with the French bean and the bush bean, crossed the bush bean with the scarlet runner, and got the same 3:1 ratio, though in the last case, he could not obtain the same ratio for the white and red colors. He spoke about his work at two meetings of the Naturforschenden Verein (natural science society) and was asked to publish his lecture in 1866. Only a few of the forty copies made have been recovered: One of the most important recipients was Carl von Nägeli, a leading botanical researcher who had written about the work of preceding experimenters. Nägeli found it impossible to accept Mendel's explanation but did engage in discussion with him; the two corresponded from 1866 to 1873. Nägeli's influence was not altogether salutary, for he set Mendel on a futile track experimenting with *Hieracium*, which, as was established later, breeds slightly differently.

In 1868, Mendel was promoted to abbot of the monastery. He became involved in a controversy about taxes on the monastery and eventually, in 1871, abandoned his studies of hybrids. A heavy smoker toward the end of his life, Mendel developed kidney problems, which led to a painful illness. Theresia, the sister who had helped him pay for his education with her dowry, was also there for his last days, taking care of him until he died in January of 1884.

Summary

Gregor Johann Mendel's work was not rediscovered for thirty years, by which time three other researchers—Hugo de Vries, Carl Erich Correns, and Erich Tschermak von Seysenegg—had, working independently, drawn some of the same conclusions. Thus, Mendel's work in itself did not directly influence the history of science, for it was not well known. Even his original explanations of meteorologic phenomena, particularly of a tornado which struck Brno in 1870, was ignored. He died without achieving the full recognition he deserved.

The explanation for his contemporaries' lack of appreciation for his work can only be speculative. For example, Mendel's successor destroyed his private papers; furthermore, scientists at the time considered Mendel's experiments to be a hobby and his theories the "maunderings of a charming putterer." In part, Mendel's use of numerical analysis, so different from the conventional working procedures of biologists up to that time, may have been suspect. Mendel's personal qualities, which enabled him to reduce a puzzling problem to its bare essentials, may also have been a contributing factor to his obscurity. Though widely read in scientific literature and an active participant in the affairs of his community, he was a modest and reticent man, who compressed twenty years of scientific work into four short papers.

This lack of fanfare concerning his discoveries was not rectified until a young priest discovered Mendel's official documents, preserved in monastery archives, in the first decade of the twentieth century. Only then were Mendel's conscientious, careful, painstaking work and the results that he achieved fully appreciated. As L. C. Dunn notes, there had been several experiments with hybridization before Mendel. Among his predecessors, Josef Gottlieb Kölreuter was an important figure, for it was he who produced the first plant hybrid with a planned experiment in 1760.

What Mendel did that no one else thought to do was to apply statistical analysis to an area of study which had not habitually conceptualized problems numerically. By so doing, he was able to discover specific and regular ratios. With this apparently simple technique, Mendel was able to formulate the rules of inheritance and thus give birth to the science of genetics.

Bibliography
Dunn, L. C. *A Short History of Genetics: The Development of Some of the Main Lines of Thought, 1864-1939.* New York: McGraw-Hill, 1965. As indicated in the subtitle, this is a study of the development of the main lines of thought in genetic studies from 1864 to 1939. Contains chapters on Mendel and on the aftermath of Mendelism. Includes photographs, a glossary, a bibliography, and an index.
Iltis, Hugo. *Life of Mendel.* Translated by Eden Paul and Cedar Paul. London: Allen & Unwin, 1932. Researched and written by the man who helped to rediscover Mendel and preserve his remaining papers. One of the best biographies of Mendel. Includes illustrations, color plates, and an index.
Mendel, Gregor. *Experiments in Plant-Hybridisation.* Foreword by Paul C. Mangelsdorf. Cambridge, Mass.: Harvard University Press, 1965. Reprinted to celebrate the centennial of Mendel's lectures on his groundbreaking experiments. The foreword contains a concise explanation of the experiments and their significance.
Olby, Robert C. *Origins of Mendelism.* New York: Schocken Books, 1966. Places Mendel's work in the context of those who came before him. Starts with Kölreuter and his hybridization experiments, includes a discussion of

Charles Darwin's genetics, and concludes with the work of the three who replicated Mendel's work independently. Contains an appendix, an index, plates, and suggested readings at the end of each chapter.

Sturtevant, Alfred H. *A History of Genetics*. New York: Harper & Row, 1965. Provides a historical background of genetics from before Mendel through the genetics of mankind. Lively discussion of the controversy over Mendel's near-perfect results. Includes a chronology of genetics history, a bibliography, and an index.

Suzuki, David T., Anthony J. F. Griffiths, and Richard C. Lewontin. *An Introduction to Genetic Analysis*. 2d ed. San Francisco: W. H. Freeman, 1981. A chapter on Mendelism provides a clear explanation of Mendel's experiments, using contemporary terminology. Includes problems, with answers, a glossary, a bibliography, and an index.

Shakuntala Jayaswal

DMITRY IVANOVICH MENDELEYEV

Born: February 8, 1834; Tobolsk, Siberia, Russia
Died: February 2, 1907; St. Petersburg, Russia
Area of Achievement: Chemistry
Contribution: Although he did important theoretical work on the physical properties of fluids and practical work on the development of coal and oil resources, Mendeleyev is best known for his discovery of the periodic law, which states that the properties of the chemical elements vary with their atomic weights in a systematic way. His periodic table of the elements enabled him to predict accurately the properties of three unknown elements, whose later discovery confirmed the value of his system.

Early Life

Dmitry Ivanovich Mendeleyev was born in 1834 at Tobolsk (modern Tyumen Oblast), an administrative center in western Siberia. He later recalled that he was the seventeenth child, although a sister claimed that he was the sixteenth and many scholars state that he was the fourteenth. His mother, Marya Dmitrievna Kornileva, came from an old merchant family with Mongolian blood. She became deeply attached to her youngest son and played an influential role in shaping his passionate temperament and directing his education. His father, Ivan Pavlovich Mendeleyev, was a principal and teacher at the Tobolsk high school, but shortly after his son's birth he became totally blind. The modest disability pension he received did not allow him to support his large family, and so Marya, a remarkably able and determined woman, reopened a glass factory that her family still owned in a village near Tobolsk. She ran it so successfully that she was able to provide for her family and complete her younger children's education.

In the Tobolsk schools, young Dmitry, an attractive curly-haired, blue-eyed boy, excelled in mathematics, physics, geography, and history, but he did poorly in the compulsory classical languages, Latin in particular. Tobolsk was a place for political exiles, and one of Dmitry's sisters wedded an exiled Decembrist, one of those who tried unsuccessfully in December, 1825, to overthrow Czar Nicholas I. He took an active interest in Dmitry, taught him science, and helped form his political liberalism.

Toward the end of Dmitry's high school education, a double tragedy occurred: His father died of tuberculosis and his family's glassworks burned to the ground. By this time, the older children had left home, leaving only Dmitry and a sister with their mother, who decided to seek the help of her brother in Moscow. After Dmitry's graduation from high school in 1849, Marya, then fifty-seven years old, secured horses and bravely embarked with her two dependent children on the long journey from Siberia. In Moscow, her brother, after first welcoming them, refused to help his nephew obtain an education on the grounds that he himself had not had one. Marya angrily left Moscow for St. Petersburg, where she again encountered difficulty in getting her son either into the university or into the medical school. Finally, through a friend of her dead husband, she secured a place for Dmitry in the faculty of physics and mathematics of the Main Pedagogical Institute, the school his father had attended. Three months later, Marya died, and not long afterward her daughter succumbed to tuberculosis. Mendeleyev, who also suffered from tuberculosis, later wrote that his mother instructed him by example, corrected him with love, and, in order to consecrate him to science, left Siberia and spent her last energies and resources to put him on his way.

Mendeleyev received a good education at the Pedagogical Institute. One of his teachers had been a pupil of Justus von Liebig, one of the greatest chemists of the time. In 1855, Mendeleyev, now qualified as a teacher, was graduated from the Pedagogical Institute, winning a gold medal for his academic achievements.

Worn out by his labors, he went to a physician, who told him that he had only a short time to live. In an attempt to regain his health, he was sent, at his own request, to the Crimea, in southern Russia. He initially taught science at Simferopol, but when the Crimean War broke out, he left for Odessa, where he taught in a local lyceum during the 1855-1856 school year and where, aided by the warm climate, his health improved. In the autumn of 1856, he returned to St. Petersburg to defend his master's thesis. He succeeded and obtained the status of privatdocent, which gave him the license to teach theoretical and organic chemistry at the University of St. Petersburg.

Life's Work

In his teaching, Mendeleyev used the atomic weights of the elements to explain chemistry to his students. This did not mean that he believed that chemistry could be completely explained by physics, but his work on isomorphism and specific volumes convinced him that atomic weights could be useful in elucidating chemical properties. To improve his understanding of chemistry, he received in 1859 a stipend for two years' study abroad. In Paris, he worked in the laboratory of Henry Regnault, famous for his studies on chlorine compounds, and at the University of Heidelberg, where he had the opportunity to meet Robert Bunsen, Gustav Kirchhoff, and other notable scientists. Because his weak lungs were bothered by the noxious fumes of sulfur compounds in Bunsen's laboratory, Mendeleyev set up a private laboratory to work on his doctoral thesis on the combination of alcohol and water. In the course of his research at Heidelberg, he discovered that for every liquid there existed a temperature above which it could no longer be condensed from the gas to the liquid form. He called this temperature the absolute boiling point (this phenomenon was rediscovered a decade later by the Irish scientist Thomas Andrews, who called it the "critical temperature," its modern descriptor). In September, 1860, Mendeleyev attended the Chemical Congress at Karlsruhe, Germany, and met the Italian chemist Stanislao Cannizzaro, whose insistence on the distinction between atomic and molecular weights and whose system of corrected atomic weights had a great influence on him.

Upon his return to St. Petersburg, Mendeleyev resumed his lectures on organic chemistry. Because he lacked a permanent academic position, he decided to write a textbook on organic chemistry, which became a popular as well as a critical success. In 1863, he began to act as a consultant for a small oil refinery in Baku. In this same year he was married to Fezova Nikitichna Leshcheva, largely because one of his sisters insisted that he needed a wife. The couple had two children, a boy, Vladimir, and a girl, Olga. The marriage was not happy, however, and quarrels were frequent. Eventually, Mendeleyev and his wife separated. He continued to live in their St. Petersburg quarters, while his wife and children lived at their country estate of Boblovo. In 1864, Mendeleyev agreed to serve as professor of chemistry at the St. Petersburg Technical Institute while continuing to teach at the university. A year later, he defended his doctoral thesis on alcohol and water, arguing that solutions are chemical compounds indistinguishable from other types of chemical combination.

A turning point in Mendeleyev's career occurred in October, 1865, when he was appointed to the chair of chemistry at the University of St. Petersburg. While teaching an inorganic-chemistry course there, he felt the need to bring to this subject the same degree of order that had characterized his earlier teaching of organic chemistry. Since he could find no suitable textbook, he decided to write his own. The composing of this book, eventually published as *Osnovy khimii* (1868-1871; *The Principles of Chemistry*, 1891), led him to formulate the periodic law. It was also one of the most unusual textbooks ever written. Unlike most textbooks, it was not a recycling of traditional material. It had instead a novel organization and an abundance of original ideas. It was also a curious blend of objective information and personal comment in which footnotes often took up more space than the text.

In organizing his ideas for the book, Mendeleyev prepared individual cards for all sixty-three elements then known, listing their atomic weights and properties, which showed great dissimilarities. For example, oxygen and chlorine were gases, whereas mercury and bromine were liquids. Platinum was very hard, whereas sodium was very soft. Some elements combined with one atom, others with two, and still others with three or four. In a search for order, Mendeleyev arranged the elements in a sequence of increasing atomic weights. By moving the cards around, he found that he could group certain elements together in already familiar families. For example, in the first table that he developed in March of 1869, lithium, sodium, potassium, and the other so-called alkali metals formed a horizontal row. In some groups he left empty spaces so that the next element would be in its proper family.

Mendeleyev's analysis of his first arrangement convinced him that there must be a functional relationship between the individual properties of the elements and their atomic weights. One of the many interesting relationships he noticed concerned valence, the ability of an element to combine in specific proportions with other elements. He observed a periodic rise and fall of valence—1, 2, 3, 4, 3, 2, 1—in several parts of his arrangement. Because valence and other properties of the elements exhibited periodic repetitions, he called his arrangement in 1869 the periodic table. At the same time he formulated the periodic law: Elements organized according to their atomic weights manifest a clear periodicity of properties. He had been thinking about information relevant to the periodic law for fifteen years, but he formulated it in a single day. Mendeleyev would spend the next three years perfecting it, and in important ways he would be concerned with its finer points until his death.

When his paper was read by a friend at the Russian Chemical Society meeting in 1869, the periodic table did not evoke unusual interest. Its publication in German met with a cool reception. Mendeleyev's opponents, who were especially censorious in England and Germany, were suspicious of highly imaginative theoretical schemes of the elements; many scientists before Mendeleyev had proposed such systems, which resulted in little of practical benefit for chemists.

Mendeleyev believed that if he could convince scientists of the usefulness of his system, it would attract followers. Therefore, he tried to show how his table and periodic law could be used to correct erroneously determined atomic weights. More significant, he proposed in an 1871 paper that gaps in his table could be used to discover new elements. In particular, he predicted in great detail the physical and chemical properties of three elements, which he called eka-aluminum, eka-boron, and eka-silicon, after the Sanskrit word for "one" and the name of the element above the gap in the table. These predictions were met with great skepticism, but when, in 1875, Paul Lecoq de Boisbaudran discovered eka-aluminum in a zinc ore from the Pyrenees, skepticism declined, especially after chemists learned that the element's characteristics had been accurately foretold by Mendeleyev. When, in 1879, Lars Nilson isolated eka-boron from the ore euxenite, even fewer skeptics were to be found. Finally, in 1879, when Clemens Winkler in Germany found an element in the ore argyrodite which precisely matched Mendeleyev's predictions for eka-silicon, skepticism vanished. In fact, Winkler used Mendeleyev's predictions of a gray element with an atomic weight of about 72 and a density of 5.5 in his search (he found a grayish-white substance with an atomic weight of 72.3 and a density of 5.5). These new elements were given the names gallium (1875), scandium (1879), and germanium (1886), and their discovery led to the universal acceptance of Mendeleyev's periodic law.

In addition to campaigning for his periodic system, Mendeleyev during the 1870's spent time on his technological interests. He was a patriot who wanted to see such Russian resources as coal, oil, salt, and metals developed properly. With this in mind, he visited the United States in 1876 to study the Pennsylvania oil fields. He was critical of the American developers' concentration on the expansion of production while ignoring the scientific improvement of industrial efficiency and product quality. Upon his return to Russia, he was sent to study his country's oil fields, and he became very critical of the way they were exploited by foreign companies. He urged Russian officials to develop native oil for the country's own benefit. From his experience in the oil fields, Mendeleyev developed a theory of the inorganic origin of petroleum and a belief in protective tariffs for natural resources.

In the year of his American trip, Mendeleyev underwent a domestic crisis. At a sister's home he had met Anna Ivanovna Popov, a seventeen-year-old art student, and fallen desperately in love with her. Anna's family opposed the relationship and made several attempts to separate the pair, resorting finally to sending her to Rome to continue her art studies. Mendeleyev soon followed her, leaving behind a message that if he could not wed her, he would commit suicide. She was mesmerized by this passionate man who, with his deep-set eyes and patriarchal beard, looked like a biblical prophet. She agreed to return to Russia and wed him, but the couple discovered that, according to the laws of the Russian Orthodox church, Mendeleyev could not be remarried until seven years after his divorce. He eventually found a priest who was willing to ignore the rule, but two days after the marriage the priest was dismissed and Mendeleyev was officially proclaimed a bigamist. Despite the religious crisis, nothing happened to Mendeleyev or his young wife. As the czar told a nobleman who complained about the situation: "Mendeleyev has two wives, yes, but I have only one Mendeleyev." The second marriage proved to be a happy one, and the couple had two sons and two daughters. Anna Ivanovna introduced her husband to art, and he became an accomplished critic and an astute collector of paintings.

During the 1880's and 1890's, Mendeleyev became increasingly involved in academic politics. Ultimately, conflict with the minister of education prompted him to resign from the University of St. Petersburg. At his last lecture at the university, where he had taught for more than thirty years, the students gave him an enthusiastic ovation. His teaching career at an end, Mendeleyev turned to public service, where he was active in many areas.

When the Russo-Japanese War broke out in February, 1904, Mendeleyev became a strong supporter of his country's efforts, and Russia's defeat disheartened him. By this time, Mendeleyev was not only the grand man of Russian chemistry but also, because of the triumph of the periodic law, a world figure. In 1906, he was considered for a Nobel Prize, but the chemistry committee's recommendation was defeated by a single vote, mainly because his discovery of the periodic law was more than thirty-five years old. Though he missed winning the Nobel Prize, he was showered with many awards in Russia and in many foreign countries. His end came early in 1907, when he caught a cold that developed into pneumonia. His chief consolation during his final illness was the reading of *A Journey to the North Pole* by Jules Verne, his favorite author.

Summary

Dmitry Ivanovich Mendeleyev's name has become inextricably linked with the periodic table, but he was not the first to attempt to develop a systematic classification of the chemical elements. Earlier in the century, Johann Döbereiner, a German chemist, had arranged several elements into triads—for example, calcium, strontium, and barium—in which such properties as atomic weight, color, and reactivity seemed to form a predictable gradation. John Newlands, an English chemist, arranged the elements in the order of atomic weights in 1864 and found that properties seemed to repeat themselves after an interval of seven elements. In 1866, he announced his "law of octaves," in which he saw an analogy between the grouping of elements and the musical octave. Several other attempts at a systematic arrangement of the elements were made before Mendeleyev, some of which were known to him. Many scholars credit the German chemist Lothar Meyer as an independent discoverer of the periodic law, since in 1864 he published a table of elements arranged horizontally so that analogous elements appeared under one another. Other scholars, however, contend that Mendeleyev's table was more firmly based on chemical properties than Meyer's and it could be generalized more easily. Furthermore, Mendeleyev was a much bolder theoretician than Meyer. For example, he proposed that some atomic weights must be incorrect since their measured weight caused them to be placed in the wrong group of the table (Meyer was reluctant to take this step). In most instances Mendeleyev's proposals proved to be correct (although the troublesome case of iodine and tellurium was not resolved until the discovery of isotopes). Finally and most notably, Mendeleyev was so impressed with the periodicity of the elements that he took the risk of predicting the chemical and physical properties of the unknown elements in the blank places of his table. Although his table had imperfections, it did bring similar elements together and help make chemistry a rational science and the periodic law an essential part of chemistry.

The periodic table grew out of the theoretical side of Mendeleyev's scientific personality, but he also had a practical side. He made important contributions to the Russian oil, coal, and sodium-carbonate industries. He served the czarist regime in several official positions. Nevertheless, he did not hesitate to speak out against the government's oppression of students, and his sympathy for the common people led him to travel third-class on trains. Though he held decidedly liberal views, it is wrong to see him as a political radical. Perhaps he is best described as a progressive, since he hoped that the czarist government would correct itself and evolve into a more compassionate regime.

Had Mendeleyev lived a few more years, he would have witnessed the complete and final development of his periodic table by Henry Moseley, whose discovery of atomic number by interacting X rays with various elements led to the use of the positive charge of the nucleus as the true measure of an element's place in the periodic table. Throughout the twentieth century, the periodic table, which owed so much to Mendeleyev, continued to be enlarged by the discovery of new elements. It was therefore appropriate that a new element (atomic number 101), discovered in 1955, was named mendelevium, in belated recognition of the importance of his periodic law.

Bibliography
Farber, Eduard, ed. *Great Chemists*. New York: John Wiley & Sons, 1961. This collection of more than one hundred biographies of chemists contains an excellent short biography of Mendeleyev. Nontechnical and contains ample references to both primary and secondary literature.
Ihde, Aaron J. *The Development of Modern Chemistry*. New York: Harper & Row, 1964. Ihde traces the development of chemistry largely through its disciplines, for example, inorganic chemistry, organic chemistry, physical chemistry, and the like. Discusses Mendeleyev's life and work in a chapter on the classification of elements. Contains an excellent and extensive annotated bibliography.
Jaffe, Bernard. *Crucibles: The Lives and Achievements of the Great Chemists*. New York: Simon & Schuster, 1930. This book tells the story of chemistry through the lives of some of its greatest practitioners. The approach is popular, uncritical, and accessible to young readers and those with little knowledge of chemistry. The chapter on Mendeleyev contains a good basic treatment of his life and his discovery of the periodic law.
Van Spronsen, Johannes W. *The Periodic System of Chemical Elements: A History of the First Hundred Years*. Amsterdam: Elsevier, 1969. Several books have been written about the periodic system of chemical elements and its history, but this one, written to commemorate the hundredth anniversary of the periodic system, is the best. Spronsen analyzes Mendeleyev's achievement in great detail. Based on original sources, the book requires some knowledge of chemistry for a full understanding of the analysis. Generously illustrated with diagrams, photographs, and graphs.

Weeks, Mary Elvira. *Discovery of the Elements*. 7th ed. Edited by Henry Leicester. Easton, Penn.: Journal of Chemical Education, 1968. This book, which has served chemists as a rich source of information about the elements—chemical, technical, historical, and biographical—has been made even more valuable by this new edition prepared by Leicester. The material on Russian chemists, including Mendeleyev, has been expanded. Extensively illustrated and thoroughly understandable to readers with a modicum of chemical knowledge.

Robert J. Paradowski

FELIX MENDELSSOHN

Born: February 3, 1809; Hamburg
Died: November 4, 1847; Leipzig, Saxony
Area of Achievement: Music
Contribution: Mendelssohn was one of the great composers of the Romantic period. His music is noted for its exceptionally melodic qualities and its ability to capture a mood. It has been continually performed and studied.

Early Life

Felix Mendelssohn was an unusually gifted and precocious child musically and was the most prominent member of an exceptionally talented family. He worked long and diligently, absorbed in his music, aware of his subtle talent and discernment in music. He loved taking walks in the woods and often wrote down the notes he heard the birds singing. His first musical influence was his mother, Leah, an expert pianist and vocalist. When Felix was only four years old, she gave him five-minute piano lessons, soon extended as the music capivated Felix's imagination. At age eight, Felix began music lessons with Karl Friedrich Zelter, the director of Berlin's Singakademie. Before long, the young musical genius was composing fugues, songs, operettas, violin and piano concerti, and piano quartets. He performed Sunday concerts in his home and even conducted a small orchestra.

Abraham Mendelssohn, Felix's father, was a prominent German banker, and his fashionable home was one of the intellectual and musical centers of Berlin. The excitement of learning reigned in Felix's "childhood castle," a home bustling with activity, servants, and tutors. Rebecka sang, Paul played the violoncello, and the eldest child, Fanny, played the piano almost as well as Felix. The children wrote their own newspaper, called at first "The Garden Paper" and, later, "The Tea and Snow Times." They made paper lanterns to decorate the trees in the garden for dances. Felix particularly loved the park, where he rode his horse. He played billiards and chess and practiced the piano, organ, and violin. He learned landscape drawing and calligraphy.

Felix, a gentle, cheerful, kindly person, was handsome, self-confident, and even-tempered. His hair was dark black and his eyes, dark brown. He dressed elegantly, was very sociable, and loved good meals and stimulating companionship. He was sharply critical of his own work, revising five or six times pieces that had already been performed successfully.

Life's Work

In a sense, Mendelssohn began his life's work before he was ten years old, inasmuch as he was already busily composing music by that age. It was, however, the composition of his early masterpiece, *A Midsummer Night's*

Dream (1826), at the age of seventeen that launched him into a serious career as a composer.

An early extended trip throughout Germany and Switzerland gave Mendelssohn a love of travel. He visited most of the beautiful, historical, cultural, and scenic places of Europe, carrying his sketchbook with him. His first visit to England and Scotland in 1829, at the age of twenty, began his lifelong attraction to English culture. The English were similarly enchanted with both Mendelssohn and his music. Even on this first visit he conducted the London Philharmonic.

Also in 1829, Mendelssohn helped to revive the singing of Johann Sebastian Bach's *Saint Matthew Passion*, which he had studied for years. Beginning in 1827, Mendelssohn and his friends assembled a small, dependable choir which met one evening a week for practice of rarely heard works. They secured permission to present the work at the Berlin Singakademie. Mendelssohn shortened the work drastically. He omitted many of the arias and used only the introductory symphonies of others. He edited passages for greater brevity. The performance was a historic success. The chorus numbered 158 and the orchestra included many from the Royal Orchestra. The king was in the royal loge with members of his court. And twenty-year-old Mendelssohn conducted without a score, as he knew the music and lyrics from memory. The historical effect was a Bach revival in Europe.

Despite his many musical activities, Mendelssohn had a very active social life and was often invited by families with girls of marriageable age. He was wealthy, cultured, courteous, handsome, of good moral character, and had a promising future. Mendelssohn chose for his wife Cécile Jeanrenaud, the daughter of a leading Huguenot minister in Frankfurt, who had died in 1819. Mendelssohn became acquainted with Cécile on one of his extended musical engagements in Frankfurt and finally realized that he was in love with this beautiful, charming girl, nine years his junior. Cécile and Mendelssohn were married on March 28, 1837, in the Reformed French Church in Frankfurt. The ceremony was performed in French. A friend wrote special music for the wedding; Mendelssohn's "Wedding March" from *A Midsummer Night's Dream* had yet to come into fashion. The couple spent their honeymoon in the upper Rhine valley and in the Black Forest. It was a wondrous and creative time: Mendelssohn sketched the outlines of half a dozen works. Mendelssohn was a devoted and content husband and Cécile an ideal wife. She loved her domestic life and was an excellent and charming hostess and a cheerful companion to her husband. She was a pious and orthodox Protestant, as was Mendelssohn. The couple had five children, one of whom died at the age of nine.

In 1833, Mendelssohn wrote the *Italian* Symphony and his oratorio on the life of the Apostle Paul. In 1835, he became conductor of the Leipzig Gewandhaus Orchestra and continued in that post for the rest of his life.

Mendelssohn loved the Psalms and set many of them to music. In 1840, he finished *Hymn of Praise* (Second Symphony), with its delicate melodic contrasts so characteristic of Mendelssohn. The choral movement is mostly from scripture, "Let everything that hath life and breath praise the Lord!" Mendelssohn also wrote the melody for "Hark, the Herald Angels Sing," and his *Reformation* Symphony (Fifth Symphony) expands on Martin Luther's "A Mighty Fortress Is Our God." In 1846, Mendelssohn completed and directed his oratorio *Elijah* to enthusiastic response. He soon began the opera *Lorelei* and his oratorio on the life of Christ, *Christus*, but he was unable to complete either. In May of 1847, his sister Fanny suddenly died. Mendelssohn lived only six months longer and died of a cerebral hemorrhage on November 4, 1847, at the age of thirty-eight.

Summary

Felix Mendelssohn excelled in Romantic musical scene painting. His two most important symphonies are geographically identified: the *Italian* and the *Scotch*, which was dedicated to Queen Victoria, whom he met during his concert tours of England. The *Italian* pictures the spirited and sunny, vibrant south, while the *Scotch* has its own peculiar northern beauty. His works *The Hebrides* (1830-1832) and *Meeresstille und glückliche Fahrt* (1828-1832; calm sea and prosperous voyage) continue to influence musical seascapes. The listener can almost hear the sounds of the sea. Mendelssohn in fact listened to the waves and the gulls and ships and the water rushing into Fingal's Cave and recorded the sounds he heard in musical transcription, just as he had recorded the songs of birds in the gardens of his boyhood home.

It was no doubt an advantage to Mendelssohn to be born into a family of wealth so that he could concentrate unreservedly on his art. He worked exceptionally hard, however, and was motivated by a sense of duty and a desire to excel. He was Jewish by birth but had been baptized into the Christian faith. His philosophy of life, morals, and music all reflected a sincere orthodox faith. Mendelssohn agreed with Bach's philosophy of sacred music, that music should "form an integral part of our service instead of becoming a mere concert which more or less evokes a devotional mood."

How is music different from verbal communication? When someone asked Mendelssohn the meanings of some of his songs in "Songs Without Words," he responded: ". . . genuine music . . . fills the soul with a thousand things better than words. . . . Only the song can say the same thing, can arouse the same feelings in one person as in another, a feeling which is not expressed . . . by the same words." Mendelssohn's music continues to evoke strong feelings.

Bibliography

Blunt, Wilfrid. *On Wings of Song: A Biography of Felix Mendelssohn.* New

York: Charles Scribner's Sons, 1974. A particularly interesting biography because of the many illustrations, anecdotes, and quotations from primary sources. An excellent introduction for the general reader. Includes cultural and scenic descriptions by Mendelssohn himself during his early nineteenth century travels in Switzerland, Germany, and Scotland.

David, Hans T., and Arthur Mendel, eds. *The Bach Reader: A Life of Johann Sebastian Bach in Letters and Documents*. New York: W. W. Norton, 1945. Valuable for a study of Mendelssohn because of the chapter on Mendelssohn's revival of the *Saint Matthew Passion*. Part of the eleven-page account is Edward Devrient's first-person account of the revival.

Kaufman, Schima. *Mendelssohn: "A Second Elijah."* New York: Thomas Y. Crowell, 1934. This occasionally laudatory biography contains some dated material. Alludes to Mendelssohn's masterpiece, *Elijah*, and considers Mendelssohn himself to have called Western civilization from "Baal-worship of the false," the banal, and the cacophony and confusion of "mere sound" that passes for music.

Kupferberg, Herbert. *The Mendelssohns: Three Generations of Genius*. New York: Charles Scribner's Sons, 1972. Places Mendelssohn in historical context by giving a one-hundred-page biographical sketch of his father, Abraham Mendelssohn, and his grandfather Moses Mendelssohn. Kupferberg also gives brief sketches of the lives of many others in the Mendelssohn family and shows them to be, men and women, a remarkable clan. The last chapter follows the Mendelssohns into the twentieth century. Includes a genealogical chart.

Marek, George R. *Gentle Genius: The Story of Felix Mendelssohn*. New York: Funk & Wagnalls, 1971. A very interesting biography. The lengthy quotations from the Mendelssohn correspondence and the many pictures enhance the book's value. Some of Mendelssohn's charming landscape drawings are also reproduced. "A Mendelssohn Calendar" is included.

Mendelssohn, Felix. *Letters*. Edited by G. Seldon-Goth. New York: Pantheon Books, 1945. A fascinating collection of personal letters. Indispensable in giving insights into the personality, character, and thinking of Mendelssohn.

Radcliffe, Philip. *Mendelssohn*. London: J. M. Dent & Sons, 1954. A standard biography for many years. Quite technical, but brief. Includes excerpts of musical scores and a catalog of Mendelssohn's works.

Werner, Eric. *Mendelssohn: A New Image of the Composer and His Age*. Translated by Dika Newlin. London: Free Press of Glencoe, 1963. The longest and most complete biography of Mendelssohn. Includes detailed technical and artistic discussions of all Mendelssohn's major works, including musical scores as examples.

William H. Burnside

MENELIK II
Sahle Mariam

Born: August 17, 1844; Ankober, Shoa
Died: December 12, 1913; Addis Ababa, Ethiopia
Areas of Achievement: Monarchy, government, and politics
Contribution: Menelik II unified Ethiopia after centuries of political fragmentation, consolidated the ancient Christian heritage against the growth
of Muslim influence, and saved Ethiopia from European colonialism. He
laid the foundations for Ethiopia's transformation from a medieval, feudal
empire to a modern state.

Early Life

Menelik II was born Sahle Mariam in the court of his father, Haile Malakot, a leading prince of the province of Shoa. Chronicles and oral tradition
reflect some uncertainty as to the details of the birth: Sahle Mariam may
have been born out of wedlock, possibly the result of Haile Malakot's infatu-
ation with a concubine. Yet the traditional sources, while almost ignoring
Sahle Mariam's father—whose reign appears to have been less than illustrious—often make much of the piety and reputation of the child's mother.
In Ethiopia, where the nobility put much importance on genealogy, these
were matters of enormous concern for Sahle Mariam's career. These concerns caused Haile Malakot's father, the mighty Sahle Sellasie, who had led
the resurgence of the Christian, Amharic-speaking nobles in Shoa earlier in
the nineteenth century, to intercede. Sahle Selassie and his influential queen,
Bezzabbesh, saw that the parents of Sahle Mariam were married in a civil
ceremony shortly after the child's birth. In order to erase any further question of Sahle Mariam's pedigree, Sahle Selassie rechristened the child Menelik II. He prophesied that Menelik would restore the empire of Ethiopia to
the ancient greatness wrought by Menelik I, the offspring of a legendary
union between Solomon, the King of ancient Israel, and Sheba, Queen of
south Arabia.

In Menelik's youth, however, there were others with similar aspirations.
Ethiopia was just emerging from the *Zamana Masafent* (age of the princes),
a long period of disunity and internal chaos. The most notable of the early
unifiers was Theodore, ruler of the province of Gonder. In 1856, Theodore's
forces defeated the Shoan levies and incorporated the province. Menelik's
father died of malaria during the final campaign against Theodore. Menelik
himself, now the designated heir to the throne of Shoa, became a ward of
Theodore at his fortress capital of Magdela. There, Menelik received the
favored treatment and education due a noble. He completed religious training and developed excellent military skills. Above all, Menelik obtained the
practical experience necessary for success as a ruler and statesman in his

own right. He also formed lasting alliances with other noble children from far-flung parts of Ethiopia.

Theodore's enterprise began with great promise. He envisioned an Ethiopia of law and order and of conciliation between Muslims and Christians. As his reign progressed, however, he resorted increasingly to force, infuriated by the resistance of Muslim principalities and deeply suspicious of intrigue. Theodore may well have been demented in his final years. After 1864, he executed members of the court on a whim and imprisoned members of the British diplomatic mission. The latter indiscretion brought a British military expedition; Theodore committed suicide as it was about to storm Magdela in 1868.

Life's Work

The disintegration of Theodore's authority set the stage for Menelik's emergence. In 1865, the Shoan nobles revolted and beseeched Menelik to return. He escaped Magdela under cover of darkness to return to Ankober. By 1866, Menelik was firmly in command in Shoa. From the moment of his return, Menelik dreamed of succeeding where Theodore had failed, in ruling a united Ethiopian empire.

In 1872, after four years of intrigue and dynastic struggles, Yohannes IV was crowned Emperor of Ethiopia at the ancient capital of Aksum in the north. Yohannes managed to hold together the tenuous unity imposed by Theodore. Only Menelik's homeland of Shoa remained outside the empire.

Menelik's ambitions—indeed his durability as an independent ruler—required outside support. Theodore's notoriety, and the British punitive expedition of 1868, had shattered Ethiopia's isolation and exposed the country to outside pressures. The opening of the Suez Canal in 1869 greatly increased European interest in the countries along the Red Sea. Egypt, ruled by the ambitious modernizer Ismail Pasha, pushed its authority deep into the Sudan, west of Ethiopia, and in 1865 occupied the old Turkish port of Mesewa on the Ethiopian coast. Menelik cultivated an alliance with the Egyptians in the hope of forcing Yohannes IV to divide his attention between two opponents rather than concentrate on Shoa. The Egyptians, however, were decimated by Yohannes' forces when they attempted to move inland in 1875. Yohannes' predominantly Greek advisers urged him to articulate a pan-Christian front in the Middle East against both Egyptian and Turkish ambitions. Yohannes also had reached an understanding with the British, who were alarmed at the pace of Egyptian expansion in northeast Africa.

In 1883, tribes in the Sudan rose in rebellion against Egyptian rule. Under the leadership of a Muslim cleric who styled himself as *Mahdi* (savior), tens of thousands of Sudanese Muslims invaded western Ethiopia in 1887 and sacked Gonder, massacring its inhabitants. Yohannes retaliated the following year by butchering sixty thousand Mahdist troops, but he was wounded in the battle and died shortly thereafter.

The throne now went to Menelik II, and his reign proved among the greatest in Ethiopian history. Menelik immediately set about pushing Ethiopia's frontiers west toward the Nile and south toward Lake Victoria. He incorporated vast quantities of trade into the empire, thus filling his usually extended exchequer. Menelik departed from the crusading ways of his predecessors by restoring religious liberty and ending the persecution of Muslims and pagans. His method of establishing a dominant culture in Ethiopia was economic and diplomatic rather than military. When new regions were added to the empire, he sowed them with strategically placed settlements of lesser Amhara nobles and Christian clergy, whose increasing control of commerce provided an incentive for the Christianization of many areas. Even tribes who remained Muslim adopted the trappings of Christian, Amhara noble etiquette and fashion.

One of Menelik's most lasting contributions to modern Ethiopia was the establishment of a new capital at Addis Ababa (new flower) in a relatively sheltered location on the central plain. The region around Addis Ababa contained many of the oldest and most venerated Christian monasteries in the country. Founding the capital there not only reiterated Menelik's commitment to the Christian tradition of Ethiopia but also brought to an end the practice of changing capitals each time a new dynastic line or regional nobility assumed power. Eucalyptus trees, imported by Menelik to provide shade for government buildings in Addis Ababa, soon spread throughout Ethiopia and helped reforest some of the barren and denuded hillsides of the country. Telegraph communication, and later the beginnings of a telephone system, tied together the outlying regions of the huge, mountainous country. In 1897, a French firm completed a direct railway link between Addis Ababa and the Red Sea coast at Djibouti.

Menelik is best known for transforming Ethiopia's role in international affairs from that of potential prey of European colonialism to that of a factor in the regional balance of power. He did so by successfully confronting Italy's bid to incorporate Ethiopia into its colonial domain. In 1882, the Italians purchased the port of Aseb from a private trading company and began to expand along the Red Sea coast. Italian ambitions triggered British occupation of northern Somalia and a French landing at Djibouti in 1885. At first, Menelik deferred to the Italians. Under the Treaty of Uccialli of May, 1889, Menelik recognized Italian sovereignty on the coast and agreed to link his foreign policy with that of Italy. Four years later, however, with Italian columns steadily pushing inland and nearby provincial governors calling for assistance, Menelik prepared for war. After several inconclusive skirmishes, the decisive battle came at Adwa on March 1, 1896, where the Ethiopian army crushed an Italian force.

The news of Adwa electrified the world; it was a stunning reverse of the forces of colonialism hitherto judged irresistible. Within months, a new treaty finalized the Italian colonial frontier with Ethiopia. Emboldened, Menelik pushed his borders westward, joining with France in 1898 in an effort to control the Upper Nile by planting his flag alongside the French at Fashoda (modern Kodok). Ethiopia thus became a factor in a major Anglo-French diplomatic crisis. In 1902, Menelik agreed to the Treaty of Addis Ababa, in which Great Britain and Ethiopia, negotiating ·on equal terms, reached agreement on placement of the western frontier.

Menelik grew frail in his final years. In 1909, he relinquished the government to a regency in the name of his grandson, Lij Yasu, whose Muslim leanings led to renewed strife and political intrigue. Menelik's new imperial administration and cultural latticework of Christian-Amhara tradition survived the crisis, however, and continued to support Ethiopia as a nation.

Summary

Menelik II ruled Ethiopia at a crucial time in its history, when the country was emerging from its own dark age and opening itself up to the world. He accomplished the rarest of feats in assimilating the military and technological advances of Europe while turning religion, tradition, and an antiquated class structure toward productive ends. In doing so, he saved Ethiopia from the fate of the rest of Africa, which fell under European rule. For nearly a century, the culture, economy, and political system of Ethiopia bore his stamp.

Bibliography

Abir, Mordechai. *Ethiopia: The Era of the Princes, the Challenge of Islam, and the Reunification of the Christian Empire, 1769-1855*. New York: Praeger, 1968. Analyzes the crucial period of disunity from the mid-eighteenth to the mid-nineteenth century, when the power of the traditional Christian nobility was in decline and Ethiopia faced the challenge of a revitalized Islam. Excellent on the importance of trade expansion and fiscal control.

Berkeley, George Fitz-Hardinge. *The Campaign of Adowa and the Rise of Menelik*. Reprint. New York: Negro Universities Press, 1969. A reprint of a 1902 edition which examines the enormous impact of the Ethiopian victory at Adwa, and the consequent rise of the country's international prestige on the intellectual and political environment of Afro-American society.

Caulk, Richard A. "Minilik II and the Diplomacy of Commerce." *Journal of Ethiopian Studies* 17 (1984): 63-76. Discusses the emperor's commercial and diplomatic aplomb in gaining control of the productive means of his country and in balancing the opportunities and dangers of increased trade with Europeans.

Darkwah, R. H. Kofi. *Shewa, Menilek, and the Ethiopian Empire, 1813-1889*. London: Heinemann, 1975. Monographic coverage of the period with emphasis on the later portion. Extensive coverage of agriculture and other economic issues, suppression of the slave trade, and military organization. Contains a useful bibliography.

Horvath, R. J. "The Wandering Capitals of Ethiopia." *Journal of African History* 10 (1969): 205-219. Discusses the locations of the capital in various periods; also useful as a brief synopsis of Ethiopian politics and society prior to the nineteenth century.

Marcus, Harold G. "Ethio-British Negotiations Concerning the Western Boundary with Sudan, 1896-1902." *Journal of African History* 4 (1963): 81-94. Reveals changed British attitudes toward Ethiopia in the wake of Adwa, which led to the bilateral Treaty of Addis Ababa in 1902.

_____. *The Life and Times of Menelik II of Ethiopia: 1844-1913*. Oxford, England: Clarendon Press, 1975. The primary focus is on Menelik's relations with Ethiopian noble dynasties and European powers. Extensive political narrative. Excellent bibliography.

Rosenfeld, Chris Prouty. *A Chronology of Menilek II of Ethiopia, 1844-1913*. East Lansing, Mich.: African Studies Center, 1976. A diary of the life and reign of Menelik gleaned from many different sources. Major foreign developments correlated with those in Ethiopia. A must for research on the period.

Ronald W. Davis

MENNO SIMONS

Born: 1496; Witmarsum, Friesland
Died: January 31, 1561; Wüstenfeld, Holstein
Areas of Achievement: Church reform, religion, and theology
Contribution: Menno contributed a stabilizing influence to the Anabaptist movement of the sixteenth century and also to a defense of religious toleration. His most lasting contribution has been his emphasis on the Bible as the authority in religion and theology.

Early Life

Menno Simons was born in the Dutch village of Witmarsum, between the cities of Franeker and Bolsward, less than ten miles from the North Sea. His parents were devout Roman Catholics who consecrated their son to the service of their church. Menno's education for the priesthood was most likely at the Franciscan Monastery in Bolsward. While there, he performed the duties of a monk but never took the vows. He studied Roman Catholic theology, learned to read and write Latin, acquired a basic knowledge of Greek, and became familiar with the writings of the early church fathers. Conspicuously absent from Menno's studies was the Bible.

Menno was ordained as a Roman Catholic priest in 1524 and remained faithful to that calling for twelve years. The last five years (1531-1536) he served as parish pastor in his home village of Witmarsum. Outwardly, he was the average country priest of the sixteenth century, performing his duties faithfully but with the least possible effort. With two fellow priests, his leisure time was spent ". . . playing [cards] . . . , drinking, and in such diversions as, alas, is the fashion . . . of such useless people." Inwardly, Menno was troubled by doubts concerning the ceremony of the Mass. He could not escape the thought, which he first attributed to Satan, that the bread and wine were not really transformed into the body and blood of Christ as he had been taught. Menno's doubts may have been prompted by the Sacramentists, a group which denied the physical presence of Christ in the Lord's Supper. Two years after becoming a priest, Menno sought and found his answer in the Bible. He later wrote, "I had not gone very far when I discovered that we were deceived. . . ." Menno then faced the same decision that faced other reformers: Would he rely on his church for authority, or would he take the Bible as his sole authority for doctrine and practice? His decision to accept the latter came in 1528.

Privately rejecting Roman Catholic authority did not mean an immediate break between Menno and the Church. Although not in agreement, he was willing to continue performing the Mass in the traditional way; at the same time, he became more deeply involved in personal Bible study.

Menno's second question concerning the traditions of his church, and the one which eventually led to his departure from it, concerned infant baptism. In 1531, a man was beheaded in nearby Leeuwarden because of Anabaptism (rebaptism based on baptism for believers only). Menno's Bible study soon convinced him that believers' baptism was the biblical position. By this time, small groups of Anabaptists were forming throughout the Netherlands, but Menno did not join any of them, partly because he enjoyed the comfortable life of a priest and partly because of the radical nature of some Anabaptists, such as those who violently captured Münster in 1534.

The greatest change in Menno's life came in April, 1535, when he accepted, as a ". . . sorrowing sinner, the gift of His [God's] grace. . . ." He then rejected both the Roman Catholic Mass and infant baptism. On January 30, 1536, Menno renounced the Roman Catholic church and joined the Anabaptists.

Life's Work

Following his break with Rome, Menno began a period of wandering that would last about eighteen years, in which he served as an underground evangelist to the scattered Anabaptist communities. In late 1536, he settled briefly in the northern Dutch province of Groningen, where at least a semblance of religious freedom existed. While there, he was baptized with believers' baptism and ordained as an elder in the Anabaptist movement. Soon thereafter, Menno was forced to resume his wandering. His exact points of residence can be traced only by noting those who were executed for sheltering him. On January 8, 1539, Tjard Reynders, a God-fearing Anabaptist in Leeuwarden, was executed solely because he had given a temporary home to Menno.

Until late 1543, Menno's work was concentrated in the Netherlands. The authorities in Leeuwarden, the capital of West Friesland, seemed determined to be rid of Menno, whose hometown of Witmarsum was in their province. In 1541, they offered a pardon to any imprisoned Anabaptist who would betray him, but the offer was not accepted. On December 2, 1542, with the support of Charles V, Emperor of the Holy Roman Empire, as well as ruler of the Netherlands, they offered a reward of one hundred gold guilders, plus a pardon for any past crime, to anyone who would deliver Menno. These efforts testify to the importance ascribed by that time to Menno's leadership of the movement.

The exact time and place when Menno married Geertruydt are not known; in 1544, however, he wrote ". . . to this hour I could not find in all the country . . . a cabin or hut . . . in which my poor wife and our little children could be put up in safety. . . ." Menno continued throughout these years to express concern for his family, all of whom, except one daughter, preceded him in death. From 1541 to 1543, Menno concentrated his labor farther south around Amsterdam, but details of this work are scarce. He evidently baptized many, although the names of only two have been preserved.

The most enduring part of Menno's work is his writing. By 1543, at least seven books from the pen of Menno Simons were circulating throughout the Netherlands, including *Dat fundament des christelycken leers* (1539; *A Foundation of Plain Instruction*, 1835), *Van dat rechte christen ghelooue* (c. 1542; *The True Christian Faith*, 1871), and *Verclaringhe des Christelycken doopsels* (c. 1542; *Christian Baptism*, 1871). Rather than being academic treatises designed for theologians, they are commonsense presentations for the average layman. Precisely because Menno's works were so accessible, church authorities were particularly determined to destroy them.

In the fall of 1543, Menno and his family left the Netherlands, and for the last eighteen years of his life he labored primarily in northwest Germany. His first German refuge was Emden, in East Friesland, ruled by the tolerant Countess Anna of Oldenburg. Menno had visited the province, which had become a haven for all Anabaptists, many times previously. By this time, however, Anna was being pressured by Charles V to suppress all the outlawed sects.

The superintendent of the East Friesland churches, on whose advice Anna relied, was John a'Lasco, a Zwinglian reformer of Polish descent. Although on friendly terms with Menno, a'Lasco's goal was a state-controlled Reformed church. Countess Anna decided to suppress those whom a'Lasco declared to be heretical. To this end, a theological discussion was held on January 28-31, 1544, involving a'Lasco, who hoped to bring the Anabaptists into the state church, and Menno, who hoped to preserve the tolerant spirit in East Friesland. The discussion revealed three irreconcilable differences. First, Menno strongly opposed the concept of a state-controlled church, which he believed always led to compromise and spiritual lethargy. Second, a'Lasco could not reconcile believers' baptism to a state church. The final point concerned Menno's unique understanding of the Incarnation of Christ; he taught that the body of Christ, to be completely sinless, had to be given completely to the Virgin Mary by the Holy Spirit. A'Lasco interpreted this as a denial of the humanity of Christ, weakening His position as the Saviour of mankind; he therefore declared that Menno was guilty of heresy. In 1545, Anna issued a decree that the more radical Anabaptists were subject to execution, while the "Mennisten" were to be examined and, if they did not conform to the state church, were to leave the province. This decree was the first official document to recognize Menno's leadership by applying his name to the peaceful branch of the Anabaptist movement.

Menno Simons left East Friesland in May, 1544, for the lower Rhine area of Cologne and Bonn, where he spent two fruitful years; the last fifteen years of his life were spent in the province of Schleswig-Holstein. There, in 1554, Menno finally found a permanent home for his weary family in Wüstenfelde, between Lübeck and Hamburg.

Menno's final years were productive in that he had time for more writing, including revising some of his earlier books. They were also troublesome years in which Menno had to settle disputes and defend himself within the Anabaptist movement. The most serious dispute concerned the ban and shunning of excommunicated members; Menno took the strict position that all human ties, even those of marriage and family, had to be broken under the ban of the church.

By 1560, Menno's health was failing. The years of hardship and privation, as well as the burden of the church, had taken a heavy toll. He often used a crutch as a result of an injury suffered in Wismar at about 1554. Menno died in his own home on January 31, 1561, exactly twenty-five years after his break with Rome, and was buried in his own garden. Unfortunately, Wüstenfelde was destroyed during the Thirty Years' War, and the site of Menno's grave could only be approximated in the early twentieth century, when a simple memorial was erected.

Summary

The Anabaptist movement began in 1525; for the next eleven years, Menno Simons was a Roman Catholic priest. Therefore, he was only a leader, not the founder, of the church that bears his name. Menno's role in the Reformation is not as obvious as that of his contemporaries, Martin Luther, Huldrych Zwingli, and John Calvin; yet his true significance is revealed in three areas of influence: his character, his message, and his work.

The character of Menno was ingrained with a sensitivity for the truth, an unswerving devotion to his convictions, and a deep trust in God. These traits enabled him to have a steadying influence on the diverse Anabaptist communities of the Netherlands and northern Germany.

The foundation of Menno's message was the Bible. He declared that he ". . . would rather die than to believe and teach my brethren a single word or letter . . . contrary to the plain testimony of the Word of God. . . ." He identified the heart of his message when he said, "I strive after nothing . . . but . . . that all men might be saved . . ."; although as a reward for this message, ". . . we can expect nothing from them (I mean the evil disposed) but the stake, water, fire, wheel, and sword. . . ."

The significance of Menno's work is that he united the northern wing of the Anabaptist movement, thus preventing its disintegration through persecution. Unlike other reformers, he did this without the aid of the state. The endurance of the Mennonite church throughout the centuries is the best testimony that his work was in the providence of God.

Bibliography

Estep, William R. *The Anabaptist Story.* Grand Rapids, Mich.: Wm. B.

Eerdmans, 1975. Emphasizes the calming influence of Menno on the diverse Anabaptist groups in the Netherlands. Estep argues that Menno's leadership enabled the movement to survive the persecution, as well as the violent and visionary elements within the movement.

Horsch, John. *Mennonites in Europe*. Scottdale, Penn.: Mennonite Publishing House, 1942. Includes an account of Menno's doubts about Roman Catholic doctrine. Covers his early contacts with the Anabaptist movement. Identifies sources of information about Menno's early labors as an Anabaptist evangelist.

Littell, Franklin H. *A Tribute to Menno Simons*. Scottdale, Penn.: Herald Press, 1961. Written to recognize the historical significance of Menno Simons on the quadricentennial of his death. Emphasis on his contributions to the Anabaptist movement, in particular, and to Protestantism, in general. Author's position is that Menno has great significance to twentieth century Christianity.

Menno Simons. *The Complete Writings of Menno Simons*. Edited by J. C. Wenger, Scottdale, Penn.: Herald Press, 1956. Complete English translation of Menno's literary works. Includes an introduction and a good brief biography. Also includes the location of the writings in other editions. Contains books, tracts, letters, hymns, and all other available writings. Gives direct insight into the philosophy and theology of Menno. Good illustrations.

Smith, C. Henry. *The Story of the Mennonites*. Bern, Ind.: Mennonite Book Concern, 1941. Includes a good summary of the inner conflicts experienced by Menno in his relationship to the Roman Catholic church.

Glenn L. Swygart

GERARDUS MERCATOR
Gerhard Kremer

Born: March 5, 1512; Rupelmonde, Flanders
Died: December 2, 1594; Duisburg, Duchy of Cleves
Areas of Achievement: Cartography and geography
Contribution: Mercator invented a map projection that is particularly useful for ocean navigation. He was the first person to use the name "atlas" for a volume of maps. His maps represented the best geographic knowledge available at his time.

Early Life

Gerardus Mercator was born in Rupelmonde, Flanders, near the modern city of Antwerp, Belgium. He was christened Gerhard Kremer but took, as did many scholars of his day, the Latinized form of his given name and surname. In the process, he upgraded his name. *Kremer* was the German word for "trader," and *mercator* is the Latin word for "world trader." Mercator's parents both died while he was young. He was provided for by his uncle, Gisbert Kremer, who financed his way at the University of Louvain, where he studied philosophy, mathematics, astronomy, and cosmography (geography of the cosmos).

After graduation, he established a workshop in Louvain, where he made globes, sundials, mathematical instruments, armillary spheres, astrolabes, and other measuring instruments. He drew, engraved, and colored maps. His first known map was of the Holy Land. In 1538, he engraved and published his first world map. It was drawn on a double, more or less heart-shaped projection that was interrupted at the equator. The Northern Hemisphere was drawn in the left-hand heart, and the Southern Hemisphere in the right. This map claims the distinction of being the first known map to give two names to the Americas: *Americae pars septemtrionalis* and *Americae pars meridionalis*, North and South America respectively. While in Louvain, he also published a map of Flanders that was based on his own survey rather than being an edited copy of another's map or a compilation of data reported by others. He also made celestial and terrestrial globes, several of which have a certain renown because of their large size and the fact that they belonged respectively to Emperor Charles V and his prime minister.

Mercator lived at the time of the Protestant Reformation and the reactionary Counter-Reformation of the Roman Catholic church. This religious conflict was particularly strong in the Low Countries. For some reason, Mercator was arrested for heresy in 1544. After Mercator was in prison for several months, some influential friends obtained his release, which very possibly may have saved his life. This experience caused Mercator to move his business to Duisburg, Germany, where he spent the rest of his life.

Life's Work

Mercator's 1554 map of Europe was one of the largest maps available at that time. It was enlarged on fifteen copper plates, and, when assembled, it was 132 by 159 centimeters in size. Mercator used italic lettering for the first time on a map drawn in northern Europe. These changes were important but superficial. The map is more important in three items of content that it corrected. A careful study of the accounts of navigators on the Mediterranean Sea and travelers in Eastern Europe led him to shorten the length of the Mediterranean Sea ten degrees of longitude. He increased the distance between the Black and the Baltic seas by several degrees of latitude and made the Black Sea several degrees longer. These corrections made his map of Europe the most accurate of his day.

In 1564, Mercator produced a 129-by-89-centimeter map of the British Isles. This map seems unusual to a modern map-reader in that it was orientated with West instead of North to the top of the map. Mercator is best known for his world map of 1569, which he drew on a projection that he invented and is known by his name. It was another large map in the Mercator tradition measuring 131 by 208 centimeters. It contained the latest geographic information known by 1569. The map showed three land masses, Africo-Eur-Asia, the New Indies (North and South America), and a large southern continent antipodal to Africo-Eur-Asia. In the latter case, Mercator seems to have been perpetuating the belief of ancient philosophers rather than reporting the findings of explorers.

South America is more rectangular on this map than it is in reality, and North America is much wider. Baja California is shown as a peninsula in this map, correcting other maps of the time that showed it as an island. Little was known of the interior of North America, so Mercator used this space to explain the features of his projection. Mercator drew North America as separated from Asia, which encouraged explorers to mount efforts to find the Northwest Passage to China. Europe, the best-known part of the world to Mercator, was drawn with the most accuracy. The coastline of Africa and Asia is easily recognized, except for eastern India, southeast Asia, and China.

The interior of Asia was not well known. The Caspian Sea is not recognizable except for its general location. This map shows that Mercator was aware that the magnetic north pole was not located at the geographic North Pole. He placed it where the Bering Strait now appears. Mercator inserted items within cartouches placed in what would have been blank spaces in the area occupied by the great southern continent. These items included notes on measuring distances on this projection, a map of the North Polar Region, and the like. Today the map is an important historic document in that it reveals what was known about the world in the mid-sixteenth century.

The projection Mercator invented for this map was a very important cartographic invention that is still being used with modifications today. Yet the importance of this projection was not appreciated until almost one hundred years after his death. The Mercator projection draws the spherical earth within a rectangular frame. It is characterized by equally spaced parallel lines of longitude and parallel lines of latitude that become farther and farther apart as the distance from the equator increases. Since lines of longitude are not parallel and lines of latitude are equally spaced, the projection introduces two errors which magnify each other. The result is that the areas of places located away from the equator are significantly distorted. The Mercator projection is soundly rejected by editors of modern-day textbooks, magazines, and atlases. It must be remembered, however, that Mercator drew this map for navigators, not geographers. The remarkable thing about his map was that every straight line drawn on this map plotted a course of constant compass direction. Thus, if the true locations of two places were known and correctly plotted on this projection, the navigator could connect the two places with a straight line and find the compass direction to follow in order to reach the place at the other end of the line. Mercator knew that this would not be the shortest possible course between two places, but he believed that the ease with which the course could be found fully compensated for the extra distance that would have to be traveled as the result of not following a great circle route.

While Mercator's projection is little used for world maps, several forms or derivations of his projection are still in common use, and his name can still be seen on many large-scale maps of small areas and on many aeronautical maps. When Mercator drew his world map in 1569, he drew it as if a cylinder were placed around the globe, tangent at the equator. Today, it is common to place this cylinder tangent to the earth at the North and South poles. When this is done, it is called a transverse Mercator projection. This form is used for most United States military maps. It is also used for medium-scale topographic maps published by the United States Geological Survey and by the Canadian Department of Mines and Technical Surveys. Aeronautical maps are drawn with the cylinder tangent to the earth along the great circle, connecting the starting place with its destination.

Mercator had what could be called a life's goal. He believed that the world needed a cosmography. His cosmography was made of three parts: The first part was about the beginnings of the world; the second part was the geography of the ancient world; and the third part was about the world geography of his day. The year 1569 marked the publication not only of his world map but also of the first part of his cosmography, *Chronologia* (1569). Mercator tried to establish the beginning of the world and to reconcile the chronologies of the ancient Hebrews, Greeks, Egyptians, and Romans with that of the Christian world.

In 1578, he published his version of Ptolemy's *Geōgraphikē hyphēgēsis*

(*Geography*), which contained twenty-seven plates engraved especially for this edition that are generally agreed to be the finest ever prepared for this work. This edition became the second part of his cosmography.

Mercator envisioned that the third part of his cosmography, *Atlas sive cosmographicae meditationes de fabrica mundi et fabricati figura* (1595; *Historia mundi: Or, Mercator's Atlas*, 1635), would include some one hundred maps, and he spent the last sixteen years of his life working on it. Since this work contained many maps bound together in one volume, it has given its name to all other such map collections.

Mercator's atlas was long in coming. In fact, it was published in parts, the first of which covered France, Belgium, and Germany. The second part contained twenty-two maps covering Italy, Yugoslavia, and Greece. The last section, which contained thirty-four maps, twenty-nine drawn by Mercator and five by his son Rumold and two grandsons, was published in the year after his death.

Summary

Gerardus Mercator is renowned for four things: his terrestrial and celestial globes of 1541; his large map of Europe in 1554 and of the British Isles in 1564; his world map of 1569, particularly the projection on which it was drawn; and his three-part cosmography, which included a chronology of the world from creation to his day, an edition of the works of Ptolemy, and his atlas of the then-known world.

Few if any books in English are dedicated to Mercator and his work. What little is known about Mercator's life comes from a very short biography written by a neighbor and fellow mapmaker, who described him as "a man of calm temperament and exceptional candor and sincerity." While little is known about Mercator, much is known about his works, many of which have been preserved in rare-book libraries around the world. Mercator was the leading cartographer of the last half of the sixteenth century. He was more than a skilled engraver and publisher of maps. He was an innovator and geographer as well.

Bibliography

Brown, Lloyd A. *Map Making: The Art That Became a Science*. Boston: Little, Brown, 1960. This book contains a portrait of Mercator and a reproduction of his world map that first used separate names for North and South America. It also tells the story about his book of maps.

_____. *The Story of Maps*. Boston: Little, Brown, 1949. A scholarly book on the history of cartography that contains information on the life and work of Mercator. It puts Mercator into the historical context of his time. Contains extensive notes, bibliographic data, and several illustrations of Mercator's maps.

Crone, Gerald R. *Maps and Their Makers: An Introduction to the History of Cartography.* London: Hutchinson University Library, 1966. This book contains some biographical material. It is more concerned, however, with Mercator's works, particularly the geographic contents of his world map of 1569 and his cosmography. Illustrated, with bibliographic references.

Greenhood, David. *Mapping.* Chicago: University of Chicago Press, 1951. Contains little information about Mercator himself. Instead, the chapter of projections describes Mercator's projection and how it is constructed in accurate yet not overly technical terms. Well illustrated.

LeGear, C. E. "Gerardus Mercator's Atlas of 1595." In *A La Carte: Selected Papers on Maps and Atlases*, compiled by Walter W. Ristow. Washington, D.C.: Library of Congress, 1972. This chapter is a reprint of an article that originally appeared in the *Library of Congress Quarterly Journal of Acqusitions* in May, 1950. It describes the contents of Mercator's atlas and provides a short biography of Mercator. Contains three reproductions of illustrations that appeared in his atlas, Mercator's portrait, and two of his maps, one of the New World and one of the British Isles.

Stevenson, Edward Luther. *Terrestrial and Celestial Globes: Their History and Construction Including a Consideration of Their Value as Aids in the Study of Geography and Astronomy.* New Haven, Conn.: Yale University Press, 1921. In addition to the usual short biography and the study of Mercator's projection and atlas, this book contains a lengthy description of Mercator's globes.

Thrower, Norman J. W. *Maps and Man.* Englewood Cliffs, N.J.: Prentice-Hall, 1972. A short history of cartography. The unique contribution of the chapter on Renaissance cartography is Thrower's description of Mercator's map rather than the projection on which it is drawn. Contains bibliographic citations.

Theodore P. Aufdemberge

MARIN MERSENNE

Born: September 8, 1588; Soultière, France
Died: September 1, 1648; Paris, France
Areas of Achievement: Physics, mathematics, music, philosophy, and theology
Contribution: Mersenne is best known as the priest-scientist who facilitated the crossfertilization of the most eminent minds of his time. He is widely commemorated for helping to establish modern science by promoting the new ideas of Nicolaus Copernicus, Galileo, and René Descartes and by attacking the pseudosciences of alchemy, astrology, and natural magic.

Early Life

Mersenne was born at Soultière, a small town near Oizé in the region of Maine, about 120 miles southeast of Paris. His mother and father, both laborers, were devout Catholics, and their son was baptized on the day he was born and received the unusual name Marin because his birth date fell on the feast of the Nativity of Mary. From his earliest years of schooling, Mersenne showed a disposition for piety and study. His parents, despite their modest condition, were able to send him, first, to the Collège de Mans, where he studied Latin, Greek, and grammar, and, later, to the new Jesuit college at La Flèche, where he went through the already famous course of studies of the Society of Jesus, with its emphasis on the humanities, rhetoric, and philosophy. At this school, Mersenne also studied Aristotelian physics, mathematics, and astronomy. The philosophy he learned was Scholasticism. René Descartes was also studying at La Flèche at this time, but they did not become close friends until 1623.

After finishing his studies at La Flèche in the summer of 1609, Mersenne went to Paris, where he spent two years studying theology. There he came into contact with the Minims, a mendicant order of friars founded in 1435 by Saint Francis of Paola. Their rule, modeled on Saint Francis of Assisi's, emphasized humility, and they were encouraged to regard themselves as the least (*minimi*) of all religious persons. Mersenne, impressed by their piety and asceticism, decided to enter the order. He became a Minim friar in 1611, and after a short novitiate professed his vows of poverty, chastity, and obedience at the age of twenty-four. He returned to Paris and was ordained soon afterward, celebrating his first mass in 1613.

The provincial of the Minims assigned Mersenne in 1614 to teach philosophy to young friars at the convent at Nevers. During his five years there, he became interested in mathematics and science. Religious reasons were inextricably bound up with the development of this interest, because he saw the contemporary proliferation of the occult arts of alchemy, astrology, and magic as a danger both to science and to religion. Followers of the occult arts were sometimes called naturalists, because they believed that nature had a soul. Modern scholars call them Hermeticists, because their inspiration was Hermes Trismegistus, the legendary author of works on astrology, alchemy, and magic. Mersenne fought this animistic world with every weapon at his disposal, because to him it was false religion and false science. According to Saint Thomas Aquinas and other Catholic theologians, God created a hierarchical world, from angels through human beings to animals, plants, and the inanimate world. Hermeticists attacked this system. For them the world existed on a single level, and therefore religious and natural facts were blended, a pantheistic view that Mersenne found abhorrent. In the Hermeticists' system, the causality that was once assigned to God or spirits became the province of plants, animals, metals, and especially stars. Certain stones could provoke storms, the position of the sun in the zodiac at a person's birth could determine his character and destiny, and the like. Since physical contact was no longer necessary for one thing to have an effect on another, occult influences could be multiplied endlessly.

Life's Work

By the time he began to teach philosophy at the Priory of the Annunciation in Paris in 1619, Mersenne had taken up his life's task to oppose the superstitions of the Hermeticists. He lived at the Minim convent near Place Royale, which would remain his home, except for travels to the Netherlands, Spain, Italy, and the south of France, for the rest of his life. A contemporary engraving depicts him in friar's robes, his face lightly bearded, his high forehead capped by a receding hairline, and his widely separated eyes in a gaze both piercing and kindly.

Mersenne's literary career began in the 1620's with the publication of a group of massive polemical works that he directed against the enemies of science and religion—atheists, Deists, skeptics, alchemists, astrologers, and Hermeticists. His first major publication was *Quaestiones celeberrimæ in Genesim* (1623; the most famous questions of Genesis), a formidable folio of nearly two thousand columns. On the surface, this book seemed to be a biblical commentary, but Mersenne had a broader apologetic intent: He wished to defend orthodox theology against the magical interpretations of the world presented by such Hermeticists as Giovanni Pico de la Mirandola, Tommaso Campanella, and especially Robert Fludd, whom he called an evil and heretical magician.

Mersenne continued his attack on these believers in the occult in *L'Impiété des déistes, athées, et libertins de ce temps* (1624; the impiety of modern Deists, atheists, and libertines). His purpose was to defend the teachings of the Catholic church against those who denied the existence of a loving creator. He was particularly disturbed by Giordano Bruno, whom he called one of the wickedest men whom the earth has ever supported. Mersenne's refutation of Bruno's doctrines of a plurality of worlds, the infinity of the universe, and the universal soul, as well as his defense of the rationality of nature, attracted the attention of Father Pierre Gassendi, whom he met in 1624 and who became his closest friend.

By 1625, Mersenne's defense of religion increasingly involved a defense of science. This approach characterized *La Vérité des sciences, contre les sceptiques ou Pyrrhoniens* (1625; the truth of the sciences against the skeptics or Pyrrhonists), a long book in the form of a discussion involving an alchemist, a skeptic, and a Christian philosopher. The philosopher argues that a genuine science of nature will develop only after mathematics and experimentation replace the false magical approach of the alchemists, who even propose that the creation of the world can be understood through chemistry. The skeptic tries to convince everyone that nothing is certain. The philosopher, though conceding that some things cannot be known, believes that many things are not in doubt, for example, relationships discovered by the scientists and equations discovered by the mathematicians.

Despite his opposition to the occult sciences, Mersenne was attracted to the modern sciences by their marvelous character. For example, he was more favorably disposed than Gassendi to comets' presaging the death of kings. Mersenne could also be gullible, as when he accepted the story of a dog's giving birth to a puppy with a human head. These lapses aside, Mersenne strongly believed that both religion and science had a rational basis but that it was important to keep religious and scientific facts separate. As time went on, however, science, which first had only influenced his religious thought, gradually came to dominate it. An example of this development was his growing acceptance of the Copernican theory that the sun rather than the earth was at the center of the universe. In 1623, he had opposed the Copernican theory because sufficient evidence was lacking, but by 1624 he was claiming that this theory was irrefutable.

During these years, Mersenne's circle of friends and correspondents was widening. He began to exchange letters with Descartes, who became an important influence on his thought. He also had much to do with advancing Descartes' ideas, particularly after Descartes went to the Netherlands. In the 1620's, Mersenne's correspondence increased to such an extent that he was soon playing the role of communication link to a wide variety of European scientists and philosophers. His friendliness, curiosity, and eclecticism made him the ideal intermediary. His religious house in the Place Royale became a meeting place for such eminent thinkers as Pierre de Fermat, France's foremost mathematician; Girard Desargues, the founder of descriptive geometry; and Pierre Gassendi. Because no scientific journals and no international societies existed then, these meetings at Mersenne's residence and his widely circulated letters helped to create a genuine scientific community that would later be formalized in the French Academy of Sciences. Although his intent in his gatherings and correspondence was still basically apologetic, his visitors and correspondents did not have to be Catholic, for it was becoming increasingly clear to him that the cause of science was the cause of God. He even became friendly with Thomas Hobbes at a time when his work was being viciously attacked for its materialism but which Mersenne interpreted as a genuinely new science of man.

The decade of the 1630's was important in the evolution of Mersenne's thought. He did significant work in music and mathematics, embraced mechanism (the doctrine that the world can be explained in terms of matter and motion), and came to the defense of Descartes and Galileo, whose works were being attacked by officials of the Catholic church. In 1634, he published four books on music. His scientific analysis of sound and its effects on the ear and soul began with his demonstration that pitch is proportional to frequency and that the intensity of sound is inversely proportional to the distance from its source. He discovered, in a law that now bears his name, that an increase in mass and a decrease in tension produce lower notes in a string of given length. He went on to discover similar relations for wind and percussion instruments. He offered quantitative explanations for consonance, dissonance, and resonance, and also measured the speed of sound, which he showed to be independent of pitch and loudness, and pioneered the study of the upper and lower limits of audible frequencies.

In his acoustical studies, Mersenne recognized the importance of mathematical and mechanical models. He believed that using mechanical models to imitate the workings of nature could also serve as a weapon against the Hermeticists, since these models revealed that the world was a machine and not an ensouled body. In this way, Mersenne withdrew the soul from the world of the animists and gave it back to the theologians. Mersenne the scientist provided Mersenne the priest with those principles necessary to save the religious values he held most dear. The spread of the mechanical philosophy owed much to Mersenne and Descartes, who relied on Mersenne as a theological consultant.

Despite Galileo's difficulties with the Church, Mersenne came to see his discoveries as superlative illustrations of the rationality of nature governed by mechanical laws. He was largely responsible for making Galileo's work known in France through his translations of Galileo's studies in mechanics into French. Nevertheless, he did not accept Galileo's ideas and experiments uncritically. He commented on the lack of precision in Galileo's experiments using inclined planes to investigate the acceleration of falling objects. His doubts about whether Galileo had actually performed these experiments led him carefully to repeat them. He discovered discrepancies and doubted the relationship between the distance traveled by an object under acceleration and the square of the time that Galileo had discovered.

The Roman Catholic church's condemnation of Galileo's Copernicanism occurred in 1633, but this did not stop Mersenne from defending Galileo's work. This might seem odd for a person of Mersenne's piety, until one realizes the naïve simplicity with which Mersenne blended his conceptions of faith and science, both of which led to the truth. Nevertheless, the Galileo affair had a profound effect on both Mersenne and Descartes, but whereas Descartes timidly refrained from publishing, Mersenne continued to issue works on Galileo, and in 1634 he even published a summary account of part of Galileo's *Dialogo sopra i due massimi sistemi del mondo, tolemaico e copernicano* (1632; *Dialogue Concerning the Two Chief World Systems, Ptolemaic and Copernican*, 1661). Mersenne agreed with the Church's need to preserve Scripture from error, but he saw no conflict between Scripture, which instructed man on how to go to Heaven, and science, which showed man how the heavens moved.

Mersenne's publication of the complete text of *Harmonie universelle* (1636-1637; universal harmony) marked the culmination of his achievements in music and science. This work, greatly valued by modern musicologists, contains a useful summary of Renaissance knowledge about acoustics and detailed information on a host of musical instruments.

During the last years of his life, Mersenne worked on mathematics. His most important studies were in number theory, especially on prime and perfect numbers. In 1644, he proposed a formula for generating primes, and although his formula produces only some of them, it inspired other mathematicians to devise better ways of finding prime numbers.

Mersenne fell seriously ill at the end of August, 1647. He became worse as a result of the ineptitude of a surgeon, who cut an artery in his right arm, allowing gangrene to set in. Despite his crippled arm, on a warm day at the end of July, 1648, he left to visit Descartes in the Netherlands. He arrived ill and tired at a Theatine monastery on the route and was quickly returned to Paris and confined to bed. The doctors eventually diagnosed an abscess on the lungs. The surgeons made an incision which caused him much suffering, without discovering his malady. Understanding that the end was near, Mersenne ordered his affairs: He gave instructions on his unfinished manuscripts, made a general confession, and arranged for an autopsy to discover the cause of his approaching death. On the first day of September, 1648, at three o'clock in the afternoon, Mersenne died in the arms of his friend Gassendi. At the autopsy, the surgeons found that their incision had been made too low. This knowledge was Mersenne's last contribution to science.

Summary

Despite his vital role in the scientific revolution of the seventeenth century, Marin Mersenne has been largely neglected and misunderstood. In his study of Mersenne and the birth of mechanism, Father Robert Lenoble did much to rescue Mersenne from oblivion for French scholars, but Mersenne is still remembered principally because of his friendship and correspondence with Descartes, Fermat, and other scientists. In the modern view, these friendships, rather than his ideas, constitute his significance. In contrast to this view, Lenoble sees Mersenne as one of the most important figures in the history of modern thought. Mersenne's life, which adventitiously placed him on the watershed between the medieval and modern worlds, allowed him to play a pivotal role in the scientific revolution. Throughout his career, Mersenne's devotion to religion and to science were in constant interaction. Indeed, his career involved him in several dual roles: priest and scientist, Renaissance man and modern, naïve believer and skeptic of the occult. Through his vast correspondence and many contacts with the makers of the scientific revolution, Mersenne not only called on specialists in every branch of science to work together but also kept these scientists attuned to religious and moral principles. In this way he did much to foster the new scientific movement and to prevent it from developing initially in an antireligious direction.

Mersenne helped to place science in its modern context. A new type of outlook arose with Mersenne, a science without metaphysics, a science that was verifiable and useful. He was an apostle of this new view, and he had the rare ability to serve the ideas of others. He contributed more than any of his contemporaries to expanding the knowledge of, and interest in, the scientific achievements of his time. Blaise Pascal once said that Mersenne had the very special talent for posing the right questions, and he posed these questions to the right people.

Mersenne believed deeply that false science pulled people away from God whereas true science led people to Him. Although his intention was to place religion first in whatever he said and did, he was living in an age that was leaving theology for science, and ironically, in attempting to do the opposite, he encouraged this trend. He fought the Hermeticists, encouraged the mechanists, and was the catalyst for the spread of many important scientific ideas. He did all this for the greater glory of God. From the vantage point of the modern world, one can see that what he actually did was to help separate science from its religious roots.

Bibliography

Boas, Marie. *The Scientific Renaissance, 1450-1630*. New York: Harper & Row, 1962. Boas, a competent scholar, presents a valuable summary of a significant period in the evolution of science. She sees Renaissance science as developing in an era of profound change, but she does not deny its connections with medieval science. She discusses Mersenne's role in organizing scientists through his extensive correspondence. Intended for general readers. Contains photographs and diagrams.

Debus, A. G. *Man and Nature in the Renaissance*. New York: Cambridge

University Press, 1978. An introduction to science and medicine during the early phase of the scientific revolution, from the mid-fifteenth to the mid-seventeenth century.

Popkin, Richard H. *The History of Scepticism from Erasmus to Descartes.* Assen, the Netherlands: Vangorcum, 1964. Treats the influence that skeptical philosophy had on the evolution of modern thought. In several of his works, Mersenne attacked skepticism, and so Popkin refers to him many times. Mersenne saw the skeptics as the enemies of both science and religion, for they put the foundations of truth in jeopardy. Scholarly but readable.

Thorndike, Lynn. *A History of Magic and Experimental Science.* Vol. 7, *The Seventeenth Century.* New York: Columbia University Press, 1958. This volume is the penultimate one in the massive eight-volume work that took Thorndike more than fifty years to write. He bases his work on the examination of numerous manuscripts in several languages; hence, this series is quite valuable as a reference tool. The chapters are thematically arranged, and the chapter on Mersenne and Gassendi contains much of interest on these two priest-scientists. Thorndike is not always accurate, and some of his work has been superseded by later scholarship, but his many translations of original materials scattered throughout his presentation make this a valuable and fascinating compendium.

Yates, Frances A. *Giordano Bruno and the Hermetic Tradition.* Chicago: University of Chicago Press, 1964. Yates emphasizes the importance of Hermeticism in Renaissance thought. She provides another strand in the story of how the late Renaissance turned into the scientific revolution. In particular, Yates believes that Bruno's philosophy has been misunderstood. She sees him as a thoroughgoing Hermeticist. Because Mersenne fought Bruno and Hermeticism, he forms an important part of Yates's story, for he stands on the modern side of the watershed separating modern science from its medieval and magical forebears.

Robert J. Paradowski

METTERNICH

Born: May 15, 1773; Coblenz, Archbishopric of Trier
Died: June 11, 1859; Vienna, Austro-Hungarian Empire
Areas of Achievement: Diplomacy, government, and politics
Contribution: As Europe's preeminent champion of post-French Revolution conservatism, Metternich was the chief architect in the reconstruction of the European map after the fall of Napoleon I. As minister of foreign affairs, and, later, as state chancellor to the Austrian emperor, Metternich presided for more than three decades over the political and diplomatic workings of the continent he had restored until the Revolutions of 1848 swept him from power and ushered in a new generation of leaders.

Early Life

Clemens Wenzel Nepomuk Lothar von Metternich was born, not within the vast hegemonous region that comprised the Austro-Hungarian Empire, but in the small German state of Trier, ruled by prince-bishops, one of whom, in the early seventeenth century, had been a Metternich. His father, Count Franz Georg Karl von Metternich, had represented the elector of Trier at the Imperial Court of Vienna, and, at the time of his son's birth, had reversed that role and was representing the Austrian emperor in his homeland. As a result, young Clemens was reared in the Rhineland, and he remained fond of this region all of his life. His mother, Countess Beatrix Kagenegg, was a woman of considerable culture, intelligence, and charm, whose sophistication and elegance were more French than Germanic. These qualities she passed on to her son, who was always more at home with the language and Old World manners of the country of his greatest adversary, Napoleon I, then he was with his own.

In 1788, at the age of fifteen, he was sent to study diplomacy at the University of Strasbourg. There, he studied under a celebrated professor, Christoph Wilhelm Koch, who was an ardent proponent of creating a conservative counterbalance that would oppose the growing nationalist sentiment in Europe. The following year saw the outbreak of the French Revolution, which spread to Strasbourg in 1790. Abhorring the destructive violence of the Revolution, Metternich left Strasbourg for Mainz, where he enrolled in the university. He abandoned that city before the arrival of the French revolutionary troops to join his father in Brussels, where the count was prime minister of the Austrian Netherlands. From there, young Metternich was sent on a minor diplomatic mission to England in 1794, the first of his career. Upon his return later that year, he rejoined his family in Vienna, where they had fled after the ever-growing fury of the French Revolution had deprived them of their position in Brussels and their home in Coblenz.

In September, 1795, Metternich married Eleonore von Kaunitz, but it was not a love match. While a student at Mainz, Metternich had been initiated into the erotic privileges of a young nobleman, and he was to show a lifelong predilection for the company of a great variety of attractive women that his steadily increasing political status made available to him, even using some of these amorous liaisons to great diplomatic advantage. His was not merely a marriage of convenience but of opportunity as well, for his bride was the granddaughter of the powerful Wenzel von Kaunitz, state chancellor to the late Empress Maria Theresa. By marrying into this family of tremendous political and social prestige, Metternich at last had entrée into the exclusive imperial inner circle of influence from which he could make his bid for high office.

Life's Work

During his first ten years of service as an ambassador for the Austrian emperor, Metternich witnessed the final dissolution of the ancient Holy Roman Empire, whose (by this time) symbolic and powerless crown had traditionally rested on the head of the reigning Habsburg monarch in Vienna. After serving as Austrian minister to the Saxon court in Dresden and the Prussian court in Berlin, where his anti-French efforts were thwarted, Emperor Francis I placed his young ambassador in the front ranks of the battle, and in 1806 Metternich presented his credentials to France's newly self-declared emperor, Napoleon, at Saint Cloud.

In Paris, he became very well informed as to the internal workings of the French Empire through his many important connections and his vast network of spies, which became legendary. For all of these advantages, his initial diplomatic efforts with the brilliant French tyrant proved to be a costly failure to his own country. Overestimating the effect of the 1808 Iberian uprising against the Bonapartes, he precipitated Austria into a war against France that ended disastrously for the Austrians in the Battle of Wagram (1809). Recalled to Vienna by the emperor, Metternich was appointed minister of foreign affairs, in which capacity he bought time for an exhausted Austria by giving Napoleon one of Francis' daughters as a bride. The match with the Archduchess Marie Louise (ironically a grand niece of Louis XVI's tragic queen, Marie Antoinette) was a calculated psychological maneuver to flatter Napoleon, whose character Metternich had closely studied during his tenure in Paris. Austria could now remain independent from the seemingly invincible French Empire, preserving the autonomy it needed to recoup its losses.

While Napoleon turned his attention and his Grande Armée from Austria to Russia, Austria quietly rearmed and Metternich tried to preserve the shaky balance of power in Europe, striving to keep the momentary status quo he had bought at so high a price. Austria now needed France to remain strong. Fearing the creation of a Prussian empire after French assault had awakened a dormant sense of German nationalism, and mindful of the threat of a Russian invasion of Europe if France collapsed, Metternich needed to counterbalance these threats with French power until Austria was again fit to face its dangerous adversary.

Metternich found his moment with France's catastrophic and surprising defeat in Russia in 1812. Confident of Austria's rejuvenation, he concluded a treaty with Russia and Prussia in June, 1813. Metternich negotiated with France for a separate peace treaty, but Napoleon hesitated, and in August of that year Austria declared war on France. That October, Francis bestowed on his most illustrious subject the hereditary title of prince. Holding close the South German states as allies to block any Russo-Prussian aggrandizement during this final conflict with France, Metternich arrived in Paris in May, 1814, after Napoleon's defeat at Waterloo and subsequent abdication, with the upper hand to sign the Treaty of Paris and open the way to the Congress of Vienna (September, 1814, to June, 1815).

Employing his own great charm and worldliness along with the music for which Vienna is legendary, Metternich attracted Europe's most powerful and glamorous figures to the Austrian capital for the "Congress that Danced," giving that city for the first and only time in its history the distinction of being the center of European politics. It was a splendid social occasion with an unending round of balls and festivities. It was also the most important political congress in a generation, and Europe's future hinged on the negotiations that took place there during those nine months.

Conservative by temperament, upbringing, and education, Metternich was further persuaded by the horror of two decades of pan-European war to restore the Continent to its pre-Napoleonic form. Additionally, he sought to replace the Habsburgs' traditional but meaningless role as the preeminent monarchs of Europe by establishing for them a very real leadership over loose confederations of German and Italian states. To this end he proposed the creation of an imperial German title to be borne by the Austrian emperor. Furthermore, he wanted to restore France to its pre-Revolutionary status with the old royal house of Bourbon, giving it equal footing with its conquerors to counter the threat of Russian dominance. Metternich failed in Germany and in Italy, primarily through the archconservatism of his own emperor. Francis embraced the idea of power in Italy, where Austria was initially welcomed with enthusiasm, but he mishandled it and only succeeded in agitating the feeling of national unity that his foreign minister had thereby tried to avoid; he refused the title of German emperor, leaving Austrian influence in the German states on an equal footing with Prussia. With France, Metternich was successful. France's Talleyrand and England's Castlereagh concluded an alliance with Metternich to keep in check the Russo-Prussian pact that had taken place.

That was the essential balance of power when the Congress broke up, and it established a European order that lasted well into the middle of the century. During most of that time Metternich was custodian of that order, making him the virtual prime minister of Europe. With patience, insight, and an uncanny ability to see through the heated rhetoric and quickly shifting currents of the time, Metternich triumphed over the more imposing figures of his generation, yet he was unable to defeat the new ideas that they had helped unleash. With England withdrawn from continental politics, republican restlessness in France, and nationalistic fervor in the German and Italian states, Metternich, by now Austrian state chancellor, could not prevent in 1848 the eruption of revolutions that swept through the great European capitals. Hated by now as a reactionary and the leading figure of repressive government, Metternich was forced to resign on March 13, 1848. He went into exile in England for three years but returned to Vienna, where he died in 1859 in his eighty-sixth year.

Summary

A cursory investigation of Metternich's many and varied achievements could give the impression that the subject was a genius. This, however, would do him an injustice because, though he may have possessed a kind of genius, the genius of his day was Napoleon and Metternich was his enemy. Although Metternich and his ilk eventually triumphed over Napoleon, it was the more prosaic qualities of patience, industry, and levelheadedness that won for him the war after losing most of the battles. He was not a visionary, but a practical man. Imagination, great style, and charm he did possess; indeed, he often depended on these qualities. Beyond this, however, Metternich was built to last long after the dust had settled and there was work still to be done. He saw his age through to its end and beyond, living long enough to see himself vilified by the very generation whose future he had striven to preserve. The conservatism he reimposed on Europe lasted nearly forty years until it was swept away forever by men such as Napoleon III, Giuseppe Garibaldi, and Otto von Bismarck, who were, if not his political heirs, certainly his successors. Seen from a modern, liberal perspective, it is easy to label those four decades as reactionary and oppressive. They were also four decades of a desperately needed peace, perhaps the longest such period that Europe has ever known.

Bibliography

Bertier de Sauvigny, G. de. *Metternich and His Times*. Translated by Peter Ryde. London: Darton, Longman & Todd, 1962. Written one hundred years after its subject's death, this biography is a good introduction to Metternich and his world. Most of this work is devoted to the comments of Metternich himself and his contemporaries, while the author serves as a guide to the Austrian minister's life.

Cecil, Algernon. *Metternich, 1773-1859: A Study of His Period and Personality.* London: Eyre & Spottiswoode, 1933. A thorough and engaging biography of Metternich and his times. The great statesman's life is recounted with an imagination that counterbalances its frequently difficult scholarly approach. Inaccessible to the lay reader, this book of moderate length is a good in-depth account of Metternich's professional life.

Haas, Arthur G. *Metternich, Reorganization, and Nationality, 1813-1815: A Story of Foresight and Frustration in the Rebuilding of the Austrian Empire.* Wiesbaden: Franz Steiner Verlag, 1963. For those interested in a detailed, documented, blow-by-blow account of the crucial negotiations and renegotiations that followed the resettlement of Europe after Napoleon's fall, this book is thorough and easy to understand.

Kissinger, Henry A. *A World Restored: Metternich, Castlereagh, and the Problems of Peace, 1812-22.* Boston: Houghton Mifflin, 1957. A biography of a celebrated nineteenth century statesman by a celebrated twentieth century statesman before the latter was well known. This is a good, if somewhat dry, introduction to Europe after Napoleon.

Metternich, Prince Clemens von. *Memoirs of Prince Metternich, 1773-1835.* 5 vols. Edited by Prince Richard Metternich. Translated by Mrs. Alexander Napier and Gerard W. Smith. New York: Charles Scribner's Sons, 1880-1884. Completed in 1844 by Metternich himself and brought to publication twenty years after his death by his son, Prince Richard, here is an account of his life from his birth to the Congress of Vienna. Recounted with the clarity and arrogance for which he was well known. Contains important documents and correspondence.

Schroeder, Paul W. *Metternich's Diplomacy at Its Zenith, 1820-1823.* Austin: University of Texas Press, 1962. An account of Metternich's years of diplomatic supremacy following the Congress of Vienna. Using maps to help illustrate this history, Schroeder describes the first years of Metternich's chancellory when his plan for Europe was most successful.

Pavlin Lange

MICHELANGELO

Born: March 6, 1475; Caprese, Tuscany
Died: February 18, 1564; Rome
Areas of Achievement: Art and architecture
Contribution: Michelangelo was a true Renaissance man, excelling in sculpture, painting, architecture, and poetry. He was the supreme master of the human body, especially the male nude, and his idealized and expressive treatment of this theme was enormously influential, both in his own day and in subsequent centuries.

Early Life

Michelangelo Buonarroti was the second of five sons of an aristocratic but impoverished Florentine family. He was born in the village of Caprese, near Arezzo, where his father was serving as magistrate, but before he was a month old the family returned to Florence.

From childhood Michelangelo was strongly drawn to the arts, but this inclination was bitterly opposed by his father, who considered artistic activity menial and hence demeaning to the family social status. The boy's determination prevailed, however, and at the age of thirteen he was apprenticed to the popular painter Domenico Ghirlandaio. From Ghirlandaio he presumably learned the technique of fresco painting, but his style was formed on the study of the pioneers of Renaissance painting, Giotto and Masaccio. It was, in fact, while copying a Masaccio fresco that he was punched in the face by another apprentice. The resulting broken nose gave his face its distinctive bent profile for the rest of his life.

About a year after entering his apprenticeship, Michelangelo's precocious talent attracted the notice of Lorenzo de' Medici, the unofficial ruler and leading art patron of Florence, and the boy was invited to join the Medici household. There he had the opportunity to study both classical and modern masterpieces of sculpture and to absorb the humanistic culture and Neoplatonic philosophy that pervaded the Medici court. From this period date Michelangelo's two earliest surviving works, both reliefs, *The Battle of the Centaurs* (c. 1492) and *The Madonna of the Steps* (c. 1492). When Lorenzo died in 1492, Michelangelo left the Medici palace and undertook the study of anatomy based on the dissection of corpses from the Hospital of Santo Spirito, for which he carved a wooden crucifix in gratitude.

In 1494, the populace of Florence, stirred by the puritanical monk Girolamo Savonarola, ousted the Medici family and reestablished a republic. Michelangelo, although he seems to have admired Savonarola and supported the republic, evidently felt threatened because of his close ties to the Medici family and fled the city, staying briefly in Venice and then in Bologna. There he supported himself with relatively minor sculpture commissions.

The year 1496 found him in Rome, where he undertook two important projects, the *Bacchus* (1497), which effectively replicated the Hellenistic style, and the Vatican *Pietà* (1499), an image of the Virgin Mary supporting the dead Christ. In this work Michelangelo minimizes the painful aspect of the subject by showing the Virgin as a lovely, surprisingly youthful woman gazing down serenely at the classically beautiful body of her son. To overcome the awkwardness of balancing an adult male body on the lap of a woman, he enlarges the Virgin but masks her size with billowing drapery and wraps the body of Christ around her to create a compact, pyramidal group. The contract called for the *Pietà* to be "the most beautiful work in marble which exists today in Rome." When, at the age of twenty-five, Michelangelo completed the piece, there was no question that he had met this requirement.

Life's Work

In 1501, Michelangelo returned triumphantly to Florence and to a new challenge. An enormous marble block that had been abandoned decades earlier because its tall, shallow proportions seemed unsuitable for a figure sculpture was assigned to him, and from it he carved the *David* (1501-1504). David was a favorite Florentine subject, but Michelangelo's treatment broke with tradition in representing the shepherd boy as a Herculean nude, twice life-size, before, rather than after, the battle so as to incorporate greater physical and psychic tension. The statue was placed in the square outside the governmental palace, but it has since been moved inside to protect it from the weather. Contemporary with the *David* or slightly later are several powerful representations of the Madonna and Child, including the artist's only unquestioned panel painting, the *Doni Madonna* (c. 1503-1505).

In 1504, the Florentine republic ordered two large battle scenes for its council chamber, one from Leonardo da Vinci and the other from Michelangelo. Neither fresco was actually painted, and even Michelangelo's preliminary drawing survives only in a copy. It shows a group of bathing soldiers struggling out of a stream at the battle alarm, and the treatment of the straining, foreshortened bodies was to provide instruction and inspiration to a whole generation of Italian artists.

This painting and a series of sculpted apostles for Florence Cathedral were interrupted when the recently elected pope, Julius II, called Michelangelo to Rome. The pope's first commission was for his tomb, a grandiose, multi-level structure that was to include more than forty figures. Michelangelo had hardly begun this project when the pope changed his mind and ordered the artist instead to paint the ceiling of the Sistine Chapel. Michelangelo vigorously objected that he was a sculptor, not a painter, but in the end he spent the years 1508-1512 covering the surface, approximately fifty-eight hundred square feet, seventy feet above the floor, with scenes from Genesis, enframed by nude youths and surrounded by enthroned prophets and Sibyls. In keeping with his preference for sculpture, emphasis is placed on the monumental figures with rather minimal background. Nevertheless, as cleaning of the fresco has revealed, the coloring is both subtle and brilliant.

Upon completion of the ceiling, Michelangelo resumed his work on the pope's tomb, producing *The Dying Slave* (1513-1516), *The Rebellious Slave* (1513-1516), and *Moses* (1505-1545). Julius, however, died in 1513, and his successors would include two members of the Medici family, both boyhood companions of Michelangelo, Leo X (1513-1521) and Clement VII (1523-1534). Both preferred to keep Michelangelo employed largely on family projects in Florence, so that progress on the Julius tomb was slow and sporadic. The first Medician commission, an elaborate façade for the family church of San Lorenzo, was never executed, but the next, a new sacristy in the same church containing tombs of the Medici dukes, although never finished, was to be the artist's most complete architectural and sculptural ensemble. Probably the most celebrated figures from this complex are the personifications of *Night* and *Day*, *Dawn* and *Dusk* (1520-1534), which recline uneasily on the curved and sloping sarcophagus lids. Above them sit idealized effigies of the dead dukes, who turn toward a statue of the Madonna and Child, the so-called *Medici Madonna* (1525). There is a noticeable change in Michelangelo's style in the 1520's, the decade of this chapel. His figures become more restless, with spiraling rhythms and sometimes elongated or otherwise distorted proportions, the overall effect of which is disturbing. The same quality is found in the architecture that Michelangelo executed in the same decade, especially the vestibule of the Laurentian Library, which includes a number of unconventional and even bizarre features. This change corresponds to a more general anticlassical and antinaturalistic trend in Italian art at this time which is often characterized as Mannerism.

When, in 1527, the Florentines again expelled their Medici rulers and restored the republic, Michelangelo sided against his patrons and supported it. During the ensuing conflict he played a major role in designing the fortifications of the city, and when Medici forces recaptured it in 1530 he went into hiding. Pope Clement amnestied the artist, but Michelangelo felt threatened and estranged under the new autocratic regime and spent increasing amounts of time in Rome. Finally, in 1534, he left Florence forever. Two days after he arrived to settle in Rome, Clement VII died.

Michelangelo expected now to be free to return to the long-delayed and repeatedly scaled-down Julius tomb, but again he was frustrated. The new pope, Paul III, declaring that he had waited thirty years to have Michelangelo work for him, induced Julius' heirs to accept a modest wall tomb featuring *Moses*, from the original project, and two more female figures from Michelangelo's hand. The monument was completed in 1545, and Michelangelo was at last free of what he himself described as "the tragedy of the tomb."

Meanwhile, he was engaged on several major projects for Pope Paul III, beginning with the fresco of the *Last Judgment* on the altar wall of the Sistine Chapel, painted between 1536 and 1541. The expressionist tendency in Michelangelo's art, already noted, is dominant here. Clusters of swirling figures alternate with empty sky and the scale of the figures changes unaccountably, with the more distant becoming larger. A poignant personal note is the inclusion of a grimacing self-portrait of the artist on the discarded skin of one of the saints.

The *Last Judgment* was followed by two more frescoes painted during the 1540's for Paul III's private chapel, *The Conversion of Saint Paul* (1542-1545) and *The Crucifixion of Saint Peter* (1542-1550). The pope also placed Michelangelo in charge of several architectural projects, including the rebuilding of the cupola at St. Peter's Basilica and the remodeling of the Piazza del Campidoglio. Neither, however, was to be completed in the artist's lifetime.

In his last years Michelangelo returned to sculpture with two devotional and deeply personal works. The Florence *Pietà* (1550-1556) was intended for Michelangelo's own tomb and contained his self-portrait. In 1555, however, he attacked and damaged the piece in a fit of frustration. Thereafter he sculpted the Rondanini *Pietà* (1552-1564), on which he was still working six days before his death, in 1564, when he was eighty-eight.

Summary

Michelangelo gave eloquent expression, in sculpture, painting, and poetry, to his own ideals and those of his contemporaries as they moved from the confident Humanism of the High Renaissance to the anxious spirituality of the Counter-Reformation period. His early work seems to harmonize the pagan sensuality of antiquity with Christian themes and to celebrate human beauty as a reflection of divine creation. As his art and thought evolved, however, he increasingly conveyed a tension between spirit and body, form and matter, and he came to depreciate physical perfection in favor of psychological and spiritual expression. In his late Roman years he became associated with the Catholic reform movement, and his growing religious fervor gives a highly personal and sometimes mystical flavor to the art of this period.

Michelangelo's genius was recognized and venerated by his contemporaries, and he exerted enormous influence on generations of younger artists. It was, however, the superficial aspects of his style—serpentine poses and muscular anatomies—that were easiest to assimilate. None of his followers was able to match his profundity of thought and feeling.

Bibliography

Condivi, Ascanio. *The Life of Michelangelo*. Edited with an introduction by

Hellmut Wohl. Translated by Alice Sedgwick Wohl. Baton Rouge: Louisiana State University Press, 1976. An essential primary source, this biography was written during Michelangelo's lifetime by one of his students and is based on the artist's own recollections. Illustrations and bibliography.

De Tolnay, Charles. *Michelangelo*. 5 vols. Princeton, N.J.: Princeton University Press, 1943-1960. The definitive scholarly study of the artist in five volumes, each devoted to a particular aspect of his life or work. Catalog of works, extensive notes, illustrations, and bibliography.

Hartt, Frederick. *Michelangelo*. New York: Harry N. Abrams, 1965. Limited to Michelangelo's paintings, which are dealt with in an introductory essay, followed by color plates with interpretive comments. Biographical chronology and bibliography.

_____. *Michelangelo, the Complete Sculpture*. New York: Harry N. Abrams, 1969. Contains lavish illustrations, many in color, with fine interpretive text geared to plates. Includes biographical chronology and bibliography.

Hibbard, Howard. *Michelangelo*. 2d ed. New York: Harper & Row, 1974, 1985. A highly readable, unobtrusively scholarly survey of Michelangelo's life and career. Illustrations and bibliography.

Murray, Linda. *Michelangelo: His Life, Work, and Times*. New York: Thames and Hudson, 1984. Focus on the artist's historical setting, with extended quotes from contemporary sources. Numerous illustrations relate both to Michelangelo's works and to his background. Bibliography.

Vasari, Giorgio. "Michelangelo." In *Lives of the Artists*, translated by George Bull. New York: Penguin Books, 1965. A major primary source, this biography by a friend and fellow artist was written shortly after Michelangelo's death and includes firsthand impressions and recollections.

Jane Kristof

JULES MICHELET

Born: August 21, 1789; Paris, France
Died: February 9, 1874; Hyères, France
Areas of Achievement: Historiography and philosophy
Contribution: Michelet was France's greatest national historian and one of the guiding forces of modern historical writing.

Early Life

Jules Michelet was the only child of a poor Parisian printer. His early life was one of material privation but deep familial love. Forced to work in his father's establishment from an early age, the youth lived a solitary life and experienced few of the common joys of childhood. His only pleasure came from his long walks after hours in the famous cemetery, Père Lachaise, and his occasional visits to Lenoir's Museum. It was from the latter that he first experienced a vivid realization of history and a fascination with the past.

Michelet's antagonism toward the Church and toward monarchy, which would loom so large in his later writings, stemmed, in part, from his youth. The family of the future historian, already in dire poverty, was reduced to absolute destitution during the Reign of Terror as Robespierre's henchmen combed the streets of Paris, jailing and executing men whose manuscripts his father had published. Fearing for his life, the elder Michelet first curtailed his printing projects and was finally forced to terminate his business by the government. Unemployment led to debts for which his father was arrested in 1808 and incarcerated for nearly a year. The collapse of his father's occupation and his ensuing imprisonment engendered in Jules a hatred of Napoleon I, clerics, and the empire that endured to his death. In his last work, *Histoire du XIXᵉ siècle* (1872-1875; history of the nineteenth century), he continued to spew forth the vitriolic opinions inculcated during his childhood.

Although financial problems led to marital strife, both parents agreed on one thing; Jules should be formally educated whatever the cost. After being tutored in Latin by a family friend, Michelet entered Lycée Charlemagne in 1812, which proved to be socially disastrous. His life of solitude had not prepared him for the competitive academic world, and the small, sensitive, shy lad became the object of endless verbal and physical abuse. The owl in daylight, as one source described him, endured the abuse and, capitalizing on his native intelligence, innate writing skills, and untiring work habits, became the top student in his class.

His brilliant academic career won for him a teaching position at the Collège Sainte-Barbe in 1822. In 1827, he published a translation of Giambattista Vico's *Principi di scienza nuova d'intorno alla comune natura delle nazione* (1744; *The New Science*, 1948) that brought him both public acclaim and an appointment to teach history and philosophy at the École Normale Supérieure, a position he held until 1838, when he accepted a chair at the Collège de France. In addition to his academic positions, he served as head of the history section of the National Archives from 1830 to 1852.

Life's Work

The philosophical foundation for Michelet's seventeen-volume *Histoire de France* (1833-1867; partial translation as *The History of France*, 1844-1846) and the seven-volume *Histoire de la Révolution française* (1847-1853; *History of the French Revolution*, 1972), his life's work, slowly evolved in 1827 as he came under the influence of German Romanticism. Vico, the little-known Neapolitan philosopher, taught Michelet that all history was universal, constantly in motion, and that humanity was the common element unifying all ages. Men die, but humanity, the receptacle for human wisdom, lives on. The still-embryonic scholar first expressed his historical philosophy in *Introduction à l'histoire universelle* (1831; introduction to universal history), maintaining that history was nothing more than the story of liberty: man's ongoing struggle to free himself from nature and fatality. As history was constantly in motion, he likened it to the movement of the sun. It rose in the east, in India, moved westward to Persia, Greece, Rome, and culminated in France. In his typically unabashed, chauvinistic manner, Michelet explained that France was superior to the rest of Europe in culture and civilization and, being such, was the new apostle of liberty. Along this line of reasoning, France became synonymous with humanity, and France alone would control the destiny of mankind. Thus, in Vico, Michelet found both a philosophy of history and a mission. His life's work would be to show how the French people fostered and nourished the spirit of liberty.

The History of France filled seventeen volumes, took thirty-four years to write, and was a labor of love. Of the seventeen volumes, only the first six merit serious consideration. These six, written between 1833 and 1844, are based on primary sources, contain no obvious bias, and reflect a unique historical method. Michelet's objective was to treat the "whole of the parts"—the land, its people, events, institutions, and beliefs—but it was the people who were the important element. The remaining eleven volumes (written between 1854 and 1867), covering the end of the Middle Ages to the Revolution, are inferior, as Michelet was forced to write them without full benefit of manuscripts and documentation. Michelet, having been relieved of his professorship and archival position for refusing to swear an oath of allegiance to Napoleon III, voices in volumes seven through thirteen his hostility toward the monarchy and toward Christianity.

In the interval that divided his work on *The History of France*, Michelet turned his attention to the French Revolution. Using the turmoil of 1789 as a backdrop, he painted a gloomy picture of the state of affairs in France; he maintained that the Church, supported by the monarchy, was threatening education, which had been an essential reform of the Revolution. In both *History of the French Revolution* and *Le Peuple* (1846; *The People*, 1846), he maintained that France was once again suffering under the tyranny of Christian monarchy and it was time for the people to sally forth and rekindle the light for justice and liberty. In *History of the French Revolution*, the voice is that of a revolutionary as Michelet becomes one of the common people who won the triumph for law and justice in 1789. His objective was to stir the masses. So effective was his effort that he has been credited with being instrumental in instigating the Revolution of 1848, which, in addition to his refusal to swear allegiance to Napoleon, cost him his academic post at the Collège de France as well as his archival position.

Deprived of rank and income, Michelet was forced to move to the countryside with only the company of his young wife, Athenais, to comfort him. As his own suffering paralleled his father's at the hands of the government, it is not surprising that when he resumed work on *The History of France* an obvious bias against the government ran through the remaining volumes. In January, 1874, the great historian fell ill, and a month later, on February 9, 1874, he died of a heart attack. Although initially interred at Hyères, France, in May, 1875, his body was later exhumed, and, before thousands of public officials, students, and friends, he was buried a second time at Père Lachaise, where he had spent his happiest moments as a child.

Summary

Jules Michelet was a product of the Romantic movement, the world of color, passion, and poetry, but his love for France became excessive. So intense were his emotions that he could not see life as it was. As his patriotism turned into idolatry and as he deified the French people and the Revolution, it became impossible for him to explain the terror of the age. While his work must be admired for its novelty and beauty, it must be scorned for its mysticism. Yet his labors were not without merit. He was the first to use the term "Renaissance" to refer to a specific period in history. He was the first to insist that geography was a determining factor in shaping a state. He was the first to make widespread use of artifacts in interpreting the past. He was the first to assign a major role to the common man as the molder of his own destiny. If his excessive love for France distorted his analysis, his historical method was destined to play a major role in inspiring future historians to view the past in its totality.

Bibliography
Geyl, Pieter. *Debates with Historians*. Rev. ed. Cleveland: World Publishing, 1958. Provides good balance to Gooch's work, as Geyl is very critical of Michelet. Although attention is given to both *The History of*

Great Lives from History
1602

France and *History of the French Revolution*, the latter is emphasized. The major criticism is Michelet's attempt to use emotionalism and senti- mentality to make wrong appear right.

Gooch, G. P. *History and Historians in the Nineteenth Century.* 2d ed. New York: Barnes & Noble Books, 1952. The best work on nineteenth century historiography in English. Gives one of the more favorable views of Mi- chelet. Gooch notes the historian's bias toward the monarchy, his anti- clerical position, and his excessive adoration of France.

Kippur, Stephen A. *Jules Michelet: A Study of Mind and Sensibility.* Albany: State University of New York Press, 1980. The only full biography of Michelet in English. The work considers Michelet's childhood, social sta- tus, and intellectual development as they contributed to Michelet's work as a historian and professor. Kippur examines Michelet's ideas on France, religion, and "the people." Gives a good analysis of Michelet's major works and is a balanced account.

Orr, Linda. *Jules Michelet: Nature, History, and Language.* Ithaca, N.Y.: Cornell University Press, 1976. Orr provides excellent coverage of Miche- let's nonhistorical writings. Gives particular attention to his writings on natural science. Traces Michelet's search for patterns of coherence in nature, which influenced his historical works. Draws upon Michelet's jour- nal to provide fascinating insight into the personal aspects of his private life.

Thompson, J. W. *A History of Historical Writing.* Vol. 2. Magnolia, Mass.: Peter Smith, 1967. This good source gives a chronological account of the major aspects of Michelet's life. Particularly good on the problems leading to Michelet's anticlerical stance in his history of the Revolution. Advocates dividing Michelet's works into two categories for analysis.

Wayne M. Bledsoe